A HISTORY OF
CHINESE PHILOSOPHY

中國哲學史

馮友蘭

A HISTORY OF CHINESE PHILOSOPHY

Vol. I

THE PERIOD OF THE PHILOSOPHERS

(FROM THE BEGINNINGS TO CIRCA 100 B.C.)

BY

FUNG YU-LAN

Translated by

DERK BODDE

With introduction, notes, bibliography and index

PRINCETON

PRINCETON UNIVERSITY PRESS

1952

Second Edition in English, 1952

This first volume of Fung Yu-lan's history was published in Chinese in 1931 by the Shen Chou Publishing
Company, Shanghai. It was reissued in 1934, together
with the Chinese edition of Vol. II, by the Commercial
Press, Shanghai. The present English edition is repro-
duced without change, except for the indicated new material and corrections on pp. xxi *et seq.*, from the translation by Mr. Bodde published in 1937 by Henri Vetch,
Peiping. This reissue of Vol. I coincides with first publi-
cation of the English of Vol. II. Both volumes are published by arrangement with Henri Vetch.

Printed in the United States of America
Fourth Printing, 1966

TABLE OF CONTENTS

MAP

TRANSLATOR'S PREFACE

Despite the fact that at the present time modern inventions are bringing the world into closer and closer physical relation, the truth remains that serious intellectual barriers still exist to prevent mutual understanding between nations and peoples. Now, as so often in the history of the world, the development of mental contacts lags behind that of physical ones, and this at a time when the very existence of these rapid methods of communication makes a sympathetic understanding of other peoples all the more imperative.

Only too often it is still possible to find even notable western scholars making such statements as : " The Dark Ages in Europe brought the world to its lowest cultural level," quite oblivious to the fact that at that very period one of the most brilliant flowerings of human culture was taking place in China under the T'ang dynasty, and that the world's first printed book was produced in that country in the ninth century. Too many of us in the West still possess the viewpoint described by the Chinese Taoist philosopher, Chuang Tzŭ, as that of the well-frog, who could see only the little circle of sky above his well, and imagined this to be the whole world. For too many of us the cultural heritage of Greece and Rome is still the world, at a time when comparative studies of other civilizations are more needed than ever before, not only for gaining an understanding of these alien cultures, but also for the understanding of our own culture, which to-day stands in serious need of an impartial evaluation.

It is for such reasons that the present translation is offered, in the hope that it will show to the West how a Chinese scholar, who has had the advantage of western training, views the philosophy of his own country. The book is a translation of the first volume of the two volume work, *Chung-kuo Che-hsüeh Shih* 中國哲學史 (A History of Chinese Philosophy), by Dr. Fung Yu-lan 馮友蘭, Ph.D. of Columbia University, and at the present time Professor of Philosophy at the National Tsing Hua University, Peiping. This first volume covers what is perhaps the most brilliant period of Chinese philosophy, extending from its earliest beginnings down to about 100 B.C., when Confucianism became orthodox. Of all works written on the subject, this one is certainly the most complete, and in many ways, it is hoped, one of the best. The second volume of the Chinese edition, not yet translated, continues the history of Chinese philosophy from this point down to the present day.

It will be noticed that the author, to a large degree, uses the method of direct quotation from original sources. This makes of his work not only a valuable source-book of Chinese philosophy, but is advantageous because it allows the ancient texts to speak for themselves, a feature of particular importance in a field like Chinese philosophy, in which many interpretations are often possible. In rendering these quoted texts into English, the translator has attempted to adhere as closely as possible to the original, and while making full use of existing translations in western languages, to which, for the sake of convenience, references are made, he has rarely accepted them without making modifications of his own which he thought would render the translation more accurate.

When not translating original quotations, however, he has not hesitated here and there to make such minor changes as would, without disturbing the meaning, improve the English style. The somewhat long paragraphs of the Chinese original have sometimes been re-divided, and for the sake of the western reader he has occasionally made slight changes or additions (such as those of the reign dates that follow the names of rulers). He has also added a number of explanatory footnotes that are marked *Tr.* . Any major alterations, all of which have been made with the consent of the author, are indicated in the footnotes. Throughout his work, the translator has had the advantage of personal advice from the author, who has read the English manuscript and made corrections and suggestions.

Those acquainted with the original work will notice several points of difference in the translation. Thus the Historical Introduction, the Chronological Table of the Philosophers, the Bibliography and the Index are not found in the original, and are additions of the translator. The map of China under the Warring States is also new. In the Bibliography will be found a list of all writings mentioned in the text, as well as the editions to which references are made. The Chinese characters of important names and terms (save those of the books listed in the Bibliography), appear in the Index. The reader who compares the English translation with the Chinese original will notice also that Chapter I of the English edition is only a partial translation of the corresponding chapter in the original. Portions of the original chapter have been combined to form one essay, which here serves as the author's Introduction, whereas other portions which it was felt would be of less interest to westerners, have been omitted. The chronology followed, unless otherwise noted, has been that given in Mathias Tchang's *Synchronismes chinois.*

In conclusion, the translator is happy to give his hearty thanks to Dr. Fung Yu-lan, who read the manuscript and carefully checked it with the original, thus helping to make this work possible. To Mr. Henri Vetch, his publisher, he is deeply grateful for a great deal of valuable advice and criticism. To his many predecessors in the field of Chinese translation, beginning with Legge, he is under a great debt, as well as to such men as Mr. Arthur Probsthain, who through his many publications of translations of Chinese philosophy, has done more than almost any other man to make this little known field of human thought accessible to the western world. To the staff of the National Library of Peiping he is greatly indebted for the obtaining of biographical information concerning certain modern Chinese scholars, for inclusion in the Bibliography. Others who have read the manuscript and to whom thanks are due, include the translator's mother and his wife.

DERK BODDE

PEIPING, CHINA,

    May 18, 1937.

NOTICE

This volume was first published in Chinese by the Shen Chou 神 州 Publishing Co., Shanghai, 1931. In 1934 it, together with Vol. II, was re-issued by the Commercial Press, Shanghai, to whom thanks are due for permission to publish the English edition.

HISTORICAL INTRODUCTION

BY THE TRANSLATOR

For those unfamiliar with Chinese history, a brief outline of the period covered in this volume may be helpful. Traditionally, Chinese history commences in very early times with the Five Emperors: Fu Hsi, Shen Nung or the Divine Farmer, Huang-ti or the Yellow Emperor, Shao Hao and Chuan Hsü. These semi-divine beings were followed, according to tradition, by Yao, the first really human ruler (supposed to have reigned 2357-2256 B.C.). Yao was succeeded upon his death, not by his son, who was considered 'unworthy' to receive the empire, but by Shun (2255-2206), who had already been Yao's minister. During Shun's reign China was troubled by a terrible flood, conquered only after nine years through the heroic efforts of the Great Yü, who constructed dikes and made waterways. Yü became emperor after Shun's death, and founded the first Chinese dynasty of Hsia. With him, too, the Empire became hereditary, the throne passing after his death to his son.[1]

Gradually, however, the Hsia dynasty fell into decay, reaching its lowest depths with its tyrannical last ruler, Chieh (1818-1766 B.C.), who is supposed to have engaged in the most abandoned debauches in a park containing, among other things, a lake of wine. A revolt broke out and Chieh was overthrown by a new hero, T'ang, who founded the Shang, also known as the Yin, dynasty (1766-1123 B.C.). This dynasty later also slowly declined, and its last ruler, Chou (1154-1123), is said to have rivalled Chieh in cruelty and debauchery.

Meanwhile, the small state of Chou (not to be confused with the name of the ruler Chou, just mentioned), had been gaining power in western China under its ruler, King Wen (1184-1157). King Wen was followed by King Wu (1156-1116), who revolted against the tyrant, Chou, overcame him, and so founded the Chou dynasty (1122-256 B.C.), the longest in Chinese history. After his death the work of consolidating the empire was greatly furthered by his brother, the Duke of Chou, who acted as regent during the early years of the young succeeding king.

Such is the traditional account of early Chinese history. Yet actually, the first authentic date in China is that on which an eclipse of the sun occurred in 776 B.C., and which is recorded in one of the

---

[1] Yü has sometimes been criticized in later times for this fact. *Cf.* pp. 115-116, where the traditional account of Yao, Shun and Yü is given.

earliest classics, the *Shih Ching* or Book of Odes (II, iv, Ode 9). All chronology prior to this date is questionable. Through archæology, however, and the deciphering of the archaic inscriptions scratched upon bone or tortoise shell by the Shang people for divination purposes, we are now learning more and more about the Shang dynasty.[1] We know, for example, that the list of Shang kings as traditionally given is correct, although their exact dates cannot yet be determined; and gradually we are realizing that many features of Chinese civilization that were formerly supposed to have originated in the Chou dynasty, actually go back to the Shang.

For the ages preceding the Shang dynasty, even archæology does not help us very greatly, and the actual existence of such figures as Yao, Shun, Yü, etc., is highly problematical. Several of them, and the Five Emperors preceding them, are probably culture heroes. Thus Fu Hsi is supposed to have invented nets and traps for hunting and fishing; the Divine Farmer, Shen Nung, to have invented the plough; and Huang-ti or the Yellow Emperor, to have invented wheeled vehicles, boats, etc.. Mythical though these heroes may be, however, a knowledge of them is highly important to the reader of ancient Chinese philosophy, because of the frequency with which they are referred to in philosophical writings. Thus Yao and Shun, together with T'ang, founder of the Shang dynasty, and Kings Wen and Wu and the Duke of Chou of the early Chou dynasty, are the sages and heroes *par excellence* of the Confucians, who always speak of them when referring to the golden age of antiquity. The wicked tyrants Chieh and Chou, last rulers of the Hsia and Shang dynasties, are often opposed to them. Yü, the conqueror of China's great flood, and founder of the Hsia dynasty, while also well spoken of by the Confucians, is the particular hero of the Mohist school established by Mo Tzŭ. And Huang-ti or the Yellow Emperor was adopted, if not invented, by the Taoist school as its patron.[2]

Our knowledge of Chinese history prior to the sun eclipse of 776 B.C. is thus rather uncertain, whereas following that date, the historical records become increasingly rich and reliable. When the Chou dynasty came into power, it elaborated a feudal system that was analogous in many ways to feudalism in Europe, being composed of a large number of feudal states, all of them of comparatively small size.[3] These were supposed to render homage to the House of Chou, whose capital was situated near the present city of Sian in Shensi. We must remember that the China of that time was very small, and was largely confined to the north China plain and the Yellow river basin.

---

[1] For this method of divination, *cf.* pp. 27-28 and 379-380.
[2] For the relations of these semi-mythical figures with the various philosophic schools, *cf.* p. 283.
[3] For a traditional account of the feudal system, *cf.* pp. 109-110.

For a while this system seems to have operated reasonably well, but before long the Chou dynasty, like its predecessors, began to deteriorate, and in 771 the capital was sacked during a sudden attack of barbarians from the west, the king was killed, and the seat of government moved to what is to-day Loyang, in Honan. The Chou rulers never recovered from this blow, and during the centuries that followed they became more and more helpless, until they were nothing more than figure-heads.

The period from 722 to 481 B.C. is generally known as the Ch'un Ch'iu period, a term derived from the *Ch'un Ch'iu* or 'Spring and Autumn Annals,' an historical chronicle of the state of Lu during these years. During this time more and more power was usurped from the House of Chou by the feudal lords, who became completely independent, and several of whom assumed the title of ' king'. An attempt at preserving order was made by establishing the institution of *Pa* or feudal Leader. This was a title assumed at various times by whoever happened to be the most powerful feudal lord at the time, and who had the power to convoke the other lords to assemblies, and to discharge many of the functions formerly performed by the Chou kings. The first of these *Pa* was Duke Huan of Ch'i (685-643).[1]

Despite these efforts at maintaining the *status quo*, it was evident that the feudal system, and with it the old institutions and ways of life, were changing under the impact of many new and irrepressible social and economic forces. The use of iron, which seems to have become fairly general in China about 600 B.C., may have been one of these forces.[2] Many feudal states were swallowed up by the few more powerful ones, who were ever extending their territories through constant warfare. It was an age of uncertainty and of expansion, both geographically and intellectually. The confines of what was known as China became greatly increased with the rise to power of a state like the semi-barbaric Ch'u in the south, which came to occupy much of present Honan, Hupeh and Anhuei. In this age of unrest there began, toward the end of the Ch'un Ch'iu period, the Period of the Philosophers, as it is called in this book, a period inaugurated by Confucius (551-479), and largely coincident in time with what in political history is known as the period of the Warring States.

This Warring States period, which followed the Ch'un Ch'iu period, began in 403 B.C., when the state of Chin split up into the three states of Han, Wei and Chao, and ended in 221 B.C. with the complete unification of all China. All the social and economic movements that had begun during the preceding age acted throughout this period with ever increasing violence. Thus many of the former

---

[1] For the names of the other four *Pa* traditionally listed, *cf.* p. 112.
[2] For an account of these movements during the Ch'un Ch'iu period, and during the age that followed, see ch. 2.

feudal aristocracies lost their power, while the peasants, who had been the virtual serfs of their overlords, gained independence. Terrific and continuous wars were waged between the seven large states that still remained on the stage, striving for supremacy. At the same time the age was one of philosophical activity such as has perhaps been unparalleled elsewhere in the world, save in classical Greece. Literally thousands of scholars, belonging to every school of thought, travelled about from state to state offering their services to the different rulers.

Finally, this political and intellectual anarchy was brought to an end by Ch'in, a barbaric state occupying much of present Kansu and Shensi. This state had never contributed a scholar of importance, but by ruthless methods, and the skilful utilization of astute advisors recruited from other parts, it succeeded, from its strategic position in the west, in making enormous increases in its territory. In 256 B.C. it put an end to the long impotent House of Chou, thus extinguishing the Chou dynasty and establishing the Ch'in dynasty in its place; and in 221 B.C. its great ruler, Ch'in Shih-huang-ti, conquered the last of the feudal states, and so unified China, actually for the first time in history. Feudalism was abolished, and replaced by a central government with a system of provincial administration essentially the same as the provincial system used to-day.

Despite these good measures, Ch'in Shih-huang has gained the undying hatred of later Chinese because of his notorious decree of 213 B.C., ordering the burning and destruction of most books throughout the empire. This was the logical culmination of his attempt toward intellectual as well as geographical unification, and of making a complete break with the past. Though the importance of this Burning of the Books has probably been exaggerated, it nevertheless dealt a blow to the hitherto flourishing philosophical schools from which they never fully recovered.

The ruthlessness that had brought the Ch'in dynasty into being, however, also led to its speedy collapse. Rebellion broke out soon after Ch'in Shih-huang's death in 210, and lasted for several years until China was again unified in 206 by a man who, though of peasant origin, rose to become Emperor and to found the Han dynasty (206 B.C.-A.D. 220). This dynasty resembled in several respects the contemporary Roman Empire in the West. It was an age of unifying and codification, which saw the beginnings of the Chinese examination system and of many other social and political institutions that have existed since that time with only minor modifications almost down to the present day. Though the feudalism abolished by the Ch'in dynasty was at first revived, it was later greatly restricted by the central government, so that never since then has it played a part in China in any way comparable to that in the West.

It is natural that with this political and social unification, the tremendous philosophical activity of the preceding feudal period, already seriously crippled by the Burning of the Books, should be still further curtailed. Unlike the Ch'in dynasty, the Han dynasty fostered scholarship and was not anti-cultural, but for various reasons this scholarship was encouraged to move along specified lines dominantly Confucian, and the final triumph of Confucianism over the other schools was largely brought about by the Han ruler, Wu-ti (140-87 B.C.), at the suggestion of the noted Confucianist, Tung Chungshu (179 ?-104 ? B.C.).[1]

This does not mean that since then other forms of thought have not been important in China. Buddhism, introduced from India during the succeeding centuries, has been particularly influential. The fact remains, however, that Confucianism since that time has usually been accepted as orthodox, at least by China's ruling and intellectual classes, even if it has no longer been the pure Confucianism of Confucius, but one into which many other streams of thought have been assimilated. And with the supremacy of Confucianism, the various historical, poetical and philosophical texts used by Confucianism, most of them written during the Chou dynasty (though not put into final form until the Han), have played a dominant rôle in Chinese thought. These are now generally known as the Chinese Classics.

For this reason Chinese philosophy may be conveniently divided into two periods. One is that period beginning with Confucius, and lasting until about 100 B.C., when Confucianism gained acceptance as the official orthodoxy. This is termed in the present work the Period of the Philosophers. The other period extends from about 100 B.C. until recent times, and is termed the Period of Classical Study. It is the first of these two periods that is dealt with in the present volume.

---

[1] See p. 403.

REVISIONS AND ADDITIONS
FOR THE SECOND EDITION

By the Translator

Save for the present added section, the text of this edition remains unchanged from that of the first edition as published by Henri Vetch in Peiping in 1937.

Were the translation to be prepared now, instead of fifteen years ago, there is little doubt that it could be improved in both style and accuracy, and that inconsistencies between it and the translation of Volume II, now being published for the first time, could be avoided. For example, Chinese words, which in Volume II are consistently romanized as *yi*, are thus romanized in the present volume only when occurring in the first syllable of proper names; otherwise they appear as *i*.

To retranslate the entire volume would, however, entail an effort and expense incommensurate with the resulting gains. Therefore, the present section has been prepared as a more feasible alternative. In it will be found not only corrections of typographical errors and errors in translation or interpretation, but also suggestions for stylistic improvement and changes designed to ensure greater consistency with the second volume. Finally, it contains a fair amount of bibliographical and other information that is totally new, including a summary of Fung Yu-lan's *Supplement to a History of Chinese Philosophy*.

I. General Comments

(1) Early references to *yin* and *yang*, the Five Elements, etc. (ch. 3): Many scholars would be skeptical of the attempt here made to prove the early existence of these and other philosophical concepts on the basis of conversations quoted from such works as the *Tso Chuan* and *Kuo Yü*. Though the events described in these works are probably for the most part historical, their recorded conversations probably contain many literary embroideries, especially when referring to concepts which, to judge from other works, became generally current only in later times. The same caution applies to the ostensibly early references to the trigrams and hexagrams of the *I Ching*, as cited on pp. 380-383, though less forcibly, since the original corpus of that work itself dates back to the beginning of the Chou dynasty.

(2) Life of Confucius (p. 43): What is here given is the traditional account, which is probably not accurate on all points, especially when it says that Confucius became Prime Minister of Lu. Cf. H. G. Creel, *Confucius, the Man and the Myth* (New York: John Day, 1949), ch. 4, esp. pp. 37 ff.

(3) Confucius and the Rectification of Names (pp. 59-62): This doc-

trine, though attributed to Confucius in the *Lun Yü*, is believed by many scholars to be a later Confucian elaboration. Cf. Creel, *op. cit.*, pp. 221, 321-322.

(4) Confucius and the *I Ching* (pp. 65, 381, 400): Here again many scholars doubt that Confucius himself had any particular connection with this work, though it became closely associated with Confucianism in later times. Cf. Creel, *op. cit.*, pp. 105-106.

(5) Mencius and the so-called "Right of Revolution" (ch. 6, sect. 3, esp. pp. 113, 117): This famous doctrine is not explicitly named here or described with the clarity that other scholars might think it deserves. Baldly stated, Mencius' theory seems to have been that a sovereign is confirmed in his rule by receiving from Heaven its Mandate or Decree (*Ming*); that should he rule badly, however, he then forfeits this Mandate; and that it thereupon becomes legitimate for the people to revolt and establish another ruler in his place, to whom Heaven then transfers its Mandate. Cf. the *Mencius*, Ib, 6 and 8; Va, 5-6; Vb, 9; VIIa, 31. This theory has had important practical results in later Chinese political history.

(6) Dating and identification of Lao Tzŭ (pp. 170-172): See also the articles by H. H. Dubs in *Journal of the American Oriental Society*, Vols. 61 (1941), 215-224, and 62 (1942), 300-304; also by D. Bodde in *ibid.*, Vols. 62 (1942), 8-13, and 64 (1944), 24-27. According to Dubs, Lao Tzŭ's son, Tsung (mentioned in the *Shih Chi* quotation cited on p. 171 as having been enfeoffed at Tuan-kan), is to be equated with a Tuan-kan Ch'ung 崇 who is mentioned in another text under the year 273 B.C. This would mean that Lao Tzŭ himself lived around the year 300 B.C. or somewhat earlier.

(7) Confucian political philosophy as representing the point of view of the people (p. 312, first sentence): This statement seemingly conflicts with the obvious aristocratic bias of early Confucianism. What Professor Fung undoubtedly means is that Confucianism, though intended primarily as a way of life for the ruling class, has nevertheless always defined good government as one that serves the needs of the people as a whole, and not merely those of the ruler.

II. Terms

Chü tzŭ, "Leader" (pp. 76, 82, 195, 246, 248), more literally means "Great Master."

Ch'un Ch'iu period (p. xvii and passim) = Spring and Autumn period.

Emperor and empire (pp. 59, 96-97, and passim) are respectively renditions of *T'ien Tzŭ*, "Son of Heaven," and *T'ien hsia*, "all under Heaven." Politically speaking, they are anachronistic for periods prior to the creation of the first genuine Chinese emperor and empire in 221 B.C. Ideologically speaking, however, the belief was already prevalent before this time that the Chinese sovereign, in theory at least, was ruler of the entire civilized world. This concept, in fact, is implied by the very term *T'ien hsia*. Cf. Tjan Tjoe-som, "On the Rendering of the Word Ti as 'Emperor,'" *Journal of the American Oriental Society*, Vol. 71 (1951), 115-121.

Fu-yung="attached territory" (p. 110).

Huo jan chih ch'i, "moving force" (p. 131), is a mistake for *hao* 浩 *jan chih ch'i*, "all-embracing force." This serious error occurred because of the graphic similarity between the characters *huo* and *hao*.

Jen, "human-heartedness" (pp. 69 f. and passim), also translated as benevolence, love, perfect virtue, etc., is in Vol. II almost always translated as "love," for reasons indicated in the Preface of that volume.

Mao ts'ai and *hsiao lien* (p. 17) respectively mean "abundantly talented" and "filial and incorruptible."

Pa, "feudal Leader" (pp. xvii, xxxvi, 112, 299-300, 312), is in Vol. II translated as "Lord-Protector" or "Tyrant" (in the ancient Greek sense).

Period of Classical Study (p. xix) or Period of Study of the Classics (pp. 17, 403) are renditions of a term which in Vol. II is translated as Period of Classical Learning.

Po shih, "scholars of wide learning" (pp. 15-16, 404), is in Vol. II translated as "erudits."

San t'ung, "Three Systems" (p. 27), is in Vol. II translated as "Three Sequences."

Scholar (pp. 52, 54, 109-110, 335) is not a good translation for *shih*, which in Chou feudal times was a general term for the lesser members of the ruling aristocracy, especially those trained for specific official positions. Thus there were at that time military *shih* as well as civil *shih*, and it was only in post-feudal times that the word came to be primarily applied to men of letters.

T'ai chi, "Great Ultimate" (p. 384), is in Vol. II translated as "Supreme Ultimate."

Wu wei, "non-activity" (p. 186 and passim), does not really mean the complete absence of all activity, but only of such as is forced, artificial, and unspontaneous. Hence another possible rendition for the term is "non-assertion."

III. BIBLIOGRAPHY

Unless otherwise indicated, the entries in this section are arranged according to their sequence in the Bibliography of this volume, pp. 410-422.

(1) *Corrections and Additions*

Sect. Ia (pp. 410-416):

I Ching: Legge's 1899 translation is the 2nd edition. For a new English version of the German translation by Richard Wilhelm, see Bibliography of Vol. II.

Kung-sun Lung-tzŭ: Full reference for Forke's translation is vol. 34 (1901-02), pp. 1-100.

Li Yün: Full reference for Legge's translation is Vol. 27, pp. 364-393.

Lieh-tzŭ: Full title of the Giles translation is *Taoist Teachings from the Book of Lieh Tzŭ.*

Lun Heng: Full reference for Alfred Forke's translation is *Lun-Heng*, 2 vols. (London: Luzac & Co., 1907; Berlin: Georg Reimer, 1911).

Lun Yü: Add translation of Arthur Waley, *The Analects of Confucius* (London: Allen & Unwin, 1938).

Mencius: Correct "six books" to "seven books."

Shih Ching: Add translation of Arthur Waley, *The Book of Songs* (London: Allen & Unwin, 1937).

Shu Ching: Legge's 1899 translation is the 2nd edition. For "first millennium B.C." read "beginning of the first millennium B.C." For a new English translation by Bernhard Karlgren, see Bibliography of Vol. II under *Shu Ching.*

Ta Hsüeh: Full reference for Legge's translation is Vol. 28, pp. 411-424. For the new translation by E. R. Hughes of this and the *Chung Yung* (listed earlier on p. 411), see Bibliography of Vol. II.

Yüeh Ling: Full reference for Legge's translation is Vol. 27 (not 17), pp. 249-310.

Sect. Ib (pp. 416-418):

Han-fei-tzŭ: Add translation of chs. 1-30 by W. K. Liao, *The Complete Works of Han Fei Tzŭ, a Classic of Chinese Legalism* (London: Probsthain, 1939), Vol. 1. Vol. II published 1959. The very important ch. 49 has been separately translated by Liao as "Five Vermin" in *T'ien Hsia Monthly*, Shanghai, Vol. 10 (1940), pp. 179-196, and the similarly important ch. 50 as "Learned Celebrities" in *Harvard Journal of Asiatic Studies*, Vol. 3 (1938), pp. 161-171.

K'ung-tzŭ Chia-yü: Add translation of sects. 1-10 (*chüan* 1-2) by R. P. Kramers, *K'ung Tzŭ Chia Yü, the School Sayings of Confucius* (Leiden: E. J. Brill, 1950). Dr. Kramers believes that the work in its present form was compiled in the third century A.D., though it incorporates earlier materials.

Kung-yang Chuan: If the author, as reputed, was actually a disciple of Tzŭ-hsia (himself a disciple of Confucius), this would date his work earlier than the beginning of the Han dynasty.

Li Chi of Elder Tai: Add translation of Richard Wilhelm, *Li Gi, das Buch der Sitte des älteren und jüngeren Dai* (Jena: E. Diederichs, 1930).

Sect. IIb (pp. 419-422):

Ch'e Yü-feng, *Lu Chai Chi.* The character for *Chai* is a misprint for 齋. The same misprint occurs on p. 422 under Wang Po.

Ku Shih Pien (cited on p. 421 under Fung Yu-lan, Ku Chieh-kang, and Liu Chieh, and on p. 422 under Yü Yung-liang) : Published in Peiping as follows: Vols. 1, 1926; 2, 1930; 3, 1931; 4, 1933; 5, 1935.

Hsia Tseng-yu: Add 3 vols., 1904. Republished as *Chung-ƙuo Ku-tai Shih* (History of Ancient China), Shanghai: Commercial Press, 1933.

Hu Shih, *Chung-ƙuo Che-hsüeh Shih Ta-ƙang*: Add Shanghai: Commercial Press, 1st ed., 1919 (many later editions).

Hui Tung: *Hsü Ching Chieh* is an abbreviation for *Huang-Ch'ing Ching-chieh Hsü-pien*, on which see Bibliography of Vol. II under *Po Hu T'ung*.

Liu Ju-lin: Add Peiping, 1929. Correct page reference is 171, not 172.

Tai Tung-yüan: For edition used, see Bibliography of Vol. II. The quotation cited on p. 287 of the present volume is from *chüan* 2, p. 91 of that edition.

Wang Fu: Correct *Chien Fu Lun* to *Ch'ien Fu Lun*.

Wang Ming-sheng: The fourth character of the title, inadvertently omitted, should be 商

(2) *English Titles*

All titles of Chinese works cited in Vol. II have been translated into English, whereas this practice has been followed only in part in the present volume. The following are English equivalents for some (not all) of the remaining untranslated titles:

Sect. Ia (pp. 410-416):

I-wen Chih = Treatise on Literature
Li Sao = Encountering Sorrow
Lü-shih Ch'un Ch'iu = Spring and Autumn of Mr. Lü
Lun Heng = Critical Essays

Sect. Ib (pp. 416-418):

Ch'u Tz'ŭ: Yü Fu = The Fisherman; *Yüan Yu* = The Distant Wandering
Ch'un-ch'iu Fan-lu = Luxuriant Dew of the Spring and Autumn Annals
K'ung-tzŭ Chia-yü = The School Sayings of Confucius [not "Sayings of the Confucian School"]
Shuo-wen Chieh-tzŭ = Explanation of Script and Elucidation of Characters
Shuo Yüan = Park of Discourses

Sect. IIb (pp. 419-422):

Ch'en Chung-fan, *Chu-tzŭ T'ung-i* = A General Survey of the Philosophers
Ch'eng Fu-hsin, *Meng-tzŭ Nien-p'u* = A Chronological Biography of Mencius
Ch'eng Yüan-ying, *Nan-hua Chen-ching Chu-su* = Commentary on the *Chuang-tzŭ*
Chia I, *Lun Shih Cheng Su* = A Memorial on Timeliness in Government

Chiao Hsün, *Lun-yü Pu-su* = A Supplementary Commentary on the *Analects*

Chiao Hsün, *Meng-tzŭ Cheng-i* = Correct Meaning of the *Mencius*

Chu Hsi, *Meng-tzŭ Chi-chu* = Collected Commentaries on the *Mencius*

Huang Pai-chia, *Sung Yüan Hsüeh-an* = Writings of Sung and Yüan Philosophers. [Pai-chia's father, Huang Tsung-hsi, was the main compiler of this work, and it is under Huang Tsung-hsi that it is listed in the Bibliography of Vol. II.]

K'ang Yu-wei, *Hsin-hsüeh Wei-ching K'ao* = Study of the Classics Forged During the Hsin Period

Kao Heng, *Lao-tzŭ Cheng-ku* = Correct Commentary on the *Lao-tzŭ*

Ku Chieh-kang, *Ku Shih Pien* = A Symposium on Ancient Chinese History

Ku Yen-wu, *Jih Chih Lu* = Daily Record of Knowledge

Liu Chieh, *Hung Fan Su-cheng* = Survey of the *Grand Norm*

Ma Hsü-lun, *Chuang-tzŭ Nien-piao* = Chronology of Chuang Tzŭ

Ou-yang Hsiu, *I T'ung Tzŭ Wen* = Questions by Young People on the *Changes*

Sun I-jang, *Mo-tzŭ Hou-yü* = Further Remarks on the *Mo-tzŭ*

Tai Tung-yüan, *Meng-tzŭ Tzŭ-i Su-cheng* = General Survey of the Meaning of the *Mencius*

Teng Kao-ching, *Mo Ching Hsin-shih* = A New Interpretation of the Mohist Canons

Ts'ui Shih, *Shih-chi T'an-yüan* = Investigation of the Origins of the *Historical Records*

Wang Chung, *Hsün-tzŭ Nien-piao* = Chronology of Hsün Tzŭ

Wang Chung, *Lao-tzŭ K'ao-i* = Study of Variants in the *Lao-tzŭ*

Wang Kuo-wei, *Han Wei Po-shih K'ao* = Study of the Erudits of the Han and Wei Dynasties

In addition to the foregoing, the following are the translations of a few other Chinese titles not listed in the Bibliography, but mentioned elsewhere in the text:

p. 44: *T'uan* = Decisions; *Hsi* = Hsi *Tz'ŭ* = The Great Appendix; *Hsiang* = Images; *Shuo Kua* = Discussion of the Trigrams; *Wen Yen* = Words of the Text.

pp. 161, 169: *Chü Yün* (for which read *Chu Yün*) = Dominant Cycles

p. 228: *Chiu Shao* = The Nine Chants; *Hsien Ch'ih* = The Hsien Pool.

p. 320: *Ku Fen* = Solitary Indignation; *Wu Tu* = The Five Vermin; *Nei Wai Chu Shuo* = Inner and Outer Congeries of Sayings; *Shuo Lin* = Collected Persuasions; *Shuo Nan* = Difficulties in the Way of Persuasion.

IV. Proper Names and Dates

In accordance with common Chinese practice, a few persons are referred to in this volume by their "style," instead of by personal name. The following list gives them their correct personal names (after the equation signs), and also corrects misspellings of other names:

An, prince of Chiao-hsi = Ang, prince of Chiao-hsi (p. 171)
Ch'e Yü-feng = Ch'e Jo-shui 若水 (pp. 368, 419)
Chi Tiao = Ch'i-tiao (p. 150, twice)
Hsieh Hsi-shen = Hsieh Chiang 絳 (p. 208)
Kuan I Wu (p. 50) = Kuan Chung (cf. p. 19, etc.)
Lu Hui-ch'ing = Lü Hui-ch'ing (p. 180)
Meng Chang = Meng-ch'ang (p. 314)
Tai Tung-yüan = Tai Chen 震 (pp. 287, 421)
Wang Yang-ming = Wang Shou-jen 守仁 (pp. 2, 4-5, 72, 281, 363)

The Chinese characters for two names (not listed in the Index) have been omitted:

Chiang Mou 江袤 (p. 225, note 1)   Li I 李頤 (p. 219)

The following titles of rulers and legendary culture heroes (for which see the Index) could, for the sake of greater clarity, be consistently translated as follows:

Fu Hsi = Subduer of Animals (pp. xv-xvi, xxxvi, 317, 379)
Shen Nung = the Divine Farmer or Divine Husbandman (pp. xv-xvi, xxxvi, 138, and passim)
Huang-ti = the Yellow Emperor (pp. xv, xxxvi, 138, and passim)
Ch'in Shih-huang-ti = the First Sovereign Emperor of Ch'in, or simply the First Emperor (pp. xviii, 10, 13, and passim)
Wen-ti = Emperor Wen (pp. 16, 171, 174)
Wu-ti = Emperor Wu (pp. xix, 17-18, 403-405)

Some names, such as Ch'un Shen, Hsin Ling, Tzǔ Hsia, Tzǔ Kung, Tzǔ Ssǔ, etc., would be better hyphenated as Ch'un-shen, Hsin-ling, Tzǔ-hsia, Tzǔ-kung, Tzǔ-ssǔ, etc.

The dates of a few persons, given incorrectly or unprecisely in the text, are corrected in the following table:

Hsieh Hsi-shen (i.e., Hsieh Chiang, see above) = 995-1039 (p. 208)
Huang Pai-chia = born 1643 (pp. 294, 420)
Kuo Hsiang = died A.D. 312 (pp. 198-199, 226, 236, 240, 242)
Liu Hsiang = 79-8 B.C. (pp. 150, 412, 418)
Liu Hsin = ca. 46 B.C.-A.D. 23 (pp. 16, 21, 412)
Lu Chiu-yüan = 1139-93 (pp. 72, 281, 363)
Teng Hsi = died 501 B.C. (p. 194)
Wang Ch'ung = A.D. 27-ca. 100 (pp. 147, 213)
Wang Mang = usurped the throne A.D. 9-23 (p. 19)
Wang Yang-ming (i.e., Wang Shou-jen, see above) = 1472-1529 (pp. 2, 4-5, 72, 281, 363)

The following table slightly corrects the chronology of a few dynasties in accordance with the dates used in Vol. II:

Former Han = 206 B.C.-A.D. 24 (p. 280)
Chin = 265-419 (pp. 1, 6, 19, 133, 219, 244)
Ming = 1368-1643 (pp. 1, 244)
Ch'ing = 1644-1911 (pp. 1, 76)

Rather than speak of 776 B.C. as the first authentic date in Chinese history (pp. xv-xvi, xxxvi), it would be better to say that all systems of chronology agree after 841 B.C.

V. Other Revisions and Additions

l. or ls.=line or lines; n.= note; para.=paragraph; sect.=section; bot.= bottom. For example, bot. l. 3=third line from bottom of page (not counting footnotes). Items prefixed by asterisks are those for which the corrections are factually important.

p. 3, bot. l. 7: have we mentioned = we have mentioned
p. 4, para. 1, bot. l. 4: than of the West = than that of the West
*p. 15, middle: books of poetry = *Book of Odes* [i.e., the *Shih Ching*]; books of history = *Book of History* [i.e., the *Shu Ching*]
*p. 17, middle: the Marquis Wei Ch'i and Wu An = the Marquises of Wei-ch'i and of Wu-an
p. 19, sect. 5, l. 5: criticial = critical
p. 29, bot. l. 10: Wu Nu = Wu Nü
p. 42, bot. l. 5: historians = officials
p. 47, l. 3: common people = people in general
p. 49, bot. ls. 14-13: for bringing culture to large masses of people = who popularized them
p. 53, bot. l. 13: whether certain three disciples = whether a certain three disciples
*p. 54, ls. 5-6: Since Heaven is not yet ready to destroy this cause of truth = Since Heaven has not yet destroyed this culture [Cf. pp. 56, 58, where the same passage is quoted.]
p. 55, bot. l. 4: on th = on the
pp. 61, below, and 62, above: *Cheng* = *Ch'eng; Tao Wu* = *T'ao Wu* [three occurrences of each]
p. 69, n. 2: Lucuis = Lucius
p. 72, l. 17: ownselves = own selves
p. 74, middle para., l. 1: it self = itself
p. 78, bot. l. 7: were not descended from the House of Chou = were descended from the Hsia
p. 85, bot. l. 3: common people = people
p. 90, l. 12: *she* = *se*
p. 91, ls. 14-15: alternatively = alternately

*p. 114, l. 11: IIa = IIIa

*p. 119, sect. 4, ls. 3-4: But why should such a government function? How is it possible? = But how ought such a government to function? How is it possible for it to do so?

*p. 120, l. 17: Ib, 6 = Ib, 5

p. 121, l. 13: or of a spring = or a spring

p. 129, bot. l. 19: passes through = passes

p. 146, ls. 21-22: delete "and is subjective, or internal."

p. 146, bot. l. 13: *ch'ang* = *chang*

*p. 162, middle: each one follows that one which it cannot overcome = each one follows that one by which it cannot be overcome

p. 163, bot. ls. 6-5 and 2: crooked and straight = crooked or straight

p. 170, bot. l. 5: (school of) = (schools of)

p. 174, bot. ls. 2-1: the dynasty = a dynasty

p. 176, bot. l. 13: the the people = the people

p. 177, bot. l. 9: appelation = appellation

*p. 178, para. 4, ls. 4-5: Of the invariable Non-being, we wish to see its secret essences. Of the invariable Being, = Therefore through the invariable Non-being, we wish to see its (*Tao's*) secret essences. Through the invariable Being,

*p. 181, bot. l. 9: (ch. 74) = (ch. 79)

*p. 186, bot. l. 11: (ch. 39) = (ch. 75)

p. 199, l. 18: speak of ocean = speak of the ocean

p. 215, n. 2: *Chen-shing* = *Chen-ching*

*p. 223, sect. 2, ls. 7-9: How can it be so low? = Where can it be lower than this?; How can it be still lower = Where can it be still lower?; How can it be even lower? = And where even lower?

p. 231, para. 2, bot. l. 3: would all be unable = are all unable

p. 237, ls. 8-9: child and a mature man = child or a mature man

*p. 241, bot. l. 4: 'I have abandoned my body,' said Yen Hui, 'and discarded = 'My limbs are nerveless and my intelligence is dimmed,' said Yen Hui. 'I have abandoned my body and discarded

*p. 246, ls. 5-6: The words translated "the Five Princes" are quite possibly a proper name, in which case the phrase, "followers of the Five Princes," should be translated "followers of Wu Hou"

*p. 250, ls. 6-7: is beneficial = is for what is beneficial; is harmful = is for what is harmful

p. 252, l. 4: the qualities = all the qualities

*p. 256, bot. l. 16: are each separate kinds, and can respond = are the same in that they can respond

p. 259, middle: comparison (*pi*) = comparison (*p'i*)

*p. 263, ls. 14, 17-18, 24-25, and bot. l. 4; also p. 264, bot. l. 17: part and whole relationship = corporeal relationship

p. 267, bot. l. 9: are 'multiple = are a 'multiple

*p. 273, ls. 19-21: Huo and Tsang are not proper names, but mean "bonds-man" and "bondswoman" (i.e., male and female slave) respectively. Hence the text should read: "A bondsman (*huo*) is a man. To love a bondsman is to love a man. A bondswoman (*tsang*) is a man (i.e., a person). To love a bondswoman is to love a man," etc.

*p. 279, ls. 13-14: Hsün Ch'ing lost his Lan-ling position = Hsün Ch'ing lost his position, whereupon he remained a resident of Lan-ling

p. 283, bot. ls. 5-4: nature of a thousand = natures of a thousand; begin-ning of Heaven = beginnings of Heaven

p. 285, l. 19: and to desire = and yet to desire

p. 287, middle para., and l. 1 of next para.: man on the street = man in the street

p. 291, bot. l. of middle para.: What does not allow that to harm this = What does not allow one thing to harm another

*p. 294, middle: erects artificialities, like a boat that cuts through the water = creates artificialities, just as a boat creates waves through its movement.

p. 296, bot. l. 3: Because = In the fact that

p. 308, lower para., ls. 1-2: Propositions are that which combine the names of several actualities in order to express one idea = Propositions are the combination of names of different actualities wherewith to dis-cuss one idea [Cf. middle of same page, where this is quoted.]

*p. 313, bot. l. 4: 543 B.C. = 536 B.C.

*p. 314, n. 1: pp. 558 and 732 = pp. 609 and 732

p. 315, ls. 12-14: discrimination = particularism [two occurrences]

p. 316, sect. 2, l. 3: changes to the old order = changes in the old order

p. 331, l. 6: is concerned in something he is especially proficient in = has that in which he is especially proficient

p. 331, bot. l. 14: free and spontaneous = self

p. 332, bot. ls. 14-13: manifestation of rewards = manifestations of rewards

p. 338, bot. l. 16: not coming up to = falling short

p. 339, bot. l. 13: differentiated = distinguished

p. 341, l. 5: Because they = Because these

p. 341, l. 15: feel resentment and revolt = are resentful and rebellious

p. 354, ls. 7-8: with a benignity = benignly

p. 360, bot. l. 2: Institute filial piety = "Institute filial piety

p. 361, n. 1, l. 1: scource = source

p. 362, bot. ls. 16-15: became complete . . . being complete = became ex-tended . . . being extended

p. 363, para. 1, bot. l. 2: that later scholars = than later scholars

p. 364, middle: without knowing to stop = without knowing where to stop

p. 364, bot. ls. 4-3, and p. 365, ls. 3 and 20: empire = the world [four oc-currences]

p. 368, l. 11: not confused = unconfused

p. 378, bot. l. 1: Delete "and Sun Yat-sen"

p. 379, bot. l. 6: to substitute = to substitute for

*p. 382, bot. l. 10: wood and rain = wood and wind

p. 391, bot. l. 10: offer mankind with ways = offer mankind ways

p. 391, bot. l. 17: He also points out = He further points out

p. 392, middle: he will be as safe if bound to a = he will be as safe as if bound to a

*p. 397, para. 3: therefore fire is bright externally . . . therefore water is bright internally = therefore the fire of the sun is bright externally . . . therefore the water of the moon is bright internally

*p. 397, para. 4: Hence the furred and feathered classes of creatures, and those that fly and walk, pertain to *yang*; while the armored, scaled and hibernating classes of creatures pertain to *yin* = The furred and feathered classes of creatures are those that fly and walk, and therefore pertain to *yang*; while the armored and scaled creatures are those that hibernate, and therefore pertain to *yin*

p. 405, l. 15: Ch'un Ch'ui = Ch'un Ch'iu

p. 440, 2nd column, next-to-last entry: unbending mind = unbearing mind

p. 450, entry under *Te*, l. 2: 226 = 227

p. 453, entry under "war, opposition to, of Mencius": 195 = 95-6, 195

p. 455: the first character in *yü ching* is incorrect (cf. p. 262); the character for *yüan* (analogy) is incorrect (see under analogy)

VI. FUNG YU-LAN'S *SUPPLEMENT TO A HISTORY OF CHINESE PHILOSOPHY*[1]

This *Supplement* is a reprint of several articles, some of which it may be useful to summarize here. Two are in English,[2] the remainder in Chinese. Among the latter, that entitled "The Philosophy of History of the Ch'in and Han Dynasties" deals with the theories of history associated with the Five Elements, Three Sequences, and Three Ages.[3]

All three of these theories, the author points out, agree on the following points: (1) History is not static, but ever moves through a determined sequence of epochs or phases. (2) This movement does not imply divine purpose, but is the result of non-spiritual forces. (3) The changes generated by it do not occur in piecemeal fashion, but are integrated; that is to say, they affect the institutions of each successive epoch in their totality. (4) History is always right; that is to say, the institutions of each epoch

[1] *Chung-kuo Che-hsüeh Shih Pu* (Shanghai: Commercial Press, 1936). The following discussion will be more meaningful if read after the reading of the main text of this volume.

[2] A brief paper, "Philosophy in Contemporary China" (originally read before the Eighth Congress of International Philosophy, Prague, 1934), and the longer "Why China Has No Science" (originally published in *International Journal of Ethics*, Vol. 32, no. 3, April, 1922).

[3] See respectively the present volume, pp. 159 ff., and Vol II, chap. 2, sects. 11-12.

are inevitable and fitting for that epoch. (5) The Five Element and Three Sequence theories are both cyclical, whereas that of the Three Ages is evolutionary or progressive. All three, however, agree that the process of history is dialectical; that is, that whatever happens in one epoch is inevitably the result of what happened in the preceding epoch. (6) Underlying these changes, however, there are certain cultural values that remain unchanged and eternally valid, without which human society could not exist. In discussing these six common concepts, the author points out that several are reminiscent of Western materialistic philosophies of history, notably Marxism.

Most of the *Supplement*, however, is devoted to three articles in which the author presents his theory of the origin of the six major schools of ancient Chinese thought: Confucian, Mohist, Names (or Dialectician), Legalist, *Yin-yang*, and Taoist. All these schools, he believes, arose out of the disintegration of the old fixed feudal society that characterized the latter centuries of the Chou period. Many men, as the result of this disintegration, lost their hereditary positions in the various states, and thus were obliged to become professional educators, politicians, military experts, and the like, who offered their specialized skills to anyone who would support them. The result was that education, formerly almost entirely restricted to men attached to specific public offices, became broadened to reach a wider circle. Confucius is the first man of this sort known to have spent part of his life as a "private" teacher rather than a public official.[4]

More specifically, the six major schools originated as follows:

(1) *Confucian school*: This arose from the *ju* or literati (see the present volume, p. 48) who were specialists in the rituals or *li* that played such an important part in the lives of the aristocracy. The result is that Confucianism became the rationalized expression of upper-class morality. This explains its emphasis on correct ritualistic behavior, on such cultural activities as music, on a graded love (stemming from the familial relationships of the strongly hierarchical feudal society of Chou times), and on the ruler as a moral example to his people. The author devotes considerable space to refuting the alternative theory of Hu Shih, according to which the *ju* were the descendants—cultured but politically impotent—of the people of the earlier Shang dynasty.

(2) *Mohist school*: This arose from men who had specialized in the military arts. Though, like the *ju*, these professional warriors had originally belonged to the aristocracy, they in late Chou times were increasingly recruited from the lower classes, becoming known as the *hsieh* or "knights" (on whom see this volume, pp. 83-84). Thus the Mohist phi-

---

[4] See also Fung Yu-lan, *A Short History of Chinese Philosophy*, edited by D. Bodde (New York: Macmillan, 1948), chap. 3, where the author indicates wherein his theory differs from the somewhat similar but more rigid theory originally advanced by Liu Hsin (ca. 46 B.C.-A.D. 23).

losophy which arose from this group was a rationalized expression of the ethics of the lower classes in general, and of the professional military class in particular. This appears in the Mohist doctrine of universal and egalitarian love (stemming from the "share-and-share alike" psychology of the professional *hsieh*), in its doctrine of Agreement with the Superior (characteristic of military groups the world over, and exemplified in its own closely knit organization), in its unsophisticated belief in spirits (contrasting with the upper-class skepticism of the Confucianists on the subject), in its utilitarianism and insistence upon simplicity of living, and in its opposition to the ceremonials and music of the Confucianists.

On one important point, however, the Mohists differed sharply from the ordinary *hsieh*, for whereas the latter were bravos willing to fight for anyone who would employ them, the former preached universal love and condemned all warfare save that waged in self-defence. This is why nine chapters in the *Mo-tzŭ* are devoted to the techniques of defensive war, including the building of instruments for resisting the siege of cities, which in turn explains the interest of the Later Mohists in mathematics and physics. When the Mohists finally disappeared as an organized school, it was because their lower-class ethics were far less palatable to the ruling group than were those of the Confucianists. Traces of somewhat similar ideas, however, have survived among the members of Chinese secret societies of later times, as well as among such groups of Robin Hood-like bandits as those portrayed in the famous novel, *Shui Hu Chuan* (All Men Are Brothers).

(3) *School of Names*: This originated from men who had specialized in the art of debate, and who used their talents on behalf of clients engaged in lawsuits. Through their tricks of sophistry, we are told, they were able to turn right into wrong, and wrong into right. A famous early "lawyer" of this sort is Teng Hsi (died 501 B.C.), who, though himself earlier than the actual School of Names, has become linked to it in later times (see this volume, pp. 194-195).

(4) *Legalist school*: This originated from men who were professional politicians, dedicated to the creating of a strong and centralized machinery of state for the rulers they served. As active statesmen themselves, their approach to politics was more direct and practical than that of any of the other schools. Hence it is wrong, despite their title, to regard them as primarily jurists, since they used law as only one of several practical techniques for achieving their purpose. The statesman Kuan Chung (died 645 B.C.), though living prior to the Legalist school, came to be regarded as a Legalist, owing to his achievements in the field of practical statesmanship.

(5) *Yin-yang school*: This, as pointed out in the present volume (p. 159), originated from men who had specialized in such occult arts as astrology and divination. The fact that the activities of this group were

in some ways analogous to those of the ritualists from which the Confucian school originated, helps explain, perhaps, the synthesis of the two schools that took place during the Han dynasty.

(6) *Taoist school*: This, as pointed out in the present volume (pp. 133 ff.), originated from educated men who, unlike those of the other schools, tried to escape the disorders of their day by retiring into the world of nature. Among such men, living amid natural surroundings, there gradually developed the concept of *Tao* as the eternal Way of Nature which all men should follow, and the consequent distrust of all human institutions as perverters of the natural order.

The Five Emperors :
Fu Hsi
Shen Nung, the Divine Farmer
Huang-ti, the Yellow Emperor
Shao Hao
Chuan Hsü
Yao (2357 ?-2256 ? B.C.)
Shun (2255 ?-2206 ?)

The Three Dynasties (*San tai* 三 代, Hsia, Shang, Chou) :

1—Hsia dynasty (2205 ?-1766 ?) :

Yü (2205 ?-2198 ?)
Chieh (1818 ?-1766 ?)

2—Shang or Yin dynasty (1766 ?-1123 ?) :

T'ang (1783 ?-1754 ?)
Chou (1154 ?-1123 ?)

3—Chou dynasty (1122 ?-256 B.C.) :

King Wen (1184 ?-1135 ?)
King Wu (1134 ?-1116 ?)
Duke of Chou is regent to young king following King Wu.
Sun eclipse of 776 B.C., the first authentic recorded date.

Ch'un Ch'iu or ' Spring and Autumn ' period (722-481)

Duke Huan of Ch'i (685-643) is first *Pa* (feudal Leader).
Confucius (551-479)

---

[1] For the chronology from Confucius onward, see the more detailed Chronological Table of the Philosophers, pp. 408-409.

CHAPTER I

INTRODUCTION

There are three questions that must often occur to all persons interested in the history of Chinese thought. First, what is the nature of Chinese philosophy, and what contribution has it to make to the world? Secondly, is it true, as is often said, that Chinese philosophy lacks system? And thirdly, is it true that there is no such thing as growth in Chinese philosophy?

The first of these questions can best be answered by briefly comparing Chinese with western philosophy. If we examine the problems studied by what, in China, during the Wei (A.D. 220-265) and Chin (265-420) dynasties, was called the 'learning of the mystery' (*hsüan hsüeh* 玄 學); by what during the Sung (A.D. 960-1279) and Ming (1368-1644) dynasties was called the 'learning of the truth' (*tao hsüeh* 道 學); and by what during the Ch'ing dynasty (1644-1912) was called the 'learning of the principles' (*i li chih hsüeh* 義 理 之 學), we find that these problems resemble to a considerable degree those of western philosophy.

In the West, philosophy has been conveniently divided into such divisions as metaphysics, ethics, epistemology, logic, etc. . And likewise in China already in the fifth century B.C., we find reference being made to the discourse of Confucius on 'human nature and the ways of Heaven' (*Lun Yü*, V, 12). Thus already in this quotation there are mentioned two of the divisions of western philosophic thought: 'human nature' corresponds roughly to ethics, and the 'ways of Heaven' to metaphysics. As for the other divisions, such as logic and epistemology, they in China have been touched on only by the thinkers of the Period of the Philosophers (extending from Confucius to about 100 B.C.), and have been neglected by later Chinese thinkers (for example, those of the Sung and Ming periods). In one way, to be sure, this later philosophy can be said to have developed a methodology, when it discussed what it called 'the method of conducting study.' This method, however, was not primarily for the seeking of knowledge, but rather for self-cultivation; it was not for the search of truth, but for the search of good.

Chinese philosophy, then, as far as regards methodology in the western sense, holds a humble position when compared with the philosophy of the West or of India. This arises more from the fact that the Chinese have paid little attention to methodology, than from their incapacity to develop it. Chinese philosophers for the most part have not regarded knowledge as something valuable in itself, and so have not sought knowledge for the sake of knowledge; and even in the case of knowledge of a practical sort that might have a direct bearing upon human happiness, Chinese philosophers have preferred to apply this knowledge to actual conduct that would lead directly to this happiness, rather than to hold what they considered to be empty discussions about it. For this reason the Chinese have not regarded the writing of books purely to establish doctrines, as in itself a goal of the highest importance. Most Chinese philosophic schools have taught the way of what is called the ' Inner Sage and Outer King.' The Inner Sage is a person who has established virtue in himself; the Outer King is one who has accomplished great deeds in the world. The highest ideal for a man is at once to possess the virtue of a Sage and the accomplishment of a ruler, and so become what is called a Sage-king, or what Plato would term the Philosopher-king.

In China, therefore, it was only when a Sage had failed to gain the position of a ruler (or at least of an official), in which he might carry his principles into practice, that he turned to the writing of books as a means of establishing his doctrines; and hence this last course was looked upon by Chinese philosophers as one to be followed only when no other alternative offered. For this reason there are comparatively few works in Chinese philosophical literature written in a complete form and offering a unified presentation; the case has generally been that the philosopher himself, or his disciples, have simply grouped together a series of miscellaneous writings into an unconnected whole. Because of this fact, even though the doctrines of a Chinese philosopher may in themselves be quite justifiable, the arguments used to support them often fall short because they are too simple or disconnected.[1]

Chinese philosophy, in short, has always laid stress upon what man is (i.e., his moral qualities), rather than what he has (i.e., his intellectual and material capacities). If a man is a Sage, he remains a Sage even if he is completely lacking in intellectual knowledge; if he is an evil man, he remains evil even though he may have boundless knowledge. The philosopher Wang Yang-ming (A.D. 1473-1529) has compared the Sage to pure gold, holding that a man need only have a pure quality to be a Sage, regardless of the extent of his knowledge or his other abilities. These may differ among different persons, just as eight pounds differs from nine pounds of gold in weight,

---

[1] Another possible explanation for this fact is that in ancient times, before the invention of paper, writings were made in China by being scratched out on strips of bamboo. Because of the clumsiness of the material, these writings were naturally made as brief and concise as possible. And so by the time of the invention of paper, supposedly in A.D. 105, this style of writing had become a habit, a fact which helps to account for the extreme ellipticity of the Chinese classical written language.

whereas the quality of the gold remains in both cases the same. The quality of gold pertains to the ' what it is ' aspect of things, whereas its amount pertains to the side of ' what it has.' Chinese thinkers stress ' what it is,' and not ' what it has,' and so have not greatly emphasized pure knowledge. This is one reason why China has had only the beginnings of science, and has lacked a properly developed system of science.[1]

Epistemology has likewise not formed an important part of Chinese philosophy, not only because Chinese philosophy has not cared to pursue knowledge purely for its own sake, but also because it does not demarcate clearly the distinction between the individual and the universe. A very important feature of modern western history has been the consciousness by the ego of itself. Once it has consciousness of itself, the world immediately becomes separated into two : the ego and the non-ego, or what is subjective and what is objective. From this division arises the problem of how the subjective ego can have knowledge of the objective non-ego, and from this arises the great emphasis which western philosophy has laid upon epistemology. In Chinese thought, however, there has been no clear consciousness by the ego of itself, and so there has been equally little attention paid to the division between the ego and the non-ego ; therefore epistemology has likewise not become a major problem.[2]

Logic is a requirement for dialectic discussion, and hence since most schools of Chinese philosophy have not striven greatly to establish arguments to support their doctrines, there have been few men, aside from those of the School of Names, who have been interested in examining the processes and methods of thinking ; and this school, unfortunately, had but a fleeting existence. Hence logic, like epistemology, has failed to be developed in China.

Chinese philosophy also, because of its special stress on human affairs, has not put equal emphasis on metaphysics. In all of the divisions of philosophy which have we mentioned, western philosophy has made great developments, whereas this has not been the case with all of them in China. Chinese philosophy, on the other hand, because of its emphasis upon the way of the ' Inner Sage,' has delved deeply into the methods of self-cultivation, that is, what it calls ' the method of conducting study.' And in this respect China truly has a great contribution to offer.

---

[1] Cf. my ' Why China has no science,' in the International Journal of Ethics, Vol. 32, No. 3.

[2] It is true that certain schools of Buddhism have in China delved quite deeply into the problem of the ego and the non-ego. These schools represent primarily Indian rather than Chinese thought, however, and hence have failed, in their original form at least, to become an integral part of the main current of Chinese thought, which has continued for the most part to pay little attention to the problems arising from the recognition of the distinction between ego and non-ego.—Tr.

The above already partially answers the second of our three questions: Is it true that Chinese philosophy lacks system? As far as the *presentation* of ideas is concerned, it is certainly true that there are comparatively few Chinese philosophical works that display unity and orderly sequence; therefore it is commonly said that Chinese philosophy lacks system. Nevertheless, what is called system may be divided into two categories, the *formal* and the *real*, which have no necessary connection with one another. It may be admitted that Chinese philosophy lacks formal system; but if one were to say that it therefore lacks any real system, meaning that there is no organic unity of ideas to be found in Chinese philosophy, it would be equivalent to saying that Chinese philosophy is not philosophy, and that China has no philosophy. The earlier Greek philosophy also lacked formal system. Thus Socrates wrote no books himself, Plato used the dialogue form in his writings, and it was not until Aristotle that a clear and ordered exposition was given on every problem. Hence if we judge from the point of view of formal presentation, Aristotle's philosophy is comparatively systematic, yet in so far as the actual content of the philosophy is concerned, Plato's philosophy is equally systematic. According to what has just been said, philosophy in order to be philosophy, must have *real* system, and although Chinese philosophy, formally speaking, is less systematic than of the West, in its actual content it has just as much system as does western philosophy. This being so, the important duty of the historian of philosophy is to find within a philosophy that lacks *formal* system, its underlying *real* system.

This search for the real system underlying any philosophy leads us to the third of our questions: Is it true that there is no such thing as progressive growth in Chinese philosophy? When we study history, we see that social organization tends to move from the less complex to the more complex, and knowledge from the less distinct to the more distinct. Men of later times base themselves on the experience of earlier men, and thus can utilize all that has happened before them. For this reason the movement of history is one of progress, a tendency which we can also perceive at work when we come to examine Chinese philosophy. The problems and scope of Chinese philosophy from the Han dynasty onward are not so numerous and comprehensive as those of the philosophy that preceded it, and yet the later philosophy is certainly more clearly expounded than the earlier one. Those who have not studied the question carefully, upon seeing how Confucius discusses the ideas of the ancient semi-mythical Emperors, Yao and Shun; how later philosophers, such as Tung Chung-shu (179?-104? B.C.), Chu Hsi (A.D. 1130-1200), and Wang Yang-ming (1473-1529), discuss those of Confucius; and how even in modern times Tai Tung-yüan (1723-1777) and K'ang Yu-wei (1858-1927) have continued to discuss Confucius, may conclude that the ancients have contributed all and the moderns nothing. Actually, however, when we think that such men as Tung Chung-shu and Wang Yang-ming are not merely commentators, and that their philosophic works represent their own philosophy and not that preceding them, the progressive growth of Chinese philosophy becomes apparent.

Some persons say that the ideas of such men as Tung Chung-shu and Wang Yang-ming are already to be found in germ in earlier Confucian writings. Hence, they reason, since these ideas are merely further developments made by these men, how can they be accepted as forming a philosophy of their own? What new contribution can they make? Even granted, however, that the philosophies of these two men are mere developments of earlier thought, we cannot regard them lightly. For development means progress. When the child grows into the mature man, the adult merely develops the capacities already inherent in the child; and when the chicken's egg becomes the chicken, the chicken merely develops the capacities already inherent in the egg. Yet how can we, on the basis of this fact, conclude that the child is therefore the adult, and the chicken egg is the chicken? One might point out that, using Aristotle's terminology, a great difference exists between potentiality and actuality. Movement from such potentiality toward actuality constitutes progress. If we wish to see the progressive growth of Chinese philosophy, we must first relegate the material of each period to that period, and the doctrines of each man to that man. Once this has been done, the true aspect of the philosophy of each school becomes evident, and the growth of Chinese philosophy also becomes manifest.

Former scholars of Chinese civilization have either not known how to separate genuine ancient writings from forgeries, or when they did, they have considered such forgeries to lack any value. This, too, has been one cause for the apparent lack of growth in Chinese philosophy. We historians of Chinese philosophy maintain that such a distinction between false and genuine writings must be made, because only after this has been done can the true aspect of the thought of each period be made evident. If we are merely studying philosophy, and not the history of philosophy, we need only trouble ourselves about whether or not the doctrines appearing in a certain work are valuable in themselves, and need not bother about discovering to what man and period they actually belong. The mere fact that a book is a forgery, does not, in such a case, destroy that book's value, provided that the ideas it expresses have value in themselves. Nor does the mere genuineness of a book make that book valuable, if what it says is in itself of no value.

Even from the viewpoint of the historian of philosophy, however, a forgery may have value. For though it cannot be used to represent the thought of the period to which it has been falsely attributed, yet it remains as the thought of the period when it was actually produced, and so can be utilized as material for the philosophic history of that period. The chapter in the *Lieh-tzŭ*, for example, which supposedly describes the doctrines of Yang Chu (who lived probably in the fourth century B.C.), does not, as a matter of fact, represent his true doctrines ; and yet it remains a systematic exposition of a much later current of thought existing during the Wei (A.D. 220-265) and Chin (265-420) dynasties, thus becoming excellent material for the study of the philosophy of these dynasties. Therefore to say that this chapter is a forgery does not destroy its value, but merely necessitates moving its period to a later time. And the necessity for thus shifting it consists only in the desire to make written history accord with actual history, that is, to gain the truth.

CHAPTER II

A GENERAL SURVEY OF THE PERIOD OF THE PHILOSOPHERS

1—BEGINNINGS OF THE PERIOD

It was not until the Chou dynasty (1122 ?-256 B.C.) that the civilization of China assumed a definite pattern. Confucius has said : " Chou had the advantage of surveying the two preceding dynasties. How replete is its culture ! I follow Chou " (*Lun Yü*, III, 14). In his mind, the Chou literature and institutions could, indeed, serve to " transmit the spirit of the Sages of the past, and open the way to scholars to come." Confucius, in fact, as we know from the *Lun Yü*, strove his entire life to perpetuate the achievements of King Wen and the Duke of Chou, two of the Chou dynasty founders.[1]

While material is not lacking from which we may study the culture, literature and institutions of the early Chou, yet up to the time of Confucius (551-479 B.C.) there appears to have been no one who composed any sort of literary work in a private capacity, that is to say, who wrote books under his own name expressing his own opinions, in contradistinction to authorship of historical works or other writings directly connected with official position.[2] The historian, Chang Hsüeh-ch'eng (1738-1801) points this out as follows :

" During the early period there were no instances of the (private) writing of books. The officials and teachers preserved the literary records, and the historians made record of the passage of events. The purpose of written words was already sufficiently fulfilled if by their means the various officials might govern, and the common people be kept under surveillance. . . . . . It was only when the times were out of joint that teachers and scholars set up their (own private) teachings, and it was in so doing that our Master (i.e., Confucius) was superior to (the legendary Emperors) Yao and Shun." [3]

Save for the tendency in this quotation to idealize the past, these words seem close to the truth. China's ancient period was essentially

---

[1] *Cf.* ch. 4, sect. 2, pp. 54 f.

[2] The books traditionally ascribed to non-official writers living prior to Confucius are all later forgeries, and the *Tao Te Ching*, supposedly written by Lao Tzŭ before the time of Confucius, is also much later. *Cf.* ch. 8, sect. 1, pp. 170-172.

[3] *Cf. Wen-shih T'ung-i, Shih-chiao* section, pt. I, in the *Chang-shih I-shu, chüan* 1, p. 23.

one of aristocratic rule, in which those who held political power were, at the same time, the possessors of material wealth and held a monopoly on education. In other words, the political and economic hierarchy, and the hierarchy of learning, coincided, so that between officials and scholars there was no real distinction. This ruling nobility, occupied as it was with political matters, had little time left for the writing of books; while because it held the political authority, it could directly express its ideals, when these existed, in concrete action, out of which could later be formulated the texts used in government instruction. There was, then, no real need for literary writings (i.e., those unconnected with the government administration). Such writing was regarded as something to be done only when there remained no other alternative of action. This is an attitude that has been characteristic of many of the philosophic schools of China.

Philosophy, however, if it is to be the systematic manifestation of thought, must necessarily find expression in the writings of private individuals. Prior to Confucius there were no such writings, and we, to-day, cannot know whether or not any kind of systematic philosophy actually did exist. Although Confucius himself did not compose any literary works, there was a period during his life when he neither held office nor engaged in any other activity, but devoted himself exclusively to the exposition of his teachings. To-day, there is nothing exceptional in such conduct, but at that early time it was truly an unheard of precedent. Confucius, furthermore, according to what his disciples have recorded of him, was the first to develop a true system of thought.[1] In these respects, then, he certainly occupies a pioneer's position in the history of Chinese philosophy, and hence the fact that later generations have honored him as The Teacher, although perhaps not entirely justified, was also not wholly unreasonable. Confucius is, therefore, the first individual to be studied in this history of Chinese philosophy, because prior to him there existed, in all probability, no system of thought worthy of being called philosophy.

2—CAUSES FOR THE DEVELOPMENT OF PHILOSOPHY DURING THE PERIOD

Among the subdivisions in the history of Chinese philosophy, that of the Period of the Philosophers occupies a primary position, whether it be in the number of its schools, the variety of problems discussed by these, its broad scope, penetrating interest of investigations, or dynamic richness of its manifestations. Special causes must

---

[1] What have been considered as the writings of private individuals prior to the Warring States period (403-221 B.C.) need not necessarily have been written by these individuals themselves. *Cf.* sect. 5, pp. 19-20.

have existed to give it such unique qualities, and these will be taken up later.[1]

In Chinese history, the age extending from the Ch'un Ch'iu period (722-481 B.C.) down to the beginning of the Han dynasty (206 B.C.—A.D. 220) is one of general emancipation, in which political institutions, social organization, and economic structure all undergo fundamental changes. The early Chou dynasty had been a time of rule by a feudal aristocracy, under which each of the feudal states was either a fief created by the Royal House of Chou, or a state that had already existed before the Chou. The ministers and great officers within these states were also all members of the ruling houses, and held their offices in hereditary perpetuity, whereas the common people were denied all share in the political power. The Tso Chuan,[2] under the year 535 B.C., states : "As the days have their divisions in periods of ten each, so men have their ten ranks. It is by these that inferiors serve their superiors, and that superiors perform their duties to the spirits. Therefore the king has the ruler (of each feudal state) as his subject ; the rulers have the great prefects as their subjects ; the prefects have their officers ; the officers have their subalterns ; the subalterns have their multitude of petty officers ; the petty officers have their assistants ; the assistants have their employees ; the employees have their menials. For the menials there are helpers, for the horses there are grooms, and for the cattle there are cowherds. And thus there is provision for all things " (p. 616). With a government thus maintained by a feudal aristocracy holding hereditary offices and fiefs, it was inevitable that the social organization should also be based on an elaborately graded hierarchy.

The outstanding characteristic of the Warring States period (403-221 B.C.), however, was the gradual collapse of the feudal system, resulting in marked changes in the earlier rigid social system. This phenomenon was marked, on the one hand, by the rise during the Warring States period of many men, of comparatively lowly origin, to positions of great political importance ; while on the other

---

[1] Dr. Hu Shih, in discussing the trends of the period prior to Lao Tzŭ and Confucius, comes to the conclusion that at that time " the government was especially dark and unenlightened, society was especially disordered, poverty and wealth were especially unequally distributed, and the life of the people was extremely bitter. With the existence of such conditions, it was natural that these should have produced reactions of thought of many kinds." Cf. his Chung-kuo Che-hsüeh Shih Ta-kang, p. 42. But there has hardly been a dynasty in China's history when such conditions have not to some extent been present. Hence while not without bearing upon the appearance of the ancient philosophy, they cannot, in themselves, be held sufficiently to account for its unique qualities. Liang Ch'i-ch'ao (1873-1929) has already pointed this out, but the factors which he in his turn holds to be of special importance, also existed during later ages, and so are likewise insufficient explanations in themselves. Cf. Liang Jen-kung Hsüeh-shu Chiang-yen Chi, pp. 11 and 16 of the first collection.

[2] A detailed history, written probably during the third century B.C., which covers the same period as, and greatly elaborates upon, the brief chronicles found in the Ch'un Ch'iu history from which the Ch'un Ch'iu period derives its name.—TR.

it was marked by the fall from power of many of the former ruling families. This movement reached a climax in 221 B.C., when Ch'in Shih-huang succeeded in unifying all China under the rule of the House of Ch'in, and dealt feudalism a decisive blow by relegating the royal families of all states except that of Ch'in to the level of the common people.

During the several years of civil warfare following the death of Ch'in Shih-huang in 210, it is true, several of the members of the former ruling families succeeded in raising armies and returning to power. And when unification was once more effected through the founding of the Han dynasty in 206, the first Han ruler, despite the fact that he was of plebeian origin, allowed feudalism to be revived by granting fiefs to his meritorious ministers and to members of his own family, as well as by allowing several of the former nobles to retain their rank. The feudalism thus revived was only a shadow of its former self, however, and especially after a revolt of several nobles occurring in 154 B.C., it was greatly circumscribed by restrictive measures, among them one that all governing officials should be directly appointed by the Emperor. The final blow was dealt by the gradual establishment of the examination system under Emperor Wu-ti (140-87 B.C.), so that after that time feudalism almost ceased to exist.

We can find evidence of the breakdown of feudalism beginning already during the Ch'un Ch'iu period. Thus it is recorded that Ning Ch'i, a mere carter, while feeding his oxen, attracted the attention of Duke Huan of Ch'i (685-643) and so obtained office, and that Po-li Hsi, while a prisoner of war, was ransomed by Duke Mu of Ch'in (659-621) for the price of five ram skins, and so became the latter's counsellor. At the same time there was a corresponding decline of the aristocracy. The *Tso Chuan*, for example, under the year 539 B.C., makes the statement: " The Luan, the Ch'i, the Hsü, the Yüan, the Hu, the Hsü, the Ch'ing and the Po (all descendants of great families of the Chin state) are reduced to the position of menials " (p. 589). Confucius himself originally belonged to the nobility of the state of Sung, but because of poverty entered office and was ' once a keeper of stores,' and ' once in charge of the public fields,' both lowly offices. All this indicates how the nobles were gradually losing their positions and becoming a part of the common people. Institutions that had been based upon a graded hierarchy likewise gradually fell into oblivion, so that by the time of the founding of the Han dynasty, it was possible for a man of the common people to become Emperor.

Intimately connected with feudalism was the economic system known as the ' well-field ' or *ching t'ien* 井 田 system. According to this, all land was divided into large squares, each subdivided into

---

[1] *Cf. Mencius*, Vb, 5.

nine smaller squares.   Each of the eight outer of these nine squares
was cultivated by one family for its own use, while the produce of
the ninth central square, cultivated in common by the eight families
and called the ' public field,' went to the support of the overlord.'
Under this system all land was ultimately the possession of the ruler.
Thus the *Shih Ching* (Book of Odes) says :   " Under the whole heaven,
every spot is the sovereign's ground ; to the borders of the land,
every individual is the sovereign's subject " (II, vi, Ode 1, 2).   The
Tso Chuan also states, under the year 535 :   " The dominion of the
Son of Heaven extends everywhere.   The feudal lords have their own
defined boundaries.   Such is the ancient rule.   Within the state
and the kingdom, what ground is there which is not the ruler's ?
What individual of all whom the ground supports is there who is
not the ruler's subject ? " (p. 616).

Such terms as ' king's land ' and ' king's subject ' were in later
times regarded merely as political concepts, but during the ancient
feudal period they had economic meaning as well.   The graded
ranks of society which have been described above, were likewise
not merely political and social, but also economic.   In short, under
the feudal system of ancient China, the Emperor (Son of Heaven),
feudal lords, and ministers and great officers, were all overlords of
the people, not only politically but also economically, and so when
the Royal House of Chou invested the male branches of its family
with land grants, those so invested acted both as political rulers and
as economic landholders.   These feudal lords, in their turn, divided
this land among their relatives, and these relatives again among the
common people for cultivation.   The common people could not
themselves own land, and so were mere agricultural serfs of their
political and economic overlords.   Consequently we find that the
records of government of that time, as found in the *Tso Chuan* and
Kuo Yü,[2] describe no more than the activities of a few noble families.
As for the common people, they were required to labor for their
lords in time of peace, while in time of war they had to be ready to
sacrifice their lives.   The relationship of serf to overlord is described
by the historian Hsia Tseng-yu (died 1924), in his discussion of the
question of the *ching t'ien* system :

" The truth of the matter probably is that the land was exclusively
the possession of the nobles, and that the peasants were all attached
to this land as serfs, this forming the basis of the distinction between
the ordinary people and those who belonged to the Hundred Names
(i.e., who bore a recognized family name, in contradistinction to the

---

[1] The word *ching* 井 or ' well,' as used here, represents the square ⊞ fields, into
which the land was divided under this system.—Tr.

[2] ' Sayings of the States,' a collection of historical conversations which cover about
the same period as does the *Tso Chuan*, but are grouped geographically according to states,
rather than chronologically.—Tr.

nameless serfs). Such a condition lasted until Lord Shang,¹ of the
state of Ch'in, abolished it. This act marked one phase of social
progress." ²

The histories tell us that Shang Yang " destroyed the *ching t'ien*
system, and opened up the paths and furrows between the fields ......
The (ancient) imperial regulations thereupon disappeared, there was no
limit upon encroachments, and among the common people there
were wealthy men who accumulated millions (of coins)." ³ This
suffices to indicate how the agricultural serfs, following their emancipation, seized power and came into control of large land areas. The
decay of the so-called *ching t'ien* system was undoubtedly one of the
main tendencies of that age, and Shang Yang, by making especial
use of political power, did no more than give it a conscious and
exemplary impetus.

Another of the tendencies of the time was the changing status
of the merchant class, which gradually rose till it acquired great
power. Thus the *Ch'ien Han Shu* (History of the Former Han
Dynasty) says :

" With the decline of the House of Chou, the rites (*li* 禮) and
laws fell into decay. ...... This falling away (from the old standards)
reached the point where, among the officials and common people,
there were none who did not set the (old) regulations aside and spurn
what is fundamental (i.e., agriculture). The peasants became few
and the merchants numerous. Of grain there was an insufficiency,
and of (commercial) goods a superfluity. ...... Thereupon the
merchants circulated goods difficult to obtain (i.e., rare and expensive
luxuries) ; the artisans produced objects of no real utility ; and the
scholars instituted conduct subversive to morality, in their pursuit
for immediate benefits and search for worldly wealth. ...... The
grounds and groves of the rich underwent elaborate adornment,
and their dogs and horses had a superabundance of meat and grain. ...
While among the common people, though all were (theoretically)
of equal rank, some by the power of their wealth could become the
masters of others " (ch. 91, p. 3).

Looked at from the economic point of view, it is evident that
the collapse of feudalism was brought about through this continual
increase of economic power of the former agricultural serfs and of
the merchants, with the result that ' the imperial regulations disappeared,' and ' the rites and laws fell into decay.' The rise of
the merchant class may be illustrated by such men as Hsien Kao,
who, while a mere merchant, successfully protected the state of Cheng

---

¹ Shang Yang (died 338 B.C.), the famous legalist statesman who introduced many
new economic measures into Ch'in. For his ideas, see ch. 13, sect. 3, p. 319.—TR.

² Cf. his *Chung-kuo Li-shih* (A History of China), I, 258.

³ *Ch'ien Han Shu*, ch. 24, pt. i, p. 7.

from the surprise attack of the state of Ch'in ; [1] and Lü Pu-wei, who, from the position of a great trader, became minister of the Ch'in state.[2] These are examples of ' capitalists ' who became directly involved in the political affairs of their day. Summing up, we may say that the breakdown of the system of hereditary revenues, and of the *ching t'ien* organization ; the emancipation of the common people ; and the amassing of private fortunes, were the outstanding changes in the economic structure during the ancient period.[3]

These great changes began during the Ch'un Ch'iu period, and came to an end about the middle of the Han dynasty. During these several centuries the novelty of the conditions which the Chinese were called upon to face, and the scope of the freedom obtained from former restrictions, stand, with the sole exception of present-day conditions, unparalleled in China's history. Even in world history, in fact, excepting again the present era, they are at least fully comparable to similar phenomena elsewhere.

During this gradual collapse of the old institutions of an entire society, it is natural that there should have been a tendency among con-servatives, seeing that " the spirit of the age is not that of antiquity, and men's hearts daily decline," to arise as upholders of these ancient institutions. Confucius was a man of this sort. Before these in-stitutions had been shaken, the mere fact of their antiquity was sufficient to awaken in men's hearts a feeling of reverence. But once that they were actually in danger, their preservers, if they wished to gain a genuine following among the rulers and men of their time, were

---

[1] When the Ch'in army was marching to attack Cheng in 627 B.C., he frightened it away by meeting it with twelve oxen which he presented on behalf of the Cheng ruler, thus indicating that the intended surprise attack was already known to Cheng. *Cf. Mém. hist.*, II, 39.—Tr.

[2] While a merchant, Lü Pu-wei attached himself to one of the Ch'in princes, and became guardian of the latter's son when the prince died. This son, who is said actually to have been Lü's own son, later became the famed Ch'in Shih-huang-ti, China's first unifier. Lü himself, after being regent, eventually became involved in a court intrigue, and died 235 B.C.—Tr.

[3] The *Tso Chuan*, under the year 526 B.C., records an interesting story :

Hsüan Tzŭ had a ring of jade, the mate of which belonged to a merchant of Cheng, and he begged it from the Earl of Cheng. Tzŭ Ch'an (Prime Minister of Cheng) refused it, ... saying : " Our former ruler, Duke Huan (806-771), came with (some) merchants from Chou. Thus they were associated in cultivating the land, together clearing and opening up this territory, and cutting down its tangled southernwood and orach. They dwelt in it together, and made a covenant of mutual faith, to last through all generations, which said : 'If you (the merchants) do not revolt against me, I will not forcibly interfere in your trade, nor will I demand or seize anything from you. If you derive profit from selling precious objects, I will take no notice of it.' Through this attested covenant, (our rulers and the de-scendants of the merchants) have preserved their mutual relations down to the present day. But now Your Excellency, having come to us on a friendly mission, has told our state forcibly to despoil this merchant. Such would be teaching us to violate a covenant. Would it not be improper ? " (p. 664).

The terms of this covenant, so solemnly recorded, strike us to-day as remarkable, and indicate the humble position of the merchants in early China, when their oppression by the nobility was an ordinary occurrence.

obliged to supply reasons for upholding the past and its institutions. Confucius had already begun this sort of work ; the later Confucians continued it ; and in this rests one of their great contributions.

The general tendency of the time was such, however, that these ancient institutions continued to disintegrate despite the attempts of the Confucians to uphold them. From the age of Confucius onward, there arose men who criticized or opposed these institutions ; who wished to revise them ; who wished to establish new institutions in their place ; or who were opposed to all institutions whatsoever. The age was one of transition, during which the institutions of the past had lost their authority, and those of the new age had not yet been definitely formulated. It was inevitable, then, that it should also be one of uncertainty and divergence. Thus when the Confucians had advanced their arguments for the preservation of the past, other philosophers, holding divergent views, were forced, if they wished to gain a following, to explain in their turn the reasons why they considered their own doctrines superior. The Confucian philosopher, Hsün Tzŭ, refers to this situation when he says about the doctrines of twelve opposing philosophers : " What they support (all) seems reasonable ; their teachings are (all) plausible " (*Hsün-tzŭ*, pp. 78, 79).

In this way men became accustomed to emphasis being laid upon logical presentation, a fact which resulted in the rise of the School of Dialecticians, with its discussions on such subjects as ' the hard and the white, similarity and difference,' and its purely logical interest. Thus we see that the beginnings of rationalism coincide with the beginnings of philosophizing.

A number of quotations from contemporary literature allude to the prevailing intellectual anarchy of the time. The *Mencius* states :

" Sage-kings cease to arise, the feudal lords give rein to their lusts, and unemployed scholars indulge in unreasonable discussions " (III*b*, 9.)

The *Chuang-tzŭ* (ch. 33) says similarly :

" The world is in great confusion, the virtuous and the sage are obscured, morality and virtue have lost their unity, and there are many in the world who have seized a single aspect of the whole for their self enjoyment. . . . . Everyone in the world does what he wishes and is a rule unto himself " (p. 439).

And the *I-wen Chih* (catalogue of the Imperial Han library, forming Chapter XXX of the *Ch'ien Han Shu*) states :

" The various philosophers belonged to ten schools, but there are only nine worthy of notice. They all began when royal control was lessening and the feudal nobles were becoming more powerful and differed widely in what they preferred and disliked. Just so the differing practices of the nine schools swarmed forth and had a common development. Each school picked a single point which was exalted as the good and was discussed so as to win the favor of the feudal lords " (*Aids*, p. 64).

All this serves to indicate the breakdown of the institutions and organization of that time, because of which ' morality and virtue lost their unity,' ' the feudal lords. . . . . differed widely in what they preferred and disliked,' and ' everyone in the world did what he wished and was a rule unto himself.' The philosophy of the Chou dynasty arose out of the freedom of thought and speech of that time, which was itself brought about by the fact that it was also an age of transition and of liberation from former restrictions.[1]

3—THE CLOSE OF THE PERIOD

The end of the Warring States period, which took place in 221 B.C., when Ch'in unified China, is usually regarded as also marking the close of the ancient period of Chinese philosophy. Because Ch'in Shih-huang (in 213 B.C.), ordered the Burning of the Books, and forbade the storage throughout the empire of ' books of poetry, books of history, and the teachings of the various philosophers,' many people consider the Ch'in dynasty as a barbaric time, in which the learning of the past was completely destroyed. Actually, however, Ch'in Shih-huang " merely burned the books which existed among the people, but did not burn those in the official archives. He merely prohibited private teaching, so that (people) would turn toward (the official class of) 'scholars of wide learning' for instruction." [2] Ch'in Shih-huang's aim, in short, and that of his Prime Minister, Li Ssŭ, the man who had first suggested the Burning of the Books, was more to create a standardization of thought, than completely to wipe out the learning of their time.[3] This is indicated by the fact that the ' scholars of wide learning ' [4] whom Ch'in Shih-huang established, included men belonging to all schools of thought.[5]

---

[1] What the *I-wen Chih* says here about the feudal nobles, that they " differed widely in what they preferred and disliked," is, itself, one cause for the flowering of thought that took place during the Warring States period (403-221 B.C.). This becomes evident when we compare this attitude with that of later Emperors, great officials and rich merchants, toward literature and scholarship. Why there should have been this difference between the early and later attitudes, however, cannot be understood without taking into consideration the political, social and economic background of the Ch'un Ch'iu and Warring States periods. The mere support, by rulers and society, of literary activities, is, in itself, not an exclusive characteristic of either of these two periods, and hence need not be dwelt upon.

[2] Ts'ui Shih (1851-1924), *Shih-chi T'an-yüan*, *chüan* 3. *Cf.* also Cheng Ch'iao (1104-1162), *T'ung-chih Hsiao-ch'ou Lüeh*, and K'ang Yu-wei (1858-1927), *Hsin-hsüeh Wei-ching K'ao*.

[3] Present historians are still undecided as to the exact scope and purpose of this Burning of the Books. But even if Ch'in Shih-huang and Li Ssŭ really did intend to destroy all learning of their time, ' so as to make ignorant the common people,' as the traditional account states, the fact that only a few years elapsed between the Burning of the Books in 213, and the establishment of the Han dynasty in 206, would have made such an attempt unsuccessful.

[4] *Po shih* 博士, an official title given to the scholars.—TR.

[5] *Cf.* Wang Kuo-wei (1877-1927), *Han Wei Po-shih K'ao*, *chüan* 4 of the *Kuan T'ang Chi Lin*.

No doubt the regulations made to ensure absolute conformity did cause thought and speech to lose their former freedom, while literary activities received a similar check. Nevertheless the fall of the Ch'in dynasty, occurring soon after the book burning, in 207 B.C., means that the influence could not have been very profound. The philosophic schools again flourished, as a result, during the early part of the Han dynasty, and there are many records in the histories of that time of both rulers and officials who showed the greatest catholicity of thought. We need only cite as an example the Prince of Huai-nan (died 122 B.C.), who induced his entourage to write a book (now known under his name as the *Huai-nan-tzŭ*), in which the doctrines of most of the philosophic schools are indiscriminately accepted.[1]

Liu Hsin (died A.D. 23), the noted compiler of the catalogue of the Han Imperial library, also states in a letter : " Under Wen-ti (179-157), the many books in the empire (which, if not destroyed, had been placed in hiding after Ch'in Shih-huang's order for their destruction), largely reappeared. All the teachings of the philosophers which had been handed down, were placed in the places of official teaching, and 'scholars of wide learning' were appointed to teach them." [2] From this statement we may see that the ' scholars of wide learning ' of Wen-ti's time, like those of Ch'in Shih-huang, included followers of most, if not all, the philosophic schools.

Furthermore, as regards Confucianism, we find that certain important Confucian texts, such as the *Li Chi* (Book of Rites), and the Appendices to the *I Ching* (Book of Changes), contain sections not written by Confucianists until the early years of the Han dynasty ; while it is also not until the beginning of the Han that the study of the *Kung-yang Chuan*[3] becomes important. Confucianism thus does not reach full maturity until the beginning of the Han dynasty. A memorial written by the prominent Confucianist, Tung Chung-shu (179?-104? B.C.), gives us some idea of the character of the time. The memorial (presented probably 136 B.C.), reads :

" The principle of unification in the *Ch'un Ch'iu* is a permanent warp passing through the universe, and an expression of what is proper extending from the past to the present. But the teachers of to-day have diverse standards (*tao* 道), men have diverse doctrines,

---

[1] The *Yen T'ieh Lun* (ch. 8) states : " It is but recently that the princes of Huai-nan and Heng-shan, encouraging literary studies, invited wandering scholars from the four corners of the empire. The Confucianists and Mohists from east of the mountains all congregated between the Chiang and Huai rivers, expounding, arguing, compiling and epitomizing, producing books by the score " (p. 51). From this, it may be seen that, in the time of the Prince of Huai-nan (died 122 B.C.), the Mohist school (*cf.* below, ch. 5) was still in existence.

[2] *Cf.* his biography in the *Ch'ien Han Shu* (ch. 36).

[3] A commentary on the *Ch'un Ch'iu* much studied at that time, until, owing to the influence of Liu Hsin, it was replaced in popular estimation by the *Tso Chuan*.—TR.

and each of the philosophic schools has its own particular position, and differs in the ideas which it teaches.   Hence it is that the rulers possess nothing whereby they may effect general unification, the government statutes having often been changed; while the ruled know not what to cling to.   I, your ignorant servitor, hold that all not within the field of the Six Disciplines [1] or the arts of Confucius, should be cut short and not allowed to progress further. Evil and licentious talk should be put a stop to.   Only after this, can there be a general unification, and can the laws be made distinct, so that the people may know what they are to follow " (*Ch'ien Han Shu*, ch. 56. pp. 20-21).   Again he says :

" Among the things paramount for the upbringing of scholars, none is more important than a university (*t'ai hsüeh* 太 學).   A university is intimately related to (the fostering of) virtuous scholars, and is the foundation of education. . . . . . Your servant desires Your Majesty to erect a university and appoint illustrious teachers for it, for the upbringing of the empire's scholars " (*ibid.*, p. 13).

The *Ch'ien Han Shu* goes on to tell us that " from the beginning of Wu-ti's reign (140-87 B.C.), when the Marquis Wei Ch'i and Wu An had been appointed as prime ministers, Confucianism began to flourish.   With Tung Chung-shu's memorial, Confucius was elevated, and the other schools of philosophy were degraded.   The establishment of officials for education, and the provincial and pre-fectural (degrees of) *mao ts'ai* 茂 材 and *hsiao lien* 孝 廉, all began with Tung Chung-shu " (*ibid.*).   From this time onward, if one wished to gain official position, one had to be an advocate of Confucianism, and this Confucianism furthermore had to be of a sort conforming to that decided upon by the government.   Thus ' the empire's out-standing men were all caught in a single snare,' and the atmosphere of complete freedom of speech and thought, which had been such an outstanding characteristic from the Ch'un Ch'iu time onward, now completely disappeared.

With the putting into practice of Tung Chung-shu's suggestion, the Period of the Philosophers came to an end, and that of the Study of the Classics commenced.[2]   With him also the school of the *Yin-yang* 陰 陽 (the male and female principles of Chinese cosmology), and the Five Elements or Powers (earth, wood, metal, fire and water), was combined with Confucianism and systematized.   After this time Confucius changed from the status of a man to that of a divine being, and the Confucianist school changed into the Confucianist religion.   It was not until the appearance of the so-called ' Old Text ' school of scholarship, that the position of Confucius gradually

---

[1] The *Ch'un Ch'iu, I Ching*, and books of poetry, history, rites, and the music.—TR.

[2] For more about Tung Chung-shu and the rise of Confucianism, see pp. 403 f.

reverted to that of a human being, and the Confucianist religion became once more the Confucianist school.[1]

4—THE CLOSE OF THE ANCIENT PERIOD OF TRANSITION

The political measures taken by Wu-ti and Tung Chung-shu to make all thought conform to a single standard, were the same in purpose as those of Ch'in Shih-huang and Li Ssŭ. How is it, then, that the one group succeeded where the other failed? There are many causes for this, but one certainly worthy of mention is the fact that the great political, social and economic changes, beginning during the Ch'un Ch'iu period, had by the middle of the Han dynasty gradually ceased. And when the characteristic elements of these movements disappeared, the distinctive features of the literary activity of the time also lost the basis for their existence.

It has been said above that these changes all arose out of the disintegration of the old culture and institutions. As this disintegration became more pronounced, contemporary thought became more independent. But after Ch'in conquered the other six states, and in 221 B.C. unified China, the former nobles, except those belonging directly to the House of Ch'in, were all reduced to the level of the common people, and superficially, one might say that the changes taking place from the Ch'un Ch'iu time onward had here come to a conclusion. In reality, however, the dispossessed descendants of these nobles still held a measure of influence, so that when Ch'in Shih-huang died, the aristocratic class again arose, and during the wars preceding the founding of the Han dynasty, the six former states once more raised their old rulers to power. This second recrudescence of the nobility was but a sunset glow, however, coming at the end of the feudal regime, so that when the Han founder pushed his way up from the common people, he was finally able to overthrow all opponents and gain an undivided allegiance. And although he, like his predecessors, gave fiefs to his relatives and meritorious ministers, these fiefs from this time on had only political and not economic significance.

By the middle of the Han, the new political and social order had already gradually become stabilized, and in the sphere of economics the people had become accustomed to the changed conditions arising from the natural economic tendencies of the time. The *Ch'ien Han Shu* says : " Among the common people, though all

---

[1] The question of the ' Old Text ' and ' New Text ' schools of classical interpretation, which, from its rise, about the time of the birth of Christ, down to the present day, has been one of the most hotly debated in Chinese scholarship, is too complicated to be discussed here. Suffice it to say, that the divinity of Confucius, and the authenticity of miraculous deeds attributed to him, has been one of the points of contention between the two schools, and that in this respect, at least, the Old Text school has been more rational and less superstitious than the New Text school. *Cf.* Vol. II of the Chinese edition of the present work, ch. 4, sect. 1.—TR.

were (theoretically) of equal rank, some by the power of their wealth could become the masters of others, while even should they become slaves, they were without resentment " (ch. 91, p. 3). This quotation indicates how, by that time, the people were already amenable to the new economic situation. Although the Han dynasty's policy was one favoring agriculture and restricting commerce, it did not result in any radical changes being made in the social and economic order. The period of transition that had begun during the Ch'un Ch'iu time now reached its close, and with it, its characteristic wealth of thought also disappeared. From the Han dynasty down to the present day, China's political and economic institutions and social organization—excepting for the remarkable socialistic innovations forcibly introduced by Wang Mang, who usurped the throne from A.D. 6 to 23—underwent no fundamental modifications ; and, therefore, the unique qualities of thought that had characterized the Period of the Philosophers did not reappear [1]

5—The Forms of the Early Literature

If we wish to study the development of Chinese philosophy, we must first determine the period and authorship of its texts. In this respect the ancient period presents special difficulties. Among the works formerly supposed to belong to the Ch'un Ch'iu and Warring States epochs, for example, criticial scholarship has now determined that the *Lieh-tzŭ* must in all probability be assigned rather to the Wei (A.D. 220-265) or Chin (265-420) dynasties, and, as such, may be used to exemplify the thought of that time, rather than of the Chou period. On the other hand, there are works generally recognized as being authentic, such as the *Mo-tzŭ* and *Chuang-tzŭ*, which may justifiably be assigned to the ancient period. And yet it is very difficult to determine how much of the thought they contain actually represents the philosophy of Mo Tzŭ and Chuang Tzŭ themselves, the men after whom they are named. As regards this point, a clear understanding of the inherent characteristics of the ancient texts is necessary.

The historian, Chang Hsüeh-ch'eng, has pointed out that the *Kuan-tzŭ*, for example, mentions events occurring after the death of Kuan Chung (noted statesman who died 645 B.C., to whom the work is attributed), while the *Han-fei-tzŭ* (attributed to Han Fei, a Legalist writer who died 233 B.C.), contains a speech made by Li Ssŭ disapproving of Han Fei's policy. It is, therefore, evident that these and other works contain sections that could not have been written by their

---

[1] To many who read these lines, such innovations as those of the statesman Wang An-shih (1021-1086), and China's early use of paper money, will probably come to mind to prove the contrary. These innovations cannot be compared in their lasting effect, however, with such radical changes as the abolition of feudalism and rise of the examination system in the Han dynasty, or with the beginnings of industrialism to-day.—Tr.

supposed authors, but were probably composed by later followers of the same school. Chang suggests that the primary purpose of a writer of ancient times, was to expound the doctrines of his school, so that the question of who was the actual author of the writing, was considered as relatively unimportant. And for this reason the writings of any school were the collective work of that school, rather than the work of any one individual.[1]

This theory is probably correct. The conception of authorship was evidently not wholly clear in early China, so that when we find a book named after a certain man of the Warring States period, or earlier, this does not necessarily mean that the book was originally actually written by that man himself. What part of it was the addition of his followers, and what part was by the original author, was not at that time looked upon as requiring any distinction, and hence to-day cannot for the most part be distinguished any longer.[2]

The books now generally attributed to various Chou dynasty writers should, therefore, be regarded as the products of their schools, rather than of the men themselves. Much has already been done in the critical analysis of such works, so that, for example, we recognize to-day that such portions as the ' Canon ' and ' Exposition of Canon ' of the *Mo-tzǔ* (chs. 40-41 and 42-43 respectively), were probably not written by Mo Tzǔ himself. In the case of such sections as the ' Will of Heaven ' (chs. 26-28) and ' Agreement with the Superior ' (chs. 11-13) of the same book, however, no one dares to decide which parts of them came first and which were later additions. In treating the philosophy of the ancient period, therefore, the present work will simply try to indicate that, during this period, there existed certain schools of philosophy and systems of thought ; but it will not attempt to determine absolutely whether these systems are always actually representative of the individuals by whom they were founded, or have been affected by later modifications.

The philosophy of this latter Chou period, includes chiefly what have long been known as the doctrines of the various philosophers

---

[1] *Cf.* Chang Hsüeh-ch'eng, *Yen-kung* sect., pt. I, in *op. cit.*, *chüan* 4, p. 5.

[2] This has already been frequently noted by Chinese scholars. In all probability what have been handed down to us as pre-Ch'in works, have all passed through the revisions made by the Han scholars. Such books as the *Mo-tzǔ* and *Chuang-tzǔ*, for example, probably did not exist prior to the Ch'in dynasty in the form in which they have come down to us to-day. What existed during the pre-Ch'in period were simply disconnected chapters, and the Han scholars, in arranging this literature, made a selection of all chapters belonging to a certain school, compiled these into one book, and gave this the name of the founder of the school, intending thereby to indicate that the book in question was a product of that school. Besides writings of this type, however, there also exist one or two works that do go back in their present form to the pre-Ch'in period, and have existed as complete books since their beginning. An example of this is the *Lü-shih Ch'un Ch'iu*, a compilation made under the auspices of Ch'in's Prime Minister, Lü Pu-wei (died 235 B.C.). After its completion, we are told, Lü Pu-wei had it hung up on the gate of the city wall so as to show off his own cleverness, a fact from which we may infer that the writing of a full-length book was at that time a rare achievement.

(*chu tzŭ* 諸 子), and, therefore, its age may be fittingly designated as the Period of the Philosophers. These philosophers have been classified by Ssŭ-ma T'an (died 110 B.C.), the father of Ssŭ-ma Ch'ien (compiler of the *Shih Chi*, China's first great general history), as belonging to six schools : that of the *Yin-yang* 陰 陽, that of the literati or Confucians (*ju* 儒), the Mohists (*mo* 墨), that of Names (*ming* 名), the Legalists (*fa* 法), and the Taoists (*tao te* 道 德).[1] To these six schools, Liu Hsin has added those of Agriculture (*nung* 農), Diplomatists (*tsung-heng* 縱 橫), Miscellaneous (*tsa* 雜), and Story-tellers (*hsiao-shuo* 小 說), thus bringing the total up to ten.[2] Some of these schools have no conceivable relationship with philosophy, however, and so in the following pages I shall select only those having philosophical interest, and describe their doctrines in their chronological appearance.

---

[1] In *Shih Chi* or ' Historical Records ' (ch. 130). *Cf.* translation in *Aids*, pp. 51 f.
[2] *Ibid.*, pp. 61 f.

CHAPTER III

PHILOSOPHICAL AND RELIGIOUS THOUGHT PRIOR TO CONFUCIUS

As I pointed out in the preceding chapter, there was in China probably no one before Confucius (551-479 B.C.) who had written any books in a private rather than official capacity. Hence we are dependent upon statements found in the *Shih Ching* (Book of Odes),[1] *Shu Ching* (Book of History),[2] *Tso Chuan* and *Kuo Yü*, to show us the religious and philosophical thought of the period prior to, and including the time of, Confucius, and to give a general picture of the state of human knowledge in China at that period.

1—DIVINE BEINGS

In the time of primitive man the belief was general, not only in China but in other parts of the world, that natural phenomena and human affairs are all under a divine and supernatural control. The *Kuo Yü* gives an example :

"King Chao (of Ch'u, reigned 515-489) asked Kuan I Fu, saying : 'What is meant when the Book of Chou says that Chung and Li succeeded in bringing about that there would no longer be communication between Heaven and Earth ? If such had not been done, would it have been possible for people to ascend to Heaven ? '[3]

"The reply was : 'This is not the meaning. In ancient times people and divine beings did not intermingle. Among the people there were those who were refined and without wiles. They were, moreover, capable of being equable, respectful, sincere and upright. Their knowledge, both in its upper and lower ranges, was capable of conforming to righteousness. Their wisdom could illumine what was distant with its all-pervading brilliance. Their perspicacity could illumine everything. When there were people of this sort, the illustrious spirits (*shen* 神) would descend in them. If men, such

---

[1] A group of three hundred and five court and popular poems, collected from the various feudal states of China, which form one of China's earliest literary remains.—TR.

[2] A collection of speeches, prayers, etc., given on various historical occasions. Many of these are later forgeries, but a few go back to the first millenium or earlier B.C.—TR.

[3] This question has reference to a statement made in the *Shu Ching*, in the section entitled 'The Marquis of Lu on Punishments,' which supposedly dates from the reign of King Mu of Chou (1001-947). *Cf.* p. 257, where Legge translates : "Then he commissioned Chung and Li to make an end to the communications between earth and heaven ; and the descents (of spirits) ceased."—TR.

people were then called sorcerers (*hsi* 覡), and if women, they were called witches (*wu* 巫). It was through such persons that the regulation of the dwelling places of the spirits, their positions (at the sacrifices), and their order of precedence were effected ; it was through them that their sacrifices, sacrificial vessels and seasonal clothing were arranged. . . . .

" ' Thereupon there were officials for Heaven, Earth, spirits, people, and the various creatures, who were called the Five Officials. They had charge over the orderly arrangement of things, so that they should not be mutually confused. This made it possible for the people to be true to themselves and sincere to others, and for the spirits to have illustrious virtue. The people, having their duties differentiated from those of the spirits, were respectful and not unduly familiar. Therefore the spirits conferred prosperous harvest upon them and the people offered things up out of gratitude. Natural calamities did not arrive, and there was an inexhaustible supply of what would be useful.

" ' But with the decline which came under (the legendary Emperor) Shao Hao, the nine Li (tribes) threw virtue into disorder. People and spirits became confusedly mingled, and things could no longer be properly distinguished. Ordinary people then performed the sacrifices, and each family had its own witches, who were utterly lacking in the necessary qualifications. The people exhausted themselves in the sacrifices, without coming to know the happiness (that should result from sacrifice properly performed). Sacrifices were offered up without any order, and people and spirits occupied identical positions. The people disregarded their solemn oaths, and were without a sense of awe. The spirits followed the customs of the people, and were impure in their practice. Prosperous harvest was no longer conferred, and there was nothing to offer for the sacrifices. Natural calamities occurred repeatedly, until there was no one who could complete his natural span of life.

" ' When (the legendary Emperor) Chuan Hsü received (the throne), he commanded Nan Cheng Chung to hold the office of Heaven so as to assemble the spirits there, and Huo Cheng Li to hold the office of Earth so as to assemble the spirits there.[1] They brought about a return of the old standards, and there were no longer any mutual encroachments or over familiarity (between men and spirits). And this is what is meant by the *cutting short of the communication between Heaven and Earth* ' " (*Ch'u Yü*, II, 1).

What is said here shows in a general way the forms of superstition of the early Chinese. From the fact that sorcerers and witches were considered necessary to regulate the dwelling places, positions at the sacrifices, and order of precedence of the spirits, we may see how

---

[1] These are the Chung and Li mentioned above.—Tr.

numerous these spirits were. The fact that the spirits were supposed to be able to bestow happiness, receive sacrifices, and to enter into human beings, shows that they were regarded as anthropomorphic beings. And the statements that " people and spirits were confusedly mingled," " people and spirits held the same position," and " the spirits followed the customs of the people," show us that the actions of these spirits were looked upon as being quite indistinguishable from those of human beings. The Chinese of that time were superstitious and ignorant; they had religious ideas but no philosophy; so that the religion and spirits which they believed in were exactly like those of the Greeks. With the coming of the Hsia and Shang dynasties, when the concept of ' Heaven ' (*T'ien* 天) and ' God ' (*Ti* 帝) arose, a monotheistic belief seems gradually to have gained influence, but at the same time there was no weakening of the old polytheism.

Thus the *Tso Chuan* and *Kuo Yü*, although frequently referring to a Heaven, also continue to speak often about the spirits. For example, in the time of King Li of the Chou dynasty (878-842), someone is reported by the *Kuo Yü* as having said :

" He who is king over men must direct what is beneficial and distribute it to those above and below ; he must bring it about that among spirits, men and creatures, there are none who do not attain their apogee " (*Chou Yü*, I, 4).

The *Tso Chuan*, under the year 706 B.C., records a speech :

" What is meant by morality (on the part of a ruler), is to show loyalty toward the people and sincerity toward the spirits. When the ruler thinks of benefiting the people, that is loyalty. When the priest is truthful in his words, that is sincerity " (p. 48). Again, under the year 684 :

" When there is but small kindness, which does not reach to all, the people will not follow you. . . When there is but small sincerity, which is not perfect, the spirits will not give you happiness " (p. 86).

And the *Kuo Yü* records a speech made apropos of the descent of a divine being which occurred in Hsin in 662 :

" When a state is about to flourish, its ruler is equable, perspicacious, sincere and upright. He is refined, pure, kind and in harmonious equilibrium. His virtue is sufficient to make his sacrifice manifest, and his kindness is sufficient to unify the people. The spirits enjoy his offerings, and the people listen to him. People and spirits are without resentment. Therefore illustrious spirits descend in it (his state), to survey his virtuous government, and scatter happiness to all alike.

" But when a state is about to perish, its ruler is covetous, reckless, perverted and depraved. He is licentious, lazy, rude and careless. . . . . . People and spirits feel hatred (toward the ruler), and have nothing to cling to. Therefore the spirits then also go (to such a country), to watch his dissoluteness and send down calamity. . . . . Looking at the affair from this angle, is not this the spirit of Tan Chu ? " [1] (*Chou Yü*, I, 12).

Likewise in the *Tso Chuan* under the year 655 : " The spirits, regardless who is the man, accept only virtue. . . . . Thus without virtue, the people will not be harmonious and the spirits will not accept the offerings. If the state of Chin seize Yü, and with illustrious virtue present fragrant offerings, will the spirits indeed reject them ? " (p. 146).

In the *Kuo Yü*, under the year 647, it is said that the ruler should : " Pacify the multitude of spirits and put in harmony the myriad of people. Therefore the Ode (III, i, Ode 6, 6,) says : ' He conformed to the example of his ancestors, and the spirits had no occasion for complaint ' " (*Chin Yü*, IV, 22).

The same work reports King Hsiang of Chou as having said in the year 634 B.C. : " Of old, when the early kings of my family held the empire, they marked out a territory of one thousand *li* for their own imperial domain, so as thereby to offer sacrifices to the Supreme Emperor (*Shang Ti* 上 帝), and to the various spirits of the mountains and rivers "
(*Chou Yü*, II, 2).

The same idea is expressed in the *Tso Chuan* under the year 569 : " The ruler is the host of the spirits and the hope of the people " (p. 466). Again under the year 541 : " . . . . . Might this not refer to Chao Meng ? . . . . . He has cast himself off from both spirits and men. The spirits are incensed against him and the people revolt. How can he last long ? " (p. 578).

These quotations indicate how numerous the ancient Chinese considered the spirits to be. Spirits and men are named in the same breath, and the primary duty of the ruler is said to be " pacifying the multitude of spirits and putting in harmony the myriad of people," for if this is not done, " the spirits will be incensed against him and the people will revolt," with the result that he will be unable to maintain his position for long. Moreover, the fact that King Hsiang of Chou speaks of the ' Supreme Emperor ' (*Shang Ti*, i.e., God) at the same time with, but as a being distinct from, the various spirits, indicates that *Shang Ti* was not himself included in their number. Again, the suggestion that the spirit which descended in Hsin might be that of Tan Chu, indicates that some spirits, at least, were supposed to have once been human beings.

Not only do the *Tso Chuan* and *Kuo Yü* contain abundant references to spirits, but the *Mo-tzŭ*, in its section ' On Ghosts ' (ch. 31), gives a number of ancient legends about them. Later, however, this belief in spirits diminished. Confucius, for example, said that

---

[1] Tan Chu was the son of the legendary Emperor Yao, and because of his unworthy conduct, was deprived of the succession, which passed on to the next Sage, Shun.—TR.

" One should respect the spirits, but keep them at a distance " (*Lun Yü*, VI, 20). He " sacrificed (to his ancestors) *as if* they were present, and sacrificed to the spirits *as if* they were present " (*ibid.*, III, 12). Again he is recorded as saying : " When you are still unable to do your duty to men, how can you do your duty to the spirits ? " (*ibid.*, XI, 11). Thus Confucius already adopted a skeptical attitude toward spirits, and believed that even if they did exist, it was better not to discuss them. And Mo Tzŭ, who came after Confucius and who was a believer in spirits, lamented that in his time men's disbelief in spirits had led the world into grave disorder, thus necessitating him to spend much effort attempting to prove their existence.

2—DIVINATION AND MAGIC

The belief was common among the ancient Chinese that a close mutual influence existed between things in the physical universe and human affairs ; therefore all sorts of divination methods were used, through which, by observing noteworthy natural phenomena, future misfortune or prosperity could be predicted. Thus the *I-wen Chih*, the catalogue of the Imperial Han dynasty library, now found in the *Ch'ien Han Shu* (ch. 30), says :

" The arts of divination (*shu shu* 術 數) were all supervised by the historian-diviners, Hsi and Ho, of the Ming T'ang palace.[1] This post of historian has long since fallen into disuse, and the books pertaining to it cannot be complete. Nevertheless, there are still some of these books extant, whereas the men themselves no longer exist. The *I* (Book of Changes) says : 'If there be not the proper men, the Way should not be emptily pursued without them' (p. 399). During the Ch'un Ch'iu period, the state of Lu had Tzŭ Shen, Cheng had Pei Tsao, Chin had Pu Yen, and Sung had Tzŭ Wei. During the period of the Six States (i.e., Warring States), the state of Ch'u had Kan Kung and Wei had Shih Shen Fu. The Han dynasty has had T'ang Tu. These are all men who have obtained a general (knowledge of these magic arts). . . . . When arranged, the arts of divination fall into six classes " (ch. 30, p. 50).

Of these six classes, the first is astrology, of which the *I-wen Chih* says :

" Astrology (*t'ien wen* 天 文) is used to arrange in order the twenty-eight ' mansions ' [2] and note the progressions of the five planets and of the sun and the moon, so as to record thereby the manifestations of fortune and misfortune. It is in this way that the Sage-king conducts government. The *I* says : ' Looking at the signs in the heavens, one thereby ascertains the changes of the seasons ' (p. 231) " (p. 43).

---

[1] The Ming T'ang 明 堂 was the palace in which the Emperor offered sacrifices and gave audience to princes. Hsi and Ho seem to have been two brothers who, according to the traditional account, had charge of the calendar under Emperor Yao.—TR.

[2] *Hsü* 宿, i.e., the twenty-eight Chinese constellations.—TR.

The second is connected with the almanac, of which the *I-wen Chih* says :

" Almanacs (*li p'u* 歷 譜) serve to arrange the positions of the four seasons in order, to adjust the times of the equinoxes and solstices, and to note the concordance of the periods of the sun, moon, and five planets, so as thereby to examine into the actualities of cold and heat, life and death. Therefore the Sage-king must keep the almanac in proper order, so as to define the clothing and color regulations of the Three Systems.[1] Furthermore, by his investigations, he knows the times of the conjunctions of the five planets and the sun and moon, while through his arts, the miseries of calamities and the happinesses of prosperity all appear manifest. These are the arts through which the Sage comes to know the decrees (of Heaven) " (p. 44).

The third is connected with the Five Elements (*wu hsing* 五 行), which are earth, wood, metal, fire and water :

" The Five Elements are the corporeal essences of the Five Constant Virtues.[2] The *Shu* (Book of History) says : 'The first category is called the Five Elements. The second is called reverent practice of the five functions ' (p. 140).[3] This means that the five functions should be used in consonance with the Five Elements. If one's personal appearance, speech, vision, hearing and thought lose their proper order, the Five Elements will fall into confusion and changes will arise in the five planets. For these all proceed from the numbers connected with the almanac, and are divisions of one thing (i.e., of the movements of the Five Elements). Their laws all arise from the revolutions of the Five Powers (i.e., Elements), and if they are extended to their farthest stretch, there is nothing (in the universe) which they will not reach to " (p. 46).

The fourth method is that connected with the stalks of the divination plant, and with the tortoise shell. The first of these was the milfoil: its stalks were manipulated to give various diagrams which could be interpreted by means of the *I Ching* (Book of Changes). In the tortoise shell method, a hole was partly bored through the shell, so that the application of heat would form cracks which could be interpreted as an answer to the question asked. The *I-wen Chih* says of these two divination methods :

" The divination plant (*shih* 蓍) and the tortoise shell (*kuei* 龜) are used by the Sages. The *Shu* says : 'When you have doubts

---

[1] *San t'ung* 三統. This was an idea promulgated by Tung Chung-shu of the Former Han dynasty, who declared that the Hsia dynasty had assumed black as its ruling color, the Shang dynasty had assumed white, and the Chou red, and that these colors and their accompanying clothing would recur in succeeding dynasties in endless succession. *Cf.* the chapter on him in Vol. II of the Chinese edition of this work.—TR.

[2] *Wu ch'ang* 五常. These are the Confucian virtues of benevolence, righteousness, propriety in demeanor, wisdom and good faith (*jen* 仁, *i* 義, *li* 禮, *chih* 智 and *hsin* 信).—TR.

[3] These are personal appearance, speech, vision, hearing and thought.—TR.

about any great matter, consult the tortoise shell and divination
stalks ' (p 146). And the *I* says : ' For making certain of good
and bad fortune, and accomplishing things requiring strenuous
effort, there is nothing better than the divination plant and tortoise
shell. Therefore, when the Superior Man is about to do something or
carry out some action, he asks, making his enquiry in words.
They receive his order, and the answer comes as the echo's response.
Be the subject remote or near, mysterious or deep, he forthwith
knows what will be the coming result. If these were not the most
exquisite things under Heaven, would they be concerned in such an
operation as this ?' (p. 369) " (p. 47).

The fifth consists of miscellaneous divinations :

" Miscellaneous divinations (*tsa chan* 雜 占) serve to keep records
of the phenomena of various things and to observe the manifestations
of good and evil. The *I* says : 'By making divinations about affairs,
one may know the future ' (pp. 464-465). These various methods of
divination are not all of one kind, but that of the dream is most important. Therefore, the Chou dynasty had officials for this form,
and the *Shih* (Book of Odes) has records of dreams about bears,
serpents, and assembled fish and banners, clear signs of (the coming of)
a great man, whereby one may examine good and bad fortune. These
are all collated with the tortoise shell and divination plant " (p. 48).

The sixth is the system of forms :

" The system of forms (*hsing* 形) deals with general statements
about the influencing forces in the entire nine provinces, in order
to erect a walled city, its outer wall, a house or a hut. In this
system of forms, the measurement and number of the bones of men
and of the six domestic animals (the horse, ox, pig, sheep, dog and
fowl) ; also the containing capacities of vessels ; are examined, so as
to find out whether their sound and matter are noble or mean, and
are of good or evil omen. This is like the pitch-pipes, each of which,
according to whether it is long or short, produces its own special
sound. This is not because of the existence of divine beings, but is the
natural result of their own measurement. Thus form and matter are
like the head and tail (of an animal). There are some things which
have form but are without matter ; and some which have matter
but no form. These are fine and abstruse differences " (pp. 49-50).

The most frequently recorded of these six kinds of divination
in the *Tso Chuan* are those of the divination plant, tortoise shell and
the miscellaneous group. The first two are often mentioned, while
the miscellaneous class would include all the divinations of dreams
which the *Tso Chuan* records. The ' system of forms ' is also referred
to in the *Tso Chuan* when it speaks of one Shu Fu, Historian of the
Interior of Chou, who was able to read human physiognomy.'

---

[1] *Tso Chuan*, p. 267.

Likewise, Hsün Tzŭ has a chapter, ' Against Physiognomy,' in which he says : " Among the ancients there was Ku-pu Tzŭ-ch'ing, who examined men's figures and features, and told their good or bad fortune, while, at the present time, there is T'ang Chü of Liang. And the common people praise them " (*Hsün-tzŭ*, p. 67).

The remaining three methods, those connected with astrology, the almanac and the Five Elements, are likewise all mentioned in the *Tso Chuan*. For example, under the year 534 B.C., when the state of Ch'u had annihilated the state of Ch'en :

" The Marquis of Chin asked the historian Chao : ' Is Ch'en now going to disappear ? ' The answer was : ' Not yet. . . . . The House of Ch'en is a branch of the descendants of Chuan Hsü (one of the earliest legendary Emperors). When the year star (i.e., Jupiter, which completes one circuit around the sun every nineteen years) was in the constellation of Shun Huo, (Chuan Hsü's dynasty) was thereby extinguished, and Ch'en will go the same way. At present it is in the Hsi Shui constellation, at the ford of the Milky Way, and (Ch'en) will once again arise' " (p. 623).

Under the year 533 B.C. :

" In summer, in the fourth month, there was a fire in Ch'en. Pei Tsao of Cheng said : ' In five years the state of Ch'en will be re-established ; and after fifty-two years of re-establishment it will finally perish. . . . . Ch'en belongs to the element water. Fire is antagonistic to water, and is under the control of the state of Ch'u. Now the Fire planet (i.e., Mercury) has appeared and kindled this fire in Ch'en, (indicating) the expulsion of Ch'u and re-establishment of Ch'en. Antagonistic elements come to their completion under the number five, and therefore I say it will be five years. The year star (Jupiter) must come five times to the constellation Shun Huo, after which Ch'en will finally perish, and Ch'u will succeed in keeping it in its possession. This is the Way of Heaven, and therefore I say fifty-two years' " (p. 626).

In 532 :

" In spring, in the king's first month, a (strange) star appeared in the constellation of Wu Nu. Pei Tsao of Cheng said to Tzŭ Ch'an : ' In the seventh month, on the cyclical day *wu-tzŭ*, the ruler of Chin will die' " (p. 628).

In 527 :

" In spring, when there was about to be a great sacrifice in the temple of Duke Wu, orders had been given to all the officers to fast. Tzŭ Shen said : ' I fear some misfortune will happen on the day of the great sacrifice, for I have seen a red and black halo which is inauspicious for it ; it is a vapour of death. Will it take effect on the officer in charge of the affair ? ' " (pp. 658-659).'

---

¹ *Cf.* also under the years 525, 524 and 510 (pp. 668, 670, 740).

Some of the methods described in the foregoing quotations are obviously astrological, whereas others are combinations of methods based on the almanac and on the Five Elements. In all of them we find stress laid upon the mutual influence supposed to exist between the 'Way of Heaven' and human affairs. In later times the *Yin-yang* and Five Elements school further elaborated these ideas, which were to exert a profound influence upon the succeeding period of Chinese philosophy.[1]

3—HEAVEN AND GOD

Besides the multitude of ordinary spirits, a Heaven (*T'ien* 天) or God (*Ti* 帝) was supposed to exist, to both of which the *Shu Ching* (Book of History) makes reference in its section, 'The Speech of T'ang':

" The sovereign of Hsia has many crimes and Heaven (*T'ien*) has commanded me to destroy him..... Fearing the Supreme God (*Shang Ti* 上 帝), I dare not but punish him..... and carry out the punishment appointed by Heaven (*T'ien*) " (p. 85).

Here in a speech of less than one hundred and fifty characters, we find Heaven and God referred to three times. Similarly in the *Shih Ching* (Book of Odes):

" Heaven commissioned the swallow to descend and give birth to (the father of our) Shang..... Of old, God (*Ti*) appointed the warlike T'ang (founder of the Shang dynasty) to appoint the princes of each quarter..... He received the appointment without any uncertainty in it..... That Yin (i.e., Shang) should have received the Appointment (of Heaven) was entirely right. ..." (IV, iii, Ode 3).

Within the less than one hundred and fifty characters of this ode of eulogy, we find five references to Heaven, God, and to the receiving of Heaven's Appointment (*ming* 命). Again, in the *Kuo Yü*:

" The Duke of Kuo dreamed that while he was in his ancestral temple, there appeared a supernatural being with a human face, white hair, and tiger's claws grasping a halberd, who stood on the roof ridge of the western corner. The Duke was frightened and started to run away, but the spirit said: 'Do not run away. God (*Ti*) has commanded, saying that (the forces of) Chin have been ordered to enter your gate.' The Duke bowed to the ground. On awakening, he summoned the historian Yin to divine the matter. The latter said to him: 'According to what Your Lordship says, this is Ju Shou (the spirit of the western quarter), who is Heaven's divine executioner. For each of Heaven's affairs there is its proper official' " (*Chin Yü*, II, 4).

In the *Shih Ching*, *Shu Ching*, *Tso Chuan* and *Kuo Yü* there are, then, frequent references to Heaven and God, among them many indicative of an anthropomorphic *Shang Ti*, so numerous that they cannot

---

[1] *Cf.* ch. 7, sect. 7, pp. 159-169.

all be quoted here. From the *Kuo Yü* quotation just given, however, we can form an idea of the relationship supposed to exist between *T'ien* and the spirits. *Shang Ti*, a name which literally translated means 'Supreme Emperor,' seems to have been the highest and supreme authority, who presided over an elaborate hierarchy of spirits (*shen* 神), who were secondary to him and paid him allegiance. This was the religious belief of a large part of the common people of China, and had probably existed since early times.

As for Heaven or *T'ien*, this word occurs in Chinese writings with five different meanings :

(1) A material or physical *T'ien* or sky, that is, the *T'ien* often spoken of in apposition to earth, as in the common phrase which refers to the physical universe as 'Heaven and Earth' (*T'ien Ti* 天 地).

(2) A ruling or presiding *T'ien*, that is, one such as is meant in the phrase, 'Imperial Heaven Supreme Emperor' (*Huang T'ien Shang Ti* 皇 天 上 帝), in which anthropomorphic *T'ien* and *Ti* are signified.

(3) A fatalistic *T'ien*, equivalent to the concept of Fate (*ming* 命), a term applied to all those events in human life over which man himself has no control. This is the *T'ien* Mencius refers to when he says : "As to the accomplishment of a great deed, that is with *T'ien*" (*Mencius*, I*b*, 14).

(4) A naturalistic *T'ien*, that is, one equivalent to the English word Nature. This is the sort of *T'ien* described in the 'Discussion on *T'ien*' in the *Hsün-tzŭ* (ch. 17).

(5) An ethical *T'ien*, that is, one having a moral principle and which is the highest primordial principle of the universe. This is the sort of *T'ien* which the *Chung Yung* (Doctrine of the Mean) refers to in its opening sentence when it says : "What *T'ien* confers (on man) is called his nature."

The references to *T'ien* in the *Shih Ching*, *Shu Ching*, *Tso Chuan* and *Kuo Yü*, excluding those to the purely physical sky of type one, seem generally to designate the ruling or presiding anthropomorphic *T'ien* of type two ; which also seems to be the type of *T'ien* spoken of by Confucius in the *Lun Yü*.

4—Beginnings of Enlightenment

During the Ch'un Ch'iu period there were also a few literati who were more enlightened, and who gradually came to lose their belief in supernatural spirits and in the so-called 'Way of Heaven.' The *Tso Chuan* records speeches by several such men, as for example under the year 662 B.C. :

"It is when a state is about to flourish that (its ruler) listens to his people ; when it is about to perish, he listens to the spirits" (p. 120).

Under the year 524 :
" The Way of Heaven is distant, while that of man is near. We cannot reach to the former ; what means have we of knowing it ? "
(p. 671).

And under the year 509 :
" The state of Hsieh makes its appeal to men, while that of Sung makes its appeal to spirits. The offence of Sung is great "
(p. 744).

Though these statements do not absolutely deny the existence of a ' Way of Heaven ' and of supernatural spirits, they already adopt the skeptical attitude expressed by Confucius that one " should respect the spirits, but keep them at a distance " (*Lun Yü*, VI, 20).

Even in early times there were also other attempts to explain the phenomena of the universe through the theory of the *yin* 陰 and the *yang* 陽, that is, the two forces which represent, respectively, female and male, darkness and light, soft and hard, inactivity and activity, etc., the interactions of which were generally supposed by later Chinese thinkers to produce universal phenomena.[1] An explanation of this sort appears in the *Kuo Yü*, for the year 780 B.C., when three river valleys belonging to the House of Chou suffered from an earthquake :

" Chou is about to perish. For the fluids (*ch'i* 氣) of Heaven and Earth do not, of themselves, lose their proper order, and if they transgress this order it is because the people have put them into confusion. When the *yang* is concealed and cannot come forth, and when the *yin* is repressed and cannot issue out, then there are earthquakes. At the present time these three rivers have suffered from an earthquake, which is because the *yang* has lost its proper place and has dominated the *yin*. The *yang* having lost its place and occupying that of *yin*, rivers and streams must necessarily be obstructed "[2]
(*Chou Yü*, I, 10).

Likewise in the *Tso Chuan* (under the year 644 B.C.) appears the record : " Six fish-hawks flew backwards past the capital of Sung, which was caused by the wind." An historian of Chou comments on this : " This is something pertaining to the *yin* and the *yang*, which are not the producers of good and bad fortune. It is from men themselves, that good and bad fortune are produced. . . . ." (p. 171).

Again, the *Kuo Yü* records a speech under the year 494 :
" The Way of Heaven is something which is filled yet not overflowing, flourishing yet not arrogant. It labors to the utmost and yet boasts not about its accomplishments. The Sage observes the proper time for his actions, which is called keeping the proper time. In the times when Heaven does not take the initiative, he (the Sage)

---

[1] *Cf.* ch. 7, sect. 7, pp. 159 f.
[2] The *yang* has control over what is dry, whereas the *yin* is moist and so controls water.—TR.

does not make a start for men.   When human troubles do not arise, he does not begin them. . . . .

"It is only Earth which is able to embrace the ten thousand creatures so as to make them one, unfailing in its affairs.   It gives birth to the ten thousand creatures, and bears and nourishes the birds and beasts, after which it accepts the fame (achieved by them) and combines their usefulness.   Those that are beautiful and that are ugly are both brought to maturity through its nourishing and life-giving. And until the proper time has arrived, things cannot be forcibly produced.   If affairs are not ready, they cannot forcibly be brought to completion. . . . .

"One must have that whereby one may know the eternal laws of Heaven and Earth, in order to enjoy Heaven and Earth's complete usefulness. . . .   One must make use of the regularities of the *yin* and the *yang*, and comply with the regularities of Heaven and Earth ; be soft yet not yielding, strong yet not hard. . . . .   Heaven lets man have his course, and the Sage accords himself with Heaven.   Man is his own propagator ;   Heaven and Earth give him form ; the Sage lets him develop and completes him " (*Yüeh Yü*, II, 1).

The attempt to explain the phenomena of the universe through the *yin-yang* theory, though still primitive, is a step forward compared with explanations based on a *T'ien*, a *Ti*, and a multitude of spirits. The 'heaven' described in this last quotation is a naturalistic one bearing strong resemblance to that of Lao Tzŭ, and seems to be a forerunner of Taoist philosophy.

5—THE RISE OF RATIONALISM

Human institutions were also believed by the early Chinese to be controlled by a *T'ien* and a *Ti*.   Thus the *Shu Ching*, in its section on ' The Counsels of Kao Yao,' says :

" Let him not have his various officers cumberers of their places. Men must act for the work of Heaven !   From Heaven come the relationships with their several duties ; we are charged with those five duties, and lo ! we have the five courses of honorable conduct ! From Heaven come the several ceremonies ; from us come the observances of these five ceremonies, and lo ! they appear in regular practice ! . . . . .   Heaven confers its decree on the virtuous, and there are the five habiliments and five decorations !   Heaven punishes the guilty, and there are the five punishments to be severally used for that purpose ! " (pp. 55-56).   Again it says :

" Heaven having produced the people below, appointed for them rulers and teachers." [1]   And yet again :

" Imperial God (*Ti*) in a pure manner carried his enquiries among the people below. . . . .   He thereupon charged the three princes

---

[1] Quoted in *Mencius*, I*b*, 3.

to labor with compassionate anxiety on the people's behalf. Po I presented his statutes to prevent the people from rendering themselves liable to punishment; Yü reduced to order the water and the land, and presided over the naming of the hills and rivers; Chi spread abroad a knowledge of agriculture for the extensive cultivation of the admirable grains. When the three princes had accomplished their work, it was abundantly well with the people " (p. 258).

Similarly the *Shih Ching* says :

" Heaven gave birth to the multitudes of people, so that they had faculties and laws " (III, iii, Ode 6, 1).

" Without consciousness, without knowing, be in accordance with the pattern of God " (III, i, Ode 7, 7).

By this ' pattern of God ' (*ti chih tse* 帝 之 則) is meant the political and social regulations instituted by *Shang Ti*. The ancient Greeks similarly supposed that the institutions of their city-states had been created by divine beings, a belief probably general among early peoples.

With the coming of the Ch'un Ch'iu period in China, however, or perhaps even before, there were men who tried to give a human interpretation to the laws and statutes, which they declared were established wholly by human beings for man's own benefit. Thus the *Kuo Yü*, under a section that refers to Duke Huan of Cheng (806-771), records an historian as saying :

" Harmony (*ho* 和) results in the production of things, but identity (*t'ung* 同) does not. When the one equalizes the other there comes what is called harmony, so that then there can be a luxurious growth in which new things are produced. But if identity is added to identity, all that is new is finished.

" Therefore, the early kings mixed the element earth with the elements metal, wood, water and fire, so as to bring various things to completion. The five tastes were thereby harmonized so as to become blended in the mouth; the four limbs were strengthened to protect the body; the six pitch-pipes were harmonized so as to make sound for the ear; the seven 'bodies' [1] were put into proper adjustment so as to regulate the mind; the eight 'rules' [2] were regulated so as to make man complete; the nine 'laws' [3] were established for the setting up of pure virtue; the ten ranks (of feudalistic society) were harmonized so as to lead the various organizations into orderliness; the thousand kinds of things were produced, the ten thousand roads were completed, the hundred thousand things were calculated, the hundred million creatures were estimated, and the billion sources of

---

[1] i.e., seven orifices : the two eyes, two nostrils, two ears, and the mouth.—TR.

[2] Those regulating the head, stomach, feet, thighs, eyes, mouth, ears and hands.—TR.

[3] Those governing the nine internal organs : the heart, liver, spleen, kidneys, lungs, stomach, groin, intestines and gall.—TR.

income were received, this being carried out to the last extreme, reaching an infinite number. [1]

" Thus, the kings, living on the lands of their nine provinces, received the billion sources of income for feeding the multitude of people. These being in orderly arrangement, they could make use of them, and there was harmony and happiness among them as if they were one. Such a condition is the ultimate of harmony.

" Thereupon the early kings married queens from different families, sought their riches from those of different regions, selected ministers and received expostulations from officials who could offer them different opinions, and held discussions about all sorts of things. They did so because they wanted harmony. If there is only one sound, it is not worth listening to. A thing entirely the same lacks decorativeness. If there is only one taste, there is no satisfaction. And if things are made of one material, there is no solidity " (*Cheng Yü*, 1).

When it is said that " when the one equalizes the other, there is what is called harmony," this means that if something salty, for example, is added to something sour, the resulting flavor will differ from its two constituents and be entirely new. What is salty is the 'other' of what is sour, and vice versa. This explains the opening words : " Harmony results in the production of things." But if what is salty is added to what is already salty, or, as the quotation says, " If identity is added to identity," then there can be no production of anything new.

In the same way, if there be only one kind of sound, there can be no music no matter how often the sound be repeated; and if only one color, no decorative pattern can be produced no matter how many times the color be applied. Everything must have its 'other' or contrast to act upon it, before there can be any process of production. By thus distinguishing between 'harmony' and 'identity,' the speaker explains why ceremonials, music and social institutions of all kinds must inevitably become ever more elaborate.

Later on, similar ideas were to be propounded by Yen Tzǔ (died 493 B.C.), a noted statesman of the state of Ch'i. Thus the *Tso Chuan* describes an incident under the year 522 :

" After the Marquis of Ch'i had returned from his hunt, Yen Tzǔ was with him in the tower of Ch'uan, when Tzǔ Yü drove up to it at full speed. The Marquis said : ' It is only Chü (i.e., Tzǔ Yü) who is in harmony with me ! ' Yen Tzǔ replied : ' Chü merely identifies himself with you ; how can he be considered to be in harmony with you ? ' 'Are harmony (*ho*) and identity (*t'ung*) different ? ' asked the Marquis.

---

[1] This passage is a good example of the Chinese fondness for classifying various things under numerical categories of fives, sixes, nines, etc., and of dealing with infinite quantities.—TR.

" Yen Tzǔ said : ' They are. Harmony may be illustrated by soup. You have the water and fire, vinegar, pickle, salt and plums, with which to cook fish. It is made to boil by the firewood, and then the cook mixes the ingredients, harmoniously equalizing the several flavors, so as to supply whatever is deficient and carry off whatever is in excess. Then the master eats it, and his mind is made equable. So it is in the relations of ruler and minister. When there is any impropriety in what the ruler approves of, the minister calls attention to that impropriety, so as to make what has been approved entirely correct. When there is anything proper in what the ruler has disapproved of, the minister brings forward that propriety, so as to remove occasion for the disapproval. In this way the government is kept in equilibrium, with no infringement of what is right, and there is no quarrelling with it in the minds of the people. . . . .

" ' As the early kings established the doctrine of the five tastes, so they made the harmony of the five notes, to make their minds equable and to perfect their government. There is an analogy between sounds and flavors. There are the breath, the two kinds of dances, the three kinds (of songs), the materials from the four quarters, the five notes, the six pitch-pipes, the seven sounds, the winds of the eight directions, and the nine songs, which united form perfect (music).

" ' Then there are the clear and the thick, the small and the large, short and long, fast and slow, solemn and joyful, hard and soft, lingering and rapid, high and low, the commencement and ending, the close and diffuse, by which the parts are all blended together. The Superior Man listens to such music that his mind may be composed. His mind being composed, his qualities become harmonious. . . . .

" ' Now it is not so with Chü. Whatever you say *yes* to, he also says *yes*. Whatever you say *no* to, he also says *no*. If you were to try to give water a flavour with water, who would care to partake of the result ? If lutes were to be confined to one note, who would be able to listen to them ? Such is the insufficiency of mere identity ' " (p. 684).

Another speech in the *Tso Chuan*, under the year 710 B.C., describes the rise of rites, music, government and laws :

" He who is a ruler of men makes it his object to manifest virtue and suppress what is wrong, that he may shed an enlightening influence on his officials, and is afraid lest he should fail in this. Therefore he seeks to display excellent virtue to show an example to his posterity. Thus his ancestral temple has a roof of thatch ; the mats in his grand chariot are only of grass ; the grand soups (used in his sacrifices) are without condiments ; and the millets are not finely cleaned. All this is to show his frugality. His robe, cap, knee-covers and mace ; his girdle, lower robe, buskins and shoes ; the crosspiece of his cap, its stopper pendants, its fastening strings and its crown : all these show his observance of the statutory measures. His gem-mats and his scabbard, with its ornaments above and below ; his belt, with its descending ends ; the streamers of his flags and the ornaments at his horses' breasts : these show his attention to the regular degrees (of rank).   The flames, the dragons, the axes and the symbol of distinction (represented on his robes) : these show the elegance of his taste.   The five colors laid out in accordance with the appearance of nature : these show with what propriety his articles are made.   The bells on his horses' foreheads, their bits, and those on the carriage pole and on his flags : these show his taste for harmony.   His flags, on which are represented the sun, moon and stars : these show the brightness of his intelligence.

" Now when by virtue he is frugal and observant of the statutes, attentive to the degrees of high and low ; his character stamped on his elegant robes and his carriage ; sounded forth also and brightly displayed—when thus he presents himself for the enlightenment of his officials, they are struck with awe and dare not depart from the rules and laws " (p. 40).

The theory here is that the ruler's chief use of ceremonials is to awe his officials so that they will not transgress the laws.

Again, under the year 536, the *Tso Chuan* records a letter sent by Shu Hsiang to the famous statesman, Tzŭ Ch'an, apropos of the latter's promulgation of a law code in the state of Cheng :

" The early kings deliberated on all the circumstances (of each crime) to make their ruling on it, and did not make (general) laws of punishment, fearing lest this should give rise to a contentious spirit among the people.   But still, as crimes could not be prevented they set up for them the barrier of righteousness, sought to rectify them with government, set before them the practice of propriety and the maintenance of good faith, and cherished them with benevolence.   They also instituted emoluments and (official) positions to encourage their allegiance, and strictly laid down punishments and penalties to awe them from excesses.   Fearing lest these things should be insufficient, they therefore inculcated them with sincerity, urged them on by their conduct, instructed them in what was most important, employed them in a spirit of harmony, came before them in a spirit of reverence, met exigencies with vigor, and gave their decisions with firmness.   And in addition to this, they sought to have sage and wise persons in the highest positions, intelligent discriminating persons in all offices, true hearted and sincere elders, and gentle and kind teachers.   In this way the people could be successfully dealt with, and miseries and disaster be prevented from arising.

" When the people know what the exact laws are, they do not stand in awe of their superiors.   They also come to have a contentious spirit, and make their appeal to the written words (of the laws), hoping peradventure to be successful in their argument. They can no longer be managed. When the government of the Hsia dynasty fell into disorder, the penal code of Yü was made ; under the same circumstances of Shang, the penal code of T'ang ; and in Chou, the code of the nine punishments. These three codes all originated in times of decay. And now in your administration of the state of Cheng, you have constructed dikes and ditches, you have established a government which has been much spoken against, and you have framed (a law code like that of) those three codes, casting in metal a record of the punishments it provides. Will it not indeed be difficult with this to keep the people in order ? " (p. 609).

Despite its conservative tone, this letter supplies a human explanation for the existence of law codes.

Another speech is recorded in the *Tso Chuan* under the year 517 :

" I have heard our late great officer, Tzŭ Ch'an, say : ' Ceremonials (*li* 禮) constitute the standard of Heaven, the principle of Earth, and the conduct of man. Heaven and Earth have their standards, and men take these for their pattern, imitating the brilliant bodies of Heaven and according with the natural diversities of Earth. (Heaven and Earth) produce the six atmospheric conditions and men make use of the Five Elements. These conditions produce the five tastes, make manifest the five colors, and make evident the five notes. When these are in excess, obscurity and confusion ensue, and the people lose their original natures.

" ' Therefore ceremonials were framed to reinforce (that nature). The six domestic animals, the five beasts (of the chase), and the three kinds of sacrificial victims, existed to maintain the five tastes. The nine forms of decoration, with their six colors and five methods of display, were made to maintain the five colors. The nine songs, the winds of the eight directions, the seven sounds, and the six pitch-pipes were made to maintain the five notes (The distinctions of) ruler and subject, superior and inferior, were formed to follow the pattern of Earth's principle. Those of husband and wife, of the home and the outside world, were formed to regulate the two kinds of work (those inside and outside the home). There were instituted the relationships of father and son, elder and younger brother, aunt and sister, maternal uncles and aunts, father-in-law and connections of one's children with other members of their mother's family, and brothers-in-law : to resemble the bright luminaries of Heaven.

" 'The duties of government, requisitions of labor, and conduct of affairs were made to accord with the four seasons. Punishments and penalties, and the terrors of legal proceedings were instituted to make the people stand in awe, resembling the destructive forces of thunder and lightning. Mildness and gentleness, kindness and harmony, were made in imitation of the creating and nourishing action of Heaven. The people had feelings of love and hatred, pleasure and anger, grief and joy, produced by the six atmospheric conditions.

" 'Therefore (the early kings) carefully imitated these relations and analogies, to regulate these six impulses. To grief there belong wailing and tears ; to joy, songs and dancing ; to pleasure, beneficence ; to anger, fighting and struggling. Pleasure is born of love, and anger of hatred. Therefore (the early kings) were careful in their conduct and sincere in their commands, decreeing misery and happiness, rewards and punishments, to control life and death. Life is a good thing ; death is an evil thing. The good thing brings joy ; the evil thing gives grief. When there is no error (in the apportionment of) joy and grief, there results a state of harmony with the nature of Heaven and Earth, which consequently can endure long' " (pp. 708-709).

The idea expressed here, as we see, is that the practical value of ceremonials and music, punishments and penalties, lies in preventing the people from falling into disorder, and that these have originated from man's capacity for imitating Heaven and Earth.

Human interpretations of the sacrificial rites were also offered by certain men during this period. The *Kuo Yü* gives an example :

" Sacrifice is that through which one can show one's filial piety and give peace to the people, pacify the country and make the people settled. It cannot be put an end to. For when the desires of the people are given free rein there comes a stoppage ; with such a stoppage there comes a wasting away ; and when this wasting away continues for long without any stimulus to it, life does not prosper, so that there is no obedience (to the commands on high). When life is not prosperous, the granting of feudal fiefs can no longer take place.

" This is why of old the early kings performed daily, monthly, seasonal and yearly sacrifice. The feudal lords omitted the daily sacrifices ; the ministers and great officials omitted the monthly ones ; and the lesser officials and common people omitted the seasonal ones. The Son of Heaven performed all-inclusive sacrifices to the various divinities and various classes of creatures. The feudal lords sacrificed to Heaven and Earth, and to the three luminaries,[1] as well as to the mountains and rivers in their territories. The ministers and great officials performed sacrifices to the spirits of the house and to the ancestors. The lesser officers and common people did no more than sacrifice to their ancestors. . . . .

" Among the common people, men and women, according to days of good fortune, offer their sacrificial victims. They are reverent with the sacrificial grain contained in the vessels, show care in cleaning up, are prudent in the decorations of their clothing, and cautious in their wine offerings. They give guidance to their sons and blood relatives, follow the seasonal sacrifices, are pious in their ancestral worship, and conduct their words along harmonious paths,

---

[1] The sun, moon, and the stars considered as one group.—TR.

so as to make illustrious their sacrifices to the early ancestors. They are reverent and solemn as if someone were overlooking them.

" Thereby local friends and relatives through marriage, elder and younger brothers and blood relations, are united. Thereby all sorts of abuses are stopped ; the evils of slander are rooted out ; those who are friends are united ; relatives are drawn into a common bond ; and both superiors and inferiors are put at rest, so as thus to extend and strengthen the family. It is through these sacrifices that those above teach the people proper respect, and those below make manifest their service to their superiors.

" When the Son of Heaven performs the great sacrifice and the suburban sacrifice, he must himself shoot the sacrificial victims, and his queen must herself pound the sacrificial grain. The feudal lords when they perform their ancestral sacrifices, must themselves shoot the ox, stab the sheep, and kill the pig, and their consorts must themselves pound the grain for the vessels. All the more, then, among those below, who would dare not be reverent and full of awe in serving the various spirits ?. . . . . It is through the sacrifices that the unity of the people is strengthened, and why, then, should they abandon them ? " (*Ch'u Yü*, II, 2).

' Reverent and solemn *as if* someone were overlooking them ': that is, there need not be a supernatural being actually overlooking the ceremony at all. If sacrifice is performed with this knowledge, its only use would seem to be to serve as a pretext for bringing the local clan members and relatives together into one assembly ; training them at the same time into a proper feeling of respect and reverence. Under such circumstances the real value of sacrifice lies in the fact that through it ' the unity of the people is strengthened.' Looked at from this viewpoint, sacrifice becomes the sort of thing which the Confucian philosopher, Hsün Tzŭ, describes as : " Among superior men it is considered to be a human practice ; among common people it is considered to be a serving of the spirits " (*Hsün-tzŭ*, p. 245). Another speech in the *Kuo Yü* runs in similar strain :

" Sacrifices are the great institutions of a state, and institutions are what enable a government to be successful. Therefore the sacrifices are carefully regulated so as to serve as institutions for the state. . .

" The regulations drawn up by the Sage-kings governing sacrifice, provide that to those whose laws had permeated among the people, there should be offered sacrifice ; to those who had died through their industriousness, there should be sacrifice ; to those through whose efforts the country had been pacified, there should be sacrifice ; to those who had warded off great natural calamities, there should be sacrifice ; and to those who had resisted tribulations, there should be sacrifice. Those not in these classes were not put on the sacrificial records. . . . "

The account lists a large number of historical and legendary worthies who through their actions had merited a place at the sacrifices, and then continues :

" The great sacrifice, the suburban sacrifice (made to Heaven in winter and Earth in summer), the sacrifices to those ancestors who have done great deeds, and to those who have displayed remarkable virtue, and sacrifices performed to show gratitude : these five are the sacrifices on the statute books of the state. In addition are the spirits of the soil and grain, and of mountains and rivers, all of whom have accomplished outstanding deeds on behalf of the people. As to the sage and virtuous men of former times, it is through them that shining sincerity has been created. As to the three luminaries in Heaven, they are what the people look up to with reverence. As to the Five Elements on Earth, these are what induce life and propagation. As to the famous mountains, rivers and marshes of the nine provinces, it is from these that useful natural resources are derived. Anything not in the above classes is not put in the records to be sacrificed to " (*Lu Yü*, I, 9).

Here it is a feeling of gratitude that supplies the motive for sacrificing. Thus looked at, sacrifice becomes indeed a ' human practice,' rather than a ' serving of the spirits.'

With such human interpretations being given to social institutions, it is not surprising that the ruler likewise tended to become divested of that divine right which had formerly rendered him incapable in the eyes of the people of committing any wrong. The *Kuo Yü* gives an instance :

" The people of the state of Chin killed Duke Li (580-573), and the people of the frontier announced the news (to the state of Lu). Duke Ch'eng (590-573) was then at court. The Duke said : ' When a subject has killed his ruler, whose is the blame ? ' None of the great officials made reply, but Li Ko said : ' It is the fault of the ruler. For the awesome power of a ruler is great, and when this power to awe is lost to such an extent that he is killed by someone, his blame must be great. Moreover the ruler exists to shepherd his people and rectify their errors. If he, himself, pursues secret debauches and disregards the affairs of his people, the people will not be rectified when they are in error, so that the evil will become greater. If with evilness he supervises the people, he will fall and be unable to get up. And if he is unwilling to employ the virtuous exclusively, he will find himself unable to employ anyone. When such (a ruler) comes to his doom, there is no one to mourn for him, and of what good then is he ? ' " (*Lu Yü*, I, 15).

Also the *Tso Chuan*, under the year 510 B.C. :

" Chao Chien Tzŭ asked the historian Mo, saying : ' The head of the Chi family expelled his ruler, yet the people submitted to him, and the feudal lords assented to what he had done. His ruler has died outside (of his state of Lu), and no one has incriminated him (i.e., the head of Chi).'

" Mo replied : ' Things are produced in twos, in threes, in fives and in pairs. Hence Heaven has three luminaries, Earth has the Five Elements. The body has the left and right (sides), and everyone has his mate or double. Kings have their dukes, and princes have their ministers who are their assistants. Heaven produced the Chi family to be the assistant of the Marquis of Lu, and this has been the case for long. Is it not right that the people should submit in this case ? The rulers of Lu have, one after another, followed their mistakes, and the heads of the Chi family have, one after another, diligently improved their position. The people have forgotten their ruler, so that, though he has died abroad, who pities him ? The altars of the grain and soil are not always maintained (by the same ruler), and the positions of rulers and ministers are not ever unchanging ; from of old it has been so. . . . . The surnames of the sovereigns of the three (previous dynasties) are now borne by men among the common people ; as you know' " (p. 741).

Certainly such approval of a minister murdering his ruler is a revolutionary idea for that time. Despite the occasional grandiloquence of the *Tso Chuan* and *Kuo Yü*, and their literary elaborations, the fundamental ideas expressed in the speeches which have been quoted from them all undeniably show a human bent. In ancient Greece the Sophist Protagoras said that " Man is the measure of all things," which is an idea also implied in the foregoing quotations. The men who made these speeches, however, were all either hereditary historians, or were nobles active in government, and so, unlike the Greek Sophists, were not in a position to discuss and propagate their ideas. Hence for the important contributions to Chinese thought, we must continue to look to such men as Confucius, Mo Tzŭ and the other later philosophers.

CHAPTER IV

CONFUCIUS AND THE RISE OF CONFUCIANISM

More is known about the life of Confucius than of any other early Chinese philosopher, owing chiefly to the long chapter (ch. 47) devoted to him in the *Shih Chi* (Historical Records). According to this chapter, he was born in 551 B.C. in the state of Lu, somewhere near the present town of Chüfu in Shantung. His ancestors were of the Royal House of Sung (a state south-west of Lu in present Honan), but his great grandfather had moved to Lu, where the family became impoverished. Thus Confucius, like many of the travelling philosophers and politicians of succeeding centuries, came from a class of society which, while of noble origin, had fallen upon hard times. The name, Confucius, is a latinization of K'ung Fu Tzŭ 孔 夫 子, meaning Master K'ung; his given name is Ch'iu 丘; and his cognomen Chung-ni 仲 尼.

Confucius is supposed to have lost his father, who had been a military officer of considerable prowess in Lu, when he was but three years old, and to have been brought up by his mother. When he was nineteen he married, and about the same time entered upon his official career in Lu, being first a keeper of grain stores and then in charge of the public lands. After passing through many experiences, the authenticity of which is doubtful—among them being a prolonged stay of several years in the neighboring state of Ch'i—he reached his highest position in 501 B.C. by becoming Prime Minister of Lu. So great was his success in this post, that the state of Ch'i, according to the *Shih Chi*, fearing his growing influence, sent a present of female dancers and musicians to the Lu ruler, who thereupon neglected the affairs of state. Full of disappointment, Confucius resigned his position and, accompanied by many of the disciples who had now gathered around him, set out in 497 upon wanderings which were to last for thirteen years. During this time, he travelled through many of the feudal states of China, staying now in one and then in another, and undergoing many hardships and dangers. At last he returned to his native state, where he spent the last three years of his life engaged in literary studies and in teaching his disciples. He died in 479 B.C., and was buried in the district of Chüfu, where his tomb is still to be seen.[1]

---

[1] These two paragraphs do not occur in the original text, but have been added for the benefit of westerners who are not so familiar with the life of Confucius as is the Chinese reader.—Tr.

Besides the above general sketch, the *Shih Chi* supplies us with considerable detailed information concerning his activities as a teacher and his character :

" In the time of Confucius, the House of Chou had declined and the rites and music had fallen into neglect. The *Shih* (Book of Odes) and *Shu* (Book of History) had become defective. (Confucius) made researches into and transmitted the rites of the Three Dynasties (Hsia, Shang and Chou), and arranged in order the recitals in the *Shu*. Starting from the epoch of T'ang and Yü (i.e., the legendary Emperors Yao and Shun), and coming down to that of (Duke) Mu of Ch'in (659-621), he grouped and classified their events. . . . . Observing the suppressions and additions (in the rites) made by Yin and Chou, he said : ' Even after one hundred generations they will still be known.' . . . . ' Chou had the advantage of surveying the two preceding dynasties. How replete was its culture ! I follow Chou.' [1] Thus the records of the *Shu* and the *Li Chi* (Book of Rites) both come to us from Confucius.

" Once, when talking to the great music master of Lu, Confucius said : ' Music may be understood. The attack should be prompt and united, and as the piece proceeds, it should do so harmoniously, with clearness of tone and continuity of time, until its conclusion (III, 23). It was only after my return from Wei to Lu that the music was revised, and the secular and sacred pieces were properly discriminated ' (IX, 14).

" In ancient times the *Shih* comprised more than three thousand pieces, but when it reached Confucius he threw out duplications, retaining those which could be used to exemplify the rites and justice. . . . . Confucius played on the zither and sang the three hundred and five pieces (comprising the present Book of Odes). . . . It was from this time that the rites and music could be obtained and transmitted, wherewith to complete the Kingly Way, and to perfect the Six Disciplines.[2]

" In his later years Confucius delighted in the *I* (Book of Changes), and arranged in order the *T'uan, Hsi, Hsiang, Shuo Kua* and *Wen Yen*.[3] He read the *I* (so assiduously) that the thongs which bound it wore out three times, and said : ' Give me a few more years like this, and I will come to a perfect knowledge of the *I*.' [4] Confucius took

---

[1] *Cf.* the *Lun Yü* (Confucian Analects) II, 23, and III, 14, which is a collection of sayings by Confucius as recorded by his disciples, and is the most reliable source concerning him. All the following quotations in this chapter, unless otherwise indicated, are from the *Lun Yü*.—Tr.

[2] These were the Books of Odes, History, Rites, Changes, Spring and Autumn Annals, and Music, which formed the basis of Confucian learning. On them see especially ch. 16. It is uncertain whether ' Music ' was actually the name of a book, or was simply a subject of study.—Tr.

[3] These, with their subdivisions, comprise the ' Ten Wings ' or Appendices to the text of the *I Ching* proper. See ch. 15, sect. 1, pp. 379-382.—Tr.

[4] *Cf. Lun Yü*, VII, 16, but there the text differs somewhat and presents special difficulties.—Tr.

the *Shih*, *Shu*, rites and music to teach to his disciples, who numbered about three thousand.   Those who, in their own person, became conversant with the Six Disciplines, numbered seventy-two. . . . .

" 'When he (Confucius) was in his native village, he bore himself with simplicity, as if he had no gifts of speech.   But when in the ancestral temple or at court, he expressed himself readily and clearly, yet with a measure of reserve ' (X, 1).   ' At court, when conversing with the higher great officials, he spoke respectfully.   When conversing with the lower great officials, he spoke out boldly ' (X, 2).   ' When he entered the palace gate, he appeared to stoop ' (X, 4).   ' When he hastened forward, it was with a respectful appearance ' (X, 3).   ' When the prince summoned him to receive a visitor, his expression seemed to change ' (X, 3).   ' When his prince commanded his presence, he did not wait for the carriage to be yoked, but went off on foot ' (X, 13).   ' Fish that had spoiled, or meat that had gone bad, or something improperly cut, he would not eat ' (X, 8).   ' He would not sit on his mat unless it was straight ' (X, 9).   ' When he dined by the side of a mourner, he never ate to repletion.   On the same day that he had been mourning, he never sang ' (VII, 9).   ' Whenever he saw a person in mourning, or one who was blind, even though it were a young boy, he always changed countenance ' (IX, 9 ; X, 16).   (The Master said :) ' When walking in a party of three, my teachers are always present ' (VII, 21).   (Again :)   ' Neglect in the cultivation of character ; lack of thoroughness in study ; inability to move toward recognized duty ; and inability to correct my imperfections : these are what cause me solicitude ' (VII, 3).   ' When he had induced a person to sing, if the song were good he would have it repeated, joining in the melody himself ' (VII, 31).   ' The Master would not discuss prodigies, prowess, lawlessness, or supernatural beings ' (VII, 20). . . .

" Then, utilizing the historical records, he composed the *Ch'un Ch'iu* (Spring and Autumn Annals), going back to Duke Yin (of Lu, 722-712) and coming down to the fourteenth year of Duke Ai (481 B.C.), (a total of) twelve dukes   (In his history) he took the state of Lu as his basis, kept close to Chou, dealt with Yin as a time of the past, and circulated (the principles of) the Three Dynasties.   His style was concise, but his meaning rich.   Thus, when the rulers of Wu and Yüeh (improperly) style themselves Kings, the *Ch'un Ch'iu* reproves them by giving them (their proper title of) Viscount.   And at the meeting of Chien-t'u (in 632), when the Chou Emperor had actually been ordered to attend (by Duke Wen of Chin), the *Ch'un Ch'iu* avoids mentioning this fact by saying : 'The celestial King went hunting at Ho-yang.'   (Confucius) offered examples of this sort to serve as rules for his own age.   And if later on there be kings who will arise and bring out the meaning of the censures and abasements, so that the meaning of the *Ch'un Ch'iu* becomes generally known, at that time rebellious subjects and criminals in the world will become seized with terror " [1]   (*Mém. hist.*, V, 390-398, 400-403, 406-412, 420-422).

Such is the concept of Confucius that has held sway in China for the last two thousand years ; yet a study of this biography, to-day, reveals many points which cannot possibly be in accordance with facts. It nevertheless remains noteworthy that Ssŭ-ma Ch'ien (145-c. 86 B.C.), the author of the *Shih Chi*, still regarded Confucius as a human person at a time when many men were already coming to look upon him as a divine being. Where he bases himself on the *Lun Yü*, his statements are for the most part trustworthy. What remains an open question, however, is the relation of Confucius to the Books of Changes, Odes, History, Rites, and Spring and Autumn Annals, and to the Music, which comprise the so-called Six Disciplines. This problem will be discussed in the following section.

1—The Position of Confucius in Chinese History

It has long been maintained by the New Text school of classical study that the Six Disciplines were composed by Confucius himself, whereas the Old Text school has maintained that he was merely their transmitter, so that both schools have at least agreed in saying that Confucius was closely connected with them. My own opinion on this subject is that they could not possibly have been originated by Confucius himself, because they were almost certainly already in existence during the Ch'un Ch'iu period, that is, prior to his time.

Much evidence has already been brought forward by past and present-day scholars to prove this point, and I, myself, have also discussed the matter elsewhere,[2] and hence need not take it up in detail here. Though Confucius could not have composed the Six Disciplines himself, however, he did use them to teach his disciples, which is probably why later ages have supposed, not entirely without reason, that Confucius had a special connection with them.

Yet even this use of the Six Disciplines for teaching need not necessarily have commenced with Confucius, for the *Kuo Yü* informs us concerning a crown prince of Ch'u, son of King Chuang of Ch'u (613-591), that the prince was given instruction in such works as the ' Odes,' ' Rites,' ' Music,' ' Spring and Autumn,' and ' Old Records.'[3] Both the *Kuo Yü* and *Tso Chuan* record numerous conversations between important personages, in which the ' Odes ' and ' History ' are frequently mentioned ; while the ' Rites ' (*Li*) were used in diplomatic relations, and the ' Changes ' (*I*) in divination. This

---

[1] *Mencius*, IIIb, 9, has a sentence similar to these last words. Down to the present day, most Chinese have clung to this ·' praise and censure ' theory of the *Ch'un Ch'iu*, and many commentaries have been written to explain the esoteric meanings to be found beneath its concise phrases.—Tr.

[2] Cf. *K'ung Tzŭ tsai Chung-kuo Li-shih chung chih Ti-wei* (The Position of Confucious in Chinese History), in the *Ku Shih Pien*, Vol. 2.

[3] Cf. *Ch'u Yü*, I, 1.

indicates that an education of this sort was acquired by a portion, at least, of the nobility of that time. Confucius was the first man, however, to use the Six Disciplines for teaching the common people. This point will be taken up in detail later.

Here I need only say that in his method of teaching, Confucius differed from the philosophic schools which followed him, inasmuch as these all emphasized the fact that they taught doctrines originating in their own school. Chapter XXXIII of the *Chuang-tzŭ* (p. 442), for example, tells us that the disciples of the Mohist school all intoned the ' Mohist Canons.' Confucius, on the other hand, was an educationalist. His aim in teaching was to nurture and develop a person so that he might become someone who would be useful to his state, rather than to produce a scholar belonging to any one philosophic school. Hence he taught his pupils to read and study a wide variety of books and subjects, so that we find a disciple saying of him : " He has broadened me by culture and restrained me by the usages of good conduct " (IX, 10). Likewise the *Chuang-tzŭ* (ch. 33) says with reference to the Confucians : " The *Shih* describes aims ; the *Shu* describes events ; the *Li* (Rites) directs conduct ; the *Yüeh* (Music) secures harmony. The *I* (Book of Changes) shows the principles of the *yin* and the *yang*. The *Ch'un Ch'iu* shows distinctions and duties " (p. 439). These were the six works which were the subjects of study of the Confucian school.

Because of such catholicity, the accomplishments of the disciples of Confucius were also not all of one pattern. Thus the *Lun Yü* says : " Noted for moral character were . . . . (here and below follow names of disciples) ; for gifts of speech, ... ; for administrative ability, ... ; and for literature and learning, ..." (XI, 2). Again, the *Lun Yü* tells us that there was one disciple who " might be appointed to the administration of revenues " ; another who " might be appointed as Controller " ; and another who " might be appointed (at court) to converse with the guests," all alike being able to manage affairs in " a state of a thousand chariots " (V, 7). This indicates that Confucius, in teaching his disciples, wholeheartedly wished them to become ' men,' in the full sense of the term, rather than sectarian scholars belonging to any one particular school.

While teaching, Confucius no doubt would sometimes make selections from the existing literature, or expand upon it according to the occasion, as will be described in the following section. If we allow such selections and explanations, made upon the spur of the moment, to represent the process traditionally spoken of as ' expunging and rectifying the Six Classics,' then there is no reason to doubt this tradition ; but on the other hand there is nothing remarkable in expunging and rectifying of such a sort. Because of conservatism, however, the later Confucians continued to use the Six Disciplines for teaching, unlike other schools of thought which taught only new doctrines originated by their own particular schools; and for this reason these Six Disciplines have come to be considered as the exclusive property of the Confucians, and even as having been composed by Confucius himself, while this 'expunging and rectifying' (if ever there really was such), has assumed an exaggerated importance.

The *I-wen Chih* chapter of the *Ch'ien Han Shu* says of the various philosophic schools that they sprang from the heritage of the Six Disciplines, a view which seems to be shared by the account of them given in *Chuang-tzŭ* (ch. 33). Such a theory is not wholly unjustified; for as has just been said, the Six Disciplines were originally a literature common to all, and it was only when each of the schools came to expound its own particular doctrines, that they came to be more definitely associated with the Confucians. It would be incorrect to say for this reason, however, that the ideas of each of the schools are therefore already all to be found in the Six Disciplines.

There exists no special word in Chinese meaning 'Confucian' or 'Confucianist,' members of the Confucian school having always been called *ju* 儒, a word which may be translated as 'literati.' Concerning this term, the *Shuo-wen Chieh-tzŭ*, one of the earliest Chinese dictionaries, appearing about A.D. 100, says: "The word *ju* means 'yielding' (*jou* 柔). It is a term applied to scholars versed in the arts." And the *Lun Yü* says: "The Master speaking to Tzŭ Hsia said, 'Be you a *ju* of the nobler type, not a *ju* of the inferior type'" (VI, 11). This would indicate that *ju* was originally a term applied in general to all persons who possessed education and were versed in the arts, so that in the time of Confucius it was still possible to speak in a general way of *ju* or scholars of the nobler type (*chün tzŭ* 君子) and inferior type (*hsiao jen* 小人), whereas later on, the use of the term was restricted exclusively to the Confucian school.

Confucius was, in short, primarily an educationalist. "A transmitter and not a creator, a believer in and lover of antiquity" (VII, 1). "Striving unwearingly (in study) and teaching others without flagging" (VII, 33). These are Confucius's own words about himself.

Thus looked at, Confucius would be nothing more than an old pedant; yet in Chinese history he has been placed in a most exalted position. I would therefore maintain that:

(1) Confucius was the first man in China to make teaching his profession, and thus popularize culture and education. It was he who opened the way for the many travelling scholars and philosophers of succeeding centuries. It was also he who inaugurated, or at least developed, that class of gentleman in ancient China who was neither farmer, artisan, merchant nor actual official, but was professional teacher and potential official.

(2) The activities of Confucius were similar in many ways to those of the Greek Sophists.

(3) The activities of Confucius and his influence in Chinese history, have been similar to that of Socrates in the West.

*

I have already mentioned the *Kuo Yü* passage which states that even before the time of Confucius, such works as the ' Odes,' ' Rites,' ' Music,' ' Spring and Autumn ' and ' Old Records ' were included in the educational curriculum of one of the crown princes of Ch'u. Yet it is evident that such a thorough education must have been inaccessible to the common people of the Ch'un Ch'iu period, and furthermore, was denied even to many of the nobility. The *Tso Chuan*, for example, under the year 540 B.C., states of Han Hsüan Tzŭ, a hereditary minister of the state of Chin, that it was only after he came on a diplomatic mission to the state of Lu, one of the most cultured regions in China, that he ' examined the books of the Grand Historian ' and saw ' the symbols of the *I* ' and ' the *Ch'un Ch'iu* of Lu ' (p. 583). Again, under the year 544, it is stated of a member of the Royal House of Wu that he had to come to Lu before he could hear the odes and music of the various states (p. 549). We may infer from this that at that time such works as the ' Book of Changes,' ' Spring and Autumn Annals,' ' Music ' and ' Odes ' were literary possessions highly prized.

Confucius, on the other hand, held as his aim that " in teaching there should be no class distinctions " (XV, 38). He said that " from him who has brought his simple present of dried meat, seeking to enter my school, I have never withheld instruction " (VII, 7). The acceptance of large numbers of students in this way, and the taking in of everyone who would pay for tuition, without personal questions about them or their families ; the giving of equal instruction in each subject, and the teaching of how to read every kind of literary treasure, truly constituted a great step toward emancipation. Thus, even though the use of the Six Disciplines for teaching purposes may not have commenced with Confucius, it was certainly he who originated their use for general teaching and for bringing culture to large masses of people.

I maintain this statement because in none of the more reliable ancient writings have I heard of men before Confucius who gave instruction to large numbers of students, nor of anyone saying that " in teaching there should be no class distinctions."

According to the *K'ung-tzŭ Chia-yü* (Family Sayings of Confucius), a work which purports to contain the words of Confucius, but which was compiled many centuries after his death, there is said to have been contemporary with him a certain Shao Cheng Mao " whose dwelling place could assemble followers and form cliques ; whose conversations were sufficient to elicit admiration and bewilder the multitude ; and whose power of resistance was sufficient to overthrow the truth and establish his own individual ideas " (sect. 2).

This man's success was such that "the disciples of Confucius three times filled (the school of Confucius), and three times left it empty. It was only Yen Yüan who did not go away."¹ Again, the *Chuang-tzŭ* (ch. 5) says : "In the state of Lu there was a man, named Wang T'ai, who had had his toes cut off. His disciples were as numerous as those of Confucius " (p. 56). The story in the *K'ung-tzŭ Chia-yü*, however, which also says that Confucius had Shao Cheng Mao executed, has already been discredited by earlier scholars, and we are even uncertain whether this man ever actually existed or not. Likewise the contents of the *Chuang-tzŭ* are ' nine-tenths fantastic tales,' so that the statement that Wang T'ai ' divided with Confucius the state of Lu in half ' is even less credible. Hence Confucius remains as the first to carry on extensive instruction, and is probably primarily responsible for inaugurating the movement which led many later philosophic schools to compete with one another in attracting followers.

Confucius, furthermore, spent many years in the company of his disciples, travelling unceasingly from one feudal state to another and talking with their rulers. This, too, was a form of activity unheard of before him, whereas afterward it became a common practice.

I have also said that I have never heard of anyone prior to Confucius who, being neither farmer, artisan, merchant nor official, made teaching his sole means of livelihood. Excluding those members of the nobility who earned their bread by holding official posts, there are frequent references to other men who rose to importance from very humble positions, yet in every case they supported themselves, when not in office, by engaging in agriculture, manual labor or trade. Mencius tells us, for example :

" Shun (one of the legendary Emperors) rose from among his channelled fields. Fu Yüeh was called to office from the midst of his building frames; Chiao Ko from his fish and salt ; Kuan I Wu from the hands of his jailer ; Sun-shu Ao from (his retreat by) the seashore ; and Po-li Hsi from the market place " (*Mencius*, VI*b*, 15).

Though Mencius is not always reliable, there is, in fact, no record of anyone prior to Confucius who did not hold office, and who at the same time did not engage in some other kind of materially productive work. Confucius himself, according to Mencius, held office during his early years because he was poor. " He was once a keeper of stores," and " once in charge of the public fields," both lowly offices (*Mencius*, V*b*, 5). But as soon as he had reached the position of " following behind the great officers of state " (*Lun Yü*, XI, 7), and when there were many students coming to him, he devoted himself wholly to the exposition of his doctrines. Moreover, not only did he himself not engage in activities materially productive, but he did not wish to teach his disciples how to do so. For example, we are told that

¹ *Cf. Hsin Lun (chüan* 4, *Hsin Yin* sect.), by Liu Hsieh (sixth century A.D.), in *Han Wei Ts'ung-shu*, p. 8.

when a disciple " requested to be taught agriculture," and " requested to be taught gardening," Confucius said :   " What a little-minded man is Fan Hsü ! " (XIII, 4). And of another engaged in commerce, Confucius said disparagingly :   " Tz'ŭ is not content with his lot, yet his goods increase abundantly. Nevertheless in his judgments he often hits the mark " (XI, 18). It was because of this refusal to engage in materially productive enterprises, that Confucius was particularly criticized by his contemporaries. An instance occurs in the *Lun Yü*, which describes how an old man who was once met on the road, carrying a basket on his staff, said of Confucius :   " His four limbs know not toil, and he cannot distinguish the five grains " (XVIII, 7). The *Shih Chi's* biography of Confucius also records a noted statesman of the time as saying :

" The literati (*ju*) are sophists and cannot be taken as model or norm. Arrogant and following only their own opinions, they cannot be made subordinates. They attach great importance to the mourning rites, give themselves over to grief, and ruin great fortunes in funerals, a practice which cannot become common usage. Sophists who travel from place to place begging for loans, they are incapable of directing a state " (*Mém. hist.*, V, 307-308).

The *Chuang-tzŭ* likewise records a fierce diatribe on Confucius :

" You are a mere word-monger, who talks nonsense about Kings Wen and Wu (founders of the Chou dynasty). . . . You have many words, which only mislead. You do not sow and yet you are clothed. Your lips patter and your tongue wags, and you produce your own rights and wrongs, with which to mislead the rulers of the world and prevent scholars from reverting to the fundamentals of things. You make a deceiving show of filial piety and brotherly love, so that by good chance you may secure some fat fief or post of power " (p. 389).

While criticisms of this sort may never actually have been made by the persons to whom they are attributed, their existence during that time is at least very possible.

There were certain other men of education living in the Warring States period, who held no office but produced the food they ate through their own efforts. There was Hsü Hsing, for example, " whose disciples, amounting to several tens, all wore clothes of haircloth, and made sandals of hemp and wove mats for a living " (*Mencius*, IIIa, 4). And there was Ch'en Chung Tzŭ, who earned a living by " himself weaving sandals of hemp, while his wife twisted hempen threads " (*ibid.*, IIIb, 10). Mencius condemned such men, however, and it is recorded of Mencius himself that " he was followed by several tens of carriages, and attended by several hundred men, getting his food from one prince after another " (*ibid.*, IIIb, 4). Since such conduct was regarded even by one of his disciples as ' excessive,' it is probable that other men of the time made even sharper criticisms. On another occasion, too, Mencius gives an elaborate account of the proper etiquette to be followed by a ruler when he gives presents to a Confucian.[1]

These passages give an insight into the characteristics of the Confucian school, through which there arose a class of 'scholars' (shih 士) who were neither farmers, artisans nor merchants, and who did not engage in any kind of productive activity, but depended entirely upon others for their support. This class seems to have been non-existent prior to Confucius, and when the word shih occurs in earlier texts, it usually refers either to someone who holds official position, or to a military officer. In this way it differs from the shih of later times, who were so called in apposition to the farmer, artisan and merchant classes.[2]

Such shih were capable of engaging in only two kinds of activity : that of holding governmental office and that of teaching. Even down to the present day, in fact, the graduates of any school in China, whether it be agricultural or technical, have usually had only two ways of livelihood : that of becoming an official or of being a professor. The Lun Yü means exactly this when it says : "The occupant of office, when his duties are finished, should betake himself to study ; the student, when his studies are finished, should betake himself to office" (XIX, 13). Confucius was, if not the originator of this type of person, at least its great patron.

Such men were fiercely criticized by the Legalist school of later times. For example, the Legalist, Han Fei Tzŭ (died 233 B.C.) :

"There are those of varied and dialectical learning, such as Confucius and Mo Tzŭ. But Confucius and Mo Tzŭ did not sow or cultivate the land, and so what could the state obtain from them ? There are those who practice filial piety and reduce their desires, as did Tseng and Shih. But Tseng and Shih would not go to war, and so of what profit were they to their country ? " (Han-fei-tzŭ, chüan 18, p. 5). Again (ch. 49) :

"The literati (ju), with their learning, throw the laws into confusion. The knights-errant (hsieh 侠), with their pugnaciousness, transgress the prohibitions. . . . Now if one pursues literary studies and practises the arts of conversation, one has none of the labor of cultivating the soil and has the actuality of possessing riches ; one has none of the dangers of war and has the honor of noble position. Who, then, would not do this ? " (chüan 19, pp. 3-4).

* *

The second point which I made was that Confucius closely resembles the Greek Sophists in his activities. Both alike broke earlier

---

[1] Mencius, Vb, 6.

[2] The word shih, mentioned in the Kuo Yü (Ch'i Yü, 1) in apposition to the farmer, artisan and merchant classes, seems to have reference there simply to a military shih. Cf. my article on Confucius, cited above, p. 46.

conventions by being the first to teach students on a large scale. The Sophists were dependent for livelihood upon the tuition fees which they thus received (one of the major criticisms levelled against them in their time), and Confucius likewise says : " From him who has brought his simple present of dried meat seeking to enter my school, I have never withheld instruction " (VII, 7). Such tuition was probably not received in any fixed amounts, but given to Confucius in the form of ' gifts.' While he was not wholly dependent on this tuition for his livelihood, and could also look to the state rulers for a certain amount of support, it was the very fact that his disciples were numerous which made this support from the state rulers forthcoming. Thus Confucius remains truly the first in China who made his living through teaching, but this fact should not in any way disparage him, since any sort of existence requires some means of support.

Another respect in which Confucius closely resembles the Sophists, is that though these were all men of wide learning and talents, and hence capable of giving instruction in all fields of study, yet their primary aim was to enable their students to lead lives of government activity. So it was with Confucius, who possessed an equally wide learning, and of whom someone said : " What a great man is Confucius ! His learning is vast, yet in nothing does he acquire a reputation " (IX, 2). And on another occasion a great minister inquired of one of the disciples : " ' Your master is surely a Sage ? What varied acquirement he has ! ' Tzŭ Kung replied : ' Of a truth Heaven has lavishly endowed him to the point of being a Sage, and his acquirements are also many.' " (IX, 6).

Thus Confucius, like the Sophists, offered instruction in many subjects (in his case the Six Disciplines). Yet at the same time his primary emphasis was on government activity, so that ' in a state of a thousand chariots ' his disciples might ' be appointed to the administration of its revenues,' or ' be appointed as Controller ' (V, 7). Once, when someone asked whether certain three disciples were suited for official employment, Confucius replied : " Yu is a man of decision. . . . Tz'ŭ is a man of penetration. . . . Ch'iu is a man of much proficiency. . . . What difficulty would they find therein ? " (VI, 6). In the same way it is customary for heads of schools even to-day to recommend their graduates for employment in various branches of the Chinese government.

*   *   *

Thirdly, I have stated that Confucius in many ways resembles Socrates. Socrates was considered by some of his contemporaries as a Sophist, though he differed from them inasmuch as he did not take tuition fees from his students and did not sell his knowledge. He had no interest in metaphysical problems, and accepted a traditional attitude toward supernatural beings ; on these questions Confucius held a similar viewpoint. Socrates regarded himself as a person who had been given a divine mission, and considered it his duty to bring enlightenment to the Greeks. So also with Confucius, who once exclaimed: "Heaven begat the virtue that is in me" (VII, 22). And again: "Since Heaven is not yet ready to destroy this cause of truth, what can the men of K'uang do to me?" (IX, 5).

Again Socrates, according to Aristotle, sought through inductive reasoning to frame universal definitions, from which standards might be made for human conduct. Confucius, likewise, expounded the doctrine of the Rectification of Names (*cheng ming* 正名), believing that once the meanings of names were made fixed, they would serve as standards for conduct. Socrates laid emphasis upon man's ethical nature, and Confucius also looked upon a man's 'complete virtue' (*jen* 仁) as of even greater importance than his capacity for government service. Therefore, although 'in a state of a thousand chariots' he granted his disciples the ability to be 'appointed to the administration of its revenues,' 'appointed as Controller,' or 'appointed (in court) to converse with the guests,' we are told that he refused to admit that they had 'complete virtue' (V, 7). Socrates wrote no works himself, but his name was made use of by many of the men who followed him (as by Plato in the *Dialogues*). Likewise in the case of Confucius, so that the phrase, 'The Master said,' occurs with extreme frequency in books of all sorts since his day. After the death of Socrates, his school of thought was further developed by Plato and Aristotle, thus becoming the orthodoxy of western philosophy. And in the same way the school of Confucius was developed by Mencius and Hsün Tzŭ, and became the orthodoxy of Chinese philosophy. This general statement will be examined in detail later.

Viewed as the counterpart of Socrates in China, Confucius occupies a very exalted position. Add to this the fact that he was the first in China to popularize learning and culture, and that he was the prototype, or at least the developer, of the *shih* or scholar class, and his achievements perhaps even exceed those of Socrates.

2—ATTITUDE OF CONFUCIUS TOWARD TRADITIONAL INSTITUTIONS
AND BELIEFS

It has already been stated that it was not until the Chou dynasty that Chinese civilization assumed a definite shape, and while the dynasty's literary records and institutions were probably not entirely the work of its founders, King Wen and the Duke of Chou, these two men were nevertheless the most important creators of Chou culture. The Lu state was ruled by the descendants of the Duke of Chou, and so the Chou culture remained more in evidence in this state than in the others. The *Tso Chuan* says under the year 506 B.C.:

"The Duke of Chou helped the Imperial House to rule the empire, he being most dear to the sovereign. The Duke of Lu (descendant of the Duke of Chou) received for his part a great carriage and a grand flag. . . . that thus the brilliant virtue of the Duke of Chou might be made illustrious. (The Duke of Lu) had been given a very wide stretch of territory, with priests, superintendents of the ancestral temple, diviners, historians, all the appendages of state, the tablets of historical records, the various officers, and the instruments of their office " (p. 754).

The *Tso Chuan* also tells us concerning an envoy from Wu, that it was when he visited Lu that " he observed the music of Chou " (p. 549), and again that when Han Hsüan Tzŭ was visiting Lu, he " examined the books of the Great Historian, and saw the symbols of the *I* and the *Ch'un Ch'iu* of Lu, whereupon he said : ' The ceremonials of Chou are complete in Lu, and now I comprehend the virtue of the Duke of Chou and how it was that the Chou became kings' " (p. 583). Culturally speaking, it is evident that Lu must have been a miniature reflection of the ancestral Chou. Especially was this the case when, after the first few centuries of its rule, the House of Chou so declined in power that a raid of western barbarians forced King P'ing (770-720) to move his capital from the west to the east, where he established the Eastern Chou dynasty. On this occasion many objects of cultural importance must have been lost, with the result that Chou culture from that time on became centered in the state of Lu.

During his entire lifetime Confucius clung to his love for study, as evidenced by several statements :

" I am not one who has innate knowledge, but one who, loving antiquity, is diligent in seeking it therein " (VII, 19).

" Even in a hamlet of ten houses there must be men as conscientious and sincere as myself, but none as fond of learning as I am " (V, 27).

" I can describe the civilization of the Hsia dynasty, but the descendant state of Ch'i cannot render adequate corroboration. I can describe the civilization of the Yin dynasty, but the descendant state of Sung cannot render adequate corroboration. And all because of the deficiency of their records and wise men. Were those sufficient then I could corroborate my views " (III, 9).

Because he was a native of Lu, where the Chou civilization was still much in evidence, Confucius had a deep knowledge and love for this ancient culture, and once he exclaimed : " Chou had the advantage of surveying the two preceding dynasties. How replete was its culture ! I follow Chou " (III, 14).

As a follower of Chou, the life aim of Confucius was to perpetuate the achievements of King Wen and the Duke of Chou, so that on th famous occasion when he was menaced at K'uang, he declared :

" Since King Wen is no longer alive, does not his culture (*wen* 文) rest, with me ? If Heaven were going to destroy this culture, a later mortal like me could not have gained such a close association with it. Since Heaven has not yet destroyed this culture, what can the men of K'uang do to me ? " (IX, 5).

Describing his mission, he said : " If there were one willing to employ me, might I not create an Eastern Chou ? " (XVII, 5). By an Eastern Chou he meant the revival in eastern China of the old Chou culture. On another occasion Confucius made a lament over his own degeneracy : " For long I have not dreamed as of yore that I saw the Duke of Chou " (VII, 5).

During the Han dynasty the Old Text school of classical scholarship maintained that it was the Duke of Chou who originated the Six Disciplines and that Confucius was only their transmitter, whereas the New Text school maintained that Confucius had composed the *Ch'un Ch'iu* to make himself in this way comparable to King Wen. While both views are probably wrong, Confucius does seem to have considered as his special duty the perpetuation of the achievements of King Wen and the Duke of Chou.

Because of this, Confucius has been mentioned by all later Confucians in conjunction with the Duke of Chou. Mencius says of someone : " Pleased with the doctrines of the Duke of Chou and Confucius, he came northward to the Middle Kingdom " (*Mencius*, IIIa, 4). And Hsün Tzŭ : " Confucius possessed the qualities of human-heartedness and wisdom, and was not prejudiced. Hence his scholarship and mastery over all teachings were sufficient to be those of the early kings. He possessed the whole of the Way (*Tao* 道); he brought it to people's notice, and he used it ; he was not prejudiced in the carrying out of it. Hence his virtue was equal to that of the Duke of Chou, and his reputation was abreast of that of the Three Kings " [1] (*Hsün-tzŭ*, p. 265).

Likewise during the Han dynasty, as in the *Huai-nan-tzŭ* : " Confucius practised the ways of Kings Ch'eng (1115-1079) and K'ang (1078-1053), and transmitted the precepts of the Duke of Chou" (ch. 21, p. 8). And the *Shih Chi* : " Five hundred years after the death of the Duke of Chou there came Confucius " (ch. 130, p. 8).

Confucius was ' a transmitter and not a creator, a believer in and lover of antiquity ' (VII, 1). What he transmitted was the Chou civilization.

Because of his knowledge and love of Chou culture, Confucius could not restrain himself from laments when he observed its decay. Thus when he saw the eight rows of dancers performing in the temple of the usurping House of Chi, a rite reserved in normal times to persons of ducal rank, he remarked that this was something which " could not be endured " (III, 1). And when he saw " the chief of the

---

[1] These were Yü, first ruler of the Hsia dynasty ; T'ang, founder of Shang ; and Kings Wen and Wu, counted as one.—Tr.

Chi family going to sacrifice on Mount T'ai," which was a royal prerogative, he exclaimed : " Alas ! Is that not saying that Mount T'ai is not the equal of Lin Fang ? " [1] (III, 6). Confucius said of the noted statesman, Kuan Chung, who " used a stand for his inverted pledge-cup," also a noble prerogative, that " he did not understand etiquette " (III, 22). And on another occasion when the ruler of the neighboring state of Ch'i had been assassinated, Confucius bathed himself and went to court, where he petitioned the Duke of Lu, saying : " Ch'en Heng has slain his ruler. I beg you to punish him " (XIV, 22). Of his own conduct, it is said that from the time when he " followed behind the great officers of state, he could not go afoot " (XI, 7). Indeed, the descriptions of his habits of living, eating and drinking, as given in the *Lun Yü* (Bk. X), seem almost those of a nobleman. This does not necessarily mean that Confucius was fond of luxury, but that he felt that if he did not live in this way, he would not be in accord with the etiquette that the ancient Chou ceremonials required.

Toward the traditional beliefs of his time Confucius was also a conservative. There are several passages in the *Lun Yü* recording his views about Heaven (*T'ien* 天) :

" Wang-sun Chia inquired : What is the meaning of the saying, ' It is better to pay court to the god of the hearth than to the god of the hall ? ' ' Not so,' said the Master. ' He who sins against Heaven has no place left where he may pray' " (III, 13).

" Once when the Master was seriously ill, Tzŭ Lu set the disciples to act as if they were a statesman's officers. During a remission of the attack Confucius observed : ' For what a long time has Yu been carrying on his impositions ! In pretending to have retainers when I have none, whom do I deceive ? Do I deceive Heaven ? ' " (IX, 11.)

" When Yen Yüan (the favorite disciple of Confucius) died, the Master exclaimed : ' Alas ! Heaven has bereft me ! Heaven has bereft me ! ' " (XI, 8).

" The Master said : 'I make no complaint against Heaven, nor blame men, for though my studies are lowly my mind soars aloft. And that which knows me, is it not Heaven ? ' " (XIV, 37).

These passages show that Heaven, for Confucius, meant a purposeful Supreme Being or ' ruling Heaven.' [2]

---

[1] A disciple of Confucius, who was skilled in asking Confucius questions about the rites. See *Lun Yü*, III, 4.—Tr.

[2] The words of Confucius : " What speech has Heaven ? The four seasons run their round and all things flourish, yet what speech has Heaven ? " (XVII, 19), have been used to prove that Confucius's Heaven was a spontaneous unpurposeful one. Yet really this passage simply means that Heaven ' rules through non-activity,' a Taoistic idea, rather than that Heaven itself is spontaneous. For if we once say of Heaven that it does not speak, we are implying that Heaven could speak if it wished, but deliberately does not do so. Otherwise such a statement would be meaningless. In the same way we would not say of a stone or a table that they do not speak, because these are objects which have always been incapable of speech. See also p. 31 for five possible interpretations of the word ' Heaven.'

The *Lun Yü* also contains several passages which mention heavenly Fate or Will (*ming* 命) :

" The Master said : 'At fifteen I set my mind upon learning. At thirty I stood firm. At forty I was free from doubts. At fifty I understood the Will of Heaven. . . .' " (II, 4).

" When Po Niu was ill the Master went to inquire about him. Having grasped his hand through the window he said : 'We are losing him. Alas ! It is Fate. That such a man should have such a disease ! That such a man should have such a disease ! ' " (VI, 8).

" The Master said : 'If my principles are going to prevail, it is through Fate. If my principles are going to fail, it is through Fate. What can Kung-po Liao do against Fate ? ' " (XIV, 38).

" Confucius said : 'The Superior Man holds three things in awe. He holds the Will of Heaven in awe ; he holds the great man in awe ; and he holds the precepts of the Sages in awe ' " (XVI, 8).

For Confucius, Heaven was a purposeful Supreme Being ; hence Fate or *ming* was the purpose of that Supreme Being. As for himself, he believed that he had a holy mission which had been conferred on him by Heaven. Hence his words : " Since Heaven has not yet destroyed this culture, what can the men of K'uang do to me ? " (IX, 5). This belief was one also shared by some of his contemporaries, among them an officer in charge of a small frontier town, who once said : " The world for long has been without principles. But now Heaven is going to use the Master as an arousing tocsin " (III, 24).

Toward spirits, however, Confucius had a more skeptical attitude. There are several passages in the *Lun Yü* on the subject :

" He sacrificed (to the ancestors) *as if* they were present. He sacrificed to the spirits *as if* the spirits were present " (III, 12).

" The Master said : 'To devote oneself earnestly to one's duty to humanity, and, while respecting the spirits, to keep away from them, may be called wisdom' " (VI, 20).

" When Chi Lu asked his duty to the spirits, the Master replied : ' When still unable to do your duty to men, how can you do your duty to the spirits ? ' When he ventured to ask about death, Confucius answered : 'Not yet understanding life, how can you understand death ? ' " (XI, 11).

Since ' while respecting the spirits, to keep away from them ' constitutes wisdom, the reverse of this of course shows lack of wisdom. But if such is the case, why should spirits be respected at all ? This question was answered by the later Confucianists, who formulated a systematic conception of sacrifices which will be discussed in detail in Chapter XIV. Here we need only stress the fact that Confucius introduced the word ' wisdom ' on this problem, and displayed a rationalist attitude, making it probable that there were other superstitions of his time in which he also did not believe. Hence the words : " The Master would not discuss prodigies, prowess, lawlessness or the supernatural " (VII, 20).

3—THE RECTIFICATION OF NAMES

For Confucius, ' a world without order (*Tao*) ' was the result of the breakdown of the social institutions of his time, and his constant hope was that this condition might be remedied, so that he said :

" When good order prevails in the world, ceremonials, music and punitive expeditions proceed from the Son of Heaven. When good order fails in the world, ceremonials, music and punitive expeditions proceed from the nobles. When they proceed from a noble, it is rare if his power be not lost within ten generations. When they proceed from a noble's minister, it is rare if his power be not lost within five generations. But when a minister's minister holds command in the kingdom, it is rare if his power be not lost within three generations. When there is good order in the world, its policy is not in the hands of ministers. And when there is good order in the empire, the people do not even discuss it " (XVI, 2).

" The revenue has departed from the Ducal House (of Lu) for five generations, and the government has devolved on ministers for four generations. Alas ! That is why the descendants of the three Huan families (who originally ruled Lu) are so reduced ! " (XVI, 3).

It was Confucius's belief that the degeneration of political and social states originates from the top. " When ceremonials, music and punitive expeditions proceed from the nobles," within ten generations there must be a further decline so that they then " proceed from a noble's minister." Given five generations of this condition, the result must be that " a minister's minister holds command in the kingdom," which is why, in the case of Lu, " the descendants of the three Huan families are so reduced." The consequence is that a revolution must take place among the people within three generations. Mencius similarly said : " If righteousness be put last, and profit be put first, they (the people) will not be satisfied unless they are snatching (everything) " (*Mencius*, Ia, 1).

Confucius believed that under these circumstances the only way to restore order would be so to arrange affairs that the Emperor would continue to be Emperor, the nobles to be nobles, the ministers to be ministers, and the common people common people. That is, the actual must in each case be made to correspond to the name. This theory Confucius called the Rectification of Names (*cheng ming* 正 名), a doctrine which he recognized as being of the utmost importance :

" Tzŭ Lu said : ' The prince of Wei is awaiting you, Sir, to take control of his administration. What will you undertake first,

Sir ?' The Master replied : 'The one thing needed is the rectification of names ' ' ' ' (XIII, 3).

" When Duke Ching of Ch'i inquired of Confucius the principles
of government, Confucius answered saying : ' Let the ruler be ruler,
the minister minister ; let the father be father, and the son son.' ' Excellent ! ' said the Duke. ' For truly if the ruler be not ruler, the
minister not minister ; if the father be not father, and the son not
son, though grain exist, shall I be allowed to eat it ?' " (XII, 11).

Every name possesses its own definition, which designates that
which makes the thing to which the name is applied be that thing and
no other. In other words, the name is that thing's essence or
concept. What is pointed out by the definition of the name ' ruler,'
for example, is that essence which makes a ruler a ruler. In the
phrase : ' Let the ruler be ruler,' etc., the first word, ' ruler,' refers
to ruler as a material actuality, while the second ' ruler ' is the name
and concept of the ideal ruler. Likewise for the other terms : minister,
father and son. For if it is brought about that ruler, minister, father
and son all act in real life in accordance with the definitions or concepts of these words, so that all carry out to the full their allotted
duties, there will be no more disorder in the world. Confucius considered his time as a period when, on the contrary, " the ruler is not
ruler, the minister not minister ; the father is not father, and the son
not son." To him this confusion was symbolized by one of the
types of drinking goblets that was then in use :

"The cornered vessel (*ku* 觚) has no longer corners. What
a ' cornered ' vessel ! What a ' cornered ' vessel ! " (VI, 23).

It was because the actualities of things no longer corresponded to
their names, Confucius believed, that the world was suffering from
disorder, and therefore the names must be rectified. Not only
this, but this rectification must begin from the top, because it
was at the top that the discrepancy between actualities and names had
originated :

"When Chi K'ang Tzŭ (who had usurped the power in Lu)
asked Confucius for the way to govern, Confucius replied : 'To
govern (*cheng* 政) means to rectify (*cheng* 正). If you, Sir, will lead
in the rectification, who will dare not to be rectified ?' " (XII, 17).

" Chi K'ang Tzŭ being plagued with robbers, consulted Confucius, who answered him saying : ' If you, Sir, be free from the love
of wealth, although you pay them they will not steal ' " (XII, 18).

" Chi K'ang Tzŭ asked the opinion of Confucius on government
and said : ' How would it do to execute the lawless for the good
of the law-abiding ?' ' What need, Sir, is there of capital punishment
in your administration ?' responded Confucius. ' If your desire is
for good, the people will be good. The moral character of the ruler
is the wind ; the moral character of those beneath him is the grass.
When the grass has the wind upon it, it assuredly bends ' " (XII, 19).

In other words, in a government through nobility, the mass of the people are uneducated, and hence the ruler's personal conduct inevitably has a great shaping influence upon that of the common man.

It has been traditionally supposed that Confucius composed the *Ch'un Ch'iu* in order to carry his rectification of names into actual practice. Mencius, for example, says that Confucius ' made ' (*tso* 作) the *Ch'un Ch'iu*, with the result that " rebellious ministers and villainous sons were struck with terror " (*Mencius*, III*b*, 9). Yet the *Tso Chuan* states under the year 607 B.C., at the time when Duke Ling of Chin was murdered :

" The Grand Historian (of Chin) wrote the entry, ' Chao Tun has murdered his prince,' and showed it to the court. Hsüan Tzŭ (i.e., Chao Tun) said that this was not true. (The historian) replied : ' Sir, you are the highest minister. Flying from the state, you did not go beyond its frontiers. When you returned you did not punish the assassin. If it is not you (who are responsible), who is it ? ' .... Confucius said of this : ' Of old, Tung Hu was an excellent historian. In his writings he had the rule of not concealing (the truth) ' " (pp. 290-291). Again, under the year 548, when Duke Chuang of Ch'i was murdered :

" The Grand Historian (of Ch'i) made a record of the fact which said : 'Ts'ui Shu has murdered his prince.' Ts'ui Tzŭ thereupon had him executed. Two of his brothers did the same after him, and were also executed. A third wrote the same and was spared. The historian in the south, learning that the Grand Historian and his two brothers had died in this way, took his tablets and went (to record also that Ts'ui Tzŭ had murdered his prince). But learning on the way that the affair had already been recorded (by the third brother), he returned " (pp. 514-515).

These quotations indicate that during the Ch'un Ch'iu period the Grand Historians of at least two states, those of Chin and Ch'i, could by what they recorded cause ' rebellious ministers and villainous sons to be struck with terror,' so that it is not only of the *Ch'un Ch'iu* of Lu that this statement was true. Probably certain standard rules existed for the recording of events, which were followed by all the historians of this early period. Thus Mencius says :

" The *Cheng* 乘 of Chin, the *Tao Wu* 檮杌 of Ch'u, and the *Ch'un Ch'iu* of Lu were books of the same character. Their subject was the affairs of (Dukes) Huan of Ch'i and Wen of Chin, and their style was historical. Confucius said : ' Their righteous principles I ventured to take ' " (*Mencius*, IV*b*, 21).

The phrase, ' righteous principles,' refers with as much force to the *Cheng* and *Tao Wu* as to the *Ch'un Ch'iu*, though it has been commonly interpreted as referring only to the latter, in consonance with the theory that Confucius had a special connection with the *Ch'un Ch'iu*. According to this passage, Confucius only ' took ' (*ch'ü* 取)

principles from works already written, but did not make them himself, a statement which seems close to the facts, even though Mencius elsewhere says that Confucius actually composed the *Ch'un Ch'iu*.[1]

But it is also possible that because the Lu rulers were descendants of the Duke of Chou, and their state was noted for its ceremonials and justice, the *Ch'un Ch'iu* of Lu, in comparison with similar histories in other states, was recognized as being especially accurate as regards 'principles.' Thus when Han Hsüan Tzŭ, as noted above, came to Lu on a diplomatic mission and saw there the books of the Grand Historian, he particularly noticed the ' *Ch'un Ch'iu* of Lu.' From this it would seem that the work possessed special qualities as compared with such histories as the *Cheng* of Chin and *Tao Wu* of Ch'u, because of which there were already persons before Confucius who had been using it for teaching purposes. Thus when the question arose as to what should be taught to the crown prince of Ch'u, son of King Chuang (613-591), the answer came :

" Teach him the *Ch'un Ch'iu* and by it encourage goodness and censure evil, so as to restrain and admonish his mind " (*Kuo Yü, Ch'u Yü*, I, 1).

From this we may see that the *Ch'un Ch'iu* had already in early times become a subject for instruction, so that its use in this way has no direct connection with Confucius.

Confucius did, no doubt, approve of the idea that the *Ch'un Ch'iu* should ' encourage goodness and censure evil,' punish rebellious ministers and villainous sons, and, as the *Chuang-tzŭ* (p. 439) says, serve to ' show distinctions and duties.' Nevertheless it would seem that the traditional account which says that Confucius actually composed the *Ch'un Ch'iu* himself, so as to carry out in this way his rectification of names, is erroneous, and that he probably did this simply by ' taking ' principles from such works as the *Ch'un Ch'iu*, in the manner that Mencius relates.

4—Confucius as a Creator through being a Transmitter

Confucius, according to his own words, was ' a transmitter and not a creator,' and we have seen how none of the works traditionally ascribed to him, even the *Ch'un Ch'iu*, could have come from his

---

[1] Liu Shih-p'ei (1884-1919), in his *Tso An Chi* (*chüan* 2), gives a detailed analysis of the word 作 *tso*, as used in the phrase in *Mencius*, IIIb, 9, which is usually translated as : " Confucius was afraid and made (*tso*) the *Ch'un Ch'iu*." This word *tso*, he shows, may have one of two meanings : the usual one of ' make ' or ' originate,' and another one of ' to practice.' He proves this by quotations from many early works showing that the word *tso* occurs in such phrases as ' to play (*tso*) music,' or ' to sing (*tso*) odes.' Similarly when Mencius says that " Confucius *tso* the *Ch'un Ch'iu*," he may have meant that he ' lectured ' or ' expounded ' it. When doing so, Confucius would no doubt have emphasized the rectification of names by such means, which would explain the words : " Their principles I ventured to take." And if such a hypothesis is true, this would be the way in which, as Mencius says, Confucius caused " rebellious ministers and villainous sons to be struck with terror."

hand. I have suggested the alternative hypothesis that Confucius took the principles underlying the writing of the *Ch'un Ch'iu* and of the other early histories, and drew from them the doctrine of the Rectification of Names, thus rationalizing the *Ch'un Ch'iu*. The great contribution of Confucius to Chinese civilization, indeed, has been the rationalization he has given to its originally existing social institutions. The *Lun Yü* offers an example :

" Tsai Wo, asking about the three years' mourning, suggested that one year was long enough.¹ ' If,' said he, ' a cultivated man be three years without exercising his manners, his manners will certainly degenerate, and if for three years he make no use of music, his music will certainly go to ruin. (In a year), the last year's grain is finished and the new grain has been garnered ; the fire-making friction sticks have been changed . . . a year would be enough.'

" ' Would you, then, feel at ease in eating good rice and wearing fine clothes ? ' asked the Master. ' I should,' was the reply. ' If you would feel at ease, then do so ; but a cultivated man, when mourning, does not relish good food when he eats it, does not enjoy music when he hears it, and does not feel at ease when in a comfortable dwelling. Therefore he avoids those things. But now if you would feel at ease, then go and do them.'

" When Tsai Wo had gone out, the Master said : ' The unfeelingness of Tsai Yü ! Only when a child is three years old does it leave its parents' arms, and the three years' mourning is the universal mourning everywhere. And Yü, .. was not he the object of his parents' affection for three years ? ' " (XVII, 21).

This serves as an example of how Confucius gives a rational basis to a social institution.²

In the course of teaching the Six Disciplines, Confucius also sometimes gave to them a new significance. The doctrine of the Rectification of Names, as already described, he arrived at by a synthesis of the principles of writing in the *Ch'un Ch'iu* and other old histories. He treated the *Shih Ching* (Book of Odes) in the same way. Thus apropos of the passage (Odes, I, v, 3) : " As she artfully smiles, what dimples appear ! Her bewitching eyes show their

---

¹ This was for the death of a parent, and at that time, as now, actually meant twenty-five or twenty-seven months during which the son must put aside all duties, eat poor food, and wear sackcloth.—Tr.

² Some say that it was Confucius who first established the custom of three years' mourning. But the *Tso Chuan*, under the year 527, states : " The King in the space of one year has had two deaths, for each of which he should have mourned three years. . . . . When a death that should be mourned for three years has occurred, even the nobles should complete the mourning for it : this is the etiquette. Even if it is the King who does not complete it and who holds feasts so soon, it is not the proper etiquette " (p. 660). This indicates that the three years of mourning had originally been a general custom, though by the time of Confucius those who practised it were already less numerous, so that even this King did not complete it. Confucius once more advocated it, and gave it a rational basis.

colors so clear," a disciple was made to understand that: "Then manners (*li* 禮) are secondary?" Confucius granted his approval to this, saying: "Now I can begin to discuss the Odes with him" (III, 8). Again:

"Though the Odes number three hundred, one phrase can cover them all, namely, 'with uncorrupted thoughts' "[1] (II, 2).

"The odes can stimulate the mind, can train the observation, can encourage social intercourse, and can alleviate the vexations of life. From them one can learn how to fulfil one's more immediate duties to one's father, and the more remote duties to one's ruler. And in them one may become widely acquainted with the names of birds, beasts, plants and trees" (XVII, 9).

This shows how Confucius, when teaching, stressed the ethical significance of the *Shih Ching*, rather than mere drill in repetitive replies. He aimed at more than merely making his disciples men who "wherever they might be sent, would not disgrace their ruler's commission" (XIII, 20).

Again, concerning the *Shu Ching* (Book of History):

"Someone asked Confucius, saying: 'Why, Sir, are you not in the public service?' The Master answered: 'Does not the *Shu* say concerning filial piety: Filial piety and friendliness toward one's brethren can be displayed in the exercise of public service? (p. 232). These qualities then are also public service. Why should only that idea of yours be considered as constituting public service?'" (II, 21).

This is the germ of the concept that harmony within the family is the root of good government in the state, an idea later developed in the *Ta Hsüeh* (Great Learning).[2] It shows us that in his exposition of the *Shu*, as of the *Shih*, Confucius elaborated its moral precepts, and did not merely transmit its words and records.

Again, concerning the rites (*li*) and music: "Lin Fang asked what was the chief principle in ceremonial observances. The Master answered: 'A great question indeed! In ceremonials, it is better to be simple than lavish; and in the rites of mourning, heartfelt distress is better than observance of detail'" (III, 4).

"In the usages of ceremonial, it is harmoniousness which is of value. In the regulations of the ancient kings this was the admirable feature" (I, 12).

Confucius said: "'Ceremonials!' they say, 'Ceremonials!' Can mere gems and gowns be called ceremonials? 'Music!' they say, 'Music!' Can mere bells and drums be called music?" (XVII, 11). Again: "Music may be readily understood. The attack should be prompt and united, and as the piece proceeds it

---

[1] This phrase occurs in the Odes, IV, ii, Ode 1, 4.—Tr.
[2] *Cf.* ch. 14, sect. 7, especially pp. 362, 364-365.

should do so harmoniously, with clearness of tone and continuity of time, until it reaches its conclusion " (III, 23).

This shows that already with Confucius, emphasis was laid upon the fundamental meaning and principles of ceremonial and music, rather than upon the mere expounding of their outer form and manner of presentation.

Confucius also said about the *I Ching* (Book of Changes) : " The men of the south have a saying : 'A man without constancy will make neither a soothsayer nor a doctor.' How well put ! (The *I Ching* says) : ' If he be inconstant in his moral character, someone will bring disgrace upon him ' (p. 126). The Master said : ' All because he did not calculate beforehand ' " (XIII, 22).

The exact meaning of this passage is admittedly unclear, but it at least indicates that also in expounding the *I Ching*, Confucius was interested in the meaning contained in its phrases rather than in the mere use of the book for divination.

This is no longer to be simply ' a transmitter and not a creator.' It is in fact to be a creator *through* being a transmitter. It was such a spirit and attitude, as handed down to the later Confucians such as Mencius and Hsün Tzŭ, that enabled the Confucian school to forge a unified system of thought.

Thus the *I Ching* had existed long before Confucius, and was handed down by the Confucian school; but it is primarily its Appendices, written by Confucians, which make it important in the history of thought. The *Ch'un Ch'iu* existed early, and was transmitted by the Confucians; but it is the *Kung-yang Chuan*, a commentary written on it by the Confucian school (together with other commentaries), which make it important. So with the *I Li* (Book of Etiquette and Ceremonial). It, too, was an early work transmitted by the Confucianists ; whereas the *Li Chi* (Book of Rites) was written by Confucianists who utilized material based on the *I Li*, and far surpasses the latter in importance in the history of thought.

The Old Text school is not far wrong, then, in maintaining that originally the Six Disciplines all formed part of the official literature, which Confucius merely transmitted but did not create. Yet the New Text school, too, has some reason for saying that Confucius was a creator rather than a transmitter ; and there has been cause for later generations holding up Confucius not only as ' the most perfect Sage,' but as ' the first Teacher.' For the *I Ching*, deprived of its Appendices, is no more than a book of divination ; the *Ch'un Ch'iu*, without such commentaries as those of Kung-yang, is only a collection of dry-as-dust brief court records ; and the *I Li*, separated from the *Li Chi*, is only a book of etiquette. In themselves these works could not possibly have possessed the influence which they have exercised during the last two thousand years. It is not the books themselves, but the writings based upon them, that have been of outstanding influence in Chinese history from the Han dynasty down to the late Ch'ing or Manchu dynasty. When the New Text school speaks of Confucius as 'the perfect Sage and first Teacher,' however, we must remember that the Confucius it is thinking of is not the historical figure, but rather a legendary Confucius standing as the ideal representative of the Confucian school.

5—The Virtues of Uprightness, Human-Heartedness, Conscientiousness and Altruism

Confucius, as said above, when expounding ceremonials or good manners (*li*), emphasized the underlying reasons for their existence. The *Lun Yü* says:
  " Tzǔ Hsia asked : 'What is the meaning of the passage,

> As she artfully smiles,
> What dimples appear !
> Her bewitching eyes
> Show their colors so clear.
> Ground spotless and candid
> For tracery splendid ! (Odes, I, 5, 3) ? '

  " ' The painting comes after the groundwork,' replied the Master. ' Then manners (*li*) are secondary ? ' said Tzǔ Hsia. ' It is Shang who unfolds my meaning,' replied the Master. ' Now indeed, I can begin to discuss the Odes with him ' " (III, 8).
  Confucius here means that a man must have a nature of sincere genuineness before he may practise ceremonial and etiquette, just as a beautiful woman must first have a bewitching smile and lovely eyes, before she may make use of powder and rouge. If not, ceremonial observances or *li* will be a false and empty form, and as such are not only unworthy of being prized, but are actually cheapening. Therefore Confucius says :
  " When a man is not virtuous (*jen* 仁), of what account are his ceremonial manners (*li*) ? When a man is not virtuous, of what account is his music ? " (III, 3).
  If a man lacks inner virtue and genuineness of nature, though he practise the outer adornments of fine manners and music, they but add to his emptiness and artificiality. Confucius says again :
  " The Superior Man (*chün tzǔ* 君 子) takes righteousness (*i* 義) as his ' basic stuff ' (*chih* 質) ; practises it with the rules of correct usage (*li*) ; brings it forth with modesty ; and renders it complete with sincerity : such is the Superior Man " (XV, 17).
  The idea here is that proper manners or *li*, and the ' basic stuff ' which is a man's genuine nature, must operate in mutual co-ordination.
  Confucius laid emphasis on the importance of man's possessing the quality of genuineness or truth, and hated all emptiness and false-

ness. He esteemed the 'basic stuff' and its accompanying quality of straightforwardness or uprightness (*chih* 直), concerning which the *Lun Yü* contains many passages. Thus Confucius says :
"Man's life is to be upright (*chih*). If one makes crooked this life, one is lucky to escape (disaster)" (IV, 17).

To have uprightness or *chih*, a man must neither deceive himself nor deceive others. . He must give true outward expression to what his mind likes and dislikes, as is shown in another passage :
" The Duke of She observed to Confucius : ' In my part of the country there is a man so upright (*chih*) that when his father appropriated a sheep he bore witness to it.' Confucius said : ' The upright people in my part of the country are different from that, for a father will screen his son, and a son his father. In that there lies uprightness ' " (XIII, 18).

Uprightness or *chih* is what comes from within. It is the direct expression of one's heart. When a father has appropriated someone's sheep, the son ordinarily would certainly not wish the fact to become known. This is simply human nature. But in the above story the son bore witness to the fact that his father had appropriated a sheep. In this case the son either wished to get the name of uprightness through sacrificing his father, or lacked feeling toward his father. Hence this could not be true uprightness.

Again in the *Lun Yü* : " The Master said : ' Who says Wei-sheng Kao is upright (*chih*) ? Someone begged vinegar of him, whereupon he begged it of a neighbor who gave it him ' " (V, 23).

The man who is upright acts according to his own feelings, whereas the man who is crooked acts according to the feelings of others. When one's own family has no vinegar, it is permissible to refuse another man's request for it. But in the present case the request was granted solely because it was feared that the other person would not be pleased with a refusal. In so doing the giver failed to be able inwardly to set himself his own standard, while at the same time he could not avoid betraying himself in order to retain the good opinion of another. Pushed to the extreme, such a man becomes false and artificial, and hence an act of this kind cannot be called *chih*.

Confucius said : " Plausible speech, an ingratiating demeanor, and fulsome respect : Tso Ch'iu Ming was ashamed of them, and I, Ch'iu, am also ashamed of them " (V, 24). Confucius was ashamed of such conduct because it shows a lack of uprightness.

The *Lun Yü* says again : " Tzŭ Kung asked : ' What would you say of the man who is liked by all his fellow-townsmen ? ' The Master replied : ' That is not sufficient.' ' Then what would you say of him who is hated by all his fellow-townsmen ? ' The Master replied : ' Nor is that sufficient. What is better is that the good fellow-townsmen should like him, and the bad hate him ' " (XIII, 24).

A man hated by all his fellow-townsmen would inevitably be one deficient in natural feelings. On the other hand the man liked by all his fellow-townsmen would be a man who tries to please everybody, striving thereby to make them pay court to his own goodness. This would also be empty falseness, and hence unacceptable.

While *chih* is a quality to be prized, there must still be a code of proper manners (*li*) to put it into practice. The *Lun Yü* says :

" The Master said : ' Respectfulness uncontrolled by the rules of propriety (*li*) becomes laboured effort, caution uncontrolled becomes timidity, boldness uncontrolled becomes insubordination and uprightness (*chih*) uncontrolled becomes rudeness ' " (VIII, 2).

Again he said : " Love of uprightness (*chih*) without a love to learn finds itself obscured by harmful candor " (XVII, 8). By learning, he here means the learning of correct manners or *li*. The meaning of the word *li* 禮 as used in ancient China was very wide, signifying then, in addition to its usual present-day definition of ' politeness ' or ' courtesy,' the entire body of usages and customs, political and social institutions. Thus a noted statesman of the sixth century B.C. said of it : " The *li* constitute the warp of Heaven, the principle of Earth, and the conduct of the people." [1] And the *Chuang-tzŭ* (ch. 33) says : " The *li* direct conduct " (p. 439). In short, all the rules for everything pertaining to human conduct may be included under the term *li*.

Confucius, in his rôle of preserver of the *li* of the Chou civilization, not only imparted knowledge to his disciples, but also taught them the *li* with which to restrain themselves. This is what a disciple meant when he said : " He has broadened me by culture and restrained me by *li* " (IX, 10). But it was because Confucius at the same time laid stress on what is ' at the foundation of *li*,' that he also spoke on the quality *chih*. At such times he was emphasizing the independence and freedom of the individual, whereas when he discussed *li*, he was stressing the restraint placed by the rules of society upon the individual. The former were Confucius's new ideas ; the latter was the traditional mould formulated from ancient times. Confucius's concept of the *chün tzŭ* 君 子, a term originally applied to the feudal princes, but which in the Confucian sense came to be applied to the man possessing ' princely ' moral qualities, that is, to the ' Superior Man,' is that of a person who, having a nature of genuineness, can by means of it carry the *li* into practice. Therefore he says :

" When the ' basic stuff ' (*chih* 質) exceeds training (*wen* 文), you have the rustic. When training exceeds the ' basic stuff,' you have

---

[1] *Cf.* above, p. 38.

the clerk. It is only when the 'basic stuff' and training are proportionately blended that you have the Superior Man" (VI, 16).
   "Since I cannot obtain men who pursue the due medium, to
teach to, they must be the ambitious and the discreet. The ambitious
push themselves forward and seize hold of things, whereas as to the
discreet, there are things they will not do" (XIII, 21).
   "Your good careful people of the villages are the thieves of
virtue" (XVII, 13).
   'Basic stuff' and training proportionately blended set man on
the median way. Although the ambitious and the discreet do not
conform in their conduct to such a medium, they at least display their
true natures, and Confucius could therefore accept them for teaching.
But as for the rustic type of moral goody-goody, these are false
'Superior Men,' and hence inferior to the lesser sort of person
who is at least genuine and without pretence.[1]
   It has been said above that the man who is not virtuous
(*jen* 仁) is one who lacks a genuine nature. There are many
passages in the *Lun Yü* which discuss this quality of *jen* or
'perfect virtue.' The word *jen* 仁, one of the most important in
Confucian thought, is composed of the character meaning 'man'
(*jen* 人), combined with the character for 'two' (*erh* 二). Thus
it is a word embracing all those moral qualities which should
govern one man in his relations with another. As such it may
perhaps be best translated into English as 'human-heartedness,'[2]
though it is often also equivalent to such words as 'morality' or
'virtue.' Briefly defined, it is the manifestation of the genuine
nature, acting in accordance with propriety (*li*), and based upon
sympathy for others.
   Thus the *Lun Yü*: "The Master said: 'Artful speech and
ingratiating demeanor rarely accompany *jen*'" (I, 3). Again:
"'The firm of spirit, the resolute in character, the simple in
manner, and the slow of speech are not far from *jen*'" (XIII, 27).
   Those of artful speech and ingratiating demeanor try through
pretence to be seductive to others, and do not display their true
natures. Such qualities 'rarely accompany *jen*,' whereas the persons
characterized in the second quotation have a simplicity and
straightforwardness which show them to be of genuine nature, so
that they 'are not far from *jen*.'
   The *Lun Yü* says again: "Once when Fan Ch'ih asked the
meaning of *jen*, the Master replied: 'It is to love your fellow

---

[1] Some ideas in the above paragraphs, beginning with the quotation, 'Man's life is
to be upright,' etc., on p. 67, down to this point, have been suggested by Professor Ch'ien
Mu and by the article by Homer H. Dubs, 'The Conflict of Authority and Freedom in
Ancient Chinese Ethics,' in the *Open Court Magazine*, Vol. 40, No. 3.
[2] This translation for *jen* has been suggested by Dr. Lucuis C. Porter, professor of
philosophy at Yenching University, Peiping.—Tr.

men ' " (XII, 22). *Jen* takes sympathy as its basis. Therefore it is love of others. Again :

" Hsien asked : . . . . ' If a man refrain from ambition, boasting, resentment and desire, it may, I suppose, be counted to him for *jen* ? ' The Master said : ' It may be counted as difficult, but whether for *jen*, I do not know ' " (XIV, 2).

The noted scholar Chiao Hsün (1763-1820) writes on this passage : "Mencius said of Kung Liu that he loved wealth, and of King T'ai that he loved feminine beauty, and that yet by allowing the common people also to gratify these feelings, they were able to maintain their ricks and granaries, while there were no dissatisfied women or unmarried men.' In his learning, Mencius succeeded in fully comprehending the doctrine of Confucius, and his idea in this statement is (the same as that expressed in the *Lun Yü*) : ' Developing oneself one develops others, and maintaining oneself one maintains others ' (VI, 28). To insist on having no desires oneself, and at the same time to be indifferent to the desires of others, is to be nothing more than a ' dried-up gourd.' Therefore men who refrain from ambition, boasting, resentment and desire, are ascetics whom Confucius did not like. Such men are not equal to those who through their own desires come to know the desires of others, and who through their own dislike come to know the dislikes of others. To make analogies (in this way) is not difficult, and yet *jen* already consists in this.. But if one cuts short one's own desires, one will be unable to comprehend the desires of others, and such is not to be considered *jen*." [2]

Confucius said on one occasion : " A man's faults all conform to his type of mind. Observe his faults and you may know his virtues (*jen*) " (IV, 7). The manifestations of a man's true nature may go too far and become faults, but nevertheless they remain manifestations of truth, and so by observing them one may know the virtues as well.

The *Lun Yü* says again : " When Yen Yüan asked the meaning of *jen*, the Master replied : ' *Jen* is the denial of self and response to the right and proper (*li*). Deny yourself for one day and respond to the right and proper, and everybody will accord you *jen*. For has *jen* its source in one's self, or is it forsooth derived from others ? ' ' May I beg for the main features ? ' asked Yen Yüan. The Master answered : ' If not right and proper (*li*), do not look ; if not right and proper, do not listen ; if not right and proper, do not speak ; if not right and proper, do not move ' " (XII, 1).

" Uprightness (*chih*) uncontrolled by the rules of good taste (*li*) becomes rudeness " (VIII, 2). Thus *jen* is the manifestation of

---

[1] *Cf. Mencius*, Ib, 5.—Tr.
[2] *Cf.* his *Lun-yü Pu-su.*

what is genuine in human nature, and which at the same time is in accordance with *li*.

The *Lun Yü* says again: "When Chung Kung asked the meaning of *jen*, the Master said: 'When abroad, behave as if interviewing an honored guest; in directing the people, act as if officiating at a great sacrifice; do not do to others what you do not like yourself. Then neither in your state nor in your private home will there be any resentment against you.' 'Though I am not clever,' replied Chung Kung, 'permit me to carry out these precepts' " (XII, 2).

"Tzǔ Kung said: 'Suppose there were one who conferred benefits far and wide upon the people, and who was able to succour the multitude, what might one say of him? Could this be called *jen*?' 'What has this to do with *jen*?' asked the Master. 'Must he not be a Sage? Even (the sage Emperors) Yao and Shun felt their deficiency therein. For the man of *jen* is one who desiring to maintain himself sustains others, and desiring to develop himself develops others. To be able from one's own self to draw a parallel for the treatment of others: that may be called the way to practise *jen*' " (VI, 28).

If the practice of *jen* consists in being 'able from one's own self to draw a parallel for the treatment of others,' this means simply that it consists in putting oneself into the position of others. In the maxim, "Desiring to maintain oneself, one sustains others; desiring to develop oneself, one develops others," there is the Confucian virtue of ' conscientiousness to others ' or *chung* 忠.[1] And in the maxim, "Do not do to others what you do not like yourself," there is the Confucian virtue of *shu* 恕 or altruism. Genuinely to practise these virtues of *chung* and *shu* is genuinely to practise *jen*. The *Lun Yü* states:

"The Master said: 'Shen! My teaching contains one all pervading principle.' 'Yes,' replied Tseng Tzǔ. When the Master had left the room the disciples asked: 'What did he mean?' Tseng Tzǔ replied: 'Our Master's teaching is conscientiousness (*chung*) and altruism (*shu*), and nothing else' " (IV, 15).

To say that the all pervading principle of Confucius is *chung* and *shu*, is the same as saying that it is *jen*. As simple as this is the

---

[1] The Confucian virtue of altruism or sympathy for others (*shu* 恕), which is discussed immediately below, may be defined as: "Do not do to others what you do not like yourself" (XV, 23). But the meaning of *chung* is not very clearly defined in the *Lun Yü*, so that later it has come to be interpreted as meaning the 'exhaustion of one's self' in the performance of one's moral duties (*chin chi* 盡己). But let us see how the term is used in the *Lun Yü* itself: "In planning for others have I failed in conscientiousness (*chung*)? " (I, 4); "In dealing with all men, be conscientious (*chung*) " (XIII, 19); "A minister serves his prince with loyalty (*chung*) " (III, 19); "Be filial and kind and they (the people) will be loyal (*chung*) " (II, 20); "Can loyalty (*chung*) refrain from admonition? " (XIV, 8). In these passages *chung* seems to have a positive meaning of acting in behalf of others, whereas nowhere does the *Lun Yü* suggest *chung* as meaning the 'exhaustion of one's self,' which would hence not seem to have been the meaning Confucius intended by the word.

method of practising *jen*, and so Confucius says : "Is *jen* indeed far off? I crave for *jen* and lo ! *jen* is at hand " (VII, 29).

The idealistic philosophers of the Sung and Ming dynasties, followers of the school of Lu Chiu-yüan (A.D. 1139-1192) and Wang Yang-ming (1473-1529), maintain that all men originally possess an 'intuitive knowledge' (*liang chih* 良 知), so that 'throughout the streets everyone is a Sage.' They therefore believe that men need only follow this 'intuitive knowledge' in their conduct, in order never to fall into error under any circumstances. Confucius never believed in such a doctrine, however. For him the true manifestations of man's nature are not in themselves necessarily to be followed under all circumstances. This is why he stated emphatically that "*jen* is the denial of self and response to the right and proper (*li*) " (XII, 1).

Thus the *li* are imposed on man from outside. But besides this outer mould, we each still have within us something which we may take as a model for our conduct. If we " can find in our ownselves a rule for the similar treatment of others " ; if we do to others what we wish for ourselves, and " do not do to others what we do not like ourselves," then the outpourings of our nature will of themselves be in accord with what is proper. Hence while there still exist occasions on which one's own natural uprightness (*chih*) cannot be followed, there is none upon which *jen* (which is one's own uprightness conforming to what is proper) may not be acted on. This is why *jen* is the 'all pervading' principle of Confucius's teaching, and the center of his philosophy.

For this reason the *Lun Yü* also frequently uses *jen* as the term for man's virtue in its entirety, as when it says : " They sought *jen* and attained to *jen*. Why then should they repine ? " (VII, 14). Again : " As to being a Sage or a man of *jen*, how can I presume to such a claim ! " (VII, 33). And yet again : " Do not seek life at the expense of *jen*. Some even sacrifice their lives to complete their *jen* " (XV, 8). The *jen* in these passages means complete human virtue.[1]

As *jen* is a name for virtue in its entirety, Confucius often used it to include all kinds of different individual virtues. Thus when Tsai Wo suggested that for the three-year mourning period one year would be enough, Confucius said that he lacked *jen* (XVII, 21), so that *jen* may include the virtue of filial piety. Later Mencius also said : " There has never been a man of *jen* who has neglected his parents " (*Mencius*, Ia, 1). The man of *jen*, in other words (that is,

---

[1] There is no doubt that in many cases the word *jen* in the *Lun Yü* contains both of the two meanings given above. In later ages, however, no distinction has been made between them, which is the reason for the many arguments about the word which have been raised in recent times.

the man who practises *chung* and *shu*), must necessarily be one who is filial.¹

Again, we hear that "the Viscount of Wei withdrew from serving (Chou, the last tyrant ruler of the Shang or Yin dynasty); the Viscount of Chi became his slave; Pi Kan remonstrated with him and suffered death." Confucius said of these that "Yin had three men of *jen*" (XVIII, 1), so that *jen* may include loyalty (*chung* 忠). Confucius said of certain ancient worthies : "Not being wise, how could they be men of *jen*?" (V, 18), so that *jen* may include wisdom. "A man of *jen* must necessarily be courageous" (XIV, 5), so that *jen* includes courage. "When Yen Yüan asked the meaning of *jen*, the Master replied : '*Jen* is the denial of self and response to the right and proper (*li*)'" (XII, 1), so that *jen* may include *li*. "Tzŭ Chang asked Confucius the meaning of *jen*, whereupon Confucius replied : 'To be able wherever one goes to carry five things into practice constitutes *jen*.' On begging to know what they were, he was told : 'They are respect, magnanimity, sincerity, earnestness and kindness. With respect you will avoid insult; with magnanimity you will win over everyone; with sincerity men will trust you; with earnestness you will have achievement; and with kindness you will be well fitted to command others'" (XVII, 6). Thus *jen* may include sincerity and the other virtues just mentioned.

6—RIGHTEOUSNESS, UTILITARIANISM AND HUMAN NATURE

In the preceding section it has been shown that Confucius laid considerable emphasis upon giving free expression to man's nature. The true manifestations of a man's nature, he said, need only be blended with good form or *li* to reach the highest excellence (*jen*), which is hence something which it is possible for all of us to follow and practise.

The *Lun Yü* states :

"The Master was entirely free from four things : he had no preconceptions, no predeterminations, no obstinacy and no egoism" (IX, 4).

"The Master said : 'There are some with whom one can associate in study, but who are not yet able to make common advance toward the Way (*Tao* 道); there are others with whom one can make common advance toward the Way, but who are not yet able to take with you a like firm stand; and there are others with whom one can take such a firm stand, but with whom one cannot make emergency decisions'" (IX, 29).

---

¹ The *Lun Yü's* reference to filial piety (*hsiao* 孝) as consisting in obedience, fostering the will of the parents, and occasional admonition, relates in particular to the method of carrying out filial piety, rather than to its general principle, and so the word is not discussed here, but will be taken up later. *Cf.* ch. 14, sect. 6, pp. 357-361.

" The men noted for withdrawal into private life were : (here follows a list of seven names). The Master observed : ' Neither abating their high purpose nor abasing themselves : were these not Po I and Shu Ch'i ? As to Hui of Liu-hsia, and Shao Lien, while they abated their high purpose and abased themselves, what they said corresponded with reason, and what they did corresponded to what men were anxious for . . . and that is all. As to Yü Chung and Yi Yi, though in their seclusion they were immoderate in their utterances, yet they sustained their personal purity, and their self immolation was in accord with the emergency. But I am different from these. With me there is no inflexible *may* or *may not* ' " (XVIII, 8).

According to what has been said above, the standard for human conduct comes at least partly from within rather than from without ; is living rather than dead ; and is capable of modification rather than immovable. Therefore in following the tendencies of our nature, we may differ in our conduct according to time and place. This is what is meant by having ' no preconceptions, no predeterminations, no obstinacy and no egoism,' and by Confucius saying of himself : " With me there is no inflexible ' may ' or ' may not.' " Those who hold to a fixed standard to guide them under all circumstances are those ' with whom one can take a firm stand, but with whom one cannot make emergency decisions.'

When the genuiness in man's nature expresses it self,it need only be kept in accordance with propriety (*li*) to be of the highest excellence. There is no need of asking whether the human conduct that follows will result in something profitable or not. As a matter of fact, all human conduct of this kind is either beneficial to society as a whole, or at least can be of no harm. Confucius, however, did not greatly stress this last point. For example, when a disciple said : " Solicitude on the decease of parents, and the pursuit of them (with sacrificial offerings) for long after, would cause an abundant restoration of the people's morals " (I, 9), Confucius might have used this as a utilitarian type of argument in favor of the three-year mourning period. Yet he preferred to say that if men did not follow the three-year mourning, their hearts would not be at rest ; and he would not admit that any benefit thereby to be derived could supply a sufficient rational basis for this custom. Never did he lay emphasis on what would be the result of an action, either in his own life or otherwise. A disciple, arguing on his behalf, once said :

" The reason why the Superior Man tries to go into office is that he holds this to be right (*i* 義), even though he is well aware that his principles cannot prevail " (XVIII, 7).

It was because of his stress on the right or righteousness (*i*), regardless of material result, that someone once said of Confucius : " Is he not the one who knows he cannot succeed and keeps on trying to do so ? " (XIV, 41). The same idea is expressed by Tung Chung-shu, the Han Confucianist: "Be correct in righteousness without considering the profitableness (of the result of action); be pure in one's principles without considering whether they bring material return." As to whether one's principles really do prevail or not, this question concerns their 'profitableness,' their 'material return,' and so need not be considered. Hence the *Lun Yü* says: "The Master seldom spoke of what was profitable" (*li* 利)¹ (IX, 1). And Confucius himself says: "The Superior Man is informed in what is right (*i*). The inferior man is informed in what is profitable (*li*)" (IV, 16).

This stress on righteousness (*i*) for the sake of righteousness is one of the doctrines which connect Confucius with Mencius, and at the same time it constitutes the fundamental point of difference between these men and the Mohist school.²

From what has been said in the foregoing pages it may be seen that Confucius's philosophy calls special attention to human psychology, with the result that psychology has been stressed by all the later Confucians also. Confucius himself says:

"In their original natures (*hsing* 性) men closely resemble each other. In their acquired practices (*hsi* 習) they grow wide apart" (XVII, 2).

Even though Confucius does not give an absolutely clear-cut answer to this problem of human nature, it is because of the importance he attached to human psychology that the question of whether man's nature is good or evil was later to become the major problem of the Confucian school.

---

¹ This *li* 利, such an important term in Mohist philosophy, is a different word from the *li* 禮, meaning the rules of propriety, discussed on p. 68.—Tʀ.

² Many persons discussing this fact point out that when Confucius was discoursing on the method of governing a state, he said that "the people having grown numerous, ... one should enrich them," and "having been enriched, ... one should educate them" (XIII, 9). Likewise Mencius emphasizes the economic aspects in the life of the people when he discusses kingly government, so that, according to this argument, it is wrong to hold that the Confucian school did not actually speak about what is profitable. In maintaining the contrary, however, I only mean to say that in any given matter the Confucians would simply ask whether it was right or not, without necessarily inquiring as to what would be the material advantage. I do not mean to say that they refused altogether to talk about what would be profitable in the life of the people. Here is where the Confucian doctrine of righteousness rather than utilitarianism, clashes with the advocacy only of what is profitable in itself, as held by the Mohist school. *Cf.* chs. 5 and 6.

CHAPTER V
MO TZŬ AND THE EARLY MOHIST SCHOOL

1—Concerning the Study of Mo Tzŭ

Mo Tzŭ 墨 子 is one of the most important figures in Chinese history, a man whose name was constantly linked with that of Confucius from the Warring States period down to the beginning of the Han dynasty. Yet Ssŭ-ma Ch'ien devotes but twenty-four words in his *Shih Chi* to this remarkable man, whereas he treats the life of Confucius at length in the section of the *Shih Chi* devoted to the lives of noble families, thus leading us to the conclusion that by about 100 B.C., when this history was written, the world of thought had already become dominantly Confucian. It has only been from the latter part of the Ch'ing dynasty (1644-1912) onward that interest in Mo Tzŭ's philosophy has slowly revived, and that information gained through scholarly researches concerning him has gradually increased beyond the little given in the *Shih Chi*. The latter account says only: "Mo Ti 墨 翟[1] seems probably to have been a great officer in the state of Sung. He was skilful in maintaining military defenses, and taught economy of use. Some say that he was contemporary with Confucius, others that he was after him" (ch. 74, p. 6).

It has now been definitely established that Mo Tzŭ must have lived after Confucius. The noted textual critic, Sun I-jang (1848-1908), has made a chronological table for Mo Tzŭ which begins in 468 and extends to 376 B.C.[2] The present-day scholar, Ch'ien Mu, on the other hand, has made a chronological table beginning with the year 479 (the year in which Confucius died), and coming down to 381 B.C. (the year in which Wu Ch'i, a noted military general, died).[3] According to the *Lü-shih Ch'un Ch'iu*, the 'Leader' (*Chü tzŭ* 鉅 子) of the Mohist school at the time of the death of Wu Ch'i was Meng Sheng,[4] which means that Mo Tzŭ must already have died before this time. For this reason the earlier chronology of Professor Ch'ien would seem more nearly correct. The fact that the time

---

[1] Ti is here the personal name of Mo Tzŭ. The word Tzŭ 子 appearing in the names of many philosophers, such as Mo Tzŭ, Chuang Tzŭ, etc., is not a part of their name, but a courteous appellation, which may be translated as 'Master Mo,' 'Master Chuang,' etc.—Tr.

[2] *Cf.* his *Mo-tzŭ Hou-yü, chüan* 1.

[3] *Cf.* his *Mo-tzŭ*, ch. 1, in the *Kuo-hsüeh Hsiao-ts'ung-shu*.

[4] See below, sect. 3, pp. 81-84.

included within his table (479-381) covers almost one hundred years, does not mean that Mo Tzŭ necessarily lived to such an age, but only that his life probably fell within this period.

Some scholars hold Mo Tzŭ to have been a native of the state of Sung (in present Honan); others that he belonged to Lu. Of the two hypotheses, the latter, which is maintained by Sun I-jang,[1] seems more probable. Concerning the origins of Mo Tzŭ's doctrines, the *Lü-shih Ch'un Ch'iu* (II, 4) has this to say : " Duke Hui of Lu (768-723) sent the minister Jang to the Son of Heaven to request the rules of proper etiquette for the (sacrifices made) in the suburbs and in the ancestral temple. King Huan sent the historian Chiao back. Duke Hui detained him, and his descendants remained in Lu. It was from these that Mo Tzŭ got his education " (p. 24). Also the *I-wen Chih* chapter in the *Ch'ien Han Shu* states : " The Mohist teaching began with the guardians of the temples " (*Aids*, p. 62). This statement seems to be derived, however, from that in the *Lü-shih Ch'un Ch'iu*, and it is regrettable that there is no other corroborative evidence. The *Huai-nan-tzŭ* also states : " Confucius and Mo Ti practised the arts of the ancient Sages and were learned in all the discourses on the Six Disciplines " (ch. 9, p. 24). Again it says : " Mo Tzŭ studied the profession of the Confucians (*ju*) and received the arts of Confucius. But he considered that the rites (of the Confucian school) were troublesome and displeasing, its stress on elaborate funerals was wealth-consuming and impoverished the people, and its practice of lengthy mourning periods was injurious to the living and harmful to human affairs. Thereupon he turned his back on the Chou dynasty practices and made use of the methods of government of the Hsia dynasty " (ch. 21, p. 8).

In the work called after Mo Tzŭ, the *Mo-tzŭ*, there are many quotations from the Books of Odes and History. Confucius, through his extensive teaching, had set his stamp on the intellectual atmosphere of the time, so that it is but natural that Mo Tzŭ, being a native of Lu, and hence living in this atmosphere, should have been influenced by Confucius in his studies of the *Shih* and *Shu*. Confucius, furthermore, was, like Mo Tzŭ, an advocate of economy, as when he said : " To conduct the government of a state of a thousand chariots, there must be a proper respect for business and good faith, economy of expenditure, and love of the people " (*Lun Yü*, I, 5). Again : " In ceremonies, it is better to be economical than lavish " (III, 4). And yet again : " In Yü [2] I can find no room for criticism. Simple in his own food and drink, he was unsparing in his filial offerings to the spirits. Shabby in his (everyday) clothing, he was most scrupulous as to the elegance of his kneeling apron and sacrificial crown. Humble

---

[1] *Op. cit., chüan* 1.
[2] The legendary first ruler of the Hsia dynasty, who by his prodigious labors is supposed finally to have saved China from a flood which ravaged it for nine years.—TR.

as to the character of his palace, he spent his strength in the draining and ditching of the country. In Yü I find no room for criticism" (VIII, 21). Thus it would seem quite possible that Mo Tzŭ, in his emphasis on economy, belief in spirits, and honoring of the Emperor Yü, was simply elaborating certain aspects already found in Confucius's own teachings.

The Mohist philosophy, according to such a theory, must, like Confucianism, have originated in Lu. Yet there are also certain scholars who hold that a connection exists between Mo Tzŭ's philosophy and the state of Sung. Yü Cheng-hsieh (1775-1840), for example, quotes the *Kuan-tzŭ* (ch. 4), which says : " If the doctrine of universal love (one of the most prominent Mohist tenets) prevails, military leaders will not go to war." Again Chapter LXV says : "We cannot prevent the other side from fighting us, they being trained soldiers, we being a mob of followers ; they having good generals, we being without ability. The defeat must be one in which the army is overthrown and the general is killed." These, Yü points out, are exactly the ideas of Duke Hsiang of Sung (650-637), who, because he refused to wound the enemy twice or to take grey-haired men as prisoners, was criticized in the *Tso Chuan* as follows : " If one wants not to wound a second time, would it not be better not to wound at all ? If one spares the old men, would it not be better to make one's submission ? " (p. 183). These concepts of universal love and antimilitarism would thus seem to have been characteristic of the people of Sung. They are reflected in the *Lü-shih Ch'un Ch'iu* (XVIII, 1) when it says : " The idea in ceasing war springs out of a mind holding universal love toward the world " (p. 292). The *Tso Chuan* tells us that after the death of Duke Hsiang, his efforts toward peace were continued by other men of Sung, some of whom proposed a disarmament for all states. After advancing these examples, Yü concludes that " Mo Tzŭ was surely a great official of Sung," and points out how Mo Tzŭ's follower, Sung K'eng (who was of Sung), later also attempted to stop conflict by saying that war is unprofitable.

Yü goes on to quote from the *Mo-tzŭ* (ch. 48), in which Mo Tzŭ criticizes a Confucian by saying : " You are only following the Chou, and not the Hsia dynasty. Your antiquity does not go back far enough " (p. 233). From this Yü concludes that it was because Mo Tzŭ was a native of Sung (the rulers of which, unlike those of Lu, were not descended from the House of Chou), that he followed the Hsia customs, whereas the Confucians, being centered in Lu, followed those of Chou.[1]

The people of Sung were, in fact, noted for their naïve simplicity, and often appear as the heroes in stories in which Chou dynasty writers wish to describe simpletons. Thus the *Chuang-tzŭ* relates : " A man of Sung carried some ceremonial caps to the Yüeh state.

[1] *Cf.* his *Kuei-ssŭ Lei-kao, chüan* 14.

But the men of Yüeh used to cut off their hair and paint their bodies, so that they had no use for such things " (p. 8). Mencius says: " There was a man of Sung who was grieved that his growing corn was not longer, and so he pulled it up " (*Mencius*, IIa, 2). And the *Han-fei-tzŭ* (ch. 49) gives the anecdote of a farmer of Sung, in whose field a rabbit once killed itself by running against the stem of a tree standing there, whereupon the man abandoned his plough and stood waiting at the tree in the hope that he would catch another rabbit. Of Mo Tzŭ himself the *Chuang-tzŭ* (ch. 33) says: " He would have men toil through life, with a bare funeral at death. Such teaching is too barren. . . . He considered self suffering as the ideal " (pp. 441-442), which suggests some of the Sung characteristics just given. A possible explanation for the whole question is that Mo Tzŭ was originally a native of Lu, where he was influenced by Confucius in the several ways described above ; that later he became an official in Sung, where he adopted the Sung ideals of universal love and anti-militarism ; and that he thus combined the two influences to form the Mohist philosophy.

Another problem centers around Mo Tzŭ's name. Formerly it was said that Mo 墨 was his family or clan name, and Ti 翟 his personal name. A recent scholar, however, has suggested that Mo is not a clan name, but rather the name of the philosophic school founded by Mo Tzŭ.[1] This argument is based upon the fact that in ancient China the word *mo* was used as the name for one of the punishments, that of branding, so that a person bearing such a designation would be one who had undergone the punishment of branding and had become a slave.[2] Mo Tzŭ himself, by his emphasis on economy and opposition to music and to long mourning, shows himself diametrically opposed to the official and ruling class of his day ; in his asceticism he lived a life similar to that of a common laborer. According to this theory, then, his disciples were designated by their contemporaries as ' men of Mo ' to indicate that they were the followers of a criminal-slave. The *Mo-tzŭ* (ch. 47), for example, tells us that King Hui of Ch'u " sent Mu Ho to receive Mo Tzŭ. Mo Tzŭ talked to Mu Ho and Mu Ho was greatly pleased. He said to Mo Tzŭ : ' Your words are quite good. But our Lord is a great Lord in the empire, and may he not refuse to employ you because they indicate the practice of the humble man ? ' " (p. 223). It was because what Mo Tzŭ advocated was in fact ' the practice of the humble man ' that it was referred to as the way of Mo, i.e., of a branded slave. If this hypothesis is true, however, it is conceivable that Mo Tzŭ may even have enjoyed having his school called by this name, in which case he would be like Antisthenes in Greece, who was called ' downright dog ' (*haplocyon*), and was so pleased with

---

[1] *Cf.* Chiang Ch'üan, *Lun Mo Tzŭ fei Hsing Mo,* in *Tu Tzŭ Chih Yen.*
[2] See Ch'ien Mu, *op. cit.,* ch. 1.

this name that after his death the figure of a dog was cut out of stone to mark his tomb.[1]

Because he was opposed to the aristocratic class, Mo Tzǔ was inevitably opposed to the Chou institutions which gave them support. The Confucians were always proclaiming themselves as the followers of Chou. Hence Mo Tzǔ, as their opponent, declared that he based his ideas on the Hsia culture. The Emperor Yü, for example, who was the legendary founder of the Hsia dynasty, was also noted for his extreme frugality and self-sacrifice.[2] Mo Tzǔ delighted in acclaiming these characteristics, not because they belonged to the Hsia dynasty, but because they fitted in with his own doctrines. Thus it is wrong to suppose that Mo Tzǔ advocated the Hsia institutions *per se*. Rather it was a case of his extolling them because, his philosophy being based on a democratic point of view, he could thus show his opposition to the Chou institutions, in which the power of the ruling class was lodged.

2—THE CANONS AND THE MAJOR AND MINOR ILLUSTRATIONS IN THE *Mo-tzǔ*

There are six chapters in the *Mo-tzǔ* : the Canons or *Ching* 經 (chs. 40-41) ; Expositions of Canons or *Ching Shuo* 經 說 (chs. 42-43) ; Major Illustrations or *Ta Ch'ü* 大 取 (ch. 44) and Minor Illustrations or *Hsiao Ch'ü* 小 取 (ch. 45), which differ markedly from the other chapters in *Mo-tzǔ*, and are most probably the product of the later followers of the Mohist school. During the latter part of the Warring States period there were a great many travelling philosophers and politicians who went about from one state to another reciting their writings. The result of the rivalries of these men was the formulation by each philosophic school of its own orthodox ' canon.' Thus the Mohist school had its Mohist Canon (*Mo Ching* 墨 經), the *Hsün-tzǔ* contains references to a Taoist Canon (*Tao Ching* 道 經), and the *Han-fei-tzǔ* (chs. 30-35) has its canons of the Inner and Outer Discussions (*Nei Wai Chu Shuo* 內 外 儲 說). During the earlier half of the Warring States period, however, when Mo Tzǔ was still alive, this type of writing had not yet come into existence.[3]

So far as we know to-day, the earliest work to have been composed by anybody, in a private rather than official capacity, is the *Lun Yü*, which is a record, of the most simple and abbreviated type, of Confucius's sayings. Later in the *Chuang-tzǔ* and the *Mencius* there is a distinct advance from disjointed conversations of this kind to records of conversations of considerable length, displaying a definite story-like structure. This was the first great development in

---

[1] *Cf.* Diogenes Laertius, *The Lives and Opinions of Eminent Philosophers*, Bk. VI, ch. 6.
[2] *Cf.* the *Lun Yü* quotation above.
[3] This view is upheld by Ku Chieh-kang. *Cf.* his *Lun Shih Ching Ching-li chi Lao-tzǔ yü Tao-chia Shu* (A Letter concerning the History of the *Shih Ching*, and the Connection of the *Lao-tzǔ* with the Taoist School), in *Ku Shih Pien*, I, sect. 1, p. 56.

style of the writings of the Warring States philosophers. Still later such records were replaced by true essay writing, such as we find in the *Hsün-tzŭ*, a change marking the second step in the prose development of these philosophers.[1] Such chapters as the Major and Minor Illustrations exemplify this change, being written in true essay form, so that they, like the Canons, could not possibly date from the time of Mo Tzŭ himself.

Further proof of the lateness of these six chapters in *Mo-tzŭ* is the fact that the dialectical subjects which they discuss, such as ' the hard and the white,' ' similarity and difference,' and ' an ox and a horse are not an ox,' are all to be found only in comparatively late works. Mencius (371 ?-289 ?), for example, though he himself indulged in argument, makes no reference to them whatsoever. These reasons suffice to indicate that these six chapters can only date from the latter part of the Warring States period, for which reason they will not be discussed here, but will be taken up later in Chapter XI.

3—The Mohists as an Organized Body

The *Mo-tzŭ* (ch. 50) states :

" Kung Shu Pan (a noted mechanical inventor of the time) had completed the construction of Cloud-ladders for the state of Ch'u, and was going to attack Sung with them. Mo Tzŭ heard of it . . . and saw Kung Shu Pan. . . . Mo Tzŭ untied his belt and laid out a city with it, using a small stick for weapon. Kung Shu Pan set up nine different machines of attack, and Mo Tzŭ nine times repulsed him. Kung Shu Pan came to the end of his machines of attack, while Mo Tzŭ was far from being exhausted in the defence. . . . Mo Tzŭ said : ' . . . . My disciples Ch'in Ku Li and others, numbering three hundred men, are already armed with my implements of defence, waiting on the city wall of Sung for the invaders from Ch'u. Though I be murdered, you cannot exhaust (the defence of Sung).' The King of Ch'u said : ' Well indeed ! Let us not attack Sung any more' " (pp. 257, 259).

This story indicates two things : The first is that this is the only recorded instance of Mo Tzŭ actually seeking to protect a state suffering from aggression, and so is indicative of the special relationship which apparently existed between him and Sung. Secondly, the story indicates that the Mohists were an organized body, capable of concerted action on such an occasion as this. Thus, while Mo Tzŭ was going to Ch'u to see Kung Shu Pan, his three hundred disciples were already at Sung ready to defend the city. Again, Chapter XLVI states :

" Mo Tzŭ sent Kuan Ch'in Ao to recommend Kao Shih Tzŭ to the state of Wei. The Wei ruler gave him large emoluments and

---

[1] This has been suggested by Professor Fu Ssŭ-nien.

ranked him among the ministers. Kao Shih Tzŭ came to court three times and gave his counsels, but none of them was carried out. So he left for Ch'i, where he saw Mo Tzŭ, and said : ' On your account the Lord of Wei gave me large emoluments and ranked me among the ministers. I went to court three times and gave all my counsels, but none of them was carried out. So I left. Will not the Lord of Wei think I am foolish ? ' Mo Tzŭ said : ' If you left to be in accordance with the true Way (*Tao*), what harm is it to be considered a simpleton ? . . . .' Kao Shih Tzŭ said : ' How dare I have gone if it were not in accordance with the true Way ? . . . .' Mo Tzŭ was pleased " (pp. 217-218).

The same chapter gives another story :

" Mo Tzŭ had recommended Keng Chu Tzŭ to Ch'u. Some (other) pupils went to visit him (Keng Chu Tzŭ). They were given only three pints (of grain) each meal and were not generously entertained. The pupils returned and reported to Mo Tzŭ, saying : ' We are not profited by Keng Chu Tzŭ's staying in Ch'u. When we visited him we were given only three pints each meal and were not generously entertained.' Mo Tzŭ said : ' Still you cannot tell.' Not long after (Keng Chu Tzŭ) sent ten pounds (of gold) to Mo Tzŭ, saying : ' Your junior disciple, who is unworthy even to die, sends ten pounds herewith, which he hopes the Master will use.' Mo Tzŭ said : ' So indeed, one really could not tell ' " (p. 214).

And Chapter XLIX :

" Mo Tzŭ sent Sheng Cho to serve Hsiang Tzŭ Niu. Hsiang Tzŭ Niu invaded Lu territory three times, and Sheng Cho three times accompanied him. Hearing of it, Mo Tzŭ sent Kao Sun Tzŭ to recall him " (p. 254).

These passages indicate how the employment and activities of Mo Tzŭ's disciples were all under his direct control. If the rulers whom they served could not follow the Mohist doctrines, they must refuse to serve them, as in the case of Kao Shih Tzŭ. If the disciples acted unethically, Mo Tzŭ could demand their recall from the prince they served, as in the case of Sheng Cho. And after disciples had gone forth to take office, they must contribute a portion of their income to the support of the Mohists, as in the case of Keng Chu Tzŭ. The *Huai-nan-tzŭ* says : " Those who followed Mo Tzŭ amounted to one hundred and eighty men, all of whom he could have made enter fire or tread on knife blades, and whom even death would not have prevented from following one another " (ch. 20, p. 14). This shows the absolute obedience rendered Mo Tzŭ by his disciples.

The Mohist organization was presided over by a Leader or 'Pope,' called *Chü tzŭ* 鉅子, so that the *Chuang-tzŭ* (ch. 33) says of the Mohists : " They regarded the *Chü tzŭ* as a Sage, and each group wished him to be its leader and hoped to be his successor " (pp. 442-443). Mo Tzŭ himself, of course, must have been the first *Chü tzŭ*, but after him, according to stories in the *Lü-shih Ch'un Ch'iu*, this post was filled by at least three different men. One of these stories (XIX, 3) tells us :

" Meng Sheng, the *Chü tzŭ* of the Mohists, was on good terms with the prince of Yang-ch'eng in Ching (i.e., the state of Ch'u). The prince commissioned him to defend the state, and broke in half a piece of jade to make the two sides of a tally. The agreement made between the two men was : 'Listen to him who can unite the two pieces of the tally into one.' When the King of Ching died, his ministers attacked Wu Ch'i, and fighting occurred at the place where the coffin was kept, the prince of Yang-ch'eng being also involved. The state of Ching blamed him for this, whereupon he fled, and Ching sent to take over his state. Meng Sheng said : ' When one has received a state from a man, and has held a tally (of recognition) with him ; and when now one does not see the tally (which must be offered for identification), and lacks the power to prevent (what is being done by force without the authorization of the tally), one cannot but die.'

" His disciple Hsü Jo remonstrated with Meng Sheng, saying : ' If it is a death that will be of advantage to the prince of Yang Ch'eng, it is a permissible death. But if it is one that is of no benefit to him, and that cuts short the line of Mohists in the world, it is not permissible.' Meng Sheng said : ' Not so. If I am not the teacher of the prince of Yang Ch'eng, I am his friend. If I am not his friend, I am his minister. If I do not die, those looking for an honorable teacher will from now on never look for one among the Mohists ; those looking for a worthy friend will never look for one among the Mohists ; those looking for a good minister will never do so among the Mohists. I am dying so that I may carry out the Mohist principles and bring onward their work. I am going to confer the position of *Chü tzŭ* on T'ien Hsiang Tzŭ of the state of Sung. T'ien Hsiang Tzŭ is a worthy person, so what danger is there that the (line of) Mohists may be cut off in the world ? '

" Hsü Jo said : ' If my Master speaks so, I beg to die first in order to prepare the way.'

" Then stepping backward, he cut off his head in front of Meng Sheng, who sent two men to confer the position of *Chü tzŭ* on T'ien Hsiang Tzŭ. Thereupon Meng Sheng himself died, and of the disciples who died with him there were eighty-three. When the two men had brought the decree to T'ien Hsiang Tzŭ, they too wished to return and die with Meng Sheng in Ching. But T'ien Hsiang Tzŭ stopped them, saying : ' Meng Tzŭ has already passed on the position of *Chü tzŭ* to me.' They refused to listen, however, but returned and died. The (other) Mohists considered that in this they had not listened to their (new) *Chü tzŭ* " (pp. 327-328).

In this story the conduct of the Mohists shows similarities with that of the class of so-called ' knights-errant ' (*hsieh* 俠), professional fighters who travelled about China offering their services to feudal lords, and of whom the *Shih Chi* says : " Their words are always sincere and their actions decisive. They are always true to what they have promised. Without regard for their own persons, they will rush into dangers threatening others " (ch. 124).

The *Lü-shih Ch'un Ch'iu* (I, 5) gives another story which throws light on the Mohist organization :

" There was Fu Tun, who was *Chü tzŭ* of the Mohists. He was living in the state of Ch'in when his son killed a man. King Hui of Ch'in (337-311) said : 'You, Sir, are old, and have no other sons, and so I have already given orders not to punish him. You must listen to me in this.'

" Fu Tun replied : 'According to the laws of the Mohists, he who has killed a man must die, and he who has wounded a man must receive corporeal punishment. This is done to prevent murdering and wounding. Now not to kill or injure others is the great duty in the world. Even if Your Highness were to reward him by giving orders not to punish him, I could not but carry out the laws of the Mohists.' He did not accede to what King Hui had requested, and executed his son ' " (p. 12).

This shows the extreme severity of the regulations governing the Mohist organization, which gave to the *Chü tzŭ* the power of life and death over those who violated the Mohist laws.

4—Mo Tzŭ's Utilitarianism

Frugality, universal love and condemnation of war had all existed as ideas prior to Mo Tzŭ. Mo Tzŭ's great contribution to Chinese philosophy is that he not only practised these ideas himself, but that he gave them a rational foundation and welded them into a unified philosophy.

There are many places in Mo Tzŭ's writings where he stands opposed to the Confucian school, the philosophy of which differed radically from his own. The Confucians " tried to be correct in righteousness, without considering whether profit (would result); tried to be pure in their principles, without considering whether this would bring material return." The Mohist school, on the other hand, laid exclusive emphasis on ' profitableness ' (*li* 利) and ' accomplishment ' (*kung* 功). Neither Confucius nor Mo Tzŭ can be reproached for his conduct, for each was working tirelessly to rescue the world from its ills. They differed radically, however, in the explanation they gave to their activities. Thus a disciple explained Confucius by saying :

" The reason why the Superior Man tries to go into office is that he holds this to be right, even though he is well aware that his principles cannot prevail " (*Lun Yü*, XVIII, 7).

That is, Confucius tried to participate in government simply because he felt morally that he ought to do so, regardless of whether his principles made progress or not. Mo Tzŭ, however, regarded his own conduct differently. The *Mo-tzŭ* (ch. 47) says :

" On his way from Lu to Ch'i, Mo Tzŭ met an old friend who said to him : ' Nowadays no one in the world practises any right-eousness. You are merely inflicting pain on yourself by trying to practise righteousness. You had better give it up.' Mo Tzŭ replied : ' Suppose a man has ten sons. Only one cultivates the ground, while the other nine stay at home. Then the one who cultivates must work all the more vigorously. Why ? Because many eat and few cultivate. To-day, if no one in the world practises righteous-ness, you should all the more encourage me. Why do you stop me ? ' " (p. 222).

Again in Chapter XLVIII :

" Kung Meng Tzŭ said to Mo Tzŭ : ' . . . . Now you go about, trying to talk over everybody. Wherefore all this fuss ? ' Mo Tzŭ said : ' . . . . Suppose here are two people good at fortune telling. One travels about to tell people's fortunes, and the other stays at home and does not go abroad. Which of these two will have more grain ? ' Kung Meng Tzŭ said that he who travelled about to tell people's fortunes would have more grain. Mo Tzŭ said : ' So with human-heartedness (*jen*) and righteous-ness (*i* 義). He who travels about and urges the people achieves more also. Why not, then, let us travel about and urge the people ? ' " (p. 231).

That is, though there are but few who practise righteousness, the material accomplishment will be greater if even only one or two do so, than if none practise it at all. Confucius was ' doing for nothing.' Mo Tzŭ was ' doing for something.'

The concepts of ' accomplishment ' (*kung* 功) and ' profitableness' or ' benefit' (*li* 利) are fundamental in Mohist philosophy, as shown in the *Mo-tzŭ* (ch. 35) :

" Some standard of judgment must be established. To expound without regard for the standard is similar to deter-mining the directions of sunrise and sunset on a revolving potter's wheel. By this means the distinction of right and wrong, benefit (*li*) and harm, cannot be known. Therefore any statement must have three tests. What are the three tests ? Mo Tzŭ said : ' Its basis, its verifiability and its applicability. On what is it to be based ? It should be based on the deeds of the ancient Sage-kings. By what is it to be verified ? It is to be verified by the senses of hearing and sight of the common people. How is it to be applied ? It is to be applied by adopting it in government and observing its benefit (*li*) to the country and the people. This is what is meant by the three tests of every doctrine ' " (pp. 182-183).¹

Of these three tests, the most important is the third. ' Its benefit to the country and the people ' was the standard by which Mo Tzŭ determined all values. Everything must have its usefulness, and all doctrines must have their applicability, before they can have any value. Chapter XLVIII says :

" Mo Tzŭ asked a Confucian, saying : ' What is the reason for performing music ? ' The reply was : ' Music is performed for music's sake.' ² Mo Tzŭ said : ' You have not yet answered me. Suppose I asked : Why build houses ? And you answered : It is to keep off the cold in winter, and the heat in summer, and to separate men from women. Then you would have told me the reason for building houses. Now I am asking : Why perform music ? And you answer : Music is performed for music's sake. This is like saying : Why build houses ? And answering : Houses are built for houses' sake ' " (p. 237).

Chapter XLVI states :

" Lord Tzŭ Kao of She asked Confucius about government, saying : ' What is a good governor like ? ' Confucius replied : ' A good governor is one who will attract those who are distant and renew old friendships.' ³ Mo Tzŭ heard of it and commented : ' Lord Tzŭ Kao of She did not put the question right, nor did Confucius give the right answer. For, did not Lord Tzŭ Kao of She understand that to be a good governor is to attract the distant and to renew old friendships ? The question was really *how* to do this. The answer told only what the inquirer understands, but did not tell what he does not understand. Therefore (I say), Lord Tzŭ Kao of She did not put the question right, neither did Confucius give the right answer ' " (p. 216). Again :

" Mo Tzŭ said : ' Doctrines that can be translated into conduct may be taught frequently. Doctrines that cannot be translated into conduct should not be taught frequently. To talk frequently about what cannot be carried out is merely to tire out one's mouth ' " (p. 217).

The two questions : " What is music ? " and " Why should there be music ? " were one in Mo Tzŭ's eyes. The Confucians said that music was for the sake of music, that is, for pleasure. Mo Tzŭ

---

¹ The *Mo-tzŭ* (ch. 36) says : " There must be three tests for a doctrine. What are the three tests ? They are the test of its basis, the test of its verifiability and the test of its applicability. To test the basis of a doctrine we examine the Will of Heaven and of the spirits, and the deeds of the Sage-kings. . . . " (p. 189). Here we find the Will of Heaven and of the spirits added to the deeds of the Sage-kings as a basis, a fact not surprising in Mo Tzŭ, who was such a strong believer in ' Heaven's Will.'

² There is a play on words here. The word 樂 means both music and pleasure, so that the sentence may also be translated : " Music is performed for pleasure's sake."—Tʀ.

³ This seems to be an echo of *Lun Yü*, XIII, 16.—Tʀ.

refused to recognize that music in itself can have any use. For him the making of music gives merely momentary pleasure, and cannot lead to any result having permanent future benefit. Any doctrine which cannot be carried out, or which cannot be imparted to others for them to carry out, is for him merely an intellectual exercise. Although it may provide us with immediate enjoyment, it can have no future use, and so is of no value.

5—WHAT IS THE GREAT PROFIT FOR THE PEOPLE?

Anything must be of profit to the country and the people before it can possess value, and it is the wealth and populousness of a country, Mo Tzŭ believed, which constitute its greatest profit. Hence everything that can bring about wealth and populousness is useful, while everything that does not do so either is of no benefit or is even harmful. All value is to be determined by this scale. The *Mo-tzŭ* (ch. 20) says:

" When a Sage rules a state, the benefits of that state may be increased twice. When he governs the empire, those of the empire may be doubled. This increase is not accomplished by appropriating land from without, but by cutting out useless expenditures. . . . What, then, is difficult to increase? To increase the population is difficult, and yet it is possible. . . . In ancient times the Sage-kings formulated laws saying: ' No man of twenty should dare to be without a family; no girl of fifteen should dare to be without her master.' Such were the laws of the Sage-kings. Now that the Sage-kings have passed away, the people have become loose. Those who like to have a family early sometimes marry at twenty. Those who like to have a family later sometimes marry at forty. When the late marriages are made up by the early ones, (the average) is still later by ten years than the legal requirements of the Sage-kings. Supposing births are given to children on an average of one in three years, then there would be two or three children born (by the time men now marry). Will not this fact show that if families are established early, the population can be increased twice? " (pp. 117-119).

This passage exemplifies the strong utilitarian basis in Mo Tzŭ's philosophy. The wealth and populousness of the people are the great benefit of the nation and the people. Therefore everything that does not directly further these two ends, or that tends to injure them, must be discarded. Hence, as the following quotation indicates, we must exalt frugality and oppose all forms of extravagance. Chapter XXI states:

"Therefore the ancient Sage-kings authorized the laws of economy, saying: 'All you artizans and workers, cartwrights and tanners, potters and smiths, each do what you have the capacity for.' They went on: 'Stop when the needs of the people are satisfied.' What

causes extra expense, but adds no benefit to the people, the Sage-kings
would not undertake. . . . The ancient Sage-kings authorized the laws
regarding clothing, saying: 'Be satisfied with clothes of blue or grey
silk in winter which are light and warm, and with clothes of grass linen
in summer which are light and cool.' What causes additional expenditure,
but does not add benefits to the people, the Sage-kings would not allow.

" Because ferocious and cunning animals were destroying men
and injuring the people, the ancient Sage-kings taught the people
the use of weapons, saying : ' Carry a two-edged sword which
penetrates when it pierces and severs when it cuts. When struck
with the flat side it does not break : this is the utility of a sword. To
be light and strong and to afford convenience of action, such is the
utility of armor.'

" A vehicle is used to carry weight and to travel great distances.
It should be safe to ride in and easy to pull ; safe so as not to hurt
the rider, and easy to pull so as to reach the destination speedily.
This is the utility of the vehicle. Because the wide rivers and broad
valleys were once not crossable, the Sage-kings ordered boats and
oars to be made. And these were made to suffice for crossing. Even
though one of the Three Chief Ministers or a feudal lord should arrive,
the boat and oars were not changed, and the ferryman put on no
decorations. Such is the utility of the boat.

"The ancient Sage-kings authorized the laws limiting funeral expenditure, saying: 'Of shrouds there shall be three pieces, sufficient to
hold the rotting flesh. The coffin shall be three inches thick, sufficient to
hold the rotting bones. The pit shall be dug not deep enough to reach
water, but just deep enough so that the gases will not escape. When the
dead are buried, the living shall not mourn too long.'

" In those ancient days, at the beginning of the race, when there
were no palaces or houses, people lived in caves dug in the side of
hills and mounds. The Sage-kings felt concerned over this cave
digging, and said : ' In winter they serve to keep out wind and cold,
but in summer they are wet below and steaming above, and we fear
may injure the health of the people.' Thereupon they built palaces
and houses which were useful. Now, what is the standard in building
palaces and houses ? Mo Tzŭ said : ' Just so that on the sides they
can keep off snow, frost, rain and dew ; within they are sufficiently
clean for sacrificial purposes ; and that the palace partitions are high
enough to separate men from women.' Anything that caused extra
expenditure, but did not add to the benefit of the people, the Sage-
kings would not undertake " (pp. 120-122).

This shows that Mo Tzŭ did not oppose extra expenditure
in itself, but only such extra expenditure as would add no benefit to
the people.

For the same reason we should avoid lavish funerals and shorten the period of mourning. Chapter XXV reads :

" (At present) if the mourner is a high official, he is expected to be supported when he rises, and to lean on a cane when he walks. And this continues for three years. Adopting such a doctrine and practising such a principle, rulers and great officials cannot come to court early. If the farmers practise this they cannot start out early and come back late, to cultivate the land and plant trees ; the artizans cannot build boats and vehicles, and make vessels and utensils ; and the women cannot rise early and retire late to spin and weave. So then, in elaborate funerals much wealth is buried, and in extended mourning abstention from work is prolonged. Wealth already produced is carried away into the grave. Productive (enterprise) is prohibited. To seek wealth in this way is like seeking a harvest by prohibiting farming. The way to wealth is not thus found.

" Now that the practice of elaborate funerals and extended mourning has failed to enrich the country, can it yet perhaps increase the population ? Again it is powerless. For if elaborate funerals and extended mourning are adopted as the rule, then upon the death of the ruler there will be three years' mourning ; upon the death of a parent there will be three years' mourning ; upon the death of the wife or the eldest son there will be three years' mourning. There will be three years' mourning for all five (relations). Besides, there will be one year for uncles, brothers and the other sons ; five months for the near relatives ; and also several months for aunts, sisters, nephews, and uncles on the mother's side. Further, there are set rules to make oneself emaciated. The face and eyes are to look sunken, and the complexion is to appear dark. Eyes and ears are to become dull, and hands and feet are to become weak and useless. Again it is said that if the mourner is a high official he has to be supported to rise and lean on a cane to walk. And this is to last three years if such a doctrine is adopted and such a principle is practised. Being so hungry and weak, the people cannot stand the cold in winter and the heat in summer. And countless numbers will become sick and die. This practice destroys the sexual relations between husband and wife.' To seek to increase the population in this way is like seeking longevity by stabbing one's self with a sword " (pp. 126-127).

The elaborate funerals and long mourning periods advocated by the Confucians were serious obstacles, both in the attempt to gain riches and to increase the population, and hence were condemned by Mo Tzŭ.

For the same reason Mo Tzŭ opposed music. Chapter XXXII reads :

" Boats are to be used on water and vehicles on land, so that gentlemen can rest their feet and lesser people can rest their shoulders

---

' Sexual relations were forbidden during the mourning period.—TR.

and backs.   Thus, why is it that the people produced wealth and contributed it, and did not dare to grumble about it ?   It was because
these things contributed to the benefit of the people.   Thus if musical
instruments equally contribute to the benefit of the people, even I
shall not dare condemn them.   Nor if musical instruments are
as useful as the boats and carts of the Sage-kings shall I dare to
condemn them.

" The people have three worries : that the hungry will not be
fed, that the cold will not be clothed, and that the tired will not get
rest.   These three are the great worries of the people.   Now suppose
we strike the great bell, beat the sounding drum, strum the *ch'in* and
the *she*, and blow the *yü* and the *sheng*, how can the material for food
and clothing then be procured for the people ?   Even I do not think
this is possible.   Its purpose is beside this.   To-day big states attack
small states, and large houses molest small houses.   The strong plun-
der the weak, the many oppress the few, the clever deceive the stupid,
and the honored disdain the humble.   Bandits and thieves rise all
together and cannot be suppressed.   But how can the chaos of the
world be put in order by striking the big bell, beating the sounding
drum, strumming the *ch'in* and *she*, and blowing the *yü* and *sheng* ?
As for me, I do not think it is possible.   Therefore Mo Tzŭ said :
' The levy of heavy taxes on the people to construct the big bell, the
sounding drum, the *ch'in*, *she*, *yü* and *sheng* is of no help in endeavor-
ing to procure the benefits of the world and destroy its calamities.'
Therefore Mo Tzŭ said :   ' To have music is wrong ' " (pp. 176-177).

Since music is without practical use, and so is to be eliminated,
all the other fine arts are naturally to be eliminated as well.   Being
products of the emotions, they are capable only of appealing to these
emotions.   By condemning such things as music on the ground that
they are of no practical value, Mo Tzŭ reveals his attitude toward
the emotions.   According to his positive utilitarianism, man's numerous emotions are not only of no practical value, but moreover of
no significance.   Hence they should be eliminated, so as not to be
impediments to human conduct.   The Confucians, on the other
hand, valued the mourning rites, mournful countenance, and sound
of wailing as expressions of human emotion.   The difference between
the two views becomes clear in a passage in Chapter XLVIII :

" Kung Meng Tzŭ (a Confucian) said :   ' I mourn for three
years in imitation of the affection that my son shows to his parents.'
Mo Tzŭ said :   ' The baby knows only to love its parents.   Therefore when the parents are no longer to be had, it continues to cry
without ceasing.   Why is this ?   It is the height of foolishness.   And
so, then, is the intelligence of the Confucian any higher than that
of the baby ? ' " (pp. 236-237).

The Confucian school, or at least part of it, did not believe in
the existence of supernatural beings, yet at the same time stressed the

performance of sacrifices in order to give emotional satisfaction. Looked at from the point of view of Mohist utilitarianism, performance of sacrifices under such circumstances is meaningless. The same chapter states again :

"Kung Meng Tzŭ said : 'There are no ghosts and spirits.' Again he said : 'The Superior Man should learn sacrifice and worship.' Mo Tzŭ said : 'To hold that there are no spirits and learn sacrificial ceremonies, is like learning the ceremonials of hospitality when there is no guest, or making fish nets when there are no fish'" (p. 236).

And Chapter XLVII :

"One must get rid of the six depravities. When silent, one should deliberate ; when talking, one should instruct ; when in action, there should be accomplishment. He who employs these three alternatively must become a Sage. One must get rid of joy and anger, pleasure and sadness, love and hatred. When hands, feet, mouth, nose, ears (and eyes) are employed for righteousness, one will surely become a Sage" (p. 224).

These all belong to man's emotional nature, called by Mo Tzŭ the 'six depravities,' which must be done away with in order that one's every act may be rationally guided. Mo Tzŭ's advocacy of the elimination of the emotions is clearly stated here.

6—UNIVERSAL LOVE

Luxury and adornment, Mo Tzŭ held, are of no benefit to the country and the people, yet at the same time they are not its greatest harm. The latter is rather the incessant fighting of people and states among themselves, caused, so Mo Tzŭ held, by the fact that men do not love one another. Chapter XVI reads :

"The purpose of those who are virtuous lies in procuring benefits for the world and eliminating its calamities. Now among all the current calamities, which are the most important ? I say that the attack on the small states by the large ones, disturbances of the small houses by the large ones, oppression of the weak by the strong, misuse of the few by the many, deception of the simple by the cunning, disdain toward the humble by the honored : these are the misfortunes in the world. Again, the lack of kindliness on the part of the ruler, the lack of loyalty on the part of the ruled, of affection on the part of the father, and of filial piety on the part of the son : these are further calamities in the world. Also, the mutual injury and harm which the unscrupulous do to one another with weapons, poison, water and fire are still another calamity in the world.

"When we come to think about the cause of all these calamities, how have they arisen ? Have they arisen out of love of others and benefiting others ? We must reply that it is not so. We should say that they have arisen out of hate of others and injuring others.

If we should classify one by one all those who hate others and injure others, should we find them to be universal or partial (in their love) ? We should have to say that they are partial. Now, since partiality against one another is the cause of the major calamities in the world, then partiality is wrong. . . . .

"Whoever criticizes others must have something to put in the place of (what he criticizes). . . . Therefore Mo Tzǔ said : 'Partiality is to be replaced by universality.' But how is partiality to be replaced by universality ? I say that when everyone regards the states of others as he regards his own, who would attack the others' states ? Others would be regarded like self. When everyone regards the capitals of others as he regards his own, who would seize the others' capitals ? Others would be regarded like self. When everyone regards the houses of others as he regards his own, who would disturb the others' houses ? Others would be regarded like self. Now, when states and capitals do not attack and seize each other, and when clans and individuals do not disturb and harm one another, is this a calamity or a benefit to the world ? We must say that it is a benefit. When we come to consider the origins of the various benefits, how have they arisen ? Have they arisen out of hate of others and injuring others ? We must say not so. We should say that they have arisen out of love of others and benefiting others. If we should classify all those who love others and benefit others, should we find them to be partial or universal ? We must say that they are universal. Now since universality is really the cause of the major benefits in the world, therefore Mo Tzǔ proclaims universality to be right.

"Moreover, we said in the beginning that the purpose of those who are virtuous lies in procuring benefits for the world and eliminating its calamities. Now we have established that universality is the cause of the great benefits in the world, and partiality is the cause of its major calamities. . . . When we try to develop and procure benefits for the world with universality as our standard, then attentive ears and keen eyes will respond in service to one another, limbs will be strengthened to work for one another, and those who know the proper course will untiringly instruct others. Thus the old and those who have neither wife nor children will have support and nourishment to round out their old age with, and the young and weak and orphans will have a place of support for them to grow up in. When universality is adopted as the standard, then such are the consequent benefits. It is incomprehensible then that people should all object to universality when they hear of it. What can be the reason ?

"Yet their objections to it are not all exhausted. It is asked : 'It may be morally good, but can it be of any use ?'

"Mo Tzǔ replied : 'If it were not useful then even I would disapprove of it. Moreover, how can there be anything *good* which cannot be of use?' Let us consider the matter from two sides. Suppose there are two men. Let one of them hold to partiality and the other to universality. Then the partial one would say: 'How can I take care of my friend as I do myself, and how can I take care of his parents as my own?' Therefore, when he found his friend hungry he would not feed him, and when he found him cold he would not clothe him. In his illness he would not minister to him, and when he would be dead he would not bury him. Such would be the word and deed of the advocate of partiality. But the words of the universal one would not be like this, nor would his actions. He would say: 'I have heard that to be a lofty man in the world one should take care of one's friend as one does of oneself, and take care of one's friend's parents as one does one's own. Only after this can one be a lofty man in the world.' Therefore when he found his friend hungry he would feed him, and when he found him cold be would clothe him. In his sickness he would minister to him, and when he was dead he would bury him. Such is the word and deed of the advocate of universality.

"These two persons, then, are opposed to one another in word and also in deed. Suppose they are sincere in word and decisive in deed, and that their word and deed are made to agree like the two parts of a tally, so that there is no word which is not realized in deed. Then we should like to ask: 'Here is a flat and wide expanse of open land, on which, clothed in armor and helmet, one is about to join battle, and life and death are not predictable. Or suppose one has been commissioned a deputy by one's ruler to far countries such as Pa, Yüeh, Ch'i and Ching, and whether one will arrive or return is quite uncertain. Then let us ask upon whom would one lay the trust of one's family and parents? Would it be upon the *universal* friend or upon the *partial* friend?' It seems to us, on occasions like these, even a fool in the world, although he himself were a person who objected to universality, would all the same lay the trust upon the universal friend. Such is verbal objection to the principle but actual selection of it, which is self-contradiction between one's word and deed. It is incomprehensible, then, why people should object to universality when they hear of it.

"Yet the objection is not all exhausted. It is objected: 'Maybe it is a good criterion for making a choice among ordinary men, but may not apply to rulers?'

"Let us again consider the matter from both sides. Suppose there are two rulers. Let one of them hold universality and the other partiality. Then the partial ruler would say: 'How can I take care of the people as I do of myself? This would be quite contrary to common sense. A man's life on earth is of short duration; it is like a galloping horse passing by a crack (in a wall).' Therefore when he found his people hungry he would not feed them, and when

he found them cold he would not clothe them. When they were
sick he would not minister to them, and upon their death he would
not bury them. Such would be the word and such the deed of the
partial ruler. But the words of the universal ruler are not like this,
nor are his deeds. He would say : ' I have heard that to be an
enlightened ruler in the world, one should first attend to one's people
and then to oneself. Only after this can one be an enlightened ruler
in the world.' Therefore when he found his people hungry he would
feed them, and when he found them cold he would clothe them.
In their sickness he would minister to them, and upon their death
he would bury them. Such would be the word and such the deed
of the universal ruler.

" These two rulers, then, are opposed to each other in word and
also in deed. Suppose they are sincere in word and decisive in deed,
so that their word and deed are made to agree like the two parts of
a tally. Then we should ask : ' Suppose this year that there is a
disastrous pestilence, that most people are in misery and privation,
and that many lie dead (and unburied) in the water-courses. Then if a
person could choose one of the two rulers, which would he prefer ? '
It seems to us that on such occasions even a fool in the world, although
he himself were a person who objected to universality, would choose
the universal ruler. This is verbal objection to the principle but
actual selection of it, which is self-contradiction between one's word
and deed. It is incomprehensible, then, why people should object
to universality when they hear of it " (pp. 87-92).

The major calamities in the world come from the failure of men to
love one another, and hence can only be solved through the doctrine
of universal love (*chien ai* 兼愛). The practice of universal love
not only benefits the one who is loved, but the one who loves, on
the principle of reciprocity. Thus Mo Tzŭ employs pure utilitarianism
to prove the necessity for universal love. Herein lies the difference
between his doctrine and the Confucian advocacy of human-
heartedness or *jen*.

The great benefits to the world come from men practising universal love, and its major calamities come from them fighting with
one another. Therefore we should condemn warfare. Chapter
XVIII says :

" Suppose soldier hosts arise. If it is in winter it will be too
cold, and if in summer it will be too hot. So it should be done neither
in winter nor in summer. But if it is in spring it will take people
away from sowing and planting, and if in fall it will take them from
reaping and harvesting. Should they be taken away in any of these
seasons, innumerable people would die of hunger and cold. And,
when the army sets out, the bamboo, arrows, plumed standards,
house tents, armor, shields and sword hilts will break and rot in
innumerable quantities and never come back. Again with the spears,

lances, swords, poniards, chariots and carts : these will break and rot in innumerable quantities and never come back. Innumerable horses and oxen will start out fat and come back lean, or will die and never come back at all. And innumerable people will die because their food will be cut off and cannot be supplied on account of the great distance of the roads, while other innumerable people will get sick and die from the constant danger, the irregularities of eating and drinking, and the extremes of hunger and over-eating. Then the army will be lost in large numbers or in its entirety ; in either case the number will be innumerable. Which means that the spirits will lose their worshippers, the number of these being also innumerable.

"Why, then, does the government deprive the people of their opportunities and benefits to such a great extent ? It has been answered : 'I covet the fame of the victor and the possessions obtainable through conquest, and therefore I do it.'

"Mo Tzŭ said : 'But when we consider the victory as such, there is nothing useful about it. When we consider the possessions obtained through it, it does not even make up for what has been lost. . . .'

"Those who endeavor to gloss over wars of aggression would say : 'In the south there are the kings of Ching and Yüeh, and in the north there are the lords of Ch'i and Chin. When their states were first assigned to them they did not extend to a few hundred *li* square, and to less than a few hundreds of thousands of people. But by means of wars and attacks their areas have increased to several thousand *li* square and the people to several million. So, then, offensive wars are not to be condemned.'

"Mo Tzŭ said : 'Although there be four or five states which may have reaped benefits, it is still not acting in accordance with the Way (*Tao*). It is like the physician giving his drugs to his patients. If a physician should give all the sick in the world the same drug, among the ten thousand people who took it there might be four or five who would be benefited. Still it is not to be said to be an efficacious medicine. Hence a filial son would not give it to his parent and a loyal subject would not give it to his ruler. Of the states into which the empire was divided in early times, an innumerable number have disappeared through wars. The earlier cases we have heard of through the ear, and the recent cases we have seen with our own eyes. . . .' " (pp. 101-104).

Bentham held that the purpose of morality and laws is to procure the greatest happiness for the greatest number, a doctrine shared by Mo Tzŭ. Mo Tzŭ condemned war, and the Confucian, Mencius, likewise says : "Those who are skilful in warfare should suffer the highest punishment" (*Mencius*, IV*a*, 14). Mo Tzŭ, however, condemned war because it is not profitable (*li*), whereas Mencius's condemnation is because it is not righteous (*i*). This distinction appears clearly in the argument between Mencius and another philosopher, Sung K'eng.[1] Sung K'eng told Mencius that he wished to see the kings of Ch'in and Ch'u and turn them from war by saying that it 'was not profitable (*li*).' Mencius, on the other hand, urged that these kings should be appealed to on grounds of human-heartedness (*jen*) and righteousness (*i*). Even though it is not certain that Sung K'eng was a Mohist himself, the incident well illustrates the difference between the Confucian and Mohist viewpoints.

7—RELIGIOUS SANCTIONS

Although Mo Tzŭ held that the doctrine of universal love is the only way to save the world, he did not believe that men through their original natures can love one another. The *Mo-tzŭ* (ch. 3) says:

" Watching a dyer of silk at work, Mo Tzŭ sighed, saying: ' What is dyed in blue becomes blue ; what is dyed in yellow becomes yellow. When the silk is put in a different dye its color becomes also different. Having been dipped five times, it has changed its color five times. Therefore dyeing must be attended to with care ! ' " (p. 9).

Man's nature, Mo Tzŭ believed, is like pure silk, and its goodness or evil is dependent entirely upon what it is ' dyed ' with. We must strive to ' dye ' others with the doctrine of universal love, so as to bring about mutual benefit in place of mutual harm. But because of the short-sightedness of the mass of the people, it is very difficult to make them see the benefits of universal love and substitute these for what is harmful. Therefore Mo Tzŭ laid stress on all kinds of sanctions which would induce men to love one another.[2] Among these were religious sanctions, Mo Tzŭ holding that there is a Supreme God above, who rewards people who practise universal love and punishes the perverse. Chapter XXVI states :

" The Son of Heaven (Emperor) is the most honorable in the world and richest in the world. Hence those who wish to be rich and honorable cannot but obey the Will of Heaven. Those who obey the Will of Heaven, love universally and benefit others, and will then be inevitably rewarded. Those who oppose the Will of Heaven, are partial and unfriendly and harming others, and will inevitably incur punishment. Thus, then, who were those who obeyed the Will of Heaven and obtained rewards, and who were those who opposed the Will of Heaven and incurred punishment ?

" Mo Tzŭ said : ' The ancient Sage-kings of the Three Dynasties, Yü, T'ang, Wen and Wu, were those who obeyed the Will of Heaven and obtained reward. And the wicked kings of the Three

---

[1] *Cf. Mencius*, VI*b*, 4.

[2] Bentham somewhat similarly maintains that man's pleasures and pains have four sources : physical, political, moral and religious. Laws and rules for conduct can only have force when they advantageously utilize the pleasure and pain arising from these four sources with which to exhort and repress. For this reason Bentham calls these sources the four sanctions. *Cf.* his *Introduction to the Principles of Morals and Legislature*, p. 25.

Dynasties, Chieh, Chou, Yu (781-771) and Li (878-842), were those who opposed the Will of Heaven and incurred punishment.'

" This being so, how did Yü, T'ang, Wen and Wu obtain their reward? Mo Tzŭ said: ' In the highest sphere they revered Heaven, in the middle sphere they worshipped the spirits, and in the lower sphere they loved the people. Thereupon the Will of Heaven proclaimed: All those whom I love they love also, and all those whom I benefit they benefit also. Their love to men is all-embracing, and their benefit to men is most substantial. And so they were raised to the honor of being Sons of Heaven, and enriched with the heritage of the empire. They were succeeded by descendants for ten thousand generations to continue the spread of their goodness all over the world. And people praise them unto this day, calling them Sage-kings.'

" This being so, how did Chieh, Chou, Yu and Li incur their punishment? Mo Tzŭ said: ' In the highest sphere they blasphemed against Heaven, in the middle sphere they blasphemed against the spirits, and in the lower sphere they oppressed the people. Thereupon the Will of Heaven proclaimed: Those whom I love they turn away from and hate, and those whom I would benefit they oppress. Their hate of men is without limit and their oppression of men is most severe. And so they were not permitted to finish out their (natural) span, and their posterity were cut off. People unto this day condemn them, calling them wicked kings.'

" But how do we know Heaven loves the people? Because it gives all of them enlightenment. How do we know it enlightens them all? Because it possesses them all. How do we know it possesses them all? Because it accepts sacrifice from them all. How do we know it accepts sacrifice from all? Because within the four seas all grain-eating (*i.e.*, civilized) people feed oxen and sheep with grass, and dogs and pigs with grains, and prepare clean cakes and wine to do sacrifice to Supreme God (*Shang Ti*) and the spirits. Possessing all the people, how could Heaven not love them? Moreover, as I have said, for the murder of any one innocent individual there will be one calamity. Who is it that murders the innocent person? It is a man. Who is it that sends down the calamity? It is Heaven. If Heaven should be thought of as not loving the people, why should it send down calamities for the murder of a man by a man? From this I know that Heaven loves the people " (pp. 137-139).

Through such arguments Mo Tzŭ sought to establish the existence of God and the nature of His Will. Shallow these proofs certainly are, but we must remember that Mo Tzŭ had no interest in metaphysics as such, his purpose being merely to establish religious sanctions with which to induce men to love one another. Chapter XXVII states:

" The Will of Heaven abominates the large state which attacks small states, the large house which molests small houses, the strong who oppress the weak, the clever who deceive the simple, and the honored who contemn the humble : these are what Heaven abominates. But more than this, it wishes people having energy to work for each other, those knowing the way to teach each other, and those possessing wealth to share with each other. Moreover, it desires the superior diligently to attend to government and the subordinates diligently to attend to their work. When the superior attends to the government diligently, the country will be orderly. When the subordinates attend to work diligently, wealth will be abundant. When the country is orderly and wealth is abundant, within the state there will be wherewith to prepare clean cakes and wine to sacrifice to Heaven and the spirits, and in relationships with outside countries there will be wherewith to furnish rings, stones, pearls and jades with which to befriend surrounding neighbors. Then grudges will not arise among the feudal lords, and fighting along the frontiers will be suspended. When the people within are provided with food and rest, then ruler and minister, superiors and subordinates will be respectively gracious and loyal ; father and son, elder and younger brothers will be respectively affectionate and filial. Therefore when the principle of obeying the Will of Heaven is understood and widely practised in the world, then justice and government will be orderly, the multitudes will be harmonious, the country will be wealthy, the supplies will be sufficient, and the people will be warmly clothed and sufficiently fed, peaceful and without worry. Therefore Mo Tzŭ said : ' If the gentlemen of the world to-day really desire to follow the true way and benefit the people, and fundamentally examine the roots of human-heartedness (*jen*) and righteousness (*i*), they cannot but pay careful attention to the Will of Heaven ' " (pp. 142-143).

Besides a Supreme God, however, there exist supernatural beings who likewise have the power to reward goodness and punish evil. Chapter XXXI states :

" With the passing of the Sage-kings of the Three Dynasties, the world lost its righteousness and the feudal lords took might as right. Rulers and ministers, superiors and subordinates are no longer gracious and loyal ; father and son, elder and younger brother are no longer affectionate and filial, virtuous and kind. Rulers do not attend diligently to government and humble folk do not attend diligently to their work. The people practise immorality and wickedness and become rebellious. Thieves and brigands with swords, poison, water and fire hold up innocent people on the highways and by-paths, robbing them of their carts and horses, coats and fur overcoats, to enrich themselves. It was with this (passing away of the Sage-kings) that the world began to fall into confusion. Now what is the reason for this ? It is all because of doubt as to the existence or non-existence of ghosts and spirits, and failure to understand that they can reward virtue and punish vice. If now all the people in the world could be made to believe that the spirits can reward virtue and punish vice, how could the world be in chaos ? " (p. 160).

But although spirits exist, men must seek for happiness through their own efforts, rather than merely sit back and implore the spirits for help. Chapter XLVIII says :

" Mo Tzŭ was ill. Tieh Pi came and inquired : ' Sir, you hold that ghosts and spirits are intelligent and control calamities and blessings. They will reward the good and punish the evil. Now you are a Sage. How can you be ill ? Is it that your teaching is not entirely correct or that ghosts and spirits are after all unintelligent ? ' Mo Tzŭ said: ' Though I am ill, in what way would the ghosts and spirits be unintelligent? There are many ways (besides that of offending the spirits) by which a man can contract diseases. Some are contracted from cold or heat, some from fatigue. If there are a hundred gates and only one be closed, where could robbers not enter ? ' " (p. 240).

Because Mo Tzŭ invoked all kinds of sanctions to induce men to love one another, he opposed the concept of an impersonal Fate (*ming* 命). For if rewards and punishments are sent down by God and the spirits, they are determined by the conduct of men themselves, rather than by Fate. But if they are decreed by Fate, quite regardless of human conduct, these rewards and punishments lose all coercive power over men. Chapter XXXV states :

" Therefore the ancient Sage-kings promulgated laws and issued orders to be standards of reward and punishment, and to encourage the virtuous and obstruct the evil. And so the people were filial to their parents at home and respectful to the elders in the village or district. They observed propriety in conduct, moderation in going out and coming in, and decency between men and women. Therefore when they were employed to look after the court they would not steal ; when they were put in defence of a city they would not revolt ; when their lord fell into difficulties, they would die for him ; and when he was banished they would follow him. This is what superiors will reward and people will applaud.

" Now those who hold that there is a Fate say : ' Whoever is rewarded by his superior was destined by Fate to be rewarded, and it is not because of his virtue that he is rewarded.' If this were the case, the people would not be filial to their parents at home or respectful to the elders in the village or district. They would not observe propriety in conduct, moderation in going out and coming in, or decency between men and women. If employed to look after the court they would steal, and when put in defence of a city they would revolt. When their lord fell into difficulties they would not die for him, and when he was banished they would not accompany him. This is what superiors will punish and people will condemn.

" Now those who hold that there is a Fate say : ' Whoever is punished by his superior was destined by Fate to be punished, and it is not because of his vice that he is punished.' If this were the case, the ruler would not be righteous, the minister would not be loyal, the father would not be affectionate, the son would not be filial, the elder brother would not be brotherly, and the younger brother would not be respectful. The tenacious holding to this doctrine is responsible for pernicious ideas and is the way of the wicked " (pp. 185-186).

8—Political Sanctions

Besides religious sanctions, Mo Tzŭ emphasized the importance of political ones, maintaining that if we wish the world to be in a state of harmony and the people to be happy, we not only must have a Supreme Ruler in Heaven above, but a Supreme Ruler amongst men. The *Mo-tzŭ* (ch. 11) states :

" In the beginning of human life, when there was yet no law and government, the custom was : ' Every man according to his own idea.' Thus when there was one man there was one idea, when two men two ideas, and when ten men there were ten different ideas. The more people there were, the more were the different concepts. Hence each man approved of his own view and disapproved of that of others, and so there arose mutual disapproval among men. As a result, father and son, and elder and younger brothers became enemies and estranged from each other, and were unable to reach any agreement. The people of the world worked against each other with water, fire and poison. Surplus energy was not spent for mutual aid ; surplus goods were allowed to rot without sharing ; excellent teachings were kept secret and not taught to one another. The disorder in the (human) world was like that among birds and beasts. Yet it was evident that all this disorder was owing to the want of a ruler.

" Therefore there was a selection of the person in the world who was virtuous and able, and he was established to be Son of Heaven. . . . When the rulers were all installed, the Son of Heaven issued a mandate to the people, saying : ' Upon hearing good or evil one shall report it to a superior. What the superior thinks to be right, all shall think to be right. What the superior thinks to be wrong, all shall think to be wrong ' " (pp. 55-56).

This passage reminds us of Thomas Hobbes, who believed that in the beginning no nations existed and man lived in a state of nature. At this period all men were mutual enemies ever struggling with one another. Being dissatisfied with this condition, they had no alternative but to set up an absolute ruler and agree to obey him. Because of this origin the state necessarily required great authority ; otherwise it would disintegrate and men would again return to a condition of nature. The absolutism of the state's authority was equal to that of God's, the only difference being that God exists eternally, whereas the state may die.[1]   Such a doctrine approaches closely the political philosophy of Mo Tzŭ.[2]

Before states, laws and governments existed, Mo Tzŭ says, there was great confusion because standards of right and wrong were uncertain.   Therefore after the establishment of the state the commands of the Emperor had to be made absolute standards of right and wrong, with none other permitted.   For this reason there is in Mo Tzŭ's philosophy no need for social sanctions in addition to political ones.   Chapter XIII states :

" Why are superiors to-day unable to govern their subordinates, and subordinates unwilling to serve their superiors ?   It is because of a mutual disregard.   What is the reason for this ?   The reason is that there is a difference in standards.   Whenever standards differ there will be a party.   The ruler may think a man good and reward him.   The man, though rewarded by the ruler, yet by the same act (for which he was rewarded) provokes the condemnation of the people.   Therefore those who do good are not necessarily encouraged by rewards.   The ruler may think a man evil and punish him. This man, though punished by the ruler, at the same time receives the approval of the people.   Because of this those who do evil are not necessarily obstructed by punishments.   Thus reward and honor from the ruler are not enough to encourage the good, and his denunciation and punishment are insufficient to prevent the evil.   What is the reason for this ?   The reason is a difference in standards " (p. 72).

Hobbes believes that among the causes of evil in a commonwealth is " the poison of seditious doctrines ; whereof one is, That every private man is Judge of Good and Evill actions." [3]   Mo Tzŭ holds exactly the same viewpoint, and hence maintains that all people must without the slightest divergence put themselves in agreement with their superior.   Chapter XIII says :

" How can the standards in the world be unified ? . . . Why not let the patriarch give laws and proclaim to the clan : ' Whoever discovers a benefactor to the clan shall report it ; whoever discovers a malefactor to the clan shall report it.'   Then whoever sees and

---

[1] *Cf.* his *Leviathan*, Pt. I, ch. 17.

[2] The *Mo-tzŭ* (ch. 12) states : " This is to say that of old when God and the spirits established the state and its capital and installed rulers, it was not to make their rank high, their emolument substantial, give them wealth and honor, and let them live in comfort and free from care.   It was to procure benefits for the people and eliminate their adversities ; to enrich the poor and increase the few ; and to bring safety to danger and order to confusion " (pp. 65-66).   Here God and the spirits are made the founders of the state, a doctrine not surprising from a person like Mo Tzŭ, who believed in the existence of a purposeful Heaven.

[3] *Leviathan*, Pt. II, ch. 29.

reports a benefactor of the clan, will be equivalent to being a benefactor of the clan himself. Knowing him, the superior will reward him; hearing of him, the group will praise him. Whoever fails to report a malefactor of the clan upon seeing one, will be equivalent to being a malefactor to the clan himself. Knowing him, the superior will punish him; hearing of him, the group will condemn him. Thereupon all the members of the clan will wish to obtain reward and honor, and avoid denunciation and punishment from their superior. Seeing the good, they will report; seeing the evil, they will report. And the patriarch can reward the good and punish the evil. With the good rewarded and the evil punished, the clan will surely have order. Now, why is it that the clan becomes orderly? Just because the administration is based upon the principle of Agreement with the Superior (*shang t'ung* 尚 同). . . .

"Therefore the clan patriarchs should again bring together the ideas of the clan and make them similar to those of the state ruler. . . . And therefore the state ruler should again choose from the ideas of the state and make them similar to those of the Emperor. The Emperor also should give laws and proclaim to the empire: 'Whoever discovers a benefactor of the empire shall report it; whoever discovers a malefactor of the empire shall report it.' Then whoever sees and reports a benefactor of the empire will be equivalent to being a benefactor of the state himself. Knowing him, the superior will reward him; hearing of him, the people will praise him. Whoever fails to report a malefactor upon seeing one, will be equivalent to being a malefactor to the empire himself. Knowing him, the superior will punish him; hearing of him, the people will condemn him. Thereupon all the people in the empire will wish to obtain reward and honor, and avoid denunciation and punishment from their Emperor. Seeing the good and the evil they will report them. Then the Emperor can reward the good and punish the evil. With the good rewarded and the evil punished, the empire will surely have order. Now why is it that the empire becomes orderly? Just because the administration is based on the principle of Agreement with the Superior.

"Now that the empire becomes orderly, the Emperor will further bring together the ideas of the empire and put them in agreement with Heaven. . . . " (pp. 72-75).

When subordinates have all become one with their superiors, and rulers have ordered that there be mutual love and benefit, nothing else but these will be possible in the world. When the apogee of 'Agreement with the Superior' is reached, there remains no place outside of the standard pattern in which the individual man's nature may express itself. Hsün Tzŭ criticized this aspect of Mo Tzŭ's philosophy, saying: " Mo Tzŭ had vision regarding uniformity, but no vision regarding individuality " (*Hsün-tzŭ*, pp. 184-185).

We should further note that though Mo Tzŭ says that all men are to follow the Will of Heaven, yet it is only the Son of Heaven (*i.e.*, the Emperor), according to this doctrine of 'Agreement with the Superior,' who can actually identify himself with Heaven. As the representative of Heaven on earth, the Son of Heaven issues his orders, and the people can do nothing but obey them. Hence, according to Mo Tzŭ, not only can there be no social sanctions beyond political ones, but even religious sanctions become mere appendages of the political ones. Here, again, Mo Tzŭ comes close to Hobbes, who maintained that the Church cannot hold any independent authority outside that of the state, for if this be not the case, the state will become divided and can no longer exist. Hobbes also maintained that if people merely hold to their own personal beliefs without obeying the laws, the state must likewise be destroyed.[1] According to Mo Tzŭ's doctrine of the identity of the Son of Heaven with Heaven, the Will of God and of the sovereign are the same, and so cannot conflict with one another. Thus his Emperor is not only a ruler, but becomes the final arbiter of all teachings and ideas.

9—ADDITIONAL REMARKS

In order to gain enrichment and an increased population, Mo Tzŭ held that everything else should be sacrificed. Such a doctrine is not wholly unjustified, for biologists tell us that all living creatures seek to protect their individual existence and that of their species, and psycho-analysts tell us that among human desires the strongest are those of self-interest and sex. Already in ancient times in China there was the saying : " (Concern with) food and sex : this is (human) nature."[2] Mo Tzŭ, too, wished only that men might maintain their individual existence, and through productive marriages might make the human race more and more numerous. His doctrine of universal love, his political institutions and his other ideas all tend toward this aim.

These doctrines are fundamentally sound, but go too far when they say we must sacrifice all immediate gain so as to attain a future and very distant aim. The *Chuang-tzŭ* (ch. 33) criticizes Mo Tzŭ as follows :
" To show no extravagance for future generations, to show no wastefulness in the use of things, to make no display in measures and institutions, to keep themselves under the restraint of strict rules so as to be prepared for the emergencies of the world : such were some of the aspects of the Way (*Tao*) in ancient times. Mo Ti and Ch'in Ku Li (his disciple) heard of these and delighted in them. But in practising them they went to extremes, and in following them they were too strict. They wrote an essay 'Against Music,' and another entitled 'Frugal Expenditure.' There was to be no singing in life,

---

[1] *Op. cit..*
[2] *Cf. Mencius*, VIa, 4.

no mourning garments at death. Mo Tzŭ taught universal love and mutual benefit, and condemned fighting. His teaching excluded anger. He was fond of study and had wide learning. Some points in his teachings were not different from those of others, whereas at other points he did not agree with the early kings. He attacked the rites and music of the ancients. . . .

"In the ancient mourning ceremonials there were distinctions between the nobles and common folk, and different degrees between high and low. For the Son of Heaven there should be a seven-layer coffin; for the feudal lords one of five layers; for the great officials three layers; and for lower officials two layers. Now Mo Tzŭ alone held as a rule for all that there should be no singing in life, no mourning garments at death, and that the coffin should be of *t'ung* wood, three inches in thickness, without any outer case.

"I fear that to teach men thus is not to love them, while to practise this oneself is certainly not to love oneself. These objections do not suffice to overthrow Mo Tzŭ's system. Yet though men sing, he condemns singing. Though men mourn, he condemns mourning. Though men enjoy music, he condemns music. Is this truly in accord with man's nature? He would have men toil through life, with a bare funeral at death. Such teaching is too barren. It would lead men into sorrow and lamentation. Its practice would be too difficult. I fear it cannot be regarded as the Way of the Sage. It is contrary to human nature and would not be tolerated. Mo Tzŭ himself might be able to do it, but what about the rest of the world? If one separates from the rest of the world, one's position is far indeed from the (Sage-)kings" (pp. 440-441).

This is a fair criticism, and perhaps indicates one reason why the Mohist school failed to survive.

Hsün Tzŭ also criticized Mo Tzŭ, saying: "Mo Tzŭ was blinded by utility and did not know the value of culture" (*Hsün-tzŭ*, pp. 263-264). Nevertheless, Liu Hsiang (77—6 B.C.) writes in his *Shuo Yüan*:

"Ch'in Tzŭ asked Mo Tzŭ: 'How are embroidered silks and fine and coarse linens to be used?' Mo Tzŭ said: '. . . . . Suppose that in a year of bad times, someone wished to give you the pearl of the Marquis of Sui, yet would not allow you to sell it, but only to keep it as a valuable decoration. Or that he wished to give you a *chung* of grain. If you would get the pearl you would not get the grain, and vice versa. Then which would you choose?' Ch'in Tzŭ said: 'I would choose the grain, for with this I could rescue myself from my extremity.' Mo Tzŭ replied: 'Truly so. So then why strive after lavishness? The Sage does not hasten to exalt what is without use and to delight in frivolity and licence. Therefore one's food should always be sufficient before one seeks to have it fine tasting; one's clothing should always be warm before one tries to make it beautiful ; and one's dwelling should always be safe before one tries to make it pleasure giving.   To do what will endure, and practise what may be long continued ; to put what is fundamental first and external decoration secondary : this is what the Sage concerns himself with.' " [1]

If this story is true, it shows that Mo Tzŭ did not recognize that luxury, lavishness and decoration are evil in themselves.   Decoration is one kind of good, only we must ' put what is fundamental (i.e., human necessities) first, and external decoration secondary.'   We must first be able to live, only after which may we seek for the amenities of life, an idea which no one would dispute.   It is extremely difficult, however, to make life for all people in the world possible. This is why Mo Tzŭ maintained that everyone, without exception, should toil and practise frugality.   This does not mean that he did not know that the refinements of life are also good, but that he simply felt that men lack the leisure for developing them.

---

[1] *Cf.* the *Fan Chih* sect., in *chüan* 20, pp. 3-5.

CHAPTER VI

MENCIUS AND HIS SCHOOL OF CONFUCIANISM

1—The Mission of Mencius and his Position in Chinese History

What happened to the Confucian school after the death of Confucius ? The *Shih Chi* gives us considerable information in its chapter devoted to the Confucians :

" After the death of Confucius, his seventy disciples scattered and travelled among the feudal lords. The important ones became teachers and ministers (of the feudal lords). The lesser ones became friends and teachers of the officials or went into retirement and were no longer seen. Thus Tzŭ Lu lived in Wei, Tzŭ Chang in Ch'en, Tan-t'ai Tzŭ-yü lived in Ch'u, Tzŭ Hsia lived in Hsi-ho, and Tzŭ Kung spent the rest of his life in Ch'i. As for such men as T'ien Tzŭ Fang, Tuan-kan Mu, Wu Ch'i and Ch'in Ku Li, these all received instruction from the school of Tzŭ Hsia and became the instructors of kings. At this time the only man who delighted in learning was Marquis Wen of Wei (403-387), and this (neglect of learning) later became more and more pronounced down to the time of (Ch'in) Shih-huang (246-210). During this period there was fighting everywhere throughout the empire between the Warring States, and Confucianism declined. Only in the states of Ch'i and Lu did learning still continue. During the reigns of Kings Wei (357-320) and Hsüan (319-301) of Ch'i [1] there were such persons as Meng Tzŭ 孟 子 (Mencius) and Hsün Ch'ing (Hsün Tzŭ), who followed the teachings of the Master (Confucius) and developed them, becoming famous in their generation for their learning " (ch. 121, pp. 1-2).

Confucius had been the first to make teaching his profession, and his example was followed by the later Confucians. Of these the greatest were easily Mencius and Hsün Tzŭ. Confucius, as I pointed out in Chapter IV, holds a place in Chinese history comparable to that of Socrates in the West. The position of Mencius in Chinese history is comparable to that of Plato, his temperament and philosophy both being idealistic ; while Hsün Tzŭ's is similar to that of Aristotle, both his temperament and philosophy being realistic.

---

[1] For these dates, see Maspero, ' La chronologie des rois de Ts'i,' in *T'oung Pao*, 1927, no. 5.—Tr.

The *Shih Chi* says in its biography of Mencius :

" Meng K'o 孟軻 was a native of Tsou. He received his education from the disciples of Tzŭ Ssŭ (the grandson of Confucius). When his learning had become comprehensive, he travelled to serve King Hsüan of Ch'i, but the latter was unable to employ him. He then went to the state of Liang, but King Hui of Liang (370-319) was insincere in his words and considered (Mencius) as pedantic and far from reality. At this time the state of Ch'in was employing the Lord of Shang to enrich its state and strengthen its soldiers ; Ch'u and Wei were employing Wu Ch'i to fight and conquer their weaker opponents ; and Kings Wei and Hsüan of Ch'i were employing Sun Tzŭ and T'ien Chi, with the result that the feudal lords faced the east so as to pay homage to Ch'i. The empire was then engaged in forming vertical (north-to-south) and horizontal (east-to-west) alliances (among the states), and held fighting as something worthy. Whereas Meng K'o was (intent on) transmitting the virtues of T'ang (i.e., Yao), Yü (i.e., Shun), and the Three Dynasties, so that those whom he visited were not willing to listen to him. So he retired and together with his disciple, Wan Chang, and others, put the *Shih* and *Shu* into order, transmitted the doctrines of Confucius, and composed the *Mencius* in seven books " (ch. 74, p. 1).

The *Shih Chi* fails to give the years of birth and death of Mencius, but according to the chronological table of Mencius' prepared by Ch'eng Fu-hsin (fourteenth century A.D.), he was born in 371 and died in 289 B.C. . The state of Tsou in which he was born was a tiny state bordering that of Lu in present Shantung, and like the latter was renowned as a center of Confucianism, so that the *Chuang-tzŭ* speaks of the Confucians as ' gentlemen and teachers of Tsou and Lu '
(p. 438).

Throughout his life the mission of Confucius had been to perpetuate the teachings of King Wen and the Duke of Chou ; that of Mencius was to perpetuate those of Confucius, so that Mencius said :

" In former times, Yü repressed the vast waters and the world was reduced to order. The Duke of Chou took in hand the barbarous tribes of the west and north and drove away ferocious animals, and the people enjoyed repose. Confucius made the *Ch'un Ch'iu*, and rebellious ministers and villainous sons were struck with terror. . . . . . I also wish to rectify men's hearts, and to put an end to perverse doctrines ; to oppose their one-sided actions and put away their licentious expressions, thus to carry on the work of the (above) three Sages. In what way do I like disputation ? It is simply that I have no alternative " (*Mencius*, IIIb, 9).

" From Yao and Shun down to T'ang there were five hundred years and more. As to Yü and Kao Yao, they saw (these earliest Sages) and so knew their doctrines, while T'ang heard their doctrines

---

[1] *Meng-tzŭ Nien-p'u.*

(as transmitted) and so knew them. From T'ang to King Wen were five hundred years and more. As to Yi Yin and Lai Chu, they saw (T'ang) and knew his doctrines, while King Wen heard them (as transmitted) and so knew them. From King Wen to Confucius there were five hundred years and more. As to T'ai-kung Wang and San-i Sheng, they saw (Wen) and so knew his doctrines, while Confucius heard them (as transmitted) and so knew them. From Confucius downward to today there have been one hundred odd years. Thus I am not yet far from the generation of that Sage, and am extremely close to his residence. Under these circumstances is there no one (to transmit his doctrines) ? Yea, is there indeed no one ? " (VIIb, 38).

Here Mencius definitely conceives of himself as the only man, in a time of disorder and intellectual confusion, able to perpetuate Confucius's teachings. He says elsewhere in similar vein : " If there is a desire that the world should enjoy tranquility and good order, who is there today, besides myself, to bring it about ? " (IIb, 13). And again : " Now what I desire to do is to study to be like Confucius " (IIa, 2, para. 22).

2—ATTITUDE TOWARD THE CHOU INSTITUTIONS

Confucius had utilized the Six Disciplines for teaching purposes, a practice continued by the later Confucians. Thus of Mencius the *Shih Chi* says that he " put the *Shih* and *Shu* in order and transmitted the doctrines of Confucius." That Mencius was well versed in the classics is proved by the fact that in the present *Mencius* the Book of Odes is quoted no less than thirty times and discussed four times ; the Book of History is quoted eighteen times, discussed once, and several times quoted without the prefacing words, ' The *Shu* says ' ; and the books of rites (*Li*) and the *Ch'un Ch'iu* are also frequently referred to.[1] In expounding the *Shih* and *Shu*, moreover, Mencius, like Confucius, chiefly emphasized the developing of their ideas. Thus he says :

" The *Shih* (III, iii, Ode 6, 1) says :

' Heaven produced mankind,
Having faculties and having laws.
These are invariable for the people to hold,
And they love this admirable virtue.'

" Confucius said : ' The maker of this ode knew indeed the Way.' Every faculty must have its law, and since these are invariable for the people to hold, they consequently love this admirable virtue " (VIa, 7). Again :

" The dissatisfaction expressed in the *Hsiao Pien* Ode (II, v, Ode 3, 3) is that of affection between relatives, and that affection shows human-heartedness (*jen*). Bigoted indeed was old Kao's explanation of the ode " (VIb, 3).

---

[1] *Cf.* Ch'en Li (1801-1882), *Tung-shu Tu-shu-chi, chüan* 3, pp. 9-10.

Because explanations of the Odes should not be thus bigoted, Mencius said:

" Therefore those who explain the Odes may not insist on one term so as to do violence to a sentence, nor on a sentence so as to do violence to the general idea. They must try with their thoughts to meet that idea, and then they shall apprehend it " (V*a*, 4).

In expounding the Book of History, Mencius held the same attitude:

" It would be better to be without the *Shu* than to give entire credence to it. In the ' Completion of the War ' ¹ I accept only two or three passages which I believe. The man of human-heartedness has no enemy under heaven. And when (the prince), the most human-hearted, was engaged against him who was the least human-hearted, how could blood have flowed till it floated the pestles of the mortars (as described in this chapter) ? " (VII*b*, 3).

A free interpretation of the Odes and History according to one's own opinion : such was the way in which the Confucian school used the Six Disciplines with which to ' create through transmitting'. Being the perpetuator of Confucius's teachings, Mencius's attitude toward the traditional institutions of his own times was conservative. The *Mencius* contains an elaborate description of the social structure of the early Chou dynasty:

" Pei-kung I asked : ' What was the arrangement of dignities and emoluments as determined by the House of Chou ? '

" Mencius replied : ' Its particulars cannot be learned, for the feudal lords, disliking their injuriousness to themselves, have all done away with the records of them. Still I have heard the general outline of them.

" ' The Emperor (*T'ien-tzŭ* 天子) constituted one dignity ; the Duke (*Kung* 公) one ; the Marquis (*Hou* 候) one ; the Earl (*Po* 伯) one ; and the Viscount (*Tzŭ* 子) and Baron (*Nan* 男) each one of equal rank : a total of five ranks. Again the ruler (*chün* 君) constituted one dignity ; the chief minister (*ch'ing* 卿) one ; the great officer (*ta fu* 大夫) one ; the scholars (*shih* 士) of the first class one ; those of the middle class one ; and those of the lowest class one : a total of six ranks.

" ' To the Emperor there was allotted a territory of a thousand *li* square. A Duke and a Marquis each had a hundred *li* square ; an Earl had seventy *li*, and a Viscount and a Baron had each fifty *li* : a total of four gradations.² Where the territory did not amount to fifty *li*, its ruler could not himself have access to the Emperor,

---

¹ Pt. V, bk. iii of the *Shu Ching*.—TR.
² Three *li* 里 are roughly equivalent to one English mile. The figures given here show the extreme smallness and consequent numerousness of the feudal states of China during the early Chou dynasty. This condition changed rapidly in later times as some states conquered and absorbed others, until in the period of the Warring States there were only a few large principalities remaining.—TR.

and his land was attached to some marquis, and was called a *Fu-yung* 附 庸. The chief ministers of the Emperor received territory equal to that of a marquis ; a great officer received as much as an earl ; and a scholar of the first class as much as a viscount or a baron.

" ' In a large state, where the territory was a hundred *li* square, the ruler had ten times as much income as his chief ministers ; a chief minister four times as much as a great officer ; a great officer twice as much as a scholar of the first class ; a scholar of the first class twice as much as one of the middle ; a scholar of the middle class twice as much as one of the lowest ; the scholar of the lowest class, and such of the common people as were employed about the government offices, had the same emolument : as much, namely, as they could have made by tilling the fields.

" ' In a state of the next order, where the territory was seventy *li* square, the ruler had ten times as much revenue as his chief minister ; a chief minister three times as much as a great officer ; a great officer twice as much as a scholar of the first class ; a scholar of the first class twice as much as one of the middle ; a scholar of the middle class twice as much as one of the lowest ; the scholars of the lowest class, and such of the common people as were employed about the government offices, had the same emolument : as much, namely, as was equal to what they would have made by tilling the fields.

" ' In a small state, where the territory was fifty *li* square, the ruler had ten times as much as his chief minister ; a chief minister twice as much as a great officer ; a great officer twice as much as a scholar of the highest class ; a scholar of the highest class twice as much as a scholar of the middle class ; a scholar of the middle class twice as much as one of the lowest ; and scholars of the lowest class, and such of the common people as were employed about the government offices, had the same emolument : as much, namely, as was equal to what they would have made by tilling the fields.

" ' As to those who tilled the fields, each husbandman received one hundred acres (*mou* 畝). When these acres were manured, the best husbandmen of the highest class supported nine individuals, and those ranking next to them supported eight. The best husbandmen of the second class supported seven individuals, and those ranking next to them supported six ; while husbandmen of the lowest class only supported five. The salaries of the common people who were employed about the government offices were regulated according to these differences ' " (V*b*, 2).

We need not suppose that this account is historically exact, nor can these regulations ever have been so uniform for every feudal state as here described. On the other hand, there is no reason to suppose that the account is not correct in its general principles. Mencius says :

" The power of vision of Li Lou, and the skill of hand of Kung Shu, without the compass and square, could not have been able to form squares and circles. The acute ear of the music master K'uang, without the pitch-pipes, could not have been able to determine correctly the five notes. The principles of Yao and Shun, without a virtuous government, could not have been able to secure a peaceful order in the empire. There are now (rulers) who have virtuous hearts and a reputation for virtue, while yet the people do not receive any benefits from them, nor will they leave any example to future ages : all because they do not put into practice the ways of the early kings. . . . . Never has there been anyone who followed the laws of the early kings and who fell into error " (IV*a*, 1).

The virtuous government here referred to would be one embodying the political and economic regulations described above. Mencius says again :

" Now, the first thing toward a virtuous government must be to lay down the boundaries. If the boundaries are not defined correctly, the division of the land into squares will not be equal, and the produce and emoluments therefrom will not be equal. . . . . When the boundaries have been defined correctly, the division of fields and regulations of allowances may be determined by you, sitting at your ease " (III*a*, 3, para. 13).

In all these passages Mencius gives approval to the Chou regulations, and shows a conservative attitude toward the traditional institutions of his time.

3—IDEAL POLITICAL AND ECONOMIC MEASURES

According to what has been said, Mencius remained ' a transmitter and not a creator,' but for the Confucian school this did not mean genuine uncreativeness, but creating *through* transmitting, as has already been explained in Chapter IV. Confucius had established the basis for this attitude, and Mencius further developed it, so that while the political and economic regulations advocated by him appear outwardly to be ' following the laws of the early kings,' they would more exactly be described as idealizations of these ancient laws.

Thus while Mencius continued to uphold the Chou regulations determining ranks and emoluments, his basic political and economic conceptions differed widely from the traditional ones. According to the traditional view, all political and economic institutions have been established primarily for the benefit of the ruling aristocracy. Mencius, on the other hand, maintains that these have rather been established on behalf of the people, a concept which is the basis of all his political and social philosophy.

Mencius exalted government of the ideal ' King,' and deprecated that of the *Pa*, or feudal leader.[1]   Hence he pointed out that " none of the disciples of Confucius spoke about the affairs of Huan (of Ch'i) and Wen (of Chin) " (*Ia*, 7, para. 2).   As a matter of fact, Confucius had especially extolled Huan of Ch'i, the first *Pa*, and his famous prime minister, Kuan Chung: " Duke Huan nine times convened the feudal lords without resorting to chariots of war, and all through the ability of Kuan Chung.   Whose virtue was like his!   Whose virtue was like his!" (*Lun Yü*, XIV, 17).   Again: " After Kuan Chung became minister to Duke Huan, he made the Duke *Pa* of the feudal lords, and entirely reduced the world to order, so that people down to the present day are recipients of his benefactions.   But for Kuan Chung we should be wearing our hair loose and folding our garments to the left (as do the barbarians) " (*ibid.*, XIV, 18).

For Mencius, on the other hand, government of a King and of a *Pa* are completely at variance with one another—a distinction which has been maintained in all later Chinese political philosophy.   This, Mencius says, is because the regulations promulgated by the ideal King are all on behalf of the people, with the result that the people delight in and obey him ; whereas the *Pa* only gains the allegiance of the people through military force :

" He who, using force, makes a pretense at virtue, is a *Pa*. . . . . He who, using virtue, practises human-heartedness (*jen*), is a King. . . . .   When one subdues men by force, they do not submit in their hearts, (and submit outwardly only because) their strength is insufficient.   When one subdues men by virtue, in their hearts' core they are pleased and sincerely submit, as was the case with the seventy disciples in their submission to Confucius " (II*a*, 3).

The reason why the ideal King acts on behalf of his people is that he has a heart which cannot bear to witness the sufferings of others, and this he develops into a government which likewise cannot endure that there be any suffering.[2]   The *Pa*, on the contrary, though he may at times promulgate measures which appear to be made for the people, does so merely to obtain a good name, profit or honor. Mencius says again :

" (Human-heartedness and righteousness) were innate in Yao and Shun.   T'ang and Wu made them corporate parts of themselves. The five *Pa* feigned them.   Their feigning was for long, and for

---

[1] As the power of the Chou ruling house declined, many of its powers and prerogatives were usurped by the more powerful of the feudal lords, who were called *Pa* 霸, and held the hegemony over the other feudal lords.   They were acknowledged as leaders, and at various times convened these lords into conferences.   According to the traditional reckoning, there were five such *Pa* during the Ch'un Ch'iu period : Duke Huan of Ch'i (685-643) ; Duke Mu of Ch'in (659-621) ; Duke Hsiang of Sung (650-637) ; Duke Wen of Chin (635-628) ; and King Chuang of Ch'u (631-591)—Tr.

[2] This will be explained in detail later.   See pp. 119 f..

long they did not relinquish them, so how could one know that they did not (really) possess them ? " (VIIa, 30).

Because, says Mencius, all economic and political measures have been established on behalf of the people, even the ruler himself is a man who has been put in office only that he may serve them :

" The people are the most important element (in a state) ; the spirits of the land and grain (she-chi 社稷) are secondary ; and the sovereign is the least.   Therefore to gain the peasantry is the way to become Emperor ; to gain the Emperor is the way to become a feudal lord ; and to gain a feudal lord is the way to become a great officer " (VIIb, 14).

In this passage we see how Mencius, although advocating the maintenance of an Emperor, feudal lords, great officials, and all the other feudal paraphernalia of the Chou, believes that their *raison d'être* lies solely in their capacity to ' gain the peasantry.'   Should a so-called ruler fail to do this, he has lost that which makes him a ruler, which is the same as not being a ruler at all.   Mencius says :

" He who outrages human-heartedness (*jen*) is called a robber ; he who outrages righteousness (*i*) is called a ruffian.   The robber and ruffian we call a mere fellow.   I have heard of the putting to death of the fellow Chou (last tyrannical king of the Shang dynasty), but I have never heard that this was assassinating a ruler " (Ib, 8).

Here again appears the Confucian doctrine of the Rectification of Names.   When Confucius and the early historians rectified the names, ' rebellious ministers and villainous sons were struck with terror.' Similarly when Mencius came to rectify the names, we might say that disordered sovereigns also became terrified.'

Although Mencius believed that a social distinction must be maintained between the sovereign and the peasants, and between ruler and ruled, he held that this existed solely in order to make a cooperative division of labor possible.   Criticizing the ideas of an opponent, Hsü Hsing, who had contended that ' ruler and subject should both till the soil,' Mencius says :

" Then, is it the government of the empire which alone can be carried on in conjunction with farming ?   There is the business of the great man, and the business of lesser men.   Moreover in the case of any single individual, (whatever articles he might require) are ready to his hand, having been produced by the various artisans. But if he must himself first make them before he could use them, this would be keeping the whole world running about on the roads.

' This principle, Mencius held, cannot be extended to the relationships of father and son, however.   Thus although the father of Shun was unkind, Shun continued to be filial toward him, which, Mencius said, displayed great filial piety.   It was inevitable that Mencius, holding in politics the concept that ' the people are the most important element,' should advocate the doctrine described above.   In his attitude toward the relationships of father and son and elder and younger brother, however, he retained the traditional viewpoint.

Therefore it is said : ' Some labor with their brains and some labor with their brawn. Those who labor with their brains govern others ; those who labor with their brawn are governed by others. Those governed by others, feed them. Those who govern others, are fed by them.' This is a universal principle in the world. . . . . When Yao and Shun governed the empire, what did they not employ their brains upon ? Yet certainly they did not employ them on farming." (IIIa, 4). Again :

" If there were no men of a superior grade (*chün tzŭ*), there would be no one to rule the countrymen. If there were no countrymen, there would be no one to support the men of superior grade " (IIa, 3, para. 14).

Human society being what it is, the life of any one individual requires for its support many varied articles produced by the labor of a large number of different workers. Hence it is impossible for an individual ' first to make them (these articles) himself before he can use them,' and therefore a cooperative division of labor is necessary. Although the activities of the ruler and of the ruled differ, they are mutually indispensable, so that neither can exist without the other.

Taking this cooperative division of labor as a basis, who is to rule and who is to be ruled ? Mencius maintains :

" When right government prevails in the world, persons of little virtue are submissive to those of great, and those of little worth to those of great. When bad government prevails in the world, persons of small power are submissive to those of great, and the weak to the strong. Both these cases are through Heaven. Those who accord with Heaven are preserved, and those who rebel against Heaven perish " (IVa, 7).

While both these conditions come from Heaven, the consequence of the second is mutual strife instead of mutual cooperation. Hence if we wish to continue on the principle of a cooperative division of labor, we must make that man a ruler who is capable of ruling, just as a person who is capable of making pottery is made a potter. In a discussion with a feudal lord, Mencius said :

" If you are going to build a large mansion, you will surely have the master of the workmen look out for large trees, and when he has found such large trees, you will be glad, thinking that they will answer for the intended purpose. Should the workmen hew them so as to make them too small, Your Majesty will be angry, thinking that they will not answer the purpose. Now, a man spends his youth in studying, and being grown up to vigor, wishes to put this into practice. If Your Majesty says to him, ' For the present put aside what you have studied and follow me,' what shall we say ?

" Here now you have an uncut gem. Although it may be worth 240,000 (taels), you will surely employ a lapidary to cut and polish it. But when it comes to the government of the state you say, ' For

the present put aside what you have learned, and follow me.' Yet why should this differ from teaching the lapidary to cut the gem ? "
(*Ib*, 9).

State and society are like a great tree or a gem. To rule them one must belong to the class of specialists who ' spend their youth in studying.' It is the men of great virtue and worth who comprise this class of specialists capable of governing the state and society.

According to such a principle, governmental office is the highest of all positions, and must be filled by persons of the greatest virtue. He who is called Emperor must necessarily be a Sage (*sheng* 聖) before he may be Emperor, and therefore the examples of Yao and Shun, who resigned from their thrones in favor of the Sages who succeeded them, become the models for Mencius's ideal government. The *Mencius* states :

" Wan Chang said : ' Is it true that Yao gave the empire to Shun ? ' Mencius said : ' No. The Emperor cannot give the empire to another.'

" ' Yes, but Shun had the empire. Who gave it to him ? ' Mencius replied : ' Heaven gave it to him.'

" ' Heaven gave it to him : was its Decree (*ming* 命) conferred on him with specific injunctions ? '

" Mencius replied : ' No. Heaven does not speak, but simply indicated its will through his personal conduct and his conduct of affairs'.

" ' Showed its will through his personal conduct and his conduct of affairs : how was this ? ' Mencius said : ' The Emperor can present a man to Heaven, but he cannot cause Heaven to give that man the empire. A feudal lord can present a man to the Emperor, but he cannot cause the Emperor to make that man a feudal lord. A great officer can present a man to a feudal lord, but he cannot cause that feudal lord to make that man a great officer. Of old Yao presented Shun to Heaven, and Heaven accepted him. He showed him to the people, and the people accepted him. Therefore I say : Heaven does not speak. It simply indicated its will through his personal conduct and his conduct of affairs.'

" (Wan Chang) said : ' I presume to ask in what way he was presented to Heaven, and Heaven accepted him ; how he was shown to the people, and the people accepted him ? ' (Mencius) replied : ' He caused him to preside over the sacrifices and all the spirits were well pleased with them : thus Heaven accepted him. He caused him to preside over human affairs and these affairs were well administered : thus the people accepted him. Heaven gave him (the empire). The people gave it to him. Therefore I say : The Emperor cannot give the empire to another.

" ' Shun assisted Yao for twenty-eight years, which was more than man could have done, and was from Heaven. After the death of Yao, when the three years' mourning was completed, Shun withdrew from the son of Yao to the south of South River. The feudal lords, however, going to Court, went not to the son of Yao, but to Shun. Litigants went not to the son of Yao, but to Shun. Singers sang not to the son of Yao, but to Shun. Therefore I say that this was through Heaven. It was after this that he went to the Middle Kingdom (China) and occupied the Emperor's seat. If he had already occupied Yao's palace and had applied pressure on Yao's son, it would have been usurpation, and not the gift of Heaven. . . . .'

"Wan Chang asked : 'People say that when it came to Yü, there was a decline in virtue (from that of Yao and Shun), and that he did not transmit (the empire) to the worthiest but to his own son. Is this true ? ' Mencius replied : ' No, it is not so. When Heaven gave the empire to the worthiest, it was given to the worthiest. When Heaven gave it to a son, it was given to a son. Shun had presented Yü to Heaven. Seventeen years elapsed and Shun died. When the three years' mourning was expired, Yü withdrew from the son of Shun to Yang-ch'eng. The people of the empire followed him, just as after the death of Yao they had not followed Yao's son but had followed Shun. Yü presented Yi (Yü's minister) to Heaven. Seven years elapsed and Yü died. When the three years' mourning had elapsed, Yi withdrew from the son of Yü to the north of Mount Chi. But those who went to Court, and litigants, went not to Yi but went to Ch'i (son of Yü), saying : He is the son of our sovereign. The singers did not sing to Yi but to Ch'i, saying : He is the son of our sovereign.

" ' That Tan Chu (son of Yao) was not equal to (Yao), and Shun's son also not equal to him ; that Shun assisted Yao and Yü assisted Shun over a period of many years, long conferring benefits on the people ; that Ch'i (Yü's son) was worthy and capable of respectfully carrying on the way of Yü ; that Yi did not assist Yü for a long period and did not long confer benefits on the people, whereas the assistance given by Shun and Yü had been far longer ; and that the sons of these rulers were some inferior, and some not inferior : all this was from Heaven, and not something which could have been brought about by man. That which is done without man's doing it, is from Heaven. That which happens without man's causing it to happen, is from Fate (*ming*).

" ' When it is a private individual who obtains the empire, his virtue must be equal to that of Shun and Yü, and in addition to this he must have the Son of Heaven presenting him (to Heaven). This is why Confucius did not obtain the empire.

" ' When the empire is held through hereditary succession, the Emperor must be like a Chieh or a Chou to be displaced by Heaven. This is why Yi, Yi Yin, and the Duke of Chou did not obtain the empire' " (V*a*, 5 and 6).

In Mencius's ideal government, as here described, the ruler of the empire must be a Sage. When this Sage becomes old, he must before his death select a Sage who is younger than himself, and try him out by first making him his assistant. When he has proved his worth, he must present him to Heaven, so as to indicate that this is a succession authorized by himself. Then when the older Sage dies, the younger one replaces him as Emperor. Yet Heaven's Will is unfathomable, and actually it is only the will of the people which can be known. Therefore if the people really turn to this younger Sage, this is an indication that Heaven has given him the empire. In other words, presenting him to Heaven really means presenting him to the people.

But " when it is a private individual who obtains the empire, his virtue must be equal to that of Shun and Yü, and in addition to this he must have the Son of Heaven presenting him (to Heaven)." That is, if the Emperor does not present him, he will lack the opportunity of first assisting the Emperor and so of being tried out, and consequently will be unable to confer benefits on the people, with the result that they will not turn to him. This doctrine comes close to that advanced in Plato's *Republic*. The Confucian school, however, because it ' created through transmitting,' was forced to represent its ideas through events supposedly historical; furthermore, because it supported the Chou institutions, and revered their founders, King Wen and the Duke of Chou, it could not attack the principle of hereditary succession. Hence it was unable to formulate its doctrine in a logical way, so that it could only say that " that which is done without man's doing it, is from Heaven; that which happens without man's causing it to happen, is from Fate."

Mencius's ideas on economics are also clearly expressed in the *Mencius*, as when he says :

" I would ask you, in the country where the nine-squares division is observed,[1] to reserve one division to be cultivated on the system of mutual aid ; and in the city to make the people themselves offer a tenth part of their produce as taxes.

" From the highest officers down to the lowest, each one must have his holy field (the produce from which is used for his sacrifices), consisting of fifty acres. Let the supernumerary males have their twenty-five acres.

" When there are deaths or moving from one house to another, there will be no quitting of the district. In the fields of one district, those who belong to the same nine squares are helpful and friendly to one another in their goings and comings, aid one another in keeping watch and ward, and sustain one another in sickness. Thus the people are brought to live in affection and harmony.

" A square *li* covers nine squares of land, and these nine squares contain nine hundred acres (*mou* 畝). The central square is the public

---

[1] This is the famous *ching t'ien* 井 田 or ' well-field ' system. *Cf.* p. 11.—Tr.

field (*kung t'ien* 公 田), and eight families, each having its private hundred acres, cultivate this public field in common. And not till public work is finished, may they presume to attend to their private affairs. This is the way of keeping the countrymen distinct (from their overlords) " (IIIa, 3).

" If the seasons for farming are not interfered with, the grain will be more than can be eaten. If close-meshed nets are not allowed to enter the pools and ponds, the fish and turtles will be more than can be consumed. If axes and bills enter the mountain forests only at the proper time, the wood will be more than can be used. When grain, fish and turtles are more than can be eaten, and there is more wood than can be used, the people are enabled to nourish their living and bury their dead without any dissatisfaction. This nourishing of the living and burying of the dead without any dissatisfaction marks the beginning of the Kingly Way (*Wang Tao* 王 道).

" Let mulberry trees be planted around five-acre homesteads, and persons of fifty years may be clothed with silk. In rearing fowls, pigs, dogs and swine, do not neglect their times (for breeding), and persons of seventy years may eat meat. Do not take away the time proper for the cultivation of a farm of one hundred acres, and its family of several mouths will not suffer from hunger. Let careful attention be paid to education in the schools, with stress on the inculcation of filial piety and fraternal duty, and there will be no gray-haired men on the roads carrying burdens on their backs or heads. There has never been a case of one who did not become a (real) king when (under his rule), persons of seventy wore silk and ate meat, and the common people suffered neither from hunger nor cold " (Ia, 3).

In these passages, by giving a new twist to the long existing *ching t'ien* or ' well-field ' system, Mencius converts it into an economic institution having socialistic implications. The viewpoint is a new one, inasmuch as in early times all land was the private possession of the state rulers and nobles, by whom it was parcelled out to the peasants, who were nothing more than serfs. The original *ching t'ien* system thus served to benefit the noble class. According to Mencius, however, land is the public property of the state, and is to be given by the state to the people, who cultivate it in a condition of liberty. The produce from the central ' public field ' in each group of nine fields continues to constitute the revenue of the ruler, nobles and officials, who therefore do not need to cultivate themselves ; but this produce is in the nature of a tax to the state, rather than of something given by agricultural serfs to their overlord. Such an institution enables the people to ' nourish their living and bury their dead without any dissatisfaction,' and so is beneficial to them.

It is equally incorrect, therefore, either to say that the *ching t'ien* system as conceived by Mencius is identical with that which actually operated in ancient times, or to say that his system is entirely imaginary.

Actually Mencius accepted the existing system, while giving it a new interpretation—another example of the way in which the Confucians created through transmitting. Mo Tzŭ, holding the viewpoint of the common people, was opposed to the Chou institutions ; Mencius, also holding this viewpoint, gave them a new interpretation. Herein lies one of the differences between the two schools.

According to Mencius, the state should not only ensure a constant livelihood to the people and give them economic security, but should also establish organizations for their education.   He says :

"Establish *hsiang* 庠, *hsü* 序, *hsüeh* 學 and *hsiao* 校 for their instruction.   The *hsiang* is to nourish, the *hsiao* is to teach, and the *hsü* is for archery.   The Hsia dynasty used the name *hsiao*, the Yin dynasty the name *hsü*, and the Chou dynasty the name *hsiang*.   The *hsüeh* has been common to all three dynasties.   These all serve to make clear the (basic) human relationships.   When these human relationships are made clear by superiors, there will be kindly feeling among the lesser people below " (IIIa, 3).

The stage in which it is possible for all men to live so that they may ' nourish their living and bury their dead without dissatisfaction ' marks merely ' the beginning to the Kingly Way.'   This becomes complete only when all have received an education and come to an understanding of the basic human relationships.   Here we find a recurrence of the idea expressed by Confucius, when in talking about the common people, he admonished one of his disciples :   " Enrich them, educate them " (*Lun Yü*, XIII, 9).

4—THE GOODNESS OF HUMAN NATURE

The ideal institutions described in the foregoing section constitute what Mencius calls the Kingly Way (*Wang Tao* 王 道), that is, a kingly or virtuous government.   But why should such a government function ?   How is it possible ?   Mencius says :

" All men have a mind which cannot bear (to see the sufferings of) others.   The early kings, having this ' unbearing ' (*pu jen* 不 忍) mind, thereby had likewise an ' unbearing ' government " (IIa, 6).

An ' unbearing,' that is, a commiserating, government, is a virtuous one.   When " all men have a mind which cannot bear (to see the sufferings of) others," virtuous government must necessarily follow.   Such a feeling of commiseration is, then, the basis which makes good government possible.   As an instance of this, the *Mencius* records that on one occasion when an ox was being led to sacrifice, King Hsüan of Ch'i could not endure its ' frightened appearance, as if it were an innocent person going to the place of death,' and that Mencius used this fact to prove to the king that he was capable of governing like a true king.   Mencius continued his argument by saying :

" Treat as befits old age the elders in your own family, so as to extend this treatment to the elders of others ; treat as befits youth the young in your own family, so as to extend this treatment to the young of others : do this and the empire may be made to revolve in your palm.   It is said in the Book of Odes (III, i, Ode 6, 2) : ' His example affected his wife and reached to his brothers.   Thereby he governed his home and the state.'   These words show how (King Wen) extended his mind (to embrace) others.   Thus if one extend one's kindliness to others, it will suffice to protect all within the four seas.   If one does not extend this kindliness, it will be insufficient to protect one's own wife and children.   The way in which the ancients came greatly to surpass other men was no other than this : simply to extend proficiently what they did so as to affect others " (I*a*, 7).

King Hsüan replied, however, that he loved wealth and feminine beauty, and therefore was incapable of carrying out the government of a true king.   Mencius said : " If Your Majesty loves wealth and. . . . . beauty," then " let the people all be able to gratify the same feelings, and what difficulty will there be in attaining to the Kingly Way ? " (I*b*, 6).   Here is an example of extending what one does oneself to apply to others, or in other words, of ' extending one's own mind (to embrace) others.'   If such a mind is given true expression in government, the resulting government will be a virtuous one.   " To extend proficiently what one does so as to affect others " sums up the virtues of human-heartedness (*jen*), conscientiousness to others (*chung* 忠), and altruism (*shu* 恕).   In his exposition of these virtues, Confucius had limited himself to their development in the self-cultivation of the individual, whereas Mencius extends their application to his philosophy of government and society.   Confucius had taught them as being for the ' Inner Sage ' ; Mencius expands them to apply to the ' Outer King.' [1]

To say that " all men have a mind which cannot bear (to see the sufferings of) others," is the same as saying that man's nature (*hsing* 性) is good.   Mencius states :

" All men have a mind which cannot bear (to see the sufferings of) others. . . . .   If to-day men suddenly see a child about to fall into a well, they will without exception experience a feeling of alarm and distress.   This will not be as a way whereby to gain the favor of the child's parents, nor whereby they may seek the praise of their neighbors and friends, nor that they are so because they dislike the reputation (of being unvirtuous).

" From this case we may perceive that he who lacks the feeling of commiseration (*ts'e yin* 惻隱) is not a man ; that he who lacks a feeling of shame and dislike (*hsiu wu* 羞 惡) is not a man ; that he who lacks a feeling of modesty and of yielding (*tz'ŭ jang* 辭 讓) is not a

---

[1] These are terms often used in Chinese philosophy, the one referring to the man who has attained to complete self-cultivation, and so made of himself a Sage ; the other referring to the man who through his virtues and abilities gains the necessary qualifications of a ruler. *Cf.* p. 2.—Tr.

man ; and that he who lacks a sense of right and wrong (*shih fei* 是 非) is not a man. The feeling of commiseration is the beginning of human-heartedness (*jen*). The feeling of shame and dislike is the beginning of righteousness (*i*). The feeling of modesty and yielding is the beginning of propriety (*li*). The sense of right and wrong is the beginning of wisdom (*chih* 智). Man has these four beginnings just as he has his four limbs. When, having these four beginnings, he says of himself that he is incapable (of developing them), he is injuring himself. And when he says of his sovereign that he is incapable, he is injuring his sovereign.

" Since all men have these four beginnings in themselves, let them know to give them their full development and completion, and the result will be like fire that begins to burn, or of a spring which has begun to find vent. Let them have their complete development, and they will suffice to protect all within the four seas. Let them be denied that development, and they will not suffice to serve his parents with " (II*a*, 6).

Ch'en Li (1801-1882) remarks on this passage : " When Mencius says that human nature is good, he means that the natures of all men have goodness, not that men's natures are all entirely good." [1] By saying that human nature is good, Mencius only means that all men possess the ' beginnings ' (*tuan* 端) of *jen, i, li* and *chih.* If these four beginnings are allowed to reach their complete development in a man, he becomes a Sage. A man's lack of goodness does not come from the fact that his nature is basically opposed to that of the man of goodness, but simply that he has not allowed these four beginnings inherent in him to develop fully. Thus Mencius says :

" In its (human nature's) reality,[2] it is possible to be good. This is what I mean by saying that it is good. If men do what is not good, it is not the fault of their natural powers.[3]

" The feeling of commiseration belongs to all men ; so does that of shame and dislike ; that of reverence and respect ; and that of right and wrong. The feeling of commiseration is human-heartedness ; that of shame and dislike is righteousness ; that of reverence and respect is propriety ; and that of right and wrong is wisdom. These are not fused into us from without. We originally are possessed of them. (We neglect them) simply because we lack reflection. Hence I say, ' Seek and you will find them ; neglect and you

---

[1] Ch'en Li, *op. cit., chüan* 3, p. 1.

[2] In translating the word *ch'ing* 情 as ' reality,' we are following the authority of Yü Cheng-hsieh (1775-1840), who quotes as support what the commentator Cheng Hsüan (A.D. 127-200) says about the word, where it occurs in the phrase, ' Those devoid of *ch'ing,*' in the *Ta Hsüeh* (p. 416). *Cf.* Yü Cheng-hsieh, *op. cit., chüan* 2, p. 30.

[3] The great Sung philosopher Chu Hsi (1130-1200) states : "The term 'natural powers' (*ts'ai* 才) is analogous to ' raw material ' (*ts'ai chih* 才質)." *Cf.* his *Meng-tzŭ Chi-chu.* Thus this word *ts'ai,* roughly translated as ' natural powers,' conveys the idea of stuff or material.

will lose them.' (Men differ from one another) some twice as much as
others, some five times as much, and some to an incalculable amount.
It is because they cannot fully carry out their natural powers" (VI*a*, 6).

This means that when a man is not good, it is not because he is
actually lacking in the basic stuff or material whereby to be good, or
that he lacks the four ' beginnings ' described above. His badness
results simply from the fact that he has either not developed, or has
suppressed and destroyed these beginnings, but this ' is not the fault of
his natural powers.'

Yet why should man develop these beginnings of goodness ?
This is another question. Utilitarians would say that man should
develop them because their development is beneficial to society,
whereas their suppression is harmful. This is the reasoning used by
Mo Tzŭ in his advocacy of universal love. Mencius, however, says
that they should be developed because it is through them that man
is human : " That whereby man differs from the birds and beasts
is but slight. The mass of people cast it away, whereas the Superior
Man preserves it " (IV*b*, 19).

That which makes man a man is the essence of humanity, or the
definition of the term, ' man,' which also is what distinguishes him
from the other animals. This distinguishing essence is the human
mind. The *Mencius* states :

" Kung Tu Tzŭ asked : ' All are equally men, yet some are
great men and some are small men. How is this ? ' Mencius replied : ' Those who follow that part of themselves which is great
are great men, and those who follow that part of themselves which
is small are small men.'

" (Kung Tu Tzŭ) continued : ' All are equally men, but some
follow that part of themselves which is great, and some follow that
part which is small. How is this ? ' (Mencius) answered : ' The
senses of hearing and seeing do not think, but are obscured by things
(of the outside world). When a thing comes into contact with another
(i.e., with one of our senses), it simply leads it away (from the right
path). But the faculty of the mind is thinking. By thinking, it
seizes (the correct view of things), whereas by not thinking it fails
to do this. This (i.e., the mind) is what Heaven has given to us.
Let a man first firmly establish the nobler part of his constitution,
and the inferior part will not be able to take it from him. It is simply
this which constitutes the great man ' " (VI*a*, 15).

Aristotle states in his *Ethics* that the appetites and desires are shared
in common by man and animals, whereas that which differentiates
man from animals is the fact that man possesses reason. Mencius
means the same thing when he says : " The faculty of the mind is
thinking." A mind capable of reasoning is man's special prerogative
and is ' what Heaven has given to us.' Hence it constitutes what
Mencius calls the part of man which is great (*ta t'i* 大 體). The senses

of hearing and seeing are shared by man in common with animals, and hence constitute that part of man which is small (*hsiao t'i* 小 體). Therefore the person who follows that part of himself which is small is not merely an inferior man, but becomes a mere animal.[1] " The senses of hearing and seeing do not think, but are obscured by things. When a thing comes into contact with another, it simply leads it away." Once one permits oneself to be led away, one will "allow one's mind to be ensnared and drowned" (VI*a*, 7). This explains why some men are evil.

What the mind likes, however, is reason and righteousness. Mencius says:

" Thus all things which are the same in kind resemble one another. And why should we doubt this solely when we come to man ? The Sage and ourselves are the same in kind. Therefore Lung Tzǔ said : ' If a man make hempen sandals without knowing the feet (for which they are intended), yet I know he will not be making baskets of them.' For sandals are all like one another because all men's feet are like one another.

" (The same way) with the mouth and flavors : all mouths have the same relishes. Yi Ya (a noted cook) only knew first what our mouths relish. Suppose that his mouth in its relish for flavors differed from that of other men, as is the case with dogs and horses which are not the same in kind with us, why should all men be found following Yi Ya in their relishes ? In the matter of tastes the whole world models itself after Yi Ya ; that is, the mouths of all men are like one another.

" And so also is it with the ear. In the matter of sounds the whole world models itself after the music master K'uang ; that is, the ears of all men are like one another.

" And so also is it with the eye. In the case of Tzǔ Tu (a man noted for his beauty), there is no man but who would recognize that he was beautiful. Anyone who would not recognize the beauty of Tzǔ Tu must have no eyes.

" Therefore I say : Men's mouths agree in having the same relishes ; their ears agree in enjoying the same sounds ; their eyes agree in recognizing the same beauty. Shall their minds alone be without that which they similarly approve ? What is it, then, of which they similarly approve ? I say it is the principles of reason (*li* 理) and of righteousness (*i*). The Sages only apprehended ahead of us what our minds mutually approve of. Therefore the principles of reason and righteousness are agreeable to our minds just as the flesh of grass-fed and grain-fed animals is agreeable to our mouths " (VI*a*, 7).

Man, then, must act in accordance with reason and righteousness so that he may ' follow that part of himself which is great.' Thus

---

[1] *Cf.* below, p. 125.

will he preserve that which makes of him a man, and be in accordance
with the essential definition of the word man.   If not, he will lose that
whereby he is human, and become one with the beasts.   Mencius says :
    " And so of what properly belongs to man, shall it be said that
his mind is lacking in human-heartedness and righteousness ?   The
way in which a man loses his goodness of mind (*liang hsin* 良 心) is
like the way in which trees are denuded by axes and bills.   Hewn
down day after day, can they retain their beauty ?   But there is a
restoration of its (the mind's) life every night, and in the calm atmosphere of early morning it feels to a close degree those desires and
aversions which are proper to humanity, but the feeling is not strong,
and is fettered and destroyed by what takes place during the day.
This fettering taking place again and again, the restorative influence
of the night is not sufficient to preserve (the mind's natural goodness),
and when this proves insufficient it becomes not much different from
that of the irrational animals, and is then held never to have possessed
those powers (which I assert).   But is this the reality regarding
humanity ? " (VI*a*, 8).
    ' The restorative influence of the night ' means man's ' heart of
human-heartedness and righteousness ' which has not yet been completely destroyed.   And if man does not preserve this, he loses that
whereby he is human, and so becomes no more than an animal.   The
reason why Mencius stressed the need for seeking for one's lost mind,
and not losing one's fundamental mind is because these are necessary before one can really be a man.
    That men all have the mind proper to man, is the reason why
man's nature is good.   When Mencius speaks of nature as good,
he draws special attention to the fact that this nature which he
speaks of is ' human nature.'   The *Mencius* states :
    " Kao Tzŭ said : ' That which at birth is so is what is called nature.' '
    " Mencius asked him : ' Is *that which at birth is so* to be called
nature just as white is called white ? '   The reply was : ' Yes.'
    " Mencius continued : ' Is the white of a white feather like
the white of white snow ?   And is the white of white snow like the
white of white jade ? '   Kao Tzŭ replied : ' Yes.'
    " ' Very well,' pursued Mencius, ' Is the nature (*hsing* 性) of a dog
like the nature (*hsing*) of an ox ?   And is the nature of an ox like the
nature of a man ? ' " (VI*a*, 3).
    Whiteness is the same throughout the world, whereas the natures
(*hsing*) of things are not the same.   The ox is not the same in kind

---

¹ 生 之 謂 性.   This ambiguous sentence is one of the most difficult in all Chinese
philosophical literature to translate exactly.   For an enumeration of several possible
interpretations, see I. A. Richards, *Mencius on the Mind*, pp. 23-28.   Kao Tzŭ's doctrine,
however, was that the nature is neither good nor bad, but morally indifferent, and hence
he here seems to be saying that the nature is simply whatever happens to exist at birth, and
so lacks the moral qualities ascribed to it by Mencius.   For Kao Tzŭ's ideas, see ch. 7,
sect. 4, pp. 145-148.—Tr.

as man, and so its nature also differs from that of man. Man's nature implies all that whereby man is human, and when this nature is lost he becomes one with the beasts. Mencius says again : " Human-heartedness (*jen*) is the mind of man ; righteousness (*i*) is man's path " (VI*a*, 11). That is, *jen* is the mind that the ' man ' who is truly human should possess ; *i* is the path that he should follow. If one does not ' dwell in *jen* and proceed from *i* ' (IV*a*, 10), one is not a real man.'

From this we can understand that Mencius is not merely making indiscriminate criticisms when he says :

" Yang's² principle is, ' Each one for himself,' which is to be without (the allegiance due to) a sovereign. Mo (Tzŭ's) principle is ' universal love,' which is to be without (the peculiar affection to) a father. Without sovereign and without father : this is to be the same as a beast " (III*b*, 9, para. 9).

The Confucian school maintains that it is man's four ' beginnings,' as manifested in the organization of human society, that constitute what are called the human relationships (*jen lun* 人 倫). Therefore Mencius says :

" The actuality of human-heartedness is to serve one's parents. The actuality of righteousness is to obey one's elder brother. The actuality of wisdom (*chih*) is this : to know these two things and not depart from them. The actuality of propriety (*li*) is this : the ordering and adorning of these two things. The actuality of music is this : to rejoice in these two things " (IV*a*, 27). Again : " The Sage is the apogee of the human relationships " (IV*a*, 2).

If we proceed according to the morality of Yang Chu and Mo Tzŭ, however, which would obliterate the human relationships, we lose ' that whereby a man is a man,' and hence are no longer in accord with the real concept of the term man, so that we become as birds and beasts. Aristotle maintained that man is a political animal, and said that if man's nature can be fully developed, a state and society must come into being. In stressing that mankind must necessarily have the relationships of ruler and subject, parent and child, the Confucian school expresses the same idea.

Men all have the beginnings of goodness, and the Sage is simply a man who has expanded these beginnings until he reaches ' the apogee of human relationships.' Therefore men are all potentially capable of becoming Sages. Mencius quotes the words of a disciple of Confucius : " What kind of a man was Shun ? What kind of a

---

' If by man's nature one exclusively means that whereby a man is a man, and whereby he differs from the animals, there is no alternative but to say that man's nature is wholly good. For, speaking with logical strictness, that portion of man's nature which is the same as the nature of animals, such as Mencius refers to when he speaks of ' the part of man which is small,' is not *man's* nature, but *man's animal* nature. Hence if we are speaking of *man's* nature, this can in fact contain nothing which is not good.

² i.e., Yang Chu. *Cf.* ch. 7, sect. 1, pp. 133 f.—Tʀ.

man am I? He who exerts himself will also become such as he was " (III*a*, 1). But if, on the contrary, one believes that "one cannot dwell in *jen* and proceed from *i*," this is " to throw oneself away " (IV*a*, 10).

Mencius regarded the individual as of extreme importance, and therefore stressed individual liberty. As for the traditional rules of etiquette (*li*), he believed that if these are at any time recognized by men to be wrong, they need no longer be acknowledged and may be revised. The *Mencius* states :

" Mencius said to King Hsüan of Ch'i : ' When the prince regards his ministers as his hands and feet, his ministers regard their prince as their belly and heart. When he regards them as his dogs and horses, they regard him as any other man of the state. When he regards them as the ground or the grass, they regard him as a robber and an enemy.'

" The King said : ' According to the rules of propriety (*li*), a minister wears mourning for a prince under whom he has formerly served. How is (the prince) to behave that he will thus go into mourning ? '

" Mencius replied : ' When the admonitions (of a minister) have been followed and his advice listened to, so that blessings have descended upon the people, if for some reason he leaves, the prince sends him an escort to conduct him beyond the boundaries. He also anticipates (with recommendations) his arrival in the country to which he is proceeding. And only after he has been gone three years without having returned, does he take back his fields and residence. This treatment is what is called a thrice repeated display of consideration. When a prince acts thus, his former minister will wear mourning for him.

" ' Nowadays, the remonstrances of a minister are not followed, and his advice is not listened to, so that no blessings descend on the people. When for any cause he leaves the country, the prince tries to seize him and hold him a prisoner. He also casts blame on him in the country to which he has gone, and on the very day of his departure, he takes back his fields and residence. This treatment shows him to be what we call a robber and an enemy. What mourning can be worn for a robber and an enemy ? ' " (IV*b*, 3).

In this quotation we see how Mencius refused to recognize the validity of an old rule of etiquette under certain circumstances. He says again : " Acts of propriety (*li*) which are not really proper (*li*), and acts of righteousness (*i*) which are not really righteous (*i*), the great man does not do " (IV*b*, 6).

This also implies that the authority of decisions made by the individual are superior to what are customarily accepted as being propriety and righteousness. It has been stated above that Confucius stressed the liberty of the individual, while at the same time he stressed the moulding of human conduct from without. The former represented Confucius's new ideas; the latter the ready standard formulated already in the age preceding him.[1] Mencius, on the other hand, lays comparatively greater emphasis on individual liberty, for maintaining, as he did, that man is by nature good, he believed that human-heartedness, righteousness, propriety and wisdom are not " fused into us from without. We originally are possessed of them." Therefore it is inevitable that he should have strong respect for the moral decisions made by the individual.

Every man is justified in assuming that all have it within them to become Sages. Yet the success or failure, profit or loss arising from other aspects of human life cannot and should not be taken into consideration. Mencius says : " As to the accomplishment of a great result, that is with Heaven. What has the ruler to do with that ? He tries his best to do good, and that is all " (I*b*, 14). Again : " Weeping for the dead should be from (sincere) sorrow, and not because of the living. The path of virtue should be followed without any bend, and not to seek emolument. The words should all be necessarily sincere, and not so as (to gain the reputation of) doing what is right. The Superior Man simply follows the law (of right) and then waits for his Fate (*ming*) " (VII*b*, 33).

This Heaven and Fate both denote something that is beyond the scope of human power. In the words of Mencius : " That which is done without man's doing it, is from Heaven. That which happens without man's causing it to happen, is from Fate " (V*a*, 6). When we consider a course of conduct, we should simply ask ourselves whether it is right or not, and if it is right, do it. We " must try our best to do good, and that is all." The success or failure resulting from such conduct depends upon the varied conditions of environment, over which man can never have complete control, and which is called Heaven or Fate. Such is the fatalistic Heaven which was described in Chapter III. The Mohist school, in its opposition to the Confucians, strongly attacked the concept of Fate ; and yet what the Confucians, or at least Mencius and Hsün Tzŭ, actually mean by Fate, contains no superstitious elements, and hence differs from the idea of Fate criticized by the Mohists.

5—Opposition to Utilitarianism

From the above we may understand why Mencius opposed the idea of utility (*li* 利). He believed firmly that all men possess the four fundamental feelings of commiseration, shame and dislike, modesty and yielding, and right and wrong, which if developed become the four virtues of human-heartedness, righteousness, propriety and wisdom. These four virtues are the natural result of the development of man's

---

[1] *Cf.* ch. 4, sect. 5, p. 68.

nature, a development which must necessarily proceed along these lines if man is to possess that which makes him man. Hence these virtues are not to be practised merely because they are materially beneficial, though their practice will in fact automatically produce a result beneficial to society. While such a beneficial result is to be highly prized, it remains only a by-product, just as when an artist produces a work of art, the latter will no doubt give other people feelings of pleasure, yet such feelings are only secondary results. Primarily, the artistic production is done to express the ideals and feelings of the artist himself, rather than with intent to give pleasure to others.

Although Mencius advocated righteousness (*i*) as opposed to the profitable (*li*), he failed to explain distinctly the difference between righteousness and profitableness ; nor did he analyse clearly the division between public and private profitableness, on which account he has laid himself open to much criticism from later scholars. We can clearly see the main ideas underlying his opposition to utilitarianism, however, in his debate with the Mohist, Yi Chih, over the question of elaborate funerals, in which he says :

" In the most ancient times, there were some who did not inter their parents. When their parents died, they took them up and threw them into some water channel. Afterwards, when they passed them by, there would be foxes and wild cats devouring them, and flies and gnats biting at them. Their perspiration started out upon their foreheads, and they looked away, unable to bear the sight. The emotions of their hearts affected their faces and eyes, and instantly they went home and came back with baskets and spades and covered the bodies. If the covering of them thus was indeed right, the filial son and human-hearted man (to-day) also certainly have their proper way to inter their parents " (IIIa, 5).

Again he says :

" Anciently there was no rule for the size of either the inner or outer coffin. In middle antiquity, the inner coffin was made seven inches thick, and the outer one the same. This was the same from the Emperor down to the common people, and was not done simply for the beauty of appearance, but because complete satisfaction was thus given to men's hearts " (IIb, 7).

The Mohist school opposed elaborate funerals and long mourning periods purely on a utilitarian basis, whereas Mencius rejects the idea of utilitarianism entirely. Elaborate funerals and long mourning periods may indeed be said to be beneficial to society, for " solicitude on the decease of parents, and the pursuit of them (with sacrificial offerings) for long after, will cause an abundant restoration of the people's morals " (*Lun Yü*, 1, 9). Yet Mencius simply says of them that " complete satisfaction is thus given to men's hearts," and here shows the characteristic spirit of the Confucian school.

6—HEAVEN, HUMAN NATURE AND THE 'MOVING FORCE'

Mencius's Heaven at times seems to be a ruling or personal one, as when he says that 'Yao presented Shun to Heaven.' At times he seems to designate a fatalistic Heaven, as has already been described above. And at still other times it is an ethical Heaven. All men, Mencius maintains, possess the four beginnings of human-heartedness, righteousness, propriety and wisdom, and therefore human nature is good. But the reason why man should have these four beginnings and his nature should consequently be good, is because that nature is 'what Heaven has given to us' (VI*a*, 15). This gives the metaphysical basis for the doctrine of the goodness of human nature. Mencius says :

" He who has exercised his mind to the utmost, knows his nature (*hsing*). Knowing his nature, he knows Heaven. To keep one's mind preserved and nourish one's nature is the way to serve Heaven. To be without doubleness of mind, whether one is to have untimely death or long life ; and having cultivated one's personal character, to wait with this for whatever there may be : this is to stand in accord with Fate (*ming*) " (VII*a*, 1).

The mind (which in Chinese is expressed by the same word which means 'heart,' *hsin* 心), constitutes 'that part of man which is great' (*ta t'i* 大 體) ; hence ' he who has exercised his mind to the utmost, knows his nature.' This is ' what Heaven has given to us.' Therefore through exercise of our minds and knowledge of our natures we may also come to ' know Heaven.'

Mencius says again :

" Wherever the Superior Man passes through, transformation follows ; wherever he abides, there is a spiritualizing influence. This flows abroad above and below together with Heaven and Earth. How can it be said that he mends society but in a small way ! " (VII*a*, 13). Again :

" All things (literally, ' the ten thousand things ') are complete within us. There is no greater delight than to find sincerity (*ch'eng* 誠) when one examines oneself. If one acts with a vigorous effort at altruism (*shu* 恕) in one's seeking for human-heartedness (*jen*), nothing will be closer to one " (VII*a*, 4).

Such phrases as ' all things are complete within us,' and references to an influence which ' flows abroad above and below together with Heaven and Earth,' definitely suggest mysticism. Unfortunately Mencius speaks here only sketchily, so that his original meaning cannot be exactly determined.

The term mysticism may, of course, have several different meanings. As used here, it designates a belief in that state in which all things form one body. In such a state the individual becomes one with the whole of the universe, and all distinctions between the self and non-self, between what is internal and what is external, are obliterated. It is usually said that this sort of mysticism must necessarily become merged with pure idealism. The universe must be an idealistic one, and the whole must have an inner connection with the spirit of the individual. According to such a doctrine, the spirit of the individual has originally been one with the spirit of the universe, but through obstructions and divisions which arose later, the individual and the universe have become separated. What some Buddhist sects designate as ignorance or *avidya*, and what the Sung dynasty Confucianists call ' selfish desires ' (*ssǔ yü* 私 欲), both refer to these later occurring obstructions. By ridding ourselves of these obstructions, each of us may return to oneness with the universe, a state called by the Buddhists the *Tathagata* or Absolute (*Chen Ju* 眞 如), while the Sung Confucianists speak of it as ' selfish desires completely finished and the Law of Heaven freely flowing.' [1]

Yet mysticism need not necessarily be linked with idealism. The Taoist, Chuang Tzǔ (see ch. 10) is a mystic, even though for him the universe is not an idealistic one. In China, the school of Mencius in Confucianism, and the school of Chuang Tzǔ in Taoism, have both held mysticism as the supreme state, and mystical experience as the highest aim of individual self-cultivation. The methods used by these two schools to attain this supreme state and aim have differed, however. Through a life of ' pure experience ' to forget the self : this has been the Taoist method. Through ' the work of love ' (a term used by Schopenhauer) to get rid of selfishness : this has been that of the Confucians. Being without self and without selfishness, the individual can become one with the universe.

If the philosophy of Mencius really contains mystical elements, his statement that all things are complete within us means that we are fundamentally one with the universe. This being so, if because of certain obstructions we seem to be separated from the universe, such a condition is equivalent to not being ' sincere ' (*ch'eng* 誠). If ' one finds sincerity when one examines oneself,' and so has returned to the state of oneness with the universe, ' there is no greater delight.' If one wishes to revert to such a state, one must use the ' work of love ' as a method. Hence the words : " If one acts with vigorous effort at altruism in one's seeking for human-heartedness, nothing will be closer to one." Through altruism one seeks human-heartedness, and through human-heartedness one seeks sincerity. This is because the qualities of altruism and human-heartedness both emphasize the lessening of the division between others and the self, and when this division is lessened, the self becomes one with the rest.

It is impossible to know whether such an interpretation is actually in accord with Mencius's original thought or not, but at least it may

---

[1] 人 欲 浄 盡, 天 理 流 行.

be said that it was an idea developed and expanded by the Confucianist philosophers of the Sung dynasty, who in fact based themselves to a considerable extent upon Mencius.[1]

If Mencius's philosophy really does contain a doctrine of mysticism, then what he calls the 'moving force' (*huo jan chih ch'i* 浩 然 之 氣), is the spiritual quality of those individuals who have attained to this highest state.   Mencius says :

"Such is the force (*ch'i* 氣) : it is most great and most strong. Being nourished by uprightness (*chih* 直), and sustaining no injury, it fills up all between Heaven and Earth " (IIa, 2, para. 13).

As to how to develop this force, Mencius says :

"Such is the force : it is the correlate of righteousness (*i*) and morality (*Tao*).   Without it, (man) is in a state of starvation.   It is produced by the accumulation of righteous deeds, and not to be obtained by incidental acts of righteousness.   If one's mind does not feel satisfaction in one's conduct, there results this state of starvation.   I have therefore said : ' Kao Tzŭ (the great opponent of Mencius on the question of human nature) has never understood righteousness, because he makes it something external.'   There must be its constant practice, without stopping.[2]   The mind must not be forgetful of it, and yet must not (deliberately strive to) help it grow " (*ibid.*, paras. 14-16).

What is here called ' righteousness ' (*i* 義) is a term probably including all the four ' beginnings ' of virtue existing in man's nature. It is something fundamental and internal; this is why Mencius says : "Kao Tzŭ has never understood righteousness, because he makes it something external."   These ' beginnings ' all have a tendency to lessen the division between others and the self.   When this process is developed, not with undue haste, but also without cessation, so that there is a long continued ' accumulation of righteous deeds,' one may reach a spiritual state in which there is no act in which ' one's mind does not find satisfaction,' and which ' fills up all between Heaven and Earth.'   When one has reached this state, then :

"To dwell in the wide house of the world, stand in the correct position in the world, and follow the great Way (*Tao*) of the world ; when having obtained one's desire (to hold office), to practise one's principles for the good of the people ; and when that desire is disappointed, to practise them alone ; when riches and honors cannot make one dissipated, poverty and mean condition cannot make one swerve, and power and force cannot make one bend oneself : these are the characteristics of the great man " (IIIb, 2).

---

[1] The above four paragraphs appear as a footnote in the original Chinese edition.—Tr.

[2] The word *cheng* 正 (proper) is here interpreted as equivalent to *chih* 止 (stopping), according to the reading of it given by Chiao Hsün (1763-1820), in his *Meng-tzŭ Cheng-i*.

CHAPTER VII

THE 'HUNDRED SCHOOLS'

Mencius's geographical environment was practically the same as that of Confucius, but the intellectual tendencies of China had already undergone great changes during the hundred odd years intervening between him and Confucius. In the days of Confucius there existed no philosophic groups of any consequence, other than that of Confucius himself and the three or four negative 'recluses' whom he encountered; with the coming of Mo Tzŭ there still existed only the two opposing schools of Confucians and Mohists. By the time of Mencius, however, many divisions of thought had already evolved, referred to in the *Chuang-tzŭ* (ch. 33) as 'the doctrines of the Hundred Schools.'[1] Mencius characterizes the spirit of his age when he says : " Sage-kings cease to arise, and the feudal lords give rein to their lusts. Unemployed scholars indulge in unreasonable discussions " (*Mencius*, IIIb, 9, para. 9).

One of the centers for scholars during this time was in the capital of the state of Ch'i, at a place known as Chi-hsia 稷下, that is, 'below Chi,' Chi being perhaps the name of a gate. In its biography of Mencius and Hsün Tzŭ, the *Shih Chi* states :

" From Tsou Yen 騶 衍 down, and including the (other) gentlemen of Chi-hsia in Ch'i, there were such men as Shun-yü K'un 淳 于 髡, Shen Tao 慎 到, Huan Yüan 環 淵, Chieh Tzŭ 接 子, T'ien P'ien 田 駢 and Tsou Shih 騶 奭, each of whom wrote books about the order and confusion of human affairs.

" Shen Tao was a native of Chao. T'ien P'ien and Chieh Tzŭ were men of Ch'i. Huan Yüan was a native of Ch'u. These all studied the arts of the Way (*Tao* 道) and the Power (*Te* 德) of Huang and Lao,[2] and put foward and arranged their ideas according to these. Thus Shen Tao was the author of twelve discussions, Huan Yüan composed an upper and a lower chapter, and T'ien P'ien and Chieh Tzŭ both had subjects which they discussed. . . . From Shun-yü K'un down, all these men were ranked as great officers and were honored and courted by having large houses built for them on the main road. This was to show to all the pensioned guests of the feudal lords of the empire, that it was the state of Ch'i which could attract the most eminent scholars in the empire " (ch. 74, 3-5).

---

[1] 百 家 之 學. *Cf. Chuang-tzŭ*, p. 439.
[2] i.e., Huang-ti, the legendary Yellow Emperor, whom the Taoists claimed as the founder of their school ; and Lao Tzŭ, the supposed author of the *Tao Te Ching*.—Tr.

The *Shih Chi* says elsewhere :

" King Hsüan (of Ch'i, reigned 319-301) delighted in travelling scholars who could talk on literary matters. Thus he conferred honors upon a total of seventy-six men, including such as Tsou Yen, Shun-yü K'un, T'ien P'ien, Chieh Tzŭ, Shen Tao and Huan Yüan, giving them houses and making them all great officers of the upper grade, who could carry on their discussions without having any administrative duties. This is how the scholars at Chi-hsia in Ch'i became numerous, until they amounted to several hundreds and thousands of men " (ch. 46, pp. 12-13).

The *Shih Chi* furthermore states of Mencius in his biography that he 'travelled to serve King Hsüan of Ch'i,' a statement confirmed by the conversations between the two men recorded in Mencius's own writings, and which makes it probable that Mencius was also, for a time, included among those who lived at Chi-hsia. Unfortunately the works of these scholars have all been lost to-day, so that for information about their doctrines we are forced to rely upon fragmentary records contained in such works as the *Mencius*, *Chuang-tzŭ*, *Hsün-tzŭ*, *Lü-shih Ch'un Ch'iu* and *Shih Chi*.

1—YANG CHU AND THE RISE OF THE TAOIST SCHOOL

Mencius says of his age that " the doctrines held by the world, if they do not approach those of Yang, approach those of Mo " (*Mencius*, IIIb, 9, para. 9). It was these two men, Yang Chu 楊 朱 and Mo Tzŭ, who were his greatest opponents, so that of his self-assumed tasks, he himself says that the most important was " to oppose Yang and Mo " (*ibid.*, para. 14). The doctrines of Mo Tzŭ have already been described. Those of Yang Chu, save for the wide publicity given them by Mencius through his attacks, have been little touched on. The chapter entitled ' Yang Chu ' in the Taoist compilation, *Lieh-tzŭ*, is a product of some unknown writer of the Wei (A.D. 220-265) or Chin (265-420) dynasties, and its theory of complete hedonism differs considerably from Yang Chu's own doctrine, which Mencius describes as :

" The principle of Yang Tzŭ is, ' Each one for himself.' Though he might have benefited the whole world by plucking out a single hair, he would not have done it " (VIIa, 26).

The *Lü-shih Ch'un Ch'iu* (XVII, 7) says :

" Yang Sheng 陽 生 valued self " (p. 285).

The *Han-fei-tzŭ* (ch. 50) contains a reference :

" Here is a man. His policy is not to enter a city which is in danger, nor to remain in the army, and for the great profit of the world he would not give one hair of his shank. Rulers inevitably follow and pay him courtesy. They value his knowledge and exalt his conduct, because he is a scholar who has slight regard for mere things and holds life as something important " (*chüan* 19, p. 8).

And the *Huai-nan-tzŭ* (ch. 13) :

" The orchestra, drum and dance for the performance of music ; obeisances and bowing for the cultivation of good manners (*li*) ; generous expenditure in funerals and protracted mourning for the obsequies of the dead : these were what Confucius established and were condemned by Mo Tzŭ. Universal love, exaltation of the worthy, assistance to the spirits and anti-fatalism : these were what Mo Tzŭ established, and were condemned by Yang Tzŭ. Completeness of living (*ch'üan sheng* 全生), preservation of what is genuine, and not allowing outside things to entangle one's person : these were what Yang Tzŭ established, and were condemned by Mencius " (p. 155).

Chinese scholars have clearly shown that the Yang Sheng of the *Lü-shih Ch'un Ch'iu* quotation is the same person as the Yang Chu of Mencius, while Mencius's account of Yang Chu's doctrine as being ' every one for himself ' (*wei wo* 為我), is obviously analogous to the *Lü-shih Ch'un Ch'iu's* statement that Yang Sheng ' valued self ' (*kuei chi* 貴已). So, too, is the *Huai-nan-tzŭ*, when it speaks of ' completeness of living, preservation of what is genuine, and not allowing outside things to entangle one's person.' [1] This gives us Yang's fundamental doctrine, and once we accept it, we may see that when the *Han-fei-tzŭ* speaks of ' a scholar who has slight regard for mere things and holds life as something important,' it, too, is evidently referring to some follower of Yang Chu.

According to this *Han-fei-tzŭ* quotation, a follower of Yang, even were he to be given the world as a return for pulling out one of his hairs, would not do so.[2] Such a person ' has slight regard for mere things and holds life as something important ' ; he ' does not allow outside things to entangle his person.' This is because the world, though large, is still something external, whereas a hair, though small, is still part of one's own person and life. Therefore the former may be regarded lightly, whereas the latter should be looked upon as important.

---

[1] 全生保眞，不以物累形.

[2] Professor Ku Chieh-kang holds that the account in *Mencius* of Yang Chu, that " though he might have benefited the world . . . he would not have done it," should be interpreted as meaning : " Though he might have been benefited by having the world . . . he would be unwilling." The conciseness and lack of inflection in the Chinese language makes either reading possible, depending on whether we take the word *li* 利, meaning benefit, to be an active verb (to benefit) or passive (to be benefited by). *Cf.* his *Ts'ung Lü-shih Ch'un Ch'iu T'ui-tse Lao-tzŭ chih Ch'eng-shu Nien-tai*, in the *Ku Shih Pien*, Vol. IV, pp. 493-494. But it seems hardly right to interpret this sentence differently from the sentence in the *Mencius* which immediately follows, a sentence which has exactly the same structure, and which reads : " Mo Tzŭ loved all alike. If by wearing away his whole body from the crown to the heel he could have benefited the world, he would have done so." Acquaintance with Mo Tzŭ's doctrines proves that this interpretation of this sentence is the only one possible, so that, by analogy, the verb ' benefit ' in the Yang Chu clause must also be active. It is probable that the words : " If one would benefit him by giving him the whole world, and hope thus that he would pluck out one of his hairs, he would not do so," represent Yang's actual doctrine ; whereas the words : " Though he might have benefited the whole world by plucking out a single hair, he would not have done it," are Mencius's interpretation of this doctrine.

The *Huai-nan-tzŭ* passage is valuable furthermore as showing the historical order of development of the doctrines of Confucius, Mo Tzŭ, Yang Chu and Mencius. Between Confucius and Mencius there had intervened the philosophies of Mo Tzŭ and of Yang Chu, so that by the time of Mencius, the Confucians, Mohists and the followers of Yang had become like the three legs of a tripod. It was natural, therefore, that Mencius, as the perpetuator of Confucianism, should exert all his strength to ' oppose Yang and Mo.'

From the above quotations, it may be seen that nowhere in the writings of the pre-Ch'in dynasty era is there to be found any such doctrine of complete hedonism directly attributed to Yang Chu as that contained in the chapter bearing his name in the *Lieh-tzŭ*; a chapter which, therefore, cannot be ascribed to him, even though hints of such hedonistic thought may be found scattered in other writings of the Warring States period.' It remains for us to ask why, if Yang's ideas were so widespread in the time of Mencius as Mencius says, have they been mentioned so rarely by later writers ? At first glance, it would seem that these doctrines vanished as soon as they appeared ; that they did not exist before Yang, and that they have left no traces after him. For this reason certain modern scholars have gone so far as to suggest that Yang Chu is nothing else than a different name of the Taoist, Chuang Tzŭ. There is no evidence at all for such a theory, however, and it is a mistake furthermore to say that no earlier expressions or later traces of Yang's ideas can be found.

Already in the age of Confucius there existed a class of men who had ' escaped from the world.' These were educated men, but ones who, seeing the difficulty of rescuing the world from its troubles, adopted a negative attitude toward it and were unwilling to take part in social and political affairs. Confucius said of such men :

" Some men of worth retire from the world ; those next to them (in worth) withdraw from their fatherland ; the next from uncongenial looks ; and the next from the uncongenial language (of their rulers) " (*Lun Yü*, XIV, 39).

The *Lun Yü* relates several instances in which Confucius was criticized by men of this kind :

" On one occasion when Tzŭ Lu happened to spend the night at Stone Gate, the gate opener asked him : ' Where are you from ? ' ' From Confucius,' replied Tzŭ Lu. ' Is he not the one who knows he cannot succeed and yet keeps on trying to do so ? ' was the response (XIV, 41).

" The Master was playing on a stone chime one day in Wei, when a man carrying a basket passed the door of the K'ung abode and remarked : ' With what feeling he is playing the chimes ! ' Presently he added : ' How contemptible is this ting-tinging. If

---

¹ For details, see below, pp. 140-141.

there is no one who knows him, let it be.' 'If the water is deep you strip up to the waist; if shallow, you tuck up your skirt!' (XIV, 42).

"Chieh Yü, a 'madman' of Ch'u, one day came singing past Confucius, saying: 'Oh, Phœnix! Oh, Phœnix! How your virtue has fallen! As to the past, reproof is useless, but the future may still be overtaken. Desist! Desist! Great is the peril of those who now fill office'" (XVIII, 5).

Another recluse, Chieh Ni, is recorded as having said to a disciple of Confucius:

"All the world is a swelling torrent, and who is there to change it? As for you, instead of following a gentleman who flees from one man (i.e., prince) to another, had you not better follow those who flee the world entirely?" (XVIII, 6).

Again, the *Lun Yü* records:

"Once when Tzŭ Lu was following the Master on a journey, he happened to fall behind. Meeting an old man carrying a basket on his staff, Tzŭ Lu asked him: 'Have you seen my Master, Sir?' 'You,' said the old man, 'whose four limbs know not toil, and who cannot distinguish the five grains, who may your Master be?' With that he planted his staff in the ground and commenced weeding.

"Tzŭ Lu joined his hands together in salutation and stood waiting. The old man kept Tzŭ Lu for the night, killed a fowl, prepared millet, and gave him to eat, introducing also his two sons.

"Next morning Tzŭ Lu went his way and reported his adventure. 'He is a recluse,' said the Master, and sent Tzŭ Lu back again to see him, but on his arrival the old man had gone. Whereupon Tzŭ Lu said (to the sons): 'It is not right to refuse to serve in office. If the regulations between old and young in family life may not be set aside, how is it that he (your father) sets aside the duty that exists between a ruler and his ministers? In his desire to maintain his own personal purity, he subverts the great relationships of society. The reason why the Superior Man tries to go into office is that he holds this to be right, even though he is well aware that his principles cannot prevail'" (XVIII, 7).

Mencius had in mind the negative attitude toward life held by recluses of this type, when he said: "The principle of Yang Tzŭ is, 'Each one for himself.' Though he might have benefited the whole world by plucking out a single hair, he would not have done it." Tzŭ Lu said of the old man carrying a basket that 'in his desire to maintain his own personal purity, he subverts the great relationships of society'; and Mencius meant the same when he remarked on another occasion: "Yang's principle is, 'Each one for himself,' which is to be without (the allegiance due to) a sovereign" (*Mencius*, IIIb, 9, para. 9). The negative recluses who appear in the *Lun Yü*, would seem, therefore, to have been the forerunners of Yang Chu.

In the age of Confucius, however, such recluses tried merely to keep themselves in a state of individual purity, and apparently made no attempt to justify their conduct by formulating any systematic philosophy. Yang Chu appears to have been the first recluse to attempt this, causing Mencius to exclaim : " The words of Yang Chu and Mo Ti fill the world, so that if the doctrines of the world do not approach those of Yang, they approach those of Mo " (IIIb, 9, para. 9). This, too, would explain the lament of Mencius : " Why should I be fond of disputing! It is because I have no alternative that I am compelled to do it " (ibid., para. 13).

Yet why, we must still ask, did Yang's doctrines seem to disappear after Mencius ? Did Mencius's opposition really result in such complete success ? The explanation probably lies in the fact that Yang Chu was followed by such Taoist philosophers as Lao Tzŭ and Chuang Tzŭ, both of whom, while in one way continuing the line of Yang Chu, formulated at the same time many ideas which had certainly not been conceived of by the latter. Yang Chu, as a consequence, became overshadowed by Lao Tzŭ and Chuang Tzŭ, which would explain why outwardly his doctrines seemed to have completely disappeared. Actually, this was not at all the case, and the Lü-shih Ch'un Ch'iu gives several accounts of ideas which were probably handed down from Yang. For example (I, 3) :

" Now, my life is my own possession, and its benefit to me is also great. If we discuss what is noble and mean, even the honor of being Emperor could not compare with it. If we discuss what is unimportant and important, even the wealth of possessing the empire could not be exchanged for it. If we discuss peace and danger, were we to lose it for only one morning, we could never again bring it back. These three are points on which those who have understanding are careful. There are those who care too much about life and so injure it. This is because they have not reached an understanding of the qualities of human life. Without such an understanding, of what avail is caution ? . . . Among the rulers and nobles of the world, whether worthy or unworthy, there are none who do not desire to live long and see many days. Yet if they daily obstruct the course of their life, of what avail is such a desire ? All long life consists in non-resistance to it. What cause such resistance are the desires. Therefore the Sage must first of all put his desires into proper harmony " [1] (pp. 6-7).

Here again recurs Yang's ' slight regard for mere things and holding of life as something important.' Such stress on the importance of life does not mean an uncontrolled giving in to the desires, however, for desires which are uncontrolled are injurious to life. For this

---

[1] The commentator Kao Yu (alive during years A.D. 205-212), says that the word shih 適, in the last sentence, means chieh 節, to ' restrain ' the desires, i.e., put them in proper harmony.

reason the same passage states that " rich meats and strong wines " are " foods which will spoil the stomach," and the " tender cheeks and white teeth " of women are " axes which destroy our natures " (*ibid.* p. 6). Persons who, on the contrary, believe that emphasis on living means the uncontrolled gratification of desire, are those who ' care too much about life and so injure it.' Hence the Sage who has a proper regard for life ' must first of all put his desires into proper harmony.' Another passage (I, 2) says :

" Therefore the Sage, as regards sounds, colors and tastes, accepts those that are beneficial to his nature and avoids those that injure his nature. This is the way to achieve complete preservation of one's nature "[1] (p. 5). Again (II, 2) :

" The Sage, thinking deeply about the world, values nothing more than life. The ears, eyes, nose and mouth are the servants of life. Although the ears desire sounds, the eyes desire colors, the nose desires sweet fragrances, and the mouth desires rich tastes, if these are injurious to life they must be halted. As regards these four organs, whichever one does not wish to benefit the life, should not be exercised " (p. 16).

The same work (II, 3) says :

" Heaven has produced mankind endowed with longings and desires. These desires have their natural tendencies (*ch'ing* 情). The natural tendencies have their restraints. The Sage cultivates these restraints to halt his desires, and, therefore, does not allow his natural tendencies to run to excess. Thus the ear's desire for the five tones, the eye's desire for the five colors, the mouth's desire for the five tastes : these constitute the natural tendencies. In these three things the desires of noble and humble, foolish and wise, worthy and unworthy, are as one. Even were it Shen Nung and Huang-ti (legendary Sage Emperors), their desires would be the same as those of (the tyrants) Chieh and Chou. The way in which the Sage is different, is that he keeps control over his natural tendencies. By acting in accordance with the principle of valuing life, one keeps control over one's natural tendencies. By not acting in this way, one loses control over them " (p. 19).

This tells us that if we are to value life, we must first restrain the desires. But the reason why life is something to be prized is exactly because through it we may enjoy sounds, colors and tastes. Therefore we restrain the desires because we hope in this way to gain long life, and thus to have still further time for enjoyment ; not because such enjoyment is improper, or because the desires are evil. The same chapter continues :

" When the ear does not delight in sounds, the eye does not delight in color, and the mouth finds taste no longer sweet, there is no

---

[1] *Ch'üan hsing* 全 性.

choice between this life and death. The men of old who attained to the true Way lived their lives to a great old age, so that they might long enjoy sounds, colors and tastes. How was this? It was because their principles were early determined upon. Their principles being early determined, they early knew how to be sparing of themselves. And knowing early how to be sparing of themselves, they did not exhaust their vital forces " (p. 20).

It is only when the ears and eyes are able to enjoy external things, that life assumes meaning. Not to do so is to value, not life, but death. If we wish to have this enjoyment for long, however, we must already at an early age decide not to enjoy to excess.

The *Lü-shih Ch'un Ch'iu* (II, 2) also quotes a certain Tzŭ Hua Tzŭ 子 華 子 as saying:

"Completeness of living (*ch'üan sheng* 全 生) is the best. Life which is incomplete is second to this. Death comes next. And constrained life is the worst. Therefore what is called the exalting of life means completeness of living. What is called completeness of living is a life in which the six desires all reach a proper harmony. What is called a life which is incomplete is one in which the six desires only obtain to a halfway degree their proper harmony. Life which is incomplete is one in which a person fails to value what he should value. The more incomplete it is, the less he values it. What is called death is a condition in which one knows nothing and reverts to the state preceding birth. What is called constrained life, is one in which none of the six desires reaches a proper harmony in any degree, and all get what they dislike. Such are submission and shame.

" There is no greater shame than a lack of righteousness. Therefore to be unrighteous means to have a constrained life, but a constrained life does not mean only what is unrighteous. Therefore I say that a constrained life is not equal to dying. How do I know this is so? When the ear hears what it dislikes, this is not as good as not hearing at all. When the eye sees what it dislikes, this is not as good as not seeing at all. Thus, when there is thunder we cover the ears, and when there is lightning we cover the eyes. This is an example. And so for all the six desires. When they are conscious of what they deeply dislike, and have no way of freeing themselves, this is not so good as for them to be unconscious of everything. And this state of being unconscious of everything is what we call death. Therefore a constrained life is not as good as death. When someone likes meat, it does not mean decayed meat, and when someone likes wine, it does not mean spoiled wine. Likewise with the exaltation of life : this does not mean a constrained life " (pp. 18-19).

This, too, is a doctrine of the Yang school. There is ' completeness of living ' when ' the six desires all reach a proper harmony,' whereas there is ' constrained life,' which is worse than death, when none of them reaches a proper harmony. For death is merely a state of ' being unconscious of everything,' whereas constrained life is a life of suffering and, as such, certainly not equal to death. Restraint of desires is again implied in the phrase, ' When the six desires all reach a proper harmony,' but such restraint does not mean absence of desire. The *Lü-shih Ch'un Ch'iu* (XXI, 4) says again :

" The states of Han and Wei were fighting with each other for territory. Tzŭ Hua Tzŭ saw Marquis Chao-li (of Han, 358-333 B.C.), who had a lugubrious look. Tzŭ Hua Tzŭ said : ' Suppose that to-day the whole world agreed before Your Highness to an epigram which said : ' If your left hand grasps it, you will lose your right hand, and if your right hand grasps it, you will lose your left. But if you do grasp it, you will gain the world.' Then would your Highness grasp it or not ? '

" Marquis Chao-li replied : ' I would not.' Tzŭ Hua Tzŭ continued : ' Very good. From this we can see that the two arms are of more importance than the world, whereas the body is still more important than two arms. The state of Han in comparison with the world is far removed in importance, and what you are now fighting for is still less important than Han. Yet Your Highness has been embittering his person and doing harm to his life to the point of chagrin, still without obtaining it.' . . .

" Prince Mou of Chung Shan in conversation with Chan Tzŭ said : ' How would it be if your body were living on the rivers and seas (i.e., in freedom), but your mind remained in the kingly palace (i.e., besieged with cares) ? ' Chan Tzŭ replied : ' I would lay more stress on life. By so doing I would come to regard material profit lightly.' Prince Mou of Chung Shan said : ' But suppose although you realized this, you still were unable to conquer yourself (in your desire for wealth) ? ' Chan Tzŭ said : ' If one cannot conquer oneself, one should give oneself free rein. For will not the spirit then be without injury ? But if, when unable to conquer oneself, one still forcibly refuses oneself any gratification, this is known as double wounding of oneself. Men who thus doubly wound themselves are not of the kind who live long ' " (pp. 380-381).

The Prince Mou of Chung Shan who appears here, has been identified by many Chinese commentators with the philosopher, Wei Mou 魏 牟, of whom Hsün Tzŭ says :

" There are those who give free rein to their passions, are satisfied with indulgence, and act like beasts. They are not qualified to develop culture or conduct government. Nevertheless their views have some foundation and their statements some reason, quite enough to deceive and confuse the ignorant masses. Such are To Hsiao and Wei Mou " (*Hsün-tzŭ*, pp. 77-78).

Wei Mou, according to Hsün Tzŭ's criticism, apparently clung to the same hedonistic doctrine of complete gratification of desire that is expressed in the Yang Chu chapter in the *Lieh-tzŭ*, with the result that we find Chan Tzŭ telling him that, by laying more stress on life, one may come to regard material profit lightly. When Prince Mou replies to this that although he realizes the fact, he is unable to carry it out, Chan Tzŭ tells him that in that case he may do what he pleases. From these passages it would seem probable that the school of Yang Chu, even while advocating restraint of the desires, maintained, at the same time, that it is the fulfilment of these desires which gives meaning to human life, and that a living, not a deadening existence, is what we should value.

In the present-day version of the *Lao-tzŭ* there are many passages expressing this idea of prizing life and despising material things. For example :

" He who in his conduct values his body more than he does the world, may be given the world. He who in his conduct loves himself more than he does the world, can be entrusted with the world " (ch. 13). Again :

" Name or person, which is more dear ? Person or fortune, which is more important ? " (ch. 44). Here, once more, is expressed the thought of the man who ' for the great profit of the world would not give one hair of his shank.'

The present-day version of the *Chuang-tzŭ* also contains several passages in which the doctrine of ' completeness of living and preservation of what is genuine ' is expressed. For example in Chapter IV there is described a sacred oak which, because its wood was good for nothing, had been spared the ax, and which said to someone in a dream :

" There are hawthorns, pear trees, orange trees, pumelo trees, gourds and others. The fruits are knocked down when they are ripe, and the trees are maltreated. The large branches are broken, and the smaller ones torn away. The life of these plants is one of suffering, because of their productiveness. They, therefore, cannot complete their natural term of existence, but come to a premature end in the middle of their time, and bring upon themselves destructive treatment from men. It is so with all things. For a long time I was learning to be useless. There were several occasions on which I was nearly destroyed. Now I succed in being useless, which is of the greatest use to me. If I were useful, could I have become so great ? " (pp. 51-52).

A similar passage is found in the same chapter :

" There was a deformed man called Su. His chin was hidden in his navel. His shoulders were higher than the crown of his head. His spinal column pointed to the sky. The openings of his five viscera were all turned upward. His thigh bones were like ribs. By sharpening needles and washing clothes he was able to support ten individuals. When the government was calling out soldiers, he wandered among them and there was no need to hide himself. When the government had any great service to be undertaken, because of his constant ailments no work was assigned to him. When the government gave grain to the sick, he received three *chung* and ten bundles of firewood. If this man who was awkward in his bodily form was still able to make his living and complete his term of existence, how much more may the person accomplish who is awkward in his virtue ? " (p. 54). And still again :

" When Confucius went to Ch'u, Chieh Yü, the 'madman' of Ch'u, wandered to his door and said : " Oh phœnix ! Oh phœnix ! What can you do with this degenerate world ? The future cannot be waited for ; the past cannot be overtaken. When good order prevails in the world, the Sage seeks for accomplishment. When disorder prevails, he may preserve only his own life. At the present time, the best one can do is to escape from punishment. Happiness is lighter than a feather, but no one knows how to carry it. Calamity is heavier than the earth, but no one knows how to avoid it. Desist ! Desist ! Oh, approaching man with your virtue ! Dangerous ! Dangerous ! Is your following of designated regulations. I avoid notoriety, lest my path be injured. I walk crookedly, lest my feet be hurt. The mountain trees cause themselves to be cut. Grease causes itself to be fried. The cinnamon tree can be eaten and is therefore cut down. The varnish tree is useful and therefore incisions are made in it. All men know the utility of the useful, but not that of the useless " (p. 55).

All these passages stress the importance of valuing one's own life, rather than external things.

These quotations may suffice to indicate how the doctrines of Yang Chu continued to find expression in the works of Lao Tzŭ and Chuang Tzŭ. They are not their most profound ideas however. Yang Chu was concerned only with ways to prevent us from injuring our own life ; and yet living in this world as we do, there are always persons and things ready to injure us, even though we, ourselves, may not do injury to our own lives. Hence we must not only try not to injure ourselves, but must ward off the injuries inflicted by others. Here Yang Chu seems to offer only one method : that of the recluse who flees from the world of men.

Human affairs, however, are ever in a state of flux, and in the final analysis there are forms of injury which cannot be avoided. Lao Tzŭ's philosophy attempted to reveal the laws underlying the transformations of things in the universe, so that by knowing these laws we might apply them, and thus hope to ' end our lives without calamity,' as Lao Tzŭ says. The *Chuang-tzŭ* passages just quoted, also try to show how we may enter human society and yet not receive its wounds. None of these methods, nevertheless, can suffice to protect us wholly, for amidst the flux of things there are too many unseen elements. Hence Lao Tzŭ sometimes speaks with still deeper insight, as when he says :

"I suffer great disaster because I have a body. When I have no body, what disaster can there be?" (ch. 13).

Truly, these are words of great understanding; words which are further developed by Chuang Tzŭ when he speaks of 'equalizing death with life, and making others identical with oneself.' For if one does not consider injury to be injury, such injury can indeed no longer be injury. Lao Tzŭ's philosophy, then, is that of Yang Chu advanced one step forward ; while that of Chuang Tzŭ is Yang Chu's philosophy pushed yet another step forward.

2—CH'EN CHUNG TZŬ

Another individualist of this time was Ch'en Chung Tzŭ 陳仲子, of whom Mencius says :

"Among the scholars of Ch'i, I must regard Chung Tzŭ as their thumb . . . Chung Tzŭ belongs to an ancient and noble family of Ch'i. His elder brother Tai received from the region of Ko a revenue of ten thousand *chung*, but he, himself, considered his brother's emolument to be unrighteous, and so would not eat of it ; he likewise considered his brother's house to be unrighteous, and so would not dwell in it. Avoiding his brother and leaving his mother, he went and dwelt in Wu-ling" (IIIb, 10).

Hsün Tzŭ says of him:

"There were some who controlled their passions ; deep and egocentric, they wrongly thought that their differences from others constituted their superiority. They were neither qualified to unite the people nor to manifest fundamental duties. Nevertheless their views had some foundation and their statements some reason, quite enough to deceive and confuse the ignorant masses. Such were Ch'en Chung and Shih Ch'iu" (*Hsün-tzŭ*, p. 78).

The *Chan Kuo Ts'e* (Plots of the Warring States) records a conversation between Empress Wei, who was Queen of King Hui-wen of Chao (298-266), and an emissary of Ch'i, of whom she asks :

"Is Chung Tzŭ of Wu-ling still living? He is a man who does not serve his king above, does not support his family below, and does not seek contact with the feudal lords among his peers. Such is to lead the people to a state of utter uselessness. How is it that until now he has not been executed?" (*Ch'i Ts'e*, IV, 7).

Here was a man who abandoned riches and position to live in the wilds of Wu-ling, where "he himself wove sandals of hemp, while his wife twisted hempen threads" (*Mencius, op. cit.*), all because he believed that his brother's income and home were unrighteous. While we have no means of knowing why he considered them so, the fact that Hsün Tzŭ says that his views were enough to deceive the masses, and that he was execrated by the feudal lords of his time, shows that he must have been a notable figure of that period.

3—Hsü Hsing and Ch'en Hsiang

Hsü Hsing 許 行 and Ch'en Hsiang 陳 相 were what the *I-wen Chih* of the *Ch'ien Han Shu* calls ' followers of the Agricultural school.' The *Mencius* says of them :

" There came from Ch'u to T'eng one Hsü Hsing, who gave out that he acted according to the words of Shen Nung.[1] Coming right up to his gate, he addressed Duke Wen saying : ' A man of a distant region, I have heard that you, Prince, are practising a virtuous government, and I wish to receive a site for a house, and to become one of your people.' Duke Wen gave him a dwelling place. His disciples, amounting to several tens, all wore clothes of haircloth, and made sandals of hemp and wove mats for a living.

" (At this time) Ch'en Hsiang, a disciple of Ch'en Liang, together with his younger brother Hsin, with their plough handles and shares on their backs, came from Sung to T'eng, saying : ' We have heard that you, Prince, are practising the government of a Sage, which shows that you also are a Sage. We wish to become the subjects of a Sage.'

" When Ch'en Hsiang saw Hsü Hsing, he was greatly pleased with him, and, abandoning entirely whatever he had learned, became his disciple. Having an interview with Mencius, he recounted to him Hsü Hsing's words as follows : ' The Prince of T'eng is indeed a worthy prince. Nevertheless, he has not yet heard the true Way. Rulers of worth cultivate the ground in common with their people and eat (what they themselves produce). They prepare their own meals, morning and evening, while at the same time they carry on their government. But now (the prince of) T'eng has his granaries, treasuries and arsenals, which is oppressing the people to nourish himself. How can he be deemed worthy ? . . .

" ' If Hsü's doctrines were followed, there would not be two prices in the market, nor any deceit in the kingdom. If a child were sent to the market, no one would impose on him ; linen and silk of the same length would be the same in price. So it would be with the prices of hemp and silk, these being the same in quantity ; with the five kinds of grain, these being the same in amount ; and with shoes which were of the same size ' " (III*a*, 4, paras. 1-3, 17).

The *I-wen Chih* says also of the followers of the Agricultural school that " they could see no need for Sage-kings. Desiring both ruler and subject to plough together in the fields, they overthrew the order of upper and lower classes " (*Aids*, p. 63). It is evident that this school had new and startling ideas about political and social institu-

---

[1] The Divine Farmer, the name of an agricultural culture hero, who was one of the legendary emperors supposedly preceding Yao and Shun.—Tr.

tions, and even though they were not long perpetuated, their general outline appears in what Mencius describes.[1]

4—KAO TZŬ AND OTHER DEBATERS ON HUMAN NATURE

Confucius had said : " By nature (*hsing* 性) men are close together. In practice they grow wide apart " (*Lun Yü*, XVII, 2) ; while Mencius had maintained the goodness of human nature. The relation of human nature to morality thereupon became one of the problems of the time. The greatest opponent of Mencius on the subject was his contemporary, Kao Tzŭ 告 子, of whom the *Mencius* says :

" Kao Tzŭ said : ' The nature (*hsing*) is like the *chi* willow, and morality (*i* 義) is like a cup or a bowl. To make human-heartedness (*jen*) and righteousness (*i*) out of man's nature, is like making cups and bowls from the *chi* willow ' " (VI*a*, 1).

" Kao Tzŭ said : ' The nature is like whirling water. Open a passage for it to the east, and it will flow to the east; open a passage for it to the west, and it will flow to the west. Man's nature makes no distinction between what is good and what is not good, just as the water makes no distinction between east and west ' " (VI*a*, 2).

" Kao Tzŭ said : ' That which at birth is so, is what is called nature ' " (VI*a*, 3).

" Kao Tzŭ said : ' (Concern with) food and sex : this is nature. Human-heartedness (*jen*) is something internal and not external. Righteousness (*i*) is something external and not internal . . . . . . When there is another person older than myself, I give him the honor due to his age. It is not that this principle of giving honor due to age is contained within me. It is just as when there is a man who is white, I then consider him as white. This follows from the fact that this whiteness of his is something external to me. Therefore I say (of righteousness) that it is something external . . . .

" ' When it happens to be my younger brother, then I love him. But if it is the younger brother of a man of Ch'in, then I do not love him. That is, it is I who determine this feeling. And therefore I say (of human-heartedness) that it is something internal. But I give the honor due to age, to the age of a man of Ch'u, and I also give the honor due to age, to the age of one of my own people. That is, it is the fact of age which determines this feeling. Therefore I say (of righteousness) that it is something external ' " (VI*a*, 4).

" Meng Chi Tzŭ asked Kung Tu Tzŭ (a disciple of Mencius), saying : ' On what ground is it said that righteousness is internal ? ' Kung Tu Tzŭ replied : ' We put into practice our feeling of respect (through it), and therefore it is said to be internal.'

---

[1] Ch'ien Mu, in his *Mo-tzŭ* (ch. 3), suggests that Hsü Hsing was the same person as Hsü Fan 許 氾, a disciple of Mo Tzŭ in the second generation, and that the Agricultural school may have evolved out of the Mohist school.

" (Meng Chi objected) : ' Suppose the case of a villager older than your elder brother by one year, to whom would you pay respect ? ' ' I would pay respect to my older brother,' was the reply.

" ' But for which of them would you first pour out wine (at a feast) ? ' ' For the villager,' (Kung Tu) replied. ' He, to whom you pay respect is then this one, while he, to whom you pay the honour due to age is that one. So, in fact, this is determined by what is without, and does not proceed from within ' (VI*a*, 5).

" Kao Tzŭ said : ' The nature is neither good nor bad ' " (VI*a*, 6).

Kao Tzŭ holds that the nature is simply the natural constitution which man has been born with, so that ' that which at birth is so, is what is called nature.' This nature is something naturally produced, just as water or the *chi* willow, and cannot be said to be good, any more than it can be said to be not good. Its later goodness or evil is the result of education and habit. This is analogous to the *chi* willow, which may be fashioned into cups and bowls, or into other things ; or water, which may be made to run east or west according to whether a passage is made on the east or west side. The quality of human-heartedness or *jen*, Kao Tzŭ maintains, is internal, because when there is love for others, it is we who love, and therefore the feeling of love is determined by ourselves and not by the person loved, and is subjective, or internal. But the quality of righteousness or *i* is external, because when there happens to be a man who is old, it is because of his age that we pay him the respect due to age. In the same way, when there is a white object, it is because of its white color that we consider it to be something white. The quality of age lies in the aged person and not in ourselves, and therefore this quality of righteousness is objective and external.

Kao Tzŭ here makes the mistake of confusing the age of the aged person with the respect due to age which one thereupon pays to him. Here there is an interesting example of the ambiguities of which the Chinese language is capable. The ' age ' of the aged man, and ' the respect due to age which I pay him,' are both expressed in the Chinese text by the one word *ch'ang* 長, which means both ' age,' and ' to age him,' that is, to pay him the honor due to age. The age of the aged man is, indeed, a quality possessed by that man, and so pertains to him and not to us. But the honor due to age which we pay him, certainly continues to pertain to us. Therefore Mencius destroys the argument by saying : " Moreover do we say it is the age itself which is righteousness, or is it the paying of the honor due to age which constitutes righteousness ? " (VI*a*, 5).

The paying of honor due to age, contains, moreover, the idea of respect, and hence differs from the analogy of the object which is white, and which we, therefore, consider as white. Therefore Kung Tu Tzŭ says : " We put into practice our feeling of respect (through righteousness), and therefore it is said to be internal."

Again, the doctrine that human-heartedness is internal, conflicts with Kao Tzŭ's own statement that " to make human-heartedness and righteousness out of man's nature, is like making cups and bowls from the *chi* willow." Our knowledge of Kao Tzŭ's doctrines is but fragmentary, however, so that we do not know if he had other explanations for these points.

Mencius elsewhere remarks : " Kao Tzŭ had attained to a state of unperturbed mind (*pu tung hsin* 不 動 心) at an earlier period of life than I did . . . . Kao Tzŭ says : ' What is not attained to in words is not to be sought for in the mind ; what is not attained to in the mind is not to be sought for in the life-force (*ch'i* 氣) ' " (II*a*, 2, paras. 2, 9). Here Mencius distinguishes the unperturbed mind of Kao Tzŭ, which has been arrived at through forcible repressions that prevent it from being perturbed, from his own, which is the result of cultivation. This latter ' is produced by the accumulation of righteous deeds ' (*ibid.*, para. 15), so that of its own accord it is unperturbed. Kao Tzŭ advocated the externalness of righteousness, and so could not understand what Mencius meant by such a statement. Hence Mencius says of him : " I therefore say, ' Kao Tzŭ has never understood righteousness, because he makes it external " (*ibid.*, para. 15). The *Mencius* states again :

" Some say : ' The nature may be made to be good, or may be made to be evil. Therefore under Kings Wen and Wu the people loved what was good, whereas under Kings Yu and Li the people loved what was cruel.'

" Some say : ' There are those whose nature is good, and those whose nature is evil. Therefore it is that under such a sovereign as Yao there yet appeared (the evil) Hsiang ; that with such an (evil) father as Ku Sou there yet appeared Shun ; and that with Chou as their sovereign, and their elder brother's son as well, there were (such men of virtue as) Chi, the Viscount of Wei, and the Prince Pi-kan ' " (VI*a*, 6).

This passage occurs in the same chapter as that which describes Kao Tzŭ's doctrine as : " The nature is neither good nor bad," indicating that all three doctrines must have been in existence about the same time. The philosopher Wang Ch'ung 王 充 (A.D. 27-c. 97) says in his *Lun Heng* (ch. 13) : " Shih Shih 世 碩 of the Chou period (one of the seventy disciples of Confucius), held that human nature is partly good and partly bad, and that, if the good nature in man be cultivated and developed, his goodness increases ; whereas if his bad nature be cultivated and developed, his badness increases . . . . Accordingly Shih Tzŭ composed a chapter ' On Cultivation' (now lost). Fu Tzŭ Chien 宓 子 賤, Ch'i-tiao K'ai 漆 雕 開 and Kung-sun Ni Tzŭ 公 孫 尼 子 (all disciples of Confucius, whose writings are now lost), also discoursed on the emotions and the nature, partly in agreement and partly in disagreement with Shih Tzŭ " (p. 165). Is the first theory in the *Mencius*, that nature may be made to be good or bad, the same as that of this Shih Shih ?¹ And is the second theory, which says that some men are by nature good and some bad, and therefore cannot be changed, that of Fu Tzŭ Chien and his associates ? The hypothesis is quite possible, though there are no means to-day of proving or disproving it.

5—YIN WEN AND SUNG K'ENG

These two men are described in the *Chuang-tzŭ* (ch. 33) as follows :
" Not to be entangled with popular fashions ; not to make a pretentious display of things ; not to be reckless toward other men nor antagonistic to the public ; to desire the peace of the world in order to preserve the life of the people ; to seek no more than is sufficient for nourishing oneself and others, thus revealing their hearts : these are some of the aspects of the Way (*Tao*) of ancient times. Sung K'eng 宋 牼 and Yin Wen 尹 文 heard of these and were delighted with them. They adopted a Hua Shan cap (with a flat top to indicate equality) as their badge. In intercourse with all things they began with knowing the prejudices. They talked about the tolerance of the mind and called it the action of the mind. By warmth of affection they sought the harmony of joy in order to harmonize the world. They wished to establish these as their principles. They endured insult without feeling it a disgrace, so as to save the people from fighting. They checked aggression and proposed disarmament in order to save their generation from war. With this message they went everywhere counselling the high and instructing the low. Though the world would not accept this message, they insisted on stating it and would not give it up. Hence it was said : ' When high and low were wearied of seeing them they persisted in showing themselves.' However, they did too much for others, too little for themselves. They said : ' Just give us five pints of food, if you please. It will be enough.'

" With this, I am afraid, the master would not be filled and the disciples would still be hungry. Even so, they would not forget the world. Day and night they toiled without ceasing, saying : ' We can manage to live on.' How great were those who sought to save the world !

" ' The Superior Man,' they said, ' is not a faultfinder. He does not depend on others.' They thought it was better to cease

---

¹ This first theory seems in actual fact to be indistinguishable from that of Mencius, who says that all men will be good if they but develop the four ' beginnings ' of goodness inherent in their natures. Yet logically speaking, it is not the same. For Mencius specifically designates that part of man's nature which is the same as that of animals, is evil, and is ordinarily simply termed human nature, as the ' small part ' (*hsiao t'i* 小 體) of man, and hence not to be accepted as truly constituting man's actual nature.

altogether than to go on explaining what is of no good to the world. 'To check aggression and propose disarmaments' were their external achievements. 'To desire few things' was their inner cultivation. In their system there was the great and small, the fine and coarse. If these points were reached their practice stopped" (pp. 443-444).

The *Mencius* says:

" When Sung K'eng was about to go to Ch'u, Mencius met him at Shih-ch'iu and asked : ' Where, Sir, are you going ? '

" He replied : ' I have heard that Ch'in and Ch'u are fighting each other, and I am going to see the King of Ch'u and persuade him to cease. If he be not pleased with this, I shall go to see the King of Ch'in, and persuade him in the same way. Of the two kings, I shall succeed with one of them.'

" Mencius said : ' I shall not venture to ask about the particulars, but I should like to hear the general idea of your plan. How are you going to speak to them ? ' Sung K'eng replied : ' I am going to tell them their course is unprofitable ' " (VI*b*, 4).

The *Chuang-tzŭ* (ch. 1) says :

" There are some men whose knowledge is sufficient for the duties of some office. There are some whose conduct will secure unity in some district. There are some whose virtue befits them to be rulers. There are some whose ability wins credit in the country . . . . Yet Sung Yung Tzŭ 宋 榮 子 laughed at these. If the whole world should admire him he would not be encouraged thereby, nor if the whole world should blame him would he thereby be discouraged. He held fast the difference between the internal and the external. He marked distinctly the boundary of honor and disgrace. This was the best of him. In the world such a man is rare, yet there still remains something he has not established " (p. 4).

And the *Hsün-tzŭ* says :

" Sung Tzŭ had vision regarding the (fact that human desires may be) few, but no vision regarding the (fact that they may be) many " (p. 185).

" The teacher Sung Tzŭ says : ' To show clearly that to meet with insult is no disgrace will prevent people from fighting. Men all consider it a disgrace to meet with insult, hence they fight. When they know that it is no disgrace to be insulted, they will not fight ' " (p. 206).

" Master Sung Tzŭ says : ' Men's passions desire but little, but everyone supposes that his own passions desire much, which is an error.' Hence he leads his disciples, splitting hairs in his discussions, making clear his examples and terms, so as to make men understand that their passions desire but little " (p. 209).

" Sung Tzŭ was blinded by the problem of desire, and did not know the value of virtue " (p. 264).

The *Han-fei-tzŭ* (ch. 50) says :

" Ch'i-tiao preached that one should neither let one's countenance become confused by fear nor one's eye become alarmed. If his action were crooked he would shun even a servant. If his action were correct, he might show anger even to the feudal lords. The rulers of the world considered him incorruptible, and honored him.

" What Sung Yung preached was : do not fight ; do not make enemies of others ; do not feel shame because of detention in prison ; and it is no disgrace to be insulted. The rulers of the world held him as someone liberal-minded, and honored him. Now, if one approves of Chi Tiao's stubbornness, one will condemn Sung Yung's tolerance. And if one approves of Sung Yung's tolerance, one will condemn Chi Tiao's stubbornness " (*chüan* 19, p. 8).

Finally, Liu Hsiang says of Yin Wen : " He with Sung Hsing 宋 銒 both travelled to Chi-hsia " (in Ch'i).[1] Sung Hsing, Sung K'eng and Sung Yung are all different names for the same man,[2] and practically all we know about him and Yin Wen is contained in these few passages.

Hsün Tzŭ, in his chapter, ' Against the Twelve Philosophers ' (ch. 6), groups Sung K'eng with the Mohists, perhaps because he ' checked aggression and proposed disarmament,' and ' did too much for others, too little for himself,' doctrines and practices which resemble those of the Mohists. Yet the *Chuang-tzŭ* says of the two men that ' to check aggression and propose disarmament were their external achievement, and to desire few things was their inner cultivation.' Thus the former constitutes only one aspect of the school of Yin Wen and Sung K'eng, and their doctrine that men desire few things was one that had not been touched on by the Mohists. Here, in fact, Yin and Sung seem to have been influenced rather by the school of Yang Chu, so that we may say of them that they combined the ideas of both Mo Tzŭ and Yang Chu.[3] At the same time they gave to each of these schools a psychological basis.[4]

Using the passages quoted above, we may group the principles of Yin Wen and Sung K'eng under six main points :

(1) ' In intercourse with all things, to begin with knowing the prejudices.'

(2) ' In talking about the tolerance of the mind, to call it the action of the mind.'

(3) ' Men's passions desire but little.'

---

[1] This is quoted in the commentary by Yen Shih-ku (A.D. 581-645) under the notice, ' *Yin-wen-tzŭ* in one section,' in the *I-wen Chih* (*Ch'ien Han Shu*, ch. 30, p. 24).

[2] *Cf.* T'ang Yüeh, *Yin Wen ho Yin-wen-tzŭ*, in the *Ch'ing Hua Hsüeh Pao*, Vol. 4, No. 1.

[3] This has been suggested by Ku Chieh-kang, *op. cit.*

[4] This has been pointed out by Ch'ien Mu in his *Mo-tzŭ*. Professor Ch'ien, however, only mentions Sung K'eng, but not Yin Wen, as adding a psychological basis to the Mohist doctrines.

(4) ' To endure insult without feeling it a disgrace, so as to save people from fighting.'

(5) ' To check aggression and propose disarmament in order to save their generation from war.'

(6) ' To desire the peace of the world in order to preserve the life of the people ; to seek no more than is sufficient for nourishing oneself and others.'

The last point constitutes their ultimate goal, to further which ' they went everywhere counselling the high and instructing the low.' Its first half is derived from the Mohists ; the second shows the influence of Yang Chu. Disorder in the world is caused by conflict between individuals and wars between states, and Yin and Sung were only perpetuating the Mohist ideas when they attempted to end this condition through condemnation of war and proposal of disarmament. The same Mohist influence is evident on Sung K'eng when in his conversation with Mencius he says that he would prevent the kings of Ch'u and Ch'in from fighting by telling them that ' it is unprofitable.'

Yin and Sung proposed, as a means of preventing strife, their doctrine that ' to endure insult is no disgrace.' Of all their ideas, this is the best known, so that we find the *Chuang-tzŭ*, *Hsün-tzŭ*, *Han-fei-tzŭ* and *Lü-shih Ch'un Ch'iu* (XVI, 8) all mentioning it. Hsün Tzŭ (in his ch. 18) criticizes the notion that such a doctrine will prevent conflicts, pointing out that when men fight after they have been insulted, it is because they dislike to be insulted, and not necessarily because they see in the insult a disgrace to themselves.' Hence, even granted that men believe that to endure insult is no disgrace, they will continue to fight because they dislike to endure the insult. Though this is a powerful criticism, Sung's argument is still not entirely unreasonable. For ' dislike ' is only something existing within the heart of the individual who has been personally insulted, whereas ' disgrace ' is connected with what is called ' face.' There are many men who fight with others not merely because they dislike what they have undergone, but also in order to protect their ' face.' Hence the general propagation of the doctrine that insult is no disgrace would, in fact, be one way of preventing conflict. Yin and Sung's second point, furthermore, concerning the ' tolerance of the mind,' would seem to be an answer to Hsün Tzŭ's criticism.

This second point is : ' In talking about the tolerance of the mind, to call it the action of the mind.' Hsün Tzŭ says of Sung K'eng that he believed that ' humiliation and tolerance are to be borne by one's self ' (p. 209). It is not fighting and love of conquest, Yin and Sung maintained, but yielding and tolerance, which constitute what they called ' the action of the mind,' that is, its natural

---

[1] *Cf. Hsün-tzŭ*, pp. 206-209.

tendencies. The *Han-fei-tzŭ* confirms this interpretation when it speaks of Sung Yung's 'tolerance' and 'liberality.'[1] If men once understood this principle, they would automatically no longer dislike receiving insult, and so man would no longer fight with man, nor state with state. Here Yin and Sung supply a psychological basis to this aspect of Mohist philosophy.

The statement that 'men's passions desire but little,' means that it is the original nature of man to want little rather than much. For while it is true that 'the eye, the ear and the mouth desire color, sound and taste to the utmost, . . .' yet the amount of these things which one man can at one time enjoy is but limited, so that, as Chuang Tzŭ says: "The tit, building its nest in the mighty forest, occupies but a single twig. The tapir slakes its thirst from the river, but drinks only enough to fill its belly" (p. 6). When there is more than this, "the five colors confuse men's eyes, the five tones dull men's ears, and the five tastes embitter the mouth" (*Lao-tzŭ*, ch. 12). Hence when what is to be enjoyed becomes too great, it is no longer beneficial and becomes injurious. It is because men understand this principle, Yin Wen and Sung K'eng would say, that their passions seek little.

Granted that they were mistaken in this idea, their purpose in upholding it was apparently to induce each man to restrict his pursuit of enjoyment within the possible limits of enjoyment, so as not to search for anything beyond this. This is why the *Chuang-tzŭ* speaks of the two as 'seeking no more than is sufficient for nourishing oneself and others.' Yang Chu had taught that men should restrain their desires, whereas Yin Wen and Sung K'eng said that men's passions originally desire but little, a principle which, once understood, would automatically lead men to limit their desires. In this they supply a psychological basis to Yang Chu's doctrines.

The first point is: 'In intercourse with all things to begin with knowing the prejudices.' This means that men must detach themselves from the biases produced by their situation, age, government, religion, customs, etc., before they can understand the realities of things. Yin Wen and Sung K'eng seem to have felt that the fact that men take insult as a disgrace and believe that their passions desire much, is the result of custom and habit, and not something owing to man's original nature. Man is like this only because he has certain prejudices. If he can come to recognize these prejudices, he will realize that insult is no disgrace, and that the passions originally do not desire much. When all men understand this, conflict will automatically cease, the world will become peaceful, the people will be allowed to live at rest, and no one will seek for more than is necessary to nourish himself. This is why Yin Wen and Sung K'eng urged:

---

[1] This has already been pointed out by Ch'ien Mu in his *Mo-tzŭ*.

' In intercourse with all things, to begin with knowing the prejudices.' [1]

6—P'ENG MENG, T'IEN P'IEN AND SHEN TAO

The *Chuang-tzŭ* (ch. 33) states of these three men :

" To be impartial and non-partisan ; to be easy-going and un-selfish ; to be decisive but without predetermination ; to be compliant without double-mindedness ; not to pay heed to anxiety, not to plan with knowledge ; to make no discrimination in things, but simply to move with them : these were some aspects of the Way (*Tao*) of ancient times. P'eng Meng 彭 蒙, T'ien P'ien 田 駢 and Shen Tao 愼 到 heard of them and were delighted with them. They started their teaching with the equality of all things. They said : ' Heaven can cover things but cannot sustain them. Earth can sustain, but cannot cover them. The great Way (*Tao*) comprehends but cannot distinguish between them.' They knew that for everything there is that of which it is capable and of which it is incapable. Hence they said : ' Selection involves exclusion ; instruction involves incompleteness ; the Way (*Tao*) omits nothing.'

" Therefore Shen Tao discarded knowledge, abandoned self, followed the inevitable, and was indifferent to things. Such were his principles. He said : ' Knowledge is not to know.' He was one who despised knowledge and would destroy it. Stupid and irresponsible, he ridiculed the world's way of preferring the virtuous ; careless and impractical, he condemned the world's great Sages ; shifting and slippery, he changed about with circumstances ; disregarding right and wrong, he was only concerned with avoiding trouble ; learning nothing from knowledge and thinking, paying no attention to past or future, he stood loftily indifferent to everything.

" He went where he was pushed and followed where he was led, like a whirling gale, like a feather tossed in the wind, like a turning millstone. He was complete without defects ; in action or at rest he was free from mistakes and never offended others. How could this be ? Because creatures without knowledge are freed from the trouble of self-assertion and the entanglements of knowledge ; in motion or at rest they do not depart from the principles of nature and for this reason they are never praised. Therefore, he said : ' Let us be like creatures without knowledge. That will be sufficient. There is no use for Sages. For a clod of earth (i.e., a creature without knowledge) does not miss the Way (*Tao*).'

" Men of ability laughed at him and said : ' The way of Shen Tao is no practice for the living ; it is a principle for the dead. It is indeed passing strange. '

---

[1] This has already been pointed out by T'ang Yüeh, *op. cit.*. As to the work now extant under the name *Yin-wen-tzŭ*, this is a later fabrication. *Cf.* Dr. T'ang's article.

" It was the same with T'ien P'ien. He studied under P'eng Meng, and got the doctrine of teaching nothing. P'eng Meng's master said : ' Of old, the men who knew the Way (*Tao*) reached the point where no man would consider them as right, and no man would consider them as wrong.' The influence of these was one of opposition, and how can it be discussed ?

" Their teaching is contrary to the common view of men, therefore few pay attention to it. They cannot avoid being regarded as shifty and slippery. What they called the Way (*Tao*) was not the Way ; what they considered right was often wrong. P'eng Meng, T'ien P'ien and Shen Tao did not know the Way. Nevertheless, in a general way they had heard something about it " (pp. 444-447).

The *Hsün-tzŭ* (ch. 6) says of them :

" There were some who emphasized law but had no law ; they would not follow the old ways but liked to make new ones. They got a hearing from the upper classes and a following from the lower. They always made systematic statements, but if one turned to examine them, one would find them loose and without any central idea. They could not regulate government nor establish social distinctions. Nevertheless their views had some foundation and their statements some reason, quite enough to deceive and confuse the ignorant masses. Such were Shen Tao and T'ien P'ien " (p. 79). Again (ch. 17) : " Shen Tzŭ had vision regarding following, but no vision regarding leading " (p. 184).

The *Lü-shih Ch'un Ch'iu* (XVII, 8) says :

" T'ien P'ien was expounding the arts of the Way (*Tao*) to the King of Ch'i. The King replied to him saying : ' What I possess is the state of Ch'i, and it is difficult with these arts of yours to rid it of its distresses.' I should like to hear about how to govern the state of Ch'i.' T'ien P'ien replied : ' My words contain nothing on government, and yet through them one may attain to government. They are like a forest, which is without ready-cut lumber, but from which ready-cut lumber may be obtained. . . . . I am speaking only about the shallow. But if I should speak about the profound, why should it be limited to the government of the state of Ch'i alone ? All transformations and reactions have their laws. Following their natures, and according themselves with other things, there is nothing that is not in harmony. P'eng Tsu (an ancient worthy noted for his longevity) thereby lived to a great age ; the Three Dynasties thereby prospered ; the Five Emperors thereby manifested themselves ; and Shen Nung thereby made himself great " (p. 287).

---

[1] This sentence does not occur in the *Lü-shih Ch'un Ch'iu*, but is added from the *Huai-nan-tzŭ* (ch. 5), where the passage is quoted. *Cf.* Morgan's translation, p. 104.

Finally, the *Shen-tzŭ*, a work attributed to Shen Tao, but probably written much later, says :

" When birds fly in the air and fish swim in the deeps, they do
not do so through any conscious art. Therefore birds and fish do
not, themselves, know that they are capable of flying and swimming ;
if they knew this, and set their minds on doing it, they would inevitably fall down and be drowned. It is likewise with the moving
of man's feet and grasping of his hands, the listening of his ears
and seeing of his eyes. At the time of their moving, grasping,
hearing and seeing, these act so of their own accord at the proper
occasion, and do not wait for the act of thinking before doing so.
If they had to wait for thought before acting, they would become
exhausted. Hence, it is those persons who accord themselves with
the spontaneous (*tzŭ jan* 自 然) who long survive, and those who
attain to the constant norm who win out " (p. 13).

Using the *Chuang-tzŭ* as a basis, we may classify the ideas of
P'eng Meng and his followers under five points :

(1) ' To start with the equality of all things.'

(2) ' To be impartial and non-partisan; to be easy going and
unselfish ; to be decisive but without predetermination.'

(3) ' To discard knowledge, abandon self, and follow the inevitable.'

(4) ' There is no use for Sages.'

(5) ' Even a clod of earth does not miss the Way (*Tao*).'

Point one, ' To start with the equality of all things,' is based upon
the idea that ' for everything there is that of which it is capable and of
which it is incapable.' Thus looked at, even though things have each
their own peculiarity, they are in fact all equal. Looked at from the
viewpoint of ' the great Way (*Tao*),' they all become levelled to one
standard, and no distinction remains between what is called noble or
mean, good or bad. Hence ' the great Way comprehends but
cannot distinguish between them.' Such distinction means the making
of all sorts of divisions between objects, the consequence of which is a
process of accepting and rejecting of things, so that there inevitably
results a favoring of this and a disregard of that, with the consequence
that only a part is obtained and the whole is lost. Therefore ' selection involves exclusion ; instruction involves incompleteness.' For
when there is something that is selected, there must remain something
that is not selected, and when there is something that is taught, there
must remain something that is untaught. The *Chuang-tzŭ* (ch. 2)
expresses the same idea when it says : " That there are construction
and destruction is like the fact that of old Chao Wen played the lute.
That there are no construction and no destruction is like the fact
that he did not play the lute " (pp. 21-22). The ' Great Way ' or
Tao looks on all things as if they were reduced to the level of one.

It 'comprehends' them, but does not 'distinguish' between them. Hence 'the Way omits nothing.' [1]

The application of this principle to human life means, that in attending to things, men must put themselves in harmony with the spontaneous movements of these things. We must simply 'discard knowledge, abandon self and follow the inevitable.' For when every object has the same equality, and there are no divisions between nobility and meanness, and goodness and badness, we, ourselves, shall naturally have no occasion for using the principle of selection and choice. The resulting state is one in which one ' makes no discrimination in things, but simply moves with them.' Such a state was reached by the person whose speech is given in the *Chuang-tzŭ* (ch. 6) : " If my left arm should be transformed into a cock, I would mark with it the time of night. If my right arm should be transformed into a crossbow, I would look for a bird to bring down and roast. If my rump-bone should be transformed into a wheel, and my spirit into a horse, I would mount it and would have no need of any other steed " (p. 81). This is the principle expressed in the second point : " To be impartial and non-partisan : to be easy-going and unselfish ; to be decisive but without predetermination." The *Lü-shih Ch'un Ch'iu* expresses the same idea when it says : " Following their natures and according themselves with other things, there is nothing that is not in harmony." Or as the *Shen-tzŭ* says : " It is those persons who accord themselves with the spontaneous who long survive."

If we wish to reach such a state, we must ' discard knowledge, abandon self and follow the inevitable.' The reason for this is that the function of knowledge is to make distinctions between things, whereas if we discard knowledge we shall no longer make these distinctions, or in others words, shall ' make no discriminations in things.' Once the ' self' accepts something as being the ' self,' we are no longer able ' to be decisive but without predetermination ' ; whereas if we ' abandon self,' we can then accord ourselves with things and ' simply move with them.' Without knowledge and without self, ' to be indifferent to things ' : this is the meaning of ' to follow the inevitable.'

" ' Knowledge is not to know.' He was one who despised knowledge and would destroy it." We must realize the truth of this statement in order to reach a state of non-knowing in which we may be free from the world of distinctions ; a world to which men of knowledge hold themselves, and which the *Chuang-tzŭ* (ch. 2) attacks

---

[1] The reader has probably already noticed the frequency with which the word *tao* 道, usually translated as Way, has appeared in preceding quotations. In most of these, it has meant the Way of man, that is, proper conduct, morality, human truth, etc. In its use in the present passage, however, its scope is a broader one than that of mere human affairs, and it becomes the Cosmic Way of the Taoists, the school of thought to which it has given its name. For its meaning in this sense, see below, p. 177.—Tr.

when it says : " Distinctions between princes and grooms. How stupid ! " (p. 30). We should, in fact, despise and destroy such distinctions, and yet it is just the class of learned men who hold to them, whom the world calls worthies and sages. The greater a man's learning, so believes the world, the more is he a Sage. But if one knows that ' knowledge is not to know,' one is ' stupid and irresponsible, and ridicules the world's way of preferring the virtuous ; careless and impractical, one condemns the world's great Sages.'

When one has attained to this state, one is ' freed from the troubles of self-assertion and the entanglements of knowledge,' and becomes a ' creature without knowledge.' Such a man ' learns nothing from knowledge and thinking, pays no attention to past or future, and stands loftily indifferent to everything. He goes where he is pushed and follows where he is led, like a whirling gale, like a feather tossed in the wind, like a turning millstone.' He ' follows the inevitable,' and ' simply moves with things.' This is almost the same as the movement of a material thing which has no knowledge, and therefore it may be said that ' even a clod of earth does not miss the Way.'

Such doctrines come close to those of the Taoists, Lao Tzŭ and Chuang Tzŭ, especially as enunciated in ' The Equality of Things and Opinions.' (ch. 2) in the *Chuang-tzŭ*. The point of difference, however, appears in the statement that ' even a clod of earth does not lose the Way.' The *Lao-tzŭ*, for example, speaks of the man who " knows the male, yet cleaves to the female, . . . knows the white, yet cleaves to the black, . . . knows glory, yet clings to ignominy " (ch. 28). And the leading idea of Chapter II in the *Chuang-tzŭ* lies in " obtaining the center of the circle so as to respond to the endless changes " (p. 18) ; in " harmonizing the systems of right and wrong, and resting in the Evolution of Nature " (p. 21) ; and in " forgetting life, forgetting the distinctions of right and wrong, and finding enjoyment in the realm of the infinite and remaining there " (p. 31).

The meaning of these various passages will be explained later in the chapters on Lao Tzŭ and Chuang Tzŭ. Here, I need only state that although these philosophers, like Shen Tao and his circle, ' despised knowledge and would destroy it,' and ' knew not to know,' yet at the same time they maintained that this state of non-knowing differs from the non-sensibility of a material thing. The *Lao-tzŭ* several times speaks with approval of the state of the little child. Yet a child, while it lacks intellectual knowledge, is certainly not an insensible creature. And when the *Lao-tzŭ* speaks of one who ' knows the male, yet cleaves to the female,' etc., this implies that we are not to be in a state of complete absence of knowledge. Likewise the world of pure experience described by the *Chuang-tzŭ*, while containing no intellectual knowledge, does include experience,

so that in it there can be no complete non-sensibility.¹ When Chuang
Tzŭ speaks of 'forgetting life, forgetting the distinctions of right
and wrong,' the word 'forgetting' deserves our special attention.
For this forgetting does not mean a complete nothingness, but only
a special attempt to forget certain things.

Herein lies the difference between a 'clod of earth' and the
personality conceived of by Lao Tzŭ and Chuang Tzŭ. The *Chuang-
tzŭ* (ch. 33) criticizes Shen Tao, saying that his doctrine 'is no
practice for the living; it is a principle for the dead.' Such would be
the result of bringing men to the state of insensible creatures. The
fact that in the course of its criticism of various philosophers, this
chapter especially singles out the schools of Lao Tzŭ and Chuang
Tzŭ for praise, whereas it attacks Shen Tao on this one point, indicates
that it was in just this respect that Shen Tao fundamentally differed
from those two. Its view of P'eng Meng and his circle was:
"What they called the Way was not the Way; what they considered
right was often wrong. P'eng Meng, T'ien P'ien and Shen Tao
did not know the Way." Yet in many ways the doctrines of these
men closely resembled those of Lao Tzŭ and Chuang Tzŭ, and so the
criticism continues : "Nevertheless, in a general way, they had heard
something about it (the Way)." It becomes apparent that the
doctrines of Lao Tzŭ and Chuang Tzŭ are simply those of P'eng Meng
and his circle developed one step further.²

The philosophy of these men stressed methods for preserving
one's life from injury. Hence such statements as : 'Disregarding
right and wrong, he was only concerned with avoiding trouble';
'in action or at rest he was free from mistakes and never offended
others'; 'in motion or at rest he does not depart from the principles
of nature and for this reason is never praised.' All these point
to the derivation of this philosophy from that of Yang Chu.
Yet at the same time its emphasis on ways whereby one may avoid the
hurts of the outside world inflicted by others, as well as hurts done
by oneself, indicates it to be a philosophy developed one step further
than that of Yang Chu.

While the original writings of Shen Tao are no longer extant,
the *I-wen Chih* classes them under the Legalist school, and says that

---

¹ *Cf.* below, ch. 10, especially pp. 239 f., and note 3 on p. 242.
² There is a broad sense and a narrow sense for the word 'knowledge.' In its broad
sense it is as wide in scope as is experience, whereas in its narrow sense it refers exclusively
to intellectual knowledge. Thus, the knowledge discussed in epistemology is knowledge
in the broad sense, whereas that spoken of in logic is knowledge in the narrow sense.
When the *Lao-tzŭ* and *Chuang-tzŭ* speak of a state of non-knowledge, they mean knowledge
in the narrow sense, whereas the knowledge spoken of by Shen Tao is knowledge in the
wider sense. This is why his doctrine becomes 'a principle for the dead,' so that
when the *Chuang-tzŭ* still says : "Nevertheless, in a general way they had heard something
about it (the Way)," it is giving high praise indeed. For while this same chapter refers
to Mo Tzŭ as a genius, and to Yin Wen and Sung K'eng as men who sought to save the
world, it says of none of them that they had heard something of the Way or *Tao*.

"Shen (Pu-hai) and Han (Fei Tzŭ) often mentioned them." The *Hsün-tzŭ* (ch. 6) says of Shen Tao and T'ien P'ien that "they got a hearing from the upper classes and a following from the lower," which is equivalent to the *Chuang-tzŭ's* statement : "They change about with circumstances." Again, it says : "There were some who emphasized law but had no law," and yet again (ch. 21) : "Shen Tzŭ was blinded by law and did not know the value of talent" (p. 264). This makes it evident that Shen Tao did, in fact, emphasize law, all the more so since the *Han-fei-tzŭ* (ch. 40) contains a speech by him about the meaning of the word 'authority' (*shih* 勢), a Legalist term. To-day, however, it is impossible for us to know the logical connection which he made between his emphasis on law and his doctrine of the equality of things ; hence we should not forcibly try to link the two together. In the present chapter I have discussed Shen Tao's ideas only as they are found in the *Chuang-tzŭ* and in the other writings in which they are similarly presented. I shall wait for the chapter on the Legalist school (ch. 13) to discuss his ideas regarding the term *shih*.

7—Tsou Yen and the School of *Yin* and *Yang* and of the Five Elements

In Chapter III I described how in ancient times the methods of astrology, the almanac, and the Five Elements or Agents (*wu hsing* 五 行) which were used for magic and divination, all laid stress on the connection supposedly existing between men and nature ; they were based on the assumption that there is a mutual interaction between the way of nature and the affairs of man. During the Warring States period these religious ideas were developed and transformed into a unified system of cosmology, and all sorts of analogies were found between the natural and human worlds. The persons who engaged in speculations of this sort were referred to in the Han dynasty as members of the school of the *Yin* 陰 and the *Yang* 陽, which are, respectively, the female principle of darkness, cold, moisture, quiet, etc., and the male principle of light, warmth, dryness, movement, etc., the interacting activities of which are supposed to produce the natural phenomena of the universe.[1] During the latter years of the Warring States period the leader of this school was Tsou Yen 騶 衍, of whom the *Shih Chi* states :

"The state of Ch'i had three scholars named Tsou. The first of these was Tsou Chi 騶 忌, who affected King Wei (of Ch'i,

---

[1] It seems to be a fact that originally the men who talked about the Five Elements did not do so about the *yin* and *yang*, and vice versa, so that these two branches of thought were separate. Later, however, especially during the Han dynasty, they became combined, so that the Han scholars applied indiscriminately the terms, '*Yin-yang* school,' or 'School of *Yin* and *Yang* and of the Five Elements,' to those who discussed the Five Elements only, as well as those who talked only about the *yin* and *yang*.

357-320) by his playing of the lute, and thus rose to a position.in the administration of the country, being enfieffed as the Marquis Ch'eng and receiving the seal of minister. He lived prior to Mencius.

" The second was Tsou Yen, who came after Mencius. He saw that the rulers were becoming ever more dissolute and were incapable of valuing virtue, through which they might incorporate in themselves (the principles in) the *Ta Ya* Odes (of the *Shih Ching*) and diffuse them among the common people. Thereupon he examined deeply into the phenomena of increase and decrease of the *yin* and the *yang*, and wrote essays totalling more than one hundred thousand words about their strange permutations, and about the cycles of the great Sages from beginning to end. His words were grandiose and fanciful. He had first to examine small objects, and extended this to large ones until he reached what was without limit. He first spoke about modern times, and from this went back to the time of Huang-ti (the legendary Yellow Emperor), all of which has been recorded by scholars. Moreover, he followed the great events in the rise and fall of ages, and by means of their omens and (an examination into their) institutions, extended his survey backward to the time when Heaven and Earth had not yet been born, to what was profound and abstruse and not to be examined.

" He began by classifying China's notable mountains, great rivers and connecting valleys ; its birds and beasts ; the productions of its waters and soils, and its rare products ; and from this extended his survey to what is beyond the seas, and which men are unable to see.

" Starting from the time of the separation of Heaven and Earth and coming down, he made citations of the revolutions and transmutations of the Five Powers, arranging them until each found its proper place and was confirmed (by history).¹

" He maintained that what scholars call the Middle Kingdom (i.e., China) holds a place in the whole world of but one part in eighty-one. China, he named the Spiritual Continent of the Red Region (*ch'ih hsien shen chou* 赤 縣 神 州), within which are nine provinces (*chou* 州), which are the Nine Provinces which Yü (the legendary Emperor who after nine years conquered China's great flood) had laid out. But these cannot be numbered among the real continents. Besides China (there are other continents) similar to the Spiritual Continent of the Red Region, making (with China) a total of nine continents, which are the real so-called Nine Continents. Around each of these is a small encircling sea, so that men and beasts cannot pass from one to another, and these (nine continents) form one division and make up one large continent. There are

---

¹ These Powers (*Te* 德), i.e., the Five Elements, are earth, wood, metal, fire and water, each one of which is supposed to overcome the preceding, and in its turn be overcome by the next, in endless succession, and each of which is supposed to preside over one period in history.—Tr.

nine (large continents) like this, and around their outer edge is a vast ocean which encompasses them at the point where Heaven and Earth meet.

"His arts were all of this sort. Yet if we reduce them to fundamentals, they all rested on the virtues of human-heartedness (*jen*), righteousness (*i*), restraint, frugality, and the practice of the association of ruler with subject, superior with inferior, and the six relationships. It is only the beginning (of his doctrines) which is fanciful. Kings, dukes and great officials, when they first witnessed his arts, fearfully transformed themselves, but later were unable to practise them.

"This is why Tsou Tzǔ was highly regarded in Ch'i. He went to Liang, where King Hui of Liang (370-319) went out to the suburb of the city to welcome him, and acted toward him with all the etiquette of a host toward a guest. He went to Chao, where the Prince of P'ing-yüan (died 252 or 251), walking on one side of the road, personally brushed off the dust from his mat. He went to Yen, where King Chao (311-279) acted as his advance guard, holding a brush (to sweep away the dust), and asked to take the seat of a disciple and receive his instruction.

"Here in a palace built for him at Chieh-shih (a place probably between the present Taku and Shanhaikuan along the coast of Hopei), the King himself went to receive instructions. (Tsou Yen) thus composed the *Chü Yün* 主 運 (now lost). In all his travels among the feudal lords he received honors of this sort. . . .

"Tsou Shih 騶 奭 was one of the Tsou scholars of Ch'i, and especially recorded in his writings the arts of Tsou Yen. . . . The arts of Tsou Yen were pretentious and vast in scope, whereas Shih had literary ability, but (his ideas) were difficult to put into practice. . . . Therefore the people of Ch'i praised the two saying: 'For discoursing on nature there is Yen; for carving out the dragon (i.e., making literary embellishments) there is Shih'" (ch. 74, pp. 2-5).

Concerning the 'revolutions and transmutations of the Five Powers' mentioned here, the *Lü-shih Ch'un Ch'iu* (XIII, 2) has a passage:

"Whenever any Emperor or King is about to arise, Heaven must first make manifest some favorable omen among the lower people. In the time of the Yellow Emperor, Heaven first made a large (number of) earthworms and mole crickets appear. The Yellow Emperor said: 'The force of the element earth is in ascendancy.' Therefore he assumed yellow as his color, and took earth as a pattern for his affairs.

"In the time of Yü (founder of the Hsia dynasty), Heaven first made grass and trees appear which did not die in the autumn and winter. Yü said: 'The force of the element wood is in ascendancy.' Therefore he assumed green as his color, and took wood as a pattern for his affairs.

"In the time of T'ang (founder of the Shang dynasty), Heaven first made some knife blades appear in the water. T'ang said: 'The force of the element metal is in ascendancy.' Therefore he assumed white as his color, and took metal as a pattern for his affairs.

"In the time of King Wen (founder of the Chou dynasty), Heaven first made a flame appear, while a red bird, holding a red book in its mouth, alighted on the altar of the soil of the House of Chou. King Wen said: 'The force of the element fire is in ascendancy.' Therefore he assumed red as his color, and took fire as a pattern for his affairs.

"Water will inevitably be the next thing which will replace fire. And Heaven will first of all make the ascendancy of water manifest. The force of water being in the ascendancy, black will be assumed as its color, and water will be taken as a pattern for affairs. If the power of water arrives without being recognized, the operation, when its cycle is complete, will revert once more to earth" (pp. 160-161).

While the *Lü-shih Ch'un Ch'iu* does not specifically state that this passage belongs to the Tsou Yen school, corroboration is given by Li Shan (died A.D. 689), who says: "In Tsou Tzŭ's cycle of the Five Powers, each one follows that one which it cannot overcome. (The power of earth) is followed by the power of wood. The power of metal follows next; that of fire follows next; and that of water follows next."[1] Li Shan quotes also from the now lost *Tsou-tzŭ*: "The Five Powers, each of which follows that one by which it cannot be overcome, were for Yü (i.e., Shun), earth; for the Hsia dynasty, wood; for the Yin (i.e., Shang) dynasty, metal; and for the Chou dynasty, fire."[2] The order and theory of the elements as given in these two passages are the same as in the *Lü-shih Ch'un Ch'iu* quotation, which thus seems to represent Tsou Yen's actual doctrine.

According to this doctrine, the Five Elements or Powers are five natural forces, each of which has its period of rise and decay. Both natural and human events are under the control of that element which happens to be in the ascendancy, but when its cycle is finished and it declines, it is followed by the next force in the series that can overcome it, and which, in its turn, flourishes and has its cycle. Wood can overcome earth; metal can overcome wood; fire, metal; water, fire; and earth, water again; so that there is an endless cycle of elements. Changes in human history are but manifestations of these natural forces, each dynasty being represented by one 'Power' and the color and institutions which it assumes being determined by this Power. According to such a theory, the courses of nature

---

[1] Quoted by Li Shan from the *Ch'i Lüeh*, in his commentary to the *Wei Tu Fu* by Tso Ssŭ, in the *Wen Hsüan*.

[2] Quoted by Li Shan in his commentary to the *Ku-an-lu Chao-wang Pei-wen*, by Shen Hsiu-wen, also in the *Wen Hsüan*.

and of human events are interlocking, and history becomes a 'divine comedy.' Such was the viewpoint upon which were based all the various philosophies of history extant during the Han dynasty [1]

We do not know who composed the 'Grand Norm' (*Hung Fan* 洪 範) section now found in the *Shu Ching* (Book of History), or the 'Monthly Commands' (*Yüeh Ling* 月 令) which is found both in the *Lü-shih Ch'un Ch'iu* and in the *Li Chi* (Book of Rites). Both of them, however, are probably products of the *Yin-yang* and Five Elements school of the Warring States period. For example, the *Hung Fan* quotes an ancient noble as saying :

" I have heard that formerly Kun dammed up the waters of the deluge and thus disorganized the arrangement of the Five Elements. God (*Ti*) was angered by this and did not give him the Grand Norm in Nine Categories. Thus the essential social relationships were ruined. Kun was condemned to die. Then Yü (Kun's son) succeeded him and flourished. Thereupon Heaven gave to Yü the Grand Norm in Nine Categories, and set forth the proper order of social relationships. The first category is called : ' The Five Elements.' The second is called : ' Reverent practice of the five functions.' The third is called : ' Intensive practice of the eight regulations of government.' The fourth is called : ' Harmonious use of the five regulations of time.' The fifth is called : ' Establishment of the royal standard.' The sixth is called : ' Orderly practice of the three virtues.' The seventh is called : ' Intelligent practice of divination.' The eighth is called : ' Thoughtful following of various indications.' The ninth is called : ' Rewarding with five kinds of good and punishing with six forms of evil ' " (pp. 139-140).

The *Hung Fan* continues about these Five Elements :

" The first is named water, the second fire, the third wood, the fourth metal, the fifth earth. The nature of water is to moisten and descend ; of fire, to burn and ascend ; of wood, to be crooked and straight ; of metal, to yield and to be modified ; of earth, to provide for sowing and reaping. That which moistens and descends produces salt ; that which burns and ascends becomes bitter ; that which is crooked and straight becomes sour ; that which yields and is modified becomes acrid ; sowing and reaping produce sweetness " (pp. 140-141).

---

[1] An example of this is the way in which Ch'in Shih-huang (246-210 B.C.), believing that the newly established Ch'in dynasty ruled by virtue of the element water, " changed the beginning of the year and the congratulations to be made at court, both of these to begin from the first day of the tenth month. He honored black as the color for clothing, and for pennons and flags. He made six the standard number. Contract tallies and official hats were all of six inches, while the chariots were six feet. Six feet made one pace, and each equipage had six horses. The name of the (Yellow) river was changed to that of Powerful Water (*Te Shui* 德 水), because it was supposed that this marked the beginning of the power of the element water. With harshness and violence, and an extreme severity, everything was decided by the law. For by punishing and oppressing, by having neither human-heartedness nor kindliness, but conforming only to a strict justice, there would come an accord with the Five Powers." Cf. *Shih Chi*, ch. 6 (*Mém. hist.*, II, pp. 129-130).

About the five functions :

" The first is personal appearance ; the second, speech ; the third, vision ; the fourth, hearing ; the fifth, thought. Of personal appearance, let it be decorous ; of speech, let it follow reason ; of vision, let it be clear ; of hearing, let it be distinct ; of thought, let it be profound. Decorum produces gravity ; following reason produces regularity ; clearness produces intelligence ; distinctness produces deliberation ; profundity produces wisdom " (p. 141).

And about the ' thoughtful following of various indications ' :

" These are rain, sunshine, heat, cold, wind and seasonableness. When these five come fully and in their regular order, the various plants will be rich and luxuriant. If there is extreme excess in any one of them, disaster follows. If there is extreme deficiency in any one of them, disaster follows. The following are the favorable indications : gravity (of the sovereign) will be followed by seasonable rain ; his regularity will be followed by seasonable sunshine ; his intelligence by seasonable heat ; his deliberation by seasonable cold ; and his wisdom by seasonable wind. The following are the unfavorable indications : the madness (of the sovereign) will be followed by steady rain ; his insolence by steady sunshine ; his idleness by steady heat ; his haste by steady cold ; and his ignorance by steady winds " (pp. 147-148).

Thus the actions of the sovereign, if extreme or improper, can exert an influence upon the natural seasons, so that history becomes a ' divine comedy.' [1]

The author of the *Yüeh Ling*, one of the earliest Chinese almanacs, is also unknown to us. According to this work, each of the ' Five Powers ' has its period of ascendancy during the four seasons of the year. Thus the power in ascendancy in spring is wood ; in summer it is fire ; in autumn it is metal ; and in winter it is water. The places where the Emperor lives, the colors of his clothes, the kinds of food he eats, and the general conduct of his government are all rigidly determined according to the Power in ascendancy during that particular month of the year. This explains the title of this work, *Yüeh Ling* 月令, which means ' monthly commands.' If the Emperor should follow these monthly commands incorrectly, he would at once influence the seasons and cause all sorts of unusual phenomena to appear. For example :

" If in the first month of spring (the sovereign) follows the regulations pertaining to summer, the rain will be unseasonable, plants and trees will drop (their leaves) early, and the state will constantly have something of which to be afraid. If he follows the autumn regulations, his people will suffer great pestilences, violent wind and beating rain will both come together, and everywhere the orach,

---

[1] For evidence that the *Hung Fan* is a product of the Warring States period, rather than of earlier date, *cf. Hung Fan Su-cheng*, by Liu Chieh, in the *Ku Shih Pien*, Vol. V.

fescue, darnel and southernwood will spring up together. If he follows the winter regulations, excessive rains will cause great damage, snow and frost will cover everything in great abundance, and grains which have been planted will yield no harvest "(p. 257).

Here, again, we find the close connection supposed to exist between the ruler's conduct and natural phenomena. In the *Hung Fan*, however, there is mention of the existence of a Supreme God who ' would be angered ' and so send down reward or punishment. The *Yüeh Ling*, on the contrary, says that each month has its own Emperor (*Ti* 帝) and ' Spirit ' (*Shen* 神). " In the first month of spring," for example, " its sovereign is T'ai Hao, and its spirit is Kou Mang " (pp. 330-331). Are the influences imparted by human affairs upon the seasons, mechanically produced and received ? Or are they awesome manifestations produced by some God who becomes angry because the human sovereign acts in a way that is improper ? The former view implies a mechanistic universe ; the latter, a teleological one. The *Yin-yang* and Five Elements school seems never to have realized the breach lying between these two concepts, and has always vacillated between them, sometimes toward the one, sometimes the other.¹

More about the interaction of human and natural events is given in the *Kuan-tzŭ* (ch. 40) :

" Therefore the *yin* and the *yang* are the great principles of Heaven and Earth. The four seasons are the great path of the *yin* and the *yang*. Punishment and reward are the harmonizers of the four seasons. When punishment and reward are in harmony with the seasons, happiness is produced ; when they disregard them, there comes calamity. But what will (the sovereign) do in spring, summer, autumn and winter ?

" The (correlates of the) east are the stars. Its season is spring. Its influence is the wind. Wind produces wood and bone. Its characteristics are those of a time of joyousness, plenty and regular growth. The duties to be performed are to put in order and cleanse the places of the spirits, and respectfully to use presents in their worship ; to make the *yang* supreme ; to repair the dikes ; to cultivate and plant the fields ; adjust properly the bridges and dams ; repair canals ; repair rooms and gutters ; make compromises of resentments ; pardon those who have sinned ; and open communication between the four quarters. Thereupon the soft wind and sweet rains will come ; the common people will live to a great age ; and the various animals will flourish. This is the virtue of the stars. . . .

---

¹ The *Yüeh Ling* fails to designate the time when the power of earth is in the ascendancy. This is because, there being only four seasons in the year, one element necessarily remains left over, for which there can be no correlate. But in the *Huai-nan-tzŭ* (ch. 5) it is stated that the power of earth gains ascendancy in the third month of summer. This is a later modification made by the *Yin-yang* school.

" The (correlate of the) south is the sun. Its season is summer.
Its influence is *yang*. *Yang* produces fire and vapors. Its characteristics are those of giving and pleasure. . . . This is the virtue of
the sun.

" The (correlate of the) central quarter is the earth. The virtue
of earth acts back and forth throughout the four seasons as an assistant
(to the other four stable elements), and wind and rain give it additional strength. It produces skin and flesh. Its characteristics are
those of harmony and equability. It is central, correct and
impartial. It assists the four seasons. Thus through it spring
produces and engenders ; summer nourishes and matures ; autumn
collects and receives ; and winter closes up and stores away. . . .
This is the virtue for the year. . . .

" The (correlates of the) west are the stars of the zodiac. Its
season is autumn. Its influence is *yin*. *Yin* produces metal,
horns and nails. Its characteristics are those of sadness, quietude,
uprightness, severity and compliance. Occupying it, one dares not
be dissolute. . . . This is the virtue of the stars of the zodiac. . . .

" The (correlate of the) north is the moon. Its season is winter.
Its influence is that of cold. Cold produces water and blood. Its
characteristics are those of purity, scattering, mild anger and secret
storing up. . . . This is the virtue of the moon. . . .

" Therefore withering in spring, flourishing in autumn, thunder
in winter and frost in summer, are all perversions of these forces.
When punishments and rewards become mixed up and lose their
orderliness, perversions of the forces come ever more frequently.
And when this happens, the country suffers many calamities.
Therefore a Sage-king establishes government in accordance with
the seasons ; accompanies education with the art of war ; and performs
sacrifices to display virtue. It is through these three that the Sage-
king can put himself into union with the movements of Heaven and
Earth " (*chüan* 14, pp. 4-6.)

In this union of government with the movements of Heaven and
Earth, we see again the ideas of the *Yin-yang* school.

A very curious idea is expounded in the *Kuan-tzŭ* (ch. 39) :
" The Earth is the origin of all things and the root of the living.
It is the producer of the beautiful and ugly, worthy and unworthy,
stupid and eminent. Water is the blood of the Earth, and flows
through its muscles and veins. Therefore it is said that water is
something that has complete faculties. . . . It is accumulated in
Heaven and Earth, and stored up in the various things (of the world).
It comes forth in metal and stone, and is concentrated in living
creatures. Therefore it is said that water is something spiritual.
Being accumulated in plants and trees, their stems gain their orderly
progression from it, their flowers obtain their proper number, and
their fruits gain their proper measure. The bodies of birds and

beasts, through having it, become fat and large; their feathers and hair become luxuriant, and their stripes and markings are made apparent. The reason why creatures can realize their potentialities and grow to the norm is that the inner regulation of their water is in accord. . . .

" Man is water, and when the producing elements of male and female unite, liquid flows into forms. . . . Thus water becomes accumulated in jade, and the nine virtues appear. It congeals to form man, and his nine openings and five viscera appear. This is its refined essence. . . . What is it, then, that has complete faculties ? It is water. There is not one of the various things which is not produced through it. It is only he who knows how to rely (on its principles) who can act correctly. . . .

" The waters of the state of Ch'i are rapid and changeable and so its people are greedy, careless and delight in valor. The waters of Ch'u are gentle and clear, and so its people are light minded and cunning. The waters of Yüeh are turbid, heavy and rich, and so its people are stupid, jealous and dirty. The waters of Ch'in are stagnant and mixed together, and so its people are greedy, quarrelsome, deceptive and delight in trouble. . . .

" Hence the solution for the Sage who would transform the world lies in water. Therefore when water is uncontaminated, men's hearts are upright. When water is pure, the people's hearts are at ease. Men's hearts being upright, their desires do not become dissolute. The people's hearts being upright, their conduct is without evil. Hence the Sage when he rules the world, does not teach men one by one, or house by house, but takes water as his key " (*chüan* 14, pp. 1-3).

In this passage water is made the origin of all things, so that the regulation of water becomes the means for the ruling of men. If one wishes to reform the world one must reform men's hearts, which can be done by changing the quality of the water. This peculiar doctrine also seems to have originated in the *Yin-yang* school.

The *Lü-shih Ch'un Ch'iu* (XIII, 1) has a very interesting passage, further developing Tsou Yen's geographical speculations, in which it says : " Heaven has nine fields ; Earth has nine continents ; the land has nine mountains ; the mountains have nine passes. There are nine lakes, eight kinds of winds, and of waters there are six rivers " (p. 157). The same chapter continues :

" The total territory contained within the four seas is 28,000 *li* from east to west, and 26,000 *li* from south to north.[1] The water courses are eight thousand *li* long, and the recipient of these waters also extends eight thousand *li*. There are six connecting valleys, six hundred noted rivers, three thousand irrigation courses, and more

---

[1] Three *li* 里 are roughly equivalent to one English mile.—TR.

than ten thousand lesser waterways. Between the four extreme limits (of the world) there are from east to west 597,000 *li*, and from south to north also 597,000 *li*. The stars of the zodiac move with the heavens, but the axis of Heaven does not itself move. At the winter solstice the sun travels in a distant path, and moves around in a circle through all four quarters (in the sky). This is called 'mysterious light' (*hsüan ming* 玄 明). At the summer solstice the sun travels in a near path and is right above. Beneath the axis of Heaven there is no day or night. To the south of the (country of the) white people, beneath the hardwood trees, there are no shadows in the middle of the day, and when one calls there is no echo. For this is the center of Heaven and Earth.

"Heaven, Earth and all things are like the body of one man, and this is what is called the Great Unity (*ta t'ung* 大 同). The multiplicity of ears, eyes, noses and mouths and the multiplicity of the five grains and cold and heat : this is what is called the Multiplicity of Differences (*chung i* 衆 異). Thus all things are made complete. Heaven makes all things flourish. The Sage observes them, so as thereby to examine his own kind. He finds the explanation of how Heaven and Earth became concrete forms, how thunder and lightning are produced, how the *yin* and the *yang* form the essence of things, and how people, birds and beasts are in a state of peace" (pp. 159-160).

Here, again, we find theories resembling those of Tsou Yen's nine large continents, and apparently also derived from the *Yin-yang* school.

The state of Ch'i, occupying the present province of Shantung, was the center of the *Yin-yang* and Five Elements school. This was because, bordering the sea, its people had a comparatively good opportunity to see and hear new and strange things, with the consequence that they were noted for their fabulous and fanciful stories. Hence whenever such stories are referred to in the literature of the Warring States period, they are usually attributed to natives of Ch'i. For example, someone once asked Mencius about the statement that " Shun stood with his face to the south, and Yao, at the head of the feudal lords, appeared before him at court with his face to the north." Mencius replied :   " These are the words of some uncultivated person from the east of Ch'i " (*Mencius*, V*a*, 4). The *Chuang-tzŭ* (ch. 1) also states :   " The *Hsieh* 諧 of Ch'i is a record of extraordinary occurrences " (p. 1). Evidently the fantastic stories of the people of Ch'i, like the naïveté of the natives of Sung, were both notorious among the people of that time. The chapter on geography in the *Ch'ien Han Shu* states :

" The territory of Ch'i is under the divided spheres (of control) of the stars Hsü and Wei. . . . To the present time (the people of) this region have delighted in the arts of the classics, boasted of a reputation for merit, been easy-going, liberal and sufficiently learned.

Their failings have been extravagant boastfulness and clannishness. Their words and conduct do not agree. They are empty, false and do not accord with fact " (ch. 28*b*, pp. 32-33).

This indicates that even in Han times the people of Ch'i were still noted for their boastfulness and story-telling proclivities. It was these characteristics which made possible the appearance of such imaginative doctrines as those of Tsou Yen and his followers. The *Shih Chi* (ch. 28) states :

" It is from the time of Kings Wei (357-320) and Hsüan (319-301) of Ch'i that the followers of the Tsou scholars discussed and wrote about the cyclic revolutions of the Five Powers. When (the King of) Ch'in became Emperor (in 221 B.C.), the men of Ch'i offered (these theories) to him, and so Shih-huang made use of them. As for Sung Wu-chi, Cheng Po-chiao, Ch'ung Shang and Hsien-men Tzŭ-kao, these were all men of Yen (occupying the present Hopei). They practised methods to gain magical immortality, so that their bodies would escape, dissolve and be tranformed, relying for this upon their services to divine beings. Tsou Yen, with his *Chü Yün*, dealing with the *yin* and the *yang*, was famous among the feudal lords. And the magicians (*fang shih* 方 士) who lived along the shores of the sea in Ch'i and Yen transmitted his arts, but were unable to comprehend them. Thereupon there arose innumerable persons who were skilled in extraordinary prodigies, in deceiving flatteries, and who knew how to win people over by evil means " (*Mém. hist.*, III, ii, pp. 435-436).

It will be remembered that in its biography of Tsou Yen, the *Shih Chi* states that he travelled to Yen, where he received special honors. Thus the doctrines of the *Yin-yang* and Five Elements school appear to have been transmitted from Ch'i to Yen, and later with the tremendous increase of magicians of the type mentioned in the foregoing quotation, the Ch'in and Han dynasties fell largely under the influence of the school.

CHAPTER VIII

LAO TZŬ AND HIS SCHOOL OF TAOISM

1—LAO TAN AND LI ERH

The book known as the *Lao-tzŭ* 老 子, but popularly called the *Tao Te Ching* 道 德 經, is traditionally said to have been written by an older contemporary of Confucius, Lao Tan 老 聃. To-day, however, it is generally believed that the *Lao-tzŭ* was composed after Confucius, that is, sometime during the Warring States period. This has already been discussed in detail by many scholars and so need not be gone into at length here.[1] What has already been said in the present book about conditions in the world of learning in ancient China, moreover, proves that the *Lao-tzŭ* must be a product of this later time, because : (1) Prior to Confucius there was no one writing in a private, non-official capacity ; hence the *Lao-tzŭ* cannot be earlier than the *Lun Yü*.[2] (2) The literary form of the *Lao-tzŭ* is not that of question and answer, and, therefore, is probably later than the *Lun Yü* and *Mencius*. (3) The style of the *Lao-tzŭ* is clearly that of a ' canon ' (*ching* 經), for which reason it probably dates from the Warring States period.[3] If one were to bring forward but one of these three points, in addition to the proofs already give by earlier scholars, one might be justly accused of committing the fallacy of begging the question. Taking them together, however, it is surely no accident that the style and doctrines of the *Lao-tzŭ*, with the other evidence, all point to its being a product of the Warring States period.

The account of the six philosophic schools contained in the *Shih Chi* (ch. 130) states :

" The Taoist school urged men to unity of spirit, teaching that all activities should be in harmony with the unseen, with abundant liberality toward all things in nature. As to practice, they accept the orderly sequence of nature from the *Yin-yang* school, gather the good points of Confucians and Mohists, and combine with these the important points of the (school of) Names and Law. In accordance with the changes of the seasons, they respond to the development of natural objects. Their achievements fit everywhere. Their ideas are simple and easily carried out. They perform but little, yet their achievements are numerous " (*Aids*, p. 51).

---

[1] See Ts'ui Shu (1740-1816), *Chu-ssŭ K'ao-hsin Lu*; Wang Chung (1744-1794), *Lao-tzŭ K'ao-i*; and Liang Ch'i-ch'ao (1873-1929), *P'ing Hu Shih chih Chung-kuo Che-hsüeh Shih Ta-kang*, in the *Liang Jen-kung Hsüeh-shu Chiang-yen Chi*, first collection.

[2] *Cf.* ch. 2, sect. 1, pp. 7-8.

[3] *Cf.* ch. 5, sect. 2, pp. 80-81.

Here it is clearly stated that the Taoist school was of late origin, since it was in this way able to adopt the good points of each of the other schools. The fact that later ages have, on the other hand, maintained that the Taoist school was the one out of which the other schools arose, indicates the scanty attention paid to this piece of philosophic criticism, written by Ssŭ-ma T'an (died about 110 B.C.), and included in the *Shih Chi* by his son, the great historian, Ssŭ-ma Ch'ien.[1]

The mistake probably originated from the fact that Ssŭ-ma Ch'ien had confused an historical person, Li Erh 李 耳, with a legendary person, Lao Tan. The real founder of the philosophy found in the *Lao-tzŭ* is Li Erh, a man who lived during the Warring States period; the ' Vast Perfect One of old ' who is spoken of in tradition is Lao Tan. It is impossible to know whether this Lao Tan was actually an historical person or not, whereas Li Erh's genealogy is given by Ssŭ-ma Ch'ien with considerable exactness. The biography of Lao Tzŭ in the *Shih Chi* states :

" Lao Tzŭ was a native of Ch'ü-jen hamlet, in Li-hsiang, in the district of K'u, in the state of Ch'u. His proper name was Erh, his pseudonym was Tan 聃, and his family name was Li. . . . Lao Tzŭ practised the Way (*Tao*) and the Power (*Te* 德). His doctrine aimed at self-effacement and namelessness. . . . Lao Tzŭ was a recluse gentleman. His son was named Tsung. Tsung became a general of the state of Wei, and was enfieffed at Tuan-kan. Tsung's son was Chu and Chu's son was Kung. Kung's great-great-grandson was Chia, who held office under Hsiao Wen-ti (179-157) of the Han dynasty. Chia's son, Chieh, became grand tutor to An, prince of Chiao-hsi, and so moved his home to Ch'i " (ch. 63, pp. 1-4).

Such circumstantial detail shows that Li Erh must have actually existed. Ssŭ-ma Ch'ien, however, has confused him with the legendary Lao Tan, with the result that all sorts of fantastic and impossible legends have crept into Li Erh's biography in the *Shih Chi*. For example : " As to Lao Tzŭ, . . no one knows where he died. Some say that Lao Lai Tzŭ 老 萊 子 was also a man of Ch'u. . . . It seems that Lao Tzŭ lived to be more than one hundred and sixty years, and some say that he was more than two hundred years old. . . . One hundred and twenty-nine years after the death of Confucius, the histories record that the historian Tan of the House of Chou had an interview with Duke Hsien of Ch'in (384-362). . . . Some say that

---

[1] Dr. Hu Shih has said that the Taoist school mentioned in this passage is merely the Taoist school as it existed at the beginning of the Han dynasty, and hence is the same as what the *I-wen Chih* chapter in the *Ch'ien Han Shu* calls the Miscellaneous school (*tsa chia* 雜 家), rather than the original school of Lao Tzŭ and Chuang Tzŭ. Yet in the classification of schools as given in the *I-wen Chih*, both a Taoist school and a Miscellaneous school are listed. Hence it is obvious that the Miscellaneous school cannot be made to include Lao Tzŭ and Chuang Tzŭ, who are the men referred to by Ssŭ-ma T'an when he speaks of the Taoist school.

this Tan was the same as Lao Tzŭ, and others say he was not. No one in the world knows if it is correct or not." It is evident, then, that the opening and closing portions of Lao Tzŭ's biography are fact, whereas the middle part which has just been quoted is myth.¹

Yet Ssŭ-ma Ch'ien's mistake is not entirely unjustified, for as has been stated, Li Erh was ' a recluse gentleman ' and ' his doctrine aimed at self-effacement and namelessness.' Hence it is natural that when he propounded his ideas he did not wish to proclaim them under his own name. Contemporaneous with him apparently existed the legend about a certain Lao Tan, the ' Vast Perfect One of old,' and so Li Erh seized an opportunity to conceal his doctrines under the name of Lao Tan, thinking, in this way, to hide his own name, and at the same time gain for his principles the enhanced reputation that goes with antiquity. This is why the *Hsün-tzŭ*, *Lü-shih Ch'un Ch'iu* and *Chuang-tzŭ* (ch. 33) all attribute the *Lao-tzŭ's* doctrines to Lao Tan. While Ssŭ-ma Ch'ien was aware that Li Erh had been the originator of these doctrines, he was led astray by the popular talk about Lao Tan as their author, and so wrongly assumed Lao Tan and Li Erh to be one person. While accepting Ssŭ-ma Ch'ien's statement that Li Erh founded the doctrines of the *Lao-tzŭ*, therefore, we must recognize that though Li Erh is an historical figure, Lao Tan is rather legendary.

It is more than probable, however, that the *Lao-tzŭ* as it exists to-day has suffered changes through the editing and re-arranging made by the Han scholars, so that it cannot really be said to be the work of one man. In the present chapter, therefore, I discuss the ideas in the *Lao-tzŭ* as a whole, and make no attempt to distinguish in it the ideas of individual men.

2—LAO TZŬ AND CHUANG TZŬ

The doctrines of the *Lao-tzŭ* are criticized by the *Hsün-tzŭ*; described in the *Chuang-tzŭ* (ch. 33) ; ' explained ' and ' illustrated ' in the *Han-fei-tzŭ*; and quoted by travelling speech-makers mentioned in the *Chan Kuo Ts'e*.² From this we may see that its doctrines were already well-known during the Warring States period.

The term, ' Taoist school,' did not exist prior to the Han dynasty, and the philosophies of Lao Tzŭ and Chuang Tzŭ, now grouped under that name, were not without difference. It has already been said that the philosophy of Lao Tzŭ is that of Yang Chu developed one step, and that of Chuang Tzŭ is Yang Chu's philosophy advanced yet another

---

¹ In this paragraph I follow the general ideas advanced by Liu Ju-lin in his *Chou Ch'in Chu-tzŭ K'ao* (An examination of the Chou and Ch'in Philosophers).

² As in *Ch'i Ts'e*, IV, 5, which states : "Lao Tzŭ says, ' What is noble makes inferior position its root. What is high makes lowliness its foundation. That is why marquises and kings refer to themselves as The Orphan, The Needy, The Ill-provided, though they are not orphans.' " This is a quotation from *Lao-tzŭ*, ch. 39.

step.¹ For this reason the *Chuang-tzŭ* (in ch. 33), which groups together all thinkers holding similar ideas, such as Sung K'eng and Yin Wen, is careful to differentiate between Lao Tan and Chuang Chou. This chapter says:

" To regard the fundamental as the essence, and things as coarse ; to regard accumulation as deficiency ; to dwell quietly alone with the spiritual and the intelligent : these were some aspects of the Way (*Tao*) of the ancients. Kuan Yin and Lao Tan heard of these and were delighted with them. They built their system upon the principle of eternal Non-being (*wu* 無) and eternal Being (*yu* 有), and centered it upon the idea of Great Oneness (*t'ai i* 太 一). Their outward expression was weakness and humility. Pure emptiness that yet did not destroy objective things was for them actuality.

" Kuan Yin said : ' Establish nothing in regard to oneself. Let things be what they are, move like water, rest like a mirror, respond like an echo, pass quickly like the non-existent, and be quiet as purity. Those who agree are harmonious. Those who gain, lose. Do not precede others, always follow them.'

" Lao Tan said : ' Know manhood, preserve womanhood. Become a channel for the world. Conscious of one's whiteness, endure disgrace and become a valley for the world.' ²

" Men all seek the first. He, alone, sought the last. He said : ' Accept the world's refuse.' Men all seek the actual (*shih* 實). He alone took the empty (*hsü* 虛). Without storing anything, he thereby had abundance, and his abundance was unique. His actions were effortless and without waste. He did nothing and laughed at ingenuity. Men all seek happiness. He, alone, sought completion in adaptation. He said : ' Only be blameless.' He regarded the deep as the fundamental ; moderation as the rule. He said : ' The hard will be crushed ; the sharp will be blunted.' ³ He was always generous and tolerant toward things. He was not aggressive towards men. This may be called the height of perfection. Oh, Kuan Yin and Lao Tan ! They were great perfect men of antiquity ! " (pp. 447-448).

The *Chuang-tzŭ* continues about Chuang Tzŭ himself :

" Silent and formless, changing and impermanent, now dead, now living, equal with Heaven and Earth, moving with the spiritual and the intelligent ; disappearing where ? suddenly whither ? ; all things are what they are, no one more attractive than others : these were some of the aspects of the Way (*Tao*) of the ancients. Chuang Chou 莊 周 heard of them and was delighted. In strange and vague expression, wild and extravagant language, indefinite terms, he indulged himself in his own ideas without partiality or peculiar appearance. He regarded the world as submerged and unclear (ignorant), so that it

---

¹ *Cf.* p. 143.
² *Cf. Lao-tzŭ*, ch. 28, of which this is an adaptation.—TR.
³ Reminiscent of *Lao-tzŭ*, chs. 4 and 56.—TR.

could not be spoken to seriously. So he put his ideas into indefinite cup-like words, ascribing them to others for authority and illustrating with stories for variety. He came and went alone with the spirit of Heaven and Earth, but had no sense of pride in his superiority to all things.

" He did not condemn either right or wrong, so he was able to get along with ordinary people. His writings, though they have a grand style, are not opposed to things and so are harmless. His phrases, though full of irregularities, are yet attractive and full of humor. The richness of his ideas cannot be exhausted. Above he roams with the Creator (*Tsao-wu-che* 造 物 者). Below he makes friends of those who, without beginning or end, are beyond life and death. In regard to the fundamental he was comprehensive and great, profound and free. In regard to the essential he may be called the harmonious adapter to higher things. Nevertheless, in his response to change and his interpretation of things, his reasons were inexhaustible and not derived from his predecessors. Indefinite and obscure, he is not one to be exhausted ! " (pp. 448-450).

The differences between Lao Tzǔ and Chuang Tzǔ become manifest from these passages, in which only the words, ' To dwell quietly alone with the spiritual and the intelligent ' ; and, ' He came and went alone with the spirit of Heaven and Earth,' are similar in idea. In other respects, we see that Lao Tzǔ's philosophy emphasizes distinctions between what precedes and what follows, womanhood and manhood, glory and disgrace, emptiness and the actual, etc. Knowing that ' the hard will be crushed, the sharp will be blunted,' it stresses the finding of a way whereby not to be thus crushed and blunted. Chuang Tzǔ's philosophy, on the other hand, is one ' without beginning and end, beyond life and death.' What the *Lao-tzǔ* stresses, Chuang Tzǔ evidently feels requires no stressing.

During the early part of the Han dynasty, the ideas of Lao Tzǔ became widespread, whereas it was only during the latter part of the Han that those of Chuang Tzǔ became popular. Ch'en Li (1810-1882) has pointed out that coincident with the rise of the Han dynasty, the doctrines of Huang-Lao (i.e., of Huang-ti, the Yellow Emperor, whom the Taoists considered as their founder, and of Lao Tzǔ), were very widespread, and were used by both Emperors Wen (179-157) and Ching (156-141) in government. Toward the end of the Han dynasty, however, the term Huang-Lao was replaced by that of Lao-Chuang. The commentators on the *Lao-tzǔ* who lived during the Former Han period thus make no mention of Chuang Tzǔ, whereas the great commentaries on Chuang Tzǔ have all been written during the Chin period (A.D. 265-420), the dynasty which followed the Han.[1]

---

[1] *Cf.* his *Tung-shu Tu-shu Chi, chüan* 12.

In his criticism of the six philosophic schools, Ssŭ-ma T'an says of the Taoists : " In accordance with the changes of the seasons, they respond to the development of natural things. Their achievements fit everywhere. Their ideas are simple and easily carried out. They perform but little, yet their achievements are numerous." And the *I-wen Chih* defines Taoism as "the method of the ruler on his throne " (*Aids*, p. 61). From this it would seem that the Han scholars, when they spoke of Taoism, specifically had in mind the philosophy of the *Lao-tzŭ*, which is concerned with how one should respond to the world. That of Chuang Tzŭ, on the other hand, rises to a plane above human affairs. When it is said of the early Han Emperors, for example, that they ruled through quiescence (*ching* 靜) and non-activity (*wu wei* 無 為), this simply means that they were following the tenets of Lao Tzŭ. With the latter part of the Han dynasty, however, when much emphasis began to be laid on 'mysterious emptiness' (*hsüan hsü* 玄 虛), Lao Tzŭ also came to be interpreted in the spirit of Chuang Tzŭ, and was linked with him, though originally, their philosophies were quite distinct from each other.

The name, Taoism, was first coined by Han scholars, who used it to include both Lao Tzŭ and Chuang Tzŭ, because their doctrines, although not identical, were at least agreed in opposing the traditional thought and institutions of their time. Another point of agreement was the fact that the two fundamental conceptions of which they spoke, the Way (*Tao*) and the Power (*Te*), had for both men the same meaning. The fact that Ssŭ-ma T'an terms this school the School of the Way and the Power (*Tao Te chia* 道 德 家), indicates that he, too, considered these two concepts (the Way and the Power) as forming the basis of Taoism.

3—THE SPIRIT OF THE PEOPLE OF CH'U

Li Erh was a native of Ch'u, a large state on the southern periphery of the civilized China of ancient times, occupying much of present Honan, Hunan, Hupeh and Anhuei. It was in this state, according to the *Shih Chi*, that Confucius met most of the recluses who are mentioned in the *Lun Yü*. The speech about a naturalistic Heaven, which has been quoted in a preceding chapter,[1] was also made by a native of the south, and has certain similarities with the ideas of Lao Tzŭ. Ch'u was inhabited by a people largely non-Chinese in origin, who had risen to prominence later than those of the other feudal states of China, and who were comparatively lacking in culture. Mencius once speaks of "a shrike-tongued barbarian of the south, whose doctrines are not those of the early kings" (*Mencius*, IIIa, 4, para. 14), and remarks again : " Ch'en Liang was of

---

[1] *Cf.* pp. 32-33.

Ch'u extraction. Pleased with the doctrines of the Duke of Chou and of Confucius, he came northward to the Middle Kingdom and studied them. Among the scholars of the northern regions, there was perhaps none who excelled him " (*ibid.*, para. 12). This indicates how, at that time, persons of Ch'u who wished to acquire the Chou culture, had to travel northward to obtain it.

If the Ch'u people did not possess all the advantages of Chou culture, however, they also did not suffer from its restraints, with the result that many extremely novel ideas sprang up among them. The chapter on geography in the *Ch'ien Han Shu* states : " Ch'u has an abundance derived from the Chiang (Yangtze Kiang) and Han rivers, and from streams, marshes, mountains and forests. . . . .Its food products are always sufficient. Therefore (its people) make little exertion, delight in life, and neglect to store anything. They have sufficient for food and drink, without thought for cold or starvation ; on the other hand, there is no family worth one thousand ounces (of gold). They believe in witches (*wu* 巫) and spirits (*kuei* 鬼), and lay emphasis on excessive sacrifices " (ch. 28b, pp. 3-6).

Despite what this last sentence says, it was still possible for such a man as Ch'ü Yüan (died c. 288 B.C.), who was a native of Ch'u, to describe in his *Li Sao*, which is one of China's most imaginative poems, how during his long wanderings he was pulled along by supernatural beings. His attitude toward such beings is poetical rather than religious. The *T'ien Wen* (Questions on Heaven), another poem in the collection of Ch'u poems of which the *Li Sao* forms a part, shows even greater skepticism, by asking all sorts of questions about legends on men and spirits, and making inquiries as to how the universe came into being and how the sun and moon revolve. Perhaps it was precisely because the the people of Ch'u were fervent believers in witches and spirits and laid much stress on sacrifice, as described in the *Ch'ien Han Shu* quotation, that a certain group of their intellectuals arose in revolt.

All of the so-called recluses were radically opposed to the government of their time. This went so far that the followers of Hsü Hsing, who came from the south, not only opposed the particular government of their own time, but all the political and social institutions that were traditionally handed down. The so-called Taoists who lived during the latter years of the Chou dynasty and the beginning of the Ch'in, were also men of this type, and their most important writings are contained in the two books called the *Lao-tzŭ* and *Chuang-tzŭ*.[1]

---

[1] The Japanese scholar, Koyanagi Shikita, lists a large number of recluses, all natives of Ch'u, mentioned in such works as the *Ch'ien Han Shu, Lun Yü, Han-fei-tzŭ, Lü-shih Ch'un Ch'iu*, etc. He then goes on to indicate a number of similarities in thought between passages in the *Yüan Yu* and the *Yü Fu* (poems by Ch'ü Yüan or his followers), and the *Lao-tzŭ* and *Chuang-tzŭ*. Cf. his article, ' The Ancient State of Ch'u as it appears in Cultural History ' (in Japanese), in the *Toho Gakuho*, Tokyo, No. 1, March, 1931, pp. 196-228.

4—THE WAY AND THE POWER

The Heaven of early times was a ruling or presiding one. Belief in such a Heaven had been acknowledged by Confucius and advocated by Mo Tzǔ. With Mencius, however, we find that what is called Heaven is at times only ethical. That is, while it contains always a moral and idealistic significance, it is no longer an anthropomorphic God laying down moral laws. The *Lao-tzǔ* goes a step further by saying, " Heaven and Earth are not kind (*jen*)"(ch. 5), thus denying Heaven's ethical and idealistic significance altogether.

The word *tao* 道, one of the most important terms in Chinese philosophy, has a primary meaning of 'road' or 'way.' Beginning with this primary meaning, it assumed already in ancient times a metaphorical significance, as the 'Way of man,' that is, human morality, conduct or truth. During this time, its meaning was always restricted to human affairs, whereas when we come to the *Lao-tzǔ*, we find the word *tao* being given a metaphysical meaning. That is to say, the assumption is made that for the universe to have come into being, there must exist an all-embracing first principle, which is called *Tao*. The *Han-fei-tzǔ*, in its chapter on 'Explaining Lao Tzǔ' (ch. 20), says :

" *Tao* is that whereby all things are so, and with which all principles agree. Principles (*li* 理) are the markings (*wen* 文) of completed things. *Tao* is that whereby all things become complete. Therefore it is said that *Tao* is what gives principles. When things have their principles, the one (thing) cannot be the other. . . . All things have each their own different principle, whereas *Tao* brings the principles of all things into single agreement. Therefore it can be both one thing and another, and is not in one thing only " (*chüan* 6, p. 7).

Each thing, that is, has its own individual principle, but the first all-embracing principle whereby all things are produced is *Tao*. The *Lao-tzǔ* says :

" There is a thing, formless yet complete. Before Heaven and Earth it existed. Without sound, without substance, it stands alone without changing. It is all pervading and unfailing. One may think of it as the mother of all beneath Heaven. We do not know its name, but we term it *Tao*. Forced to give an appellation to it, I should say it was Great " (ch. 25).

" Great *Tao* drifts about. It may go this way or that. The ten thousand creatures owe their existence to it, and it does not disown them. Its achievements are completed while it is nameless. Like a garment it covers the ten thousand things and brings them up, but makes no claim to be master over them " (ch. 34).

What *Tao* accomplishes is not done purposefully, but is simply spontaneously so. Therefore :

"Man's standard is Earth. Earth's standard is Heaven. Heaven's standard is *Tao*. *Tao's* standard is the spontaneous (*tzŭ jan* 自 然)" (ch. 25).

Tao being the all-embracing first principle through which all things are brought into being, *Tao's* actions are the actions of all things. At the same time it is through *Tao* that all things are enabled to be all things. The *Lao-tzŭ* says: "*Tao* never does, yet through it all things are done" [1] (ch. 37).

Thus understood, *Tao*, since it is the first principle of all things, cannot itself be a 'thing' in the way that Heaven and Earth and 'the ten thousand things' are things. Objects can be said to be Being (*yu* 有), but *Tao* is not an object, and so may only be spoken of as Non-being (*wu* 無). At the same time, however, *Tao* is what has brought the universe into being, and hence in one way it may also be said to be Being. For this reason *Tao* is spoken of as both Being and Non-being. Non-being refers to its essence; Being to its function. Therefore the *Lao-tzŭ* says:

"The *Tao* that may be called *Tao* [2] is not the invariable *Tao*. The names that can be named are not invariable names. Non-being is the term given to that from which Heaven and Earth sprang. Being is the term given to the mother that rears the ten thousand things (on earth). Of the invariable Non-being, we wish to see its secret essences. Of the invariable Being, we wish to see its borders. These two have issued together but are different in name. The two together we call the Mystery (*hsüan* 玄). It is the Mystery of Mysteries, the Doorway of all secret essences" (ch. 1).

Being and Non-being have both issued from *Tao*, and thus are two aspects of *Tao*. The *Lao-tzŭ* says again:

"*Tao* produced Oneness. Oneness produced duality. Duality evolved into trinity, and trinity evolved into the ten thousand (i.e., infinite number of) things. The ten thousand things support the *yin* and embrace the *yang*.[3] It is on the blending of the breaths (of the *yin* and the *yang*) that their harmony depends" (ch. 42).

"Heaven and Earth and the ten thousand things are produced from Being; Being is the product of Non-being" (ch. 40).

The *Chuang-tzŭ* (ch. 33), in its description of Lao Tzŭ and Kuan Yin, says that they "built their system upon the principle of eternal Non-being and eternal Being, and centered it upon the idea of Great Oneness" (p. 447). Being and Non-being are the two aspects of *Tao*, and the Great Oneness is the same as the Oneness referred to in the phrase, '*Tao* produced Oneness.' When it is said that Heaven and Earth and the ten thousand things are produced from Being, this 'Being' is, perhaps, the same as the 'Great Oneness';

---

[1] *Wu wei erh wu pu wei* 無 爲 而 無 不 爲.
[2] Literally, 'that may be *tao*-ed,' the word *tao* being used here as a verb.—Tr.
[3] i.e., their every mode is determined by the interplay of these two forces.—Tr.

the duality spoken of is evidently Heaven and Earth ; and the trinity is the *yin*, the *yang*, and the harmony resulting from the interaction of these two. The same idea is found in the *Chuang-tzŭ* (ch. 21) which states : " The perfect *yin* is majestically passive. The perfect *yang* is powerfully active. Passivity emanates from Earth. Activity proceeds from Heaven. The interaction of the two forms a harmony from which things are produced " ' (pp. 266-267).

I have said that *Tao* is Non-being. Nevertheless, this only means ' Non-being ' as opposed to the ' Being ' of material objects, and so it is not a mere zero or nothingness. For how could *Tao* be nothingness when at the same time it is the first all-embracing principle whereby all things are produced ? The *Lao-tzŭ* says :

" *Tao* as a thing is impalpable, incommensurable. Incommensurable, impalpable, yet latent in it are forms. Impalpable, incommensurable, yet within it are entities. Shadowy it is and dim, yet within it there is an essence. This essence is extremely pure, but none the less efficacious " (ch. 21).

' Impalpable, incommensurable ' means that it does not have material existence ; while ' forms,' ' entities ' and ' essence ' mean that it is not the Non-being of a zero. On the words in the fourteenth chapter, ' A shape without shape, a thing without form,' the noted commentator Wang Pi (A.D. 226-249) writes in similar vein : " If we want to say it is Non-being, yet things from it gain completeness. If we want to say it is Being, yet we do not see its form."

Tao being the first all-embracing principle, it is not an individual thing, and so it is difficult to designate it by such a name as would be used to designate an object having individual existence. This is because all names have a power of limitation and determination. When we say a thing is this, it is thereby defined to be this and not that. *Tao*, on the other hand, is ' all pervading and unfailing ' ; it is here and it is also there ; it is this and it is also that. Therefore the *Lao-tzŭ* says :

" *Tao* is eternally nameless " (ch. 32).

" *Tao* is concealed in the nameless " (ch. 41).

As the *Han-fei-tzŭ* says : " *Tao* brings the principles of all things into single agreement. Therefore it can be both one thing and another, and is not in one thing only." It is fundamentally incapable of having any name applied to it, and so when we term it ' *Tao*,' we are simply forcing a name to it.

Tao, then, is the all-embracing first principle for all things. *Te* 德, a word usually translated in English as ' virtue,' but which, in many cases, would be better translated as the ' efficacy ' or ' power ' inherent in a thing, is the principle underlying each individual thing.

' In this paragraph, beginning from the words, ' The duality spoken of,' I follow the ideas expressed by Kao Heng in his *Lao-tzŭ Cheng-ku*.

It is the same as the principle (*li* 理) spoken of in the *Han-fei-tzŭ* when this says : " All things have each their own different principle."

The *Lao-tzŭ* states :

" Great *Te's* form follows only *Tao* " (ch. 21).

"*Tao* gave them birth. *Te* reared them. Becoming things, they gained forms. Through their tending forces (*shih* 勢) they became completed. Therefore of the ten thousand things, there is not one that does not honor *Tao* and prize its *Te*. No one has commanded the honoring of *Tao* and prizing of its *Te*, but this has been forever spontaneous " (ch. 51).

The *Kuan-tzŭ* (ch. 36) says : " *Te* is the dwelling place of *Tao*. Things obtain it (from *Tao*) so as to be produced. Living things obtain it so as to function ; it is the essence of *Tao*. Therefore *Te* is an obtaining.[1] This means it is that through obtaining which a thing is what it is. That which is doing nothing (*wu wei* 無 爲) is called *Tao*. The dwelling place of this is *Te*. Therefore there is no separation between *Tao* and *Te*. And, therefore, those who speak about them make no discrimination " (*chüan* 13, p. 3). That is, *Te* is *Tao* ' dwelling ' in objects, or in other words, *Te* is what individual objects obtain from *Tao* and thereby become what they are. This explanation, which is somewhat abstruse, seems to be implied by the *Lao-tzŭ* when it says : " *Tao* gave them birth. *Te* reared them " (ch. 51). Nowhere, however, does the *Lao-tzŭ* give a very clear statement.

Apropos of the words in the *Lao-tzŭ* passage just quoted : " Becoming things, they gained forms ; through their tending forces they became completed," Lu Hui-ch'ing (eleventh century A.D.) comments : " When they become things, there is simply a special shaping of them. . . . Once having forms, those which are to be naked cannot but be naked ; those which are to have scales, claws, feathers and hair, cannot but have these scales, claws, feathers and hair. And the progression through infancy, maturity, old age and death, cannot be otherwise than this progression through infancy, maturity, old age and death. For all these, it is their tending forces which must make them necessarily so."[2] The ' gaining of forms ' means the process of transformation into individual objects. Things are definitely what their tending forces make of them, which are the activities of *Tao* and *Te*, and are spontaneous. Therefore it is said : " No one has commanded the honoring of *Tao* and prizing of its *Te*, but this has been forever spontaneous."

5—Observations on Things

Running through the phenomenal change of the universe, the *Lao-tzŭ* maintains, are to be found certain general principles which

---

[1] There is a play on words here, the word ' obtaining ' 得, also being pronounced as *te* in Chinese.—Tr.

[2] Quoted by Chiao Hung (1541-1620) in his *Lao-tzŭ I*, *chüan* 5, p. 2.

may be called 'Invariables' (*ch'ang* 常). The *Han-fei-tzŭ*, in its chapter, 'Explaining Lao Tzŭ' (ch. 20), states :

"Things which are now preserved, then destroyed; which suddenly are produced and suddenly die; which are at first flourishing and then decay, cannot be called Invariables. It is only what was produced together with the separation of Heaven and Earth, and which will not die or decay until Heaven and Earth diminish and scatter, that is called an Invariable" (*chüan* 6, p. 7).

Because this word contains the idea of universality and eternity, *Tao* is described by it, as for example :

"The *Tao* that may be called *Tao* is not the invariable *Tao*" (ch. 1).

In the same way the *Te* which is derived from this invariable *Tao* is called the invariable *Te* :

"He who does not deviate from the invariable *Te*, returns to the Limitless. . . . He who has a sufficiency of the invariable *Te*, returns to a state of Unwrought Simplicity" (ch. 28).

When *Tao* is spoken of as 'Non-being' and 'Being,' it is called 'invariable Non-being' and 'invariable Being' (ch. 1). When it is stated that it cannot be conceived of as having form, it is said :

"*Tao* is invariably nameless" (ch. 32).

As to *Tao's* action, the *Lao-tzŭ* says :

"*Tao* invariably does not do, yet there is nothing that is not done" (ch. 37).

And in speaking of the honoring of *Tao* and prizing of its *Te*, it says.

"No one has commanded this, but it has been invariably spontaneous" (ch. 51).

Concerning the general laws running through human affairs, the *Lao-tzŭ* states :

"The world is invariably possessed by him who does nothing" (ch. 48).

"The people at their tasks, invariably spoil them when within an ace of completing them" (ch. 64).

"There is invariably the Lord of Slaughter (i.e., Heaven) who kills" (ch. 74).

"The *Tao* of Heaven makes no distinction between persons. It is invariably on the side of the good person" (ch. 74).

All these are general laws, which are invariably true. The ability to know these general laws is highly valuable, and is called 'enlightenment' (*ming* 明). The *Lao-tzŭ* says :

"All things, howsoever they flourish, return to their root. This return to their root is called quiescence (*ching* 靜), which is called submission to Fate (*ming* 命). Submission to Fate is called the Invariable. To know this Invariable is called enlightenment" (ch. 16).

The *Lao-tzŭ* several times speaks of enlightenment as knowledge of the Invariable, thus indicating the importance of the latter. Therefore the *Lao-tzŭ* says :

" He who knows the Invariable is liberal. Being liberal, he is without prejudice. Being without prejudice, he is comprehensive.¹ Being comprehensive, he is vast.² Being vast, he is of *Tao*. *Tao* is forever, and he who possesses it will not fail throughout his lifetime " (ch. 16).

The word *jung* 容, here translated as 'liberal,' is the same as that in the passage in *Chuang-tzŭ* which describes Lao Tzŭ : "He was always generous and liberal toward things " (p. 448). The man who comprehends the Invariable and relies upon it for his actions, does not follow his own partial opinion, and therefore is without prejudice. *Tao* is " all pervading, unfailing," and "if we were forced to designate it, we would call it Great " (ch. 25). The man who comprehends the Invariable and relies on it, may likewise become all pervading and unfailing, so that, as Lao Tzŭ says, he ' will not fail throughout his lifetime.' This is called ' practising enlightenment,'³ as in the passage :

" Therefore the Sage is invariably in the most perfect way helping men, and so does not turn his back on men. He is invariably in the most perfect way helping creatures, and so does not turn his back on creatures. This is called practising enlightenment " (ch. 27).

Sometimes the *Lao-tzŭ* speaks of a practising of the Invariable, as in the passage :

" Good sight means seeing what is small. Strength means preserving what is weak. . . . These are called practising the Invariable " (ch. 52).

If we do not understand the general laws underlying the changing phenomena of the universe and merely rely on our own caprice for conduct, harmful result must be the consequence, so that :

" Not to know the Invariable and to do blindly is to go to disaster " (ch. 16).

Of all the laws underlying phenomenal change, the greatest is that if any one thing moves to an extreme in one direction, a change must bring about an opposite result. This is called ' reversion ' (*fan* 反) or ' return ' (*fu* 復). The *Lao-tzŭ* says :

" The movement of *Tao* consists in reversion " (ch. 40).

" Vastness means passing on, and passing on means going far away, and going far away means returning " (ch. 25).

---

¹ This follows Ma Hsü-lun, who in his *Lao-tzŭ Ho-ku* says there is one edition in which the word *wang* 王 (king) reads *chou* 周 (comprehensive).

² The word *ta* 大 (vast) is substituted for the word *t'ien* 天 (heaven), at the suggestion of Ma Hsü-lun, *op. cit.*

³ Ma Hsü-lun, *op. cit.*, says that the two words *hsi* 襲 (to attack) and *hsi* 習 (to practise) were in ancient times used interchangeably.

" All things together act, and I thereby see their return " (ch. 16).

Because reversion is the movement of *Tao*, " It is upon calamity that happiness leans ; it is upon happiness that calamity rests . . . . Correctness reverts to peculiarity, and goodness reverts to evil " (ch. 58). This being so, " Be twisted and one shall be whole ; be crooked and one shall be straight ; be hollow and one shall be filled ; be tattered and one shall be renewed ; have little and one shall obtain ; but have much and one shall be perplexed " (ch. 22). It is because of this law that " a hurricane never lasts a whole morning, nor a rainstorm the whole day " (ch. 23). Therefore : " He who by *Tao* helps a ruler of men, does not with arms force a conquest of the world, for such things invite a reversal " (ch. 30). Likewise : " Is not the *Tao* of Heaven like the stretching of a bow ? What is high is brought down, and what is low is raised up. So, too, from those who have too much, (*Tao*) takes away, and those who are deficient it augments " (ch. 77). In the same way, " The world's weakest overcomes the world's hardest " (ch. 43). And " nothing under Heaven is softer or more yielding than water ; but when it attacks things hard and resistant, there is nothing superior to it " (ch. 78). Because of this truth, " Things, if one seeks to diminish them, sometimes increase ; if one seeks to increase them, sometimes diminish " (ch. 42).

All these passages are given simply to show what the Taoists believed were the natural laws underlying phenomenal change, and not merely because they are strange and startling, though by many people they have been regarded as unsolvable paradoxes. Because of their apparent perverseness, the *Lao-tzŭ* says : " True words are like their reverse " (ch. 78). Also : " The mysterious *Te*, so deep, so remote, is to things their reverse. It is from this that there comes the Great Harmonious Accord " (ch. 65). Again : " When the man of low capacity hears *Tao*, he laughs greatly at it. If he did not laugh, it would be unworthy to be considered as *Tao* " (ch. 41).

6—How to Live in the World

Since phenomenal change, according to Lao Tzŭ, is governed by the underlying laws just described, the man who knows the Invariable and hence is enlightened, must possess definite rules for living in the world and maintaining contact with things. The most important point is to realize that, in order to live in any specified manner, one must begin by living in a manner exactly the opposite. One must first go south, so that one may gain the northern road. Thus :

" What is in the end to be shrunk must first be stretched. Whatever is to be weakened must begin by being made strong. What is to be overthrown must begin by being set up. What is to be snatched away, must first be given " (ch. 36).

" He who grudges expense pays dearest in the end. He who has hoarded most will suffer the heaviest loss " (ch. 44).

This does not mean that the *Lao-tzŭ* exalts secret plotting. It merely describes what happens. Therefore :

" The Sage, putting himself in the background, is always to the fore. Remaining outside, he is always there. Is it not just because he does not strive for any personal end that all his personal ends are fulfilled ? " (ch. 7).

" He does not show himself ; therefore he is seen everywhere. He does not define himself ; therefore he is distinct. He does not assert himself ; therefore he succeeds. He does not boast of his work, and therefore it endures. He does not contend, and for that very reason no one under Heaven can contend with him " (ch. 22).

" Just because he never at any time makes a show of greatness, he, in fact, achieves greatness " (ch. 34).

" What is noble makes inferior position its root. What is high makes lowliness its foundation. That is why marquises and kings refer to themselves as ' The Orphan,' ' The Needy,' ' The Ill-provided ' " (ch. 39).

" If a large kingdom can get beneath a small kingdom, it will win the adherence of the small kingdom. It is because the small kingdoms are beneath the large kingdoms that they win the adherence of large kingdoms " (ch. 61).

" Therefore he who wishes to be above the people, must speak as though he were beneath them. He who wishes to lead them, must put himself behind them . . . . It is because he does not contend, that for that very reason no one under Heaven can contend with him " (ch. 66).

" Pitying, he is therefore able to be brave. Frugal, he is therefore able to be profuse. Not venturing to be first in the world, he is therefore able to become chief of the state " (ch. 67).

"It is only by taking illness as illness, that it is not illness" (ch. 71).

Such are the ways by which the man who knows the Invariable lives in the world. Anything which goes to one extreme must swing to its opposite. He who would control a movement and limit it to its developing phases only, without allowing it to move to its reverse, must keep control of the elements of reversal already contained within it, and thus prevent it from ever going to this extreme. Therefore :

" The Way (*Tao*) to lightness seems as if dark. The Way that goes forward seems to go back. The Way that is level seems as if it were uneven. The Power (*Te*) that is loftiest looks like an abyss. What is sheerest white looks dark. The Power that is most sufficing looks inadequate. The Power that stands firmest looks flimsy. What is in its natural, pure state, looks faded. The great square has no corners. . . " (ch. 41).

" What is most perfect seems to have something missing, yet its use is unimpaired. What is most full seems empty, yet its use is inexhaustible. What is most straight seems crooked ; the greatest skill seems like clumsiness ; the greatest eloquence seems like stuttering " (ch. 45).

Those who comprehend the Invariable understand this, and therefore : " He who knows the male, yet cleaves to the female, becomes like a ravine for the world. . . . He who knows the white, yet cleaves to the black, becomes the standard by which all things are teste l . . . . He who knows glory, yet clings to ignominy, becomes like a valley for the world " (ch. 28). In short :

" The Sage discards the excessive, the extravagant, the extreme " (ch. 29). This is because he fears that when things move to such an extreme, the reaction will carry them to the opposite extreme. Therefore the *Lao-tzŭ* says :

" Fill to the very full, and you will wish you had stopped in time. Temper to the very sharpest, and you will find it soon grows dull. When gold and jade fill your hall, it can no longer be guarded. Wealth and place breed insolence, that brings ruin in its train. When your work is done, then withdraw ! That is the *Tao* of Heaven " (ch. 9). Again :

" Those who possess this *Tao* do not try to fill themselves to the brim " (ch. 15).

Hegel has said that the progress of history is always marked by the three stages of thesis, antithesis and synthesis. When from one extreme something moves to the opposite extreme, this is the step from thesis to antithesis. " What is most straight seems crooked ; the greatest skill seems like clumsiness." Were there merely straightness and skill alone, these would necessarily have to change into crookedness and clumsiness. But it is because they are of a straightness which contains crookedness, and of a skill which contains clumsiness, that they are called the most straight and the greatest skill. They are the synthesis arising out of thesis and antithesis. Hence the most straight is not crooked, but only seems so, and the greatest skill is not clumsiness, but only looks so. Those who comprehend the Invariable, ' know the male yet cleave to the female,' and so always remain in the final position of synthesis in which they will not fail throughout their lifetime. '

'The historical order of a philosophy, that is, the way in which it evolved in the mind of its founder, need not necessarily be the same as its logical order. In describing Lao Tzŭ's philosophy, I have treated it in its logical order, and, therefore, have first described what is meant by *Tao* and *Te*, and from this have gone on to the concept of reversion or return. But it is possible that historically, the chronological order in which this philosophy was developed was quite different, and that the author of the *Lao-tzŭ* first had in mind reversions of the type mentioned in Chapter LVII : " The more laws are promulgated, the more thieves and bandits there will be," and from these inductively developed the principle of reversal and return.

7—POLITICAL AND SOCIAL PHILOSOPHY

The law described above, that things when they reach one extreme must return, is always true regardless of circumstances. Thus the five colors are pleasing to the eye in themselves, but an excess of them ' confuses the eye. ' Likewise the five notes normally please the ear, but if we strike them to excess they ' dull the ear ' (ch. 12). Extending this principle, one finds that political and social institutions often serve to produce results diametrically opposed to their original purpose. As the *Lao-tzŭ* says :

" The more restrictions and prohibitions there are in the world, the poorer the people will be. The more sharp weapons the people have, the more troubled will be the country. The more cunning craftsmen there are, the more pernicious contrivances will appear. The more laws are promulgated, the more thieves and bandits there will be " (ch. 57).

Laws were originally made to restrain criminals, but if they are made too elaborate and numerous, criminals will rise against them in even greater numbers. The man who rules an empire, similarly, is originally desirous of doing something. But if he tries to do this something *through* doing, he will in the end not do anything. Therefore :

" The empire is a holy vessel, which may not be tampered with. Those who tamper with it, harm it. Those who grab at it, lose it " (ch. 29).

" The people are difficult to keep in order because those above them interfere. That is the only reason why they are difficult to keep in order " (ch. 75).

Because, furthermore, people seek life too excessively, their seekings are sometimes not for life but for death :

" In a man's struggles for life, three out of ten are for death. How is this ? It is because men feed life too grossly " (ch. 50).

" Excessive living is ominous " (ch. 55).

" The people attach no importance to death, because they attach too much importance to life. This is why they attach no importance to death " (ch. 39).

Therefore in ruling the empire, the Sage lays emphasis on annulling all sources of disorder. He gets rid of laws and of the traditional virtues of human-heartedness (*jen*) and righteousness (*i*). He acts through non-activity (*wu wei*), and rules through non-ruling. Non-acting reverses itself to a condition in which there is nothing that is not done (*wu pu wei* 無 不 爲), and non-rule to a condition in which there is nothing that is not ruled. Therefore it is said :

" I act not and the people of themselves are transformed. I love quiescence (*ching* 靜), and the people of themselves go straight. I concern myself with nothing, and the people of themselves are prosperous. I am without desires, and people are of themselves of an Unwrought Simplicity (*p'u* 樸) " (ch. 57).

Likewise it is through non-nurture that the Sage nurtures life : " He who does not prize life does better than he who prizes life " (ch. 75).

" Man's standard is Earth, Earth's standard is Heaven, Heaven's standard is *Tao*, *Tao*'s standard is the spontaneous " (ch. 25). The spontaneous (*tzŭ jan*) is, then, also man's standard. What has been said above agrees with this principle.

Yet man, living as he does in the world, requires certain social institutions in order merely to maintain existence. He must control them, however, so that they will not go to an extreme and thus produce opposite reactions. Therefore :

" When Unwrought Simplicity (*p'u* 樸) is scattered, it is made into implements. When the Sage utilizes it, he becomes chief of all ministers " (ch. 28).

" *Tao* is invariably nameless. Unwrought Simplicity, though seemingly of small account, is greater than anything under Heaven. . . As soon as it is put under regulation, there are names. As soon as there are names, know that it is time to stop. Only by knowing when it is time to stop can danger be avoided " (ch. 32).

In the natural world, *Tao* itself is nameless ; it is the ' ten thousand things' of the universe which have names. Human society, too, was originally nameless. This is the ' Unwrought Simplicity ' spoken of by Lao Tzŭ. With the development of human institutions, however, names came into being, or in the words of Lao Tzŭ, " When Unwrought Simplicity is scattered, it is made into implements. But when the Sage utilizes it, he becomes chief of all ministers." And when names exist, "Only by knowing when it is time to stop can danger be avoided." In other words, one must not allow too many institutions to be founded, for they will produce reactions contrary to the intentions of their founders.

8—ATTITUDE TOWARD DESIRE AND KNOWLEDGE

Inasmuch as men are born with desires, for which they establish all kinds of methods for their satisfaction, the *Lao-tzŭ* frequently speaks about the desires. The more methods there are, however, the more difficult will it be entirely to satisfy all the desires, and the more will people be injured by them. Hence ' excessive living is ominous,' and ' things, if one seeks to increase them, sometimes diminish.'

Therefore, rather than establish all kinds of ways whereby to satisfy the desires, it is better to make the desires few from the beginning. The fewer they are, the more easily will they be satisfied, and the more benefit will man derive from them. This is the meaning of the words : " Things, if one seeks to diminish them, sometimes increase "; and, " He who does not prize life, does better than he who prizes life." The way to reduce the desires is to reduce the number of objects of desire. The *Lao-tzŭ* says :

" If we do not exalt the ' worthies,' the people will no longer be contentious. If we cease to set store by products that are hard to get, there will be no more thieves. If the people never see such things as excite desire, their hearts will not be confused. Therefore the Sage rules the people by emptying their minds, filling their bellies, weakening their wills, and toughening their sinews, ever making the people without knowledge and without desire " (ch. 3).

" Banish wisdom, discard knowledge, and the people will be benefited a hundredfold. Banish human-heartedness (*jen*), discard righteousness (*i*), and the people will be dutiful and compassionate. Banish skill, discard profit, and thieves and robbers will disappear. If, when these three things are done, they find life too plain and unadorned, then let them have accessories. Let them have Unadornment (*su* 素) to look upon and Unwrought Simplicity (*p'u*) to hold. Let them have selflessness and fewness of desires " (ch. 19).

" If, having been transformed, they should desire to act, we must restrain them by the Unwrought Simplicity that is without name. With Unwrought Simplicity that is without name, there comes desirelessness. Being without desires, there comes quiescence (*ching*), and the world, of itself, is at rest " (ch. 37).

These passages all speak of the complete absence of desires, but what they really mean is that the desires should be made fewer. This is evidenced by the fact that the *Lao-tzŭ's* principles particularly aim at ' filling their bellies ' and ' toughening their sinews,' since men, unless they are like the Buddhist who believes in a fundamental negation of human life, cannot be absolutely desireless. Therefore in the ideal society conceived of in the *Lao-tzŭ*, the people must " obtain their food sweet, their clothing beautiful, their homes comfortable, and their rustic tasks pleasurable " (ch. 80). These passages make it evident that human desires are not to be absolutely extinguished, and that the idea is only to " discard the excessive, the extravagant, the extreme " (ch. 29). The reason for so doing is :

" He who is content suffers no humiliation ; who knows where to stop, cannot be harmed. He is forever safe and secure (ch. 44).

" There is no disaster greater than not knowing contentment with what one has : no greater sin than having desire for acquisition. Therefore he who knows the contentment that comes simply through content, will always be content " (ch. 46).

" To rule men and serve Heaven, there is nothing better than frugality " (ch. 59).

The lessening of desires includes this idea of frugality.

Wishing to lessen the desires, the *Lao-tzǔ* opposes knowledge. This is because : (1) Knowledge is itself one of the objects of desire. (2) Knowledge enables us to know more about the objects of desire, and so causes us no longer to know contentment. (3) Knowledge can help us in our efforts to gain the objects of desire, and hence can have such an effect upon us that we no longer know where to stop, with the result that " because of study, we daily increase (in desire) " (ch. 48). The *Lao-tzǔ* says :

" When intelligence and knowledge appeared, the Great Artifice (*ta wei* 大 偽) began " (ch. 18).

" The difficulty of ruling the people is commensurate to the amount of their knowledge. Therefore those who rule by giving knowledge are despoilers of the state. Those who rule without giving knowledge, are the state's good fortune " (ch. 20).

For this reason one must " banish wisdom, discard knowledge, and the people will be benefited a hundredfold " ; " banish learning, and there will be no more grieving " (ch. 20).

" Therefore the Sage desires what is undesired, and sets no store by products difficult to get. He studies what is unstudied, and corrects the mistakes of ordinary men " (ch. 64).

' To desire what is undesired ' is to reach a state in which the desires become fewer or are entirely absent, that is, one in which it is ' the undesired ' that constitutes the object of desire. ' To study what is unstudied ' is to reach a state in which there is no knowledge, that is, one in which it is ' the unstudied ' that constitutes the object of study. The common masses mistakenly suppose that learning is in learning ; the Sage teaches that non-learning constitutes learning.

9—THE IDEAL MAN AND IDEAL SOCIETY

The child's knowledge and desires are both very simple, and so when the *Lao-tzǔ* speaks of the man who has cultivated himself, it often compares him to a little child (*ying-er* 嬰 兒). For example :

" I alone am inert, giving no indication (of activity), like an infant that has not yet smiled " (ch. 20).

" Not to part from the invariable *Te* : this is to return to the state of infancy " (ch. 28).

" Can you concentrate your breath to make it soft like that of a little child ? " (ch. 10).

" He who holds the *Te* in all its solidity, may be likened to an infant " (ch. 55).

In his rule of the empire, likewise, the Sage wishes to make all people like small children :

" The Sage, in his dealings with the world, cautiously dulls the wits of the world. The Sage treats all as children " (ch. 49).

The *Lao-tzǔ* likewise often speaks of a stupid appearance as being characteristic of the man who has cultivated himself. This is because the knowledge and desires of the ignorant and simple-minded man are, like those of the child, extremely simple. Thus it is said :

" Mine is the heart of a very idiot. So dull am I. So many people are there who shine. I alone am dark. They look lively and self-assured, I alone, depressed. I seem unsettled like the ocean, blown adrift, never brought to a stop. All men can be put to some use. I, alone, am intractable and boorish " (ch. 20).

In ruling the people, the Sage wishes to make them all like this also :

" In the days of old those who practised *Tao* with success did not do so by enlightening the people, but by causing them to be ignorant " (ch. 65).

Yet the ignorance of the Sage is the result of a conscious process of cultivation. It is the sort of ignorance described as ' great knowledge is like ignorance,' a synthesis resulting from knowledge and ignorance ; hence it differs from primeval ignorance. Of such primeval ignorance, the *Lao-tzŭ* speaks when it says : " Therefore the Sage rules the people by emptying their minds, filling their bellies, weakening their wills, and toughening their sinews, ever making the people without knowledge and without desire " (ch. 3). By so doing he causes the people to rest content in their original and primeval state of ignorance. It is such primeval ignorance, as opposed to the conscious cult of ignorance, which is the distinguishing feature between the common people and the Sage.

" The practice of *Tao* consists in subtracting day by day," and this is done in order to make both the knowledge and the desires of the people " be subtracted and yet again subtracted, till one has reached non-activity (*wu wei*) " (ch. 48). When this state has been reached, the ideal society may be established. The *Lao-tzŭ* says :

" Given a small country with few inhabitants, let it be brought about that though there should exist military implements, they would not be used. Let the people regard death seriously and not move far from their homes. Though there might be boats and carriages, no one would go in them. Though there might exist weapons of war, no one would drill with them. Let the people return to the use of knotted cords (for keeping records). Let them obtain their food sweet, their clothing beautiful, their homes comfortable, and their rustic tasks pleasurable. The neighboring state might be so near at hand that one could hear the cocks crowing in it and the dogs barking. But the people would grow old and die without ever having been there " (ch. 80).

Such is Lao Tzŭ's ideal society. It is not merely the state of savagery of a primitive society, but rather a civilization that includes primitive-ness. It is not a society in which there are no boats and carriages, but they are simply not used ; not one in which weapons of war do not exist, but there is no one who will drill with them. For if it were actually a primitive society, how, then, could the people obtain their

food 'sweet' and their clothing 'beautiful'? One may paraph-
rase Lao Tzŭ's words and say: "Great civilization looks like
primitiveness." Such a civilization is the one best able to survive.[1]

---

[1] When a race possesses a pure culture containing no elements of barbarism, this is
the first sign of its decadence. The fact that the Chinese prize refinement and pacifism
so highly, indicates that in many ways their culture is an approximation of this condition.
If, then, the Chinese race is indeed decadent, it is because of the fact that it is over civilized.

CHAPTER IX

HUI SHIH, KUNG-SUN LUNG AND THE OTHER DIALECTICIANS

1—The General Tendencies in the Dialectician Doctrines

There was one group of philosophers which was known as the School of Names (*ming chia* 名 家) by Han scholars, but which during the Warring States period was generally known as the School of Forms and Names (*hsing ming chia* 刑 名 家),[1] or as the 'Dialecticians' (*pien che* 辯 者). Thus the *Chuang-tzŭ* (ch. 12) says: "The Dialecticians speak about the 'separateness of hard and white,' as if these could be hung up on different pegs" (p. 144). Again (ch. 33): "Through such sayings Hui Shih 惠 施 made a great show in the world, and taught them to the Dialecticians. The Dialecticians in the world were delighted with them. . . . Huan T'uan 桓 圍 and Kung-sun Lung 公 孫 龍 were followers of the Dialecticians" (pp. 451-452). These quotations are evidence of the prominence of this philosophic group during the period, and of the general application to it of the term, 'Dialecticians.'

The works of the Dialecticians, with the exception of the partially preserved *Kung-sun Lung-tzŭ*, have all been lost. What we know to-day about the doctrines of Hui Shih and the other Dialecticians is mostly derived from the paradoxes recorded in Chapter XXXIII of the *Chuang-tzŭ*. These paradoxes represent only the final conclusions arrived at by the Dialecticians, leaving us with no means of knowing the steps of reasoning by which they reached their conclusions. Logically speaking, one and the same conclusion may be arrived at from different premises, so that if we know only the conclusion, it is impossible to know from which of the many possible premises it was reached. Therefore, a strictly historical study of the paradoxes of Hui Shih and the other Dialecticians is impossible, since we are left wholly free to supply our own premises and explanations for these conclusions, quite independent of the ones which were actually used. There have been comparatively few systems of thought in China, however, offering purely theoretical interest, and so if for the above reason we were to overlook this school, Chinese philosophy would seem all the more

---

[1] *Cf. Chan Kuo Ts'e, Chao Ts'e* II, 2. The word *hsing* 刑, meaning 'punishment,' is here equivalent to *hsing* 形, meaning 'form.' *Cf.* Wang Ming-sheng (1722-1797), in *Shih-ch'i-shih Shang-chüeh, chüan* 5.

one-sided. Yet if we wish to explain these paradoxes, we can only do so by first understanding the general tendencies underlying the doctrines of the Dialecticians. And to do this we must study the opinions and criticisms on the Dialecticians found in the earlier philosophical writings.

The *Chuang-tzŭ* (ch. 12) says of them :

" There are some who seem to regulate their way of life in an anomalous way. They try to prove the impossible as possible, and to affirm what others deny. The Dialecticians speak about the ' separateness of hard and white,' as if these could be hung up on different pegs. Can such men as these be called Sages ? " (p. 144). Chapter XVII :

" Kung-sun Lung said to Mou of Wei : ' When young I studied the ways of the early kings. When I grew up I understood the practice of human-heartedness (*jen*) and righteousness (*i*). I unified the like and the unlike, and separated hard and white. I proved the impossible as possible, and affirmed what others denied. I controverted the wisdom of all the philosophies. I refuted all arguments that were brought against me. I thought that I was the most wise ' " (pp. 214-215). And Chapter XXXIII :

" Huan T'uan and Kung-sun Lung were followers of the Dialecticians. They threw a deceiving glamour over men's minds and altered their ideas. They could overcome men's words but could not convince their minds. Herein lay the weakness of the Dialecticians. . . . Yet Hui Shih regarded himself as the ablest talker. . . . In reality he simply contradicted men, yet wished to have the reputation of overcoming them. Therefore he was never in harmony with others " (pp. 453-454).

The *Hsün-tzŭ* (ch. 6) says :

" There were some who would not follow the early kings and would not acknowledge the rules of proper conduct (*li*) and standards of justice (*i*), but liked to deal with strange theories and to indulge in curious propositions. They were subtle but could not satisfy real needs ; critical but useless ; worked much but with few results. Their teachings could not serve as systematic regulations for government. Nevertheless their views had some foundation and their statements some reason, quite enough to deceive and confuse the ignorant masses. Such were Hui Shih and Teng Hsi 鄧 析 " (p. 79). And Chapter XXI :

" Hui Tzŭ (i.e., Hui Shih) was blinded by phrases and did not know facts. . . . If one speaks of the Way (*Tao*) from the viewpoint of phrases, there will be nothing but arguments " (pp. 264-265).

Ssŭ-ma T'an is recorded in the *Shih Chi* (ch. 120) as stating :

" The School of Names made minute examination of trifling points in complicated and elaborate statements, which make it impossible for others to refute their ideas. They specialized in the definition of names, but lost sight of human feelings. Therefore I say : ' They lead men to a sparing use of words which makes it easy to lose the truth.' Yet to force names to express actualities, and to study logical order so that there will be no error, is a task that must be investigated " (*Aids*, p. 52).

The *I-wen Chih* states :

" The teaching of the School of Names began with the Ministry of Ceremonies. For with the ancients, where title and position differed, the ceremonies accorded to them were also different. Confucius said : ' Are not correct names necessary ? If names be incorrect, speech will not follow its natural sequence. If speech does not follow its natural sequence, nothing can be established.' ¹ Herein lies the strength of this school. But when carried out by disputatious persons, they attack each other tooth and nail and cause subtle divisions and disorder " (*Aids*, p. 62).

All these criticisms of the Dialecticians were made by their contemporaries or by comparatively early writers, and though they may not always be wholly justified or trustworthy, we can see in them the general tendencies underlying the Dialectician doctrines. In other words, these accounts and criticisms show the direction we must take in order to interpret the Dialectician doctrines, and by using this material as a guide, we may perhaps not fall short of the truth.

The *Chuang-tzŭ*, excluding its Chapter XXXIII, which gives an account of the philosophic schools, is full of fanciful stories, and the two foregoing quotations from it certainly cannot be accepted as absolutely true. The words and actions of the historical figures appearing in the *Chuang-tzŭ*, nevertheless, usually do represent in a general manner their actual viewpoints. Thus when the *Chuang-tzŭ* mentions Confucius, it usually speaks of him as talking about rites, righteousness and the classics, and while the words it quotes may not actually have been spoken by him, they at least represent what he stood for. Though we must take the *Chuang-tzŭ's* statements about historical figures with caution, therefore, we can still accept them as representing the general attitudes of these men.

The above quotations show that the Dialecticians founded their doctrines wholly on a logical basis ; as Ssŭ-ma T'an says, they ' specialized in the definition of names.' This is why the Han scholars termed them the School of Names, and to-day in explaining their teachings we shall do well to study this aspect first.

2—HUI SHIH AND CHUANG TZŬ

Hsün-tzŭ mentions Hui Shih with Teng Hsi in the same breath. Yet according to the *Lü-shih Ch'un Ch'iu*, Teng Hsi, who lived in the

¹ *Cf. Lun Yü*, XIII, 3.—TR.

sixth century B.C., long before Hui Shih's time, occupied himself solely with teaching people how to conduct lawsuits, and seems to have been the most famous lawyer of ancient times. It may be that he obtained his reputation through sophisticated argument, and that this is why he has in later times so often been associated with the Dialecticians ; but actually the latter, while exalting debate, did not necessarily encourage sophistry.

According to tradition, Hui Shih was a native of the state of Sung,' and a friend of Chuang Tzŭ. From the fact that Chuang Tzŭ is said to have visited the grave of Hui Shih,² Hui Shih appears to have lived somewhat before him. The *Lü-shih Ch'un Ch'iu* (XXI, 5) says that Hui Shih taught the 'abolition of honorable position' (p. 383), and the *Han-fei-tzŭ* (ch. 30) says that he 'wished that fighting between the states of Ch'i and Ching (i.e., Ch'u) would cease ' (*chüan* 9, p. 4). The *Chuang-tzŭ* (ch. 33) also records him as saying : " Love all things equally ; the universe is one " (p. 451). Thus Hui Shih, like the Mohists, advocated universal love and opposed war, and for this reason Dr. Hu Shih has grouped him with the Later Mohists. Chapter XXXIII of the *Chuang-tzŭ* does not put him in their school, however, because the Mohists possessed a definite organization, to enter which a person must " regard their *Chü tzŭ* as a Sage, want him as his leader and hope to be his successor " ³ ; mere preaching of universal love and opposition to militarism were insufficient to make him a Mohist. Hui Shih's doctrine of ' abolition of honorable position,' though unknown in its details, also seems to be directly opposed to the Mohist doctrine of Agreement with the Superior. During the Warring States period, owing to the fierce fighting of the time, there were many persons who preached pacifism. Thus Mencius opposed aggression, and Kung-sun Lung also advocated cessation of war. This current was general to the age, and it is certainly not because of this doctrine that Hui Shih and Kung-sun Lung became famous.

Although the *Chuang-tzŭ* (ch. 33) does not clearly state that Hui Shih was a Dialectician, it does say that " through his sayings he made a great show in the world and taught them to the Dialecticians " (p. 451). Also that " Hui Shih daily argued with others and deliberately presented strange propositions to the Dialecticians of the world . . . Hui Shih regarded himself as the ablest talker " (p. 453). Probably, then, Hui Shih was actually a Dialectician, which explains why the *Chuang-tzŭ* (ch. 5) records Chuang Tzŭ as saying to him : " Now you devote yourself to the external and wear out your vitality. You

---

¹ *Cf.* the statement made by Kao Yu (alive during years A.D. 205-212), in his commentary to the *Lü-shih Ch'un Ch'iu* (XVIII, 5).

² *Cf. Chuang-tzŭ* (ch. 24), p. 321.

³ *Chuang-tzŭ* (ch. 33), pp. 442-443.

prop yourself against a tree and mutter, or lean over a table and sleep. Nature chose for you your bodily form, and you babble about ' the hard and the white ' " (p. 67). Likewise Chapter II says : " Hui Tzŭ argued, leaning against a decayed dryandra tree . . . . So Hui Tzŭ ended with the obscure discussion of ' the hard and the white'" (p. 22). Hsün Tzŭ says of him that he " was blinded by phrases and did not know facts " (*Hsün-tzŭ*, p. 264), and the *Chuang-tzŭ* (ch. 33) corroborates this by saying :   " Hui Shih in the end had only the reputation of being a skilled debater " (p. 454).

The same chapter states :

" In the south there was a queer man named Huang Liao, who asked why the sky did not fall and the earth did not sink ; also about the causes of wind, rain and the rolling thunder.   Hui Shih answered without hesitation and without taking time for reflection.   He discussed all things continuously and at great length, imagining that his words were but few, and still adding to them strange statements " (pp. 453-454).

At the present time, unfortunately, the only surviving part of Hui Shih's many words are the ten paradoxes recorded in Chapter XXIII of the *Chuang-tzŭ*, which everyone to-day interprets differently.   To my mind, however, Chuang Tzŭ shows himself to have been greatly influenced by Hui Shih.   What the *Chuang-tzŭ* (ch. 2) says, for example : " When there is life, then there is death ; when there is death, then there is life " (p. 18), is similar in meaning to one of Hui Shih's ten paradoxes : " The sun at noon is the sun declining ; the creature born is the creature dying " (p. 450).   Again the statement in the same chapter :   " In all the world, there is nothing greater than the tip of an autumn hair ; Mount T'ai is small " (p. 23), is similar to Hui Shih's paradox :   " The heavens are as low as the earth ; mountains are on the same level as marshes " (p. 450.)   Again the words :   " The universe came into being with me together, and with me, all things are one " (p. 23), are similar to the paradox :   " Love all things equally ; the universe is one " (p. 451).   The *Chuang-tzŭ* (ch. 24) tells us how Chuang Tzŭ felt grief at Hui Shih's grave, and that he said :

" A man of Ying who had his nose covered with a hard scab, no thicker than a fly's wing, sent for a stone-mason to chip it off.   The stone-mason plied his adze with great dexterity, while the patient let him chip.   When the scab was all off, the nose was found to be uninjured, the man of Ying never having changed color.   When Yüan, Prince of Sung, heard of this, he summoned the stone-mason and said : ' Try to do the same for me.'

" ' I used to be able to do it, Sire,' replied the stone-mason, ' but my material has long since perished.'   And I, too, ever since the Master (i.e., Hui Shih) perished, have been without my material, having no one with whom I can speak " (p. 321).

The *Chuang-tzŭ* is full of fantastic stories, and these may not actually be Chuang Tzŭ's own words, any more than the several conversations between Chuang Tzŭ and Hui Shih found in the *Chuang-tzŭ* are necessarily historical. Undoubted similarities do exist, nevertheless, between Chuang Tzŭ's ideas and those of Hui Shih, as in the three instances just given, and since the *Chuang-tzŭ's* accounts of the two men contain nothing inherently impossible, we may accept them as corroboratory evidence. Once having this clue to guide us, it becomes evident that if we wish to explain Hui Shih's ten paradoxes, we can best do so by looking for their elucidation in the *Chuang-tzŭ* itself, in which way, perhaps, we may not go far wrong.

3—HUI SHIH'S TEN PARADOXES

The *Chuang-tzŭ* (ch. 33) says :
" Hui Shih . . . . examined the meanings of things and said :
' The greatest has nothing beyond itself, and is called the Great Unit (*ta i* 大 一) ; the smallest has nothing within itself, and is called the Little Unit (*hsiao i* 小 一) ' " (p. 450).

This is the first of the ten paradoxes. The *Chuang-tzŭ* (ch. 17) states : " The Spirit of the River said, ' Am I then to regard the universe as great and the tip of a hair as small ? ' ' Not at all,' said the the Spirit of the Ocean, '. . . for what man knows is not to be compared with what he does not know. The span of his existence is not to be compared with the span of his non-existence. By means of the most small to strive to exhaust the most great is to fall into confusion and not attain one's object. Looked at in this way, how can we know that the tip of a hair is the *ne plus ultra* of smallness, or that the universe is the *ne plus ultra* of greatness ? ' ' Dialecticians of the day,' replied the Spirit of the River, ' all say that the infinitesimally small has no form, and that the infinitesimally great is beyond all measurement. Is this indeed true ? ' " (pp. 202-204). Again (ch. 25) : " The infinitely small is inappreciable ; the infinitely great is beyond all measurement " (p. 350). These quotations are similar in meaning to Hui Shih's paradox, while the mention of the ' Dialecticians of the day ' is in all probability a reference to Hui Shih. Most men consider the universe as large and the tip of a hair as small. Logically speaking, however, a thing must have ' nothing beyond itself ' before it can be considered the most great, and ' nothing within itself ' before it can be the most small. Looked at from this viewpoint, neither the universe (in Chinese, ' Heaven and Earth ') nor the tip of a hair, can fulfil these requisites.

Hui Shih's second paradox is :
" That which has no thickness cannot be increased in thickness, yet in extent it may cover a thousand miles " (p. 450).

The *Chuang-tzŭ* (ch. 3) says : " The edge of a knife is without thickness " (p. 34). To be without thickness is the extreme of thinness, which carried to its farthest limits, means the ideal surface or plane of geometry. What is without thickness cannot be three-dimensional, but can be two-dimensional, and so it is possible to say of it that ' in extent it may cover a thousand miles.'

The third paradox is :

" The heavens are as low as the earth ; mountains are on the same level as marshes " (p. 450).

The *Chuang-tzŭ* (ch. 17) says : " If looking at things according to their gradated differences, we say they are relatively big, then there is nothing in the universe which is not big ; if we say they are relatively small, there is nothing in the universe which is not small. To know that the universe (' Heaven and Earth ') is but as a tare-seed, and that the tip of a hair is a mountain : this is the expression of relativity " (p. 206). When we consider as the most great only that which has ' nothing beyond itself,' and compare the universe with this, it is then, relatively speaking, but a tare-seed. Likewise if we consider only what has ' nothing within itself ' as the most small, and compare the tip of a hair with this, the tip of the hair becomes, relatively speaking, like a mountain. Using the same principle, if we take things as relatively high, there is nothing that is not high, whereas if we take them as relatively low, there is nothing that is not low. Therefore : " The heavens are as low as the earth ; mountains are on the same level as marshes."

The fourth paradox is :

" The sun at noon is the sun declining ; the creature born is the creature dying " (p. 450).

Kuo Hsiang (died A.D. 312), in his commentary on the *Chuang-tzŭ* (ch. 6), says : " Of effortless power, there is none greater than evolutionary transformation (*pien hua che* 變 化 者). It carries the universe onward toward the new ; it moves mountains away from the old. The old does not pause even for a moment ; suddenly it has already advanced to become the new. Thus there is no time when the universe and all things are not undergoing change." Because there is ever this unceasing movement of time, it is possible to say : " The sun at noon is the sun declining ; the creature born is the creature dying."

The fifth paradox is :

" A great similarity differs from a little similarity. This is called the little similarity-and-difference (*hsiao t'ung i* 小 同 異). All things are in one way all similar, in another way all different. This is called the great similarity-and-difference (*ta t'ung i* 大 同 異) " (pp. 450-451).

The *Chuang-tzŭ* (ch. 5) says : " If we see things from the point of view of their difference, even liver and gall are as far from each other as the states of Ch'u and Yüeh. If we see things from the point of view of their similarity, all things are one " (p. 57). Kuo Hsiang comments on this : " If we differentiate things according to their differences, everything is different from the other. . . . If we consider things similar according to their points of similarity, there is nothing which is not the same." This viewpoint is the same as that in the *Chuang-tzŭ* passage quoted under the third paradox. If we regard things in the universe as similar, there are points of similarity in all of them, and we can say that from one aspect they are all similar ; but if we regard them as different, they all have points of difference between one another, and we can say that from another aspect they are all different. This is what is called great similarity-and-difference. As to what ordinary people call similarity and difference, this is simply similarity and difference between one particular object and another particular object. Such is the little similarity-and-difference, not the great similarity-and-difference.

The sixth paradox is :
" The South has no limit and has a limit " (p. 451).

The *Chuang-tzŭ* (ch. 17) says : "You cannot speak of ocean to a well-frog. He is limited by his environment " (p. 201). The places to which most men have travelled are limited, and therefore they believe that the South has no limit. But this is the viewpoint of the well-frog. If we look from the viewpoint that what is most great is only what has nothing beyond it, then the apparent limitlessness of the South actually does have a limit.

The seventh paradox is :
" I go to the state of Yüeh to-day and arrived there yesterday " (p. 451).

The *Chuang-tzŭ* (ch. 17) says : "You cannot speak of ice to a summer insect. He is restricted by his time " (p. 201). Let us once realize that " the old does not pause even for a moment ; suddenly it has already advanced to become the new. Thus there is no time when the universe and all things are not undergoing change." Then let us suppose that ' I go to the state of Yüeh to-day.' I arrive there to-morrow, but what I at present call to-morrow has by that time suddenly already become something of the past. Therefore : " I go to the state of Yüeh to-day and arrived there yesterday." This paradox comes close to sophistry. For although what we call present and past have no fixed absolute standard, nevertheless they must, within any given field of discourse, each have the same relative standard as the other. Although the yesterday of ' I arrived yesterday ' can be called yesterday, it is certainly not yesterday when put in conjunction with the to-day of ' I go to the state of Yüeh to-day.' Chuang Tzŭ also seems to disagree with this paradox, so that he says in Chapter II : " The case in which there are no opinions, while yet a distinction is made between right and wrong, is as inconceivable as that one goes to Yüeh to-day, but arrived there yesterday. This is to make what is not, to be. How to make what is not, to be, even holy Yü could not know. How can I do it?" (p. 16).

The eighth paradox is:
" Connected rings can be separated " (p. 451).

The *Chuang-tzŭ* (ch. 2) says : "Separation is the same as construction ; construction is the same as destruction" (p. 20). " The sun at noon is the sun declining ; the creature born is the creature dying." Connected rings are now complete, now in dissolution. At the moment they are linked, but suddenly they may already no longer be linked. Therefore : " Connected rings can be separated."

The ninth paradox is :
" I know the center of the world ; it is north of Yen [1] and south of Yüeh " [2] (p. 451).

The *Chuang-tzŭ* (ch. 17) says : " The Four Seas : are they not to the universe but as puddles in a marsh ? The Middle Kingdom : is it not to the surrounding oceans as a tare-seed in a granary ? " (p. 202). Yet the ancient Chinese assumed China to be the center of the world, and since they believed that the center of China fell on a spot somewhere south of Yen and north of Yüeh, this for them also constituted the center of the world. Such a narrow belief is exactly what the same chapter in *Chuang-tzŭ* terms the viewpoint of a well-frog. If once we regard things from the viewpoint that ' the greatest has nothing beyond itself,' however, then "the world has no directions, and therefore wherever we may happen to be is the center; a circle has no starting point, and therefore wherever we may happen to be (on its circumference) is the beginning."[3]

The tenth paradox is :
" Love all things equally ; the universe is one " (p. 451).

" If we see things from the point of view of their difference, even liver and gall are as far from each other as the states of Ch'u and Yüeh. If we see things from the point of view of their similarity, all things are one." This tenth paradox is based upon the point of view of the identity of all things. The *Chuang-tzŭ* (ch. 2) says : " In all the world, there is nothing greater than the tip of an autumn hair ; Mount T'ai is small.[4] Neither is there anyone longer-lived than a child cut off in its infancy ; P'eng Tsu (the Chinese Methusaleh) died young. The universe came into being with me together, and with me, all things are one " (p. 23). This expresses the same idea.

---

[1] A state in north China, where Peiping now is.—Tr.
[2] A state in the south near present Hangchow.—Tr.
[3] Quoted from the commentary by Ssŭ-ma Piao (died A.D. 306), given in Lu Te-ming's (died A.D. 627) *Ching-tien Shih-wen*.
[4] T'ai Shan, the famous sacred mountain in Shantung.—Tr.

4—DIFFERENCES BETWEEN HUI SHIH AND CHUANG TZǓ

According to the explanations just given for Hui Shih's ten paradoxes, we find that he argues always from the viewpoint that 'the greatest has nothing beyond itself,' to show that all things are limited and relative. This comes close to the ideas expressed in the *Chuang-tzŭ* in such Chapters as II and XVII. Thus Chapter II says : " The universe came into being with me together, and with me, all things are one." But directly below it continues : "If then all things are one, what place is there for speech ? " (pp. 23-24). Herein lies the difference between Chuang Tzǔ and Hui Shih. Hui Shih uses only the intellect to prove that all things are in one aspect all similar, in another aspect all different, and that the universe is one. He says nothing as to how we may *experience* this state in which the universe is one. Chuang Tzǔ, on the other hand, speaks mystically of the ' wordlessness ' beyond the realm of words, and the ' non-knowledge ' beyond that of knowledge. It is through what he calls the ' fasting of the mind ' (*hsin chai* 心 齋) and ' sitting in forgetfulness ' (*tso wang* 坐 忘) that we can attain to the state of absolute freedom in which we forget the distinctions between others and self, and equate life and death, so that all things become one. Therefore Chapter XXXIII of the *Chuang-tzŭ* says of him that he " roamed with the Creator above, and below made friends of those who, without beginning or end, are beyond life and death " (p. 449). But as to Hui Shih, " Weak in virtue, strong in dealing with things, his way was dark and narrow " (p. 454). Thus looked at, Chuang Tzǔ's philosophy is actually that of Hui Shih advanced one step further, and hence while Chuang Tzǔ's writings have been used in the preceding pages to explain Hui Shih, yet in the final analysis the two men remain distinct.

The *Chuang-tzŭ* (ch. 17) records someone as criticizing Kung-sun Lung by saying :

" ' Moreover, for one whose knowledge does not reach (to what is beyond) the right and wrong domain (i.e., to where these distinctions are obliterated), to attempt to understand Chuang Tzǔ, is comparable to a mosquito trying to carry a mountain, or an ant trying to swim a river ; they cannot succeed. And is not one whose knowledge does not reach to the abstrusest of the abstruse, but is based only upon what is useful for the moment, like the frog in the well ?

" ' Moreover he (Chuang Tzǔ) moves in the realm of the Yellow Springs (i.e., the underworld) below and soars to Heaven above. For him, north and south do not exist ; the four points are gone ; he is engulfed in the unfathomable. For him, east and west do not exist. Beginning with mystery, he has reverted to the Great Thoroughfare (i.e., *Tao*). And yet you think you are going to analyse his doctrines and meet them with argument ! This is like looking at the sky through a tube, or pointing at the earth with an awl. Is it not indeed petty ? ' " (p. 216).

Although this criticism of the Dialecticians, made from Chuang Tzǔ's viewpoint, may not be entirely correct, yet Chuang Tzǔ's philosophy, as a matter of fact, does begin with words and debate, and end with wordlessness and non-debate. It transcends the ' domain of right and wrong,' and ' reverts to the Great Thoroughfare,' and thus differs from that of the Dialecticians who begin and end with ' analysis ' and ' argument.' Hence the *Chuang-tzǔ* (ch. 33), in criticizing Hui Shih, pays special attention to the fact that he delighted in debate, by saying that ' in reality he simply contradicted men, yet he wished to have the reputation of overcoming them,' and that he ' deliberately presented strange propositions to the Dialecticians of the world.' In describing Chuang Tzǔ, on the other hand, it particularly stresses the fact that he did not care for debate :

" Chuang Chou... in strange and vague expression, wild and extravagant language, indefinite terms, indulged himself in his own ideas without partiality or peculiar appearance.... He put his ideas into indefinite cup-like words, ascribing them to others for authority and illustrating with stories for variety .... He did not condemn either right or wrong, so he was able to get along with ordinary people. His writings, though they have a grand style, are not opposed to things and so are harmless. His phrases, though full of irregularities, are yet attractive and full of humor ... " (p. 449).

All this seems to be in sharp contrast to the dialectics of Hui Shih. This account of Chuang Tzǔ is only some two hundred odd words long, yet about half of it is devoted to describing his manner of expression, as if with the express purpose of differentiating him from Hui Shih. The *Han-fei-tzǔ* (ch. 22) quotes Hui Shih as saying :

" The person who flees, runs eastward, and his pursuer also runs eastward. They are both alike in running eastward, but the causes for each doing so are different. Therefore I say that one should examine those who are engaged in identical occupations " (*chüan* 7, p. 14).

The difference between Chuang Tzǔ and Hui Shih is comparable to this.

Yet Chuang Tzǔ's philosophy, as long as it remains in the sphere of ' words ' and ' knowledge,' is, after all, very similar to that of Hui Shih, and therefore when the latter died, Chuang Tzǔ lamented that he no longer had anyone with whom to talk. The *Chuang-tzǔ* (ch. 33) says :

" He (Hui Shih) might be considered as the exponent of one aspect of *Tao*. But he claimed almost to have reached *Tao* itself. Hui Shih could not content himself with the one aspect ; he diffused his energy over all things but was never satisfied. In the end he had only the reputation of being a skilled Dialectician. Alas! Hui Shih with his talents wandered about without achieving anything; he went after things without returning (to *Tao*). It was like shouting to silence an echo, or racing with his own shadow. Alas!" (p. 454).

Seen from Chuang Tzŭ's point of view, Hui Shih might, indeed, appear to have failed and to have wandered off on a side track.[1]

5—KUNG-SUN LUNG'S 'DISCOURSE ON THE WHITE HORSE'

For readers unacquainted with the special characteristics of the Chinese language, the following sections, dealing with Kung-sun Lung, will probably be particularly difficult to understand. Kung-sun Lung's main thesis appears to be that particular things in the universe are made up of an infinite number of ' universals' (to speak in modern philosophic language), which remain ever unchanging and distinct from one another, although the physical objects in which they are temporarily manifested and combined, may change or disappear. His difficulty in proving this thesis is heightened by the nature of the Chinese written language, which because it is pictographic and ideographic, and at the same time non-inflected, can express the difference between singular and plural objects, the concrete and the abstract, etc., only with difficulty. For further details on this point, see p. 206, note 1.—Tr.

Kung-sun Lung 公孫龍 was a native of the state of Chao (in the present province of Shansi).[2] The *Chuang-tzŭ* (ch. 33) says of him: " Such were the questions over which the Dialecticians argued with Hui Shih all their days, without reaching any conclusion. Huan T'uan and Kung-sun Lung were followers of the Dialecticians " (p. 453). Kung-sun Lung, according to this, would appear to have lived somewhat later than Hui Shih. Yet the fact that Chuang Tzŭ also argued on such subjects of Kung-sun Lung as ' the white horse ' and ' *chih* and things,'[3] shows that Kung-sun Lung lived not later than Chuang Tzŭ. Once he urged Kings Chao of Yen (311-279) and Hui of Chao (298-265) to cease war, saying: " The idea in ceasing war springs out of a mind holding universal love toward the world." [4] Pacifism was a tenet held by many men of that time, however, and it was not for this that Kung-sun Lung was known

---

[1] This same chapter says, describing Mo Tzŭ: " Ah! What ability he had! " And of Yin Wen and Sung K'eng: " They were men who sought to save the world." Though this is praise, it is not of the highest kind. But of Shen Tao and T'ien Pien it says: " Nevertheless, in a general way they had heard about it (*Tao*). " And of Hui Shih: " He claimed almost to have reached *Tao* itself." This greater praise is evoked by the fact that both of these two schools had points in common with the philosophy of Chuang Tzŭ. Chuang Tzŭ, for his part, spoke alike of ' words ' and of ' wordlessness '; of ' knowledge ' and of ' non-knowledge.' Shen Tao, on the one hand, stressed only the state of non-knowledge, for according to him even " a clod of earth does not miss the *Tao* "; whereas Hui Shih, on the other, stressed only words, so that ' in the end he had only the reputation of being a skilled Dialectician.' Thus each of them held but one aspect of Chuang Tzŭ's philosophy.
[2] *Cf. Shih Chi*, ch. 74.
[3] *Cf.* below, sect. 8, pp. 209-212.
[4] *Lü-shih Ch'un Ch'iu* (XVIII, 1), p. 292.

as the leader of a school. The *Kung-sun Lung-tzǔ*, a small work bearing his name which partially survives, says in its Chapter I :

"Kung-sun Lung was a Dialectician of the time of the Six States (i.e., Warring States). Dissatisfied with the divergence and confusion between names and their actualities, he used his peculiar talent to discuss the alleged inseparability of whiteness. Pointing out analogies in other objects, he argued on this theme of whiteness . . . . He wished to extend his argument so as thereby to rectify names with their actualities, and thus transform the whole world " (pp. 61-62).

Again, he says of himself : "What I have gained my reputation with, is my discourse of the white horse. If you deprive me of that, I have nothing to impart " (p. 64).

The *Chuang-tzǔ* (ch. 33) says :

"Huan T'uan and Kung-sun Lung were followers of the Dialecticians. They threw a deceiving glamour over men's minds and altered their ideas. They could overcome men's words but could not convince their minds. Herein lay the weakness of the Dialecticians " (p. 453).

This shows that it was his particular dialectic that made Kung-sun Lung famous.

About his discourse on the white horse, the *Kung-sun Lung-tzǔ* (ch. 2) states :

"A white horse is not a horse . . . . . The word ' horse ' denotes a shape, ' white ' denotes a color. What denotes color does not denote shape. Therefore, I say that a white horse is not a horse. . . . When a horse is required, yellow and black ones may all be brought forward, but when one requires a white horse, a yellow or black horse cannot be brought forward. . . . Therefore, yellow and black horses are each separate kinds, and can respond to the call for a horse, but not to the call for a white horse. Hence it results that a white horse is not a horse. . . .

"Horses certainly have color. Therefore, there exist white horses. Suppose there is a horse without color, then there is only the horse as such. But how can we get white horses ? Therefore, a white one is not a horse. A white horse is ' horse ' together with ' white.' ' Horse ' with ' white ' is not ' horse.' ¹ Therefore, I say that a white horse is not a horse.

"The word ' white ' does not specify (*ting* 定) what is white. We may disregard this last and it is all right. But the words ' white horse ' specify of the white what it is that is white. The white that is specified is not (the quality) ' white ' itself. The word ' horse ' neither excludes nor includes any color. Therefore, yellow and black ones may all respond to it. But the words, ' white horse,' exclude and include color, and yellow and black horses are all excluded owing to their

---

¹ The text reads : " ' Horse ' with ' white ' is ' horse,' " but we must insert the word ' not ' (*fei* 非), if the argument is to make sense.—Tr.

color. Therefore, it is only 'white horse' that will correspond. That in which nothing is excluded is not that in which something is excluded. Therefore, I say a white horse is not a horse " (pp. 67-70).

The word, ' horse,' only designates the characteristics common to all horses, that is, as the text says, 'only the horse as such.'[1] This has no specifying color, whereas when a white horse is spoken of, the color is specified. Hence what is specified by the words, ' white horse,' does in fact differ from what is designated by the word ' horse.' Moreover the quality ' white ' remains white, regardless of whether it is the white of one white thing or of another white thing. This is why " the word ' white ' does not specify what is white." When we speak of the ' white ' in the term ' white horse,' we mean only this white and that of nothing else. Or as the text says : " The words ' white horse ' specify of the white what it is that is white. The white that is specified is not (the quality) ' white ' itself." That is, the white of a white horse is no longer the general quality, ' white, ' and hence what is designated by the term, ' white horse,' also differs from what is designated by the word, ' white.'

6—KUNG-SUN LUNG'S CONCEPTION OF THE *CHIH*[2]

What are designated or intended by such terms as ' horse,' ' white,' etc., are what the *Kung-sun Lung-tzŭ* (ch. 3) calls *chih* 指, a term which I here interpret as being roughly equivalent to the western word ' universal.' Such *chih* or ' universals ' differ from concrete things (*wu* 物), which latter are described in the *Kung-sun Lung-tzŭ* (ch. 6) as follows :

" Heaven and Earth, together with what they produce, are things (*wu*). Each thing is what it is and no more : this means actuality. Actualities (*shih* 實) occupy what they do occupy and no less : this is position. . . . To rectify that which designates an actuality, means to rectify its name. . . . A name (*ming* 名) is what designates an actuality. If we know that ' this ' is not ' this,' and that ' this ' does not lie in ' this,' then it will not be designated (by this name). If we know that 'that' is not ' that,' and that ' that ' does not lie in ' that,' then, too, it will not be designated (by that name)" (p. 81).

According to this passage, a thing (*wu*) is that which occupies position in space and time, that is, in modern philosophical language, a concrete particular. Such would be this or that horse, this or that white horse.

Besides these concrete particulars, however, the *Kung-sun Lung-tzŭ* also speaks of something which it calls *chih* 指. These *chih*, as we

---

[1] 有 馬 如 已 耳.
[2] With the consent of the author, this section has been somewhat modified from the original text, for the sake of greater clarity, so that what was originally a footnote now appears as paragraph (2) and following.—TR.

shall see later (in sect. 8), stand in apposition to concrete particulars, and as such, I interpret them as being roughly equivalent to the western term, 'universal.' This interpretation may be arrived at in two ways:

(1) The word *chih* 指 literally means ' a finger,' ' to point out,' ' to designate,' or in the *Kung-sun Lung-tzŭ*, ' that which is designated,' meaning by this, that which is designated by a name.

The explanation is that names serve two purposes. In the first place, any name points out its corresponding particular, or as the text says : " A name is what designates an actuality." At the same time, however, a name also designates the universal which underlies this particular.

Thus besides this or that particular horse, there is the horse as such ; and besides this or that particular white, there is the ' white which does not specify what is white.' Such ' horse ' and ' white ' are universals, and names not only serve to point to their particulars, but to such universals as well. In section eight we shall see that the *chih* (literally, ' what is designated ') is placed by Kung-sun Lung in apposition to ' things,' a fact which speaks strongly for the assumption that when he speaks of *chih*, he really means the universal designated by any name.[1]

(2) Or according to a second interpretation, the word *chih* 指, as used in the *Kung-sun Lung-tzŭ*, is equivalent to *chih* 旨, another word having the same pronunciation, and written in the same way, save that the left strokes (扌) of the character, meaning ' hand,' have been omitted.[2] Now this second word, *chih* 旨, means 'idea' or 'concept.' Therefore, according to this interpretation, the first word *chih* 指, as used by Kung-sun Lung, no longer holds its primary meaning of 'a finger,' or ' to point out,' but instead means ' idea ' or ' concept.' In the latter sense it, rather than some other special term, has been used by Kung-sun Lung to designate the universal, just as Plato used the word ' idea ' for this purpose.

This second explanation is also possible, but is not so direct as to say that the word *chih*, used in its customary sense of ' to designate,' is employed by Kung-sun Lung to refer to the universal as it is ' designated ' by its name.

---

[1] Strictly speaking, names or terms are divided into those that are abstract and those that are concrete. The abstract term denotes the universal, the concrete term the particular. The particular is the denotation, and the universal the connotation, of the term. In western inflected languages there is no difficulty in distinguishing between the particular ('white ' or ' horse ') and the abstract (' whiteness ' or ' horseness '). In Chinese, however, owing to the fact that the written characters are ideographic and pictorial and lack all inflection, there is no possible way, as far as the form of individual words is concerned, of distinguishing between abstract and concrete terms. Thus in Chinese the word designating a particular horse, and that designating the universal, ' horseness,' are written and pronounced in the same way. Similarly with other terms, so that such words as ' horse ' and ' white,' being used to designate both the concrete particular and the abstract universal, thus hold two values.

[2] For the fact that these two words were in ancient times used interchangeably, see Ch'en Chung-fan, *Chu-tzŭ T'ung-i*.

7—KUNG-SUN LUNG'S 'DISCOURSE ON HARD AND WHITE'

The purpose of Kung-sun Lung's 'Discourse on the White Horse' is to prove that 'horse,' 'white,' etc., are all separate and independent universals. The *Chuang-tzŭ* (ch. 17) mentions Kung-sun Lung's 'separateness of hard and white' (p. 214), by which is meant the doctrine that hardness and whiteness are two separate universals. The fifth chapter of the *Kung-sun Lung-tzŭ*, the title of which is 'Discourse on Hard and White,' reads :
"Is it possible that hard, white and stone are three ? "   " No."
" Can they be two ? "   " Yes."
" How ? "
" When without hardness one finds whiteness, this gives two ; when without whiteness one finds hardness, this gives two [1]. . . . Seeing does not perceive hardness, but perceives that which is white, without the hardness. Touching does not perceive whiteness, but perceives hardness. It perceives hardness without the whiteness. . . . Finding its (the stone's) whiteness, or finding its hardness, lies in seeing or non-seeing (i.e., in touching). The seeing and non-seeing are separate from each other. Neither one pervades the other, and therefore they are separate. Separateness is concealment" (pp. 77-78).

The absence of whiteness or hardness here spoken of refers to these qualities as found in the concrete stone. When we look at the stone, we perceive whiteness but not hardness, and the hardness, being unperceived, is separate (i.e., distinct) from the whiteness. Likewise when we touch a stone, we perceive hardness but not whiteness, and the whiteness, being unperceived, is separate from the hardness. Hence 'neither one pervades the other.' This is epistemological proof that hardness and whiteness are separate universals.

The 'Discourse on Hard and White' continues with objections made to these propositions :
" Because the eye cannot behold hardness nor the hand grasp whiteness, one cannot say that there is no hardness or whiteness. The organs perceiving them are not the same, and cannot be interchanged. But hardness and whiteness both are in the stone, so how can they be separated ? " (p. 79).

That is, the perception or non-perception of hardness and whiteness are dependent on touch and sight respectively, but hardness and whiteness exist in the stone independently of these organs, so how can they be separate ? Kung-sun Lung replies to this :
" There are white things, but whiteness does not specify what is white. There are hard things, but hardness does not specify what is hard. Being non-specifying, they are general, and so how can they be in the stone ? " (p. 79).

---

[1] i.e., whiteness plus stone, and hardness plus stone, respectively.—TR.

Hsieh Hsi-shen, of the Sung dynasty (960-1279), says in his commentary on this : " There are myriads of things that share the quality of whiteness, which thus does not specify (only) the whiteness of the stone. But is it only the stone which hardness and whiteness do not specify ? They do not specify any of the myriads of things. When they do not specify any of the myriads of things, how can it be solely in the stone that they exist together ? " Both whiteness and hardness do not specify the things which they make white and hard, and so how can they be said to be in the stone ? Some things in the universe have hardness but not whiteness ; others have whiteness but not hardness. Thus it becomes still more apparent that hardness and whiteness are two separate universals. Here metaphysical proof is adduced for their ' separateness.'

The ' Discourse on Hard and White ' continues :

" Hardness does not ' share ' (*yü* 與) itself in the stone and thus be hard ; it is common to other things. It is not in things and thus hard ; but its hardness is necessarily hardness in itself. If it is not hard (because of) stones and things, but is hard (in itself), then no such hardness exists in the world, but it lies concealed.

" If whiteness is really not whiteness in itself, how could it be white (because of) stones and things ? If whiteness is necessarily white, it is white (in itself) without being white (because of) things. With yellow and black it is the same. When (whiteness and hardness) can exist without stone, how can one speak of a hard and white stone ? Hence (these qualities) are separate. They are separate because of this " (pp. 79-80).

Hsieh Hsi-shen comments on this : " Hardness is not hardness solely in the stone, but is also hardness in myriad other things. Therefore it is said : ' It does not share itself in the stone and thus be hard ; it is common to other things.' But even when it is not in the myriad things, it is necessarily hardness of itself. Therefore it is said : ' It is not in things and thus hard ; but its hardness is necessarily hardness in itself.' There is no such independently existing hardness in the world which can be perceived. On the other hand it cannot therefore be said that there is no such hardness. Hence it is said : ' But the hardness lies concealed.' "

Likewise with whiteness. Though such independently existing whiteness is not to be found in the world, and so cannot be perceived, yet whiteness is white in itself. For if we were to grant that whiteness could not be white in itself, it then could not make a stone or other object white ; whereas if it is white, and is so in itself, then it subsists in itself without depending on other things. Yellow, black and all other colors are the same. White may subsist without the stone, and being without the stone, there is no such thing as a hard-and-white stone. Thus from a metaphysical point of view it may be seen that hardness and whiteness are separable and self-subsistent.

That is, the universals, 'hardness' and 'whiteness,' both have independent subsistence. Though they have such subsistence, however, they can only be perceived by men when they are manifested in concrete objects ; that is, men can only perceive hardness and whiteness when these 'share' (*yü* 與) themselves in objects. Yet even when they are not manifested in objects in this way, this does not mean that they are not self-subsistent, but only that men cannot then perceive them. This is why they are said to 'lie concealed.' This concealment is self concealment, not concealment caused by something else. Hence the same chapter states :

" They conceal themselves. It is not that they are concealed (by something else) and so are concealed " (p. 78).

Plato, when he said that particulars are perceivable but not thinkable, while ideas are thinkable but not perceivable, meant exactly this. Thus the fact that hardness and whiteness are separable becomes all the more apparent ; but more than this, all universals are separate and have self subsistence. Therefore the same chapter says :

" Being separables, they are all single, which is the correct (way of) the world " (p. 80).

8—Kung-sun Lung's ' Discourse on *Chih* and Things '

Neo-realists of the present day hold that particulars exist, while universals subsist, that is, have being even though not in space and time. Thus hardness is hardness, even if not manifested in an object, and we cannot, merely because we do not then perceive it, therefore maintain that there is no hardness. To say, as Kung-sun Lung does, that hardness ' lies concealed,' seems to be another way of saying that it subsists. This point is made clear in the ' Discourse on *Chih* 指 (i.e., ' universals ') and Things (*wu* 物) ' in the *Kung-sun Lung-tzŭ* (ch. 3) :

"There are no things (*wu*) that are not *chih*, but these *chih* are no *chih*. If the world had no *chih*, things could not be things. If, there being no *chih*, the world had no things, could one speak of *chih* ? *Chih* are what do not exist in the world. Things are what do exist in the world. It is impossible to consider what does exist in the world to be what does not exist in the world. In the world there exist no *chih*, and things cannot be called *chih*. If they cannot be called *chih*, they are no *chih*.

" They are no *chih*, (and yet it has been stated above that) there are no things that are not *chih*. That there are no *chih* in the world, and that things cannot be called *chih*, does not mean that there are no *chih*. It is not that there are no *chih*, because there are no things that are not *chih*.

" There are no things that are not *chih*, but these *chih* are no *chih*. That there are no *chih* existing in the world, arises from the fact that all things have their own names, which are not themselves *chih*. When they are not *chih*, to call them *chih*, would be to take *chih* to mean also what are not *chih*. It would be impermissible to take what are not *chih* as *chih*.

" *Chih*, moreover, are what are held in common in the world. There are no *chih* existing in the world, but things cannot be said to be without *chih*. That they cannot be said to be without *chih*, means that there are none that are not *chih*. That there are none that are not *chih*, means (we return to our opening statement) that there are no things that are not *chih*. There are no *chih* that are non-*chih*. *Chih* that share themselves in things are non-*chih*. Supposing there were no thing-*chih* (*wu-chih*) existing in the world, who would there be to speak directly about non-*chih* ? If there were no things existing in the world, who would there be to speak directly about *chih* ? If there were *chih* but no thing-*chih* in the world, who would there be to speak directly about non-*chih* ? Who would there be to assert directly that there are no things that are not *chih* ? Moreover how can *chih*, which certainly in themselves become non-*chih*, depend upon things, and so only be *chih* when they share themselves in these ? " (pp. 70-72).'

If we analyse the things in the world, we find that they are simply composed of various universals. Universals, however, cannot themselves be further analysed or split up into other universals, and so it is said : " There are no things that are not *chih*, but these *chih* are no *chih*. If the world had no *chih*, things could not be things." But in order to occupy space and time and so be perceived by man, universals must have that which they ' specify ' (*ting* 定) or in which they ' share ' (i.e., reveal) themselves ; that is, they must become manifest in things. Therefore : " If. . . . . the world had no things, could one speak of *chih* ? " Again : " *Chih* are what do not exist in the world. Things are what do exist in the world." That is, when universals do not ' share ' themselves in things, they do not exist in time and space but ' lie concealed ' (i.e., subsistent or latent), whereas things do have existence in time and space, and so exist in the world.

Therefore although things can be analysed as forming various universals, as things in themselves they are not universals. Hence on the one hand it may be said : " There are no things that are not *chih*"; while on the other hand one may say : " Things cannot be called

---

' This is one of the most perplexing and ambiguous passages in all Chinese philosophy. The chief difficulty arises in connection with the Chinese word *fei* 非, which occurs constantly throughout the text linked with the word *chih*, and which seems to hold three different meanings : (1) Meaning ' not,' as in the phrase, ' There are no things that are not *chih* ' (*fei chih*). (2) Meaning ' no,' as in the phrase, ' But these *chih* are no *chih* ' (*fei chih*). (3) Meaning ' non,' as in the phrase, ' There are no *chih* that are non-*chih* ' (*fei-chih*). This third sense seems to be required in the last lines of the passage, which speak about *chih* and non-*chih* in apposition to one another, while at the same time introducing another new term, ' thing-*chih* ' (*wu-chih*), into the discussion.—TR.

chih." To say that ' in the world there exist no *chih*,' is to say that universals themselves do not exist in time and space.

Nevertheless all things in the world have their names, for as was said in a preceding passage : " A name is what designates an actuality." The actuality is a particular. The name is the representative of the universal. It is only a representative, however, and not the universal itself. Although there are names existing in the world, there are no existing universals. Therefore it is said : " That there are no *chih* existing in the world, arises from the fact that all things have their own names, which are not themselves *chih*." If names are not universals, they may not be assimilated to universals, so that : " It would be impermissible to take what are not *chih* as *chih*."

A universal is what is held in common by all members in its class. Thus the universal ' horse' pertains to all members in the class of horse, that of ' white ' to all members in the class of white, and so on. Therefore it is said : "*Chih*, moreover, are what are held in common in the world... There are no *chih* existing in the world, but things cannot be said to be without *chih*." In one way there are no things that are not universals, for all particular things are the concrete forms of universals, occupying space and time. But in another way things are not universals, for what occupies space and time is the particular, not the universal. Therefore on the one hand, " That they cannot be said to be without *chih*, means that there are none that are not *chih*. That there are none that are not *chih*, means (we return to our opening statement) that there are no things that are not *chih*." But on the other hand, " There are no *chih* that are non-*chih*. *Chih* that share themselves in things are non-*chih*." This last sentence means that when several universals are combined and become manifest in time and space, they become things. Such universals when thus manifested in things, ' share' themselves in them, that is, are ' thing-*chih*'. If there were no universals, there could exist no things, nor could there be things if there were no ' thing-*chih*' (i.e., *chih* that have become manifest by ' sharing ' themselves in concrete objects).

If there were universals but no things, there would only be subsisting universals, ' concealed ' and not manifest, and so there could exist no man who could discourse on universals and things. Therefore it is said : " Supposing there were no thing-*chih* existing in the world, who would there be to speak directly about non-*chih* ? If there were no things existing in the world, who would there be to speak directly about *chih* ? If there were *chih* but no thing-*chih* in the world, who would there be to speak directly about non-*chih* ? Who would there be to assert directly that there are no things that are not *chih* ?" The combination of universals and their manifestation in time and space as things, however, is a spontaneous process not caused from without. Therefore it is said : " Moreover how can *chih*, which certainly in themselves become non-*chih*, depend upon things, and so only be *chih* when they share themselves in these?" The 'non-*chih*' here mean concrete things.

9—KUNG-SUN LUNG'S 'DISCOURSE ON THE EXPLANATION OF CHANGE'

The universal is unchanging, but the particular is ever changing. In its 'Discourse on the Explanation of Change,' the *Kung-sun Lung-tzŭ* (ch. 4) discusses this problem of how there are changes and also no changes:

"Does two contain one?"   "Two has no one."
"Does two contain right?"   "Two has no right."
"Does two contain left?"   "Two has no left."
"Can right be called two?"   "No."
"Can left be called two?"   "No."
"Can left and right together be called two?"   "They can" (p. 73).

The universal of 'two' is simply 'two' and nothing else. Hence it is not 'one,' nor is it 'right' or 'left.' But 'right' added to 'left' is two in number, and therefore put together these can be called two. The chapter continues:

"Is it permissible to say that a change is not non-change?" "It is."

"Can 'right' which shares itself (in something) be called change?"   "It can."

"What is it that changes?"   "It is 'right'" (pp. 73-74)."

The universal does not change, but the particular ever does so. Change is not non-change. This 'sharing' (*yü* 與) of 'right' is the same as that mentioned in the 'Discourse on Hard and White,' when this says: "Hardness does not share itself in the stone and thus be hard." That is, though the universal itself does not change, the particular in which the universal is manifested certainly may do so. Hence the universal, 'right,' does not change, but right which 'shares' itself in things may do so. The right of a particular thing, for example, may become its left. When the questioner asks, "What is it that changes?", and the reply is made, "It is right," this right is one that 'shares' itself in things, and not simply the universal of right.[1]

The chapter continues with questions by the interlocutor:

"If the right has been changed, how can you still call it right? And, if it has not been changed, how can you speak of a change? If two has no right and no left, how is it that two is left together with right?" (p. 74).

---

[1] In this point I have followed suggestions made by my colleague, Professor Chin Yo-lin.

The questioner does not understand that the right which can be changed is the right in concrete things, whereas the universal, ' right,' remains unchanged. He further fails to understand that left, added to right, is two in number, and that this is why these together are called two.

Again : " A ram added to an ox is not a horse. An ox added to a ram is not a fowl " (p. 74).

This means that right added to left make the number two, whereas the universal, ' right,' and the universal, ' left,' cannot be so combined to make two, any more than can the universals of ram and ox be combined to make horse, or of ox and ram to make fowl. The same chapter continues :

" A ram and an ox are different. Because a ram has upper front-teeth, an ox none, we cannot say that an ox is not a ram, nor a ram an ox. They might not both have those particular teeth, and yet belong to the same species. Because a ram has horns and an ox has horns, we cannot say that an ox is a ram and a ram an ox. They might both have horns, and yet belong to quite different species. A ram and an ox have horns, a horse none ; a horse has a long tail, which a ram and an ox do not have. Therefore I say that a ram together with an ox are not a horse. That means that there is no horse (in the present discourse). Consequently, a ram is not two, and an ox is not two, but a ram and an ox are two. Thus it is shown that a ram and an ox are not a horse. If they were considered to be so, it would be a case of exemplifying (two) by taking quite different species. This is like the case of taking left and right " (pp. 74-75).

This shows that the universals of ox, ram and horse are entirely different, and so those of ram and ox cannot be combined to form horse. Though they cannot be thus combined, however, their number if they are counted together, will be two. Therefore it is said : " A ram is not two, and an ox is not two, but a ram and an ox are two." Though a ram and ox are not of the same species, this does not prevent them from being counted together to make two, just as right and left are added to make two. Hence : " If they were considered to be so, it would be a case of exemplifying (two) by taking quite different species. This is like the case of taking left and right."

Continuing :

" An ox and a ram have hair, while a fowl has feathers. The speaking about the leg of a fowl makes one. Its number of legs is two. Two and one make three. The speaking about the leg of an ox and ram makes one. The number of their legs is four. Four and one make five. Thus rams and oxen have five feet each, and fowls have three. Therefore when I say that an ox and a ram do not make a fowl, I have no other reason than this. If choosing for comparison a horse or a fowl, the horse is better. What has certain qualities and what has not, cannot be put in the same species. To make such

appellation is called a confusion of terms, and would be a loose
appellation (*k'uang chü* 狂 舉)" (p. 75).

This means that an ox and a ram differ even more from a fowl than
from a horse. The universal leg of a fowl, that is, 'the speaking
about a fowl's leg,' together with its actual two legs, make three. In
the same way the speaking about an ox's and ram's leg, that is,the universals, 'ox leg' and 'ram leg,' together with their actual four legs,
make five for each.' Hence the universals of ox and ram cannot be
combined to make fowl. Yet even if they could be combined in this
way, it would be better to say that they could be combined to make
horse. For compared to a fowl, a horse is closer to an ox and a ram,
and hence : " If choosing for comparison a horse or a fowl, the
horse is better." To say that a ram and an ox could make a fowl
would be a 'confusion of terms' and a 'loose appellation.'

The text that follows is not very clear, but its general idea seems
to be that green and white cannot make yellow, nor can white with
green make blue. This follows the same reasoning as that a ram and
an ox are not a horse, and an ox and a ram are not a fowl. Hence
the text says : " Yellow corresponds to horse ; blue to fowl " (p. 76).
These are simply further analogies to explain the ideas given above.

10—The 'Unity of Similarity and Difference' and 'Separateness of Hard and White'

The *Chuang-tzŭ* (ch. 5) says : " If we see things from the point
of view of their difference, even liver and gall are as far away from
each other as the states of Ch'u and Yüeh. If we see things from the
point of view of their similarity, all things are one " (p. 57). This is
spoken with reference to particulars, however. Any particular thing
is made up of many different qualities, which are themselves not
absolute. Hence Mount T'ai may be said to be small, while the tip
of an autumn hair may be said to be large. But with universals this
is not the case. A universal is simply a universal, and its quality is
absolute. Thus the universal of 'big' can only be big, and that of
'small' can only be small. Hui Shih's point of view stresses particular
things, and so he says : " All things are in one way all similar, in
another way all different," and concludes by saying : " Love all
things equally ; the universe is one." Kung-sun Lung, on the other
hand, lays stress on the universal, and so speaks of the 'separateness
of hard and white,' and summarizes by saying : " They are all single,
which is the correct (way of) the world." Having such opposing viewpoints, the doctrines of these two groups were completely different.
When persons of the Warring States period discussed the doctrines of

---

¹ The universal leg of a fowl cannot, actually speaking, be added to its two existing
legs. The Dialecticians nevertheless maintained this idea, so that in the *Chuang-tzŭ* (ch.
33) we find such paradoxes being attributed to them as : " A fowl has three legs "; and,
" A brown horse and a dark ox make three " (pp. 451-452).

the Dialecticians, they usually summarized them as 'the unity of similarity and difference, and separateness of hard and white.' This was only a general way of speaking, however. Actually the Dialecticians were divided into two schools : that of the 'unity of similarity and difference,' headed by Hui Shih ; and that of the 'separateness of hard and white,' headed by Kung-sun Lung.

Chuang Tzŭ's philosophy agreed in part with that of Hui Shih, and therefore he approved of the 'unity of similarity and difference,' but not of the 'separateness of hard and white.' The *Chuang-tzŭ* (ch. 2) says :

"To take *chih* to illustrate that *chih* are not *chih*, is not so good as to take non-*chih* to illustrate that *chih* are not *chih*. To take a horse to illustrate that horses are not horses, is not so good as to take non-horses to illustrate that horses are not horses. The universe is a *chih*; all things are a horse " (p. 19).

Kung-sun Lung holds that " there are no things that are not *chih*, but these *chih* are no *chih*." Such is 'to take *chih* to illustrate that *chih* are not *chih*.' Again, Kung-sun Lung maintains that " a white horse is not a horse." Such is ' to take a horse to illustrate that horses are not horses.' But if we ' see things from the point of view of their identity,' then *chih* or universals are identical with the myriad things that are not *chih*, so that *chih* are non-*chih*. Likewise a horse is identical with the myriads of things that are not horses, and at the same time a horse is not merely a horse. When this is the case, ' The universe is a *chih*; all things are a horse.' And then one may say with Chuang Tzŭ : " The universe came into being with me together, and with me, all things are one."

11—THE TWENTY-ONE PARADOXES OF THE DIALECTICIANS

Chapter XXXIII of the *Chuang-tzŭ*, in addition to the ten paradoxes attributed directly to Hui Shih, records twenty-one others made by ' the Dialecticians of the world.' [1] Among these twenty-one paradoxes, some are based upon Hui Shih, others upon Kung-sun Lung, and hence I shall divide them into two groups : those of the ' unity of similarity and difference,' and those of the ' separateness of hard and white.'

Those of the first group are :
" The egg has hair."
" Ying (the capital of Ch'u) contains the whole world."
" A dog may be a sheep."
" The horse has eggs."
" The frog has a tail." [2]

[1] *Cf.* pp. 451-453.
[2] Ch'eng Yüan-ying (seventh century A.D.), in his *Nan-hua Chen-shing Chu-su*, says that in the state of Ch'u people used the term here translated as frog (*ting tzŭ* 丁 子, which usually means ' nail ') as meaning frog.

" Mountains produce mouths."
" Tortoises are longer than snakes."
" A white dog is black."

The *Hsün-tzŭ* (ch. 2) contains a list of similar paradoxes : " ' Mountains are on the same level as pools ; the heavens are level with the earth.' ' The states of Ch'i (in far eastern China) and Ch'in (in far western China) are conterminous.' ' That which enters by the ear issues from the mouth.' ' A hook has a beard.' ' The egg has hair.' Utterances like these are difficult to uphold, nevertheless Hui Shih and Teng Hsi were bold enough to undertake their defence" (*Forke*, p. 85). This passage proves that all paradoxes of this type should be attributed to Hui Shih's group.

To say that ' the egg has hair,' means that out of the egg may come a hair-bearing, and not feather-bearing, creature. A dog, likewise, is not a sheep, and yet it is said : ' A dog may be a sheep.' A horse is a viviparous creature, and to say that 'the horse has eggs ' means that it may become an oviparous creature. A frog does not itself have a tail, so that to say that ' the frog has a tail ' means that it may become a creature having a tail. Likewise mountains do not produce mouths, and so to say that ' mountains produce mouths ' means that they may become such things as have mouths. On the paradox in the *Hsün-tzŭ*, 'That which enters by the ear issues from the mouth,' Yang Liang, in his commentary (published A.D. 818), gives an explanation : " Some say that this is the same as ' mountains produce mouths', that is to say, that mountains have mouths and ears." And upon the *Hsün-tzŭ's* paradox, ' A hook has a beard,' Yü Yüeh (1821-1906) suggests : " The word *kou* 鈎 (hook) may be a substitution for *ch'ü* 姁 (married woman)." According to this emendation, therefore, the meaning would be : "A married woman has a beard." All these paradoxes are based upon the principle of the similarity of all things. Seen from the point of view of their similarity, there are no things that are not similar, and hence any one thing may be said to be any other thing, and vice versa.

Hui Shih says : " The heavens are as low as the earth ; mountains are on the same level as marshes." Again : " I know the center of the world ; it is north of Yen and south of Yüeh." In the same way one may say : " Ying contains the whole world." Also : " The states of Ch'i and Ch'in are conterminous."

There is a Chinese proverb that states : " There are ways in which a foot is short, and in which an inch is long." If we say a thing is long because it is long in a certain way, then ' tortoises are longer than snakes.' As for the final paradox, the *Ching-tien Shih-wen* quotes Ssŭ-ma Piao (died A.D. 306) as saying : " A white dog with black eyes may be considered also a black dog." In other words, when we say the white dog is white, it is because his fur is white. We designate him as white according to that wherein he is white. But if we were to call him black according to that wherein he is black, this would be to say that ' a white dog is black.'

The paradoxes belonging to the ' separateness of hard and white ' group are :

" A fowl has three legs."

" Fire is not hot."

" Wheels do not touch the ground."

" Eyes do not see."

" *Chih* do not reach ; things never come to an end." [1]

" T-squares are not square ; compasses cannot make circles."

" Chisels do not surround their handles."

" The shadow of a flying bird never moves."

" There are times when a flying arrow is neither in motion nor at rest."

" A puppy is not a dog."

" A brown horse and dark ox make three."

" An orphan colt has never had a mother."

" If a rod one foot in length is cut short every day by one half of its length, it will still have something left even after ten thousand generations."

As to the paradoxes : ' A fowl has three legs ' ; and, ' A brown horse and dark ox make three,' the *Kung-sun Lung-tzŭ* (ch. 4) says : " The speaking about the leg of a fowl is one. Its number of legs is two. Two and one make three. The speaking about the leg of an ox and ram is one. The number of their legs is four. Four and one make five " (p. 75). The *Chuang-tzŭ* (ch. 2) says similarly : " One and speech make two " (p. 24). The one of this speech (or perhaps, if we proceed by another explanation, the universal idea of the ' leg of a fowl '), added to the fowl's two legs, make three. In the same way, the speaking about a brown horse and dark ox is one, and the number of them is two, making a total of three. Or, according to the other explanation, the universal of ' a brown horse and dark ox ' is one, and they themselves are two, also making a total of three.

We have seen that Kung-sun Lung's ' separateness of hard and white ' is based upon both epistemological and metaphysical arguments. The explanation for the paradox, ' Fire is not hot,' is, metaphysically speaking, that the universal of fire is fire, and the universal of hot is hot. The two are absolute and not one, and so even though a particular and concrete fire possesses the quality of hotness, fire as a universal is not hot. Or epistemologically speaking, the hotness of fire proceeds from our sensation of it, so that hotness is subjective. It pertains to us, and not to the fire.

---

[1] The actual reading in the *Chuang-tzŭ* is : " *Chih* do not reach ; the reaching never comes to an end." The present interpretation is taken from the version appearing in the *Lieh-tzŭ* (ch. 4). *Cf. Forke*, p. 83.

The paradox, 'Wheels do not touch the ground,' may be explained by saying that what is touched by the wheel is a small portion of the ground, and not the entire ground itself, just as a white horse is not a horse. Or we may say that a wheel that touches the ground is a concrete wheel, and the ground touched by it is concrete ground. But the universal, 'wheel,' does not touch the universal, 'ground,' nor is the universal, 'ground,' touched by the universal, 'wheel.'

As to the paradox, 'Eyes do not see,' Kung-sun Lung's 'Discourse on Hard and White' says : " The white is perceived through the eye seeing, by means of fire (i.e., light), but the fire does not see. So then, fire and the eye do not see, and it is the mind which sees. But the mind does not see, vision being something separate " (p. 80). That is, for us to be able to see, we must possess eyes, light, and the function of the mind. Without all these three we cannot see, so that if we have eyes alone, sight is no longer possible. This is the epistemological explanation. In metaphysics, we may say that the universals of ' eye,' ' light,' ' mind' and ' vision,' are four distinct universals. They are all ' separate ' and so cannot be combined into one.

The paradox, ' Chih do not reach ; things never come to an end,' is based on the distinction made by Kung-sun Lung between chih (universals) and things, in his chapter bearing that name. Plato said that ideas are thinkable but not perceivable. That is, what we can perceive is the particular, whereas the universal can be thought of but not perceived ; or as Kung-sun Lung says here : ' Chih do not reach (to our perception).' Things bounded by space and time, however, in which the universal becomes manifested, are ever changing and are being perpetuated in endless succession ; hence ' things never come to an end.'

The paradox, ' T-squares are not square ; compasses cannot make circles,' may be explained by saying that the absolute square and absolute circle are universals. Particular squares and circles as found in actuality cannot be absolute squares or circles, nor can particular T-squares or compasses produce such absolute squares and circles.

The same argument holds true in the paradox, ' Chisels do not surround their handles.' What surrounds the handle is a concrete and particular chisel, but the universal, ' chisel,' does not surround a handle.

We may group together the next two paradoxes : ' The shadow of a flying bird never moves ' ; and, ' There are times when a flying arrow is neither in motion nor at rest.' Three explanations are possible for this :

(1) Ssŭ-ma Piao is quoted in the *Ching-tien Shih-wen* as saying : " The form is at rest ; the tendency is in movement. When the form is apparent there is slow movement. When the tendency is

apparent there is rapid movement." That is, when we say that the shadow of a flying bird moves and that a flying arrow is not at rest, we are speaking of their moving tendency. But when we say that the shadow of a flying bird does not move and that a flying arrow does not move, we are speaking of their forms. When we say, ' There are times when a flying arrow is neither in motion nor at rest,' we are referring both to the arrow's form and to its impelling tendency.¹

(2) Or we may say that what move and what have times of motion and of rest, are the particular flying arrow, and the particular shadow of the flying bird, as they exist in actuality. As to the universals of these, they, like all universals, do not move, and so have neither movement nor rest.

(3) We may also say that an object which during one instant of time is at two points, is in movement, whereas an object which in two instants of time remains at one point, is at rest. An object which during one instant of time remains at one point, is said to be neither in motion nor at rest. Hence when it is said that ' the shadow of a flying bird never moves,' this refers to the fact that the shadow during one instant of time is not in two points. Likewise when it is said that ' there are times when a flying arrow is neither in motion nor at rest,' this refers to the fact that the flying arrow during one instant of time remains in one point. This statement has reference to the ideal shadow of the flying bird, and the ideal flying arrow, and not to shadows and arrows in actuality. The same is true in the case of the ' rod one foot in length ' described below.²

The paradox, ' A puppy is not a dog,' is analogous to the statement that a white horse is not a horse.

To explain the paradox, ' An orphan colt has never had a mother,' the *Ching-tien Shih-wen* quotes Li I of the Chin dynasty (265-420) : " A colt when it is born has a mother, but when it is spoken of as orphan, it is then without a mother. Once the term ' orphan ' is applied, that of ' mother ' must be dispensed with. The mother was the mother of a colt, and so an *orphan* colt has never had a mother." This also is said with reference to the universal, ' orphan colt.' ' Orphan colt, ' as a universal, means a colt that has no mother. But in the case of a particular orphan colt in the actual world, there must have been a time when it had a mother, and hence such a particular orphan colt cannot be spoken of as never having had a mother.

The final paradox is : ' If a rod one foot in length is cut short every day by one half of its length, it will still have something left even after ten thousand generations.' This means that matter is

---

¹ Just what Ssŭ-ma Piao means by ' form ' (*hsing* 形) and ' tendency ' (*shih* 勢), it is difficult to determine, and this quotation is given more as an example of the way the commentators have handled these texts, than as a logical explanation.—TR.

² This last explanation has been suggested by Professor Chin Yo-lin.

infinitely divisible. Thus if each day we take the half of what has been cut in half the day before, even after ten thousand generations there must remain something. Such division, however, is only an ideal operation carried out with an ideal rod. A concrete rod could not be thus infinitely divided, for division carried out in this way on an actually existing rod would be something impossible.

12—Sensation and Intellect

The preceding pages have shown us that the viewpoint of Hui Shih is one stressing the particular. The particular is ever in a state of change, and hence Hui Shih's philosophy may also be said to be one of change. Kung-sun Lung's viewpoint, on the other hand, is one stressing the universal, and the universal does not change, so that Kung-sun Lung's philosophy may be said to be one of permanency. The philosophies of these two men, though differing, are both the result of the examination of the world by the intellect, and hence what they perceived is of a sort quite different from the world that is perceived with the senses.

Our common sense is based wholly upon sensory knowledge, and from the viewpoint of such knowledge, the Dialecticians did indeed seem to "prove the impossible as possible, and affirm what others deny." What our common sense holds to be not so, they maintained was so, and vice versa. This is why the criticism was made of Hui Shih that " in reality he simply contradicted men, yet he wished to have the reputation of overcoming them," and why the Dialecticians were accused of having " made minute examination of trifling points in complicated and elaborate statements, which made it impossible for others to refute their ideas. They specialized in the definition of names, but lost sight of human feelings." Likewise it was said that " they attack each other tooth and nail and cause subtle divisions and disorder." Kung-sun Lung himself is reported to have said : " I controverted the wisdom of all the philosophies. I refuted all arguments that were brought against me." These criticisms, made by varying schools of thought, were all based upon common sense. Whether the Dialecticians did, in fact, " like to deal with strange theories and to indulge in curious propositions " merely to gain the reputation of overcoming others, or whether they really wished to reach what they believed to be the truth, we cannot know. But the value of a philosophy, in any case, exists quite independently of the motives which may have induced its founders to establish this philosophy.

CHAPTER X
CHUANG TZŬ AND HIS SCHOOL OF TAOISM

1—CHUANG TZŬ AND THE CHARACTERISTICS OF THE PEOPLE OF CH'U

The *Shih Chi* (ch. 63) gives a biography of Chuang Tzŭ :
" Chuang Tzŭ 莊 子 was a native of Meng (in present Honan).
His personal name was Chou 周. He held a small post at Ch'i-yüan,
in Meng. He was a contemporary of Kings Hui of Liang (370-319)
and Hsüan of Ch'i (319-301). His erudition was most varied, but his
chief doctrines were based upon the sayings of Lao Tzŭ. His writings,
which run to over 100,000 words, are for the most part allegorical.
His literary and dialectic skill was such that the best scholars of the
age were unable to refute his destructive criticism of the Confucian
and Mohist schools. His teachings were like an overwhelming flood
which spreads unchecked according to its own will, so that from
rulers and ministers downward, none could apply them to any
practical use.

" King Wei of Ch'u (339-329), hearing good of Chuang Tzŭ,
sent messengers to him, bearing costly gifts, and inviting him
to become Prime Minister. At this Chuang Chou smiled and said
to the messengers : ' A thousand taels of gold is valuable indeed, and
to be Prime Minister is an honorable position. But have you never
seen the sacrificial ox used for the suburban sacrifice ? When after
being fattened up for several years, it is decked with embroidered
trappings and led to the altar, would it not willingly then change place
with some uncared-for pigling ? Begone ! Defile me not ! I would
rather disport myself to my own enjoyment in the mire than be slave
to the ruler of a state. I will never take office. Thus I shall
remain free to follow my own inclinations.' " [1]

Meng was a place in Sung, so that Chuang Tzŭ was a native of
Sung ; yet at the same time the form of his thought is close to that
of the Ch'u people. The *Shih Chi* (ch. 84), for example, says of the
Li Sao (the great elegy written by Ch'ü Yüan of Ch'u, who committed
suicide about 288 B.C.) : " It is like the cicada moulting in the midst
of muck and silt, and then soaring aloft to wander beyond the dusty
world. Undefiled by the dirt of the world, its purity is untarnished
though it has passed through the mud." All the Elegies of Ch'u

---

[1] *Cf.* H. A. Giles, *Chuang Tzŭ*, pp. vii-viii. This incident is taken from the *Chuang-tzŭ*
(ch. 32), p. 434.—TR.

(*Ch'u Tz'ŭ*), of which the *Li Sao* is the most noted example, display a richness of imagination and freeness of spirit that distinguish them completely from the eulogies and songs that make up the Book of Odes. The thought and style of the *Chuang-tzŭ*, likewise, display great freedom and imagination. A passage in the fourteenth chapter gives an example :

"Does the sky turn around? Does the earth stand still? Do sun and moon compete for their positions? Who causes this? Who directs this ? Who has leisure enough to see that such movements continue ?

" Is there perhaps a mechanical arrangement that makes these bodies move inevitably as they do ? Is it perhaps that they keep revolving without being able to stop themselves ? Is it the clouds which make the rain ? Or is it the rain which makes the clouds ? Who makes it descend ? Who has leisure enough to see that such a result is achieved ?

" Wind comes from the north. It blows now east, now west ; and now it whirls aloft. Who puffs it forth ? Who has leisure enough to be flapping it this way or that ? I should like to know the cause of all this " (p. 173).

Both in form and in content this passage resembles the *T'ien Wen* (Questions about Heaven), one of the poems contained in the Elegies of Ch'u. While it may not actually have been written by Chuang Tzŭ himself, it shows at any rate the connection between his school and the Ch'u people. The position of this school was one of thorough-going opposition to all traditional thought and institutions ; attacking the Confucians and Mohists alike, it found praise only for Lao Tzŭ. Thus Lao Tzŭ, though not placed by the *Chuang-tzŭ* (ch. 33) in the same group with Chuang Tzŭ, is treated with great respect. We should keep in mind the fact that the state of Sung bordered Ch'u, making it quite possible that Chuang Tzŭ was influenced on the one hand by Ch'u, and at the same time was under the influence of the ideas of the Dialecticians. (Hui Shih, it will be remembered, was a native of Sung.) Thus by using the dialectics of the latter, he was able to put his soaring thoughts into order, and formulate a unified philosophical system.

The *Shih Chi* tells us that Chuang Tzŭ was a contemporary of Kings Hui of Liang and Hsüan of Ch'i. This would make him practically contemporary with Mencius; indeed, professor Ma Hsü-lun, in his Chronology of Chuang Tzŭ, makes his life extend from 369 to 286 B.C. [1] But, it may be asked, if Chuang Tzŭ was a contemporary of Mencius, why is it that the two seem never to have debated with each other ? The answer is that Chuang Tzŭ's philosophy is, after all, that of Yang Chu developed a step further, so that to Mencius he might have seemed a mere follower of Yang Chu.

---

[1] *Cf.* the *Chuang-tzŭ Nien-piao* in his *T'ien Ma Shan Fang Ts'ung Chu.*

Mencius, similarly, would be regarded by Chuang Tzŭ as a follower of Confucius. Hence when Mencius attacked Yang Chu and Mo Tzŭ, it is possible that with them he also included Chuang Tzŭ; while when Chuang Tzŭ criticized the Confucians and Mohists, it is possible that he also included Mencius. This may explain why, even though Mencius mentions only Yang Chu, and Chuang Tzŭ mentions only Confucius, the two may nevertheless have been perfectly aware of each other's existence.

2—The Way, the Power and Nature

Although Chuang Tzŭ's philosophy differs from that of the *Lao-tzŭ*, his concepts of *Tao* and *Te* remain the same. The *Chuang-tzŭ* (ch. 22) says of *Tao*:

" Tung Kuo Tzŭ asked Chuang Tzŭ : ' Where is the so-called *Tao* ? ' Chuang Tzŭ said : ' There is nowhere where it is not.' Tung Kuo Tzŭ said : ' Specify an instance of it.' Chuang Tzŭ said : ' It is in the ant ' ' How can it be so low ? ' ' It is in the panic grass.' ' How can it be still lower ? ' ' It is in the earthenware tile.' ' How can it be even lower ? ' ' It is in excrement.' To this Tung Kuo Tzŭ made no reply. Chuang Tzŭ said : ' Your question does not touch the fundamentals of *Tao*. When Huo, inspector of markets, asked the managing director about the fatness of pigs, the test was always made in parts least likely to be fat. You should not specify any particular thing. There is not a single thing without *Tao*. There are three terms : Completeness, All-embracingness and the Whole. These three names differ but denote the same reality ; all refer to the one thing ' " (pp. 285-286).

Tao is the all-embracing first principle through which the universe has come into being. When there are things, there must be *Tao*. Therefore ' there is nowhere where it is not.' Another passage (ch. 6) says :

" *Tao* has reality and evidence, but no action and form. It may be transmitted, but cannot be received. It may be attained to, but cannot be seen. It exists by and through itself. It existed prior to Heaven and Earth, and indeed for all eternity. It causes the gods to be divine, and the world to be produced. It is above the zenith, but it is not high. It is beneath the nadir, but it is not low. It is prior to Heaven and Earth, but it is not ancient. It is older than the most ancient, but it is not old " (p. 76).

Being the all-embracing first principle that produces the universe, *Tao* ' exists by and through itself.' Without beginning or end, it is eternal, and all things in the universe depend upon it to be constantly brought into being.

The action of *Tao* is also spontaneous. Therefore (ch. 12) :

" (Human) skill is bound up with human affairs ; human affairs are bound up with what is right ; what is right is bound up with the

Power *(Te)* ; *Te* is bound up with *Tao* ; and *Tao* is bound up with Nature *(T'ien* 天) " (p. 136).

Nature means what is spontaneous, so that :

" To act by means of non-activity *(wu wei* 無 爲) is what is called Nature " (p. 137). Again (ch. 17) :

" What is of Nature is internal. What is of man is external . . . . . That oxen and horses should have four feet is what is of Nature. That a halter should be put on a horse's head, or a string through an ox's nose, is what is of man " (p. 211).

When Chuang Tzŭ says that ' *Tao* is bound up with Nature,' his meaning is that of the *Lao-tzŭ* (ch. 25), when it says : " *Tao's* standard is the spontaneous (ch. 25)."

Tao is the all-embracing first principle of the universe, and this first principle is outwardly made manifest in the things of the universe. A passage in chapter XIII says :

" Oh, my Master ! Oh, my Master ! Thou who destroyest all things and dost not account it cruelty ; thou who benefitest all time, and dost not account it kindness ; thou who art older than antiquity and dost not account it age ; thou who supportest the universe, shaping the many forms therein, and dost not account it skill : this is the happiness of Nature ! " (p. 159).

How is this so ? *Tao* is manifested in all things, and therefore when these things are born and grow, we may say in one way that it is *Tao* that brings this about, yet in another way we may say that all things do these things by themselves. " What do I do ? What do I not do ? Things are transformed of themselves " (p. 209). Chapter II says :

" The winds as they blow differ in thousands of ways, yet all are self-produced. Why should there be any other agency to excite them ? " (p. 13).

All things are like this ; they all are transformed of themselves. Therefore, in the words of the *Lao-tzŭ* (ch. 37), " *Tao* never does, yet through it all things are done."

Because *Tao* is not a particular object, it can be spoken of as Non-being *(wu* 無). Chapter XII says :

" At the Great Beginning *(t'ai ch'u* 大 初) there was Non-being. It had neither being nor name and was that from which came the One. When the One came into existence, there was the One, but still no form. When things obtained *(te* 得) that by which they came into existence, it was called their Power *(Te).* What was formless, yet divided, though the division is not clearly made, was called Fate *(ming).* This Fate, flowing into movement, brought things into existence, and these things being brought into existence according to certain principles, had what is called form. This physical form enclosing the spiritual part, each with its own special principles, was what was called its nature *(hsing)* " (pp. 143-144).

The Non-being here spoken of is *Tao*. The *Lao-tzŭ* says : '*Tao* produced Oneness' (ch. 42), and Chuang Tzŭ similarly speaks of *Tao* as that from which came the One. As for *Te*, he says : "When things obtained that by which they came into existence, it was called their *Te*." Thus the all-embracing first principle whereby the universe is produced is *Tao*. The first principle whereby each individual thing is brought into existence is called *Te*. Therefore : "Form without *Tao* cannot have existence. Existence without *Te* cannot have manifestation" (p. 138).

It is because *Tao* and *Te* are equally that whereby things have existence, that in both the *Lao-tzŭ* and *Chuang-tzŭ* they are grouped together under a single phrase, *Tao-Te*. A commentator writes : "*Tao* and *Te* are the same in substance though different in name . . . . That which is everywhere is called *Tao*. That which is obtained from it is called *Te*. *Tao* is what all men follow. *Te* is what men individually obtain from it (*Tao*). Let us try to make comparison with water. Certainly the vast deeps of lakes and seas differ from what is contained in the hollow on top of a platform. But inasmuch as they are both water, are they different ? What pours out of a river and what flows from a ditch are as they are, because (of the water) they have received. Is it not correct, then, to say that their substance is the same though their names be different ? " [1]

This points out very well wherein *Tao* and *Te* are identical and wherein different. In order to be in accord with Chuang Tzŭ's philosophy, however, we must revise the statement to read : "*Tao* is what all things (including man) follow. *Te* is what things individually obtain from it." What brings things from formlessness into a condition in which they have form and existence is termed Fate (*ming*). Having become things, they must assume definite forms. These forms, together with their spiritual parts, must have definite organization and principles, or as was said above, 'each has its own special principles.' It is that organization and these principles which we call a thing's or a man's nature (*hsing*).

3—The Philosophy of Change

The forms of things, however, are not forever changeless, remaining always as they were when they were created. According to Chuang Tzŭ, there is never a moment when things in the universe are not in a process of change. The *Chuang-tzŭ* (ch. 2) says :

"When once we have received the corporal form complete, its parts do not fail to perform their functions till the end comes. In conflict with things or in harmony with them, they pursue their

---

[1] A statement made by Chiang Mou, quoted by Chiao Hung (1541-1620), in *chüan* 7, p. 38, of his *Lao-tzŭ* I.

course with the speed of a galloping horse. Is it not deplorable ? "
(p. 15). Again (ch. 17) :
"The existence of things is like a galloping horse. There is
no movement through which they do not become modified, no
time when they are not changed " (p. 209). And again (ch. 27) :
"Things are under different species (*chung* 種). They undergo
changes from one form to another. Their beginning and end are
like a circle, no part of which is any more the beginning than another
part. This is called the Evolution of Nature (*t'ien chün* 天 鈞).
The Evolution of Nature is the Boundary of Nature (*t'ien i* 天 倪) "
(p. 365).

This same phrase, ' Evolution of Nature,' occurs also in Chapter
II (p. 21). Its meaning is that what we call Nature, is a process of
movement. In the preceding chapter I said that the philosophy
of Hui Shih was one of change, and we see here that Chuang
Tzŭ's is similar.

4—How to Attain Happiness

All things come from *Tao*, and each obtains from it its own
individual *Te*. All things have their own spontaneous natures. Let
them once follow these, says Chuang Tzŭ, and happiness lies straight
before them, without need to seek it afar. The *Chuang-tzŭ* (ch. 1)
illustrates this idea by the story of the mythical *p'eng* bird, the
greatest of all living creatures, as contrasted with the tiny cicada
and the young dove : "When the *p'eng* is moving to the Southern
Ocean, it flaps along the water for three thousand *li*. Then it ascends
on a whirlwind to a height of ninety thousand *li*, for a flight of
six months' duration " (p. 1). But the cicada and dove laugh at the
p'eng, saying : "When we make an effort, we fly up to the trees.
Sometimes, not able to reach, we fall to the ground midway. What
is the use of climbing ninety thousand *li* in order to start for the
south ? " (p. 2). Kuo Hsiang (died between A.D. 307 and 312), in
his famous commentary on Chuang Tzŭ, says about this passage :
"He (Chuang Tzŭ) tells the story of the extremely great and
the extremely small, in order to illustrate the fitness of the nature
of things. . . . If there is satisfaction for their natures, the *p'eng*,
although large, has nothing to be proud of in comparison with the
small bird, and the small bird has no desire for the Celestial Lake.
Therefore, though there is a difference between the great and the
small, their happiness is the same." [1]

If this is the case with things, it is also the case with men, so
that the same chapter continues :
"There are some men whose knowledge is sufficient for the
duties of some office. There are some men whose conduct will
secure harmony in some district. There are some men whose virtue

---

[1] *Cf.* Fung Yu-lan, *Chuang Tzŭ*, pp. 27 and 30.

befits them to be rulers. There are some men whose ability wins credit in a country. In their opinion of themselves, they are just like what is mentioned above (i.e., the *p'eng* and the dove) " (p. 4).

Descartes has said in similar strain : " Good sense is, of all things among men, the most equally distributed ; for every one thinks himself so abundantly provided with it, that those even who are the most difficult to satisfy in everything else, do not usually desire a larger measure of this quality than they already possess." [1] That is, every man finds complete satisfaction in that with which he has been endowed by Nature. The *Chuang-tzŭ* (ch. 9) says :

" The people have a constant nature : to weave and clothe themselves, till and feed themselves. This is the common nature of all, and everyone agrees with it. This is said to be sent by Nature. And so in the age when the nature of man was perfect, men moved quietly and gazed steadfastly. At that time there were no roads over the mountains or boats and bridges to cross the waters. Things were all born and matured, each attached to its own native locality. Birds and beasts multiplied ; trees and shrubs grew up. The former could be led by the hand. One could climb and peep into the raven's nest. In this age of perfect nature, men dwelt together with birds and beasts, and the human race was one with all things. How could there be a knowledge of the distinctions of superior and inferior men ? All being equally without knowledge, their instincts (*te* 德) did not leave them. All being equally lacking in desires, they may be said to have been in a state of Unadorned Simplicity (*su p'u* 素樸). Being in this state, they had possession of their original natures " (pp. 107-108).

Another passage (in ch. 13) records an apocryphal speech made by Lao Tzŭ to Confucius :

" Do you, Sir, wish to cause the world to be well governed ? Heaven and Earth have their constants. The sun and the moon have their brightness. The stars have their groupings. Trees and shrubs have their life and growth. You, Sir, first liberate your instincts (*te* 德) and follow *Tao*. That is all. Why then these vain struggles after ' human-heartedness ' (*jen*) and ' righteousness ' (*i*), as though beating a drum in search of a lost child ? Alas, Sir ! You have thrown men's original natures into confusion ! " (p. 167).

The words, ' Heaven and Earth have their constants,' etc., are descriptive of the natural processes of the universe, and when the admonition is given : ' Liberate your instincts and follow *Tao*,' it is meant that in this way men and things can come to follow their own innate natures. The same chapter says :

" Comprehension of the qualities of Heaven and Earth : this is called the great root and the great foundation. It is to be in

---

[1] *Cf. Discours de la méthode*, p. 1.

harmony with Nature (*T'ien*). . . . To be in harmony with Nature is the happiness of Nature" (p. 159).

It is through following their natures that men and things can reach this state of harmony with Nature, called the happiness of Nature.

Political and social institutions of all kinds, as viewed by Chuang Tzŭ, serve only to impose suffering on man. This is because the natures of different things are not identical, and each individual thing has its own special likings. Hence they neither need be, nor should they be, forcibly made identical. Since things are thus different, it is right that they should remain different. In this way uniformity is made out of difference. All political and social institutions, however, decide upon a single Good as a standard for conduct, and make all men follow this standard. This is to constrain difference to a forced uniformity, in which case what is intended to help people results only in harming them. The *Chuang-tzŭ* (ch. 18) relates a story :

"Of old, when a seabird alighted outside the capital of Lu, the Marquis of Lu went out to receive it, gave it wine in the temple, and had the *Chiu Shao* music played to amuse it, and a bullock slaughtered to feed it. But the bird was dazed and too timid to eat or drink anything. In three days it was dead. This was treating the bird as one would treat oneself, and not as a bird would treat a bird. Had he treated it as a bird would have treated a bird, he would have put it to roost in a deep forest, allowed it to wander over the plain, to swim in a river or lake, to feed upon fish, to fly in formation (with others), and to settle leisurely. When it already hated hearing human voices, fancy adding music! Play the *Hsien Ch'ih* and *Chiu Shao* in the wilds of Tung-t'ing, and on hearing it birds will fly off, beasts will run away, and fish will dive below. But men will gather together to listen.

"Water, which is life to fish, is death to man. Being differently constituted, their likes and dislikes must necessarily differ. Therefore the early Sages did not make abilities and occupations uniform. Name was commensurate with actuality, and the purpose remained within the bounds of what was feasible. This was called having a due relationship with others, coupled with benefit to oneself" (pp. 226-227).

Here is an outspoken condemnation of the fixed standards which man must obey. The Sage (of the Confucian type) formulates all sorts of political and social institutions as standards, and commands everyone to obey them. Although his purpose is undoubtedly praiseworthy, and he is actuated wholly by love for his people, the result is like that in the case of the Marquis of Lu who loved the bird, and who through loving it, ended by injuring it. Hence Chuang Tzŭ violently opposes the idea of governing through government, and maintains that if one wishes to keep the world in good order, the only way is to govern through non-government. The *Chuang-tzu* (ch. 7) says :

" Bring your mind into a state of quiet, and your energy (*ch'i* 氣) into a state of indifference. Follow the spontaneity of things and hold within you no element of ego. Then the empire will be governed " (p. 93). Again (ch. 11) :

" I have heard of letting mankind alone, but not of governing mankind (with success). Letting alone springs from fear that men will pollute their innate natures, and set aside their instincts (*te* 德). When men do not pollute their natures and set aside their instincts, then is there need for the government of mankind ? " (p. 119).

It is possible to govern through non-government because regardless of how widely people may differ in their likes, they all equally desire order and peace. Chapter I says :

" Everything in the world longs for peace. Why should there be some who address themselves laboriously to govern the empire ? " (p. 8). Again (ch. 12) :

" Good order is desired by the whole world alike, so why bother to take Shun into consideration ? " (p. 152).

Since good order is generally desired, one need only let things alone, and good order will result spontaneously. Thus Chuang Tzŭ, like Lao Tzŭ, advocated government through non-government, though his basis for this doctrine differs from that of the *Lao-tzŭ*.

If one does not follow men's innate natures, but wishes to rule them forcibly through all kinds of institutions, the process is like putting a halter around a horse's neck or a string through an ox's nose ; what is natural and spontaneous is changed into the artificial. The result is misery and man-made suffering of all kinds. Chapter VIII says :

" The duck's legs are short, but if we try to lengthen them, the duck will feel pain. The crane's legs are long, but if we try to cut off a portion of them, the crane will feel grief. Therefore we are not to amputate what is by nature long, nor to lengthen what is by nature short " (p. 101).

The purpose of artificiality is largely concerned with just such cutting off of what is long and the lengthening of what is short, that is, changing what is natural. As soon as there is artificiality, therefore, the happiness that comes from according oneself with the natural is lost. The result is unhappiness and also a loss of interest in life. As an example, the *Chuang-tzŭ* (ch. 7) gives a story about the ruler of the Center, who was called Primitivity, and his two friends, Change and Uncertainty. These had often been well treated by Primitivity, and so decided to repay his kindness, saying : " All men have seven holes for seeing, hearing, eating and breathing. Primitivity alone has none of these. Let us try to bore some for him " (p. 98). So every day they bored one hole ; but on the seventh day Primitivity died.

Another passage (ch. 17) says : " Do not let what is of man obliterate what is of Nature. Do not let what is purposeful obliterate Fate " (p. 211). This is what happens when what is natural and spontaneous is changed into something artificial.

5—LIBERTY AND EQUALITY

What has already been said shows that Chuang Tzǔ's social and political philosophy is one of complete liberty. For, says Chuang Tzǔ, only when all men have complete liberty, can they follow their spontaneous natures and so obtain happiness. An advocate of complete liberty, however, must also be an advocate of complete equality. For if in the relations of man with man and thing with thing, we once recognize that there are some cases in which ' that ' is better than ' this,' and other cases in which ' this ' is better than ' that,' then what is good must work toward reforming what is not good so as to make it also good. And then the doctrine of complete liberty falls to the ground. Chuang Tzǔ, however, believed that all men and creatures should have complete liberty, and therefore also maintained that there is nothing in the world which is not good, and that there is no point of view which is not right. In this lies a fundamental difference between Chuang Tzǔ's philosphy and Buddhism. For Buddhism, on the contrary, maintains that there is nothing in the world which is good, and no point of view which is not false. The *Chuang-tzǔ* (ch. 2) says :

" Now I would ask you some questions. If a man sleep in a damp place, he will have a pain in his loins, and half his body will be as if dead. But is it so with an eel ? If a man live up in a tree, he will be frightened and all in a tremble. But is it so with a monkey ? Of these three, who knows the right way of habitation ? Men eat flesh ; deer feed on grass. Centipedes enjoy snakes ; owls and crows delight in mice. Of these four, who knows the right taste ? Monkey mates with monkey ; the buck with the doe ; male fish with female. Mao Ch'iang and Li Chi were considered by men as the most beautiful of women ; but at the sight of them fish dived deep in the water, birds soared high in the air, and deer hurried away. Of these four, who knows the right standard of beauty ? " (p. 27).

We must either admit that there is a fixed standard for beauty, in which case one of the four is correct ; but in that case we may fairly ask, which of the four ? Or we may admit that there is no fixed standard, in which case all four are correct. This is like the case of the seabird, which liked to swim in the river or lake and to eat fish, whereas the Marquis of Lu liked music and the sacrificial ox. Although the two methods of enjoyment are absolutely different, they may both be accepted as correct.

The viewpoints of men, similarly, differ in as many ways as do the sounds produced by the wind roaring through the openings in the trees of the forest, as described in the first paragraph of Chuang Tzǔ's second chapter. In the final analysis, which is right and which is wrong? Could the 'argument' of the Dialecticians of Chuang Tzǔ's day really distinguish between right and wrong? His second chapter, entitled 'The Equality of Things and Opinions,' says:

" Suppose that you argue with me. If you beat me, instead of my beating you, are you necessarily right and am I necessarily wrong? Or, if I beat you and not you me, am I necessarily right and are you necessarily wrong? Is the one of us right and the other wrong? Or are both of us right and both of us wrong? Both of us cannot come to a mutual and common understanding, and others are all in the dark. Whom shall I ask to settle this dispute? I may ask someone who agrees with you; but since he agrees with you, how can he settle it? I may ask someone who agrees with me; but since he agrees with me, how can he settle it? I may ask someone who differs from both you and me; but since he differs from both you and me, how can he settle it? I may ask someone who agrees with both you and me; but since he agrees with both you and me, how can he settle it? In this way, you and I and others would all be unable to come to a mutual and common understanding; should we wait for still another person?" (pp. 30-31).

Thus it is evident that right and wrong cannot be decided through argument. For if we select any one thing as being right, which of all the points of view in the world shall we select as being the right one? It is as impossible to decide this as it is to determine who knew the right way of habitation, the right taste, and the right standard of beauty, in the passage quoted. If we do not select some one thing as being right, the points of view of everyone in the world are all equally right. All of them being right, we can each of us follow our own individual viewpoint, and there is no need for argument. The same chapter continues:

" Referring to the right and the wrong, the 'is' and the 'is not': if the right is really right, we need not dispute about how it is different from the wrong; if the 'is' is really 'is,' we need not dispute about how it is different from the 'is not'! Regardless whether the changing sounds are relative to one another or not, let us harmonize them within the Boundary of Nature, and leave them alone in the process of natural evolution. This is the way to complete our span of years. Let us forget life. Let us forget the distinctions of right and wrong. Let us find enjoyment in the realm of the infinite and remain there!" (p. 31).

Let us regard the points of view in the world as we do the 'changing sounds' or the chirps of young birds also mentioned in this chapter. No one ever wished to dispute about the sounds of the wind or the cries of birds, as to whether they are right or wrong. Why, then, should we hold heated arguments only about the rightness or wrongness of men's words ? We should, in short, simply let them alone.

It is along such lines that the same chapter replies to the debaters of its time :

" Speech is not merely the blowing of the wind. It is intended to say something. But what it is intending to say is not absolutely established. Is there really such a thing as speech ? Or is there really no such thing as speech ? Some consider speech as different from the chirping of young birds. But is there any distinction between them, or is there no distinction ? How is *Tao* obscured that there should be a distinction between true and false ? How is speech obscured that there should be a distinction between right and wrong ? Where is *Tao* not present ? Where is speech not appropriate ? *Tao* is obscured by partiality. Speech is obscured by eloquence. Therefore, there are the contentions between the Confucians and the Mohists. Each of these two schools affirms what the other denies, and denies what the other affirms. If we are to affirm what these two schools both deny, and to deny what they both affirm, there is nothing better than to use the light (of understanding).

" There is nothing which is not the ' that ' (another thing's other) ; there is nothing which is not the ' this ' (its own self). Things do not know that they are another's ' that ' ; they only know that they are ' this.' Therefore I say that the ' that ' proceeds out of the ' this,' and the ' this ' also evolves from the ' that.' The ' that ' and the ' this ' can be spoken of as alternately producing one another. Nevertheless, when there is life there is death, and when there is death there is life. When there is possibility there is impossibility, and when there is impossibility, there is possibility. Because of the right there is the wrong, and because of the wrong there is the right. This is why the Sage does not proceed along these lines, but sees things from the point of view of Nature.

" The ' this ' is also ' that.' The ' that ' is also ' this.' The ' that ' has a system of right and wrong. The ' this ' also has a system of right and wrong. Is there really a distinction between ' that ' and ' this ' ? Or is there really no distinction between ' that ' and ' this ' ? Not to discriminate ' that ' and ' this ' as opposites, is the very essence of *Tao*. Only the essence, an axis as it were, is the center of the circle responding to the endless changes. The right is an endless change. The wrong is also an endless change. Therefore, it is said that there is nothing better than to use the light (of understanding) " (pp. 16-19).

This passage seems to be a criticism of the doctrines of Kung-sun Lung. Kung-sun Lung, in his ' Discussion of Names and Actualities,' maintained that 'that' can only be 'that,' and 'this' can only be 'this.'[1] Chuang Tzŭ, on the contrary, maintains that the two are relative. Therefore "the 'that' proceeds out of the 'this,' and the 'this' also evolves from the 'that.' The 'that' and the 'this' can be spoken of as alternately producing one another." Similarly with the contentions between the Confucians and Mohists. They each cling to one thing as being right, so that "the 'that' has a system of right and wrong ; the 'this' also has a system of right and wrong." It is like an endlessly revolving closed circle. If we once realized that there is nowhere where *Tao* is not present, and nothing in which speech is not appropriate, we would see that the contentions of Confucians and Mohists, equally with the chirps of young birds, are merely natural 'changing sounds.' Hence we must simply let them alone, which is why Chuang Tzŭ says : " This is why the Sage does not proceed along these lines, but sees things from the point of view of Nature." This 'point of view of Nature' is equivalent to the 'light of reason.'

Right necessarily implies the existence of wrong, and vice versa, so that right and wrong are purely relative. If we let the right and the wrong, the 'this' and the 'that,' alone, however, without considering them to be right and wrong or this and that, no opposition will exist between them. Therefore, "Not to discriminate 'that' and 'this' as opposites is the very essence of *Tao*." 'This' and 'that' are both alternately right and wrong. "The right is an endless change. The wrong is also an endless change." One should not keep up endless debate with the person who maintains a definite idea of right and wrong, but should stand in the center of the circle and let others alone. This is because 'only the essence, an axis as it were, is the center of the circle responding to the endless changes.' The same chapter says further :

" Therefore the Sage harmonizes the systems of right and wrong, and rests in the Evolution of Nature. This is called following two courses at once " (p. 21).

Another chapter (ch. 27) also speaks of this 'Evolution of Nature,' as well as of the 'Boundary of Nature' (p. 365). These expressions refer to the spontaneous changes of all things. To 'rest in the Evolution of Nature' means to let things follow their own spontaneity. The Sage's attitude toward the alternating right and wrong of things, is simply to let them alone. Therefore his attitude does not abolish the distinctions of right and wrong, but transcends them, an act which may be called ' following two courses at once.'

To look at things from this viewpoint is to look at them from the standpoint of *Tao*, or, as western philosophic language would express it, *sub specie aeternitatis*. Chapter XVII says :

---

[1] *Cf.* quotation on p. 205.

"From the standpoint of *Tao*, there is nothing which is valuable or worthless. Whereas from the point of view of things, each holds itself as something valuable and other things as of no account. From the point of view of the vulgar, the value or worthlessness of a man does not depend upon himself, (but upon wealth, position, etc.). If looking at things according to their gradated differences, we say they are relatively big, then there is nothing in the universe which is not big; if we say they are relatively small, there is nothing in the universe which is not small. To know that Heaven and Earth are but as a tare-seed, and that the tip of a hair is a mountain : this is the expression of relativity.

"From the viewpoint of its function, if we say that a thing exists or does not exist, in reference to the function it fulfills or does not fulfill, then there is nothing which does not exist, nothing which does exist. If we know that east and west are opposite, and yet that the one cannot be without the other, we know the due adjustment of the functions of things.

"From the viewpoint of the biases (of things), if we say that anything is right because it is right (in its own eyes), then there is nothing which is not right. If we say that anything is wrong because it is wrong (in the eyes of others), then there is nothing which is not wrong. To know that Yao and Chieh were both good and both evil from their opposite points of view : this is to see their bias . . . .

"From the standpoint of *Tao*, what is 'valuable'? What is 'worthless'? Do not hold to something bigotedly, for this would involve great opposition with *Tao*. What are 'few'? What are 'many'? They are inconstant. Do not be one-sided in your conduct, for this would be diverging from *Tao*. Be dignified, as the ruler of a state who is completely unselfish. Be dispassionate, like the worshipped spirit of the land, whose dispensation is impartial. Be all-comprehensive, like the points of the compass, to whose boundlessness no limit is set. Hold all things in your embrace, and then which will leave you? This is to be without one-sidedness. Where all things are equal, how can one be long and another short?

"*Tao* is without beginning or end, whereas things die and are born. They have no guarantee of permanence. Now empty, now full, they have no set form. Past years cannot be recalled; time cannot be arrested. Growth and decay are the succession of transformations. When there is end, there is beginning. This is the way to speak of the aspects of the great standard and to discuss the principles of all things" (pp. 205-206).

The world commonly classifies men according to the rank they hold in government or society, so that 'the value or worthlessness of a man does not depend upon himself,' but upon the way the world regards him. Each individual thing, however, thinks of itself as exceptional and other things as ordinary, as, for example, the small dove described in Chapter I, who mocked at the great *p'eng* bird. But all these see things from a finite viewpoint. If one can go beyond this finite viewpoint, one will then look at things from the standpoint of *Tao*. From such a standpoint everything is equal to everything else. And if one still further unites with *Tao*, and makes no distinctions whatsoever, one will reach the state in which ' all things with oneself are one.' This point will be taken up in detail below.

There are some who may say that inasmuch as Chuang Tzŭ holds that ' following two courses at once ' is what is right, he is in this respect still holding to a distinction between right and wrong. This point is also taken up in the *Chuang-tzŭ* (ch. 2) :

" Now I have something to say. I do not know whether or not what I shall say is of the same character as what others say. In one sense, what I say is not of the same character. In another sense, what I say is of the same character, and there is no difference between what I say and what others say . . . . I have just said something ; but I do not know whether what I have said is really something said or not really something said. In all the world there is nothing greater than the tip of an autumn hair ; Mount T'ai is small. Neither is there anyone longer-lived than a child cut off in its infancy ; P'eng Tsu (the Chinese Methuselah) died young. Heaven and Earth came into being with me together, and with me, all things are one. Since all things are one, what room is there for speech ? But since I have spoken of the oneness, is this not already speech ? One and speech make two ; two and one make three. Going on from this, even the most skilful reckoner will not be able to reach the end, so how much less able to do so are ordinary people ! If, proceeding from nothing to something, we can reach three, how much more shall we reach, if we proceed from something to something ! Let us not proceed ; let us stop here " (pp. 22-24).

Chuang Tzŭ, by holding that ' following two courses at once ' is right, also has a right and a wrong, and so is no different from others who hold to a right and a wrong. Yet by saying that this ' following two courses at once ' is what is right, he wishes to transcend ordinary right and wrong, and so after all is no longer in the same class with other people who hold to a right and wrong. Therefore he says : " I have just said something ; but I do not know whether what I have said is really something said or not really something said." If even Chuang Tzŭ fails to escape from the weakness of still having a right and a wrong, because he holds that transcending the ideas of right and wrong is what is right, then how much more do those persons who make the ordinary distinctions of right and wrong ! Therefore he says : " If, proceeding from nothing to something, we can reach three, how much more shall we reach, if we proceed from something to something ! " Hence : " Let us not proceed ; let us stop here."

6—IMMORTALITY

There is nothing that is not good, and no point of view that is not right. This is the fundamental idea of Chuang Tzŭ's second chapter on 'The Equality of Things and Opinions'. Extending this conception, there is no form of existence which is not good. What is called death is nothing more than a change from one form of existence to another. Hence if we look upon our present form of existence as something to find happiness in, there is no reason why we should not also find happiness in the new form of existence which we assume after death. The *Chuang-tzŭ* (ch. 6) says :

" To have attained to the human form is a source of joy. But, in the infinite evolution, there are myriads of other forms that are equally good. What an incomparable bliss it is to undergo these countless transitions ! " (p. 75).

Chapter II says :

" How do I not know that the love of life is not a delusion ? How do I not know that he who is afraid of death is not like a man who was lost from his home when young and therefore does not want to return ? Li Chi was the daughter of the border warden of Ai. When the state of Chin first got her, she wept until the front part of her robe was drenched with tears. But when she came to the royal residence, shared with the king his luxurious couch, and ate rich food, she regretted that she had wept. How do I know that the dead will not repent of their former craving for life ? Those who at night dream of a banquet, may the next morning wail and weep. Those who dream of wailing and weeping, may in the morning go out and hunt. When they dream, they do not know that they are dreaming. In their dream, they may even interpret dreams. Only when they are awake, they begin to know that they dreamed. By and by comes the Great Awakening, and then we shall find out that life itself is a great dream " (pp. 29-30).

Chapter XVII says : " *Tao* is without end or beginning, whereas things die and are born " (p. 209). Kuo Hsiang comments on this : " Death and life are never-ceasing transformations. They are not an end or a beginning." If we once understand this principle, we can equalize life and death. Chapter VI says :

" If my left arm should be transformed into a cock, I would mark with it the time of night. If my right arm should be transformed into a crossbow, I would look for a bird to bring down and roast. If my rump-bone should be transformed into a wheel, and my spirit into a horse, I would mount it and would have no need of any other steed. When we come, it is because we have the occasion to be born. When we go, we simply follow the natural course. Those who are quiet at the proper occasion and follow the course of nature, cannot be affected by sorrow or joy. These men were considered by the the ancients as people who are released from bondage " (p. 81).

Not to be affected by sorrow or joy, is to have transformed the emotions by means of reason. Spinoza has said that the emotions are human bondage. If there are men of true knowledge, who understand the reality of the universe, and who know that the way in which things evolve is inevitable, they will be unmoved by whatever they may meet. They will not be bound by the emotions and will attain to human freedom. Suppose, for example, that a sudden gust of wind blows down a roof tile so that it hits a small child and a mature man on their heads. The child will feel intense anger against the tile, whereas the man's emotions will not be stirred, and for this very reason his pain will be actually less. This is because the man will understand that the falling of the tile is a physical phenomenon, and therefore he will ' not be affected by sorrow or joy.' The *Chuang-tzŭ* (ch. 3) comments about someone who bitterly mourned the death of Lao Tzŭ :

" This is to violate the principle of Nature and to increase the emotion of man, forgetting what we have received (from Nature). This was called by the ancients the penalty of violating the principle of Nature " (p. 36).

Death is the natural result of life, and to feel bitterness against such a result is ' to violate the principle of Nature and to increase the emotion of man.' He who does so must pay the penalty, which is the suffering which he feels during his mourning. If we understand that ' when we come, it is because we have the occasion to be born ; when we go, we simply follow the natural course,' then we shall no longer be affected by sorrow or joy, and so shall not pay any penalty, but shall be released from bondage. This will be because we have used reason to transform our emotions. The *Chuang-tzŭ* (ch. 18) describes how when the wife of Chuang Tzŭ died, Chuang Tzŭ sang, beating time on a bowl, and when questioned by a friend, replied :

" When she first died, how could I help not being affected ? But then on examining the matter, I saw that in the Beginning she had originally been lifeless. And not only lifeless, but she had originally been formless. And not only formless, but she had original-ly lacked all substance. During this first state of confused chaos, there came a change which resulted in substance. This substance changed to assume form. The form changed and became alive. And now it has changed again to reach death. In this it has been like the passing of the four seasons, spring, autumn, winter and summer. And while she is thus lying asleep in the Great House (i.e., the Universe), for me to go about weeping and wailing, would be to show myself ignorant of Fate (*ming*). Therefore I refrain " (pp. 223-224).

This shows how Chuang Tzŭ was able to control his emotions by means of reason, until he was no longer affected by sorrow or joy.

From another viewpoint, we may not only consider life and death as equal to one another, but can even attain to a state of neither life nor death. Chapter V says :

" If we see things from the viewpoint of their difference, even liver and gall are as far from each other as the states of Ch'u and Yüeh. If we see things from the viewpoint of their similarity, all things are one " (p. 57).

Chapter XXI says :

" Grass-eating animals do not dislike to change their pasture ; creatures born in water do not dislike to change their water. These minor modifications have no effect on the general uniformity. . . . Now the universe is the unity of all things. If we attain this unity and identify ourselves with it, then the members of our own body are but so much dust and dirt, while death and life, end and beginning, are but as the succession of night and day, which cannot disturb our inner peace ; and how much less shall we be troubled by worldly gain and loss, good luck or calamity ! " (p. 267).

Chapter VI says :

" A boat may be hidden in a creek ; a net may be hidden in a lake ; these may be said to be safe enough. But at midnight a strong man may come and carry them away on his back. The ignorant do not see that no matter how well you conceal things, smaller ones in larger ones, there will always be a chance for them to escape. But if you conceal the universe in the universe, there will be no room left for it to escape. This is the great truth of things. . . . Therefore the Sage wanders amidst that which cannot escape, but wholly remains. He who can accept both early death and old age, beginning and end, will be followed by men. How much more is that (to be followed) which connects all things and upon which all phenomena depend ? " (pp. 75-76).

For everything in the universe, no matter where we may hide it, there exists the possibility of its being lost. But if the universe as a whole is hidden in the universe as a whole, there remains no place where it may be lost. Therefore if we can unite ourselves with the universe to form one ; ' if we attain this unity and identify ourselves with it '; then, since the universe has no beginning or end, so too shall we be without beginning and end. The universe is eternal, and so are we. This is the meaning of the words : ' To wander amidst that which cannot escape, but wholly remains.' The same chapter says later :

" I kept on speaking to him ; after three days, he began to be able to disregard all worldly matters. After he had disregarded all worldly matters, I kept on speaking to him ; after seven days, he began to be able to disregard all external things. After he had disregarded all external things, I kept on speaking to him ; after nine days, he began to be able to disregard his own existence. Having disregarded his own existence, he was enlightened. Having become enlightened, he was then able to gain the vision of the One. Having the vision of the One, he was then able to transcend the distinction of past and present. Having transcended the distinction of past and present, he was then able to enter the realm where life and death are no more. Then, to him, the destruction of life did not mean death, nor the prolongation of life an addition to the duration of his existence. He would follow anything ; he would receive anything. To him, everything was in destruction, everything was in construction. This is called tranquility in disturbance. Tranquility in disturbance means perfection " (pp. 79-80).

In this passage the process of forgetting or effacement is graphically described : first that of worldly things, then of the external world as a whole, and then of one's own existence, until one reaches a sudden mystical enlightenment in which one sees the unity of all things. When this unity is perceived, the distinctions between past and present, life and death, are obliterated, and one reaches eternity. Thus we can see that it is by forgetting life that one may attain to immortality, a goal which would be impossible if the distinction between existence and non-existence were not first obliterated. Such is a state in which ' the destruction of life does not mean death, nor the prolongation of life an addition to the duration of existence.' In this state, no distinctions whatsoever are made, so that ' one follows anything, and would receive anything.' The experience in this state is pure experience.

7—The World of Pure Experience

From the foregoing, we can see that the state of pure experience means a state in which the individual is one with the universe. Pure experience is the experience in which we have no intellectual knowledge, in which we accept the immediate presentation ; "the *that* in short (for until we have decided *what* it is, it must be a mere *that*)," as William James has said. We simply take " the *that* at its face value, neither more nor less ; and taking it at its face value means, first of all, to take it just as we feel it, and not to confuse ourselves with abstract talk about it." [1] The so-called intuition (*hsien liang* 現 量) of the Buddhists seems to be similar to this. So is the experience of the True Man (*chen jen* 眞 人) spoken of by Chuang Tzŭ. And the world in which he lives is a world of experience of this kind. The *Chuang-tzŭ* (ch. 2) says :

" The knowledge of the ancients was perfect. How perfect ? At first, they did not know that there were things (i.e., they had experience, but no intellectual knowledge). This is the most perfect knowledge ; nothing can be added. Next they knew that there were

---

[1] James, *Essays in Radical Empiricism*, pp. 13, 48.

things, but they did not make distinctions between them. Next they made distinctions between them, but they did not yet pass judgments upon them. When judgments were made, *Tao* was injured. With the injury to *Tao*, individual preferences came into being. Are there really construction and destruction? Or are there really no construction and destruction? That there are construction and destruction is like the fact that of old Chao played the lute. That there are no construction and destruction is like the fact that he did not play the lute" (pp. 21-22).

The less knowledge one has of things, distinctions, and of right and wrong, the more pure is the experience. When one is in a state of pure experience, the things experienced are concrete; whereas what are designated by names are abstractions. Thus what are designated by names actually form only a part of experience. For example, what is designated by the word ' man ' only comprises the general characteristics of mankind as a whole. It fails to include the specific individual characteristics of each individual man. Therefore as soon as there are names, there is apparent ' construction,' whereas actually there is ' destruction,' for the names fail fully to cover the qualities of the things to which they are applied. Kuo Hsiang says in his commentary on the above passage:

" All tunes cannot be played at once. Therefore in blowing wind instruments or plucking stringed ones, no matter how many hands take part in it, there must be some tunes left unplayed. To play music is to make the tunes known. But by making it known one gets only a part; by not making it known, one gets the whole. Therefore, the fact that Chao Wen played the lute was to destroy something by constructing something. The fact that Chao Wen did not play the lute was to destroy nothing by constructing nothing." [1]

All the distinctions of names are like this. Therefore we should only take experience's ' face value ' and not confuse ourselves with abstract verbal distinctions. The *Chuang-tzŭ* (ch. 2) says:

" The possible is possible; the impossible is impossible. *Tao* evolves and sequences follow. Things have names and are what they are. What are they? They are what they are. What are they not? They are not what they are not. Everything is what it is, and does what it can do. There is nothing which is not something. There is nothing that cannot do something. Therefore, a beam and a pillar are identical. So are ugliness, beauty, greatness, wickedness, perverseness and strangeness. Separation is the same as construction. Construction is the same as destruction. But all things, without regard for their construction and destruction, may again be united in the one. Only the truly intelligent know the unity of things, but follow the common and the ordinary. The

---

[1] Fung Yu-lan, *Chuang Tzŭ*, p. 54.

common and the ordinary are the natural functions of all things, which express the common nature of the whole. Following the common nature of the whole, they are happy. Being happy, they are near perfection. For them, perfection is to stop. They stop, yet they do not know that they stop. This is *Tao*" (pp. 19-20).

Thus each thing is what it is, and does what it does. There is no need for us consciously to make it so, or consciously make distinctions about things. With distinctions there comes ' construction,' but with such construction there must also be ' destruction.' In pure experience, however, there is neither construction nor destruction. Therefore the truly intelligent man avoids all distinctions, and rests in a state of pure experience, in which he is near perfection. The perfection is reached when although he rests in this state, he is unconscious that he rests in it. At this point, although ontologically things still have their thousands of particularities, epistemologically there are no distinctions to the knower. At this point one can truly realize that ' Heaven and Earth came into being with me together, and with me, all things are one.'

What the *Chuang-tzŭ* calls ' the fast of the mind ' (*hsin chai* 心齋) and ' sitting in forgetfulness ' (*tso wang* 坐忘) are designations for this state of pure experience. Of the former, Chapter IV says :

" Maintain the unity of your will. Do not listen with ears, but with the mind. Do not listen with the mind, but with the spirit (*ch'i* 氣). The function of the ear ends with hearing ; that of the mind, with symbols or ideas. But the spirit is an emptiness ready to receive all things. *Tao* abides in the emptiness ; the emptiness is the Fast of the Mind " (p. 43).

And of the latter, Chapter VI says in the course of a series of apocryphal conversations between Confucius, and his disciple, Yen Hui :

" ' I have made some progress,' said Yen Hui. ' What do you mean ? ' asked Confucius. ' I forget human-heartedness (*jen*) and righteousness (*i*),' replied Yen Hui. ' Very well, but that is not perfect,' said Confucius.

" Another day Yen Hui again saw Confucius and said : ' I have made some progress.' ' What do you mean ? ' asked Confucius. ' I forget ceremonials (*li*) and music,' replied Yen Hui ' Very well, but that is not perfect,' said Confucius.

" Another day Yen Hui again saw Confucius and said : ' I have made some progress.' ' What do you mean ? ' asked Confucius. ' I sit in forgetfulness,' replied Yen Hui. Confucius changed countenance and said : ' What do you mean by Sitting in Forgetfulness ? '

" ' I have abandoned my body,' said Yen Hui, ' and discarded my knowledge, and so have become one with the Infinite (*ta t'ung* 大通). This is what I mean by Sitting in Forgetfulness ' " (p. 89).

Both these terms, the Fast of the Mind and Sitting in Forget-fulness, refer to the discarding of knowledge and emptying of the mind, so as to ' become one with the Infinite,' a condition which is one of pure experience. This state is also implied in the ' disregard of all worldly matters ' and ' disregard of all external things ' mentioned in the preceding section. Chapter XII says :

" Through cultivation of one's nature (*hsing*), one returns to the Power (*Te*). Having returned to the Power, one becomes identified with the Beginning. Being thus identified, there comes emptiness. With this emptiness, there comes vastness. One is then like (birds) chirping with joined beaks.[1] Being like this, one reaches a union with the universe. Joined in this union, one is as someone stupid or confused. This is called the Mysterious Power (*Hsüan Te* 玄 德). It is identification with the great flux " (p. 144).

This so-called Mysterious Power is the condition of the True Man (*chen jen* 眞 人) in his state of pure experience. Such is the world of the True Man, which is described in the *Chuang-tzŭ* (ch. 6) :

" The True Man of old slept without dreaming and waked without anxiety. He ate without discrimination, and his breathing was deep [2] . . . . The True Man of old knew neither to love life nor to hate death. Living, he felt no elation ; dying, he offered no resistance. Unconsciously he went ; unconsciously he came ; that was all. He did not try purposely to forget what his beginning had been, or to seek what his end would be. He received with delight anything that came to him, and left without consciousness anything that he had forgotten. This is what is called not preferring the conscious mind to *Tao*, or supplementing Nature with man. Such is what we call the True Man " (pp. 69-70).

The True Man, being without thought or knowledge, empties his mind and becomes one with the infinite. Therefore he has the power to ' sleep without dreaming and wake without anxiety.' The same idea is expressed in a phrase already quoted in the preceding section : ' He would follow anything, he would receive anything.' [3]

---

[1] Kuo Hsiang comments on this : " To speak spontaneously without having the intention of speaking : this is to be like (birds) chirping with joined beaks."

[2] This seems to point toward special breathing exercises used to reach the state of mystical union.—Tr.

[3] The wordlessness that transcends words, and the absence of knowledge that transcends knowledge, of which Chuang Tzŭ speaks, and which were mentioned above (ch. 9, sect. 4, pp. 201-203), here become apparent. What Chuang Tzŭ speaks of as absence of knowledge, however, is a state coming after one has already had knowledge, and so is actually a synthesis of knowledge and primitive ignorance. As such it differs from original ignorance. In considering pure experience, we must also make this distinction. The new-born baby, for example, can have experience but no knowledge. Its experience is pure experience, which is primitive pure experience. But if someone, having already passed through a state of knowledge, attains once more to a state of pure experience, what he thus attains to a second time is already one stage higher than the primitive state of pure experience. The state of ' Mysterious Power ' in which ' one is as if stupid or confused,' is not one of actual stupidity and confusion, but only *seems* like these. Chuang Tzŭ's philosophy, however, is not entirely clear on this point.

8—ABSOLUTE FREEDOM

It is only after reaching the state of pure experience that one may attain to absolute freedom. For although each thing, if it follows its own nature, may attain happiness, yet its life still remains dependent on something else. This is described in the *Chuang-tzŭ* (ch. 1):

"Lieh Tzŭ ' could ride upon the wind and pursue his way, in a wonderful and admirable manner, returning after fifteen days. Among those who attain happiness, such a man is rare. Yet, although he was able to dispense with walking, he still had to depend upon something" (p. 5).

Lieh Tzŭ could ride on the wind, but without wind he could not move. Therefore his freedom was dependent upon wind. Extending this idea, we find that everyone in the world is dependent upon something for his happiness. Some require riches, others fame, others love, before they can be happy. Being dependent upon something, they can only reach freedom after obtaining what they are dependent upon, and hence they cannot be absolutely free. The man who ' fasts the mind ' and ' sits in forgetfulness,' however, sees that ' life and death are one, and the right and the wrong are the same ' (p. 61), and so his freedom is not dependent on anything, but is limitless and absolute. The *Chuang-tzŭ* (ch. 1) says :

" Suppose there is one who chariots upon the normality of the universe, rides upon the transformation of the six elements, and thus makes excursion in the infinite, what has he to depend upon ? Therefore, it is said that the Perfect Man (*chih jen* 至 人) has no self ; the Spiritual Man (*shen jen* 神 人) has no achievement ; the Sage (*sheng* 聖) has no name " (p. 5).²

' To chariot upon the normality of the universe,' etc., means to reach a union with the universe. One who suceeds in attaining this state does so because he has no self, no achievement and no name, but especially because of the first. Such a man is called the Perfect Man (*chih jen*), of whom the *Chuang-tzŭ* (ch. 2) says :

" The Perfect Man is spirit-like (*shen* 神). Were the great lakes burned up, he would not feel hot. Were the great rivers frozen hard, he would not feel cold. Were the mountains to be riven by thunder or the seas thrown into waves by a storm, he would not be frightened. Being such, he would mount upon the clouds, would ride upon the sun and moon, and would thus wander at ease beyond the seas. Neither death nor life can affect him ; how much less can the consideration of what is beneficial and what is harmful ? " (pp. 27-28).

---

¹ 列 子, a Taoist philosopher probably legendary, introduced by Chuang Tzŭ, and after whom a book, called the *Lieh-tzŭ*, has later been falsely attributed.—TR.

² Such terms as the Perfect Man, the Spiritual Man, and the True Man (described in the last section), occur frequently in the *Chuang-tzŭ* as designations for those who have reached the state of pure experience.—TR.

No place is there where the Perfect Man does not find his way. This is the ultimate of freedom.

Such is Chuang Tzŭ's mysticism. I discussed in Chapter VI the mysticism of Mencius, and pointed out that the method he uses to reach this mystic state is one of "acting with a vigorous effort at altruism (*shu*)" in one's "seeking for human-heartedness (*jen*)," until one reaches a state in which, as Mencius says, "All things are complete within us. There is no delight greater than to find sincerity (*ch'eng*) when one examines oneself." [1] The method of Chuang Tzŭ is to abolish all distinctions in knowledge until one reaches a state in which "Heaven and Earth came into being with me together, and with me, all things are one." These are two outstanding conceptions in the history of Chinese philosophy. That of Chuang Tzŭ, however, has been left untouched since the Wei (A.D. 220-265) and Chin (265-420) dynasties, whereas that of Mencius has been further developed by the Neo-Confucianists of the Sung (A.D. 960-1279) and Ming (1368-1644) dynasties. [2] What is particularly distinctive about Chuang Tzŭ's philosophy, is that his mysticism does not postulate an idealistic universe. In this respect he is at one with Spinoza.

9—CHUANG TZŬ COMPARED WITH YANG CHU

The foregoing sections reveal the weaknesses inherent in the methods of the 'recluses' and of Yang Chu, who clung to a doctrine of escaping from the world in order to have 'completeness of living and preservation of what is genuine.' The *Chuang-tzŭ* (ch. 20) says :

"Chuang Tzŭ was travelling over a mountain, when he saw a large tree with luxuriant branches and foliage. A woodsman had stopped beside it, not caring to hew it, and on Chuang Tzŭ's enquiring the reason, he was told that it was of no use.

"'This tree,' cried Chuang Tzŭ, 'by virtue of being good for nothing, succeeds in completing its allotted span.'

"When the Master (i.e., Chuang Tzŭ) left the mountain, he put up at the house of a friend. The friend was delighted, and ordered a servant to kill a goose and offer it.

"'One,' said the servant, 'can cackle. The other cannot. Which shall I kill?' His master said : 'Kill the one which can't cackle.'

"The next day a disciple asked Chuang Tzŭ : 'Yesterday there was that tree on the mountain, which because it was good for nothing, was allowed to complete its allotted span. But now our host's goose, because it was good for nothing, has had to die. Which alternative do you take?'

---

[1] *Cf.* p. 129.
[2] For details, see Fung Yu-lan, *Chung-kuo Che-hsüeh chung chih Shen-mi Chu-i* (Mysticism in Chinese Philosophy), in the *Yenching Journal of Chinese Studies*, No. 1.

" ' I rest,' replied Chuang Tzŭ with a smile, ' between the two. Yet this position between the two only appears to be right, whereas in fact it is not so, so that one still cannot escape entanglements.   But if one wanders about charioted upon *Tao* and *Te*, it is not so.   Without praise or blame, be now as a dragon (i.e., large), now as a snake (i.e., small) ; change with the times, without ever making a special effort ; now above, now below, using harmony as a measure, wander to the first ancestor of things, using things as things, and not being used as a thing by things.   How then can one suffer entanglement ?   Such were the methods of Shen Nung and the Yellow Emperor.

" ' But not so among the passions of things, and the traditional relationships of men.   Where there is union, there is separation ; where there is construction, there is destruction ; where there is purity, there is oppression ; where there is honor, there is disparagement ; where there is action, there is retrogression ; where there is worthiness, there is underhandedness ; and where there is unworthiness, there is deceit.   How can one be certain as to the result ?   Alas ! Take note, my disciples.   It is only in the domain of *Tao* and *Te* (that one can be completely safe) ' " (pp. 245-247).

If, then, we cannot comprehend that ' life and death are one, and the right and wrong are the same,' we can never completely escape from entanglements no matter how skilfully we cut ourselves off from the human world.   For ' where there is union, there is separation ' ; each good thing has its opposite.   Hence regardless of whether or not we are useful, none of us can receive only happiness and not bad fortune.   As for the Perfect Man, on the other hand, ' neither death nor life can affect him ; how much less the consideration of what is beneficial and what is harmful ? '   For him, these things are no longer benefit and harm, and hence, no longer injured by them, he can escape from all entanglements.   Such a man, who ' wanders about charioted upon *Tao* and *Te*,' can thus ' use things as things, and not be used as a thing by things.'   In his relations with all things, he is not passively moved, but is an active mover.

CHAPTER XI

THE LATER MOHIST SCHOOL

1—Conditions of the Mohist School during the Warring States Period

The *Han-fei-tzŭ* (ch. 50) says :
" After the death of Mo Tzŭ, there were the Mohists of Hsiang Li, the Mohists of Hsiang Fu, and the Mohists of Teng Ling " (*chüan* 19, p. 7). The *Chuang-tzŭ* (ch. 33) says :
" The disciples of Hsiang Li Ch'in, the followers of the Five Princes, and the Mohists of the south, such as K'u Huo, Chi Ch'ih and Teng Ling Tzŭ, all studied the 'Mohist Canons' (*Mo Ching* 墨 經), but they disagreed, holding opposite views and calling each other 'heretical Mohists' (*pieh Mo* 別 墨). They disputed with one another about the 'hard and white' and 'similarity and difference,' and answered each other's arguments with irregular and strange statements. They regarded the *Chü tzŭ* (the Mohist 'Leader') as a Sage, and each group wished him to be its leader and hoped to be his successor. Even now these differences are not settled " (pp. 442-443).

Such were conditions in the Mohist school during the Warring States period. To this period must be assigned the dialectical chapters contained in the *Mo-tzŭ*, known respectively as the ' Canons ' (*Ching* 經, chs. 40-41), ' Expositions of Canon ' (*Ching Shuo* 經 說, chs. 42-43), and ' Major and Minor Illustrations ' (*Ta Ch'ü* 大 取 and *Hsiao Ch'ü* 小 取, chs. 44-45). The prime reason for writing these chapters was to oppose the Dialecticians, whose doctrines were at that time generally considered to be contrary to all common sense, whereas Confucians and Mohists alike, with their stress upon the practical, agreed in using common sense to explain the universe. The fact that the Dialectician statements were all based on logic, however, forced their Mohist and Confucian opponents also to base their arguments on logic. This explains the appearance of such writings as the ' Mohist Canons ' in the Mohist works, and the chapter on ' The Rectification of Names ' in the *Hsün-tzŭ*, both written with the purpose of upholding common sense and attacking the Dialecticians.

Since both Confucians and Mohists were considerably influenced by the Dialecticians, they used more solid arguments in the development of their ideas than had their predecessors, a fact which becomes apparent when we compare the six dialectical chapters in the *Mo-tzŭ* discussed here, with the earlier chapters in *Mo-tzŭ*; or the *Hsün-tzŭ* with the *Lun Yü* and *Mencius*.

The writing of the 'Mohist Canons' stands out as a greater accomplishment than does that of the chapter on 'The Rectification of Names' in the *Hsün-tzŭ*, probably because the Mohist school from the beginning had valued dialectic more than had the Confucian. Mo Tzŭ himself had said: "To refute my words with one's own words is like throwing an egg against a stone. The eggs in the world would be exhausted without doing any harm to the stone" (*Mo-tzŭ*, p. 229). Again he said: "In speech, not quantity but wisdom, not literary refinement but detailed examination, should be cultivated" (p. 8). He further maintained that a doctrine should be subjected to three logical tests. All of this indicates his belief in the importance of the cultivation of wisdom and detailed examination.[1]

Again, the *Mo-tzŭ* (ch. 47) states: "Mo Tzŭ brought numerous books in his wagon drawers on his southern journey as an envoy to Wei" (p. 226). And in Chapter XLVI:

"Kung Meng Tzŭ said: 'The Superior Man does not create but transmits.'[2] Mo Tzŭ said: 'Not at all. . . . It seems to me that what there is good in the old should be transmitted, and what there is good in the present should be created (i.e., established), so that what is good may increase all the more'" (p. 219).

The *Chuang-tzŭ* (ch. 33) also says: "Mo Tzŭ was fond of study and had wide learning. Some points in his teachings were no different from those of others, while on other points he did not agree with the early kings" (p. 440). This 'fondness of study' is also a conspicuous feature in the 'Mohist Canons' of the Later Mohists.

It has already been suggested by Wang Chung (1744-1794), in his preface to the *Mo-tzŭ*, that the term 'Mohist Canons' was originally applied not only to the two chapters in *Mo-tzŭ* (chs. 40-41) which now specifically go by that name, but also to the two 'Expositions of Canon' and to the 'Major and Minor Illustrations.' Though there is no proof of this, the character and content of these other chapters agree unquestionably with those of the two 'Canon' chapters proper, and so they will be discussed together here as products of the Warring States period.

Lu Sheng (alive in A.D. 291) wrote a work called 'Preface to a Commentary on the Mohist Dialecticians' (*Mo Pien Chu Hsü* 墨 辯 注 敍), in which he grouped the 'Canons' and 'Expositions of Canon' under the term, 'Mohist Dialecticians' (*Mo Pien*). Dr. Hu Shih has not only followed this usage of calling the Later Mohists 'Dialecticians,' but has also suggested that the term *pieh Mo* 別 墨 should

---

[1] See above, pp. 85-86.
[2] The Confucian doctrine of 'creating through transmission.' Cf. *Lun Yü*, VII, 1.—Tr.

be interpreted as meaning ' Neo-Mohists.' ¹ Though it is true that the six chapters of the Later Mohists contain discussions about ' hard and white,' ' similarity and difference,' and other topics of the Dialecticians, these are inserted not to defend, but on the contrary to destroy, the Dialectician arguments, and the main motive in these chapters is to give an exposition of the Mohist ideas themselves ; while even the term, ' Mohist dialecticians,' is unknown before Lu Sheng's time. This means that the Later Mohists should be carefully distinguished from the Dialecticians. Not only this, but the *Chuang-tzŭ* tells us that the various Mohist groups " disagreed, holding opposite views and calling each other ' heretical Mohists,' " which means that each group was accusing the other of not being orthodox, rather than that they were applying the term *pieh Mo* to themselves in the sense of ' Neo-Mohists,' as Dr. Hu Shih believes. At the same time they ' regarded the *Chü tzŭ* as a Sage, and each group wished him to be its leader and hoped to be his successor.' This indicates that despite the differences existing between the various Mohist groups of the Warring States period, the rigid organization of the early Mohist school nevertheless persisted.

2—UTILITARIANISM IN THE ' MOHIST CANONS '

The doctrine of utilitarianism forms the basis of Mo Tzŭ's philosophy, but though Mo Tzŭ himself stressed utility, he failed to explain *why* we should thus value it. The ' Mohist Canons ' go one step further, and supply utilitarianism with a psychological basis. For example : ²

Canon, I : " The beneficial (*li* 利) is that which when obtained gives pleasure " (p. 418).

Exposition : " When one obtains it and it gives pleasure, this is what is beneficial (*li*). What is harmful is not this " (p. 446).

Canon, I : " The harmful (*hai* 害) is that which when obtained is disliked " (p. 419).

Exposition : " When one obtains it and it is disliked, this is what is harmful. What is beneficial is not this " (p. 446).

What we like is the beneficial ; what we dislike is the harmful. Therefore to move toward what is beneficial and to avoid what is

---

¹ This is the term found in the *Chuang-tzŭ* (ch. 33), which we have translated above as ' heretical Mohists.' The word *pieh* really means 'unlike' or ' different,' or, according to our interpretation, ' heretical,' whereas Dr. Hu Shih takes it as meaning ' different ' from the original school, that is, ' neo- '.—TR.

² Owing to the long neglect from which the ' Mohist Canons ' have suffered, as well as their original abstruseness, their text is frequently corrupt and makes perhaps the hardest reading in ancient Chinese philosophical writings. Much has been done toward their elucidation by such modern scholars as Sun I-jang (1848-1908), Liang Ch'i-ch'ao (1873-1929), Hu Shih and others, but their textual emendations are too numerous to be conveniently recorded here, and hence readers who are interested in them are asked to consult the original Chinese edition of the present work.—TR.

harmful is spontaneous in man's nature, and hence utilitarianism becomes the proper basis of human conduct. Bentham has stated very similarly :

"Nature has placed mankind under the governance of two sovereign masters, *pain* and *pleasure*. It is for them alone to point out what we ought to do. . . . The principle of utility recognises this subjection, and assumes it for the foundation of that system, the object of which is to rear the fabric of felicity by the hands of reason and law." [1]

What Bentham here terms pleasure and pain, the 'Mohist Canons' call the beneficial and the harmful, through which one may gain pleasure or pain ; while what Bentham terms reason, they call knowledge. Desires are blind, and must be led by knowledge, before one can obtain future benefit and avoid future harm. The *Exposition*, I, says :

"Suppose a man desires to cut off his finger. If he does not foresee the evil consequences of this, his knowledge (*chih* 智) is to blame. But if his knowledge has cautioned him not to do it, and yet he still desires to cut it off, he will suffer the consequences. This is like desiring to eat dried meat before knowing its good or bad smell. One wishes to do so even though there might be a bad smell. This means that one does not allow what one is uncertain about to deter one from what one desires. But suppose that outside one's wall there is either benefit or harm, which cannot yet be known. Though by venturing outside one might obtain some money, one does not go out. This is a case of allowing what one is uncertain about to deter one from what one desires " (p. 455).

The utility of the intellect consists in considering beforehand what will be the results of present conduct. When these results have been considered, the intellect can lead us toward the beneficial and away from the harmful, either so as to refuse the immediate small benefit in order to avoid a great future harm, or to accept immediate small harm so as to gain great future benefit. The following of such a process is what the *Major Illustrations* calls ' weighing ' or ' balancing ' (*ch'üan* 權) :

"To estimate the heaviness and lightness of bodies is called weighing (*ch'üan*). This weighing does not consist in finding out the right or wrong of things. It consists in balancing them correctly.

"When one cuts off a finger so as to preserve the hand, this is to choose the greater benefit and the lesser harm. To choose the lesser harm is not to choose harm, but to choose benefit. What one has thus chosen is because the situation is not under the control of oneself. If on meeting a robber one loses a finger so as to save one's life, this is benefit. The meeting with the robber is harm . . . . Choice of the

---

[1] *Cf.* his *Introduction to the Principles of Morals and Legislation*, p. 1.

greater benefit is not a thing done under compulsion. Choice of the lesser harm is a thing done under compulsion. The former means choosing from what has not yet been obtained. The latter means discarding from what one has already been burdened with " (pp. 503-506).

Again, in the *Canons* :

Canon, I : " Desire, when it is correctly weighed (*ch'üan*), is beneficial. Aversion, when it is correctly weighed, is harmful " (p. 420).

Exposition : " Balance (*ch'üan*) is two and not partial " (p. 458.)

That is, *ch'üan* is the objective weighing of good and bad, and hence is 'two and not partial.' This utilitarian philosophy holds that the benefit which man does and must select is not the immediate small benefit, but the future greater benefit, and likewise with the harm to be avoided. Hence whatever may happen to be desirable at the moment, may not necessarily be beneficial. It is only the desire which has been ' correctly weighed ' that can constitute true benefit, while what we dislike must also be correctly weighed before it can constitute true harm.'

In accordance with this viewpoint, the ' Mohist Canons ' establish the beneficial as the basis for all morality :

Canon, I : " Righteousness (*i* 義) consists in doing benefit (*li*) " (p. 415).

Exposition : " Righteousness consists in having one's mind set upon loving the world, and being able skilfully to benefit (*li*) it (the world), even though (one's righteousness) may not necessarily be made use of " (p. 443).

Canon, I : " Loyalty (*chung* 忠) consists in benefiting one's ruler " (p. 416).

Exposition : " Loyalty consists in exerting oneself for one's ruler and being able skilfully to benefit him, even though one does not thereby gain his favor " (p. 444).

Canon, I : " Filial piety (*hsiao* 孝) consists in benefiting one's parents " (p. 416).

Exposition : " Filial piety consists in holding love toward one's parents, and being able skilfully to benefit them, without thereby necessarily profiting " (p. 444).

Canon, I : " Meritorious accomplishment (*kung* 功) consists in benefiting the people " (p. 420).

---

¹ Exactly the same idea is found in the *Hsün-tzŭ* (ch. 2) : " The balance (*ch'üan*) between what is desired and what is disliked, what is accepted and what is refused, is, when one sees something desirable, to think of what may be undesirable in it before and afterward ; and when one sees what is beneficial, to think of what may be harmful in it before and afterward. One must weigh both sides, calculating them, before one can determine what is to be desired and what disliked, what accepted and what refused. In this way one will never meet with disaster. All men's calamities come from one-sidedness. When they see what is desirable, they do not consider what may be undesirable in it. When they see what is beneficial, they do not consider what may be harmful in it. Then when they move there must come disaster, and when they act there must come occasion for shame. This is the evil of one-sidedness " (*chüan* 2, p. 9.)

Exposition : " Meritorious accomplishment does not wait for any particular time, (but is always ready) like fur clothes (for winter) " (p. 447).

In all these cases the producing of what is beneficial is made the guiding motive of all virtue.

3—DISCUSSIONS ON KNOWLEDGE

Wishing to uphold common sense against the Dialecticians, the Later Mohists paid particular attention to the nature and origin of knowledge. Thus :

Canon, I : " Knowing (*chih* 知) is a faculty (*ts'ai* 材) " (p. 414).

Exposition : " Knowing is a faculty. This knowing is that by means of which one knows, but which of itself does not necessarily know, as in the case of light " (p. 442).

Such ' knowing ' is really the faculty or ability for knowing, the possession of which does not in itself necessarily mean the possession of knowledge. It is analogous to the eye's capacity for seeing objects, which is the eye's ' light ' ; and yet having this ' light ' does not necessarily mean that the eye will have sight. For the eye which has the capacity for seeing must also have something which is to be seen, before there can be sight. Likewise the faculty for knowing must have that which is to be known, before there can be knowledge. Again :

Canon, I : " Knowledge (*chih* 知) is a meeting " (p. 414).

Exposition : " Knowledge is that in which the knowing (faculty) meets the object and is able to apprehend its form and shape, as in seeing " (p. 442).

Such knowledge is that gained through the meeting of the faculty for knowing with the object to be known, enabling this faculty to perceive and apprehend the object. The eye, for example, originally having a capacity for seeing, sees the object to be perceived, and thereby also has vision. Again :

Canon, I : " Mind-knowledge (*chih* 想) is an understanding (*ming* 明) " (p. 414).[1]

" *Exposition* : Mind-knowledge is that in which the knowing (faculty) ' discusses ' (*lun* 論) the object and its knowing of it becomes clear, as in understanding " (p. 442).

That is, when our faculty for knowing ' meets ' the external objects which are to be known, it not only can sensually perceive their appearance, but it can know the kind of things they are. When it sees a tree, for example, it not only perceives its appearance, but it also knows that the tree is a tree. Such knowing that it is a tree consists in comparing the particular thing in question with the class of trees

---

[1] This word *chih* 想, composed of ' knowledge ' (*chih* 知) and ' mind ' (*hsin* 心), is not now found in any dictionary, indicating the long neglect from which these Mohist texts have suffered.—TR.

already existing in our former experience, a process in which "the knowing 'discusses' the object." Once this has been done, even though we have not yet seen whether the tree in question possesses the qualities generally pertaining to all trees, we can assume that it must have them. Thereupon our knowledge of the particular tree becomes distinct, or as the text says, 'its knowing of it becomes clear.'

In addition, there is another kind of knowledge which is not obtained through the senses :

Canon, II : " There is knowledge (*chih* 知) which does not come through the five roads. The reason is given under ' duration ' " (p. 427).

Exposition : " The knowing (faculty) sees through the eyes, which see because of fire (i.e., light), but the fire does not see, (the object) being known only through the five roads. But in durational (knowledge) there is no seeing with the eyes, or with fire " (p. 485).

The five roads are the five senses, called roads because it is along them that our sensations pass. Most of our knowledge is derived through the senses, so that there can be sight, for example, only when the eye and fire (that is, light) exist together. Without the eye there can be no sight. But there is also a kind of knowledge obtained independently of our senses, which is knowledge of duration. ' Duration ' (*chiu* 久) is explained as :

Canon, I : " Duration is what reaches to different times " (p. 421).

Exposition : " Duration is what unites past and present, morning and evening " (p. 448).

' Duration ' here evidently means time, and our ' durational ' knowledge, that is, our knowledge or sense of time, is not knowledge derived from the five senses.

There is yet another kind of mental activity :

Canon, I : " Cogitation (*lü* 慮) is a seeking for " (p. 414).

Exposition : " There is cogitation when there is seeking for something on the part of that which knows. But it need not obtain (what it is seeking for), as in gazing sideways (at something) " (p. 442).

What is here referred to is the activity of purposeful knowledge. We are ever using our knowledge to attain a certain end. Activity of this kind is termed *lü* (here translated as cogitation), and is ' a seeking for.' There are times when our eyes simply look upon things, without having any aim, but when we turn our heads aside in order especially to look at something, then there is a ' seeking for something on the part of that which knows.' Yet this sort of knowledge may not after all always gain what it is seeking for.

Man's capacity to know things is recognized by the Later Mohists as the primary factor in human life :

Canon, I : " Life (*sheng* 生) is body plus the knowing (faculty) " (p. 418).

Exposition : " Life : The life of bodies is ever something uncertain " (p. 446).

Canon, I : " In sleep, there is the knowing (faculty) without knowledge " (p. 418).

A body which possesses a knowing faculty is alive; without it it is dead. A state in which there is knowing without knowledge (that is, the faculty for knowing without the actual knowledge), is sleep. The state in which there is no faculty for knowing, and no knowledge, is death.

Besides the above definitions, the Later Mohists discuss from a logical viewpoint the origins and types of knowledge :

Canon, I : " Knowledge (*chih* 知) comprises hearing (*wen* 聞), inference (*shuo* 說), and personal experience (*ch'in* 親) ; there is that of names (*ming* 名), of actualities (*shih* 實), of correspondence (*ho* 合), and of action (*wei* 為) " (p. 419).

Exposition : " Knowledge : That which has been received through transmission is hearing ; that which is not hindered by distance is inference ; what is personally observed is personal experience. What designate are names ; what are designated are actualities ; when names and actualities pair with each other, this is correspondence ; will (*chih* 志) and movement (*hsing* 行) constitute action " (pp. 457-458).

' Hearing,' ' inference ' and ' personal experience' are classifications of knowledge according to how it is obtained. ' Names,' ' actualities,' ' correspondence ' and ' action ' are the various kinds of knowledge itself. These will be discussed one by one below.

(1) ' Hearing ' is knowledge which has been ' received through transmission,' i.e., through written or spoken words. All historical knowledge is of this kind.

(2) ' Inference ' is knowledge obtained by going from the known to the unknown :

Canon, II : " When one hears that what is not known is like what is known, then both are known " (p. 437).

Exposition : " What is outside is known. Then someone says : ' The color inside the room is like this color (outside).' In this case what is not known is like what is known. Thus between white and black, which would be the right one ? That which is said to be like this color. If this is white, that too must be white. Now knowing that this color is white, we therefore know that that one is white.

" Names serve by what is understood to make certain what is not known ; not by what is not known to conjecture at what is understood. It is like using a foot-rule to measure an unknown length. As to what is outside (in the above example), this is personally experienced ; what is inside is knowledge through inference " (p. 495).

We see some white objects outside a room, but do not know the color of those inside. Then if someone says that the objects inside are the same color as those outside, we shall know that they are white and not black. For since the number of white things in the world has no fixed limit, all of them can be grouped under the class of what is designated by the term, 'white thing.' Hence once we know that a certain object is designated by this term, we do not have to see it ourselves in order to know what its color is like.

Such is inference, 'which is not hindered by distance.' In other words, it is knowledge unlimited by personal considerations of time and space. Names, in the same way, enable us from what we do know to pass on to what we do not know. Hence "names serve by what is understood to make certain what is not known; not by what is not known to conjecture at what is understood."

(3) 'Personal experience' (*ch'in* 親) is knowledge obtained through the meeting that takes place between our knowing faculty and the thing to be known. All knowledge, pushed back to its origins, depends upon personal experience. For example, while we ourselves have only a 'hearing' knowledge of the events described in history, the first persons to have transmitted this knowledge must have had a personal experience of them. Likewise, even if we have not seen a particular thing, we can have a general knowledge of its nature and appearance, once we know its name. But in order to possess this knowledge, we, or others who have told us about it, must first of all have had a personal knowledge of the particular examples of the thing designated by the name. This is the type of knowledge discussed in western epistemology.

Such are the divisions of knowledge according to how it is obtained. It may also be classified as being of four different types:

(1) The knowledge pertaining to 'names' (*ming* 名), which are themselves divided into three types:

Canon, I: "Names are general (*ta* 達), classifying (*lei* 類), and private (*ssŭ* 私)" (p. 419).

Exposition: "Names: 'Thing' is a general name. All actualities (*shih* 實) must bear this term. 'Horse' is a classifying name. All actualities of that sort must have that name. 'Tsang' (a man's name) is private. This name is restricted to this actuality" (p. 457).

The name, 'thing,' is common to all things, and is the name of the *summum genus*. Hence it is a 'general' name. All particular objects must use this name, or as the text says, 'All actualities must bear this term.' 'Horse' is a term for a specific class of things, and hence a 'classifying' name. Only things in this particular class can use this name, or as the text says, 'All actualities of that sort must have that name.' 'Tsang' is the name of a person, and so is 'private.' The use of such a name is confined to only the one particular, or in the words of the text, ' This name is restricted to this actuality.' ¹

(2) Following the knowledge pertaining to ' names,' comes that pertaining to ' actualities ' (*shih* 實). These ' actualities ' are simply the particular things that names serve to designate.

(3) By ' correspondence ' (*ho* 合) is meant our knowledge of the correspondence of names to actualities, that is, the knowledge which exists ' when names and actualities pair with each other.' There are three ways in which this correspondence may be effected :

Canon, I : " In the process of designation, there is that of transference (*i* 移), of general appellation (*chü* 舉), and of direct designation (*chia* 加) " (p. 419).

Exposition : " In the process of designation, to name a ' puppy ' a ' dog,' is transference ; to name them ' puppy ' and ' dog,' is general appellation ; to call out : ' Puppy ! ' is direct designation " (p. 457).

A puppy is an immature dog, which means that it is a particular variety of dog. Hence to say that a puppy is a dog, is similar to saying that a white horse is a horse. In these cases one transfers or borrows the name, ' dog,' to designate ' puppy,' and the name, ' horse,' to designate ' white horse.'

Concerning general appellation, the *Canon*, I, says : " General appellation is a description of an actuality (*shih*) " (p. 419). The *Exposition* explains this : " General appellation consists in saying something by using a name to designate the actuality " (p. 447). That is, when we use the names, ' puppy ' and ' dog,' to designate puppies and dogs in general, this is general appellation. To designate a particular puppy, and call it, saying, ' Puppy!'; to say, that is, ' This is a puppy,' is to apply the general name, 'puppy,' to a particular puppy, which is ' direct designation.'

When we say that ' a puppy is a dog,' therefore, we must ask ourselves whether or not the puppy really is a dog, and when we say that something is a puppy, we must ask whether it really is a puppy. In other words, we must make certain that the names we use really correspond to their actualities. The knowledge which ascertains whether they do so or not is that of ' correspondence.'

(4) ' Action ' (*wei* 爲) is the knowledge whereby we know how to do a certain thing. ' Will and movement constitute action.' When we perform a certain act, we must have a purpose for doing so, together with a course of action. The former constitutes the ' will,' the

---

¹ The *Major Illustrations* (pp. 517-518, 522) states that names are classified into those which ' name according to the form and appearance ' ; which ' name according to the location ' ; and which ' name according to the measurement and number.' It groups such names as ' mountain,' ' mound,' ' house ' and ' temple ' under the first group ; and such names as ' district,' ' hamlet,' and the states of ' Ch'i ' and ' Ching,' under the second. There is no exposition of the third group, the text here being deficient, but this would probably include names of weights and measures, numbers, etc. This classification is extremely incomplete, and it is probable that part of the text has been lost.

latter, the 'movement.' The union of these two is given the general name of 'action.' Such action is of six kinds :

Canon, I : " Action consists in preservation, destruction, exchange, diminution, accretion and transformation " (p. 420).

Exposition : " Action : Fortifying a terrace is preservation; sickness is destruction ; buying and selling are exchange; emptying is diminution ; growth is accretion ; frogs and rats are (cases of) transformation " (p. 459).

This divides action according to the different purposes, that is, the variations of ' will ' (*chih* 志), that guide it. The *Canon*, I, says again : " What has taken place (*i* 已) may be constructive or destructive " (p. 419). And the *Exposition* : " What has taken place : To make clothes is constructive ; to treat sickness is destructive " (p. 456). The purpose of the former is to produce clothing ; of the latter, to get rid of sickness. Likewise the purpose in fortifying a terrace is to ensure its preservation, which is equivalent to the construction involved in the making of the clothes. The ' action ' in both of these examples is 'preservation. The purpose in treating sickness is to be without sickness, or in other words, to destroy something, so that here the action is ' destruction.' Buying and selling have mutual exchange as object, so that the action is ' exchange.' At times we wish to diminish a thing, and then diminution forms the action ; at other times to increase a thing, and then the action becomes accretion. Concerning 'transformation,' the *Canon*, I, says : "Transformation is perceptible change" (p. 422). And the *Exposition* : " Transformation is, for example, when a frog becomes a quail " (p. 449). The *Lieh-tzŭ* (ch. 1) has a passage which speaks of ' the field rat becoming a quail,' and which helps to explain this reference; it indicates that in ancient China the belief was prevalent that both frogs and rats can change into quail, i.e., can undergo transformation. There are times when we wish gradually to change a thing, and then our action becomes ' transformation.' In order to achieve our purpose in all these cases, we must have corresponding movement. Knowledge whereby we know what this movement should be, is that of ' action.'

Mo Tzŭ emphasized the practical, and the Later Mohists retained this standpoint, as may be seen from the following :

Canon, II : " A man may (seem to) know what he does not know. The reason is given under ' selection by means of names ' " (p. 428).

Exposition : " Knowing : Mix what a man knows and what he does not know together, and ask him about them. Then he must say : ' This is what I know. This is what I do not know.' If he can select and reject, he knows them both " (p. 485).

The *Mo-tzŭ* (ch. 47) says : " The statement that that which is bright is white, and that which is dark is black, even keen sighted persons cannot alter. But if we were to mix up black and white objects, and let the blind choose between them, they would not know which is which. Hence I say that the reason the blind do not know white from black does not lie in the matter of their names, but in the process of selection " (p. 225). For the Mohists, the ability to make one's selections according to the names of things, means that of being able to put knowledge to practical use in conduct.

4—Discussions on Dialectic

Our knowledge, when expressed in language, is called ' speech ' (*yen* 言), which is described as :

Canon, I : " Speech is the uttering of appellations (*chü* 舉)" (p. 419) . . . . " Speech is the service of the mouth " (p. 422). . . . " When by means of the spoken one's ideas gain expression, this is the dialectical activity of the mind " (p. 422).

Exposition : " Therefore speech is what all mouths are capable of, and that which utters names. A name is the designation of (an actuality), such as a tiger. As to speech, it is meant to say here that (the quality of) speech is extreme stoniness " (p. 447).

The *Mo-tzŭ* (ch. 47) says : " To refute my speech with one's own speech is like throwing an egg against a stone " (p. 229). Mo Tzŭ advocated : " In speech, not quantity but wisdom, not literary refinement but detailed examination, should be cultivated " (p. 8). This is why it is stated here that speech should be as firm as a stone (literally, of ' extreme stoniness '). In order to reach this goal, our speech must be guided along a definite pattern, which the *Minor Illustrations* calls ' dialectic ' (*pien* 辯). Such ' dialectic ' may have both a wide and a narrow meaning, but that mentioned in the *Canon* and *Exposition* is dialectic only in its narrow sense, in which sense it differs from what the *Canons* call ' statement ' (*shuo* 說) :

Canon, I : " Statement (*shuo*) is that whereby to bring understanding. . . . If there is one person who denies, both will deny . . . . But dialectic (*pien*) is conflict over something. In dialectic, the one who wins is right " (p. 418).

Exposition, I : " As to this ' something,' if both persons deny that all ' ox-trees ' (the name of a tree) are oxen, they will have nothing to argue about. But in dialectic, one says it is an ox, and the other says it is not. This is conflict over something. They cannot both be right, and not being both right, there must be one who is wrong, as, for example, if it were a dog " (pp. 454-455).

Exposition, II : " Dialectic is that in which one person says a thing is so, and another says it is not so. The one who is right will win " (p. 479).

This makes dialectic a conflict or argument between two parties. When it is simply a case of ' statement,' however, one person will affirm something, and the other one will likewise affirm it, or one will deny something (as when it is said, ' If there is one person who denies '), and the other will also deny it (' both will deny '). For example, one person says that an ' ox-tree ' is not an ox, and the other will also say so, with the result that ' they will have nothing to argue about.' In such a case there can be no dialectic. But if one person holds this ' ox-tree ' to be an ox, while the other denies it, then there is conflict between two persons and consequently dialectic, in which ' the one who is right will win.'

This definition, which makes of dialectic purely an argument between two parties, is a narrow one. The dialectic described in the *Minor Illustrations* has a wider meaning :

" Dialectic serves to make clear the distinction between right and wrong, to discriminate between good and disordered government, to make evident the points of similarity and difference, examine the principles of names and actualities, differentiate between what is beneficial and what is harmful, and determine what is uncertain. It describes the forms of myriads of things, and in discussions seeks to compare the various speeches. It uses names to designate actualities, propositions to express ideas, statements to set forth causes, taking and giving according to classes. What one oneself has, one should not blame others for having, and what one is oneself without, one should not blame others for not having " (pp. 526-527).

According to this passage, dialectic has six uses : (1) to distinguish between right and wrong ; (2) between good and disordered government ; (3) between similarity and difference ; (4) to examine names and actualities ; (5) to differentiate between what is beneficial and what is harmful ; (6) to settle what is uncertain. The way to do this is to ' use names to designate actualities, propositions to express ideas, statements to set forth causes.'

(1) The meaning of to ' use names to designate actualities' has been explained in the preceding section. (2) By propositions (*tz'ŭ* 辭) are meant combinations of two or more names to express one idea, or as the *Hsün-tzŭ* (ch. 22) says, " The combination of names of different actualities wherewith to discuss one idea " (p. 290).

(3) Concerning the third method (to ' use. . . statements to set forth causes') :

Canon, I : " A cause (*ku* 故) is that with the obtaining of which something becomes " (p. 413).

Exposition : " A minor cause is one with which something may not necessarily be so, but without which it will never be so. For example, a point in a line. A major cause is one with which something will of necessity be so, and without which it will never be so, as in the case of the act of seeing which results in sight " (p. 441).

The *Canon*, I, explains a point as : " A point is that part of a line [1] which is without thickness and comes at the very beginning " (p. 416). If there is once a point, this need not necessarily result in there being a line. That is, a point is a thing ' with which something may not necessarily be so, but without which it will never be so.' This ' minor cause ' is equivalent to what modern logic would call a ' necessary cause,' while the ' major cause ' includes what would today be called both ' sufficient ' and ' necessary ' cause. Of what modern logic calls a ' sufficient cause,' that is, one with which something will of necessity be so, but without which it may or may not be so, the Mohist texts make no mention. *Ku*, then, is a word comprising the various causes described above, and to use ' statements to set forth causes ' means not only to set forth the material causes of things, but also the causes (i.e., the steps of reasoning), by which we arrive at a certain statement. In other words, as said above, ' Statement is that whereby to bring understanding.'

There are seven ways of establishing a statement, which are described by the *Minor Illustrations* as follows :

" What is possible (*huo* 或) is what is not complete. What is hypothetical (*chia* 假) is what is at present not so. Imitation (*hsiao* 效) consists in taking a model (*fa* 法). What is imitated is what is taken for model. If the cause (*ku*) is in agreement with the imitation, it is correct. If it is not in agreement with the imitation, it is not correct. This is the method of imitation (*hsiao*). The method of comparison (*pi* 辟) consists in using one thing to explain another. The method of parallel (*mou* 侔) consists in comparing two propositions (*tz'ŭ* 辭) consistently throughout. The method of analogy (*yüan* 援) says : ' You are so. Why should I alone not be so ? ' In the method of extension (*t'ui* 推), when what has not been accepted is the same as what has been accepted, it is permissible. For example, when it is said that the other is the same, how can I say that it is different ? " (pp. 527-528).

(1) ' What is possible is what is not complete.' The *Canon*, I, says : " There is completeness (*chin* 盡) when there is nothing that is not so " (p. 421). A certain characteristic need not necessarily be shared by all things in a certain class. For example, not all horses need be white horses, and so it would only be permissible for us to say that it is *possible* for horses to be white, but not that they *are* white. Again, there are times when our knowledge of a thing may be incomplete, so that we can only venture a possible judgment on it. Thus if a certain horse is white, but we do not actually know whether it is so or not, we can only say that it is possibly white.

(2) ' What is hypothetical is what is at present not so.' That is, we may postulate certain conditions, and then determine that under

---

[1] Literally ' body ' (*t'i* 體), a word which in these texts means line.—TR.

these conditions there must be such and such happenings. An example of this is the statement by Confucius : " Were any prince to employ me, in a twelvemonth something could be done, but in three years the work could be completed " (*Lun Yü*, XIII, 10). When Confucius says here : " Were any prince to employ me," he is not making a statement of fact, but a hypothetical one, something, in other words, which ' is at present not so.'

(3) ' Imitation consists in taking a model (*fa* 法).' This model is described as :

Canon, I : " A *fa* is that according to which something becomes " (p. 418).

Exposition : " *Fa* : Either the concept (of a circle), or the compasses, or a finished circle may be used as the *fa* (for making a circle) " (p. 454).

Canon, II : " The mutual sameness of things of one *fa* extends to all things in that class. Thus squares are the same, one to another. The reason is given under ' square ' " (p. 435).

Exposition : " All things which are squares have the same *fa*, though (themselves) different, some being of wood, some of stone. This does not prevent their squares mutually corresponding to one another. They are all of the same kind, being all squares. Things are all like this " (p. 491).

The *fa*, in other words, is the common model which may be applied to any particular things falling in its class. In the class of squares, for example, there are such differences as that some are made of wood, others of stone, etc., but this does not prevent them from all being squares. Extending this principle, the model through the imitation of which things become like this model, is a *fa*, and the things that are modelled upon this *fa* are imitators or *hsiao* 效. The *fa* for making a circle, for example, may either be the concept of the ideal circle, or it may be the compasses used for making circles, or it may be another circle which has already been completed. Once this *fa* has been fixed, all the things which imitate it become circular in form.

The word *ku* 故 in the phrase, ' If the cause (*ku*) is in agreement with the imitation,' (a word which ordinarily means ' therefore '), here has the same significance as in the already quoted phrase, ' statements to set forth causes (*ku*) ' ; that is, it is the cause which makes things as they are, or it is the reasoning, based upon which a statement is upheld. If one wishes to know whether the cause which has been advanced is the true cause or not ; to know whether it is the cause ' with which something will of necessity be so, and without which it will never be so,' the best way is to establish this cause as a model or *fa*, and see if it ' is in agreement with the imitation (*hsiao*),' that is, see if it can produce the expected effect. *Hsiao* in this phrase is the thing which imitates the *fa*, and is also the effect of it. We must prove that the cause or *ku* is equivalent to the *fa*, ' according to which something becomes,' before we can know that it is really the cause, ' with the obtaining of which something becomes.' Hence : ' If the cause is in agreement with the imitation, it is correct ; if it is not in agreement with the imitation, it is not correct.'[1] The essential idea is that if we wish to know whether what we call a cause is a true cause or not, the best way is to apply it and see whether it can produce the expected effects. Mo Tzŭ had said that there are three tests to prove the truth of a doctrine. This corresponds to the third of his tests, which is the applicability of a doctrine, save that in these Later Mohist writings this test is not restricted exclusively to political and social arguments.

(4) The statement, ' The method of comparison consists in using one thing to explain another,' is explained by Wang Fu (*c.* A.D. 76— *c.* 157) as follows : " The use of comparison arises out of the failure of direct statement to be comprehensible. Therefore we borrow for illustration another thing which is so or not, so as to make it clear." [2]

(5) ' The method of parallel consists in comparing two propositions consistently throughout.' This is well illustrated in the *Kung-sun Lung-tzŭ* (ch. 1), in which Kung-sun Lung says :
" I have heard that when the King of Ch'u . . . lost his bow, his attendants wished to search for it, but the King said : ' Desist. The King of Ch'u has lost a bow, and a man of Ch'u will get it. What need to search further ? ' When Confucius heard of this he said : ' . . . . He might also simply have said that a man has lost it, and a man will get it. Why need it be restricted to Ch'u ? ' In this Confucius differentiated ' a man of Ch'u ' from what is called ' a man.' Now to approve of Confucius's differentiation of ' a man of Ch'u ' from what is called ' a man,' and yet disagree with my differentiation of ' a white horse ' from ' a horse,' is to be obstinate " (pp. 62-63).

This gives an example of ' comparing two propositions consistently throughout.'

(6) " The method of analogy says : ' You are so. Why should I alone not be so ? ' " This method is also found in the passage just quoted.

(7) " In the method of extension, when what has not been accepted is the same as what has been accepted, it is permissible. For example, when it is said that the other is the same, why should I say that it is different ? " Thus we say that all men are mortal. If someone asks us why we say this, we must reply that we know that all men of the past have died, and because we see that men of to-day and of the future are the same in kind as those of the past, we can through ' extension ' know that these men must also die. Having observed

---

[1] From the sentence in the previous paragraph beginning, ' Extending this principle,' down to this point, I have followed Hu Shih's *Hsiao Ch'ü P'ien Hsin-ku.*
[2] *Cf.* his *Chien Fu Lun*, ch. *Shih Nan*, *chüan* 7, p. 5.

a number of particular instances and seeing that they all act in a certain way, we can assume that other instances of the same kind will also act in this way. Those things which have been observed, constitute 'what has been accepted'; those belonging in the same class, but which have not yet been observed, are 'what has not been accepted.' Because they are of the same class as 'what has been accepted,' we are permitted the judgment that all things in this class are all alike. This is what is called 'taking and giving according to the class.' [1]

The *Major Illustrations* also has a passage touching on what the commentator, Sun I-jang (1848-1908), interprets as meaning 'the laws of speech' (*yü ching* 語 經) :

" According to the laws of speech . . . there are three things which must be complete before it may be adequately produced . . . . Propositions (*tzŭ* 辭) originate from causes (*ku* 故), grow according to reasons (*li* 理), and proceed according to classes. There will be error if propositions are established without understanding of what they grow out of. People to-day will go nowhere unless they have a path. Although one has strong limbs, if one does not know the path, one may speedily expect difficulty. (Likewise) propositions proceed according to their classes. If they are formulated without the classes they belong to being understood, there must arise difficulty " (pp. 508-509, 523).

The general idea of this passage seems to be similar to the *Minor Illustrations* passage explained in the last few pages, and it is a pity that the chapter that contains it is so corrupt that the details remain unknown.

5— Discussions on ' Similarity and Difference '

The four methods of comparison, parallel, analogy and extension are all concerned with the points of similarity between things, with the purpose of enabling us to pass from things of which we already have knowledge to those which we do not know. The similarities between things are of many kinds, however, and if one followed these four methods uncritically one might easily fall into error. The *Minor Illustrations* explains this as follows :

" There are ways in which things may be similar, without being throughout similar. The method of parallel between propositions comes to a point where it stops. Things are so, and there is a reason why they are so. They may be the same in what they are, while at the same time the reason why they are so may not be the same. Things are accepted, and there is a reason why they are accepted. They may be the same inasmuch as they are accepted, whereas the reason why they are accepted need not be the same. Hence the methods of

---

[1] From the paragraph beginning, ' The method of parallel,' down to this point, I have followed Dr. Hu Shih , *op. cit.*

comparison, parallel, analogy and extension, when they are used, may lead to differences and turn into difficulty; and when they are carried far, may lead to error. They may become loose and detached from their bases, and so cannot but be examined, and cannot always be used. Hence in speech there are many aspects, various classes and different causes, so that one cannot be one-sided " (pp. 528-529).

There are also various types of difference between things, to which the ' Mohist Canons ' give a detailed discussion :

Canon, I : " Agreement is that with respect to which separate things are as one " (p. 421).

Exposition : " There is agreement, as when two different men both alike see a pillar " (p. 448).

Canon, I : " In agreement there is that of identity (*ch'ung* 重), of part and whole relationship (*t'i* 體), of co-existence (*ho* 合), and of generic relation " (*lei* 類) (p. 420).

Exposition : " Agreement : When there are two names for the one actuality, this is identity. Inclusion in one whole is part and whole relationship. Both being in the same room is co-existence. Having some points of similarity is generic relation " (p. 459).

Canon, I : " In difference (*i* 異) there is that of duality (*erh* 二), of no part and whole relationship (*pu t'i* 不 體), of separateness (*pu ho* 不 合), and of dissimilarity (*pu lei* 不 類) " (p. 421).

Exposition : " Difference : In duality two things necessarily have variations. When things have no connection, there is no part and whole relationship. When they are not in the same place, there is separateness. When they have nothing in common, there is dissimilarity " (p. 460).

Canon, I : " When agreement and difference are jointly considered, what is present and what is absent can be set forth " (p. 421).

Exposition : " In the joint consideration of agreement and difference, . . . when it deals with measurement, it is a question of how much or little ; . . . when of an unmarried girl and of the mother of a child, it is a question of age and youth ; of two things absolutely irreconcilable, it is a question of white and black ; of the center, it is a question of the sides ; . . . of the body remaining and the mind wandering, it is a question of maintenance and loss . . ." (p. 460).

These passages indicate four ways in which things may agree or differ, and which make it possible for various things to be called similar to one another, even though the way in which they are similar differs. Thus Mo Ti and Mo Tzŭ are both names for the same actuality. This is identity. Things which are all mutually related to something, as in the case of hands, feet, head and eyes, which are all parts of a man's body, are in part and whole relationship. Things which are in the same place, as two men who live in the same room, have common co-existence. Things of the same class, all of which have characteristics in common, have generic relationship.

Likewise there are four kinds of difference. We must first know in what way things agree and differ, according to these classifications, before we can extend our knowledge concerning them, without falling into error.

Besides the above, there are things which at times may be described by the same term, even though they belong to different classes. To these we must also pay special attention :

Canon, II : " Different classes are not comparable. The reason is given under ' measurement ' " (p. 427).

Exposition : " Difference : What is longer, a tree or a night ? Of which is there more, knowledge or rice ? Of the four things, rank, parents, conduct or price, which is more valuable ? . . ." (p. 465).

A tree and a night are things of different categories, yet of both it may be said that they are long or short. Likewise with knowledge and rice. Therefore to take them as belonging to the same categories, means inevitably to fall into error.

Such is the Later Mohist concept of ' similarity and difference,' a concept differing fundamentally from that of the ' unity of similarity and difference ' held by one group of Dialecticians. While it may not necessarily have been developed as an attack upon the Dialectician stand, yet the ideas of Hui Shih and Chuang Tzŭ upon this subject were, if judged by the statements of the Later Mohists, certainly erroneous. Hui Shih's contention that ' all things are in one aspect all similar, in another aspect all different,' was based upon the belief that although all things are different, they all ' have some points of similarity,' and although all similar, they all ' have some points of difference.' When one says, however, that all things ' have some points of similarity,' this means generic relationship (the fourth type of agreement), and if because of this one says that ' all things are one,' this is to confuse this generic relationship with part and whole relationship (the second type of agreement), which is a serious error. There are four kinds of difference, likewise, and when we say that all things are different, we must distinguish of what are the differences, and not confuse them.

The *Exposition* does not explain very clearly the ' joint consideration of agreement and difference,' and the text here is apparently corrupt. The general idea seems to be that things can have opposing characteristics, such as much and little, age and youth, white and black, center and sides, maintenance and loss, etc., depending upon the aspect we are considering them from. Thus in the case of a woman who is first an ' unmarried girl,' and then becomes the ' mother of a child,' it is a human being who has been both young and old. Also a man's body may be in a certain spot, while his mind is wandering, as when it is said that ' the body remains and the mind wanders, when it is a question of maintenance and loss.' The group of Dialecticians who advocated the ' unity of similarity and difference,' made advantageous use of this argument of relativity to say that ' a white dog is black,' and ' a tortoise is longer than a snake.' To this the Later Mohists would reply that although a white dog may be said to be black, a tortoise to be long, and a snake to be short, and although what are called black and white and long and short have no fixed standards, yet there should be common standards for these qualities when they are used within the same field of discussion. Thus a tortoise may indeed be said to be long, but compared to a snake it is after all usually shorter. And although the philosophy of Hui Shih and Chuang Tzŭ has other logical bases, its arguments, when founded upon this doctrine of the ' unity of similarity and difference,' are in fact open to the criticism given above.[1]

6—Discussions on ' Hard and White '

The Dialecticians argued about the ' unity of similarity and difference ' and ' separateness of hard and white,' whereas the Later Mohists advocated exactly the reverse : the separateness of similarity and difference, and unity of hard and white. The former has already been studied Of the latter, the ' Mohist Canons ' say :

Canon, I : " Hardness and whiteness are not mutually exclusive " (p. 417).

Exposition : " Suppose there are the two, hardness and whiteness. When they are in different places, they do not pervade one another; not thus pervading, they are then mutually exclusive " (p. 453).

Canon, II : " For hardness and whiteness, the reason is given under ' interdependence ' " (p. 431).

Exposition : " When hardness has whiteness, these must pervade each other " (p. 469).

Canon, II : " They are in one. One of them is known, and one of them is not known. The reason is given under ' preservation ' " (p. 439).

Exposition : " To be in the stone is oneness. Hardness and whiteness are two, yet (they are both) in the stone. Hence it is possible that one of them is known and one of them is not known " (p. 480).

Canon, II : " When there are two, one cannot one-sidedly get rid of one of them. The reason is given under ' seeing and combining into one, one and two, width and length ' " (p. 426).

Exposition : " Since seeing and non-seeing are separable, therefore one and two do not pervade each other, and width and length (are like) hardness and whiteness " (p. 465)

This maintains the unity of hardness and whiteness (' hardness and whiteness are not mutually exclusive '), contrary to Kung-sun

---

[1] The words appearing in this section as ' identity,' ' similarity,' ' agreement,' etc., are all translations of the one Chinese word *t'ung* 同, which according to the context assumes varying meanings.—TR.

Lung's 'separateness of hard and white.' The *Kung-sun Lung-tzŭ* says in its chapter on this subject: " Seeing does not perceive hardness, but perceives that which is white, without the hardness. Touching does not perceive whiteness, but perceives hardness. It perceives hardness without the whiteness. . . . Finding its (the stone's) whiteness, or finding its hardness, lies in seeing or not seeing (i.e., in touching). The seeing and non-seeing are separate from each other. They each do not pervade the other, and therefore are separate " (p. 78). Here Kung-sun Lung attempts to prove epistemologically that hardness and whiteness are two independent universals.[1]

The same chapter gives a criticism made by an objector : " Because the eye cannot behold hardness nor the hand grasp whiteness, one cannot urge that there is no hardness or whiteness. . . . Hardness and whiteness both are in the stone, so how can they be separated ? " (p. 79). Again : " The whiteness of a stone and the hardness of a stone, the seeing and the non-seeing (i.e., touching), are two ; together with (the stone), three. They are like width and length which pervade one another. Should they not be in evidence ? " (p. 79). The Mohists follow exactly the arguments of the objector here quoted, that hardness and whiteness pervade each other and are not mutually exclusive. They both exist in the stone, which is what is meant by ' preservation.'

When we look at the stone, we see whiteness but not hardness, and when we feel the stone, we feel hardness but not whiteness. This arises, however, simply from our own capacity for perception or non-perception, and has no relation with the existence or non-existence of hardness and whiteness in the stone. Hardness is one, whiteness is two, and because seeing and non-seeing are separable, it is said that one and two do not pervade each other. However the seeing or non-seeing has no connection with the existence or non-existence of hardness and whiteness in the stone. Hardness and whiteness are both in the stone, exactly as width and length each contain the other. Hence ' when there are two, one cannot one-sidedly get rid of one of them.' This attacks Kung-sun Lung's epistemological proof that hardness and whiteness are two separables. Suppose these are not together in one place, however, as when there is whiteness (but not hardness) in white snow, or hardness (but not whiteness) in a hard stone, then ' being in different places, they do not pervade one another.' Under such circumstances they can be said to be ' mutually exclusive.' If it is a question of a hard and white stone, however, then the hardness and whiteness ' both are in the stone,' and since they are thus united, the hardness pervades whiteness and the whiteness hardness. The *Exposition* means this when it says : " When hardness has whiteness, these must pervade each other." In such a case they ' are not mutually

[1] *Cf.* ch. 9, sect. 7, p. 207.

exclusive.' This is an attack upon Kung-sun Lung's metaphysical proof that hardness and whiteness are two separables.[1]

The 'Mohist Canons' say again :

Canon, II : "'What are designated' (*chih* 指) are two, from neither of which is there escape. The reason is given under 'the interrelationship of two'" (p. 439).

Exposition : " Suppose there is 'that which is designated' (*chih*). Suppose you know it, and also know what I have not brought forward : this is duplication. But when there is a case when you know it but do not know what I have not brought forward, it is possible that of one term, some is known and some is not known. But if it is to be known, this knowledge of it must be 'designated' (*chih*) so as to inform me, and then I shall know it. This is multiple designation, in which there are two. . . . If it is said that only what I bring forward must be designated, and what I do not bring forward need not be designated, such certainly cannot be designated alone. If what one wishes to designate be not transmitted, the meaning will seem to lack sense. Moreover, when what one knows is this, and what one does not know is also this, this means to know that which one does not know. How then can it be said that of one term, some is known and some is not known ? " (p. 480).

Canon, II : " When one knows something, and it cannot be 'designated' (*chih*), the reason is given under 'stupidity'" (p. 440).

Exposition : " This is stupidity. What it grasps certainly cannot be designated " (p. 481).

While the corruptness of this text makes a satisfactory interpretation almost impossible, the general theme seems to bear upon Kung-sun Lung's discussions of the *chih*, which I have already interpreted as meaning the universal which a name designates.[2] Names, however, not only serve to designate their universals, but also to designate their concrete particulars. Hence "'what are designated' are two, neither of which can be escaped from," and are 'multiple designation, in which there are two.' Kung-sun Lung's group maintained that 'it is possible that of one term, some is known and some is not known.' This means that when we use 'one term' to speak about a universal, we know only the universal designated by that name, and not the particular designated by it. That is, as the text says, " Only what I bring forward must be designated, and what I do not bring forward need not be designated." The Later Mohists, however, held that the universal exists in the particular, and hence

---

[1] The *Canon*, II, says : " As to there being no hardness and whiteness, the reason is given under 'no duration or space'" (p. 431). This is left unexplained in the *Exposition*, but we can infer that this statement means that without time and space, hardness and whiteness cannot exist. This would seem to attack Kung-sun Lung's statement that " there exists no hardness in the world, but the hardness lies concealed " (p. 80).

[2] *Cf.* ch. 9, sect. 6, pp. 205-206.

cannot itself be the name's sole designation. For if the name designates solely the universal, its meaning is incomplete, so that 'such
certainly cannot be designated alone. If what one wishes to designate
be not transmitted, the meaning will seem to lack sense.' Hence,
'How can it be said that as regards one term, some is known and some
is not known?'

Moreover, can a universal that is designated only by a name, be
perceptible to man? If there really do exist a hardness and whiteness
which do not 'share' themselves in things (such as Kung-sun Lung's
group talks about), then it must certainly be possible for them to be
perceptible to man. Hence the Mohists remark that "if it is to be
known, this knowledge of it must be 'designated' so as to inform me,
and then I shall know it." Only the particular, however, can be
designated and shown in this way, whereas the universal is
fundamentally not perceivable. Hence the Mohists attack this viewpoint by saying: "When one knows something, and it cannot be
designated, the reason is given under 'stupidity.'" Kung-sun
Lung's universal cannot be designated and thus shown, and hence:
"What it grasps certainly cannot be designated." In its doctrine
of the universal, Kung-sun Lung's group approaches what western
philosophy would term realism, whereas the Later Mohists approach
nominalism.

The 'Mohist Canons' state elsewhere:

Canon, II : " (To say that) an ox and a horse are not an ox, and to
grant that they are, are both the same. The reason is given under
'the general'" (p. 435).

Exposition : " Therefore it is not permissible to say that an ox
and a horse are not an ox ; nor that an ox and a horse are an ox. So it
is in some ways permissible and in some ways not permissible. But
to say that an ox and a horse are an ox, this not having been allowed,
is not permissible. Moreover the ox is not two, and the horse is not
two, while the ox and the horse are two. Then there is no difficulty
(in that) an ox is nothing but an ox, and a horse is nothing but a
horse, but an ox and a horse are not an ox and not a horse "
(p. 493).

That is to say, if an ox and a horse are taken together as forming
one term, ' ox-horse,' this ' ox-horse ' cannot be said to be an ox.
This is because it is only the ox in ' ox-horse ' which is an ox, and not
the horse in the combination. Yet to say that ' ox-horse ' is not an
ox is also not permissible, since in the combination, ' ox-horse,' an ox
certainly exists. However, ' the ox is not two, and the horse is not
two, while the ox and the horse are two,' so that the ox cannot be said
not to be an ox, nor the horse not to be a horse, whereas it can be
said of the combination, ' ox-horse,' that it is neither an ox nor a
horse. This resembles Kung-sun Lung's doctrine that ' a white
horse is not a horse.' Kung-sun Lung, however, states definitely

that a white horse is not a horse, whereas this statement says that in one way it is also not permissible to say that an ox and a horse are not an ox. Kung-sun Lung, in other words, groups his arguments round the universal, that is, a name's connotation, whereas this argument bases itself upon the particular, that is, a name's denotation. Herein lies a fundamental difference between the two schools.

Although the Later Mohists differ from Kung-sun Lung on the question of the universal, they agree with him in advocating the ' rectification of names and their actualities.' The *Canon*, II, when it says, " In a loose appellation (*k'uang chü* 狂 舉), one cannot know distinctions " (p. 435), uses the term, ' loose appellation,' in the same sense as it is used in the ' Discourse on the Explanation of Change ' in the *Kung-sun Lung-tzŭ* (p. 75).[1] The *Canon*, II, says also :
" That and this : ' That ' and ' this ' agree with ' that ' and ' this.' The reason is given under ' difference ' " (p. 436).

Exposition : " That (i.e., the above statement) refers to the rectification of the names, ' that ' and ' this.' ' That ' and ' this ' are correct when the that-ness of ' that ' stops at ' that ,' and the this-ness of ' this ' stops at ' this.' ' That ' and ' this ' are not correct when ' that ' is moreover ' this,' and ' this ' is also moreover ' that.' (To say) that ' that ' is ' this,' is also correct, if that ' that ' is ' this ' stops at ' that ' being ' this.' If in this way they are ' that ' and ' this,' then ' that ' may also be ' this,' and ' this ' may also be ' that ' " (pp. 493-494).

This concept of the Rectification of Names is identical with Kung-sun Lung's, being closely similar to that expressed in the ' Discourse on Names and Actualities ' in the *Kung-sun Lung-tzŭ*. Rectification or correctness exists when that is only that, and this is only this. But if the meanings of that and this are not fixed, so that the meaning of that is sometimes this, and the meaning of this is sometimes that, then the two are loose. Yet even when the names have once been rectified, so that the meanings of the names, ' that ' and ' this,' have been fixed, the things designated by these names need not be fixed and stationary. For looked at from one angle, ' this ' thing is ' that ,' whereas from another angle, ' that ' thing is ' this.' ' This ' considers ' that ' to be ' that,' while ' that ' also considers ' this ' to be ' that.' The names, ' that ' and ' this,' in other words, are essentially relative, and hence " that ' that ' is ' this ' is also correct." What the *Chuang-tzŭ* (ch. 2) says about ' that and this ' is based upon this argument, as when it remarks : " Everything is ' that '; everything is ' this '.....Hence it is said that the ' that' and the ' this ' produce each other. This is the doctrine of the alternate existence of that and this " (pp. 17-18). If we argue solely from the viewpoint of the particulars of things, things are ever from ' that ' becoming

---

[1] *Cf.* p. 214.

'this,' or vice versa, without any fixed standard. The universals of the names, 'that' and 'this,' however, (as distinct from 'that' and 'this' particular thing), are just as equally fixed and stationary, and hence the meaning of these names ('that' and 'this'), can also be made fixed. The Rectification of Names consists precisely in such fixation.

7—Discussions on Other Problems of the Dialecticians

The *Canon*, II, says :
" Fire is hot. The reason is given under ' looking ' " (p. 427).
Exposition : " Fire : When one says that fire is hot, this does not mean that it is I who possess the hotness of the fire. It is as when one looks at whiteness " (p. 485).

This seems to be an attack upon the Dialectician paradox that ' fire is not hot.' Such a statement can be proved epistemologically by saying that the hotness of fire comes from our own sensation of the fire, and is something subjective, in ourselves and not in the fire. The Mohists, however, maintain that the hotness of fire lies in the fire itself and not in ourselves. Similarly, when we look at whiteness, the whiteness lies in the white object and not in ourselves.

Canon, II : " If it is cut in no other way except in half, then there will be no action (of cutting). The reason is given under ' point ' " (p. 433).

Exposition : " In cutting in half, what comes at the very beginning is selected. But being what comes at the beginning, its center will not be halved, as this is a point. But if one takes away what comes before and after (the point), then the point remains in the middle. The cutting off must be by halves, and unless it is by halves, there can be no cutting " (p. 490).

Though perhaps corrupt, this is an attack on the paradox : " If a rod one foot in length is cut short every day by one half its length, it will still have something left after ten thousand generations." The Mohists define a point as " that part of a line which is without thickness and which comes at the very beginning" (p. 416). The *Exposition* says on this : "A point is what has nothing within it" (p. 452). This is like the Euclidean definition that a point is without width or breadth. As such it cannot be divided. But if one continues day by day to cut the stick in half, one will finally reach a stage at which there is only an indivisible point remaining, which can no longer be cut in half. Any object, if it can be cut in two at all, must have the capacity of being cut in half. A point, however, has no halves which can be halved, and hence cannot be thus cut in two. This argument is one made from the viewpoint of the particular.

Canon, II : " There may be nothingness. But what has once existed cannot be done away with. The reason is given under ' what has happened ' " (p. 433).

Exposition : " There may be nothingness, but what is already so is something which has happened, and so cannot be non-existent " (p. 490).

This says that things in the world, if they have not already existed, may quite conceivably never exist. Once something has occurred, however, the existence of that thing will always remain as a fact which cannot be done away with. Although it is not necessary to interpret this statement as a direct attack upon the Dialectician paradox that ' an orphan colt has never had a mother,' it may well be cited in apposition to it. For let us suppose that the question of the orphan colt is discussed from the aspect of the particular. Then if from the beginning it had never had a mother, how could this particular colt have come into existence ? But if it did once actually have one, it cannot now be said never to have had a mother, even though at present it may not have one.

Canon, II : " Movement over distance requires duration. The reason is given under ' earlier and later ' " (p. 434).

Exposition : " In movement, the movement must be first toward what is near, and afterward toward what is distant. Distance and nearness constitute space. Earlier and later constitute duration. A person who moves over space, requires duration " (p. 491).

This statement, that movement over space requires duration or time, may be contrasted with that of the Dialecticians : " I go to the state of Yüeh to-day and arrived there yesterday." [1]

8—ARGUMENTS FOR UNIVERSAL LOVE

The Later Mohists, having made such a detailed study of the methods of dialectic, used these methods to oppose all persons who attacked the Mohist doctrine of universal love. These attacks, according to the Later Mohist writings, were of two kinds. One of these was : ' Infinity is injurious to universality.' That is, it was asked, since the number of people in the world is incalculable, how can one love

---

[1] The *Canon*, II, says : " A shadow does not move. The reason is given under ' changing action ' " (p. 432). The *Exposition* says : " In the case of a shadow, when the light comes, the shadow disappears. But if it (the shadow) does not disappear, it will be there forever " (p. 469). This has been generally interpreted as identical in meaning with the Dialectician paradox : " The shadow of a flying bird never moves." Actually, however, there is a difference inasmuch as in the paradox it is a question of the ' shadow of a flying bird,' whereas the Mohist statement speaks merely about a shadow. To say that the shadow of a flying bird does not move is to contradict common sense. Such is not the case, however, if one says that ' a shadow does not move.' For example, we all admit that the shadow made by a sundial at noon is not the same as that made by it at eleven a.m. . This is because the needle which produces this shadow does not itself move, and hence its shadow also does not move. The fact is, that the eleven a.m. shadow disappears because of the shifting of the light, while the noon shadow which replaces it is one newly produced. The eleven a.m. shadow, however, if it does not disappear, will continue ever fixed in its one spot, since it is itself non-moving. But the ' shadow of a flying bird,' on the contrary, is a shadow that is itself in movement, and hence differs completely from the other shadow.

all of them ?   The other was : ' To kill a robber is to kill a man.'
That is, if the Mohists advocated universal love, how could they at
the same time advocate punishment of criminals ?   The Mohists
responded to these criticisms as follows :
    Canon, II : " Infinity is not injurious to universality.   The reason
is given under ' fullness or not ' " (p. 437).
    Exposition : " Infinity : (Objection :) If the South has a limit, it
can be included in toto.   If it has no limit, it cannot be included
in toto.   We cannot know whether it has a limit or not, and hence
cannot know whether it can all be included or not.   Not knowing
whether people fill this (space) or not, we are necessarily unable to
know whether they can be included in toto or not.   This being so,
it is perverse to hold that all people can be included in our love.
(Answer :) If people do not fill what is unlimited, then people have
a limit, and there is no difficulty in including anything that is limited.
If they do fill what is unlimited, then what is (supposed to be)
unlimited is limited, and then there is no difficulty in including what
is limited " (p. 497).
    Canon, II :   " One may not know their number, but know what
it includes.   The reason is given under ' question ' " (p. 438).
    Exposition : " If one does not know their number, how can
one know to love all people inclusively ?   There are some who
ask questions (about people), and who include in their love all those
about whom they have asked.   But if without knowing their number,
one includes all in one's love, there is no difficulty " (pp. 497-498).
    Canon, II :   " When the minister (of a ruler), or a puppy or a dog
have run away, and the one who has lost them does not know where
they are, this does not prevent him from loving them.   The reason
is given under ' a lost child ' " (p. 438).
    Exposition : " When a minister has run away, one does not know
where he is, and when a puppy or a dog run away, their names are
unknown.   Even the cleverness of the one who has lost them may be
unable (to reunite) the two " (p. 481).
    These are all answers to the objection that ' infinity is injurious
to universality.'   The critic says :   If the South has a limit, it may be
entirely included, but if it is illimitable, it cannot be entirely included.
When one does not yet know whether the South is limited or not, the
possibility or not of including in one's love all the people in the South
is still less knowable.   Is it then not perverse of you to say that one
can include all people in one's love ?   The reply to this is : If the
South is illimitable, it cannot be entirely filled with people, and hence
the number of people must be limited.   If it is limited, however, what
difficulty is there in loving all men ?   Yet if people do in fact fully
occupy this supposedly illimitable South, then what appears infinite
is actually limited.   And once the territory is limited, what difficulty
is there in loving all people in it ?

The critic says again : When you do not know the number of people, how can you know that you are loving the whole people ? The reply is : If there is a doubter, let him ask questions everywhere about people, and let him love entirely those about whom he has asked. Then even though he forgets the number of the people he has asked, what is the harm ? The critic says : When you do not know where all people live, how can you love them all ? The reply is : When one does not know where they are, this does not prevent one from loving them. For example, suppose I have a puppy or a dog which have run away from me. Having lost them, I do not know where they are, nor do I know what new name has been given them, and even though I use a skilful searcher, I cannot reunite the two. This is exactly like the case of a child that has been lost. Although his father does not know where he is, this does not prevent him from loving him.[1]

The *Minor Illustrations* says :

" A white horse is a horse. To ride a white horse is to ride a horse. A black horse is a horse. To ride a black horse is to ride a horse. Huo is a man. To love Huo is to love a man. Tsang is a man. To love Tsang is to love a man. This is to affirm what is right.

" But Huo's parents are men (i.e., people). Yet when Huo serves his parents, he is not serving men. His younger brother is a handsome man. But to love his younger brother is not to love handsome men. A cart is wood. But to ride a cart is not to ride wood. A boat is wood. But to enter a boat is not to enter wood. A robber is a man. But many robbers are not many men ; and that there are no robbers does not mean that there are no men.

" How is this explained ? To hate the existence of many robbers is not to hate the existence of many men, and to wish that there were no robbers is not to wish that there were no men. The world generally agrees on this. And this being the case, although a robber-man is a man, yet to love robbers is not to love men, and not to love robbers is not not to love men. Likewise to kill a robber-man is not to kill a man. There is no difficulty in this proposition. This one and that (foregoing one) are in the same category. The world holds to that and does not consider itself wrong, but it considers the Mohists to be wrong when they hold to this . . . " (pp. 529-530).

This tries to prove that killing a robber is not killing a man, and that therefore the execution of robbers does not prevent us from universal love for men. For when we say that a white horse is a horse, we do so because the primary factor in the white horse is the fact that it is a horse, not that it is white. But when one loves a younger brother, one does so because he is a younger brother, and not because he happens to be handsome. Therefore loving a younger

---

[1] In these explanations I follow Teng Kao-ching's *Mo Ching Hsin-shih*.

brother who is handsome does not mean loving handsome men. Likewise the most important fact about a robber is that he is a robber, not that he is a man, and so, the Mohists argue, when we kill a robber it is not the same as killing a man.

This passage is followed by another in which the Mohists answer the attacks made upon their doctrine of anti-fatalism, which need not be quoted here.

9—ARGUMENTS WITH OTHER PHILOSOPHIC SCHOOLS

Besides the above, the Later Mohists directed many arguments against the various other schools of thought of their time. These will be described now one by one. For example :

Canon, II : " What is so at one time is not always so. The reason is given under ' extension from this to that ' " (p. 432).

Exposition : " Yao was a wise ruler because we judge him from the present to the past. But if the ancients were placed in the present, Yao would be incapable of good rule " (p. 469).

Canon, II : " (To say :) ' This is the righteousness of a Yao,' is to project the present into the past with difference in time. The reason is given under ' what are righteous are two (different things) ' " (p. 429).

Exposition : " As regards Yao and Ho : Sometimes we use the reputation to describe the man, sometimes the actuality to show the man. To say, ' My friend is a rich merchant,' is to describe him by reputation. To point out this Ho, is to show him by the actuality. (When we speak of) Yao's ' righteousness ' (*i*), the reputation exists to-day, but the actuality, ' righteousness,' remains a thing of the past " (p. 488).

This is an attack upon the Confucian reverence for such Sages of the past as Yao and Shun. When we say that Yao was skilled in good government, we are saying this at the present time with respect to something that was done in the past. If we were to speak of it in the past, with respect to his conducting good government in the present day, it is quite possible that he would be incapable of good rule. This is because the way in which good government is conducted differs according to the times.[1]

Canon, II : " Why a thing becomes so ; how to find it out ; and how to let others know it : these need not be the same. The reason is given under ' disease ' " (p. 428).

Exposition : " There is someone who injures : this is the way the thing is. The seeing of this (injury) is knowledge of it. The telling of it is letting others know " (p. 467).

That is, what the Confucians say about the way Yao conducted his government is simply what they themselves know, and need

---

[1] In this explanation I follow Teng Kao-ching, *op. cit.*

not be identical with Yao's actual conduct of government. Yao's reputation for ' righteousness ' is something of the present time, whereas the actuality of this righteousness is something of the past. Since present and past are two different times, we may infer that the reputation of Yao's ' righteousness ' and the actuality of this ' righteousness ' are two different things. Likewise when we call a certain man a rich merchant, we are describing him by reputation, but if we actually point out this certain man, Ho, this is to show him in his very actuality. The good name given to Yao is something of the present, whereas the actuality of this goodness is in the past. How then can the two be the same ? ¹ From these arguments we can see that the praise bestowed by the Confucians upon Yao may not correspond to Yao's actual goodness.

Canon, II : " That human-heartedness (*jen*) and righteousness (*i*) are respectively internal and external, is wrong. The reason is given under ' great contradiction ' " (p. 439).

Exposition : " Human-heartedness is to love ; righteousness is to benefit. What loves and benefits is this. What is loved and benefited is that. The loving and benefiting are not internal and external with respect to each other. Neither are what are loved and benefited external and internal with respect to each other. He who considers human-heartedness as internal and righteousness as external, is making a comparison of the act of loving with the object benefited. This is a loose appellation (*k'uang chü* 狂 舉). It is as if the left eye were coming out, and the right eye going in " (p. 498).

That human-heartedness or *jen* is internal, and righteousness or *i* is external, was the doctrine held by Kao Tzŭ and his group.² The *Kuan-tzŭ* (ch. 26) says similarly : " *Jen* comes forth from within ; *i* acts from without " (*chüan* 10, p. 1). The Later Mohists, however, maintain that it is I who am capable of loving and benefiting, whereas what is loved and benefited is another. Both the capacity to love and the capacity to benefit are thus internal, and hence one cannot say that the one is internal and the other external. In the same way what are loved and what are benefited are both external, and hence one cannot say that the first is internal and the second external. Thus to say that *jen* is internal and *i* is external, is to compare the doer, as regards love, with the one who receives the action, in the case of benefit.³ This would be like saying that the left eye comes out while the right eye goes in and would be a loose appellation or statement.⁴

Canon, II : " The Five Elements do not constantly overcome one another. The reason is given under ' quantity ' " (p. 425).

---

¹ Here I also follow Professor Teng Kao-ching.
² *Cf.* Ch. 7, sect. 4, pp. 145 f.
³ The Mohists, as already stated (pp. 84 f.), made righteousness (*i*) equivalent to the beneficial (*li*).—TR.
⁴ Here too I follow Professor Teng Kao-ching.

Exposition : " The five are metal, water, earth, fire and wood. Quite separate (from any cycle), fire may melt metal. This is because of the greater amount of fire. Or metal may reduce (fire) to cinders. This is because of the greater amount of metal. Metal may spoil wood. Wood may scatter water " (p. 483) '

This is an attack upon the doctrine of the Five Elements as held by Tsou Yen and others. When the overcoming of metal, wood, water, fire and earth by one another is simply the result of what is more abundant overcoming what is less abundant, there can be no real cyclical succession of one element by another. This argument is one based upon the concept of metal, wood, water, fire and earth as concrete and physical things, rather than as constituting five etherial Elements or Powers.

Canon, II : " Study is advantageous. The reason is given by those who oppose it " (p. 439).

Exposition : " Study : By maintaining that people do not know that study is of no advantage, one is thereby informing them of this fact. This informing them that study is of no advantage, constitutes a teaching. To hold as a teaching that study is of no advantage, is perverse " (p. 499).

Canon, II : " Non-existence is not necessarily dependent upon existence. The reason is given under ' what is meant ' " (p. 428).

Exposition : " Non-existence : Suppose there were no horses. There would be none only after they had once existed. But the collapse of the sky is something non-existent. Here there is non-existence which is simply non-existence " (p. 486).

These are attacks upon statements in the *Lao-tzŭ*. The latter says : " Banish learning, and there will be no more grieving " (ch. 20). Once one considers learning to be of no value, however, how can one *teach* that learning is of no value ? Once teaching exists, learning exists, which means that one still holds learning to be something valuable.

The *Lao-tzŭ* says again : " Existence and Non-existence grow out of one another " (ch. 2). The Mohists, on the contrary, maintained that existence and non-existence are not necessarily mutually dependent. If we say that there are no horses, their non-existence is, to be sure, dependent upon the fact that they formerly existed, for the world must at one time have had horses, in order that later it might be said that there are no horses. But when we say that there is no such thing as the collapse of the sky, non-existence of this sort is not dependent upon existence. This is because there need never actually have existed a case of the sky's collapsing, in order for us now to state that such a collapse does not exist.

Canon, II : " To say that in dialectic there is no winner is incorrect. The reason is given under ' dialectic ' " (p. 438).

' This reading follows that of Teng Kao-ching, *op. cit.*

Exposition : " In speaking, when what is said does not agree, there is dissent. There is agreement when one (of two persons) says it is a puppy, and another says it is a dog. There is dissent when one says it is an ox, and another says it is a horse. When neither of them wins, there is no dialectic. Dialectic is that in which one person says a thing is so, and another says it is not so. The one who is right will win " (p. 479).

Canon, II : " To hold that all speech is perverse, is perverseness. The reason is given under ' his speech ' " (p. 437).

Exposition : " (To hold that all speech) is perverse is not permissible. If the speech of this man (who holds this doctrine) is permissible, then speech is not perverse since there it is permissible. But if this man's speech is not permissible, then it is wrong to take it as being correct " (pp. 495-496).

Canon, II : " That knowing it and not knowing it are the same, is perverse. The reason is given under ' no means ' " (p. 438).

Exposition : " There is knowledge when there is discussion about it. When there is no knowledge, there is no means (by which to discuss it) " (p. 479).

Canon, II : " To condemn criticism is perverse. The reason is given under ' not condemning ' " (p. 440).

Exposition : " To condemn criticism is to condemn one's own condemnation. If one does not condemn it, there is nothing to be condemned. When one cannot condemn it, this means not to condemn criticism " (p. 500).

These are all attacks upon the ideas of Chuang Tzǔ, who maintained that all things and ideas are variable. Therefore, if we are to accept any one thing as being right, which, Chuang Tzǔ would ask, is it to be ? But if we do not hold to one thing as being right, then all things are right. Hence, says Chuang Tzǔ, following the spontaneity of things, " Let us harmonize them within the Boundary of Nature, and leave them alone in the process of natural evolution. This is the way to complete our span of years. Let us forget life. Let us forget the distinctions of right and wrong. Let us find enjoyment in the realm of the infinite and remain there ! " (*Chuang-tzǔ*, p. 31).

Seen from its positive aspect, this doctrine does not mean the obliteration of right and wrong, but a transcending of them ; while from its negative aspect, it is simply a refusal to hold to any one thing as being right, and an affirmation that ' in dialectic, there is no one who wins,' and that ' knowing it and not knowing it are the same.' The *Chuang-tzǔ* (ch. 2) says : " When there is argument, there is something which the argument does not reach ; great argument does not require words ; speech that argues falls short of its aim " (p. 25). Thus looked at, says Chuang Tzǔ, " All speech is perverse," and hence he condemns all criticism by one man of another. The Later Mohists, on the other hand, maintained that when people differ as to what is right and wrong, this constitutes argument, in which the person who is right will win. This has already been explained above. They further held that speech which says that ' all speech is perverse,' is itself perverse speech. For if such speech is right, then it, at least, is not perverse, which means that it is wrong to say that ' all speech is perverse.' But if, on the other hand, this speech is itself wrong, this means that other speech in general cannot be entirely perverse.

To state that ' knowing it and not knowing it are the same,' is also perverse speech. For this statement in itself represents a knowing, and such knowing is not the same as not knowing. Such a speech constitutes discussion, and discussion can exist only when there is knowledge ; when there is no knowledge there is nothing with which to hold discussion. Similarly, criticism exists whenever any person uses words to condemn words, and hence to say that criticism is wrong, is equivalent to saying that one oneself is wrong. If one does not hold one's own criticism to be wrong, however, one is arguing against the idea that ' it is wrong to criticize.'

CHAPTER XII
HSÜN TZŬ AND HIS SCHOOL OF CONFUCIANISM

1—Hsün Tzŭ as a Scholar

Of Hsün Tzŭ 荀 子, whose given name was K'uang 況, and whose cognomen was Ch'ing 卿, the *Shih Chi* (ch. 74) says :
" Hsün Ch'ing was a native of Chao (a state in the south of present Hopei and Shansi). When he was fifty, he first came to spread his teachings abroad in Ch'i. . . . T'ien P'ien and the other scholars associated with him were already all dead in the time of King Hsiang of Ch'i (283-265),· and Hsün Ch'ing was the most eminent (surviving) learned scholar. Ch'i was still repairing the gaps in the ranks of the ' great officers,' [1] and Hsün Ch'ing was three times officer for the sacrificial wine offering. Among the people of Ch'i were some who slandered Hsün Ch'ing, and he thereupon went to Ch'u, where Prince Ch'un-shen made him magistrate of Lan-ling (a place in southern Shantung). When Prince Ch'un Shen died (in 238 B.C.), Hsün Ch'ing lost his Lan-ling position. Li Ssŭ, who later became Prime Minister of Ch'in, was his disciple.[2]

" Hsün Ch'ing hated the governments of his corrupt generation, its dying states and evil princes, who did not follow the Way (*Tao*), but gave their attention to magic and prayers and believed in omens and luck. It was a generation of low scholars who had no learning. (Thinkers) such as Chuang Chou (i.e., Chuang Tzŭ), on the other hand, were specious and threw the customs into disorder. Therefore he expounded the prosperity and decay that come from putting into practice the Confucian and Mohist doctrines and virtues. By the time of his death he had written and arranged in order several tens of thousands of words. He was buried in Lan-ling." [3]

The statement that the people of Hsün Tzŭ's age ' gave their attention to magic and prayers, and believed in omens and luck,' indicates that the doctrines of the *Yin-yang* school were already prevalent at that time. It was just during this age of superstition that the Confucian school, which after Mencius had lacked eminent scholars,

---

[1] *Lieh ta fu* 列 大 夫, a title conferred on the many scholars assembled at Chi-hsia in Ch'i. See p. 132.—Tr.
[2] It was largely through the counsels of Li Ssŭ that Ch'in Shih-huang succeeded in uniting China into one empire in 221 B.C. . Li Ssŭ was also directly responsible for the famous Burning of the Books in 213.—Tr.
[3] *Cf.* Dubs, *Hsüntze, the Moulder of Ancient Confucianism*, pp. 26-28.

became rejuventated with Hsün Tzŭ, who was the most skilled of all the ancient Chinese philosophers in criticizing other philosophical schools, and whose remarkable learning and erudition contributed greatly toward the development of the classical studies that were carried on later during the Former Han dynasty (206 B.C.—A.D. 25). The *Hsün-tzŭ* (ch. 1) states :

" To miss once in a hundred shots is sufficient to prevent a person from being classed as an expert archer ; to fail to go the last half step in a thousand *li* is enough to prevent a person from being classed as an expert driver ; to fail to understand the niceties of human relationships, and not to be intent upon human-heartedness and righteousness, is sufficient to prevent a person from being classed as an eminent scholar. Scholarship means to study with intentness and singleness of purpose . . . . It is only when there is completeness and exhaustiveness that there is scholarship. The Superior Man knows that when his knowledge is not complete or refined, it is insufficient to be classed as excellent. Therefore he recites (the classics) sentence by sentence in order to make them a part of himself, seeks to penetrate them in order to understand them, and puts them into practice and lives as a man of virtue. . . " (p. 40).

This is how Hsün Tzŭ taught others, and shows too the nature of his own learning.

The critic, Wang Chung (1744-1794), in his Chronological Table, places Hsün Tzŭ between 298 and 238 B.C.,[1] and although the dates of Hsün Tzŭ's life cannot be exactly determined, the active period of his life probably falls somewhere within this sixty year period.

2—Attitude toward Confucius and Mencius

Hsün Tzŭ, like Mencius, honored Confucius as a man whose learning was most complete, exhaustive and refined. The *Hsün-tzŭ* (ch. 6) says :

" There were those who united different systems, made words and practice equivalent, unified the different groups, and gathered together the talented men of the world, to tell them of the great antiquity and to teach them perfect order. Every corner of their rooms and each mat on their floors was filled with the culture of the kings and the customs of the perfect society. . . . Such were Confucius and (his disciple) Tzŭ Kung " (*Aids*, p. 38).

Chapter XXI says :

" Confucius was benevolent and wise and was not blind. Therefore he studied the methods of government and was worthy to be ranked with the early kings. This school maintained the system of the Chou dynasty and put it into practice. He was not blind in regard to the whole. Therefore his character was equal to that of

---

[1] See his *Hsün-tzŭ Nien-piao*, in his *Shu Hsüeh Nei Wai P'ien*.

the Duke of Chou ; his fame was on a par with that of the Three Kings. This was the happiness of being free from blindness " (p. 265).

Hsün Tzŭ regarded his contemporaries as men who were clear-sighted on some points, but blind on others. In contrast to such men of 'perverted knowledge,' Confucius 'was benevolent and wise and was not blind.' On this point Hsün Tzŭ was in full agreement with Mencius, who had said : " In Confucius we have what is called a complete harmony " (*Mencius*, V*b*, 1). Mencius, however, tended to emphasize Confucius's virtue, whereas Hsün Tzŭ empha-sized his learning.

Although Hsün Tzŭ thus honors Confucius, he sharply attacks Mencius (ch. 6) :

" There were some who, in a general way, followed the early kings but did not know their fundamentals. Yet their abilities were numerous, their ambition great, their knowledge many-sided and varied. Based on ancient traditions, they developed theories which were called the Five Elements. Their views were peculiar, con-tradictory and without standards ; dark and without illustrations ; confined and without explanations. They elaborated their statements and paid honor to them saying : ' These are the true sayings of the former illustrious man (Confucius).' Tzŭ Ssŭ (grandson of Confucius) began this, and Mencius followed. The ignorant scholars of the world welcomed it and did not know that it was false. They accepted it and passed it on, thinking that because of this, Confucius and Tzŭ Yu (a disciple of Confucius) would carry authority with later generations. This was the fault of Tzŭ Ssŭ and Mencius " (*Aids*, p. 37).

Westerners are in the habit of saying that a person is born either a Platonist or an Aristotelian, and James, in his *Pluralistic Universe*, divides philosophic schools into those that are ' tough-minded ' and those that are ' tender-minded.' Mencius belongs to the ' tender-minded ' group, with a philosophy of idealistic tendencies, while Hsün Tzŭ is of the ' tough-minded ' school, with a philosophy having materialistic tendencies. From the point of view of Hsün Tzŭ's semi-materialism, therefore, Mencius's idea of apprehending Heaven through the exhausting of our own natures, and his statement that ' all things are complete within us,' would indeed seem to be ' peculiar, contradictory and without standards ; dark and without illustrations ; confined and without explanations.' Hsün Tzŭ's attack on Mencius, then, was prompted because the viewpoints and tem-peraments of the two men fundamentally differed, so that among the Confucians of the Warring States period we find a conflict between the schools of Mencius and Hsün Tzŭ, just as among the Sung and Ming Neo-Confucianists we find one between the school of Ch'eng I (1033-1107) and Chu Hsi (1130-1200) on the one hand, and that of Lu Chiu-yüan (1139-1192) and Wang Yang-ming (1473-1529) on the other.

3—Attitude toward the Chou Institutions

Hsün Tzǔ's attitude toward the institutions of the Chou dynasty might in one way be called conservative. The *Hsün-tzǔ* (ch. 9) says :
" A king's institutions should not depart from those of the Three Dynasties (Hsia, Shang, Chou) ; its methods should not differ from those of the later kings. Principles which differ from those of the Three Dynasties are loose ; methods which differ from those of the later kings are incorrect. There are models for garments ; there are rules for buildings ; there is an established grading of officials and soldiers. Mourning rites, sacrifices and their utensils all have their appropriate gradations. All music which is not correct should be totally abandoned. All colors which are not of the ancient sort should be entirely dispensed with. All utensils which are not of the ancient sort should be destroyed. This is what is meant by returning to antiquity. Such are the institutions of a King " (p. 131).

The later kings here spoken of mean the kings of the early Chou dynasty. Chapter V says :
" There is no way of human living which does not have its distinctions (*pien* 辨) ; no distinctions are greater than those of social distinctions (*fen* 分) ; no social distinctions are greater than the rules of proper conduct (*li* 禮) ; there are no rules of proper conduct greater than the Sage-kings.

" But there were many Sage-kings. Which shall I follow ? When rites are too ancient, their form becomes obliterated. When music is too ancient, its details are lost. The officers in charge fail to keep these when they are too ancient. Hence it is said : If you wish to see the footprints of the Sage-kings, then look where they are most clear, that is to say, at the later kings. These later kings were the rulers of the whole country. To give up the later kings and follow those of highest antiquity is like giving up one's own prince and serving another's prince. Hence it is said : If you wish to know a thousand years, then consider to-day ; if you wish to understand ten or one hundred thousand, then examine one or two ; if you wish to know ancient times, then examine the course of the Chou dynasty. If you wish to know the course of the Chou dynasty, you must learn from the proper man, the Superior Man (i.e., Confucius) who is honored " (pp. 72-73).

Hsün Tzǔ, like Mencius, thus paid honor to Confucius and believed in the conservation of the Chou institutions ; but where Mencius said that men should follow the examples of the early kings, Hsun Tzǔ maintained that it is the later kings who should be followed. However, what they meant by these two terms was exactly the same.

To Hsün Tzǔ, the later kings meant those of the early Chou, who must be followed because, as I have previously pointed out, the ancient institutions were fast falling into decay by the time of the Ch'un Ch'iu and Warring States periods. Among the intellectuals of this time, some tried to conserve these ancient institutions, others criticized or opposed them, and still others wished to establish completely new ones in their place.[1] When advocating their doctrines, these intellectuals were in the habit of seeking support for them in the sayings of the ancient Sages, either historical or legendary. Thus Confucius, when he upheld the early Chou institutions, often made references to King Wen and the Duke of Chou, the men who had been so important in founding it. Mo Tzŭ, who came after Confucius, wished to follow the Hsia dynasty rather than the Chou, and brought forward the even more ancient Yü, supposed founder of the Hsia dynasty, to supersede the influence of King Wen and the Duke of Chou. Mencius, following Mo Tzŭ, went back still further to the legendary Yao and Shun, to supersede Yü. Finally the Taoists, such as Lao Tzŭ and Chuang Tzŭ, went back for their heroes to an epoch preceding that of Yao and Shun, and invoked such imaginary figures as the Yellow Emperor (Huang-ti), to displace Yao and Shun. The consequence was that, though in the time of Mencius it had still been possible to speak of such men as King Wen and the Duke of Chou as the ' early kings,' by Hsün Tzŭ's time so many other supposedly earlier figures had been evoked by various debaters, that one could only speak of King Wen and the Duke of Chou as later kings.

Concerning the question of imitating antiquity, the Taoist followers of Lao Tzŭ and Chuang Tzŭ maintained that a vast difference exists between ancient and modern times, and that therefore the institutions of the early Chou could not be successfully revived. The *Chuang-tzŭ* (ch. 14) says :

" For travelling by water, there is nothing like a boat. For travelling by land, there is nothing like a cart. If, because a boat moves readily in water, you were to try to push it on land, you would never succeed in making it go. Now are not ancient and modern times like water and land, and Chou and Lu (the state of Confucius) like the boat and the cart ? To try to make the customs of Chou succeed in Lu, is like pushing a boat on land : great labor and no result, except certain injury to oneself " (pp. 180-181).

Whereas Hsün Tzŭ (ch. 3) says :

" Therefore the nature of a thousand or ten thousand men are as those of one man. The beginning of Heaven and Earth were as the present day. The ways of a hundred (early) kings are as those of the later kings. The prince who examines the way of the later kings, and then talks about what happened before these various

---

[1] *Cf.* p. 14.

kings, is like one who discusses like a courtier. To extend abroad the threads of good manners (*li*) and standards of justice (*i*), to make clear the distinctions between right and wrong, to bring the important things of the whole country into one control, and to rule the masses within the seas, is like directing a single person. Thus the scope of what one holds is narrow, but the accomplishment is great. A five inch foot-rule is the proper standard for the entire world. Hence the true ruler does not leave his hall, yet his accomplishments satisfy the sentiments of all people within the seas. This is because he has the proper way to do it " (*chüan* 2, pp. 7-8). Again (ch. 5) :

" Abandoned incorrigible people say : Ancient and present times are different in nature ; the reasons for their order and disorder differ. And many people are thus misled. Those people are stupid and without learning, ignorant and without perception. They can be deceived in what they see, and is this not all the more the case with traditions handed down through a thousand ages? The abandoned incorrigible person can thus deceive the people within the space of their doors and halls, and can he not all the more do so with regard to the traditions of a thousand ages of antiquity ?

" But why cannot the Sage be so deceived ? I say it is because the Sage measures things by himself. Hence by himself he measures other men ; by his own feelings he measures their feelings ; by his class he measures other classes ; by his doctrines he measures their merit ; by the Way (*Tao*) he can completely comprehend things. Past and present are the same. Things that are the same in kind, though extended over a long period, continue to have the self-same principles. Hence to consider wrong doctrines and not be misled, to look at a miscellany of things and not be confused, can be done by this way of measuring " (pp. 73-74).

By abandoned and incorrigible people, Hsün Tzŭ would mean such men as those who wrote the *Chuang-tzŭ* passage quoted above. His conception here is that of a static universe, in which the present day is like the beginning of the world, and in which the human race remains unchanged. Why then, he asked, could not the Chou institutions be revived, when, as he said, " Things that are the same kind, though extended over a long period, continue to have the self-same principles " ?

4—HEAVEN AND HUMAN NATURE

When Confucius spoke of Heaven, he meant a ruling or personal Heaven. The Heaven of Mencius was at times personal, at times fatalistic, and at times ethical. Hsün Tzŭ's Heaven is naturalistic, a point in which he seems to have been influenced by the *Lao-tzŭ* and by Chuang Tzŭ. The *Chuang-tzŭ* (ch. 14), for example, speaking of the movements of Heaven, Earth, sun and moon, says : " Is there perhaps a mechanical arrangement that makes these bodies move inevitably as they do ?   Is it perhaps that they keep revolving without being able to stop themselves ? " (p. 173).   This is clearly a naturalistic cosmology, and so is Hsün Tzŭ's, as shown in the following passage (from ch. 17) :

"Heaven has a constant regularity of activity.   It did not exist for the sake of Yao nor cease to exist for the sake of Chieh.   Respond to it with good government, and success will result.   Respond to it with misgovernment, and calamity will result. . . . Hence to understand the distinction between Heaven and man : this is to be a great man. To make complete without acting (*wu wei*), and to obtain without seeking : this is what is meant by the activities of Heaven.   Being like this, although it is deep, man will not give deep thought to it ; although it is great, he will not use his ability (for its investigation) ; although mysterious, he will not scrutinize it : this is what is meant by refraining from contesting in one's activities with Heaven.   Heaven has its seasons, Earth has its material resources, man has his government.   This is what is meant (when it is said that man) is able to form a trinity (with Heaven and Earth).   To give up that wherewith one can form such a trinity, and to desire that with which one forms the trinity, is to be led into error.

"The fixed stars make their round ; the sun and moon alternately shine ; the four seasons succeed one another ; the *yin* and *yang* go through their great mutations ; wind and rain are widely distributed ; all things acquire their harmony and have their lives ; each gets its nourishment and develops to its appointed state.   We do not see the cause of these occurrences, but we do see their effects : this is what is meant by being spirit-like.   The results of all these changes are known, but we do not know the invisible source : this is what is called Heaven.   It is only the Sage who does not seek to know Heaven " (pp. 173-175).

The movements of the stars, sun and moon are all represented here as natural processes.   The Sage does not seek to know the cause which makes them as they are, but instead expends all his energy " to seek for himself much happiness," after which " he will be able to control Heaven's seasons and Earth's material resources, and utilize them." [1]   It is in this way that man can form a trinity with Heaven and Earth.   Therefore :

"Instead of exalting Heaven and thinking about it, why not heap up wealth and use it advantageously ?   Instead of obeying Heaven and praising it, why not adapt Heaven's Fate (*T'ien Ming*) and make use of it ?   Instead of looking toward the propitious time and waiting for it, why not seize the opportunity and utilize it ?   Instead of relying on things to increase of themselves, why not put forth one's ability and develop them ?   Instead of thinking of things and considering

---

[1] Quoted from the commentary by Yang Liang on the above passage, published in A.D. 818.

them as things, why not set them in proper order and consider them as one's own ? Instead of wishing that things will have the wherewithal by which to live, why not hold in your possession that which makes things come to maturity ? Thus if a person neglects what man can do and thinks about Heaven, he fails to understand the nature of things " (p. 183).

This is the way to ' control Heaven's seasons and Earth's material resources, and utilize them.'

Mencius spoke of an ethical Heaven, and believed that man's nature (*hsing*) is a part of this Heaven. This is the metaphysical basis for his doctrine that man's nature is originally good. Hsün Tzŭ's Heaven, however, is a naturalistic one, and differs entirely from that of Mencius, inasmuch as it contains no ethical principle. In the same way his doctrine of human nature is diametrically opposed to that of Mencius. Thus he says (ch. 23) :

" The nature (*hsing* 性) of man is evil ; his goodness is only acquired training (*wei* 偽) " (p. 301).

Concerning the meaning of this ' nature ' and ' acquired training,' the same chapter goes on :

" That in man which cannot be learned and cannot be worked for, is what is meant by nature (*hsing*). That in man which can be learned in order to be able to act, and which can be worked for in order to have results, is acquired training (*wei*). This is the distinction between nature and acquired training " (p. 303). Again (ch. 19) :

" Nature (*hsing*) is the unwrought material of the original ; what are acquired (*wei*) are the accomplishments and refinements brought about by culture (*wen* 文) and the rules of proper conduct (*li*). Without nature, there would be nothing upon which to add the acquired. Without the acquired, nature could not become beautiful of itself " (p. 234).

" That which at birth is so, is called the nature " (p. 281).[1] *Hsing* or nature is something pertaining to Heaven. Since Heaven is mechanistic, and lacks any ideal or ethical principle, nature likewise cannot contain an ethical principle. Morality is something made by man, and so is called 'acquired.' The *Hsün-tzŭ* (ch. 23) says :

" Now man, by his nature, at birth loves profit, and if he follows this tendency, strife and rapacity come about, whereas courtesy and yielding disappear. Man at birth is envious and hateful, and if he follows these tendencies, injury and destruction result, whereas loyalty and faithfulness disappear. At birth he possesses the desires

---

[1] It is interesting to note that Hsün Tzŭ here expresses the same idea as did Kao Tzŭ, though in the Chinese, Hsün Tzŭ's wording is less concise and ambiguous than Kao Tzŭ's. See above, pp. 124, 145. Hsün Tzŭ means by this statement, however, that man's nature is definitely evil, whereas Kao Tzŭ only believed that it is morally indifferent to either good or evil.—TR.

of the ear and eye, and likes sound and women, and because he follows these tendencies, impurity and disorder result, whereas the rules of proper conduct (*li*), standards of justice (*i*),[1] and finish and orderliness disappear. Therefore to give rein to man's original nature and to follow man's feelings, means inevitable strife and rapacity, together with violations of etiquette and confusion in the proper way of doing things, and a reversion to a state of violence. Therefore the civilizing influence of teachers and laws, and the guidance of the rules of proper conduct (*li*) and standards of justice (*i*) are absolutely necessary. Thereupon courtesy results, culture is developed, and good government is the consequence. By this line of reasoning it is evident that the nature of man is evil, and his goodness is acquired " (p. 301).

But although human nature is evil, it is possible for every man to become good. The same chapter says :

" ' The man in the street can become a Yü.' [2] How about this ? I say that what gave Yü the qualities of Yü was that he put into practice human-heartedness, righteousness, obedience to law, and uprightness. So then there is a possibility for knowing and practising human-heartedness, righteousness, obedience to law and uprightness. This being so, every man on the street has the capacity for knowing human-heartedness, righteousness, obedience to law and uprightness, and the means to carry out these principles. Thus it is evident that he can become a Yü. . . .

" Suppose this man on the street directs his capacities to learning, concentrating his mind on one object, thinking and studying and investigating thoroughly, adding daily to his knowledge and long retaining it. If he accumulates goodness and does not stop, he will reach to spiritual clairvoyance, and will form a trinity with Heaven and Earth. Thus the Sage is a man who has attained to that state by cumulative effort " (pp. 312-313).

Ch'en Li (1810-1882) remarks on this : " Tai Tung-yüan (1723-1777) says : ' This, and the doctrine that human nature is good, are not only not contradictory, but even seem to illustrate one another.' [3]

---

[1] 義, a word which we have generally translated as 'righteousness,' often in conjunction with the quality of human-heartedness (*jen*). As used by Hsün Tzŭ in conjunction with the 'rules of proper conduct' (*li*), however, it seems to lose its sense of 'righteousness' as practised by the individual, and to become more general and impersonal, a thing possessed by society as a whole. Thus the *li* are the accumulated traditional *mores* as applied by society to the individual. Likewise *i* seems to be the code of what is just and proper, as held by society rather than the individual, and hence is no longer a personal virtue, as is *jen*. As such, we translate it when used in conjunction with *li*, as 'standards of justice.' See especially p. 296, where Hsün Tzŭ says that human society is based upon man's knowledge of standards of justice (*i*).—TR.

[2] A saying similar to this, but applied to Yao and Shun, appears in *Mencius*, VI*b*, 2.—TR.

[3] Tai was one of the most important Ch'ing dynasty philosophers. *Cf.* for this quotation, his *Meng-tzŭ Tzŭ-i Su-cheng*.

And I say :   That a man in the street can become a Yü, is the same
as Mencius's saying that all men can become Yao or Shun, only
Yao and Shun have been substituted for by Yü.   This being so,
why should he (Hsün Tzǔ) have had to establish a separate doctrine
for himself ? " [1]

Mencius, however, by saying that human nature is good, meant
that innate within this nature are the beginnings of goodness, which
if further developed, will make of him a Yao or a Shun.   Hsün Tzǔ,
on the other hand, by saying that human nature is evil, means that it
not only lacks any beginnings of goodness, but that it even contains
the beginnings of evilness.   At the same time, however, man possesses
the faculty of intelligence, and therefore, if once told about such
things as the proper relationships between father and son, or ruler
and subject, he can learn to acquire them himself.   The accumulation
of such learning over a prolonged period results in the formation of
habit, so that the Sage attains to his state through cumulative effort.
Hsün Tzǔ says (ch. 8) :

" It is the common man in the street who, having accumulated
goodness and wholly completed its cultivation, is called a Sage.
First he must seek and then only will he obtain ; he must do it, and
then only will he reach perfection ; he must store it up, and then only
will he rise ; he must complete its cultivation, and then only can he be a
Sage.   Thus the Sage is a man who has accumulated (goodness).   A
man who accumulates (practice in) hoeing and ploughing, becomes
a farmer ; who accumulates (practice in) chopping and shaving wood,
becomes an artisan ; who accumulates (practice in) trafficking in
goods, becomes a merchant ; who accumulates (practice in) the rules
of proper conduct (*li*) and standards of justice (*i*), becomes a Superior
Man " (pp. 115-116).

That any man in the street has a potential capacity for knowing
and practising such virtues as human-heartedness and righteousness,
is explained by his faculty of intelligence, but does not mean
that man innately has an ethical constitution.   A man becomes
the Superior Man through repeated practice in the ' accumulation '
of the rules of proper conduct and standards of justice, just as he
becomes a farmer through practice in hoeing and ploughing.   These
are both matters of knowledge and habit.   Mencius says that
man differs from the beasts inasmuch as he has the beginnings of
goodness within him, such as a mind which distinguishes between
right and wrong.   Hsün Tzǔ, on the other hand, says that man
differs from the beasts in having superior and more varied intellectual
capacities.   Thus we see that his doctrine of the evilness of human
nature is in fact quite at variance with Mencius's doctrine that
human nature is good.

---

[1] *Cf.* Ch'en Li's *Tung-shu Tu-shu Chi, chüan* 3, p. 2.

5—Hsün Tzŭ's System of Psychology

What I have discussed in the preceding section may be made even clearer by examination of Hsün Tzŭ's psychology. The *Hsün-tzŭ* (ch. 22) states :

" That which at birth is so, is called the nature (*hsing*). That which is produced by the harmony of life, essential and responding to (external) stimulus ; which is not produced by training, but exists spontaneously : this is called the nature. The love, hate, joy, anger, sorrow and pleasure of this nature are called the emotions (*ch'ing* 情). When, the emotions being so, the mind selects from among them, this is called cogitation (*lü* 慮). When the mind cogitates and can act accordingly, this is called the acquired (*wei* 偽). When, after accumulated cogitation, and the training of the abilities, there results completion, this is called the acquired (*wei*). To act for the sake of righteous gain is what is meant by having a proper occupation. To act correctly according to righteousness is good conduct. That in man by which he knows is (called the faculty of) knowing (*chih* 知). That in (the faculty of) knowing which corresponds to (external things) is called knowledge (*chih* 智). That in man by which he can do something is called his ability (*neng* 能). That by doing which he can accomplish something is called ability. An injury to the nature is called a defect. What one meets with by chance is called Fate (*ming* 命) " (pp. 281-282).

Again, in the same chapter :

"Every doctrine of government which depends on the elimination of human desires, is one which cannot guide the desires and is hampered by their presence. Every doctrine of government which waits for the lessening of the desires of man, is one which cannot curb the desires and is hampered by the great number of desires. Desire does not depend upon whether satisfaction is possible, whereas its gratification seeks what is possible. That desire does not depend upon whether attainment is possible, is something received from Nature (*T'ien* 天). That gratification seeks what is possible, is something brought about by the mind. The nature (*hsing*) possesses desires, for which the mind devises regulations and restraints . . . . What men desire most is life, and what they dislike most is death. Yet there are men who cling to life and find death, not because they do not desire life and do desire death, but because they cannot live but can only die. Therefore if a person's action stops short of his desires, it is the mind which has arrested it . . . . . If a person's desires are weak, while his actions go beyond them, it is the mind which has caused this. . . . .

" Human nature (*hsing*) is the product of Nature (*T'ien*). The emotions (*ch'ing*) are the materials of the human nature. Desires are the reactions of the emotions (to external stimuli). These emotions can never avoid assuming that what is desired can be sought and obtained. The necessary beginning of knowledge is to consider that desires are permissible and so to guide (but not wholly repress) them. . . .

" Men never obtain what they desire unadulterated, and when they reject what they dislike, it never goes away unmixed. Hence men's actions should always correspond to the standard. When the steelyard is not held properly, a heavy article suspended from it will swing up high, and people will think it is light ; a light thing will hang down low, and people will think it is heavy. In this way people are misled about weights. When the standard is not right, calamity is mixed with what is desirable and people think it is happiness; or happiness is mixed with what is disliked and people think it is calamity. And so in this way, too, people are misled about happiness and calamity. The Way (*Tao*) was the correct standard for ancient times as it is for the present. If you depart from the Way to choose your own inner standard, then you will not know what will lead to calamity or happiness.

" If a trader barters one thing for one thing, people say : ' He has neither loss nor gain.' If he barters one for two, people say : ' There is no loss, but a gain.' If he barters two for one, people say : ' There is no gain, but a loss.' The schemer gets as much as he can ; the man who plans, follows where he may. No one will exchange two for one because they know the art of counting things. To follow the Way is like exchanging one for two. How can there be loss ? To leave the Way to choose one's own inner standards is like exchanging two for one ; how can there be any gain ? " (pp. 293-295, 296-297).

Men have emotions and desires, and also mind. The desires need not be wholly eliminated, but only need to be kept in proper restraint by the mind, through its power of cogitation. The reason why the mind finds it possible to restrain the desires, is because it knows that if they are given free rein, the result will inevitably be undesirable.

What men desire and what they dislike are usually intimately bound up with one another ; neither one nor the other is ever wholly unadulterated. Therefore when men are rejecting or accepting, they must use their intellect to weigh each possible aspect of benefit or harm, and avoid being ' misled about happiness and calamity.' The Way or *Tao* gives the correct standard both for ancient times and for the present day. Hsün Tzŭ says elsewhere of this *Tao* : " The *Tao* is not the *Tao* of Heaven ; it is the *Tao* of Earth ; it is the Way followed by man " (p. 96). ' The rules of proper conduct, standards of justice, and finish and orderliness,' together with ' human-heartedness, righteousness, obedience to law and uprightness,' are what constitute this Way of man. All these are what make it possible for men to live and to satisfy their desires. Chapter XXI says :

" The Sage knows the afflictions which befall the mind, and sees the calamities which come from being prejudiced and prevented from knowing the truth. Hence he considers neither what is desired nor what is disliked, neither beginning nor end, neither nearness nor distance, neither the broad nor the shallow, and neither the ancient nor the present. He puts all things on an equal basis, and keeps the balances level. For this reason all the heterodoxies are not able to prejudice him, confusing his order.

" What can be said to be the balance ?   It is the Way (*Tao*). . . . How can a person know the *Tao* ?   Through the mind.   How does the mind know ?   By emptiness, unity and quiescence.   The mind never ceases to store away (*tsang* 臧) (impressions), yet it has that which may be called emptiness (*hsü* 虛).   The mind has always a multiplicity, yet there is that which may be called a unity (*i* 一).   The mind is always active, yet there is that which may be called quiescence (*ching* 靜).

" Man from birth has the capacity to know things ; this capacity has its memory (*chih* 志).   This memory is what is meant by stored-away (impressions).

" Yet besides this there is that which may be called emptiness.   That which does not allow what is already stored away to injure that which is about to be received is called the mind's emptiness.

" The mind from birth has the capacity for knowledge.   This knowledge contains differences.   Differences consist of knowing at the same time more than one thing.   To know more than one thing at the same time is plurality.   Yet the mind has that which may be called a unity.   What does not allow that to harm this, is called the mind's unity.

" When the mind sleeps, it dreams ; when it takes its ease, it indulges in reverie ; when it is used, it reflects.   Hence the mind is always active.   Yet it has that which may be called quiescence.   That which does not permit dreams (i.e., unrealities) and confusion to disturb one's knowledge is called the mind's quiescence.

" For one who has not found the *Tao*, but is seeking for it, emptiness, singleness and quiescence may be said to be the rules for his conduct.   Cause him who is seeking for the *Tao* to make his mind empty, and then he can receive it (*Tao*).   Cause him who is working for the *Tao* to make his mind unified, and when it is unified he can work for it in its entirety.   Cause him who is thinking of the *Tao* to make his mind quiescent, and when it is quiescent, he can perceive it (*Tao*).   He who knows the *Tao* and perceives it, who knows the *Tao* and follows it, is one who embodies the *Tao*.   Emptiness, unity and quiescence are called great pure illumination.   When there is nothing having form which he does not perceive ; nothing that he perceives which he cannot discuss ; nothing that he discusses in which he errs, . . . how can such a one have blindness ? " (pp. 265-266, 267-268).

These quotations show us that, according to the psychology of Hsün Tzŭ, there not only exist desires which seek for, and must

receive satisfaction, but also a mind capable of thought and knowledge. This mind sets up a 'standard' (*ch'üan* 權) or 'balance'
(*heng* 衡), with which to place a restraint upon the desires, so that
it may, in the words of the Later Mohists, 'choose the greater
benefit and the lesser harm.'[1] This aspect of Hsün Tzŭ's philosophy
is in complete accord with the utilitarianism of the Mohists, and marks
another difference between him and Mencius.[2] But 'how does the
mind know ? By emptiness, unity and quiescence.' Now emptiness
(*hsü*) and quiescence (*ching*) are terms often used by Lao Tzŭ and
Chuang Tzŭ, so that the *Lao-tzŭ* says, for example : "Attaining to
emptiness is the apogee ; with the preservation of quiescence there is
consolidation" (ch. 16). And the *Chuang-tzŭ* (ch. 13) states :

"The quiescence of the Sage is not quiescence merely because
quiescence is said to be something good. It is such quiescence that
nothing can disturb the mind. When water is quiescent, it mirrors
the beard and the eyebrows, and gives the accuracy of the water-
level, so that the great craftsman can take it as his model. And
if the quiescence of water is like a mirror, how much more so are the
faculties of the mind of the Sage ! These are then the mirror of the
universe and the speculum of all things.

"Emptiness, quiescence, stillness and non-activity : these are the
levels of the universe and the perfection of *Tao* and *Te*. Therefore
true rulers and Sages rest therein. Resting therein they reach emptiness, from which comes actuality, from which comes order. Also
from emptiness comes quiescence ; from quiescence comes movement ;
and from movement comes attainment. From quiescence comes non-
activity (*wu wei*) ; and with non-activity (of the ruler) comes the
possibility (of the officers) to assume responsiblity. With non-activity
there is happiness, and where there is happiness no cares can abide,
and life is long " (pp. 157-158).

Though Hsün Tzŭ also speaks of quiescence and emptiness, he
defines the latter as 'that which does not allow what is already stored
away to injure that which is about to be received' ; and the former
as 'that which does not permit dreams and confusion to disturb
one's knowledge.' Thought is the important function of the mind,
so that 'when it (the mind) is used, it reflects.' The dreams spoken
of here mean of the mind that 'when it takes its case, it indulges in
reverie,' the result of which is a flood of confused and distorted imaginings of all kinds. Quiescence is the power of preventing these distorted imaginings from obstructing the proper functioning of thought.
Hence although Hsün Tzŭ speaks of quiescence and emptiness, he
does not mean by these terms the state of mind of the Sage who 'uses

---

[1] *Cf.* p. 249.

[2] Hsün Tzŭ's philosophy contains elements of utilitarianism, and hence when he
criticizes Mo Tzŭ, he uses utilitarianism in his arguments (*cf.* his chs. 10 and 19). This
marks another difference between him and Mencius.

his mind like a mirror.'   In this respect, Hsün Tzŭ has borrowed from the Taoists, while modifying what he has taken.

Hsün Tzŭ also discusses in his third chapter the quality of sincerity (*ch'eng* 誠) :

" For developing the mind of the Superior Man, there is nothing better than sincerity (*ch'eng*).   Having attained to *ch'eng*, he will have no other concerns.   Preserve human-heartedness (*jen*) only, practice righteousness (*i*) only.   With a sincere mind preserve human-heartedness, and it will become tangibly manifested.   In such manifestation, there will be spirituality, and with such spirituality there will come transformation.   With a sincere mind practise righteousness, and there will come orderliness.   With orderliness there is clarity, and with clarity one can reform oneself.   Alternately to reform oneself and to transform others is to have a virtue like Heaven.   Heaven speaks not, yet man holds it as something lofty.   Earth speaks not, yet man holds it as something solid.   The four seasons speak not, yet the people know their times.   This is to attain sincerity through regularity.

" The Superior Man, having perfect virtue, is silent, yet his meaning is comprehensible ; he does not expand himself, yet is close to others ; he does not display anger, yet has an awesome appearance. It is through being cautious in one's own singleness of purpose that one can thus follow in harmony with Fate.

" He who would skilfully practice the *Tao*, without sincerity cannot have singleness of purpose (*tu* 獨).   Lacking singleness of purpose, he will not gain tangible manifestation.   Without such manifestation, although he has ideas and makes them known through his appearance and words, the people may not follow him, or even if they do, will be in doubt.

" Heaven and Earth are great, but without sincerity they could not have any effect upon all things.   The Sage is intelligent, but without sincerity he could not have any effect upon the people. Father and son are closely related, but without sincerity they would be wide apart.   The ruler above is honored, but without sincerity he would be contemned.

" Sincerity is what the Superior Man adheres to, and is the root of government.   Where it is, other things of the same kind will come. He who reaches for it will attain it.   He who neglects it will lose it.   He who grasps and obtains it, will become as if light (in weight). Being light, he will move with singleness of purpose.   Moving with unswerving singleness of purpose, he will be complete.   Being complete to the full extent of his ability, ever changing without returning to his original state, he will be transformed " (*chüan* 2, pp. 6-7).

The word *ch'eng*, here roughly translated as ' sincerity,' means truth and genuineness.   If we can pursue any affair with truth and genuineness, we shall be able to seek it with exclusive singleness of purpose. If we can 'with a sincere heart preserve human-hearted-ness,' and 'with a sincere heart carry righteousness into practice,' then as a matter of course we shall be able 'to preserve human-hearted-ness only, and practise righteousness only.' This is the meaning of the words : ' Having attained to sincerity, he (the Superior Man) will have no other concerns.' The result of this will be that such visible results as ' tangible manifestation,' ' spirituality, ' ' transforma-tion,' ' orderliness,' ' clarity' and ' reformation ' will automatically be produced. These are what result from the preservation of human-heartedness and the practice of righteousness.

If we cannot pursue an affair with truth and genuineness, however, we likewise cannot seek it with entire singleness of purpose. And without this, we can attain to no tangible result. Hence the words : ' Without sincerity he cannot have singleness of purpose. Lacking singleness of purpose, he will not gain tangible manifesta-tion.' He who pursues the qualities of human-heartedness and righteousness must be ' moving with unswerving singleness of purpose,' and then only will he be complete. This is because such moral qualities are not innate in man's nature, and the study of them changes his nature and erects artificialities, like a boat that cuts through the water. Hence without unswerving devotion and effort, we cannot change our nature in its attitude toward such qualities as human-heartedness and righteousness. But when through practice such a changing of the nature becomes habitual, these qualities become like a second human nature. Hence the words : ' Ever changing without returning to his original state, he will be transformed.' Such is the doctrine of a man who holds that human nature is evil ; the believer in the goodness of human nature, on the other hand, would be one who would teach men to return to their original natures. Herein lies another distinction between Mencius and Hsün Tzŭ

6—Origins of Society and the State

Hsün Tzŭ says : " Man desires to be good because his nature is evil " (p. 306). This statement has been criticized by a later scholar : " If man's nature is really bad, how can he have a mind which desires goodness ? " [1] But what has already been said would show that such a criticism is invalid. So-called goodness, says Hsün Tzŭ, is a combination of social ceremonies, institutions, culture, and moral qualities such as human-heartedness and righteousness, together with just laws. These things are not originally desired by man, but he is left no alternative but to desire them. Hsün Tzŭ says (ch. 10) :

" All things are present in the world, but have different forms. They do not of themselves have any special appropriateness, but they are put to use by man. This is art. Different classes of men

---

[1] See Huang Pai-chia (lived *ca.* A.D. 1681), *Sung Yüan Hsüeh-an, chüan* 1.

live together and seek for the same things, but with different methods. They have the same desires, but different degrees of knowledge. This is nature. Both the intelligent and the stupid are alike in having some capacities. But what they are capable of is not the same, and here the intelligent and stupid differ. If their circumstances remained the same while their degree of intelligence differed; if they could act selfishly without incurring trouble; if they could give free rein to their desires without end; then the people's hearts would be aroused to strife and there could be no satisfaction. . . . Then there would be no prince to rule the subjects, and no superior to rule the inferiors. The country would be injured and people would give free rein to their desires. People desire and hate the same things. Their desires are many, but things are few. Since they are few there will inevitably be strife.

" For the accomplishment of a hundred workmen goes to support a single individual. Yet an able man cannot be skilled in more than one line, and one man cannot hold two offices simultaneously. If people all live alone and do not serve one another, there will be poverty. If they live together, but are without social distinctions (*fen* 分), there will be strife. Poverty is a misfortune and strife is a calamity. To rescue people from misfortune and eliminate calamity, there is nothing like making social distinctions clear and forming a social organization. If the strong coerce the weak, the intelligent terrorize the stupid, and the people who are subjects rebel against their superiors; if the young insult the aged, and the government is not guided by virtue; if this be the case, then the aged and weak will suffer the misfortune of losing their subsistance, and the strong will suffer the calamity of division and strife.

" Work is what people dislike; gain and profit are what they like. If there is no distinction of occupation, then people will have difficulty in getting work done and the calamity of striving in order to obtain any desired result. If the union of male and female, the relationship of husband and wife, the match-making by the relatives of the bride and the groom-to-be, the sending of betrothal presents and the fetching of the bride, are not according to the rules of proper conduct (*li*); if this be the case, then people will have the misfortune of losing their mates and the calamity of having to struggle to gain any sex relation. Hence for this reason intelligent men have introduced social distinctions " (pp. 151-153).

This explains the origin of society and the state according to utilitarianism, and supplies all rites and institutions with a rational basis. It is similar to the doctrine of Agreement with the Superior found in the *Mo-tzŭ* (chs. 11-13). Men have intelligence, are capable of knowledge, and realize that without a social structure people cannot preserve themselves, and that such a social structure is dependent upon institutions embodying ethical principles. Such institutions are therefore established by the intelligent and accepted by the others. This term, intelligent, should be especially noted. It means that men make these institutions because of their knowledge, and not because by nature they are inclined to be moral. The *Hsün-tzǔ* (ch. 9) says again :

"Water and fire possess forces but are without life ; shrubs and trees have life but no knowledge ; birds and beasts have knowledge but no standards of justice (*i*). Man has force, life, knowledge, and also standards of justice. Hence he is the highest being on earth. His strength is not equal to that of the ox ; his running is not equal to that of the horse ; and yet the ox and horse are used by him. How is this ? I say that it is because men are able to form social organizations, whereas these others are unable.

"How is it that men are able to form social organizations ? Because of their social distinctions (*fen* 分). How can these distinctions be carried out ? Through standards of justice (*i*). Thus when there is justice in distinctions, there is harmony. When people are harmonious, they can unite ; when united, they have greater strength ; having greater strength, they become powerful ; being powerful, they can overcome other creatures. Hence they can have palaces and houses for habitation. Hence they can order their actions according to the four seasons, control all things, and take all things profitable in the whole world. They gain this for no other reason than that they have social distinctions and standards of justice.

"Hence if men are to live, they cannot get along without a social organization. If they form a social organization, but have no social distinctions, they will quarrel ; if they quarrel, there will be disorder ; if there is disorder, they will disintegrate ; disintegrating, they will become weak ; and being weak, they will be unable to dominate other creatures. Hence they will no longer have palaces and homes for habitation. All of which means that people cannot abandon the rules of proper conduct (*li*) or standards of justice (*i*) for an instant " (pp. 136-137).

From this passage it would seem that it is the possession of standards of justice that differentiates man from animals, and this fact serves as an argument to prove the necessity for social distinctions and standards of justice. But let us remember the words : "When people are harmonious, they can unite ; when united, they have greater strength ; having greater strength, they become powerful ; being powerful, they can overcome other creatures. Hence they can have palaces and houses for habitation." Here it is evident that Hsün Tzǔ still uses utilitarianism as a basis for his arguments. He says again (ch. 5) ;

"Wherein is it that man is truly man ? Because he makes social distinctions. When he is hungry he desires to eat ; when he is cold he desires to be warm ; when he is tired he desires to rest ; he likes what is beneficial and dislikes what is injurious. Man has these ways of acting from birth ; he does not depend upon something to get them. In these things Yü (the sage founder of the Hsia dynasty) and Chieh (its last evil ruler) were alike. However, man is not truly man simply because he alone has two feet and lacks hair, but rather in that he makes social distinctions. Now the yellow-haired ape also has two feet and is hairless (on the face) ; yet (in contradistinction from it), the Superior Man sips his soup and carves his slices of meat. Hence man is not truly man in so far as he, especially, has two feet and no hair, but in the fact that he makes social distinctions. Birds and beasts have fathers and offspring, but not the affection between father and son ; they are male and female, but do not have the proper separations between males and females.

" Hence there is no way of human living which does not have its distinctions (*pien* 辨) ; no distinctions are greater than those of social distinctions (*fen*) ; no social distinctions are greater than the rules of proper conduct (*li*) ; there are no rules of proper conduct greater than the Sage-kings " (pp. 71-72).

This passage tries to prove the necessity for the *li* by saying that it is these that make man truly man. In this respect Hsün Tzŭ agrees with Mencius, but he differs once more when he says of man : " He likes what is beneficial and dislikes what is injurious : man has these ways of acting from birth."

7—RITES AND MUSIC

The *Hsün-tzŭ* contains a chapter (ch. 19), on the origin of rites and rules of proper conduct (*li*) :

"From what have the rules of proper conduct (*li*) originated? The answer is that man at birth has desires. When these desires are not satisfied, he cannot remain without seeking their satisfaction. When this seeking for satisfaction is without measure or limit, there can only be contention. When there is contention there will be disorder ; when there is disorder, everything will be destroyed. The early kings hated this disorder, and so they established the rules of proper conduct (*li*) and standards of justice (*i*) so as to set limits to this confusion, to satisfy men's desires, and give opportunity for this satisfaction, in order that desires should not be stretched to the breaking point by things, nor things be used up by desires ; that both these two should mutually support one another and so continue to exist. This is how the *li* originated " (p. 213).

Here we find the *li* being used to determine proper limits, and thus restrain the desires. I have already pointed out that Confucius, in his teachings, emphasized the importance of individual freedom on the one hand, while on the other hand he attached importance to the restraining mould that is imposed from without by the *li* or *mores* upon human conduct.[1] With Mencius, comparatively greater emphasis was placed on individual freedom, for advocating as he did the goodness of human nature, it was natural that he should stress the individual's right to his own moral judgment.[2] But Hsün Tzŭ, on the other hand, with his emphasis on external standards and authority, laid stress on *li*. Thus he says (ch. 1):

" In study, what should one begin with ? What end with ? The art begins by reciting the classics, and ends in learning the *li* " (p. 36). Again (ch. 2):

" Man's emotions, purposes and ideas, when proceeding according to the *li*, will be orderly. If they do not proceed according to the *li*, they become wrong and confused, careless and negligent. Food and drink, clothing, dwelling places and movements, if in accordance with the *li*, will be proper and harmonious. If not in accordance with the *li*, they will meet with ruin and calamity. A person's appearance, his bearing, his advancing and retiring when he hastens or walks slowly, if according to the *li*, are refined. If not according to the *li*, he will be haughty, intractable, prejudiced and rude. Hence man without the *li* cannot exist ; affairs without the *li* cannot be completed ; government without the *li* cannot be peaceful " (pp. 44-45).

Hsün Tzŭ, maintaining as he did that ' the nature of man is evil ; his goodness is only acquired training,' could hardly do otherwise than stress *li* as a means of rectifying this nature.

The value of *li*, aside from serving to determine proper limits and thus restraining human desires, lies also in their use to beautify and refine the expression of human emotions. This is a point which Hsün Tzŭ examines deeply. In his emphasis on the useful, Hsün Tzŭ was at one with Mo Tzŭ, but he differed greatly in his attitude toward human emotions. Mo Tzŭ, holding a doctrine of extreme utilitarianism, believed that the various human emotions are valueless and of no significance, and so should be repressed. The result was, as Hsün Tzŭ says, that Mo Tzŭ was " blinded by utility and did not know the value of culture " (pp. 263-264). Although Hsün Tzŭ also advocated utilitarianism, he was not so extreme as Mo Tzŭ, and hence he left a place in life for the emotions and human amenities, as well as for the purely useful. This becomes apparent when we study what Hsün Tzŭ has to say about mourning and sacrificial rites. These rites, all of which originated in human superstition, received from Hsün Tzŭ, out of his naturalistic philosophy, a new and rational explanation which constitutes one of his great contributions. He also shows great understanding in what he says about music. The chapters in the *Li Chi* (Book of Rites) which deal with mourning and sacrificial rites, and with music, are in large part identical

---

[1] *Cf.* ch. 4, sect. 5, p. 68.
[2] *Cf.* ch. 6, sect. 4, pp. 126-127.

with Hsün Tzŭ's writings, and if not actually taken from the *Hsün-tzŭ*, were probably written by his followers. Hence for the sake of convenience, the two chapters in the *Hsün-tzŭ* that deal with rites and music (chs. 19-20) will not be touched on here, but will be discussed together with the *Li Chi* in Chapter XIV.

8—The King and the Feudal Leader

" There is no way of human living which does not have its distinctions ; no distinctions are greater than those of social distinctions ; no social distinctions are greater than the *li* ; there are no *li* greater than the Sage-kings " (p. 72).   Hsün Tzŭ says again (ch. 21) :

" The Sage fulfils the duties of the natural relationships ; the King fulfils the ideals of government.   He who fulfils both is worthy to be the culmination of the world " (p. 276).

The King must also be a Sage, Hsün Tzŭ says, before there can be government or society.   Thus (ch. 18) :

" Therefore to be Emperor, be the right man.   The empire is the weightiest thing there is.   Only the strongest man is able to bear its weight.   It is the largest of all.   Only the most discriminating is able to make its proper distinctions.   It is the most populous. Only the most wise is able to harmonize it.   Unless he is a Sage, he will not be able to fulfil these three requirements.   Hence unless he is a Sage, he will not be able to rule as true King " (pp. 191-192).

When a Sage is King, his government will be that of a true King. In discussing the distinction between the true King, and those Leaders (*Pa* 霸) of the feudal lords who, when the royal Chou power decayed during the Ch'un Ch'iu period, usurped many of the privileges of the legitimate ruler, Hsün Tzŭ speaks as follows (ch. 7) :

" The disciples of Confucius, and even immature menials, talked rarely about the five *Pa*.[1]   Why was this the case ?   Because they did not have a just doctrine of government ; they were not sublime ; they were not extremely refined ; and they did not satisfy people's minds.   Their course of action was well calculated ; they used judgment in seeing who worked and who was lazy ; they carefully accumulated their resources ; they prepared instruments of war ; they were able to overturn their enemies.   They conquered through a deceitful heart.   They glossed over their contentiousness by an appearance of yielding the precedence to others ; they relied on an appearance of benevolence (*jen*) to enable them to tread the path of profit seeking.   They are heroes of the small-minded man.   But how can they really be great enough to be placed in the same class with the great rulers ?

" But the true Kings were different.   They were most worthy and could therefore save the degenerate ; they were most powerful,

---

[1] For their names, see note on p. 112.—Tr.

and could therefore bear with the weak ; in war they could certainly have imperilled the weak, but they rarely fought them. They were refined and accomplished and thus displayed themselves to the whole world. Then oppressive states became peaceful and changed of themselves. They only punished the dangerous and violent. Hence punishment was used very rarely by the Sage-kings " (pp. 83-84).

Government will be that of a true King only when a Sage rules. When he does not, it is merely that of a *Pa*, and perhaps even a disordered government. Mencius makes the same distinction between King and *Pa*, but in so doing he emphasizes the motives of the ruler. Thus he says that the good government of the true King arises from the fact that ' he has a heart which cannot endure to see suffering.' Hsün Tzŭ, on the other hand, maintains that man's nature is evil, and so does not use this argument to distinguish King from *Pa*.

In describing the life of the people under kingly government, the *Hsün-tzŭ* (ch. 9) says :

" The King grades taxation and adjusts the amount of corvée to be given ; he regulates everything in order to nourish all his people. He levies a tithe on the land. At the frontier passes and market-places he examines travellers but does not levy duties. He prohibits or permits wood-cutting and fishing, according to the season ; but he does not tax them. He appraises the land and assesses its tax. He regulates tribute according to the distance of the place. There should be a circulation of valuables and grain without restriction or hindrance, enabling foodstuffs to be freely transported, and thus all within the four seas will be like one family. Then those who are near will not hide their ability, and those who are distant will not grumble at their toil. There will be no unenlightened or secluded country which will fail to fly to serve him and be satisfied and rejoice in him. This is what is called being a leader and teacher of men. These are the ways of a righteous King " (pp. 132-133).

Again in the same chapter :

" A ruler is one who is good at organizing society. If this doctrine of forming a social organization is carried out as it should be, all things will fulfil their appropriate function ; the six kinds of domestic animals will all thrive ; all living things will fulfil their destiny. For if their nourishment and growth is at the proper season, the six kinds of domestic animals will develop and increase ; if their harvesting and preservation are at the proper season, shrubs and trees will flourish. If government decrees are timely, the people will be united, the worthy and good will serve the ruler ; it will be the rule of a Sage-king.

" When shrubs and trees are in bloom and leaf, the ax must not enter the forest, and people must not cut short the life of the trees or shrubs when young, nor stop their growth. When sea tortoises, water lizards, fish, turtles, eels and sturgeons are full of roe or have spawned, nets and poison must not enter the marshes and lakes, and people must not cut short the life of these water creatures nor stop their growth. The spring ploughing, the summer weeding, the fall harvesting, and the winter storing away of the grain : these four things must not be out of season. Then the five grains will not fail, and the people will have an abundance of food. Ponds, lakes, streams and marshes should be strictly closed at the proper time, and then fish and turtles will be abundant, and the people will have a surplus for use. The cutting down and growth of timber should not be at the wrong season, and then the mountains and forests will not be bare, and the people will have a surplus of timber " (pp. 137-139).

In these ideas Hsün Tzŭ is at one with Mencius, save that he does not touch upon the ' well-field ' (*ching t'ien* 井 田) system.

The *Hsün-tzŭ* (ch. 18) speaks as follows about the punitive expeditions which were led by T'ang and King Wu (founders of the Shang and Chou dynasties), against the rulers of the preceding dynasties :

" The sophists common to-day say : ' Chieh and Chou were the legal rulers of the empire, and T'ang and Wu rebelled and took it from them by force.' This is not so. . . . T'ang and Wu did not *seize* the empire. They cultivated their own ways of truth ; they carried out their principles of righteousness ; they exalted the common benefit of the empire ; they did away with the common sources of injury to the empire ; and so the empire *turned* to them. Chieh and Chou did not *resign* the empire. They abandoned the virtue of Yü and T'ang ; they confused the distinctions of the rules of proper conduct (*li*) and standards of justice (*i*) ; their bestial actions heaped up misfortune for them and completed their evil destiny ; and so the empire *left* them. He to whom the empire turns is called King ; he whom the empire abandons is called doomed. Hence the fact that Chieh and Chou did not rightfully possess the empire, and that T'ang and Wu were not guilty of murdering a ruler, is clear from this argument " (pp. 189-191).

Hsün Tzŭ says in the same chapter, concerning the story of the abdication of the legendary Emperors, Yao and Shun :

" The sophists common to-day say : ' Yao and Shun abdicated and yielded the throne.' This is not so. . . . When the Sage-kings had died, and there was no Sage in the country, then certainly there was no one with sufficient virtue in favor of whom the empire could be abdicated. If there is a Sage in the country, and he is (the Emperor's own) son, then the empire does not leave that family ; the court does not change, the states do not alter their fealty ; the empire is submissive and turns to him without any difference. What change is there if a Yao succeeds a Yao ?

" If there is no Sage among his descendants, but there is one among the Three Chief Ministers, then it is best that the empire should go to them ; they will revive and restore it. Then the empire is sub-missive ; it turns to them without any difference. If a Yao succeeds a Yao, what change is there ? Only a change of dynasty, an alteration in the government, is difficult. Hence when the Emperor lives, that whole country exults ; it is most obedient and well-ordered ; according to people's virtue is rank determined. When he dies, the person who is able to carry the responsibility of the empire will naturally succeed him. In this, the distinctions of the rules of proper conduct (*li*) and of standards of justice (*i*) are made complete, and what need is there of abdication ? " (pp. 198-200).

In these passages Hsün Tzŭ points out : (1) that T'ang and Wu were Kings because the empire of itself turned to them, and (2) that there was no need for Yao and Shun to abdicate. On the death of a Sage-king, the rule should be continued by his son, if the son is a Sage. If not, and there is a Sage among the high nobles (such as the Three Chief Ministers), the rule should be continued by that Sage. In short, on the death of a Sage-king, the rule must be carried on by whoever is sufficiently qualified, regardless of whether he belongs to the ruling family or not. This ideal is identical with that of Mencius, only Mencius adds to it the concept of a Decree (*ming* 命) of Heaven, whereas Hsün Tzŭ remains purely rational.

Because of his belief that man's nature is evil, and his consequent failure to emphasize individual freedom, Hsün Tzŭ differs from Mencius in his political philosophy, inasmuch as he maintains that the so-called Sage-kings must have absolute power. Thus in the same chapter :

" The Emperor's authority and position are most honorable, and he has no peer in the empire. . . . His virtue is pure and com-plete ; his wisdom and kindness are most illustrious. When he faces the south (i.e., seated on his throne) and rules the empire, all living people are moved and obey, and yield to his influence. The empire then has no recluses nor any neglected good men. What is in accord with his acts is right ; what differs from them is wrong. . . . " (p. 198).

This is similar to Mo Tzŭ's doctrine of Agreement with the Superior, for though the latter did not hold man's nature to be positive-ly evil, neither did he believe, as did Mencius, that the beginnings of goodness are innate in man.

9—THE RECTIFICATION OF NAMES

Confucius, discussing the Rectification of Names (*cheng ming* 正名), said : " Let the ruler be ruler, the subject subject ; let the father be father, and the son son." Mencius said : " To be without the relationships of ruler and of father is to be like the beasts " ; in thus placing outside the pale of human kind those who disregard the relationships of ruler and of father, he was adopting this same Confucian doctrine of the Rectification of Names. By Confucius and Mencius, however, the doctrine was developed along purely ethical lines, and therefore had only ethical, but no logical, interest. A similar condition has existed in western philosophy, where Socrates, in his search for strict meanings through inductive method, had only an ethical interest ; in Plato, with his doctrine of ideas, the interest continued to be largely in ethics rather than in logic ; and it was not until Aristotle that pure logic began. Hsün Tzŭ's age was likewise one in which the Dialecticians were most flourishing, and hence his doctrine of the Rectification of Names, unlike that of Confucius and Mencius, contains great logical interest.

It has already been said that the ' Mohist Canons,' together with Hsün Tzŭ's chapter on ' The Rectification of Names ' (ch. 22), were both attacks upon the Dialecticians, and stood for common sense.' In its statements about knowledge and logic, this chapter of Hsün Tzŭ's is in fundamental agreement with the ' Mohist Canons,' and so will be discussed here in comparison with them.

I have already described how, according to the, psychological system of Hsün Tzŭ, there exists in man both a mind capable of thought and knowledge, and emotional desires which seek satisfaction. Concerning the faculty of knowing (*chih* 知), Hsün Tzŭ's chapter, ' The Rectification of Names,' says :

" That in man by which he knows is (called the faculty of) knowing. That in (the faculty of) knowing which corresponds to (external things) is called knowledge (*chih* 智). . . . Form and color are distinctions made by the eye. ' Clear ' and ' confused ' sounds, harmony, musical time and other sounds, are distinctions made by the ear. Sweet and bitter, salty and fresh, peppery and sour and other flavors, are distinctions made by the mouth. Perfumes and smells, fragrance and putrescence, the smell of fresh meat and fetid smells, the smell of the mole-cricket and the smell of decayed wood, and other smells, are distinctions made by the nose. Pain and itching, cold and heat, smoothness and roughness, lightness and heaviness, are distinctions made by the body. Liking and exertion, joy and anger, sorrow and pleasure, love, hatred and desire, are distinctions made by the mind.

" The mind also gives meaning to impressions. It gives meaning to impressions, and only then, by means of the ear, can sound be known ; by means of the eye, forms can be known. But the giving of meaning to impressions must depend on the fact that the natural senses make a classification of the particular sensations, and then only can knowledge be had. When the five senses note something but cannot classify it, and the mind tries to identify it but fails to give it meaning, then one can only say that there is no knowledge " (pp. 282, 284-285).

' *Cf.* ch. 11, sect. 1, p. 246.

The 'Mohist Canons' say: "Knowing is a faculty" (p. 414). All men have this faculty, which is described by Hsün Tzǔ as 'that in man by which he knows.'

The *Canons* say again: "Knowledge is a meeting" (p. 414). That is, there is knowledge when the faculty for knowing comes in contact with the things to be known. Hsün Tzǔ expresses the same idea when he says: "That of (the faculty of) knowing which corresponds to (external things) is called knowledge." The contact of the faculty of knowing with the thing to be known gives us knowledge, but this is only sensual knowledge. When we have merely a sensual impression of an object, we cannot, strictly speaking, be said to know it. Hence in addition to the definitions given above, the 'Mohist Canons' say that " mind-knowledge is an understanding " (p. 414). This type of knowledge is equivalent to that which Hsün Tzǔ speaks of, which comes about when ' the mind also gives meaning to impressions.'

For when the faculty for knowing comes in contact with the object to be known, one can gain a sense impression of the object's appearance; or, as the 'Mohist Canons' say: "Knowledge is that in which the knowing (faculty) meets the object and is able to apprehend its form and shape" (p. 442). The objects to be known are numerous and varied. Form, color, etc., constitute the appearances of these objects as perceived by what Hsün Tzǔ calls the ' natural senses ' (*t'ien kuan* 天官), which he defines (ch. 17) as: "The ear, the eye, the nose, the mouth and the body each receive stimuli and cannot interchange their functions. These are what are meant by the natural senses " (pp. 175-176).

When our faculty for knowing comes in contact with an external object, it not only receives a sensual impression of that object's appearance, however, but it can also know what sort of object it is. Thus when we see a tree, we not only perceive its appearance, but we can know that it is a tree. We can do this because our faculty for knowing includes the mind (taking the mind as being the organ of thought, distinct from the senses). This mind is described by the *Hsün-tzǔ* (ch. 17): " The mind is established in the central void to control the five senses. This is what is meant by the ' natural ruler ' (*t'ien chün* 天 君) " (p. 176).

' The mind gives meaning to impressions.' That is, as has just been said, it is our eyes that meet a tree and perceive it, but it is our mind that thereupon knows that the object is a tree. Since the mind has this power of giving meaning to impressions, ' then only, by means of the ear, can sound be known; by means of the eye, forms can be known.' Without such a faculty these senses would simply be able to receive sensory impressions of the objects with which they come in contact, but would be unable to let us know what these things are. When we know that a certain tree is a tree, it is because our mind places this particular object in the class of trees of which it already has knowledge. Hence, as Hsün Tzŭ says : " The giving of meaning to impressions must depend on the fact that the natural senses make a classification of the particular sensations, and then only can knowledge be had." If the class of trees has never come within our experience, we shall not know that this specific object is a tree. Or, as Hsün Tzŭ says : " When the five senses note something but cannot classify it, and the mind tries to identify it but fails to give it meaning, then one can only say that there is no knowledge."

As to the origin and use of names, Hsün Tzŭ's chapter, ' The Rectification of Names,' says :

" Names (*ming* 名) were made in order to denote actualities (*shih* 實), on the one hand so as to make evident the noble and base, and on the other to distinguish similarities and differences. When the distinction between the noble and base is evident, and similarities and differences are distinguished, under these circumstances a man's mind will not suffer from the misfortune of being misunderstood, and affairs will not suffer from the calamity of being hindered or wasted. This is the reason for having names.

" Because of what, then, are similarities and differences found ? Because of the natural senses. All (creatures) that are of the same class and have the same emotions, have the same natural senses with which to perceive things. When things are compared and some are found to be somewhat alike, then names for them are agreed upon, and so they can be recognized. Form and color are distinctions made by the eye. ' Clear ' and ' confused ' sounds, harmony, musical time and other sounds, are distinctions made by the ear. . . . These are the reasons why there are similarities and differences.

" Then, accordingly, names are given to things. When things are alike, they are named alike ; when different, they are named differently. When a simple term [1] would be sufficient to convey the meaning, a simple term is used ; when a simple term is insufficient, then a compound term [2] is used. When simple and compound concept do not conflict, then the general term [3] may be used ; although it is a general term, there is no harm in using it. The one who knows that different actualities have different names, and who therefore never refers to different actualities otherwise than by different names, will not experience any confusion. Likewise he who refers to the same actuality should never use any other but the same name.

" For although all things are innumerable, there are times when we wish to speak of them all in general, so we call them ' things.' ' Things ' is the most general term. We press on and generalize ; we generalize and generalize still more, until there is nothing more general. Then only we stop. There are times when we wish to speak of one aspect,

---

[1] A term composed of one character only, e.g., ' tree.'—Tr.
[2] A term composed of two or more characters, e.g., ' ox-tree.'—Tr.
[3] The class or common term, e.g., ' tree ' as applied to trees in general.—Tr.

so we say ' birds and beasts.' ' Birds and beasts' is the great classifying term. We press on and classify. We classify and classify still more, until there is no more classification to be made, and then we stop.

"There are no names necessarily appropriate of themselves. Things were named by agreement. When, the agreement having been made, it has become customary, this is called an appropriate designation. That which is different from what has been agreed upon is called an inappropriate designation. Names have no corresponding actualities necessarily appropriate of themselves. There was an agreement and things were named; when the agreement had been made and had become customary, these were called names appropriate to actualities. But there are names that are especially felicitous. When a name is simple, direct, easily understood and not contradictory, this is called a felicitous name " (pp. 284, 285-286).

' All (creatures) that are of the same class and have the same emotions, have the same natural senses with which to perceive things.' We are all members of the human race, have the same sensory faculties, and hence the same knowledge in regard to external objects. Therefore ' names were made in order to denote actualities,' so as thus to enable us to convey ideas to one another. But actualities are particulars, and names cannot completely denote the characteristics of a particular object. Hence they can only express the ' somewhat alike.' Since names serve to denote actualities, what they denote must be absolutely defined. Things which are identical are denoted by identical names ; those which differ, by different ones. When one ' knows that different actualities have different names, and therefore never refers to different actualities otherwise than by different names ' ; or when, ' referring to the same actuality, never uses any other but the same name,' then names can ' make distinctions between similarities and differences.' This distinction between general and classifying names is readily shown in the ' tree of Porphyry ' :

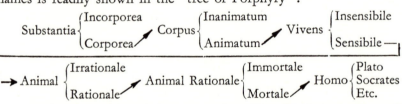

In this tree, ' substantia ' corresponds to Hsün Tzŭ's ' most general term,' extending ' until there is nothing more general,' while ' homo ' corresponds to his ' classifying term,' extending ' until there is no more classification to be made.' Such intermediate terms as ' corpus,' ' vivens,' ' animal,' etc., are, with respect to the first, classifying terms ; with respect to the second, general terms.

Names which designate things, are intended to differentiate between similarity and difference. As applied to the social relationships between man, their purpose is to differentiate between the noble and the base. Such differentiations are indicated by the terms : ruler, subject, father, son, etc. When Confucius spoke about the Rectification of Names, he had in mind only names of this type, intending thus to make the ruler accord to the name of ruler, and the subject to the name of subject. Hsün Tzŭ, as a Confucian, still keeps something of this ethical interest in his Rectification of Names, as well as a purely logical interest, so that he says : " On the one hand they are to make evident the noble and base, and on the other to distinguish similarities and differences."

By saying, " There are no names necessarily appropriate of themselves," Hsün Tzŭ means that at the time when names were first invented, a certain name was used to indicate a certain thing according to the free will of those who made these designations. For example, men agreed with one another that they would call a dog by the word ' dog,' yet in the beginning they might just as conceivably have agreed upon the word ' horse ' to designate it. When these designations had once been agreed upon, however, so that people used a certain name to indicate only that certain thing, this became customary. Thereupon names and the things they designated had their necessary appropriateness, one to the other, and could no longer be changed at pleasure. Even when the names were first being made, however, at the time when ' there were no names necessarily appropriate of themselves,' there were nevertheless some that were ' especially felicitous.' Names which could be readily pronounced, for example, would be more felicitous than difficult sounding ones.

Names must have definite meanings, only after which will ' a man's mind not suffer from the misfortune of being misunderstood, and affairs will not suffer from the calamity of being hindered or wasted.' In order that they might be made standard, all names were decided upon by the government, and once having been decided upon, they could not be changed by the people at their pleasure. Hsün Tzŭ says in the same chapter :

" Therefore when the kings had regulated names, when they had fixed terms and so distinguished actualities, and when their principles were carried out and their will everywhere known, they were careful to lead the people toward unity. Therefore making unauthorized distinctions between words, and making (new) words ; thus confusing the correct nomenclature, causing the people to be in doubt, and bringing about much litigation, was called great wickedness. It was a crime like that of using false credentials or false measures. Therefore their people did not dare to depend on making strange terms in order to confuse the correct nomenclature. Hence their people were guileless. Being guileless, they could be easily ordered. Being easily ordered, they achieved results.

" Since the people did not dare to depend on making strange terms in order to confuse the correct nomenclature, they were united in virtue and law-abidance, and respectful in obeying orders. In this way their example (i.e., that of the rulers) spread. Their example spread and results were achieved : such was the apogee of good government. This was the benefit of being careful in preserving the terms which had been agreed upon. . . . Should a true King arise, he must certainly follow the ancient terms and make the new ones " (pp. 282-283).

As human knowledge increases, names must also increase in number. And once names exist, men can use them in their speech to convey the ideas in their minds. The same chapter continues :

" The object of a name is to know the actuality when one hears the name. The combining of names consists in stringing them together to make literature. When both the usefulness and the combination of names are secured, that is called knowing these names. Names are that whereby we define various actualities. Propositions (*tz'ŭ* 辭) are the combination of names of different actualities wherewith to discuss one idea. Dialectic and explanation take one actuality and its name under discussion, so as to understand their different aspects. Designation and naming are the object of dialectic. Dialectic and explanation are that whereby the mind delineates the Way (*Tao*). The mind is the master artisan of the Way. The Way comprises the regular and necessary principles of order and good government.

" When a person's mind accords with the Way ; when his dialectic accords with his mind ; when his propositions accord with his dialectic ; when he rectifies names and so designates actualities ; when names are founded on actualities and are understood ; when he discriminates differences without making mistakes ; when he classifies things without error ; then he can listen to discussions and tell if they are in accord with a cultivated style ; he can argue and exhaust all possible reasoning ; by means of the right Way he can distinguish wickedness, as with the plumb-line one may determine the crooked and the straight. For this reason unorthodox doctrines cannot confuse him ; all the schools of philosophy cannot escape him. . . . This is the dialectic of the Sage " (pp. 290-291).

' Propositions are that which combine the names of several actualities in order to express one idea.' To say, for example, ' Man is an animal,' is to state a proposition. The *Minor Illustrations* in the *Mo-tzŭ* refers to this kind of proposition when it speaks of ' propositions to express ideas ' (p. 527). Dialectic consists in the application of such propositions to a certain thing so as to discuss it in detail. An example of this occurs in the *Hsün-tzŭ* (ch. 19), when it discusses the uses of *li* in detail, thus ' taking one actuality and its name under discussion, so as to understand their different aspects.' When Hsün Tzŭ speaks of the Sage who ' classifies things without being wrong,' and ' can argue and exhaust all possible reasoning,' he is merely touching upon topics which are discussed in much greater detail in the *Minor Illustrations* in the *Mo-tzŭ*.

None of the philosophic schools of Hsün Tzŭ's time escape his criticism, and in this same chapter, ' The Rectification of Names,' he divides into three groups what he considers to be fallacious doctrines, taking the Rectification of Names as his basis. Of the first of these, he says :

" ' To receive insult is no disgrace ' ; ' the Sage does not love himself ' ; ' to kill robbers is not to kill men ' : these are fallacies in the usage of names to confuse names. Investigate the reason for having names, observe of what sort the names are, and then you will be able to stop this confusion." (pp. 287-288).

' To receive insult is no disgrace,' is a doctrine of Sung K'eng.[1] ' The Sage does not love himself,' and ' to kill robbers is not to kill men,' are both doctrines of the Mohists, and the *Major Illustrations* in the *Mo-tzŭ* states : " The loving of men does not exclude the self. Oneself is included among those loved. If oneself is among those who are loved, one's love will include oneself. Thus loving oneself in a proper way is to love men " (p. 507). Loving oneself, that is, is the same as loving others, and hence the Sage does not say anything specifically about loving himself.

The connotation of the phrase, ' to receive insult,' however, already implies the idea of disgrace ; the connotation of the word ' robber,' implies the idea of man ; and both the denotation and connotation of the word ' self,' differ from that of the word ' men.' Hence such doctrines are ' fallacies in the usage of names to confuse names.' We can determine whether or not they are false by seeing how these names come to be what they are : whether the terms, ' receive insult ' and ' robber,' do not in fact imply the ideas of ' disgrace ' and ' men ' respectively ; and whether the meanings of ' self ' and ' men,' are not in fact distinct.

Of the second group of fallacies, Hsün Tzŭ says :

" ' Mountains and abysses are on the same level ' ; ' the desires seek to be few ' ; ' domestic animals are not included in what is considered good eating, and the great bell does not contribute to pleasure ' : these are fallacies in the usage of actualities in order to confuse the names. Investigate the means through which similarities and differences are found, and see what fits the actuality, and then you will be able to stop this confusion " (p. 288).

' Mountains and abysses are on the same level, ' is one of Hui Shih's paradoxes.[2]   ' The desires seek to be few ' is a doctrine of Sung K'eng.[3]   The last two statements appear to be those of the Mohists,

---

[1] *Cf.* p. 151.
[2] *Cf.* p. 198.
[3] *Cf.* p. 150.

who by saying that domestic animals are not of themselves good eating, and that the big bell does not contribute to pleasure, would maintain their opposition to wasteful luxury and music. In individual cases there are in fact instances when a mountain may be low or an abyss high. Thus an abyss located on a high mountain may be level with a mountain that rests on low land. Likewise there do exist men whose desires sometimes seek to be few, and others who sometimes do not find domestic animals good eating, or who do not find that the great bell contributes to pleasure. But to say that these statements are always true, Hsün Tzŭ contends, is to apply the special characteristics of individual actualities to fit the general characteristics of all things within the class designated by their name. Such are ' fallacies in the usage of actualities so as to confuse the names.' By means of our senses, we must observe directly whether these statements are in fact always true, and so determine their truth or falsity.

Hsün Tzŭ says of the third group :

" ' Even if you do not go and see, the center pillar exists ' ; ' an ox and a horse are not a horse ' : these are fallacies in the usage of names so as to confuse their actualities. Investigate the agreements about names ; take what these agreements accept, to reject what they refuse to countenance ; then you will be able to stop this confusion " (pp. 288-289).

These statements are both found in the ' Mohist Canons.' The meaning of the first is not clear, but the second is explained by saying that the phrase, ' an ox and a horse,' implies both ox and horse, and so cannot be said to mean either solely an ox or solely a horse. This has already been explained on pages 268-269. Hsün Tzŭ, on the contrary, maintains about an ox and a horse, that a horse does in fact exist, so that to say that an ox and a horse are not a horse is using names so as to confuse their actualities. We must examine the original agreements made upon names so as to see whether or not a horse is in fact a horse, and then we can determine the truth or falsity of this statement.

In the chapter on the Later Mohists, I said that this statement that an ox and a horse are not a horse reveals the basic difference of standpoints of Kung-sun Lung and the ' Mohist Canons.' In the latter it is pointed out that, although in one way an ox and a horse are not an ox, yet in another way it is not permissible to say they are not an ox. This is already closer to common sense than is Kung-sun Lung's doctrine that a white horse is not a horse, but Hsün Tzŭ follows common sense even more closely in his criticism.

Hsün Tzŭ, however, seems to have had a method still more direct than this for dealing with doctrines he regarded as fallacious. Thus he continues in his chapter on ' The Rectification of Names ' :

" All heretical doctrines and heinous teachings which are impudently fabricated and which depart from the Way (*Tao*) can be classed among these three fallacies. Hence the wise ruler, knowing to which class they belong, does not dispute about them. Thus the people can be easily united in the Way (*Tao*), although they cannot be given all the reasons for things. Hence the wise ruler deals with the people by authority, and guides them on the Way ; he orders things by his decrees, explains things by his proclamations, and restrains them by punishments. Thus his people are turned into the Way as by magic. Why should he use dialectic ?

" Now the Sage-kings are no more, the world is in disorder, wicked doctrines have arisen, the wise man has no power to compel the people to do right, and no punishments to prevent them from following wrong, and so there is dialectic. When an actuality is not understood, its name is brought forward ; when its name is not understood, it is illustrated ; when the illustration is not understood, then it is explained ; when the explanation is not understood, then dialectic comes into use. Hence the name, illustration, explanation and dialectic are the great refinements of human activity and the beginnings in the achievements of a King " (pp. 289-290).

' The people can be easily united in the Way, although they cannot be given all the reasons for things.' Confucius expresses the same idea when he says : " The people may be made to follow a course, but not to understand the reason why " (*Lun Yü*, VIII, 9). Li Ssŭ, the great Prime Minister of Ch'in Shih-huang-ti, who finally unified feudalistic China in 221 B.C., was Hsün Tzŭ's pupil, and in these words of Hsün Tzŭ lies the philosophical basis for that standardization of thought, attempted by Li Ssŭ and Ch'in Shih-huang, which culminated in the Burning of the Books in 213 B.C.

CHAPTER XIII

HAN FEI TZŬ AND THE OTHER LEGALISTS

1—The Legalist Doctrines and the Social, Political and Economic Tendencies of their Time

The Confucians, Mohists and Taoists all held political theories which, though widely differing, agreed in discussing government primarily from the point of view of the people. There was another group of thinkers, however, who discussed government wholly from the viewpoint of the ruler or the state. These were known among their contemporaries as scholars of the ' laws ' (*fa* 法) and ' methods ' (*shu* 術),[1] and by the people of the Han dynasty as the Legalist school (*fa chia* 法家). The Legalist doctrines were most flourishing in the state of Ch'i, and in the three states of Han, Wei and Chao (into which the state of Chin had been divided after 403 B.C.). This is quite possibly to be attributed to the reforms which seem to have been made in Ch'i and Chin under Dukes Huan of Ch'i (685-643) and Wen of Chin (635-628), both of whom held the position of feudal Leader or *Pa* over the other feudal lords of their time. Owing to these reforms, it was principally in their two states that a group of men succeeded in forming a new party of political theorists, based upon the practical tendencies of their time.

The collapse of the feudal system during the Ch'un Ch'iu and Warring States periods resulted, on the one hand, in the emancipation of the common people from their immediate overlords, and on the other, in the concentration of power in the hands of the state rulers. The great political tendency of the time was a movement from feudal rule toward a government by rulers possessing absolute power; from government by customary morality (*li*), and by individuals, to government by law. Under the early feudal system, a state's territory was severely limited in extent, while internally each state was again divided into many ' houses.' Within each of these states the nobles governed their people by means of the *mores* or *li* which had been handed down from generation to generation, while the agricultural serfs, on their part, simply followed the commands of their overlords. The fact that the governments of that time were conducted largely on a personal basis, seems to have given the nobles the habit of assuming

---

[1] *Cf.* the *Han-fei-tzŭ*, ch. 11.

an appearance of what was called ' awe-inspiring majesty,' with which
to impress their subjects.   For example, a speech recorded in the *Tso
Chuan* under the year 542 B.C. tells us that :

" Having an awe-inspiring majesty is what we call dignity.
Presenting a pattern which induces imitation is what we call manner.
When the ruler has the dignified manner of a ruler, his ministers fear
and love him, imitate and resemble him, so that he can hold possession
of his state, and his fame continues through long ages.   When a
minister has the dignified manner of a minister, his inferiors fear and
love him, so that he can preserve his official position, protect his
clan, and rightly order his family.   So it is with all classes downward,
and it is by this that high and low are made firm in their relations to
one another " (p. 566).   Another speech of the year 578 says :

" I have heard that men receive at birth the exact and correct
principles of Heaven and Earth, this being called (Heavenly) Decree.
There are the rules of action, propriety, righteousness and awe-
inspiring majesty for securing the (Heavenly) Decree.   Men of ability
nourish these rules and so secure blessing, while those devoid of
ability violate them and so bring on themselves calamity.   Therefore
superior men diligently attend to the rules of propriety (*li*), and men
in an inferior position do their labor.   In regard to the rules of
propriety, there is nothing like practising the greatest respectfulness.
In doing one's labor, there is nothing like being earnestly sincere.
That respectfulness consists in serving the gods ; that earnestness,
in fulfilling one's duties in life " (pp. 381-382).

The sphere and organization of the state and society of that time
were very small and simple, and therefore the relationship between
ruler and subject, overlord and serf, was a personal one.   Hence
for the feudal lords to maintain the necessary relations between
each other, all that was required was a code of social etiquette (*li*) ;
while toward their serfs they only needed to display an ' awe-inspiring
majesty ' and a manner for the latter's imitation, by means of which,
as Confucius says, they might be the wind beneath which bows the
grass.   When the feudal system began to crumble, however, the power
of the state rulers became, on the one hand, greater and more centralized, while on the other hand the common people gained more
independence from their immediate overlords.   Thus as the sphere
of the state expanded, and its organization became more and more
complex, the former close man-to-man relationships became wider and
looser.   As a consequence, difficulties automatically arose to hinder
the attempt to continue government upon a personal basis, so that one
after another, various states of the time promulgated law codes.   The
Tso Chuan, for example, tells us that in 543 B.C., Tzŭ Ch'an, a statesman
of Cheng, composed a criminal code, and that in 513 B.C., the state of
Chin " inscribed penal laws prepared by Fan Hsüan Tzŭ upon bronze
tripods which it had cast."   Both of these are evident instances of the

prevailing tendency of the age.[1] The penal code of Cheng was strongly criticized by other statesmen of the time,[2] to whom Tzŭ Ch'an replied: "I do it to save the world," thus openly recognizing the necessity of his age. The code of Chin, according to *Tso Chuan*, was also attacked by Confucius, who said:

"Chin is going to ruin! It has lost its proper rules. Chin ought to keep the laws and rules which T'ang Shu received for the regulation of his people, and the ministers and great officers ought to keep them in their several positions. Then the people would be able to honor the upper classes, and the higher classes would be able to preserve their inheritances. There would be nothing wrong with the noble or the mean. We should have what might be called the proper rule . . . . But now when those rules are abandoned, and tripods with the penal laws on them are cast instead, the people will study the tripods. How will they then honor their men of rank, and what will the nobles do? When there is no distinction of noble and mean, how can a state continue to exist?" (p. 732).

Such criticism is representative of the conservative views of that time, views, however, which were quite unable to prevent the political tendencies of the age. The causes of these tendencies lay in the changes taking place in the social and economic organization, and were such that they could not have been halted by any one group of men.

Although Confucius was conservative as regards political change, he was in other respects revolutionary. After he had established the class of travelling scholars, there was a continual increase in the number of men who gained their living in this way, instead of engaging in some productive form of occupation. We have already seen how in the Chi-hsia district in the capital of Ch'i there were 'several hundreds or thousands of men' who lived at the cost of the state, free from all duties,[3] while elsewhere there were such princes and high ministers as Meng Chang and Hsin Ling, each maintaining several thousand 'scholars.' The rise to prominence of this scholar class was coincident with the collapse of the feudal order, and came largely as the result of the repeated admonitions of both Confucians and Mohists to the nobles, urging them to give office to the deserving and the able. Among these scholars, many were undoubtedly quite worthless, and hence, from the point of view of the ruler or state, such a class of literati, engaged only in endless discussions and free from all responsibilities, should certainly be kept in check. Among the common people, of course, there were also men eager to join this non-productive, new aristocracy, and those of them who failed in this effort were almost certain to feel disappointment. This

---

[1] *Tso Chuan*, pp. 558 and 732.
[2] See the letter quoted above, pp. 37-38.
[3] See pp. 132-133.

explains why the *Lao-tzŭ* says : " Not elevating the worthy will make the people lose contentiousness " (ch. 3). Hsün Tzŭ, too, being opposed to the debates of all schools of thought, wished to "deal with the people by authority, and guide them to the Way (*Tao*) ; . . explain things by proclamations, and restrain them by punishments " (*Hsün-tzŭ*, p. 289). Though these statements are each based on different premises, they are both directed against this evil of their time.

The *Book of Lord Shang* (II, 7) says :

" During the time when Heaven and Earth were established, and the people were produced, people knew their mothers but not their fathers. Their way was to love their relatives and to be fond of what was their own. From loving their relatives came discrimination, and from fondness of what was their own, insecurity. As the people increased and were preoccupied with discrimination and insecurity, they fell into disorder. At that time, people were intent on excelling others and subjected each other by force ; the former led to quarrels and the latter to disputes. If in disputes there were no justice, no one would be satisfied. Therefore men of talent established equity and justice and instituted unselfishness, and the people began to delight in moral virtue. At that time, the idea of loving one's relative began to disappear and that of honoring talent arose.

" Now virtuous men are concerned with love, and the way of talented men is to outvie one another. As people increased, being without restraint and long following the practice of one outdoing the other, there was again disorder. Therefore a Sage, having received the administration, made divisions of land and property, and distinctions between men and women. Divisions having been established, it was necessary to have restraining measures, so he established interdicts. These being instituted, it was necessary to have those who could enforce them. Thereupon he established officials. These having been established, it was necessary to have someone to unify them. So he set up a ruler. Once a ruler had been set up, the idea of honoring talent disappeared and that of prizing noble rank arose.

" Thus in the highest antiquity, people loved their relatives and were fond of what was their own ; in middle antiquity, they honored talent and delighted in moral virtue ; and in later days, they prized noble rank and respected office. Honoring talent means outvying one another in one's conduct, but setting up a ruler means relegating talented men to unemployment. Loving one's relatives means making selfishness one's guiding principle, but the idea of equity and justice is to prevent selfishness from holding the field. But these three methods did not aim at antagonistic purposes. When the guiding principles of the people become unsuited to the circumstances, their standards of value must change. As conditions in the world change, different principles are practised " (pp. 225-227).

Though this division into three ages may be anthropologically and sociologically incorrect, it holds true to some extent when applied to the Ch'un Ch'iu and Warring States periods. The early part of the Ch'un Ch'iu period was an aristocratic age, in which everything was the possession of the ruling family. It was an age in which the aristocracy ' loved their relatives and were fond of what was their own.' Later, when the common people gained more power, Confucians and Mohists both advocated the ' exalting of the virtuous and employment of the capable ' (Mo-tzŭ, p. 30), and ' showing a comprehensive love to all men and allying with the good ' (Lun Yü, I, 6). This was a time in which people ' honored talent and delighted in moral virtue.' Still later some of the state rulers, having thus honored the talented and being in their turn aided by them, succeeded in consolidating their own power and destroying that of their adversaries.

By this time, however, the talented men whom they had employed were using their abilities to contend with one another, creating increasing disorder, the result of which was that the rulers were forced to hold them in check. Thus the latter years of the Warring States period were a time in which the people ' prized noble rank and respected office.' The establishment of absolute rulers, and the consequent relegation of the talented to unemployment, came as a reaction to the evils inherent in the preceding period of honoring the talented. This tendency toward the concentration of power was the basis upon which the governments of the latter part of the Warring States period rested.

Exaltation of absolute power by the monarch, stress on government by law, and prohibition of private teachings, were, then, the natural political tendencies of that time ; the Legalists merely supplied the theoretical arguments. At the same time the collapse of the feudal system resulted in a free competition between the newly emanicipated farmer and merchant classes, together with the amassing of great fortunes. These too were the natural social and economic movements of the age, to which the Legalists gave rational explanations.

2—THE LEGALIST CONCEPT OF HISTORY

As we have just seen, the doctrines of the Legalists were a direct response to the political and other tendencies of their age, which were making revolutionary changes to the old order. Hence the Legalists also urged the overthrow of the old, and attacked the custom, followed by all the philosophers from Confucius downward, of seeking examples in antiquity to support one's arguments. The Book of Lord Shang (I, 1), states :

" Former generations did not follow the same doctrines, so what antiquity should one follow ? The emperors and kings did not copy one another, so what rites should one follow ? Fu Hsi and Shen Nung taught but did not punish. Huang-ti, Yao and Shun punished, but without anger. Wen and Wu both established laws in accordance with what was opportune and regulated rites according to practical requirements. As rites and laws were fixed in accordance with what was opportune, regulations and orders were all expedient, and weapons, armor, implements and equipment were all practical. Therefore I say : ' There is more than one way to govern the world and there is no necessity to imitate antiquity in order to take appropriate measures for the state.' T'ang and Wu succeeded in rising to be kings without following antiquity, and as for the downfall of Yin and Hsia, they were ruined without rites having been altered. Consequently, those who act counter to antiquity do not necessarily deserve blame, nor do those who follow established rites, merit much praise " (pp. 172-173).

The *Han-fei-tzŭ* (ch. 49) states :

" If there were one who in the age of the Hsia dynasty constructed nests or instruments to produce fire through friction, Kun and Yü would laugh at him.¹ They would laugh, because their age has advanced beyond these inventions. If there were one who in the age of Yin and Chou cut the ground for water-courses, T'ang and Wu would laugh at him.² And so to-day if there were someone who lauded the ways of Yao, Shun, T'ang, Wu and Yü to the present generation, he would be laughed at by the modern Sages. Hence the Sage does not aim at practising antiquity, and does not model himself upon what is considered to be permanently correct. He discusses the affairs of his own age, and prepares for them accordingly. There was once a man of Sung who tilled his field. In the midst of his field stood the stem of a tree, and one day a hare in full course rushed against that stem, broke its neck, and died. Thereupon the man left his plough and stood waiting at that tree in the hope that he would catch another hare. But he never caught another hare and was ridiculed by the people of Sung. If, however, you wish to rule the people of to-day with the methods of government of the early kings, you do exactly the same thing as that man who waited by his tree . . . . Therefore affairs go according to their time, and preparations are made in accordance with affairs " (*chüan* 19, pp. 1-2).

The trends of the age ever change, and political and social institutions must change likewise. Some of the Taoists had already noted this principle, but it was the Legalists, supplying rational explanations for the political changes taking place in their time, and therefore opposing the doctrines of their conservative contemporaries, who really made this concept of history their own.

---

¹ The early Chinese, according to some accounts, were nest builders living in trees. Yü, first ruler of the Hsia dynasty, and Kun, his father, worked hard to bring under control a great flood which had ravaged China for many years.—Tr.

² Because by this time the flood had long passed.—Tr.

3—The Three Groups in the Legalist School

The Legalist school was divided into three groups, one of which laid stress on *shih* 勢, an important Legalist term which may be translated as 'power' or 'authority'; the second laid emphasis on the concept of law (*fa* 法) itself; and the third stressed *shu* 術, that is, 'statecraft,' or the art of conducting affairs and handling men. The first group was headed by Shen Tao 慎到, who was a Taoist as well as a Legalist, and has already been discussed.[1] He is quoted in the *Han-fei-tzŭ* (ch. 40) as saying:

"A flying dragon rides on the clouds, and a floating snake travels on the mist; but when the clouds disperse and the mist lifts, the dragon and the snake are not different from a cricket or an ant, because they have then lost the element on which they rode. If men of talent are subjected by worthless men, it is because their authority is weak and their position low, whereas if the worthless can be subjected by men of talent, it is owing to the authority of the latter being strong and their position honored. Yao as an ordinary citizen would have been unable to govern three people, whereas Chieh as the Son of Heaven was able to bring the whole empire into disorder. From this I know that it is authority (*shih*) and position that should be relied upon, whereas talent and wisdom are not respected. If a bow being weak, an arrow is yet carried high, it is because it is speeded up by the wind; if a person being of no worth, his orders yet carry, it is because they are assisted by the masses. When Yao was of low rank, the people did not listen (to his teaching); but when he was sitting with his face to the south and was king over the empire, his orders carried, and his interdicts had force. From this I see that talent and wisdom are not sufficient to subdue the masses, but that authority (*shih*) and position are able to subject even men of talent" (*chüan* 17, p. 1).

The *Kuan-tzŭ* (ch. 67) says:

"If there is an intelligent ruler above, who is the possessor of authority (*shih*) whereby he can rule with absolute certainty, his multitudes of subjects will not dare to do wrong. The reason why these multitudes of subjects do not dare to deceive their ruler, is not because they love him, but because they fear his awe-inspiring power (*shih*). The people vie with one another in offering their services, not because they love their ruler, but because they fear his laws and commands. Therefore the intelligent ruler keeps the invincible measure in his own hand, with which to govern the people who must be at his service. He rests in an authority (*shih*) requiring obligatory respect, so as to keep in order the subjects who must obey him. Thus his orders are carried out, and his interdicts serve to forbid. The ruler is honored and his subjects are meek. Therefore the 'Meaning of Laws'[2] says: 'That the ruler is honored and his subjects are

---

[1] *Cf.* ch. 7, sect. 6, pp. 153-159.
[2] Ch. 46 of the *Kuan-tzŭ*.—Tr.

meek, does not come through attempts to cousin them.   It is through the supremacy of the (ruler's) power ' " (chüan 21, p. 7).

This passage, though not directly attributed to Shen Tao, is also a glorification of shih, and as such agrees with the ideas of Shen Tao's group, which maintained that the ruler must possess awe-inspiring shih or power before he can govern his subjects.

The leader of the group which emphasized shu 術, that is, statecraft or methods of government, was Shen Pu-hai 申 不 害, who was appointed minister in Han in 351, and died in 337.   His works are now lost.[1]   The leader of the group which emphasized law (fa 法) was Shang Yang 商 鞅, a descendant of the royal family of Wei, who for many years served as minister in Ch'in, until becoming involved in an intrigue, he was killed in battle in 338 B.C., and suffered the ignominy of having his corpse torn to pieces by chariots.[2]   The Han-fei-tzŭ (ch. 43) says of these men :

"A questioner asked: 'Of the doctrines of the two schools of Shen Pu-hai and Kung-sun Yang 公 孫 鞅 (i.e., Shang Yang), which is more valuable to the state ? ' The answer was : ' This cannot be decided. If a man does not eat for ten days, he will die.   In the time when the great cold is in full sway, if he does not have clothing he will also die. If of the food and the clothing one is to ask which is more necessary to the man, the reply will be that he cannot be without either of them.   They are both articles for preserving life.'

" Now Shen Pu-hai talks about methods of government (shu), while Kung-sun Yang makes laws.   These methods consist in awarding offices according to their responsibilities, and holding actualities in accord with their names.   They consist in keeping in one's hand the power of life and death, and in examining the ability of one's subjects.   This is something a ruler of men keeps in his grasp.

" Laws serve to provide the models for the orders promulgated by the officials ; that penalties will be kept fresh in the minds of the people ; that rewards will go to those who are observant of the laws ; and that punishments will go to those who violate orders.   These are guides for the ministers.   If the ruler does not have his methods of government (shu), there will be weakness above.   If his ministers do not have their laws (fa), there will be confusion below.   Neither of these can be dispensed with.   They are both the instruments of emperors and kings " (chüan 17, pp. 4-5).

Methods (shu) are what serve the ruler to keep himself in power. Laws are what are to be obeyed by the people.   The difference between Shen Pu-hai and Shang Yang consists in their respective emphasis on these two concepts.

---

[1] Cf. the brief mention of him in the Shih Chi (ch. 63).—TR.
[2] Cf. his biography in Duyvendak's introduction to the Book of Lord Shang.—TR.

4—The Three Groups and Han Fei Tzŭ

The man who co-ordinated these three groups, and at the same time drew on the doctrines of the *Lao-tzŭ* and of Hsün Tzŭ to found his own philosophic school, was Han Fei Tzŭ 韓 非 子, who died in the state of Ch'in in the fourteenth year of Ch'in Shih-huang (233 B.C.).[1] The *Shih Chi* says in its biography of him :

" Han Fei was one of the princes of the state of Han. He delighted in the study of punishments, names, laws and methods of government, while basing (his doctrines) upon Huang and Lao.[2] (Han) Fei had an impediment in his speech, and so could not conduct discussions, but he was skilled in writing books. Together with Li Ssŭ, he studied under Hsün Ch'ing (i.e., Hsün Tzŭ). (Li) Ssŭ considered himself not equal to (Han) Fei. Seeing the weakness of the Han state, (Han) Fei several times admonished the King of Han in memorials. But the King of Han was incapable of making use of them. Thereupon Han Fei was incensed that in the government of the state he (the king) did not concern himself with cultivating and reforming his laws and institutions ; did not keep control of his power (*shih*), by means of which to rule his subjects ; did not enrich the state or strengthen the army; and that in seeking for men he did not employ able men for office, but on the contrary elevated dissolute parasites, putting them in positions above persons of real merit. . . . Observing the changing examples of success and failure of the past, he (Han Fei) therefore composed the *Ku Fen*, *Wu Tu*, *Nei Wai Chu Shuo*, *Shuo Lin* and *Shuo Nan*, running to over one hundred thousand words "[3] (ch. 63, pp. 5-6).

Han Fei believed that neither power (*shih*), methods of government (*shu*), nor laws (*fa*), can be neglected, one for another. Therefore he says in the *Han-fei-tzŭ* (ch. 48) :

" *Shih* is the means for gaining supremacy over the masses. . . . Therefore the intelligent ruler carries out his regulations as would Heaven, and employs men as if he were a spirit. Being like Heaven, he commits no wrong, and being like a spirit, he falls into no difficulties. His *shih* enforces his strict teachings, and nothing that he encounters resists him. . . . Only when this is so can his laws be carried out in concert " (*chüan* 18, p. 8).

By comparing the ruler with Heaven, Han Fei Tzŭ means that he acts only according to the law, fairly and impartially. That ' he employs men as if he were a spirit ' means that he makes use of them according to his ' methods ' or *shu*, secretly and unfathomably ; while with the awe which he inspires through the use of rewards and penalties, he ' carries out his laws in concert.' There is no state that

---

[1] *Cf. Mém. hist.*, II, 117.
[2] i.e., Huang-ti and Lao Tzŭ, supposed to be the founders of Taoism.—TR.
[3] These are respectively chs. 11, 49, 30-35, 22-23 and 12 of the present *Han-fei-tzŭ*.—TR.

cannot be governed when these three, authority, methods and laws, are practised together.

5—THE IMPORTANCE OF LAW

As the Ch'un Ch'iu period passed into that of the Warring States, laws became ever more necessary, as has already been explained. The Legalists, furthermore, contributed theories to explain the necessity for having these laws, as in the *Kuan-tzŭ* (ch. 67) :

" The intelligent ruler unifies measures and weights, sets up different standards, and steadfastly maintains them. Therefore his decrees are promulgated and the people follow them. Laws are the models for the empire and the representative standards for all affairs. Officials are those on whom the people depend for their lives (i.e., they have power of life and death over the people). Therefore the government of the intelligent ruler carries out punishments according to the law. Hence when crimes are punished according to law, the people will go to their death without resentment, and when meritorious deeds are measured according to law, the people will accept their rewards without being under a sense of obligation. This is the merit of achievement by means of law. Hence the chapter, ' The Meaning of Laws ' (ch. 46), says : ' When a state is governed by law, things will simply be done in their regular course.'

" The intelligent ruler bases his regulations on laws and standards, and therefore his multitude of ministers govern squarely and uprightly, without daring to be wicked. The people know that the ruler conducts affairs according to law, and so when the officials have law for what they enforce, the people obey them, and when they lack law, the people stop (obeying them). By means of law the people can check the officials, and superiors can conduct business together. Therefore false and deceiving men do not gain the opportunity of deceiving their superiors ; jealous men have no chance to use their destructive minds ; flatterers are unable to display their wiles ; and even a thousand *li* away no one dares to usurp or to commit evil. Therefore the chapter, ' The Meaning of Laws,' says : ' When there are regulations based on laws and standards, there cannot be any craftiness based on deception ' " (*chüan* 21, p. 10).

The *Han-fei-tzŭ* (ch. 27) states :

" Disregarding laws and methods (*shu*), and relying upon his mind for government, even Yao could not put one state in order. Throwing aside square and compass, and measuring by his own incorrect ideas, even Hsi Chung would be unable to complete a single wheel. If, while making no use of a footrule, he measured length, even Wang Erh would be unable to measure with fifty per cent of success. If it were seen to that the ruler of ordinary ability kept his laws and methods, or that a clumsy craftsman kept his compass, square and measure, among ten thousand things there would be no error. If the ruler can avoid that which even talented and clever people cannot accomplish, and continues in that in which even stupid persons can make no error amid ten thousand things, human strength will be expended to the utmost for him and his reputation for merit will be established " (*chüan* 8, p. 9). Again (ch. 38) :

" As for the laws, let them be recorded on the registers, set up in the government offices, and promulgated among the people " (*chüan* 16, pp. 5-6).

The ' intelligent ruler ' rules the state by law. Once the laws have been formulated, he makes them known to everyone so that the people of the state will all respect and obey them. Not only this, but he also guides his own conduct by legal standards. Once these standards exist, therefore, even should there later be a mediocre ruler, he would suffice to conduct government.

After the laws have been made, everyone in the state, both ruler and ruled, must obey them, and cannot change them at will. The *Kuan-tzŭ* (ch. 45) states :

" If the law is not uniform, there will be misfortune for the holder of the state . . . . Therefore it is said that the law must be kept constant. It is out of this (constancy) that preservation or destruction, order or disorder, develop, and the Sage ruler uses it as the great standard for the empire . . . . All things and affairs, if not within the scope of the law, cannot advance. Therefore law is the highest principle for the empire and of true utility to the Sage ruler . . . . . There are those who make laws, those who maintain them, and those who model themselves after these laws. The maker of laws is the ruler. The maintainers of the laws are his ministers. Those who take the laws as their models are the people. When ruler and minister, superior and inferior, noble and humble all obey the law, this is called having Great Good Government " (*chüan* 15, pp. 5-6).

The *Han-fei-tzŭ* (ch. 6) says :

" Therefore the intelligent ruler sees to it that his multitude of subjects do not allow their minds to wander beyond the scope of the law ; do not perform acts of favoritism within the scope of the law ; ¹ and make no act not in accord with the law " (*chüan* 2, p. 3). Again (ch. 37) :

" Although a ruler employs men, he must measure them according to standards, and watch them according to the function of their offices. Affairs in accord with the law he allows to proceed ; those not in accord with the law, he puts a stop to " (*chüan* 15, p. 9).

The highest ideal of the Legalist school is that ' ruler and minister, superior and inferior, noble and humble all obey the law.' This will result in ' Great Good Government,' and is an ideal which has never yet been actually attained in China.

---

¹ i.e., do not act on their own initiative to do more than the law requires.—TR.

When laws have once been established so that everyone obeys them, all heterodox doctrines of private individuals must be prohibited because they strike at the efficacy of the law.   The *Han-fei-tzŭ* (ch. 41) says :

"Someone asked : 'How does dialectic come about ?' The reply was : 'It comes about from the lack of intelligence of the superior.' The questioner asked : 'How can the superior's lack of intelligence produce dialectic ?' The reply was : 'In the state of an intelligent ruler, his orders are what are most authoritative in the words of men, and the laws are what are most appropriate to affairs. There cannot be words of two men that are equally authoritative, nor can there be two laws that are both the best. Therefore words not in accord with laws and commands must be prohibited.   If there are some who, regardless of laws and commands, by associating with craft and shifting with circumstances, produce something profitable by their research into affairs, their superior must hold them to be responsible for their words.   When their words are correct, they will have great reward ; when not correct, they will suffer heavy penalty.   This is the way whereby ignorant people will fear the penalties and not dare to speak, while learned persons will not dispute over anything.   Such is the way to be without dialectic.

"'But in an age of disorder it is not so.   The ruler promulgates his orders, and the people with their learning nullify them.   When the officials have their laws, the people through their private conduct modify them.   The ruler looks disparagingly on laws and commands, and honors the learning and conduct of the literati.   This is why there are so many men of learning in the world . . . . Therefore, when there are so many of those who wear the clothing, girdle and sword of the literati, there will be few men left for agriculture or for war. When such phrases as those of the 'hard and the white' and 'no thickness' make their appearance,[1] laws and commands come to an end.   Therefore I say that when the superior lacks intelligence, dialectic comes about'" (*chüan* 17, pp. 3-4).

Laws, then, are the highest standards by which to judge the words and actions of the people of a state.   All words and actions not in accord with the law must be prohibited.   Therefore (ch. 49) :

"In the state of the intelligent ruler, there is no literature of books and records, but the laws serve as teachings.   There are no sayings of the early kings, but the officials act as teachers" (*chüan* 19, p. 5).

6—RECTIFICATION OF NAMES AND ACTUALITIES

The 'methods' (*shu*) discussed by the Legalists are those whereby the ruler may maintain his supremacy over the ruled.   One of these

---

[1] Subjects debated on by Kung-sun Lung and Hui Shih respectively.—TR.

methods, which has comparatively greater philosophical interest, is what is called ' the examination of actualities (*shih* 實) according to their names (*ming* 名).' This was a practical application to statecraft of the rectification of names and actualities as formulated by the Dialecticians. The *Kuan-tzŭ* (ch. 38) says :

" When names are rectified and the laws made ready, the Sage has no concerns " (*chüan* 13, p. 7). Again (ch. 55) :

" Actualities are kept under strict control through the application of names. Names are fixed according to their actualities. Names and actualities mutually produce one another. This mutual interaction is their nature. When names and actualities are in agreement, good government results. When they are not in agreement, disorder results " (*chüan* 18, p. 3).

The *Han-fei-tzŭ* (ch. 8) states :

" In using the method of maintaining uniformity, names are of primary importance. When names have been rectified, things will be fixed. When names have not been rectified, things undergo change. Therefore the Sage holds to uniformity and rests in quiescence. He causes names to be self-applying, and commands that things remain fixed in themselves. His inferiors, even without seeing him, are therefore simple and correct. He employs men according to their ability, and then lets them work of themselves. They are given according to what they do, and are promoted of themselves. All things being correct and in their place, they are fixed, and are designated by the superior with names. When the name is unknown, the actuality is investigated. When the actuality and name are seen to be in agreement, what comes forth from them is utilized. When the two are both true to one another, inferiors display their natures . . . . The ruler holds the names in hand, and his subjects model their actualities after the names. When actualities and names are in agreement, superior and inferior are in harmony with one another " (*chüan* 2, pp. 6-7). Again (ch. 7) :

" When a ruler wishes to prevent wickedness, he examines into the correspondence between actualities and names, words and work. When a subject makes claims, the ruler gives him work according to what he has claimed, but holds him wholly responsible for accomplishment corresponding to this work. When the accomplishment corresponds to the work, and the work corresponds to what the man has claimed he could do, he is rewarded. If the accomplishment does not correspond to the work, nor the work correspond to what the man has claimed for himself, he is punished. Thus when subjects have made great claims, while their actual accomplishment is small, they are punished. This is not punishment because of the smallness of the accomplishment, but because the accomplishment is not equal to its name. And when subjects have made small claims while the actual accomplishment is great, they are also punished. This is not because no pleasure is taken in the larger accomplishment, but because it is not in accord with the name given to it. The injury done is greater than if the larger accomplishment had not been performed, and therefore they are punished " (*chüan* 2, p. 5).

Confucius had advocated the Rectification of Names, wishing thereby to make all classes of society accord to what they ought to be. The Legalists advocated it as a means by which the ruler might maintain control over his subjects. The Dialecticions had advocated the rectification of names and actualities, wishing thus ' to be careful in what one means '; for them ' a certain actuality must have a certain name.' The Legalists wished to maintain ' correspondence between actualities and names,' and so believed that a certain name must have a certain actuality. Thus a ruler, when he gives work to a man, must hold the man responsible for results corresponding to the name of the work, and if the subject has made some claims for himself, " the ruler gives him work according to what he has claimed, but holds him wholly responsible for accomplishment corresponding to this work." The actuality, that is, must correspond to the name. Once this system exists, all subjects who assume office will naturally strive to live up to the name of their office, and hence the ruler need only keep control of the names in order to judge the accomplishments of his officials. Hence the words : " The ruler holds the names in hand, and his subjects model their actualities after the names." Such is the ' method ' to simplify what is complex and to govern ten thousand by one. This is why " the Sage holds to uniformity and rests in quiescence. He causes names to be self-applying, and commands that things remain fixed in themselves."

7—STRICTNESS IN REWARDS AND PUNISHMENTS

From what has been said in the preceding section, it may be seen that laws and ' methods ' are equally indispensable to the ruler, so that the *Han-fei-tzŭ* (ch. 43) says : " Neither of these can be dispensed with. They are both the instruments of emperors and kings " (*chüan* 17, p. 5). With laws and methods only, however, and no controlling authority (*shih*) by which to carry them into practice, the ruler would still be unable to keep those beneath him in subjection. The *Han-fei-tzŭ* (ch. 28) says :

" When there is the ability but not the power (*shih*), even the talented will be unable to rule the evil. Thus if some timber a foot in length is set up on top of a high mountain, it will look down upon a valley eight thousand feet deep. This is not because the timber is tall, but because of the loftiness of its position. When Chieh was Son of Heaven, he was able to keep the empire in subjection. This was not because he was talented, but because of the greatness of his power (*shih*). When Yao was an ordinary citizen, he was unable to govern three families. This was not because he was unworthy, but because of the lowliness of his position. When a weight of thirty thousand catties has a boat, it floats. When a trifling weight is without a boat, it sinks. This is not because the thirty thousand catties are light while the trifling weight is heavy, but because the one possesses controlling power (*shih*), while the other does not. Thus what is short can see over what is tall, because of its position, and one who is unworthy can rule the talented because of his *shih*" (*chüan* 8, p. 11). Again (ch. 52) :

"That by which a horse can carry a weight or draw a vehicle along a distant road is its muscles. That by which the ruler of ten thousand or a thousand chariots can govern the empire and attack other feudal lords is his awe-inspiring *shih*. Awe-inspiring *shih* is the muscle of the ruler " (*chüan* 20, p. 3).

A ruler's *shih* is outwardly manifested in his rewards and punishments, which act as the ' two handles ' of his administration. The *Han-fei-tzŭ* (ch. 7) says :

" The way in which the intelligent ruler leads and governs his subjects is by means of two handles. These two handles are penalty and benevolence. What are penalty and benevolence ? By penalty is meant capital punishment, and by benevolence is meant the giving of rewards. Then subjects will stand in fear of punishment, and will receive benefit from reward. Therefore when the ruler uses penalty and benevolence, his multitude of subjects stand in fear of his majesty and rally around what is beneficial to them " (*chüan* 2, p. 4).

There is no one who does not fear capital punishment and who does not find the receiving of rewards beneficial. Therefore by utilizing this principle the ruler can profitably make use of his people and make effective his awe-inspiring *shih*. The *Han-fei-tzŭ* (ch. 48) states :

" All ruling of the empire must be done by utilizing human nature. In human nature there are the feelings of like and dislike, and hence rewards and punishments may be employed. When rewards and punishments may be employed, interdicts and commands may be established, and the way of government is completed. The ruler holds on to these handles so as to rest in his power (*shih*), and hence his orders operate and his interdicts serve to prevent. These handles consist in the control over death and life ; power (*shih*) is the means of maintaining supremacy over the masses " (*chüan* 18, p. 8).

To make use of the human feelings of like and dislike, and so to utilize rewards and punishments, is to rule people in accordance with human psychology. Therefore Chapter XXVIII says : " He who acts in opposition to the human heart, though he might be Pen or Yü, could not make men exert themselves for him; he who knows the human heart, does not himself move, yet they (the people) act of themselves " (*chüan* 8, p. 11).

8—The Evilness of Human Nature

'In human nature there are the feelings of like and dislike, and hence rewards and punishments may be employed.' That is, men's natures know only to move toward what is beneficial and avoid what is harmful. Hence they may be compelled to act simply through motives of profit and harm. Most of the Legalists believed that man's nature is evil, and Han Fei Tzŭ, as the disciple of Hsün Tzŭ, is especially clear on this point. The *Han-fei-tzŭ* (ch. 8) says : "The Yellow Emperor (Huang-ti) had a saying : 'Between superior and inferior each day there are a hundred conflicts.' Inferiors conceal their selfishness, with which to take advantage of their superiors. Superiors keep the measures and methods, with which to control their inferiors " (*chüan* 2, pp. 8-9). Again (ch. 32) : "When a man sells his services as a farm hand, the master will give him good food at the expense of his own family, and pay him money and cloth. This is not because he loves the farm hand, but he says : 'In this way, his ploughing of the ground will go deeper and his sowing of seeds will be more active.' The farm hand, on the other hand, exerts his strength and works busily at tilling and weeding. He exerts all his skill cultivating the fields. This is not because he loves his master, but he says : 'In this way I shall have good soup, and money and cloth will come easily.' Thus he expends his strength as if between them there were a bond of love such as that of father and son. Yet their hearts are centered on utility, and they both harbor the idea of serving themselves. Therefore in the conduct of human affairs, if one has a mind to do benefit, it will be easy to remain harmonious, even with a native of Yüeh.¹ But if one has a mind to do harm, even father and son will become separated and feel enmity toward one another " (*chüan* 11, p. 6). And Chapter XLVI : "Moreover as to children, a father and mother when they produce a boy congratulate one another, but when they produce a girl, they put it to death. These have both come forth from the womb of the mother, and yet when it is a boy there is congratulation, while when it is a girl it is put to death. This is because the parents think of their later convenience, and calculate about what is profitable in the long run. Thus even parents show calculating minds in their attitude toward their offspring. How much more will this be the case when there is none of the affection which exists between father and child ! " (*chüan* 18, pp. 1-2).

All men, Han Fei Tzŭ insists, act from motives of selfishness and self-profit, and so 'show calculating minds in their attitude' toward one another. It is this fact that makes the system of rewards and punishments possible.

---

¹ A barbarian state of the south occupying much of present-day Chekiang.—Tr.

In economics, Han Fei Tzŭ holds that since all men act in their own interests, it is better to leave them alone in free competition. Therefore he opposes the Confucian doctrine of the equal division of land. Chapter L says :

" Men of learning who discuss government in the present age say : ' Give land to those who are poor, so as to give something to those who are helpless.' But suppose there is a man whose circumstances are similar to those of others, and there has been no profit from a prosperous year or from other sources, yet he alone is self sustaining. This means that he must either have been industrious or economical. Now suppose there is a man whose circumstances are similar to those of others, and there has been no tribulation of famine, disease or calamity, yet he alone is poor. He must have been either wasteful or lazy. The wasteful and lazy person is poor, while the industrious and economical person is rich. Now for the superior to collect from the rich man so as to distribute to the poor home, is to take from the industrious and the economical and give to the wasteful and the lazy. To wish thus to lead the people to increased activity and frugality is impossible " (*chüan* 19, p. 8).

Free competition will cause all the people to be more active and frugal, with the result that production will increase.

The Confucian school believed that the people of antiquity were morally better than those of the present time, and that there were then more Sages. Han Fei Tzŭ agrees (ch. 49) that such a view is not entirely erroneous, though he gives his own explanation for it :

" The men of old did not till the field, for the fruits of plants and trees were sufficient for food. Nor did the women weave, for the skins of birds and animals were enough for clothing. Without working there was enough to live, there were few people and plenty of supplies, and therefore the people did not quarrel. Hence neither large rewards nor heavy punishments were used, and the people were naturally in good order. But nowadays people do not consider a family of five children as large, and, each child having again five children, before the death of the grandfather there may be twenty-five grandchildren. The result is that there are many people and few supplies, and that one has to work hard for a meagre return. So the people fall to quarrelling, and though rewards may be doubled and punishments heaped up, one does not escape from disorder.

" When Yao held the empire, his reed thatch was not trimmed, and his oak roof-beams were unsmoothed. The unhusked kernels of pannicled millet were his food, and the *li* and *huo* plants made his broth. In winter he wore deerskins, and in summer clothing of dolichos fiber. Had it been the clothing and nourishment of a porter, it could not have been worse than this.   When Yü held the empire, he himself ploughed so as to set an example to his people. His thighs were without fat and his shanks worn off of all hair. Had these been the labors of a servant or a slave, they could not have been more arduous than his.

" According to these words, those of old who abdicated as Emperor, were thereby throwing away the nourishment of a porter and parting from the labors of a servant or slave.   Those of old, therefore, who handed over the empire, are not to be praised.   But nowadays when even a district officer dies, his descendants can maintain private carriages for many generations.   Hence people value such offices.   Therefore as regards the attitude of people toward abdications, the fact that those of old lightly declined the position of Emperor, while to-day they part with reluctance from the position of a district officer, is because of the altered amount of the respective advantages.

" Thus people who dwell in the mountains and have to draw water from a valley, give water to each other as gifts at festivals. And those who live in a marsh and are troubled with water, hire labor to cut open the ground to let the water go.   In the spring of a year of famine, one is unable to feed one's younger brother, while in the autumn of a year of plenty, even distant relatives will have food.   It is not that one's own flesh and blood are neglected, while one has love for passing visitors, but it depends upon the difference in quantity of material goods.   Hence the ancient indifference to goods was not because of moral virtue, but because of the abundance of goods. Nor are the present-day struggles for acquisition due to moral decadence, but because of the scarcity of goods.   It was not because of moral excellence that (in the past) a man lightly declined the position of Emperor, but because of the limitations of his power.   And it is not because of moral decadence that (to-day) a man strives fiercely for government employment, but because of the weightiness of the authority.   Therefore the Sage governs according to quantities, such as scarcity and abundance, and hence (under his rule) lightness of punishment is not kindness, nor is severity of punishment oppression. These are carried out according to the circumstances of the occasion " (*chüan* 19, pp. 1-2.)

Men of ancient times and of the present day differ in conduct because of their altered environments, and not because of difference in their natures.   It is permissible to say that the customs of ancient people were gentle, but not to say that this means that their natures were better.

Human nature being like this, men must be led by governmental organization and kept in their place by punishments, if the world is to be properly ordered.   But if, as Confucius and Mencius urged, people were to be led by virtue and kept in place by the traditional *li*, the government would be without authority and would reach nowhere. The *Han-fei-tzŭ* (ch. 50) says :

" The severe household has no fierce slaves, while it is the affectionate mother who has the prodigal son. From this I know that awe-inspiring power (*shih*) can repress outrage, whereas virtue and kindness are insufficient to halt disorderliness. In his rule of a state, the Sage does not depend on men doing good of themselves, but makes it so that they can do no wrong. Within the frontiers of a state, there are no more than ten people who do good of themselves, whereas if one makes it so that the people can do no wrong, the entire state can be kept peaceful. He who rules a country makes use of the majority and neglects the few, and so does not concern himself with virtue but with law.

" If we had to depend upon an arrow being perfectly straight of itself, there would be no arrows in a hundred generations. If we had to depend upon a piece of wood being perfectly round of itself, there would be no wheels in a thousand generations. There is not one arrow straight of itself nor a piece of wood round of itself in a hundred generations. How is it then that everyone in the world rides carriages and shoots birds ? It is the result of applying the art of stretching and bending. Although there are arrows that are straight of themselves, and pieces of wood that are round of themselves, without depending upon the art of stretching and bending, yet the skilled workman does not value them. Why is that ? He who rides is not one man, and he who shoots does not release the bow only once. Likewise the intelligent ruler does not value people who are of themselves good without rewards and punishments. Why is that ? The laws of the state cannot be neglected and it is not one man who is being ruled. Therefore the ruler who possesses methods of government, does not follow the good that happens by chance, but practises according to necessary principles " (*chüan* 19, pp. 9-10).

Law, methods and power must be employed for government : these constitute its ' necessary principles.'

9—Non-activity

If the ruler can utilize these principles, he will be able to rule through non-activity (*wu wei* 無 爲). The *Han-fei-tzŭ* (ch. 8) says :

" Affairs lie in the four quarters (i.e., the outside world). What is important is in the center. The Sage holds what is important, and the four quarters come to imitate him. He awaits them in a state of ' emptiness ' (*hsü* 虛), and they all work by themselves. The four quarters being concealed, he leads them to activity (with his non-activity). When his aids of the left and right have been established, he simply opens the door and receives them. Without change or variation, they both become active. They act unceasingly, which is said to be acting according to principle. Things have their appropriateness and materials have their right use. It is when each rests in its appropriate place that superior and inferior are in a state of non-activity (*wu wei*). When the cock is made to preside over the night and the cat is commanded to catch rats, each being used according to its ability, then the superior is without concern. When the superior is concerned in something he is especially proficient in, affairs are no longer in their proper order. He who is vain and delights in his own ability is deceived by his inferiors. When he likes to bring forth arguments and kindliness, his inferiors take advantage of his abilities. Then the duties of superior and inferior are reversed, and so the country is not properly governed " (*chüan* 2, p. 6).

Chapter XXIX says:

" Those of old who maintained only the main features of things, surveyed Heaven and Earth, observed the rivers and seas, and made use of mountains and valleys. Just as the sun and moon shine forth, the four seasons progress, the clouds spread, and the wind blows, so did they not encumber their minds with knowledge, nor themselves with selfishness. They relied for good government or disorder upon laws and methods (*shu*); let right and wrong be dealt with by rewards and punishments; and referred lightness and heaviness to the balance of the scale. They did not oppose the natural order, and did not inflict injury upon human feelings and nature. They did not blow up the hair to seek for a small blemish beneath; [1] nor did they wash away the dirt to examine into what is hard to know. They did not go beyond the scope (of the law), or hesitate to remain within it. They did not press what is beyond the law, or let loose what is within it. They kept to the proper order, and responded to the spontaneous (*tzŭ jan* 自 然). Calamity and blessing came from a person's conforming to the law, and not from (the ruler's) likes and dislikes. The responsibilities for glory or disgrace depended upon the individual, and not on others " (*chüan* 8, pp. 11-12).

The ruler utilizes the free and spontaneous activity of his subjects, while keeping the ' two handles ' of rewards and punishments in his own hands, by means of which to hold them responsible for the result. The duties of the ruler are like those of the helmsman of a great ship. From his lofty position he makes slight movements with his hands, and the ship of itself follows his desires and moves. This is the way whereby the one may control the ten thousand, and by quiescence may regulate activity.

This idea is already to be found among some of the Taoists, as in the *Chuang-tzŭ* (ch. 13):

" The virtue of the wise ruler makes the universe its starting point, *Tao* and *Te* its essential, and non-activity (*wu wei*) its constant way. By non-activity he can administer the empire and yet have energy to spare; but by activity he is himself used by the empire and

---

[1] i.e., find fault with someone.—TR.

is yet insufficient. Therefore the men of old valued the principle of non-activity.

"But if superiors have non-activity, their inferiors will also have non-activity, which will mean that inferiors will be equal in virtue to their superiors. When they are equal to their superiors in virtue they are no longer their subjects. On the other hand, if while inferiors practise activity, superiors will also practise activity, then superiors will have the same practices as their inferiors. And when they have the same practices, they cease being rulers. The superior must practise non-activity so as to administer the empire, and his inferiors must practise activity in order to be utilized in the empire. This is an invariable law.

"Therefore rulers of old, although their knowledge spread throughout the universe, did not themselves think. Although their eloquence beautified all things, they did not themselves speak. Although their abilities exhausted all things within the limits of the seas, they did not themselves act.

"Heaven has no parturitions, yet all things are evolved. Earth knows no increment, yet all things are nourished. The wise ruler has non-activity, yet the empire's work is accomplished. Therefore it has been said: 'There is nothing more spiritual than Heaven, nothing richer than Earth, and nothing greater than the wise ruler.' Wherefore it has also been said: 'The virtue of the wise ruler makes him the peer of Heaven and Earth.' This is how he chariots upon the universe, with all things as his team, and how he keeps for his use the society of man. . . .

"Therefore those of old who made manifest the great *Tao*, first made manifest Heaven, and *Tao* and *Te* came next. *Tao* and *Te* being made manifest, the virtues of *jen* and *i* came next. These being made manifest, divisions and standards came next. Then came actualities and their names, then employment without interference, then distinctions of good and bad, then discrimination between right and wrong, and then rewards and punishments. With the manifestation of rewards and punishments, fools and wise men assumed their proper positions, the noble and the humble occupied their correct places, and the virtuous and the worthless were employed according to their nature. It was necessary to distinguish the capacities of men and give them names accordingly, in order to serve the ruler, nourish the ruled, administer things, and cultivate the self. Where knowledge and plans are not utilized, one must fall back upon the natural. This is perfect peace, the acme of good government. Therefore it has been written: 'Wherever there is an actuality, there is also its name.' Actualities and names the ancients had indeed, but they did not give precedence to them.

"Thus those of old who spoke about the great *Tao*, passed through five phases before actualities and names were reached, and

nine phases before rewards and punishments could be discussed "
(pp. 160-161, 163-164).

Because of the complexity of government affairs, the ruler,
even granted that he has the requisite energy, will inevitably be
neglecting one thing for another, if he has to administer them all
himself. The energy and time of any one man are limited, whereas
the affairs of the empire are unlimited. Hence if he insists on acting,
he will ' himself be used by the empire, and yet be insufficient ';
therefore the wise ruler makes ' non-activity his constant way.' But
if he delegates all things to others to be administered, everyone will
be active and nothing will be neglected, so that ' by non-activity he
can administer the empire and yet have energy to spare.'

The detailed methods used to carry this principle into practice
are discussed in the nine phases that follow. ' Divisions and
standards ' mean the establishing of official positions, and the exact
determination of what things are to be under the control of each
office. When these are understood, a certain man will be put in
charge of a certain position. The man is the ' actuality,' his office
is the ' name.' He should be allowed to carry on his duties without
hindrance. Thus after actualities and names have been made manifest,
there comes ' employment without interference.' But the ruler,
though indifferent to the way in which the office is conducted, must
ever examine the accomplished results. These are the ' distinctions
of good and bad.' The persons with good results are right, and
those with poor ones are wrong. Hence there is then ' discrimination
between right and wrong.' What is right is rewarded, and what is
wrong is punished, so that with the manifestation of right and wrong,
come rewards and punishments. When this state is reached, wise and
stupid, virtuous and unworthy, all occupy their proper positions, and
the empire is well governed.

The *Chuang-tzŭ* (ch. 11) says :

" What are lowly yet have to be put up with are things. What
are humble and yet cannot but be followed are the people. What are
small and yet require to be attended to are affairs. What is harsh and
yet still necessary to be set forth, is the law. Far off, but still claiming
our presence, is righteousness (*i*). Near, but still claiming extension,
is human-heartedness (*jen*). What restrain, but are still of bounteous
store, are the rules of propriety (*li*). Of middle course, but yet of
lofty scope, is Power (*Te*). One, but not to be without variation, is
Tao. Spiritual, but not to be devoid of action, is Nature (*T'ien*).

" Therefore the Sage looks up to Nature, but does not offer to
aid. He perceives his Power (*Te*), but does not involve himself.
He guides himself by *Tao*, but makes no plans. He identifies himself
with human-heartedness, but does not rely on it. He extends to
righteousness, but does not store it up. He responds to *li*, without
being tabooed thereby. He undertakes affairs without declining them.

He metes out law without confusion. He relies on the people and does not make light of them. He accommodates himself to things and does not ignore them.

"Things are not worthy to be taken into consideration, yet one cannot but accept them. He who is not enlightened by Nature will not be pure in his *Te*. He who has not a clear apprehension of *Tao* is nowhere right. And he who is not enlightened by *Tao*: alas for him!

"What then is *Tao*? There is the *Tao* of Nature and the *Tao* of man. Non-activity and compliance make the *Tao* of Nature; activity and entanglement the *Tao* of man. The *Tao* of Nature is the ruler; the *Tao* of man the subject. The distance which separates them is great. Let us all take heed thereto!" (pp. 133-134).

Han Fei Tzŭ "delighted in the study of punishments, names, laws and methods of government, while basing (his doctrines) upon Huang and Lao." [1] These words make it evident that the Legalist school has been greatly influenced by the Taoists. Taoism says that the *Tao* rests upon the spontaneous action of all things, and that therefore through non-activity there is nothing that is not done. Extending this principle to political philosophy, we find that the ruler must sit quietly above, resting upon the free and spontaneous action of his people. This is why the *Chuang-tzŭ* designates the *Tao* of Nature, which is non-activity, as that of the ruler; while the *Tao* of man, which is activity, is that of the subjects.

Yet if, among the people, each individual acts on his own, can a strifeless harmony really be reached? One group of Taoists, who idealized the natural, said that if we rely upon the spontaneity of man's nature, then everything will be right. This is the attitude of Chuang Tzŭ's school, which Hsün Tzu criticized by saying that it was "blinded by Nature and did not know man" (*Hsün-tzŭ*, p. 264). Another group said that if men can all be brought to a state of ignorance and of minimun desires, they will in this way be able to rest peacefully in a state of simplicity. This was the view of the followers of the *Lao-tzŭ*. Still another group knew that 'things are not worthy to be taken into consideration, yet one cannot but accept them.' Affairs, too, though small, must be attended to, and laws, though harsh, must be set forth. Therefore they discussed ' divisions and standards,' ' actualities and their names,' ' right and wrong,' ' rewards and punishments,' etc., such as are mentioned in the preceding quotations. Their aim was to have all people governed by law, and in this respect the group, like the Legalists, was under the influence of the political changes of its age, and hence differed from the other Taoist groups who talked only about Utopias.

The Legalists developed this phase of Taoism still further, so that the present *Kuan-tzŭ* contains two chapters (38 and 49) which

---

[1] From his biography in the *Shih Chi*. See above, p. 320 —Tr.

show strong Taoist influence, while chapters XX and XXI of the *Han-fei-tzŭ* are devoted to explanations of the *Lao-tzŭ*. Although these two Legalist works are both the compilations of later men, we can infer from them that most of the Legalist groups were versed in the Taoist doctrines. Even that group of Taoists, however, which went so far as to discuss actualities and names, rewards and punishments, still ' did not give precedence to them.' They spoke of law as something harsh, and while admitting of things that ' one cannot but accept them,' they at the same time described them as ' not worthy to be taken into consideration.' Thus they did not wholly disassociate themselves from the characteristic Taoist viewpoint, and in this respect they ultimately differed from the Legalists.

10—THE LEGALISTS AND THE NOBLES OF THEIR TIME

The political tendency of the Warring States period was one moving away from a government by feudal nobles toward absolute monarchy. The Legalists both supplied a rational basis for this movement, and used their ability and learning to aid the rulers in their thoroughgoing reforms, for which reason they fell under the particular dislike of the great ministers and hereditary nobles of their time. The *Han-fei-tzŭ* (ch. 11) says :

" Scholars versed in methods (*shu*) must see far and examine clearly. If they do not examine clearly they will be unable to unearth heterodoxy. Scholars skilled in the law must have strong resolution and unyielding uprightness. Without unyielding uprightness they will be unable to redress wickedness. . . . Scholars versed in methods, perspicacious and obedient, are able to bring to light the secret feelings of powerful men. Scholars skilled in the law, of unyielding uprightness, who are also perspicacious and obedient, are able to rectify the wicked conduct of powerful men. Hence when scholars versed in methods and skilled in the law are employed, nobles and powerful ministers will inevitably be done away with. This is why there is such an enmity between scholars versed in the law, and men who hold high offices, that they cannot exist together. . . . Hence how can scholars of the law and of methods escape danger, when what they depend upon must inevitably fail to bring them supremacy, and when their power cannot co-exist (with that of nobles and ministers) ? Those of them who can be falsely incriminated for some crime, are executed under the common law. Those who cannot be accused of some crime, are assassinated by private swords. Thus those versed in laws and methods, should they come into conflict with their superior, if not executed, inevitably meet death from private swords " (*chüan* 4, pp. 1-2). Chapter XLII says :

"T'ang-ch'i Kung said to Han (Fei) Tzŭ : ' I have heard that the practising of the rules of proper conduct (*li*), the cultivation of one's conduct and rejection of knowledge, is the way to move successfully in society. But now you, Sir, set up laws and methods (*shu*), and establish standards and measures. I hold that this is putting your person in danger. . . . You discard the way to safety and advance perilous conduct. I see no reason for you to do so ! '

" Han (Fei) Tzŭ said : ' I understand your words, Sir ! It is certainly not at all easy to set up means for governing the empire and standards for maintaining the people. Yet the reason why I discard your advice and carry out my own humble choice, is because I believe that by setting up laws and methods, and establishing standards and measures, I can benefit the people and ease their way. Therefore I fear not the calamity of incurring the wrath of a disorderly or unenlightened superior, but must think of how to make wealth and profit adequate for the people. This is the conduct of the benevolent and wise man. He who is afraid of the calamity of incurring the wrath of a disorderly or unenlightened superior, and who escapes from the doom of death, while knowing that by saving his own person he will not bring forth wealth and benefit for the people, is an avaricious and mean person. I cannot endure the report of acting avariciously and meanly, and dare not harm the course of morality and knowledge. You, Sir, have the idea of being kind to me, but would in fact be doing me great injury ! ' " (*chüan* 17, p. 4).

The state and society of that time were daily enlarging their sphere of activity, and their organization was becoming more and more complex. Since the former methods of government no longer suited, new ones were necessary. The followers of Han Fei Tzŭ believed that the ' setting up of laws and methods, and establishing standards and measures ' would ' profit the people and ease their way.' In their determined insistence upon these innovations, even in the face of death, they showed themselves indeed to be men acting in a positive way to help the world.

CHAPTER XIV

THE CONFUCIANS OF THE CH'IN AND HAN
DYNASTIES

The *Han-fei-tzŭ* (ch. 50) says about the later Confucians :
" After the death of Confucius, there were the Confucian (followers) of Tzŭ Chang, Tzŭ Ssŭ, Yen (Hui), Mencius, Ch'i-tiao, Chung Liang, Sun (i.e., Hsün Tzŭ) and Yo-cheng " (*chüan* 19, p. 7).

These comprised the Confucian schools of the latter part of the Warring States period. The writings of these men and of those of the early Han dynasty were, about the time of Christ, compiled by a certain Tai Te 戴 德 into a single work of eighty-five sections. By Tai Sheng 戴 聖, the nephew of Tai Te, this compilation was reduced to forty-six sections, and in this form comprises what is to-day known as the *Li Chi* 禮 記 (Book of Rites). This version quickly gained popular favor, while the earlier compilation by Tai Te (generally called the *Li Chi* of the elder Tai, to distinguish it from that of Tai Sheng), has come down to us only in part. Besides these two compilations, there exists another Confucian work of about the same period known as the *Hsiao Ching* 孝 經 (Classic of Filial Piety). This has been traditionally ascribed to Confucius, but it is not mentioned in the *Lun Yü*, and is first referred to only in the *Lü-shih Ch'un Ch'iu* (XVI, 6), so that it too probably dates from the latter part of the Warring States period. The contents of these two works form the subject of the present chapter.

1—General Principles of Li

It has been said in the chapter on Confucius that he discussed both ' uprightness ' (*chih* 直), and the rules of good manners or social usage (*li* 禮). In discussing the former he was stressing the freedom of the individual, while in discussing the latter he was emphasizing the mould that is imposed from without on the individual by social institutions.[1] While emphasizing the *li* or traditional *mores*, however, Confucius offered no general theories to explain their nature and bearing on human life, and in this respect, at least, was content to remain ' a transmitter and not a creator.'

It was only toward the end of the Warring States period and the beginning of the Han dynasty that the Confucians evolved general theories about *li*, among which those of Hsün Tzŭ have already

---

[1] See p. 68.

been briefly described. As to the theories of the other Confucians, the *Li Chi* contains several passages. Thus in Chapter II :

"Tseng Tzŭ said to Tzŭ Ssŭ : 'Chi, when I was in mourning for my parents, no water or other liquid entered my mouth for seven days.' Tzŭ Ssŭ said : 'As regards the *li* framed by the early kings, those who exceed them should come down to them, whereas those who do not come up to them should strain to reach them. Hence, when the Superior Man is mourning for his parents, it is for three days that no water or other liquid enters his mouth, and only with the aid of his staff is he able to rise '" (XXVII, 133-134). Again :

"When Tzŭ Hsia, having left off his mourning (for his parents), was introduced (to Confucius), a lute was given to him. He tried to tune it, but it would not be tuned. He touched it, but it would bring forth no melody. Rising he said : 'I have not yet forgotten my grief. The early kings framed the *li*, and I dare not exceed them.' But when a lute was given to Tzŭ Chang under the same circumstances, he tried to tune it, and it became tuned. He plucked it, and it gave forth melody. Rising he said : 'The early kings framed the *li*, and I dare not but come up to them '" (XXVII, 142-143). Chapter VII says :

"Drinking, eating and sexual pleasure : these are the things men greatly desire. Death, poverty and suffering : these are what they greatly dislike. Thus the feelings of like and dislike are the great (motivating) principles of men's minds. But men keep them hidden in their minds, where they cannot be fathomed or measured. When good and evil are both hidden in their minds, and there is no visible manifestation of them, if we wish to have one thing whereby to comprehend them all, what else is there except *li* ? " (XXVII, 380). Chapter XXV says :

"Once Confucius was at home at his ease, with Tzŭ Chang, Tzŭ Kung and Yen Yu by him . . . . The Master said : 'Shih, you err by excess, and you, Shang, by not coming up to . . . .' Tzŭ Kung moved across the mat and replied : 'Allow me to ask by what means it is possible to take this middle way ? ' The Master said : 'By means of the *li*, the *li*. Yes, it is by the *li* that one may hold to the mean '" (XXVIII, 270-271). Chapter XXVII says :

"The *li*, following human feelings, act as regulators and refiners of them, so as to keep the people within bounds " (XXVIII. 284).

Thus the *li* perform two functions : that of regulating (*chieh* 節) human emotions ; and that of refining (*wen* 文) them, that is, giving them a refined expression. This is necessary because human feelings and desires must be kept within proper limits, or in other words, must be kept within the proper mean. This mean is the point of exact propriety in the expression of feeling, going beyond which means conflict either with other persons or with other aspects of oneself. The *li* constitute the mould imposed from without which will maintain men in this correct mean. While Confucius laid emphasis upon the free expression of genuine nature and feelings, he at the same time said that ' these must be restrained by *li* ' (*Lun Yü*, I, 12). His concept of the function of *li* here seems to be equivalent to what I have just stated, although he does not explain it clearly.

Coming to Mencius, we find the statement : " The actuality of *jen* lies in serving one's parents ; the actuality of *i* lies in obeying one's eldest brother ; . . . . the actuality of *li* lies in the regulation and refinement of these two things " (*Mencius*, IVa, 27). Thus for Mencius also, regulation and refinement are the two functions of *li*. Mencius, however, holds the belief that man is born with a mind capable of yielding to others, and so *li* for him mean nothing more than the manifestation of this mind in concrete terms. Therefore he, like Confucius, does not say a great deal about the meaning of *li*.

Hsün Tzŭ, on the contrary, believed that man's nature is evil, and that all men have desires which, if unrestrained, will lead to mutual conflict and confusion. This is why, as he says, " The early kings established *li* and standards of justice (*i*) to set limits to this confusion" (*Hsün-tzŭ*, p. 213). For Hsün Tzŭ, however, the *li* remain solely a means to prevent conflict between man and man, and he makes no mention of how they may be also used to harmonize the conflicting emotions within the individual. The *Li Chi* (ch. 2), on the other hand, definitely expresses this latter idea when it says that the *li* serve as a restraining mould, preventing conflict between the feeling of concern for one's parents, and the desire to obtain food, drink and pleasure for oneself. Thus with Hsün Tzŭ we already find the theory of *li* being treated in considerable detail; in the quotations from the *Li Chi* just given, the Confucians finally develop a complete theory to explain their meaning and function.

There are still other passages in the *Li Chi* in which the *li* are described as a mould for defining and maintaining the various gradations of human society. Chapter I says :

" The *li* are that whereby are determined (the observances toward) close and far relatives, points which may cause suspicion or doubt are settled, similarity and difference are differentiated, and right and wrong are made clear " (XXVII, 63). And Chapter XXIV :

" Of all things by which the people live, the *li* are the greatest. Without them, there would be no means of regulating the services rendered to the spirits of Heaven and Earth; there would be no means of distinguishing the positions of ruler and subject, superior and inferior, old and young; and no means of keeping separate the relations between man and woman, father and son, elder and younger brother, and of conducting the intercourse between contracting families in a marriage, and the frequency (of the reciprocities between friends) or their infrequency (XXVIII, 261).

The *li* thus maintain the social gradations that are necessary if there is to be no conflict between man and man.

Once we comprehend the basic principle of *li*, we can understand that in their concrete manifestations they can vary according to individual circumstances, and so are not something forever fixed. Chapter VII says :

" Therefore the Sage-kings formed the lever of the standards of justice (*i*) and the ordering of the *li*, so as to regulate human feelings with them. Therefore human feelings were the field of the Sage-kings. They fashioned the *li* to plough it. They set forth standards of justice with which to plant it. They instituted learning to weed it. They made human-heartedness (*jen*) the fundamental object by which to gather all its fruits, and they employed music to give repose. Thus the *li* are the embodied expression of what is right (*i* 義). If there are rites (*li*) which, although not among those of the early kings, stand the test of being judged by the standard of what is right, they may be adopted on this ground of being right " (XXVII, 389-390). Chapter VIII says :

" In considering the *li*, their timeliness should be the great consideration . . . . Yao's resignation of the throne to Shun, and Shun's to Yü ; T'ang's dethronement of Chieh, and the overthrow of Chou by King Wu : these are all to be judged according to their time " (XXVII, 396). Chapter XVII :

" The times of the Five Emperors were different, and therefore they did not each adopt the music of his predecessor. The Three Kings belonged to different ages, and so they did not each follow the *li* of their predecessor " (XXVIII, 102). Chapter IX :

" That which is most important in ceremonies (*li*) is to understand the meaning behind them. While missing the meaning, the number of things and observances in them may still be correctly exhibited, for this is the business of the officers of prayer and recording. Hence these may all be exhibited, while the meaning remains difficult to know. The knowledge of their meaning and the reverent maintenance of it is the way whereby the Son of Heaven secures good government for the empire " (XXVII, 439).

Once the real principles lying behind the *li* are understood, they may be formulated ' in accordance with human feelings, to act as regulations and refinements of them.' The fundamental principles of the *li* remain unchanged, but their outward concrete manifestations in ' the number of things and observances ' ever change with the times.

In one of the chapters of the *Li Chi* of the elder Tai, a comparison is made between *li* and law :

" The knowledge of all men lies in being able to witness the past, but not the future. The *li* serve to put interdictions in advance on what is about to take place, while law makes interdictions on what has already occurred. Hence the use of law may be easily perceived, while it is difficult to know what the *li* will bring about. Thus in rewarding to encourage goodness, and punishing to curb evil, the early kings stood squarely on this (principle), firm as metal or stone ; they practised it sincerely, following it with a regularity like that of the four seasons ; they rested in its operation as impartially as Heaven and Earth. How could this be considered as of no use ? But why did they speak about the *li* ? Because they are valuable for cutting off evil before it has sprouted, and evoking respectfulness from the smallest beginnings, making the people daily move toward goodness and put sin at a distance, without themselves realizing it. Confucius has said : ' In hearing lawsuits, I am no better than other men, but surely the great thing is to bring about that there are no lawsuits ' (*Lun Yü*, XII, 13). This is what he meant . . . .

"When there is government through *li* and standards of justice (*i*), *li* and justice are accumulated ; when it is by punishments and penalties, there is an accumulation of these. When these last are accumulated, the people feel resentment and revolt. When *li* and standards of justice are accumulated, the people are in a state of harmony and feel affection. Thus rulers of all periods have been alike in desiring that the people be good, but the methods they have used to bring about such goodness have differed. Some have led them with virtuous teachings, while others have driven them by laws and commands. When they are led with virtuous teachings, these virtuous teachings are practised and the people are peaceful and contented. When they are driven by laws and commands, the laws and commands go to extremes and the people are sad and pitiful. The feelings of sadness or contentment are responsible respectively for calamity or blessing " (*chüan* 2, pp. 1-2).[1]

It is not always true that the *li* serve to prevent what has not yet happened, and that law condemns or punishes what has already been committed. Yet it is a fact that what *li* regulate is for the most part positive, whereas what law regulates is largely negative. Law moreover, is backed up by the state rewards and punishments, whereas the *li* do not need to depend on such support.

2—General Principles underlying Music

Though music, for Confucius, was of great importance, he said nothing about its general underlying principles, as to its origin and relation to human life. These points are first discussed in detail in the section on music in the *Hsün-tzŭ* (ch. 20), and in the *Yüeh Chi* 樂 記 (Record of Music) which forms Chapter XVII of the *Li Chi*. The *Hsün-tzŭ* says :

"Now music is the expression of joy.[2] This is something which human feelings make unavoidable. For man cannot be

---

[1] This passage is derived from the *Lun Shih Cheng Su*, by Chia I (201-169 B.C.).

[2] There is a play on words here. The words ' music ' and ' joy,' though pronounced differently in Chinese, are both designated by the same character, 樂. This indicates the deep underlying affinity existing between the two since very early times, according to Chinese thought.—Tr.

without joy.   And when there is joy, it must be expressed in sound and given embodiment through movement and repose.   In a man's conduct, his sounds, movements and pauses are expressive of all the changes in his mood.   Hence man cannot be without joy, and when there is joy, it must have a physical embodiment.   When this embodiment does not conform to right principles, there will be disorder.   The early kings hated this disorder, and so they established the music of the *Ya* and *Sung* to guide it.[1]   They caused its music to be joyful and not to degenerate, and its beauty to be distinct and not limited.   They caused it in its indirect and direct appeals, its complexness and simplicity, its frugality and richness, its rests and notes, to stir up the goodness in men's minds and to prevent evil feelings from gaining any foothold.   This is the manner in which the early kings established music " (pp. 247-248).

The *Li Chi* (ch. 17) says :

" The production of all musical sounds (of man) comes forth from the human mind.   The movements of the human mind are activated by external things.   Being acted upon by external things, it moves, and this movement finds physical embodiment in sound. . . .

" Hence when the mind is moved to sorrow, the sound is sharp and fading away.   When it is moved to pleasure, the sound is slow and gentle.   When it is moved to joy, the sound is exclamatory and scatters.   When it is moved to anger, the sound is coarse and fierce.   When it is moved to reverence, the sound is straightforward, with an indication of humbleness.   When it is moved to love, the sound is harmonious and soft.   These six sounds are not of man's nature, but arise only after there has been stimulation by external things.   Therefore the early kings were watchful in regard to what would act as a stimulus " (XXVIII, 92-93).

The function of music, according to these passages, lies in regulating human emotions, and inducing them to be expressed in accordance with right principles, or in other words, within the proper mean.   *Li* regulate human desires, while music regulates human emotions.   The purpose of both is to act as a regulator so that man will keep to the mean.   The same chapter continues :

" Therefore the early kings, when they instituted *li* and music, did not do so to gain full satisfaction for the desires of the mouth, stomach, ears and eyes.   But they intended to teach the people to regulate their likes and dislikes, and to turn them back to the normal course of humanity.   To be quiescent at birth : this is man's natural (literally, ' heavenly ') nature.   To move when acted upon by external objects : this is the desire of his nature. . . .   When man is acted upon by external things without end, and no regulation is set to his likes and dislikes, he becomes changed through the encounter

---

[1] These are two of the divisions in the *Shih Ching* (Book of Odes).—TR.

with any external object.   To be so changed by things is to
have the natural principle (*t'ien li* 天 理) within him extinguished,
and to give the utmost indulgence to his human desires.   With
this there comes the rebellious and deceitful heart, with its licentious
and wild disorder. . . .   This is the way to great disorder.   Therefore
the early kings instituted *li* and music to regulate human conduct "
(XXVIII, 96-97).

Describing the efficacy of both *li* and music, the chapter goes on :
" The *li* regulate people's minds.   Music harmonizes their sounds.
Government serves to carry this out, and punishments to guard
against its violation.   *Li*, music, punishments and government :
when these four have full play without irregularity or collision, the
Kingly Way is complete.

" Music makes for common union.   The *li* make for difference
and distinction.   From common union comes mutual affection ;
from difference, mutual respect.   Where music prevails, we find a
weak coalescence ; where *li* prevail, a tendency to separation.   It
is the business of the two to harmonize people's feelings and give
elegance to their outward manifestations. . . .

" Music comes from within ; *li* act from without.   Coming
from within, music produces the serenity (of the mind).   Acting
from without, *li* produce the finished elegance (of manner).   Great
music must be easy.   Great *li* must be simple.   Let music achieve
its full results, and there will be no resentments.   Let *li* achieve their
full results, and there will be no contentions.   The reason why bow-
ings and courtesies could set the world in order is that there are
music and *li* " (XXVIII, 97-99).

The government advocated by the Confucians is one based on
li and music, in which administrative machinery and punishments
exist only to maintain them.   The same chapter goes on to adduce
a metaphysical basis for *li* and music :

" Heaven is high, Earth is low ; all things are scattered between
them in their individual particularities ; the *li* were instituted
in accordance with these.   These things flow forth unceasingly,
and by their united action production and change ensue ; music
arose in accordance with this.   Growth in spring and maturing
in summer : these are like the quality of human-heartedness (*jen*).
Harvesting in autumn and storing in winter : these are like righteousness (*i*).   Human-heartedness is akin to music, and righteousness is
akin to *li*. . . .

" Heaven is honorable, Earth is lowly, and likewise the
positions of ruler and subject were both made definite.   The depths
and heights (of Earth) having been laid forth, noble and low position
were determined.   Movement and repose have their constant
regularities, and the small and the big are particularized.   Animals
are grouped according to their kind, and plants are divided according

to their family.   Thus the natures and endowments of things are not
the same.   In Heaven they take (ethereal) forms ; on Earth they
acquire physical bodies.   This being so, the *li* represent the distinctions of Heaven and Earth.

" The breath of Earth ascends on high, and that of Heaven
descends below.   The *yin* and the *yang* act upon one another, and
the *ch'ien* 乾 and the *k'un* 坤 agitate each other.¹   They are drummed
on by thunder, excited by wind and rain, moved by the four seasons,
warmed by the sun and moon, and all the processes of change and
growth vigorously proceed.   This being so, music represents the
harmony of Heaven and Earth.

" Transformations that are not timely produce nothing, and if no
distinction existed between man and woman, disorder would arise :
such is the nature of Heaven and Earth.

" When we think of *li* and music, how they reach the height of
Heaven and embrace the Earth ; move in the *yin* and *yang*, and establish
contact with divine beings—we must acknowledge their height as the
highest, their reach as the farthest, their depth as the deepest, and
their breadth as the broadest.

" Music appeared in the Great Beginning (*t'ai shih* 太 始), and
the *li* took their place on the completion of things.   What manifests
itself without ceasing is Heaven.   What manifests itself without
stirring is Earth.   Movement and quiescence sum up all between
Heaven and Earth.   And so the Sages would simply speak about *li*
and music" (XXVIII, 102-105).

According to these words, the universe from its beginning has
possessed a natural order or harmony, of which *li* and music are the
concrete exemplifications.

3—THEORY OF MOURNING RITES

I have already pointed out how Hsün Tzŭ said that *li* on the
one hand serves to regulate desire, and on the other to give refinement
to human feelings.²   This refinement of human feelings, according to
what the *Hsün-tzŭ* and *Li Chi* say, can most easily be observed in
the mourning rites, which I shall now discuss.

Psychologists tell us that our minds are divided into intellect
and emotion.   When someone close to us dies, our intellect realizes
that the dead person cannot be recalled to life, and that the doctrine
of personal immortality is something unprovable, uncertain and
difficult to give credence to.   Our emotional self, nevertheless,
hopes at the same time that the dead one may return to life, and that
his soul will not perish.   If, at this point, we were to follow only our

---

¹ These are other terms used to designate the male and female forces of the universe.
See next ch., pp. 382 f.—Tr.
² *Cf.* ch. 12, sect. 7, pp. 297-299.

intellect, we might well deal with the dead in the way described in the *Lieh-tzŭ's* chapter on Yang Chu : " They may burn my body, or cast it into deep water, or bury it, or leave it unburied, or throw it wrapped in a mat into a ditch " (p. 44). All rites for the dead, according to such a viewpoint, become equally meaningless. If we are to follow only the emotional aspect of our minds, however, we must be prepared to accept all kinds of superstition as true, and to refuse to recognize judgments of the intellect. This is what religion tends toward.

The *Hsün-tzŭ* and the *Li Chi*, in discussing this problem, hold to a midway course between these two alternatives, and take both intellect and emotion into consideration. The sacrificial and mourning rites described by them are, according to their explanations, poetical rather than religious, and their attitude toward the dead is likewise poetical rather than religious.[1]

In the West, Santayana has urged that religion should discard superstition and dogma and become like poetry. But a study of what the *Hsün-tzŭ* and *Li Chi* say about mourning and sacrificial rites shows us that this transformation of religion to poetry was already advocated by them. Originally, mourning and sacrificial rites were religious ceremonies, containing considerable superstition and dogma. But the *Hsün-tzŭ* and *Li Chi*, following the Confucian method of creating through transmitting, purified and re-interpreted these rites, thus changing them from religion into poetry. In ancient times, for example, utensils were given to the dead because of a belief in the immortality of the soul, which, people supposed, could make use of them. In later times, however, the Confucians gave a new interpretation to these so-called ' spiritual utensils ' (*ming ch'i* 明 器). The *Li Chi* (ch. 2) says :

" In dealing with the dead, if we treat them as if they were entirely dead, that would show lack of affection and should not be done ; or, if we treat them as if they were entirely alive, that would show lack of wisdom and should not be done. On this account the vessels of bamboo (used for burial with the dead) are not fit for actual use ; those of earthenware cannot be used to wash in ; those of wood are incapable of being carved ; the lutes are strung, but not evenly ; the reed-pipes are complete, but not in tune ; the bells and musical

---

[1] Poetry can interpret the universe and all things according to human feelings ; it can accord itself with man's emotions ; can invest reality with human imagination ; and is allowed to say even what men know to be untrue. Here is the fundamental difference between poetry and prose, art and science. Though poetry and art do not represent reality, however, they at the same time realize that they do not do so. Therefore although they are to a large degree divorced from intellect and dependent upon the emotions, they still do not conflict with intellect. Though themselves most unscientific, they do not conflict with science. We can gain emotional satisfaction from poetry and art, and at the same time not be prevented from intellectual development.

Religion is also a manifestation of emotion, but differs from poetry and art in that it holds visions based on the emotions to be actual truths, and hence refuses to recognize intellectual judgments. It is in this that it becomes dogmatic.

stones are there, but have no stands. They are called 'spiritual utensils' (*ming ch'i*), indicating that the dead are to be treated like spirits" (XXVII, 148). Again :

"He who made the 'spiritual utensils' knew the principle underlying the mourning rites. They are things complete (to all appearance), yet cannot be used" (XXVII, 172-173).

To look at the dead from an exclusively intellectual viewpoint, and so decide that they have no consciousness, would be to lack affection. To look at them from an exclusively emotional viewpoint, and so decide that they do have consciousness, would be to lack wisdom. Men steer a course between these two alternatives by making utensils that are complete in form, yet cannot actually be used. They are made complete in form with the wish that they *might* be used by the dead, and in order thus to satisfy men's emotional hopes. But they are made so that they cannot actually be used, because our intellect tells us that the dead cannot utilize them. In discussing the mourning and sacrificial rites, the *Hsün-tzŭ* and *Li Chi* both argue entirely from a subjective and emotional stand, for intellectually and objectively we certainly realize that the dead are quite dead, and that therefore there is no need to speak further of them. I shall quote here again from these two works to illustrate this point. The *Li Chi* (ch. 2) says :

"The rites of mourning are the extreme expression of grief and sorrow. The regulation of that grief in accordance with the changes (of time and feeling) was made by Superior Men who were mindful of those to whom they owe their being.

"The calling back (of the soul) is the most complete expression of love, and the mental state for it is that of prayer . . . .¹

"Filling the mouth (of the dead) with uncooked rice and cowry shells arises from a feeling which cannot bear that it should be empty. The idea is not that of giving food, but of serving beautiful things (to the dead).

"The inscription (bearing the name of the dead) is an illustrious banner. Because the dead can no longer be recognized, (the son) maintains that flag, as a mark of identification. Because of his love for him the son makes this record. His reverence for him finds in these its utmost expression . . . .

"The offerings to the unburied dead are placed in plain unornamented vessels, because the hearts of the living are full of unaffected sorrow. In the sacrifices (subsequent to the burial), the mourner does his very utmost to express his devotion. How does he know that the spirit will enjoy his offerings ? He is guided only by his pure and reverent heart . . . ." (XXVII, 167-169).

---

¹ This ceremony of calling back the soul after death, and asking it to re-enter the body, has existed until modern times in China.—Tr.

The mourner does his utmost to express his devotion in order to gain emotional satisfaction for himself, without considering whether the spirit actually accepts his offering or not. In so doing, he is not allowing his intellect to be confused by his emotions.

The *Li Chi* (ch. 32) says about the custom of not dressing the corpse until three days after the death :

" Someone asked : ' Why does the dressing not commence till three days after death ? ' The reply was : ' When his parent is dead, the filial son is sad and sorrowful, and his mind is full of trouble. He crawls about and bewails his loss, as if the dead might come back to life. How could the dead be taken away from him and be dressed ? Therefore, when it is said that the dressing does not begin till after three days, the meaning is that he is waiting during that time to see if (his parent) will come back to life. When after three days there is no such return, there is indeed no life, and the heart of the filial son is still more downcast. Moreover (during this time) the means of the family can be calculated, and the necessary clothes can be provided and made accordingly ; the relatives who live afar can also arrive. Therefore the Sages have decided in this case that three days should be allowed, and the rule has been made accordingly ' " (XXVIII, 377-378).

About the burial, which takes place only after three months, Chapter II says :

" Tzŭ Ssŭ said : ' On the third day of mourning, when the body is put into the coffin, (a son) should exercise sincerity and good faith in regard to everything that is placed with it, so as to have no cause for regret. In the third month, when the body is interred, he should do the same with regard to everything that is placed with the coffin in the grave, and for the same reason ' " (XXVII, 124).

The *Hsün-tzŭ* says (ch. 19) :

" The funeral should not take place more than seventy or less than fifty days after (the death). Why is this ? It is so that the distant may come ; that everything may be obtained ; that all matters may be attended to. The loyalty (of the son) reaches the utmost, the ceremonial regulations are complete, and the ceremonial ornament is perfect. Then on the first of the month they divine the burial place, and on the last of the month they divine the day, and then bury the dead " (p. 231).

The resumption of mourning after the burial is described in the *Li Chi* (ch. 32) :

" When (the mourners) go, accompanying the coffin (to the grave), they look forward, with an expression of eagerness, as if they were following someone and unable to catch up to him. When returning to bemoan (the departed), they look disconcerted, as if seeking someone whom they cannot find. Hence, when escorting (the coffin), they appear full of affectionate desire ; when returning, they appear full of perplexity. They have sought (the deceased) and cannot find him; they enter the gate, and do not see him; they go up to the hall, and still do not see him. He is gone! He is dead! They will never see him more! Therefore they wail, weep, beat their breasts, and leap, giving full vent to their sorrow before ceasing. Their minds are disappointed, pained, fluttered and indignant. They can do nothing more with their wills; they can do nothing but continue to be sad. In presenting sacrifice in the ancestral temple, (the son) offers it (to the deceased) in his disembodied state, hoping that his spirit will peradventure return." (XXVIII, 376-377).

Though this is done with the emotional hope that the dead might return, the term ' peradventure ' (*chiao hsing* 徼 幸) shows that even in this hope, the mourner is not being deceived by his emotions.

After the burial, there still remain three years of mourning for the death of a parent, of which the *Li Chi* (ch. 35) says :

" All living creatures between Heaven and Earth, being endowed with blood and breath, must have a certain amount of knowledge. Possessing that amount of knowledge, there is not one of them but knows to love its kind. Take the larger birds and beasts. When one of them has lost its mate, after a month or a season it is sure to return and wander around the old haunts. It turns round and round, utters its cries, now moves, now stops, and looks perplexed and uncertain in its movements, before it can leave the place. Even the smaller birds, such as swallows and sparrows, chatter and cry for a little before they can leave the place. But among all creatures that have blood and breath, there is none which has intelligence like man. Hence the feeling of man toward his parent remains unexhausted even till death.

" Will anyone follow the example of those men who are under the influence of their depraved lusts? With such a man, when a parent dies in the morning, he will forget him by evening. But if we follow the course of such men, we shall be not even equal to the birds and beasts. How could we then live with our kindred and not fall into all disorders?

" Shall we then follow the example of the cultivated Superior Man? Then the twenty-five months, after which the three years ' mourning comes to an end, will seem to pass like a carriage with four horses whirled past a crack (in a wall).[1] And if we continue to indulge this feeling, it will prove to be inexhaustible.

" Therefore the early kings determined the proper medium for mourning, and appointed its definite limits. As soon as it was sufficient for the beautified expression of the feeling, it was to be laid aside." [2]

---

[1] The three-year mourning period actually terminated at the beginning of the third year, i.e., after the twenty-fifth month.—Tr.

[2] XXVIII, 392-394. *Cf.* also *Hsün-tzŭ*, pp. 240-241.

All these quotations argue strictly from a subjective and emotional viewpoint, for the fundamental meaning of the mourning rites is simply to give satisfaction to the feelings.

Hsün Tzŭ sums up the mourning rites as follows :

" The *li* consist in being careful about the treatment of life and death. Life is the beginning of man. Death is the end of man. When the end and beginning are both good, the way of humanity is complete. Hence the Superior Man respects the beginning and venerates the end. To make the end and beginning uniform is the practice of the Superior Man, and is that in which lies the beauty of *li* and standards of justice (*i*). For to pay over-attention to the living and belittle the dead would be to respect them when they have knowledge and disrespect them when they have not . . . .

" The way of death is this : once dead, a person cannot return again. (It is in realizing this that) the minister most completely fulfils the honor due to his ruler, and the son the honor to his parents.

" Funeral rites are for the living to give beautified ceremonial to the dead ; to send off the dead as if they were living ; to render the same service to the dead as to the living ; to the absent as to the present ; and to make the end be the same as the beginning . . . . .

" Articles used in life are prepared so as to be put into the grave, as if (the deceased) were only moving house. Only a few things are taken, not all of them. They are to give the appearance, but are not for practical use . . . . Hence the things (such as were used) in life are adorned, but not completed, and the ' spiritual utensils ' are for appearance but not use . . . .

" Hence the funeral rites are for no other purpose than to make clear the meaning of death and life, to send off the dead with sorrow and reverence, and when the end comes, to prepare for storing the body away . . . . Service to the living is beautifying their beginning ; sending off the dead is beautifying their end. When the end and the beginning are both attended to, the service of the filial son is ended and the way of the Sage is completed. Slighting the dead and over-emphasizing the living is the way of Mo (Tzŭ). Slighting the living and over-attention to the dead is the way of superstition. Killing the living to send off the dead is murder.[1] The method and manner of *li* and standards of justice (*i*) is to send off the dead as if they were alive, so that in death and life, the end and the beginning, there is nothing that is not appropriate and good. The Confucian does this " (*Hsün-tzŭ*, pp. 227-228, 235-239).

Thus the clothing, coffin, etc., are all for the purpose of sending off the deceased as if he were alive. Intellectually we know that what

---

[1] i.e., through human sacrifice, a practice often condemned, but long followed, especially in the semi-barbaric state of Ch'in.—Tr.

is dead is dead, yet emotionally we still hope that the dead one may be still living. To rely at this stage entirely upon intellect would be to show lack of affection, while to depend entirely upon the emotions would be to show lack of wisdom. Hence the true way to maintain a grip upon both the intellect and the emotions, upon affection and wisdom, is to treat the dead as if they were living. In establishing these rites, the Sages were not acting arbitrarily, as is pointed out by the Li Chi (ch. 32) :

" Such is the mind of the filial son, the real expression of human feeling, the true course of li and standards of justice (i). It is not something that descends from Heaven, nor does it come out of the Earth. It is simply the expression of human feelings " (XXVIII, 379).

4—THEORY OF SACRIFICIAL RITES

The preceding section has described the theories of the Hsün-tzŭ and Li Chi on funeral rites. Their theories on sacrificial ceremonial are also based wholly on a subjective and emotional viewpoint. Sacrifices, they assert, like mourning rites, serve simply to give satisfaction to the emotions. Thus the Li Chi (ch. 21) says :

" Of all the ways for keeping men in good order, there is none more important than li. The li are of five kinds, and none of these is more important than sacrifice.

" Now the idea of sacrifice is not something that comes from without. It issues from within, being born in the heart. When the heart is deeply moved, expression is given to it in ceremonies (li), for which reason only men of virtue can completely reach the meaning of the sacrifices.

" The sacrifices of such men have their own blessing ; not indeed what the world calls blessing, for blessing here means perfection. Perfection is the name given to the complete and natural discharge of all duties. When nothing is left incomplete or improperly discharged, this is called perfection. It means that internally everything has been done that should be done, and externally everything is performed according to the proper method . . . .

" Therefore the virtuous man, when he sacrifices, exercises all sincerity and good faith, with all conscientiousness and reverence. He makes offerings of things, accompanies them with ceremonies, employs the soothing influence of music, and does everything suitable according to the season. Thus intelligently does he offer his sacrifices, without seeking for any gain therefrom. Such is the heart of a filial son . . . .

" Whatever Heaven produces, whatever Earth matures : all are exhibited in the greatest abundance. Externally all things are there, and internally there is the utmost effort of the will : such is the true spirit in sacrificing " (XXVIII, 236-238).

Here we find ' the utmost effort of the will ' being made ' without seeking for any gain therefrom.' That is, the attention is directed solely toward the sacrifice itself, and not toward the object to which the sacrifice is directed. The *Hsün-tzǔ* (ch. 19) says :

" Sacrificial rites are the expression of man's affectionate longings. They represent the height of altruism, faithfulness, love and reverence. They represent the completion of propriety and refinement. If there were no Sages, no one could understand this. The Sage plainly understands it ; the scholar and Superior Man accordingly perform it ; the official observes it ; and among the people it becomes an established custom. Among Superior Men it is considered to be a human practice ; among the common people it is considered to be a serving of the spirits . . . .

" Divination, finding the lucky days, fasting, cleaning the temple, spreading out tables and mats, offering animals and grain, praying for blessings (from the deceased) as if the deceased enjoyed the sacrifice ; selecting the offerings and sacrificing them as if the deceased tasted them ; offering the three-legged winecup without washing it ; for the one who sacrifices to have a wine-flask ready as if the deceased drank from his goblet ; when the guests leave, for the host to bow them off, change into his mourning clothes and take up his position and cry, as if the spirit of the departed had left : with such sorrow and reverence one serves the dead as one serves the living, and serves the departed as one serves those who are present. What is served has neither substance nor shadow, yet this is the completion of refinement " (pp. 244-246).

Because the sacrificer has emotions of affectionate longing, he performs the sacrifice. Yet the object toward which his sacrifice is directed ' has neither substance nor shadow,' and the sacrifice is performed simply ' *as if* the deceased enjoyed the sacrifice ' and ' *as if* the deceased drank from his goblet.' The sacrificer is careful in performing the ceremony, while at the same time he realizes that its object lacks actual reality ; ' yet this is the completion of refinement.' In this way the sacrifice becomes something poetical.

The *Li Chi* (ch. 21) describes in further detail the psychological state of the sacrificer :

" The severest vigil and purification is maintained and practised in the inner self, while a looser vigil is maintained externally. During the days of such vigil, the mourner thinks of the departed, how and where he sat, how he smiled and spoke, what were his aims and views, what he delighted in, and what he desired and enjoyed. By the third day he will perceive the meaning of such exercise.

" On the day of sacrifice, when he enters the apartment (of the temple), he will seem to see (the deceased) in the place (where his spirit-tablet is). After he has moved about (to perform his operations), and is leaving by the door, he will be arrested by seeming to hear the sound of his movements, and will sigh as he seems to hear the sound of his sighing . . . .

" It is only the Sage who can sacrifice to God (*Ti*), and only the filial son who can sacrifice to his parents. Sacrifice is a turning toward. (The sacrificer) turns (his thoughts toward the propitiated), only after which can he offer his sacrifice . . . . How well sustained is his reverence ! How complete is the expression of his faithfulness ! How earnest is his wish that the departed should enjoy the service ! . . . . .

" Still and grave, absorbed in what he is doing, he will seem to be unable to sustain the burden, and in danger of letting it fall. In this his heart reaches the height of filial piety and reverence . . . . Is not his the highest filial reverence ? . . . . Thus he manifests his mind and thought, and in his lost abstraction of mind seeks to commune with the dead in their spiritual state, if peradventure they could enjoy his offerings, if peradventure they could indeed do so. This is the aim of the filial son " (XXVIII, 210-212, 214).

Men suppose to-day that a person who sees a spirit has been deluded by his own imagination. According to this passage, however, sacrifice can advantageously make use of such hallucinations, so that by thinking of the dead in lost abstraction, a person may come to see the spirit. To gain communion with the dead through abstraction in this way, hoping that ' *peradventure* they could enjoy his offerings,' is nothing more than to give satisfaction to the emotions of 'affectionate longings.' Hence by the Superior Man, sacrifice is considered to be a ' human practice,' while among the common people it is regarded as a ' serving of the spirits.'

Hsün Tzǔ held this poetical attitude not only toward ancestral sacrifice, but toward all other kinds of sacrifice as well. He says in his Chapter XVII :

" If people pray for rain and get rain, why is that ? I answer : There is no other reason for it. It is simply as if there had been no prayer for rain, and it had nevertheless rained. When people save the sun or moon from being eaten (in an eclipse), or when they pray for rain in a drought, or when they decide an important affair only after divination, this is not because they think in this way they will get what they want, but only to make a fine appearance. Hence the Superior Man looks upon it as a fine gloss put over the matter, while the common people consider it supernatural. He who thinks it is a gloss is fortunate ; he who thinks it is supernatural is unfortunate " (pp. 181-182).

Prayer for rain serves to express one's feeling of anxiety, while the use of divination to decide great affairs serves to express one's earnestness. These are instances of putting a beautiful gloss over things. But to regard these things as supernatural is to fall into superstition, with all its disastrous consequences.

Sacrifice to the ancestors is done, on the one hand, because we possess emotions of 'affectionate longings,' but on the other it is done to demonstrate our gratitude for our parents' kindness. Hsün Tzŭ says (ch. 19) :

" The *li* are rooted in three things :   Heaven and Earth are the origin of life ; our ancestors are the origin of our group ; our rulers and teachers are the origin of ordered government.   Without Heaven and Earth, how could there be life ?   Without our early ancestors, from what could we have sprung ?   Without rulers and teachers, how could there be ordered government ?   If one of these three were lacking, men would be without peace.   Hence the rites (*li*) are to serve Heaven above and Earth below, honor our ancestors, and make eminent our rulers and teachers.   These are the three important things about the rites " (pp. 219-220).   And the *Li Chi* (ch. 9) says :

" All things originate from Heaven ; man originates from his ancestors.   This is the reason why Ch'i'[1] was associated with *Shang Ti* (in the suburban sacrifice).   This sacrifice in the suburbs (*chiao chi* 郊 祭) is to express gratitude toward the originators and recall the beginnings " (XXVII, 430-431).

Sacrifices made to other supernatural beings, like those to the ancestors, also serve to express gratitude to the originators of things. The same chapter continues :

" The great *cha* 蜡 sacrifice of the Son of Heaven consists of eight (sacrifices) . . . . (The word) *cha* expresses the idea of searching out. In the twelfth month of the year all sorts of (harvested) things are brought together, (and those who engendered them) are sought out and given them in offering.

" In the *cha* sacrifice, the principle one (sacrificed to) is the Father of Husbandry.   Offerings are also presented to (ancient) superintendents of husbandry, and to (the discoverers of) the various grains, to express thanks for the crops that have been reaped.

" The principle of the ancient wise men was that when things are given for our service, it is necessary to make some return for them. Cats are welcomed because they devour the field rats, and tigers are welcomed because they devour the boars of the fields.   These are welcomed and sacrificed to.   Offerings are also made to (the ancient inventors of) the dykes and water-channels.   (These are all) provisions for husbandry . . . . In the *cha* are expressed the highest sentiments of goodness and righteousness " (XXVII, 431-432).   Again (ch. 20) :

" According to the institutes of the Sage-kings about sacrifices, sacrifice should be offered to those who gave laws to the people ; to those who have labored unto death in the discharge of their duties ; to those who through laborious toil have strengthened the state ; to those who have succeeded in staving off great calamities ; and to those who have warded off great evils.

---

[1] The supposed ancestor of the Chou dynasty.—Tr.

" Such were the following : Nung, the son of the Lord of Li-shan, who possessed the empire and showed how to cultivate all the cereals ;[1] Ch'i, (progenitor) of Chou, who continued his work after the decay of the Hsia dynasty, and so was sacrificed to under the name of Chi ; Hou T'u, a son of the line of Kung Kung that swayed the nine provinces, who was able to reduce them all to order, and was sacrificed to as the spirit of the soil ; . . . . T'ang, who ruled the people with a benignity and rid them of their oppressor; and Kings Wen, who ruled by peace, and Wu, who achieved through war, who delivered the people from their afflictions. All these rendered distinguished services to the people.

" As to the sun and moon, the stars and constellations, the people look up to them. As to mountains, forests, streams, valleys and hills, these supply them with the materials for use which they require. Only men and things of this character are admitted into the sacrificial canon " (X X V I I I, 207-209).

This is identical with what Comte calls the ' religion of humanity.' It is based on sacrifices performed to express gratitude to men who have done great deeds in the past. In Chinese society of the old type, the members of each guild worship the divinity of that guild. Thus carpenters worship Lu Pan and wine brewers Ko Hsien. The significance is, that every handicraft has had its inventor, and that those who in later times make their living through this handicraft, when they think of its origin and wish to express gratitude, regard this inventor as a divine intelligence, and so sacrifice to him. Heaven and Earth, stars, constellations, birds, beasts, trees, etc., are likewise sacrificed to out of feelings of gratitude. This practice, while it may have originated from animism, has, because of the interpretation given it by the Confucian school, become poetical rather than religious.

Among the Confucians there was one group who especially advocated this idea of expressing gratitude because they hoped thus to increase the virtue of the people. Tseng Tzŭ, Confucius's disciple, said :

" Solicitude on the decease of parents, and the pursuit of them (with sacrifical offerings) for long after, would cause an abundant restoration of the people's morals " (*Lun Yü*, I, 9). And the *Li Chi* of the elder Tai says :

" Funeral and sacrificial rites serve to inculcate benevolence and love. By attaining to a feeling of love one can perform the rites of mourning and sacrifice, while the perpetuation of the sacrifices of spring and autumn serves to express the longing of the mind. Now sacrifice consists in making offerings. When there is a longing and a making of offerings to the dead, how much more will there be so to the living ! Therefore it is said that when the mourning and sacrificial rites are clearly understood, the people are filial " (*chüan* 8, p. 6).

---

[1] This is the Divine Farmer, Shen Nung, the supposed founder of agriculture.—Tr.

If one returns one's gratitude to the unknowing dead, how much more should one do so to the conscious living ! If men would not contend with one another, but would do good turns to each other, there would be universal peace.   Such a utilitarian doctrine, however, was not one shared by most Confucians.

Communal sacrifice, moreover, offers an opportunity to the people for rest and recreation.   The *Li Chi* (ch. 9), discussing the *cha* sacrifice, says :

" They sacrifice, wearing yellow robes and yellow caps.   It is a time of rest for the field labourers. . . . All the harvest having been gathered in by the time of the *cha*, the people have nothing to do but rest, and therefore after the *cha*, the wise ruler does not commence any new work " (XXVII, 433-434).

Chapter XVIII says :

" Tzŭ Kung having gone to see the *cha* sacrifice, Confucius said : ' Did it give you pleasure ? ' He replied : ' The people of the whole state appeared to be mad.   I do not know in what I could find pleasure.'   The Master said : ' For their hundred days' labor in the field, (the husbandmen) receive this one holiday.   This is what you do not understand.   If a bow were always drawn and never relaxed, even Kings Wen and Wu could not use it.   Nor did they leave it always relaxed and never drawn.   To keep it now strung and now unstrung was the way of Wen and Wu ' " (XXVIII, 167).

Looked at from this viewpoint, sacrifice becomes to a still greater degree poetic, rather than religious.

5—THEORY OF MARRIAGE RITES

In the preceding sections I have presented the theories on mourning and sacrificial rites found in the *Hsün-tzŭ* and *Li Chi*. There is still one point, however, which though not clearly discussed in the *Li Chi*, may nevertheless be inferred from its theories on mourning and sacrificial rites, and so will be discussed here.

The quotations given above show that at least some of the Confucians did not believe in the immortality of the soul after death.   Yet though they could not recognize personal immortality, death could still not be regarded by them as absolute extinction. In the first place, the descendants of a man constitute a portion of his body which is perpetuated, and hence a man who has descendants does not actually die.   No proof is necessary to show that this is true of all living creatures.   Secondly, the fact that there has been a certain individual who lived in a certain place at a certain time, is a definite fact in the universe which cannot in any way be wiped out.   Anything that has once existed, cannot be made to have been non-existent.   In this respect, then, an ordinary person who lived contemporary with Confucius, cannot be said to have been non-existent any more than could Confucius. The difference lies only in the fact that the one person is known to the world, whereas the other has been forgotten. The same holds true of persons of the present day. They are regarded as great or lowly men according to whether their fame is great or small. Even a man unknown to anyone else, however, cannot be said not to exist. For his existence or non-existence does not depend upon whether he is known to others or not. In this respect, then, we can say that all men are immortal. This sort of immortality differs from biological immortality, however, and may be called ideal immortality.

It is generally recognized, nevertheless, that immortality which leaves no name to be remembered by others is of no value, and hence the word immortality is usually restricted to that which leaves an enduring fame in later times. Hence in China it is said that there are three kinds of men who are immortal: the highest are those who have shown virtue; those who do great deeds are second; and those who have left great teachings behind them are the third. It is by having accomplished something that a man can be known and remembered by others, and so be immortal. But if immortality were to be restricted to these three categories, there would be very few men in the world who would succeed in obtaining such immortality through remembrance. Most people are mediocre and incapable of making society remember them, and so will be remembered only by their relatives and descendants. This explains the special emphasis laid by the Confucians on ancestor worship, by means of which everyone, because of the remembrance accorded him by his descendants, can receive his measure of the immortality of remembrance. This is the doctrine implied in the Confucian theories on mourning and sacrificial rites.

The attention paid by the later Confucians toward this question of immortality may be seen in their theories on marriage rites. In these rites, their emphasis is directed wholly on their biological function. Thus the *Li Chi* says (ch. 41):

" The ceremony of marriage is intended to be a bond of love between two (families of different) surnames, in order to secure the services in the ancestral temple for the past, and to secure the continuance of the family line for the future. Therefore the Superior Man sets great value upon it " (XXVIII, 428). Chapter XXIV:

" If there were no union between Heaven and Earth, the myriad things would not be produced. By means of the grand rite of marriage, generations of men are perpetuated through myriads of ages. How can Your Lordship say this ceremony is too great? " (XXVIII, 265).

Chapter IX, describing the marriage ceremony:

" The groom's parents descend from the hall by the steps on the west, while the bride does so by those on the east. This shows the household is given to the bride'.... There is no congratulation at the marriage ceremony, for it is something for the perpetuation of men (XXVII, 442). And Chapter V:

" The family that has married a daughter away, does not extinguish its candles for three nights, thinking of the separation that has taken place. The family that has received the wife, for three days has no music, thinking of the succession of the parents " (XXVII, 322).

Mencius has also said:

" There are three things that are unfilial, and to have no posterity is the greatest of them. Shun married without informing his parents because of this, lest he should have no posterity " (*Mencius*, IV*a*, 26).

These passages indicate that for the Confucians, the chief function of marriage is to produce offspring. Through marriage which produces children, a new self is created to replace the old self, in this way ensuring biological immortality. Thus looked at, the preparation for marriage becomes as sad an affair as the preparation of the coffin, for if there were no death, there would be no need for marriage. The fundamental purpose of sexual intercourse is to produce life, and the feelings of love and delight which arise from this act are mere supplementary emotions. From the biological viewpoint, they are of no great consequence, and so were not seriously considered by the Confucians. Hence when the Confucians discussed the relation between husband and wife, they spoke only of the distinctions that should exist between the two, and never spoke about their love.

All men die, and most men fear death. From this fact all kinds of superstition have arisen, while many religions have upheld a dogmatic belief in the immortality of the soul. But the Confucians, at least some of them, did not maintain a belief in the immortality of the soul, but laid special stress on means to enable all men to gain biological and ideal immortality. In Chinese society of the old type, a man having sons who were themselves married and had produced children, looked on them, when he reached the sunset of life, as stays for his own life. Hence he could regard his existence as already having been entrusted to someone, and so could await death calmly, without further care as to whether his soul after death would continue to exist or not. This attitude has been directly developed by Confucian thought.

6—THEORIES ON FILIAL PIETY

The Confucians, as we have seen, held that the function of marriage lies in creating a new self to replace the old. The

---

¹ The steps on the west are for the guests, those on the east for the hostess.—TR.

hope of the old self is that the new one will be able to perpetuate the life and activity of the old self down to ' ten thousand generations,' and the new self, if it can fulfil this aspiration, is a filial offspring. The way thus to meet this wish, the way to ' succeed the parents,' may be divided under two aspects : the physical and the spiritual. The physical aspect can again be divided into three factors : the care of the parents ; the bearing in mind that one's own body is something bequeathed to one by one's parents, and hence the valuing and protecting of it ; and the production of a ' new self ' to carry on the life of the parents. The *Li Chi* (ch. 21) says :

" Yo-cheng Tzŭ-ch'un injured his foot in coming down from his hall, and for some months was unable to go out. Ever after this he had a look of sorrow, so that a disciple said to him : ' Your foot, Master, is better, and though for some months you could not go out, why should you still wear a look of sorrow ? ' Yo-cheng Tzŭ-ch'un replied : ' It is a good question you ask ! A good question indeed ! I have heard from Tseng Tzŭ what he heard the Master (i.e., Confucius) say, that of all that Heaven produces and Earth nourishes, there is none so great as man. When, his parents having given birth to his body whole, he returns it to them whole, this may be called filial piety. When no member of it has been mutilated and no disgrace done to any part of the person, it may be called whole. Hence the Superior Man does not dare to take the slightest step forgetful of his filial duty.

" ' But now I forgot the way of filial piety, which is why I wear a look of sorrow. (A son) should not forget his parents in a single lifting of his feet, nor in the utterance of a single word. He should not forget his parents in a single lifting of his feet, and therefore he will walk in the highway and not take a by-way, he will use a boat and not attempt to wade through a stream ; not daring, with the body left him by his parents, to go into peril. He should not forget his parents in the utterance of a single word, and therefore an evil word will not issue from his mouth, and an angry word will not come back to his person. Not to disgrace his person and not to cause shame to his parents may be called filial duty ' " (XXVIII, 228-229).

An example of how Tseng Tzŭ, the disciple of Confucius probably most responsible for the growing emphasis laid by the Confucians on filial piety, tried to preserve his own body intact, is found in the *Lun Yü* : " When Tseng Tzŭ was taken ill, he called his disciples and said : ' Uncover my feet, uncover my arms. The Ode (II, 5, 1) says : " Be anxious, be cautious, as when near a deep gulf, as when treading thin ice." From now henceforth I know I shall escape all injury, my disciples ' " (VIII, 3).

If, however, we only succeed in returning our body intact to our parents, then, after the death of this body, the life of our parents will have no 'new self' in which to be perpetuated, and hence the son will still lack filial piety. Mencius meant exactly this when he said : " There are three things that are unfilial, and to have no posterity is the greatest of them." For if a man has no posterity, the family line (or at least his branch of it), which has been handed down from the earliest ancestors, will be cut off, and this would show the greatest lack of filial piety.

On the spiritual side, filial piety consists, during the lifetime of our parents, in conforming ourselves to their wishes, and giving them not only physical care and nourishment, but also nourishing their wills ;' while should they fall into error, it consists in reproving them and leading them back to what is right. After the death of our parents, furthermore, one aspect of it consists in offering sacrifices to them and thinking about them, so as to keep their memory fresh in our minds. This point has already been fully discussed. Another aspect consists in perpetuating the activities of our parents and carrying on their uncompleted purposes ; or for us ourselves to achieve something new, and thus make our names, and through them the names of our parents, widely known so that they will gain an immortality among others. The *Chung Yung* (Doctrine of the Mean) says :

" The Master said : ' How great was the filial piety of Shun ! His virtue was that of a Sage ; his dignity was the throne ; his riches were everything within the four seas. He offered his sacrifices in his ancestral temple, and his descendants maintained them " (p. 308). Again :

" The Master said : ' How far-reaching was the filial piety of King Wu and the Duke of Chou ! Now filial piety consists in the skilful carrying out of the wishes of our forefathers, and the skilful continuation of their undertakings. In spring and autumn they repaired the temple halls of their ancestors, set forth their ancestral vessels, displayed their various robes, and presented the offerings of the several seasons . . . . To occupy their places, practise their ceremonies, perform their music, reverence what they reverenced, love those whom they loved, serve the dead as one serves the living, and serve the departed as one serves those who are present : this is the height of filial piety ' " (pp. 310-311).

Spiritual filial piety of this sort is great and far-reaching, and is more important than the physical aspect of filial piety. The *Li Chi* (ch. 21) says :

" Tseng Tzŭ said : ' There are three degrees of filial piety. The highest is the honoring of our parents ; the second is not disgracing them ; the lowest is being able to support them.'

" Kung Ming I asked Tseng Tzŭ : ' Can you, Master, be considered as filial ? ' Tseng Tzŭ replied : ' What words are these ?

---

¹ *Cf. Mencius,* IV*a*, 19.

What words are these ? What the Superior Man calls filial piety requires the anticipation of our parents ' wishes, the carrying out of their aims, and their instruction in the proper path. I am simply one who supports his parents. How can I be considered filial ? ' " (XXVIII, 226).

In these passages we find spiritual filial piety considered as the most important kind.

The filial son wishes to return intact the body bequeathed him by his parents. He not only must not allow it to be mutilated, but also must not permit it to be disgraced. " The highest filial piety is the honoring of our parents ; the second is not disgracing them." The first of these means a positive practice of virtue, so as to give a glorious name to the parents; the second, a negative avoidance of evil conduct, so that the parents will not gain a bad name. If a man keep these two in mind, he will practise every kind of virtue naturally. In several chapters in the *Li Chi*, therefore, as well as in the *Hsiao Ching* (Classic of Filial Piety), filial piety is made the source of all the virtues. The *Li Chi* (ch. 21) says :

" The body is that which has been transmitted to us by our parents. Dare anyone allow himself to be irreverent in the employment of their legacy ? If a man in his own house and privacy be not grave, he is not filial ; if in serving his ruler he be not loyal, he is not filial ; if in discharging the duties of office he be not serious, he is not filial ; if with friends he be not sincere, he is not filial ; if on the field of battle he be not brave, he is not filial. If he fail in these five things, the evil (of the disgrace) will reflect on his parents. Dare he but be serious ?

" To prepare fragrant flesh and grain which he has cooked, tasting and then presenting them before his parents, is not filial piety ; it is only nourishing them. He whom the Superior Man pronounces filial is he whom the people of his state praise, saying with admiration, ' Happy are the parents who have such a son as this ! ' That indeed is what can be called filial. The fundamental lesson for all is filial piety. The practice of it is seen in the support (of the parents). One may be able to support them ; the difficulty is in doing so with proper reverence. One may attain to that reverence ; the difficulty is to do so without self-constraint. That freedom from constraint may be realized ; the difficulty is to maintain it to the end.

" When his parents are dead, and the son carefully watches over his actions, so as not to pass down a bad name for his parents, he may be said to be able to maintain his piety to the very end. True love (*jen*) is the love of this ; true manners (*li*) are the doing of this ; true righteousness (*i*) is the rightness of this ; true sincerity is being sincere in this ; true strength is being strong in this. Music springs from conformity to this ; punishments come from violation of this . . . . .

Institute filial piety, and it will fill the space from Heaven to Earth ; spread it out, and it will extend over all the space within the four seas ;

hand it down to future ages, and it will be forever observed ; push it on to the eastern, western, southern and northern seas, and it will everywhere be the standard " (XXVIII, 226-227).

The *Hsiao Ching* says :

" Now filial piety is the root of all virtue, and that from which all teaching comes . . . . Our bodies, in every hair and bit of skin, are received by us from our parents, and we must not venture to injure or scar them. This is the beginning of filial piety. When we have established ourselves in the practice of the Way (*Tao*), so as to make our name famous in future ages and thereby glorify our parents, this is the goal of filial piety. It commences with the service of parents ; it proceeds to the service of the ruler ; it is completed by the establishment of one's own personality . . . . Yes, filial piety is the way of Heaven, the principle of Earth, and the practical duty of man. Heaven and Earth invariably pursue this course, and the people take it as their pattern " (pp. 466-467, 473).

According to this concept, anyone who possesses the virtue of filial piety must thereby possess all the other virtues. Hence filial piety is the source of all the virtues.[1] This doctrine had great influence during the Han dynasty, under which all those who 'were filial sons and obedient brothers' were especially favored by the government. Likewise, the posthumous titles of the Han Emperors are all prefixed by the word ' filial ' (*hsiao* 孝), indicating the particular importance that was then given to this ideal.[2]

7—THE GREAT LEARNING

There are two short works that have exercised a tremendous influence upon later Chinese philosophy. They are the *Ta Hsüeh* 大 學

---

[1] The doctrine that filial piety is the scource of all virtues must have arisen comparatively late. The *Lun Yü* contains many utterances by Confucius on filial piety, and also says : " Yu Tzŭ said : ' . . . . The Superior Man devotes himself to the fundamental, for when that has been established right courses naturally evolve ; and are not filial devotion and respect for the elders in the family the very foundation of human-heartedness (*jen*) ? ' " (I, 2). This means that the way to have *jen* is to extend the self to others. The tie between one's self and one's family is the closest of all relationships, and therefore if one is unable to extend one's self to them, one will still less be able to do so toward outsiders. Hence if one wishes to extend one's self to others, one must begin with the members of one's family. This is why filial devotion and respect toward the elder members of one's family are the basis of *jen*. Both Confucius and Mencius thus laid emphasis upon filial piety, and yet neither of them made it the basis for all virtue. The real basis is *jen*, and when there is *jen* there automatically is filial piety. Mencius implies this when he says : " There has never been a man possessing *jen* who neglected his parents " (*Mencius*, Ia, 1).

[2] The *Li Chi* chapters from which I have quoted to illustrate filial piety, are traditionally supposed to contain the words of Tseng Tzŭ, and the *Hsiao Ching* also purports to record the answers of Confucius to his questions. Tseng Tzŭ was evidently famous for his own filial piety, so much so that Mencius several times refers to the way in which he took care of his father, saying : " To serve one's parents as Tseng Tzŭ served his may indeed be accepted (as the standard) " (*Mencius*, IVa, 19). Yet though Tseng Tzŭ himself practised filial piety, it is hard to determine whether or not he actually advocated it as the source for all virtues. Mencius and Hsün Tzŭ do not speak clearly on this point, and the *Li Chi's* attribution of its speeches to various historical persons is very loose, so that it is impossible to know who was actually their speaker.

(Great Learning) and *Chung Yung* 中 庸 (Doctrine of the Mean), that are contained in the *Li Chi* (chs. 39 and 29), and now, together with the *Lun Yü* and the *Mencius*, comprise the *Four Books* which for so many years have formed the classical basis of Chinese learning.

The *Ta Hsüeh* was believed by the great Neo-Confucianist Sung philosopher, Chu Hsi (1130-1200), to have been written by Tseng Tzŭ, while another Sung scholar, Wang Po (1197-1274), attributed it to Tzŭ Ssŭ, the grandson of Confucius. These assumptions are mere surmises, however, unsupported by statements in any earlier writings. The *Ta Hsüeh* itself says in its opening paragraphs:

" What the Great Learning teaches is : clearly to exemplify illustrious virtue, to love the people, and to rest in the highest good.

" The point where to rest being known, the object of pursuit is then determined ; that being determined, a calm unperturbedness may be attained to. After that calmness will follow a tranquil repose ; in that repose there will be careful deliberation ; and that deliberation will be followed by achievement. Things have their root and their branches. Affairs have their end and their beginning. To know what comes first and what comes last is to be near to the Way (*Tao*).

" The ancients who wished clearly to exemplify illustrious virtue throughout the world, first ordered well their own states. Wishing to order well their states, they first regulated their families. Wishing to regulate their families, they first cultivated their own persons. Wishing to cultivate their persons, they first rectified their minds. Wishing to rectify their minds, they first sought for absolute sincerity in their thoughts. Wishing for absolute sincerity in their thoughts, they first extended their knowledge. This extension of knowledge lay in the investigation of things.

" Things being investigated, knowledge became complete. Their knowledge being complete, their thoughts became sincere. Their thoughts being sincere, their minds were then rectified. Their minds being rectified, their persons became cultivated. Their persons being cultivated, their families were regulated. Their families being regulated, their states were rightly governed. Their states being rightly governed, the world was at peace.

" From the Son of Heaven down to the common people, all must consider cultivation of the person to be fundamental. It cannot be, when the root is neglected, that what should spring from it should be well ordered. It has never been, when what is important is slightly cared for, that what is of slight importance should be greatly cared for. This is called knowing the fundamental ; this is called the perfection of knowledge " (pp. 411-413).

This section presents the main ideas of the *Ta Hsüeh*, consisting of three aims, and eight steps toward the attaining of these aims.

Most of the ideas expressed in it are clear enough and need no further elucidation, but the two phrases, ' extension of knowledge ' (*chih chih* 致知) and ' investigation of things ' (*ko wu* 格物), which are not clearly explained in the subsequent paragraphs of the treatise, have given rise to many interpretations by later scholars. Thus much of the conflict between the two opposing schools of the Sung and Ming dynasties, led by Ch'eng I (1033-1107) and Chu Hsi (1130-1200) on the one hand, and Lu Chiu-yüan (1139-1192) and Wang Yang-ming (1473-1529) on the other, has centered over the interpretation of these two phrases. Because of their tremendous influence upon later philosophers, an attempt at their elucidation is imperative, but in doing so, we must ask which of the explanations that have later been attached to them is closest to the original context. Hsün Tzǔ was the outstanding Confucian of the latter part of the Warring States period, and the Confucians who followed him belonged for the most part to his school. For example, the fact that the *li* were much discussed by Hsün Tzǔ, makes most of the chapters in the *Li Chi* discuss *li* from his viewpoint. Likewise his ideas on education, as they appear in the *Hsün-tzǔ* (ch. 1), are copied word for word in the *Li Chi* of the elder Tai, while the ' Record on Education ' found in the *Li Chi* (ch. 16), also discusses education from Hsün Tzǔ's viewpoint. It is thus evident that his influence during the Ch'in and Han dynasties was much greater that later scholars have usually supposed. The ' Record on Education ' in the *Li Chi* says :

" According to the ancient system of education, for families there was the village school (*shu* 塾) ; for one locality there was the *hsiang* 庠 ; for the larger districts there was the *hsü* 序 ; and in the capitals there was the college (*hsüeh* 學).

" Every year some entered the college, and every second year there was a competitive examination. In the first year it was seen whether they could read the texts intelligently and explain the meaning of each ; in the third year, whether they were reverently attentive to their work and took pleasure in the community life ; in the fifth year, how they broadened their studies and became intimate with their teachers ; in the seventh year, how they could discuss what they had studied and what friends they selected. This was called the small completion (*hsiao ch'eng* 小成). In the ninth year, when they knew the different classes of subjects and had gained a comprehensive knowledge ; were firmly established and would not fall back ; this was called the great completion (*ta ch'eng* 大成). After this their training was sufficient to transform the people and change the customs, so that those near at hand would pay allegiance to them with delight, and those far off would think of them with longing. Such was the method of the Great Learning " (XXVIII, 83-84).

The words, " They were firmly established and would not fall back," are reminiscent of what Hsün Tzǔ (in his ch. 3) says of the Sage, that 'ever changing without returning to his original state, he will be transformed' (*chüan* 2, p. 7). This has already been explained.[1] The 'Record on Education' holds that Great Learning consists in knowing the different classes of subjects and in gaining comprehensive knowledge ; in being firmly established and not falling back ; and in being sufficient to transform the people and change the customs. The fundamental idea here is similar to that in the *Ta Hsüeh*, which offers a program of eight steps, beginning with the investigation of things and extension of knowledge, and culminating in the giving of peace to the entire world. In this respect it would seem that the *Ta Hsüeh*, like the 'Record on Education,' should be interpreted from Hsün Tzŭ's viewpoint. The *Hsün-tzŭ* (ch. 21) says :

" That which knows is the nature of man, and that which can be known is the laws of the material world. If a person sought to know the laws of the material world through his capacity of knowing, there being nothing to hinder him, in a lifetime he could not go all over them. In studying these laws, although he might know a myriad of them, it would be insufficient for him to embrace the changes of all things. He would remain the same as the stupid person. To study until one is old and one's children are grown, remaining yet like the stupid man, without knowing to stop, is indeed to be over ambitious. Therefore the true student learns where to rest. But where to rest ? Rest in the most perfect. What may be called the most perfect ? It is the state of the Sage " (p. 276).

The *Ta Hsüeh* also teaches men where to rest and says that this means ' to rest in the highest good.' Here, again, it agrees with Hsün Tzŭ. Elsewhere, while describing the point at which a man should stop, it says about King Wen :

" As a sovereign, he rested in human-heartedness (*jen*) ; as a minister, he rested in reverence ; as a son, he rested in filial piety ; as a father, he rested in kindness ; in intercourse with his subjects, he rested in good faith " (p. 416).

Hsün Tzŭ has also said that the state of the Sage is that in which he stops when there is perfection, and that "the Sage is one who fulfils the duties of the natural relationships " (p. 276). This idea is echoed in the *Ta Hsüeh* passage just quoted.

If a man knows where to rest, he has a definite goal before him toward which to strive. Having such a goal, his mind will be settled, and being settled, it will be calm and unperturbed. Being unperturbed, it will be in tranquil repose, will be able to deliberate, and so will attain. Mencius says :

" People have a common saying : ' Empire, state, family.' The root of the empire is in the state. The root of the state is in the family. The root of the family is in the individual " (*Mencius*, IV*a*, 5).

---

[1] *Cf.* pp. 293-294.

This is similar to the progression given in the *Ta Hsüeh*, which moves from cultivation of the person to regulation of the home, and from regulation of the home to display of virtue in the empire. Perhaps these words of the *Ta Hsüeh* were inspired by Mencius, but the *Hsün-tzŭ* (ch. 12) also states :
" Do you ask how to conduct the affairs of state ? I say, I have heard of cultivation of the person, but never of conducting affairs of state. The ruler is the form. When the form is correct, its shadow will be correct. The ruler is the basin. When the basin is round, the water in it will assume roundness. The ruler is the cup. When the cup is square, the water in it will assume squareness. When the ruler shoots, his minister will shoot also. King Chuang of Ch'u liked slender waists, and so in his palace there were people starving themselves. This is why I say : I have heard of cultivation of the person, but never about conducting affairs of state " (*chüan* 8, pp. 4-5).
This gives the Confucian doctrine that if the man at the top is correct, those below him will model themselves on him and will also be correct, and so there will be good government. The *Ta Hsüeh* says :
" Yao and Shun led on the empire with goodness, and the people followed them ; Chieh and Chou with oppression, and the people followed them. When the orders of a ruler are contrary to what he himself likes, the people do not follow them (i.e., the orders).
" Therefore the Superior Man requires from others only the qualities that he himself has, and blames others only for the qualities that he himself lacks. Never has there been a man who could teach others without having reference to what is stored up in his own person. Therefore the government of the state depends upon the regulation of the family. . . . When the ruler as a father, a son, an elder or a younger brother, is a model, then the people imitate him " (pp. 418-419).
The fact that if the ruler acts as a model, his people will model themselves upon him, means that cultivation of the person becomes the foundation for regulating the home, ruling the state, and bringing peace to the world. The ruling of a state, furthermore, consists in government of men by men, so that, as the *Chung Yung* says, " The model is not far away." Hsün Tzŭ likewise says : " The Sage measures things by himself. Hence by himself he measures other men ; by his own feelings he measures their feelings." Again : " A five inch foot-rule is the proper standard for the entire world." [1] A person who has cultivated himself will automatically be able to be a measure for others. The *Ta Hsüeh* continues :
" What is meant by ' making the whole world peaceful depends on the government of its states,' is this : When the superiors

---

[1] *Cf.* above, p. 284.

treat their aged as the aged should be treated, the people become filial; when they treat their elders as elders should be treated, the people learn the respect due to someone older; when they treat compassionately the young and helpless, the people do the same. Thus the Superior Man has a principle with which, as with a measuring-square, to regulate his conduct.

"What a man dislikes in his superiors, let him not therewith employ his inferiors; what he dislikes in his inferiors, let him not therewith serve his superiors; what he dislikes in those before him, let him not therewith precede those who are behind him; what he dislikes in those who are behind him, let him not therewith follow those who are before him; what he dislikes on the right, let him not display toward the left; what he dislikes on the left, let him not display toward the right: this is called the principle, with which, as with a measuring-square, to regulate one's conduct " (p. 419).

Such a course is like that of Hsün Tzŭ, whereby a foot-rule of five inches becomes ' the proper standard for the entire world.'

To cultivate one's person, one must first rectify one's mind. In other words, the Sage must have knowledge of the Way or *Tao*. But to know this Way, his mind must have ' emptiness, unity and quiescence.' ' The *Hsün-tzŭ* (ch. 21) says :

" The mind of man is like a tub of water. Place it upright and do not shake it, and the mud will settle on the bottom, and the clear water will be on top. Then it will be clear enough to mirror the beard and eyebrows and reveal the features. But if a light wind crosses its surface, the mud at the bottom will be stirred up and the clear water at the top will be disturbed, until a person cannot see in it his true form. The mind is also like this. Hence if it is guided by principle and nourished by purity, nothing can upset it. Then it is sufficient to determine right and wrong, and to decide what is uncertain " (p. 271).

The *Ta Hsüeh* says :

" What is meant by ' the cultivation of the person depends on rectifying the mind ' is : If a man's mind be under the influence of anger, it will not be correct. The same will be the case if he be under the influence of terror, or of fond regard, or of sorrow and distress " (p. 416).

Under such conditions the mind is like the tub of water that has been disturbed by the wind. If it cannot remain unperturbed, it will be unable to ' determine right and wrong, and to decide what is uncertain.' The *Hsün-tzŭ* continues :

" But if a little thing leads the mind astray, outwardly this man's poise is changed, and inwardly his mind is upset, so that he is not even able to decide ordinary matters.

' *Cf.* p. 291.

" Therefore there were many who liked to write, but there was only one Ts'ang Chieh (the supposed inventor of writing) who was known in later times, because of his mind's singleness. There were many who liked agriculture, but there was only one Hou Chi who could hand it down, because of his singleness. Many liked music, but only K'uei could hand it down, because of his singleness. Many liked standards of justice (*i* 義), but only Shun could hand them down, because of his singleness. Ch'ui made the bow and Fou Yu made arrows, but (the archer) Yi was expert at archery. Hsi Chung made the carriage and (Hsiang) Tu introduced the use of the team of four horses, but Tsao Fu was expert at driving. From ancient times until to-day there have not been men who without devoting themselves to a single thing, could be expert in it " (pp. 271-272).

The mind must be concentrated on one thing in order to retain its correctness. The *Ta Hsüeh* says likewise : " When the mind is not present, we look and do not see ; we hear and do not understand ; we eat and do not know the taste of what we eat " (p. 216).

To avoid this failure to concentrate we must seek for a thing earnestly. The *Ta Hsüeh* says :

" In the ' Announcement to the Prince of K'ang ' it is said : ' Be as if you were watching over an infant.' '[1] If the mind be really sincere in its seeking, though it may not hit the central mark, it will not be far. There has never been (a girl) who learned first to bring up a child, that she might afterwards marry " (p. 417).

The true protection given by a loving mother to her infant is a concrete example of sincerity (*ch'eng* 誠). The *Ta Hsüeh* says :

" What is called ' making the thoughts sincere (*ch'eng*) ' is the allowing of no self-deception. For example, when we hate a bad smell or like a beautiful color, this is called being true to one's self. Therefore the Superior Man must be watchful over himself when he is alone (*shen ch'i tu* 慎 其 獨). There is no evil to which the mean man, dwelling in retirement, will not proceed ; but when he sees a Superior Man, he tries to disguise himself, concealing his evil and displaying what is good. The other beholds him as if he saw his lungs and liver ; of what use (is his disguise) ? This is the meaning of the saying, ' What sincerely is within will be manifested without.' Therefore the Superior Man must be watchful over himself when he is alone.

" Tseng Tzǔ said : ' Ten eyes behold it. Ten hands point to it. How serious ! ' As riches adorn a house, so virtue adorns the person. When the mind becomes expanded, the body appears at ease. Therefore the Superior Man is sure to make his thoughts sincere " (p. 413).

A man's dislike of a bad smell and liking for a beautiful color are both genuine likes and dislikes, and hence are concrete examples of sincerity (*ch'eng*). The *Ta Hsüeh's* statement that ' what sincerely

---

[1] *Cf. Shu Ching*, p. 168.—TR.

is within will be manifested without,' and that one should be watchful over oneself when one is alone, are reminiscent of the *Hsün-tzŭ*. Hsün Tzŭ, however, when he speaks of ' singleness ' (*tu* 獨), means single-minded concentration. If a man, that is, can pursue an affair with sincerity, he can attend to it with single-minded devotion.' The *Ta Hsüeh*, on the other hand, when it speaks of being watchful over oneself when alone (*shen ch'i tu*), means that our inward thought must be the same as our outward conduct, and here differs slightly from Hsün Tzŭ.

Our mind must have something which it pursues with sincerity, before it can be not confused and correct. Hence the words : " The point where to rest being known, the object of pursuit is then determined," etc. This is why, " Wishing to rectify one's mind, one first seeks for absolute sincerity in one's thoughts." Such sincerity follows from knowing where to rest. Therefore, " Wishing for absolute sincerity in one's thoughts, one first extends one's knowledge." Such extension of knowledge consists in comprehending that : " Things have their root and their branches. Affairs have their end and their beginning. To know what comes first and what comes last is to be near to the Way." Therefore, as the *Ta Hsüeh* says : " From the Son of Heaven down to the common people, all must consider cultivation of the person to be fundamental. It cannot be, that when the root is neglected, what should spring from it should be well ordered. It has never been, when what is important is slightly cared for, that what is of slight importance should be greatly cared for. This is called knowing the fundamental, this is called the perfection of knowledge." [2] For one who possesses the perfection of knowledge, the cultivation of the individual is fundamental, and is something which will be done with single-minded sincere effort. Hence the saying : " Knowledge being complete, thoughts become sincere." The *Ta Hsüeh* says again : " Virtue is the root ; wealth is the branches. If he make the root secondary and the branches primary, he will only quarrel with the people and teach them rapine " (p. 420). We must know that virtue is fundamental and so strive with single-minded sincerity ' clearly to exemplify illustrious virtue throughout the world.' This is also the meaning of the saying : " Knowledge being complete, thoughts become sincere."

Yet if we wish to know the root and branches of things, we must have some correct knowledge about them. If not, what we call the root and branches may not be root and branches, and with this initial error, everything that follows will be wrong. The *Hsün-tzŭ* (ch. 21) says :

---

[1] *Cf.* quotation on p. 293, where Hsün Tzŭ uses the word 'singleness' (*tu*).

[2] The Sung scholars, Ch'e Yü-feng (lived circa A.D. 1274), and Wang Po (1197-1274), consider this paragraph to be the explanation of the phrase, 'the extension of knowledge and investigation of things.' *Cf.* their *Lu Chai Chi, chüan* 2.

" Whenever in observing things there is doubt and the mind is uncertain, then external objects are not apprehended clearly. When my thoughts are unclear, then I cannot decide whether a thing is so or not. When a person walks in the dark, he sees a stone lying down and takes it to be a crouching tiger ; he sees a clump of trees upright, and takes them to be standing men. The darkness has perverted his vision. The drunken man crosses a hundred-pace wide canal and takes it to be a half-step wide ditch ; he bends his head when going out of a city gate, taking it to be a small private door. The wine has confused his senses. When a person sticks his finger in his eye and looks, one thing appears as two ; when he covers his ear and listens, a tiny sound is taken to be a big noise. The circumstances have confused his senses.

" So when one looks down from the top of a mountain, a cow looks like a sheep ; but whoever wants a sheep does not go down and lead it away. The distance has obscured its size. When one looks up from the foot of a mountain, a ten-fathom tree looks like a chop-stick ; but whoever wants a chop-stick does not go up and snap it off. The height of the mountain has obscured its length. When the water moves, the shadows dance, and men do not then judge whether they are beautiful or ugly. The state of the water is confused. A blind man who lifts up his head and looks, does not see the stars. But people do not determine thereby the existence or non-existence (of the stars). The man is misled by his blindness. A man who would make judgments at such times would be the most stupid in the world. In forming his judgments such a simpleton would be using doubtful premises to make decisions. And when such is the case, the judgment must inevitably be incorrect. When it is incorrect, how can he avoid falling into error ? " (pp. 274-275).

If we perceive things on occasions when we have been deceived by their appearance, we cannot have a true knowledge of them. Therefore the extension of knowledge lies in the investigation of things. If the mind can penetrate beneath the external appearance of things and see their fundamental reality, then only can it have true knowledge of them. If not, the decisions rendered by a beclouded judgment must be incorrect. If we are to have such true knowledge of things, however, we must first not allow ' the mind to be uncertain.' For the extension of knowledge and investigation of things are both mental operations, and therefore are intimately and naturally connected with the mind's correctness, as interacting cause and effect.

8—THE DOCTRINE OF THE MEAN

The *Chung Yung* 中 庸 (Doctrine of the Mean), which, like the *Ta Hsüeh*, is included in the *Li Chi*, and forms one of the *Four Books*, has been traditionally ascribed to Tzŭ Ssŭ, the grandson of Confucius. Thus the *Shih Chi*, in its biography of Confucius, states that " Tzŭ Ssŭ

composed the *Chung Yung*" (*Mém. hist.*, V, 431). Also, that the
Hsün-tzŭ (ch. 6) groups Tzŭ Ssŭ and Mencius together, coupled with
the fact that the ideas expressed in the *Chung Yung*, as they exist to-day,
are in many ways similar to Mencius's doctrines, would make it seem
that Tzŭ Ssŭ was actually their author. Toward the latter part of
the *Chung Yung*, however, there occurs the sentence : " To-day
throughout the empire carts all have wheels with the same gauge ; all
writing is with the same characters ; and for conduct there exist the
same rules " (p. 324). This would seem to indicate conditions as they
were following the unification of feudal China, first under Ch'in in
221 B.C., and later under the Han dynasty. The *Chung Yung* also
remarks elsewhere : " It (the earth) sustains mountains like the Hua
peak without feeling their weight " (p. 322). This is a reference to
the sacred mountain of Hua Shan in Shensi, whereas it would be
natural to expect such a man as Tzŭ Ssŭ, who was a native of the
state of Lu (occupying what is now Shantung), to refer in such a case
to Shantung's sacred mountain, T'ai Shan. The statements made on
such philosophic concepts as Fate (*ming*), man's nature (*hsing*), sincerity
(*ch'eng*) and enlightenment (*ming* 明), are also more detailed than those
of Mencius, and would seem to be further developments of his
doctrines, whereas Tzŭ Ssŭ lived prior to Mencius. All this evidence
would seem to indicate that the *Chung Yung* was really the work of
a Confucian of Mencius's group, living in the Ch'in or Han
dynasty.

Wang Po (1194-1274) throws some light on this problem by
pointing out that the *I-wen Chih* in the *Ch'ien Han Shu* contains an
entry : " *Chung Yung Shuo* 中 庸 說 (Explanations of the Doctrine
of the Mean) in two sections." From this entry he concludes that
during the Han dynasty two separate works probably existed, and
that these were later combined to form the present *Chung Yung*,
perhaps by the younger Tai, at the time when he was compiling the
Li Chi.[1] Wang Po points out further that the words of the title,
Chung Yung, do not appear in the opening section of the work, as is
usually the case in writings of this period, and that the real subject of
this section is *Tao*. It is only in the next section that the words *chung*
and *yung* occur, a fact which would seem to throw suspicion on the
first section.[2]

Wang Po is very suggestive here, though he has not pushed
the problem to its conclusion. If we examine the ideas in the *Chung
Yung* closely, we find that the first section, beginning with the opening sentence and extending to the words : " Heaven and Earth
would have their proper positions, and all things would be nourished "
(i.e., p. 300 to p. 301) ; together with the closing section, beginning
with the words : " When those in inferior positions do not obtain

---

[1] *Cf.* Wang Po's *Ku Chung-yung Po*, in the *Lu Chai Chi*, *chüan* 5, pp. 16-17.
[2] *Ibid.*, *chüan* 2, pp. 11-12.

confidence from their superiors," to the end of the work (i.e., p. 316 to p. 329), discuss for the most part the relation of man to the universe, and seem to be a development of Mencius's mystical ideas, while the style is that of a formal essay. The intervening section (pp. 301-316), on the other hand, discusses chiefly human affairs, and seems to be a development of the doctrines of Confucius, while its style is that of recorded conversations. Thus this central section would seem to constitute the original *Chung Yung* of Tzŭ Ssŭ, as listed under his name in the *I-wen Chih*.[1] The opening and closing sections, on the other hand, have been added by a later Confucian, and so probably constitute the ' *Chung Yung Shuo* in two sections ' spoken of in the *I-wen Chih*. This assumption is strengthened by the fact that all the references to the standard cart-wheel gauge used throughout the empire, etc., occur in this latter section. The fact that the author of these opening and concluding sections named them ' Explanations of the Doctrine of the Mean ' (*Chung Yung Shuo*), shows that he must have been a follower of Tzŭ Ssŭ ; yet at the same time they contain ideas derived from Mencius, from which it would seem that their author was a follower of the latter as well. The probable explanation is that the two groups of Confucians headed by Tzŭ Ssŭ and Mencius were originally similar to each other, which would also explain why the *Hsün-tzŭ* (ch. 6) has grouped the two men together.

I shall begin by discussing the middle or original section of the *Chung Yung* (pp. 301-316). This commences :

" Chung-ni (i.e., Confucius) said : ' The Superior Man is in the state of equilibrium (*chung*) and normality (*yung*) ; the small man is the reverse of these states. The Superior Man exhibits them, because he is the Superior Man, and holds to the timely mean (*chung*) ; the small man is the opposite of them, because he is the small man, and does anything without taking (morality) into consideration ' " (pp. 301-302).

These concepts of equilibrium or the mean (*chung* 中) and normality (*yung* 庸), had already been expressed by Confucius.[2] The *Chung Yung* also speaks here of a timely mean (*shih chung* 時 中), that is, a mean in human affairs such as Aristotle would call relative and not absolute.

This mean of Aristotle is one that is taken as a guide for human emotions and actions, and that differs according to the time, place and person which are encountered, thus making it impossible to have any fixed rules that will serve as a mean under every circumstance.[3]

---

[1] This is only a general statement, for this central section also seems not to be entirely free from later additions, though for the most part it probably constitutes Tzŭ Ssŭ's original *Chung Yung*.

[2] *Cf. Lun Yü*, VI, 27, where the two terms occur.

[3] *Cf.* Aristotle's *Ethics*, Bk. II, ch. 5.

The timely mean spoken of by the *Chung Yung* is precisely like this. Mencius also emphasized timeliness, as when he said :

" Not to serve a prince whom he did not esteem, nor command a people whom he did not approve ; in a time of good government to take office, and on the occurrence of confusion to retire : such was Po I. ' Whom may I not serve ? My serving makes him my prince. What people may I not command ? My commanding them makes them my people.' In a time of good government to take office, and when disorder prevailed, also to take office : such was Yi Yin. When it was proper to go into office, then to go into it ; when it was proper to remain out of office, then to remain out of office ; when it was proper to continue in it long, then to continue in it long ; when it was proper to withdraw from it quickly, then to withdraw from it quickly : such was Confucius " (*Mencius*, IIa, 2, 22).

" Po I among the Sages was the pure one ; Yi Yin was the responsible one ; Hui of Liu-hsia was the accommodating one ; and Confucius was the *timely* one " (V*b*, 1).

" Tzŭ Mo holds to the medium. By holding that medium, he is nearer the right. But to hold it without allowing room for the exigencies of circumstance is like holding to only one point. Why I hate holding to one point is the injury it does to the Way (*Tao*). It cares for but one point and disregards a hundred others " (VII*a*, 26).

Mencius lauded Confucius for being a Sage of timeliness, in contrast to the others, who all held to a fixed and immovable rule for determining their acceptance or resignation of office. The same idea is expressed in the *Lun Yü* : " There are some with whom one can take a firm stand, but cannot associate in judgment " (IX, 29). Such is to hold to only one point. If one holds to the mean without regard for the time, this would be to ' hold the medium without allowing room for the exigencies of circumstance,' which would be to care for but one point and thereby to disregard a hundred others. The *Chung Yung* says :

" The Master said : ' The Way (*Tao*) is not far from man. When men consider as the Way, a way which is far from men, it is not the Way. The Ode (I, 15, 5) says : '' In hewing an ax-shaft, in hewing an ax-shaft, the pattern is not far off.'' We grasp one ax-handle to hew the other ; but if we look from one to the other, we still consider them as apart. Therefore the Superior Man governs men by men ; and when they change (what is wrong), he stops. Conscientiousness to others (*chung* 忠) and altruism (*shu* 恕) are not far from the Way. What you do not like when done to yourself, do not do to others.

" ' In the Way of the Superior Man there are four things, not to one of which have I attained : To serve my father as I would require my son to serve me, I am not yet able ; to serve my ruler as I would require my minister to serve me, I am not yet able ; to serve my elder brother as I would require my younger brother to serve me, I am not yet able ; to set the example in behaving to a friend as I would require him to behave to me, I am not yet able. (The Superior Man) practises the ordinary virtues and pays attention to ordinary words. If he is defective, he dares not but exert himself. He dares not also do something that is more than what it should be. His words bear respect to his actions, and his actions bear respect to his words. Is not the Superior Man characterized by a perfect sincerity ? ' " (pp. 305-306).

This is simply a development of the ideas of Confucius on *chung* (the doing to others what one likes oneself) and *shu* (the not doing to others what one does not like oneself). In practising *chung* and *shu* one draws a parallel from one's own self to treat others. This is why the Superior Man ' governs men by men', and therefore for him ' the pattern is not far off.' The way to morality is as simple as this. This explains the significance in the title, *Chung Yung*, of the word *yung* (a term which means ' usual ' or ' constant ').[1]

The *Chung Yung* says :

" The universal Way for all under Heaven is five-fold, and the (virtues) by means of which it is practised are three. There are the relations of ruler and subject, father and son, husband and wife, elder and younger brother, and of friend and friend : these five constitute the universal Way for all. Wisdom (*chih* 知), human-heartedness (*jen*), and fortitude (*yung* 勇) : these three are universal virtues for all. That whereby they are practised is one. Some are born and know it ; some study and so know it ; some through painful difficulties come to know it. But the result of their knowing is all one. Some naturally practise it ; some easily practise it ; some do so by dint of strong effort. But the result accomplished comes to one and the same thing.

" The Master said : ' To be fond of learning is to be near to wisdom ; to practise (virtue) with vigor is to be near to human-heartedness ; to know to be ashamed (of one's errors) is to be near to fortitude. He who knows these three things knows how to cultivate his own person. Knowing how to cultivate his own person, he knows how to govern others. Knowing how to govern others, he knows how to govern the empire and state " (pp. 313-314).

---

[1] The virtues of *chung* and *shu* both aim at the extension of one's self to others, so that the one quality can imply the other. Thus the *Chung Yung*, when it speaks about serving one's father as one would have one's son serve oneself, etc., is really discussing only *chung* (' Do as you would be done by '). Whereas the *Ta Hsüeh*, when it speaks about a principle, with which, as with a measuring-square, to regulate one's course, and says : ' What a man dislikes in his superiors, let him not therewith employ his inferiors,' etc. (*cf.* above, p. 366), is really discussing only *shu* (the not doing to others what one does not like oneself). If we combine these two concepts, we have the principles of *chung* and *shu*.

This again is a development of the ideas of Confucius, and makes the relations of ruler and subject, etc., the universal Way for all, while human-heartedness, wisdom and fortitude, which are the results of individual self-cultivation, become the people's universal virtues. Through following the universal Way, by means of the universal virtues, one may both cultivate one's self and govern others.

Such are the ideas found in the central or older section of the *Chung Yung*. In the opening and closing sections (pp. 300-301, 316-329), we find the anti-utilitarianism of Mencius, together with his mystical tendencies, explained and combined into a unified system. The *Chung Yung* says :

" What Heaven confers (*ming* 命) is called the nature (*hsing*).' The following of this nature is called the Way (*Tao*). The cultivation of this Way is called instruction " (p. 300).

In the *Li Chi* of the elder Tai it is stated :

" What is divided from *Tao* is called what is conferred (*ming*). What assumes form in individual things is called the nature (*hsing*). What is evolved through the *yin* and the *yang*, and manifests itself in material forms is called life (*sheng* 生). The cessation of this evolution and completion of the term of existence is called death " (*chüan* 13, p. 3).

The Heaven or *T'ien* mentioned in the *Chung Yung* is equivalent to the *Tao* in the passage just quoted. The nature (*hsing*) of each individual thing is received from Heaven, with which it has a relationship, according to the Confucians, which is similar to the Taoist conception of the *Te* and *Tao* relationship.² Heaven is the ethical first principle of the universe, while *hsing* is what Heaven ' confers ' on man, or in other words, what man receives ' divided ' from Heaven or *Tao*. Confucius emphasized on the one hand the value of the true expression of emotion and desire by the individual, and on the other hand their regulation by *li*. The *Chung Yung* likewise stresses the ' following of the nature ' on the one hand, while on the other it advocates the ' cultivation ' and ' instruction ' of this nature. The *Chung Yung* says again : " The state in which joy, anger, sorrow and pleasure have not yet made their appearance is called that of equilibrium (*chung*). When they have appeared, but are all in accordance with the proper measure, this is called the state of harmony (*ho* 和) " (p. 300). All such feelings are natural, and so must be allowed expression. But at the same time we must keep them ordered by means of ' instruction,' and must regulate their expression so that it will be neither too extreme nor too restrained.

---

¹ The word *ming*, ordinarily translated as Fate, or as the Decree (of Heaven), is here used as a verb, to confer. This is explained by the fact that the Fate of a man is what he receives from Heaven, or in other words, what Heaven confers on him.—TR.

² *Cf.* ch. 8, sect. 4, pp. 179-180 ; ch. 10, sect. 2, p. 225.

I have already pointed out how Mohist philosophy differed from the Confucian. The Confucians pursued what was right or appropriate, without consideration of any consequent benefit, in contrast to Mo Tzŭ, who considered only benefit and the result of conduct as important.' Those persons, said the Confucians, who do not consider the gain resulting from an act as the important thing, hold this attitude because they believe that the meaning and value of conduct does not go beyond it, but lies in the conduct itself. The *Chung Yung* support this attitude toward life with a metaphysical argument when it states :

" The Ode (IV, i, sect. 1, 2) says : ' The Decree (*ming*) of Heaven, how profound is it and unceasing ! ' Meaning, it is thus that Heaven is Heaven. (Again) : ' Oh ! How illustrious was the singleness of the virtue of King Wen ! ' Meaning, it was thus that King Wen was *wen* 文 (cultured). His singleness was unceasing " (pp. 322-323).

" Therefore absolute sincerity (*ch'eng* 誠) is unceasing ; unceasing, it continues long ; continuing long, it manifests itself ; manifesting itself, it reaches far ; reaching far, it becomes large and substantial ; being large and substantial, it becomes high and brilliant.

" By being large and substantial, it supports (all) things. By being high and brilliant, it overspreads (all) things. By reaching far and continuing long, it perfects (all) things. In its largeness and substantiality it is the equal of Earth. In its loftiness and brilliance, it is the equal of Heaven. In its reaching far and continuing long it is infinite.

" A person who is like this, without being seen, makes a display ; without any movement, transforms ; without any effort (*wu wei*), makes complete. The way of Heaven and Earth may be completely stated in one sentence : They are not double-minded in their creations of things, and so they produce things inexhaustibly. The way of Heaven and Earth is to be large and substantial, high and brilliant, far-reaching and long-continuing " (pp. 321-322).

' Heaven ' (in this case meaning Nature) moves unceasingly ; it acts, but not for something. The Superior Man takes this Heaven for model. Therefore he, too, must exert himself without ceasing. He also acts, but not for something.

I have already pointed out that there is a mystic tendency in Mencius's philosophy. The *Chung Yung* further develops this tendency, making the highest state of human development ' the union of the inner and the outer.' In this state, although life goes on and all things continue to exist, there is no longer any distinction between what is within and without, what is of self and of others. The ' absolute sincerity ' (*ch'eng*) described by the *Chung Yung* seems to refer to such a condition. ' Heaven ' or *T'ien* originally possessed

---

' *Cf.* ch. 5, sect. 4, pp. 84-87.

this *ch'eng*; *T'ien*, that is, originally made no distinction between what is within and without. Therefore the *Chung Yung* says :
" *Ch'eng* is the way of Heaven. To attain to that *ch'eng* is the way of man . . . . Enlightenment (*ming* 明) which comes out of *ch'eng* is to be ascribed to the nature (*hsing*). *Ch'eng* which comes out of enlightenment is to be ascribed to instruction. Given *ch'eng*, there is enlightenment ; given enlightenment, there is *ch'eng*" (pp. 318-319).

Ch'eng being the way of Heaven, man must use 'instruction' in order, through self-enlightenment, to attain to *ch'eng*. Hence such attainment constitutes the way of man. The *Chung Yung* continues :
" *Ch'eng* is the end and beginning of things. Without *ch'eng* there would exist no things. Therefore the Superior Man considers *ch'eng* as the noblest of all attainments.

" The quality of *ch'eng* does not consist simply in perfecting one's self. It is that whereby one perfects all other things. The perfection of the self lies in the quality of *jen*. The perfection of other things lies in wisdom. In this is the quality of the nature (*hsing*) ; it is the way in which comes the union of the inner and the outer. Therefore whatever always pursues it is fitting " (p. 321).

This doctrine, that the perfection of oneself and of other things is the way whereby to effect a union of inner and outer, is the same as Schopenhauer's ' work of love ' which transcends the *principium individutionis*. *Ch'eng* is the ' quality of the nature.' ' Instruction ' can add nothing to this nature which was not already there, but can only assist it to attain its fullest development. The *Chung Yung* says on this :
" It is only he in the world who has most *ch'eng* who can develop his nature to its utmost. Able to develop his own nature to its utmost, he can do the same to the natures of other men. Able to develop to their utmost the natures of other men, he can do the same to the natures of things. Able to develop these to their utmost, he can assist the transforming and nourishing operations of Heaven and Earth. Capable of assisting in these transforming and nourishing operations, he can form a trinity with Heaven and Earth " (p. 319).

The individual natures of men and of other things are all parts of ' Heaven,' and so the man who can fully develop his own nature, can do the same for the natures of other men and things. The man of perfect *ch'eng* is one without distinctions between inner and outer, self and others, and so has already attained to the state in which all things form one. In this state he can assist the transforming and nourishing operations of Heaven and Earth, and thus form a trinity with them. Such a man has the virtue of the Sage, and therefore he can accomplish wonderful things, should he furthermore hold the position of Emperor. The *Chung Yung* says :
" Therefore the course of the Superior Man (who is a ruler) is rooted in his own character, and attested by the multitudes of the

people. He examines (his institutions) by comparison with those of the founders of the Three Dynasties, and finds them without mistake. He sets them up before Heaven and Earth, and there is nothing in them contrary (to their mode of operation). He presents himself with them before spiritual beings, and no doubts about them arise. He is prepared for the rise of a Sage a hundred ages after, without any misgivings. That he can present himself (with his institutions) before spiritual beings, without any doubts about them arising, shows that he knows Heaven. That he is prepared to wait for the rise of a Sage a hundred ages after, without any misgivings, shows that he knows man.

"Therefore the movements of the Superior Man mark out for ages the way for all under Heaven ; his actions are the law for ages for all under Heaven ; his words are for ages a law for all under Heaven. Those who are afar look longingly for him, and those who are near never weary of him. . . .

"Never has a Superior Man obtained an early renown throughout the world who did not correspond to this description" (pp. 325-326).

When such a man occupies the throne, he rules the world simply through the influence of his virtue. In such a condition :

"All things are nourished together, without their injuring one another ; all courses are followed without any collision. The smaller energies are like river currents ; the greater energies are seen in mighty transformations. It is this which makes Heaven and Earth so great " (p. 326).

We may see from the foregoing that the *Chung Yung* largely follows the ideas of Mencius, while the *Ta Hsüeh* largely follows those of Hsün Tzŭ. These two works have exerted a tremendous influence upon later Chinese philosophy, and it is no pure accident that during the Warring States period they should have represented the two great Confucian groups of that time, headed, respectively, by Mencius and Hsün Tzŭ.

9—THE EVOLUTIONS OF *LI*

Later Confucianism received considerable Taoist influence.[1] In the political and social philosophy of one part of the Confucian school, this influence is well represented in the section entitled ' The Evolutions of *Li* ' (*Li Yün* 禮 運) in the *Li Chi* (ch. 7) :

"Confucius said : ' I have never seen the practice of the great *Tao*, and the eminent men of the Three Dynasties, though I have had a mind to do so. When the great *Tao* was in practice, the world was common to all ; men of talents, virtue and ability were selected ; sincerity was emphasized and friendship was cultivated. Therefore men did not love only their parents, nor did they treat as children only

---

[1] *Cf.* pp. 292-293, for the way in which Hsün Tzŭ was influenced.

their own sons. A competent provision was secured for the aged till their death, employment for the able-bodied, and a means of upbringing for the young. Kindness and compassion were shown to widows, orphans, childless men, and those who were disabled by disease, so that they all had the wherewithal for support. Men had their proper work and women had their homes. They hated to see the wealth of natural resources undeveloped, but also did not hoard wealth for their own use. They hated not to exert themselves, but also did not exert themselves only for their own benefit. Thus (selfish) schemings were repressed and found no development. Robbers, filchers and rebellious traitors did not show themselves, and hence the outer doors were left open. This was the period of Great Unity (*ta t'ung* 大 同).

" 'Now that the great *Tao* has fallen into obscurity, the world has become (divided into) families. Each loves but his own parents, and treats as children only his own children. People accumulate material things and exert their strength for their own advantage. Great men take it as the proper *li* that their states should descend in their own families. Their object is to make the walls of their cities and suburbs strong, and their ditches and moats secure. *Li* and standards of justice (*i*) they regard as the bonds whereby to keep in its correctness, the relation between ruler and subject; in its generous regard, that between father and son; in its harmony, that between elder and younger brother; in a community of sentiment, that between husband and wife. They use them to formulate institutions, lay out lands and hamlets, adjudge courageous and wise men as superior, and regulate accomplishments for their own advantage. Hence scheming practices come thereby and militarism arises.

" 'It was in this way that Yü, T'ang, Wen, Wu, King Ch'eng and the Duke of Chou obtained their distinction. Of these six great men, each paid great attention to *li*. Thus they displayed their justice, tested their sincerity, exposed errors, exemplifed virtue and discoursed about courtesy, thus showing to the people the invariable constants. All rulers who did not follow this course lost power and position, and all regarded them as pests. This was the period of Small Tranquility (*hsiao k'ang* 小 康) " (pp. 364-367).

This says that the government and society so striven for by some of the Confucians is, in the final analysis, only that of the Small Tranquility, above which there is the government of Great Unity. This idea is one plainly borrowed from the social and political philosophy of the Taoists. In recent times the philosophy of the Confucian school exemplified here has been much exalted by certain Chinese political leaders, such as the reformer, K'ang Yu-wei (1858-1927), and Sun Yat-sen.

CHAPTER XV

THE APPENDICES OF THE BOOK OF CHANGES AND THE COSMOLOGY OF THE *HUAI-NAN-TZŬ*

1—ORIGIN OF THE BOOK OF CHANGES AND OF ITS APPENDICES

The *I Ching* 易 經 (Book of Changes) was first of all a book of divination. Its original corpus is made up of the famous eight trigrams (*pa kua* 八 卦), each consisting of combinations of three broken or unbroken lines, as follows : ☰ ☱ ☲ ☳ ☴ ☵ ☶ ☷. These are traditionally said to have been drawn by the mythological Emperor Fu Hsi. There are also sixty-four hexagrams derived from the original eight trigrams by combining any two of these into diagrams of six lines each, thus making a total of sixty-four different combinations. Some scholars say they were made by Fu Hsi himself;[1] others that they were formulated by King Wen, one of the Chou dynasty founders.[2] Both the written explanations in the *I Ching* given to each of the hexagrams, and the brief descriptions of each of the six lines within every individual hexagram, are sometimes said to have been written by King Wen.[3] Others say that the former were composed by King Wen and the latter by the Duke of Chou.[4] The *I Ching's* Appendices, commonly known as the Ten Wings (*Shih I* 十 翼), are traditionally, but quite unjustifiably, ascribed to Confucius.

It is probable that during the Shang dynasty (1766 ?-1123 ? B.C.) the *I Ching's* eight trigrams were not yet in existence, since the Shang people then made divinations not by means of the divining plant (with which the *I Ching's* trigrams were originally associated), but by means of the tortoise shell.[5] The former method was an invention of the Chou people, made either to substitute, or to supplement, the tortoise shell method. The *I Ching's* trigrams and hexagrams thus would seem to have originally been made as pictorial substitutes for the cracks formed in the tortoise shell when this was heated with fire by the diviner ; while the explanations in the *I Ching* on each hexagram, and on the individual lines of each hexagram,

---

[1] This statement is given by the famous *I Ching* commentator, Wang Pi (A.D. 226-249).
[2] This is said by the historian, Ssŭ-ma Ch'ien (145—c. 86 B.C.).
[3] This is also said by Ssŭ-ma Ch'ien.
[4] This is said by the noted commentator on the classics, Ma Yung (A.D. 79-166).
[5] For these two methods, see p. 27.—TR.

would seem to correspond to the prognostications made by the Shang diviners when they examined the tortoise shell cracks. After such examination, these diviners would either make prognostications that were entirely new, or would sometimes utilize earlier prognostications. These earlier prognostications would be followed if the new cracks made in the shell were similar in form to cracks that were already known from former occasions ; but when no prototypes existed, an entirely new prognostication had to be devised.

The cracks thus formed from the heating of a tortoise shell were numerous and intricate and hence difficult to interpret. Consequently the prognostications based on them were also complicated and difficult to remember. The use of the divining plant in conjunction with the *I Ching's* diagrams, however, put an end to these difficulties. For the diagrams of the *I Ching*, formed of broken and unbroken lines in such a way that they bore a certain resemblance to the cracks appearing in the tortoise shell, were at the same time limited in number to sixty-four combinations, with the result that their prognostications were likewise limited. Thus when divination was made with the divination plant, a standard prognostication could always be obtained corresponding to whichever hexagram or line in the hexagram happened to be encountered, and the meaning of the prognostication could then be applied to the situation at hand. This was certainly a far easier method than that of the tortoise shell, in which any combination of new cracks might appear.[1] Perhaps this explains the *I Ching's* alternative name of *Chou I* 周 易. It was named *Chou* from the fact that it was composed by the people of the Chou dynasty, and *I* because its method of divination was an easy one.[2]

Originally the *I* was written to be used with the divining plant, but later, even when not used for divination, the meanings of the explanations of its hexagrams and lines continued to be quoted when support for an argument was sought for. The *Tso Chuan* gives an example under the year 597 B.C. :

" The army of Chin went to the rescue of the state of Cheng. . . . . Chih Tzŭ. . . . .crossed the Yellow River with the part of the central army that was under him. Chuang Tzŭ of Chih said : ' This army is in great danger ! The *Chou I*, under the case of the hexagram *shih* 師 ☷☵, as changed into that of *lin* 臨 ☷☱, says : " An army proceeds according to the regular rules. If these are not good, there will be evil." '[3] If the leader conforms himself to what is proper, the result is good. If not, the result is evil. A multitude divided

---

[1] These ideas, beginning with the words, " It is probable that during the Shang dynasty," etc., which begin §2, p. 379, have largely been taken from the article by Yü Yung-liang, *I Kua Hsi-tz'ŭ ti Shih-tai chi ch'i Tso-che*, in the *Ku Shih Pien*, III, pt. i.

[2] The word *i* 易 means ' easy ' as well as ' change.'—TR.

[3] *Cf. I Ching*, p. 72. *Shih* is hexagram No. 7, and *lin* is No. 19.—TR.

become weak; it is like the blocking up of a stream so as to form a marsh. The rules of service are changed so that each one goes his own way. Therefore it is said that the rules are not good. They are as it were dried up, just as the full stream is dried up and cannot follow its course. Consequently evil must ensue. Not to act is called *lin*. Is there a greater lack of action than where there is a chief who is yet not obeyed? This is the case we now have. If we really encounter the enemy, we shall certainly be defeated, and Chih Tzŭ will be responsible. Even if he now escapes and returns, great evil will await him '" (p. 316-317).

Again, under the year 545 :

" The Viscount of Ch'u will soon die. He does not practise virtue in his government, and is greedy and blind in his conduct toward the feudal lords. Can he, in order to satisfy his own desires, hope to continue for long? The *Chou I*, under the hexagram *fu* 復 ䷗, as changed into that of *i* 頤 ䷚, says : ' A blind return is of evil augury.' ' Cannot these words be applied to the Viscount of Ch'u? He wishes to return to his first desire, and reject what is fundamental. He has no place to return to. This is a blind return. Is it not inauspicious?" (p. 541).

Confucius also made use of the *I* in this way when he quoted and expanded the meaning of the thirty-second hexagram, so as thus to teach the necessity for constancy (the meaning of this hexagram).[2] Hsün Tzŭ, too, frequently quoted the hexagrams to support his arguments.[3] All these instances indicate that in later times the *I* was no longer used purely as a book of divination, but was regarded as a work having a wider significance. So too with its Appendices, which could not have been the work of any one man, but were probably written by several men who, while utilizing its varied ideas, added their own views and developed them, and thus made the *I* into a work having a unified philosophic system.

That these ' Ten Wings ' or Appendices could never have been written by Confucius, has already been made clear both by past and contemporary scholars.[4] The chapter on the Confucian school in the *Ch'ien Han Shu* says :

" During the Ch'in interdiction of learning (i.e., the Burning of the Books in 213 B.C.), the *I*, being a book of divination, was the only work not forbidden, and so its line of transmission was not interrupted. With the rise of the Han (in 206 B.C.), T'ien Ho, because he belonged to the family of T'ien, (rulers) of Ch'i, was

---

[1] *Cf. I Ching*, p. 108. *Fu* is hexagram No. 24, and *i* is No. 27.—Tr.
[2] *Cf.* p. 65.
[3] *Cf.* the *Hsün-tzŭ*, ch. 5 (*chüan* 3, p. 9), and ch. 27 (*chüan* 19, pp. 9 and 10).
[4] *Cf.* the *I T'ung Tzŭ Wen*, by Ou-yang Hsiu (1017-1072) ; *Chu Ssu K'ao Hsin Lu*, by Ts'ui Shu (1740-1816) ; various articles by Professor Ku Chieh-kang in the *Ku Shih Pien* ; and my own *K'ung Tzŭ tsai Chung-kuo Li-shih chung chih Ti-wei*, in the *Ku Shih Pien*, Vol. II.

transferred to Tu-ling, and was called Tu T'ien-sheng. Wang T'ung and his son, Chung, of Tung-wu, to whom he (T'ien Ho) gave (the *I*); Chou Wang-sun and Ting K'uan of Loyang; and Fu Sheng of Ch'i, all made commentaries on the *I* in several chapters " (ch. 88, p 7).

We have no means of knowing if these ' commentaries ' (*chuan* 傳) are among the present ' Ten Wings ' or not, but at any rate it is probable that the latter are in character similar to, and date from about the same period, as these commentaries.

2—THE EIGHT TRIGRAMS AND THE *YIN* AND *YANG*

The eight trigrams and their combinations of sixty-four hexagrams were invented in early Chou times, as I have said in the preceding section, to simulate the cracks formed in the tortoise shell of the earlier divination method. Originally these eight trigrams may not have had any specific meanings attached to them, but later on they were elaborated so that each came to be representative of certain ideas. Appendix V of the *I Ching* says :[1].

" The *ch'ien* 乾 ☰ trigram is Heaven, and hence is called father. *K'un* 坤 ☷ is Earth, and hence is called mother. *Chen* 震 ☳ by its first (i.e., lowest) line is male (i.e., an unbroken line), and so is called the eldest son. *Sun* 巽 ☴ by its first line is female (i.e., a divided line), and so is called the eldest daughter. *K'an* 坎 ☵ by its second (i.e., central) line is male, and so is called the second son. *Li* 離 ☲ by its second line is female, and so is called the second daughter. *Ken* 艮 ☶ by its third (i.e., upper) line is male, and so is called the youngest son. *Tui* 兌 ☱ by its third line is female, and so is called the youngest daughter.[2]

" *Ch'ien* is Heaven, round, and is the ruler and the father. . . . *K'un* is Earth and is the mother. . . . *Chen* is thunder. . . . *Sun* is wood and rain. . . . *K'an* is water. . . . and is the moon. . . . *Li* is fire and the sun. . . . *Ken* is mountain. . . . *Tui* is marsh. . . (pp. 429-432)."

Though this is supposed to be one of the later appendices, yet already in the Ch'un Ch'iu period, according to the *Kuo Yü* and *Tso Chuan*, people were thinking of *ch'ien* as Heaven, *k'un* as soil, *sun* as wind;[3] *li* as fire, *ken* as mountain;[4] *chen* as thunder, *k'an* as water;[5] and *chen* again as the eldest son, and *k'un* as the mother.[6] Thus what Appendix V records is simply a unification and arrangement of what had already been said.

---

[1] These appendices are here numbered according to Legge's numbering in his translation.—TR.

[2] Here, as throughout the trigrams and hexagrams in the *I Ching*, the progression is made from the lowest line up to the topmost one.—TR.

[3] Cf. *Tso Chuan* under the year 672, p. 103.

[4] *Ibid.*, year 537, p. 604.

[5] *Kuo Yü* (*Chin Yü* IV. 9).

[6] *Ibid.*

Once these fixed meanings had become attached to the eight trigrams, the present cosmologies in the *I Ching* were written. These based their speculations upon the origin of life as it is seen to occur in the case of the human being, and extended this by analogy to apply to the origins of other things. Appendix III says : " There is an intermingling of the genial influences of Heaven and Earth, and the transformation of all things proceeds abundantly. There is an intercommunication of seed between male and female, and all things are produced " (p. 393). A human being is produced by the union of man and woman, and so by extension, the universe is also considered to have two prime principles : the male or *yang*, the trigram for which is *ch'ien* ; and the female or *yin*, the trigram for which is *k'un*. Heaven and Earth are the physical representations of these principles. From the union of *ch'ien* and *k'un* comes *chen*, which has a male or unbroken lower line, and hence is the eldest son, the physical representation of which is thunder. *Sun* has a female or broken lower line, and hence is the eldest daughter, the physical representation of which is wind. *K'an*, having a central male line, is the second son, represented by water. *Li*, having a central female line, is the second daughter, represented by fire. *Ken*, having a topmost male line, is the youngest son, represented by mountains. And *tui*, having a female topmost line, is the youngest daughter, represented by low marshes.

The greatest things in the universe, in short, are Heaven and Earth. In Heaven, the objects most noteworthy to man are the sun, moon, wind and thunder ; on Earth they are mountains and marshy lowlands ; and the things most used by man are water and fire. The ancient Chinese regarded these objects as forming the constituents of the universe, made the eight trigrams correspond to them, and linked these trigrams together by giving them the relationships of father and mother, and of sons and daughters.

The objects symbolized by the eight trigrams are thus made the basic constituents of the universe. During the Chou dynasty this system seems to have existed quite independently from that of the Five Elements which has already been described,[1] so that the proponents of one system did not uphold the other. In the Han dynasty, however, the two schools were united. Thus Tsou Yen and his followers are referred to in Han times as the *Yin-yang* school, though in reality the *yin* and *yang* were originally attached to the system of the eight trigrams, which Tsou Yen had not touched.

Already in early times, however, the *yin* and *yang* had been used to explain the phenomena of the universe,[2] and were later often referred to by the Taoists, as in the *Lao-tzŭ* : " *Tao* produced Oneness. Oneness produced duality. Duality evolved into trinity, and trinity evolved into the ten thousand things. The ten thousand things

[1] Ch. 7, sect. 7, pp. 159-169.
[2] *Cf.* ch. 3, sect. 4, pp. 32-33.

support the *yin* and embrace the *yang*. It is on the blending of the breaths (of the *yin* and the *yang*) that their harmony depends " (ch. 42). Again, the *Lü-shih Ch'un Ch'iu* (V, 2) says :

" Great Oneness produced the two Forms (*i* 儀). The two Forms produce the *yin* and the *yang* " (p. 58). The *Li Chi* (ch. 7) says :

" *Li* must be rooted in the great Oneness, which divided to form Heaven and Earth, and revolved to make the *yin* and the *yang* " (pp. 386-387).

In the same manner the *I Ching* (Appendix III) says :

" In the *I* there is the Great Ultimate (*t'ai chi* 太極), which produced the two Forms (*i*). These two Forms produced the four emblems (*hsiang* 象), and these four emblems produced the eight trigrams " (p. 373). Again :

" One *yin* and one *yang* constitute what is called *Tao*. That which is perpetuated by it is good. That which is completed by it is the individual nature (*hsing*). The benevolent see it and call it benevolence (*jen*). The wise see it and call it wisdom. The common people use it daily, yet without realizing it. Thus the Superior Man's *Tao* (is seen by) few. It is manifested in acts of benevolence (*jen*), and lies stored up in things of utility. It drums all things onward, without having the same anxieties thereon that possess the Sage. Complete is the abundance of its Power (*Te*) and the greatness of its achievement ! Richly possessing it is what is meant by ' the greatness of its achievement.' The daily renewing of it is what is meant by ' the abundance of its Power ' " (pp. 355-356).

The duality spoken of in the *Lao-tzŭ*, and probably the two Forms of the *Lü-shih Ch'un Ch'iu*, both refer to Heaven and Earth. In the *I Ching*, however, the two Forms seem to be the *yin* and *yang*, as evidenced by its statement that " one *yin* and one *yang* constitute what is called *Tao*." Chiao Hsün (1763-1820) says about this : " That which is divided from *Tao* is called Fate (*ming*). That which is manifested in the individual is called his nature (*hsing*). The unity of *Tao* is divided so as to give completeness to the natures of individual men. The natures of all things are united so as to give completeness to the whole of *Tao*. One *yin* and one *yang* are what make *Tao* never ending." [1]

The relation given here between *Tao* and the individual nature is exactly that of the Taoists between *Tao* and *Te*. *Tao* is the all-embracing first principle through which all things are produced, and the natures of individual men and things are parts separated from this *Tao*. There is nothing produced by *Tao* that is evil, and so the *I* says : " That which is perpetuated by it (*Tao*) is good." It is only after *Tao* separates that it becomes defined and gives completion

---

[1] *Cf.* his *Lun-yü T'ung-shih I-kuan Chung-shu*.

to something, and therefore the *I* says : " That which is completed by it is the individual nature." The *I* then continues : " The benevolent see it and call it benevolence. The wise see it and call it wisdom." The *Lao-tzŭ* means the same thing when it says : " The *Tao* that may be called *Tao* is not the invariable *Tao* " (ch. 1), and again when it says that the *Tao* "produces but does not possess ; acts but does not depend upon anything; is leader yet does not preside " (ch. 51). Therefore, says the *I*, " The common people use it daily, yet without realizing it." The *Tao* " drums all things onward, without having the same anxieties thereon which possess the Sage." Likewise the *Lao-tzŭ* says :
" Heaven and Earth are not benevolent. They treat all things like straw dogs " (ch. 5).¹ That is, all things are produced spontaneously, without Heaven and Earth (i.e., the universe) having the intention of either being kind or unkind to them.

The Appendices of the *I Ching* thus borrow ideas from the *Lao-tzŭ*, at the same time adopting the *yin* and *yang* doctrines, and equating these to *ch'ien* and *k'un*, the male and female principles. Produced by *Tao* or the Great Ultimate, these are the two first principles of the universe. Describing their qualities, the *I* Appendices say :
" Vast is *ch'ien*, the beginner ! All things owe to it their beginning. It comprises Heaven . . . . . The way of *ch'ien* is to change and transform, so that everything obtains its proper nature (*hsing*) according to its Fate (*ming*) " (p. 213).
" Perfect is *k'un*, the beginner ! All things owe to it their birth. It receives obediently the influences of Heaven . . . " (p. 214).
" The way of *ch'ien* constitutes the male ; the way of *k'un* constitutes the female. *Ch'ien* knows the great beginning ; *k'un* gives to things their completion. It is through its ease that *ch'ien* is known ; through its simplicity that *k'un* exhibits its ability " (p. 349).
" There is *ch'ien*. In its quiescence it has concentration ; when in activity it goes straight ahead ; and it is thus that it has great productive power. There is *k'un*. In its quiescence it is self-collected and capacious ; when in activity it develops its resources ; and thus its productive power is on a wide scale " (p. 358).
" *Ch'ien* is a *yang* thing ; *k'un* is a *yin* thing. The *yin* and the *yang* unite their forces, and the hard and the soft gain embodiment, thus giving manifestation to the phenomena of Heaven and Earth " (p. 395).

Here again we find the origin of human life being taken as an example to explain by extension the origin of all things. " There is an intercommunication of seed between male and female, and all things are produced." Extending this same principle, we find :

---

¹ According to the commentators, dogs made of straw were offered as sacrifices to Heaven and Earth.—Tr.

" There is an intermingling of the genial influences of Heaven and Earth, and the transformation of all things proceeds abundantly." [1] " Heaven gives forth and Earth produces, leading to an increase without restriction " (p. 247).

Heaven and Earth are the physical representations of *ch'ien* and *k'un*, *yang* and *yin*. Of these two first principles, the one is hard, the other soft ; the one gives forth, the other receives ; to one all things owe their beginning ; to the other they all owe their birth. " There is *ch'ien*. In its quiescence it has singleness ; when in activity it goes straight ahead. . . . There is *k'un*. In its quiescence it is self-collected and capacious ; when in activity it develops its resources." " Shutting a door is like *k'un* ; opening a door is like *ch'ien* " (p. 372). In all these statements the reproductive activities of male and female are taken as examples to explain *ch'ien* and *k'un*.

Other aspects of the relation of *ch'ien* to *k'un* are explained in the *I* Appendices by making analogies between them and the relationship of man and woman in the human society of that time. Thus in Appendix I :

" Perfect is *k'un* the beginner ! All things owe to it their birth. It receives obediently the influences of Heaven. *K'un* in its thickness, supports and contains things. Its Power (*Te*) harmonizes and is unlimited. Its comprehension is wide and its breadth great. Various things obtain from it their full development. The mare is a creature of earthly kind. It moves over the earth without limits. It is mild and docile, beneficial and firm. Such is the course of the Superior Man. If it (*k'un*) goes ahead first, it will become confused and lose the way. It it follows, it will docilely gain the regular (way). . . . The good fortune arising from resting in firmness corresponds to the unlimited capacity of Earth " (pp. 214-215). And Appendix IV :

" *K'un* is most soft, yet when in movement it is hard. It is most at rest, yet its Power (*Te*) is square. By following, it obtains its lord and has the regular (way). It contains all things in itself, and its transforming power is glorious. What docility marks the way of *k'un* ! It receives the influences of Heaven and acts at the proper time. . . . Although the *yin* has its beauties, it keeps them under restraint in its service of the King, and does not claim success for itself. This is the way of Earth, of a wife, of a subject. The way of Earth is, not to claim the merit of achievement, but on another's behalf to bring things to their proper issue " (pp. 418-420).

The *ch'ien* or *yang* is master, while the *k'un* or *yin* is their helper. If the *k'un* puts itself forward, it ' will become confused and lose the way.' But if it follows the *ch'ien* or *yang*, it will ' obtain its lord and have the regular (way).' For long this has been held up in China as the ideal of wifely conduct.

---

[1] *Cf.* above, p. 383.

There must be union between man and woman to produce offspring, and likewise the *yin* and the *yang* must unite to produce all things. Appendix I says :
" When Heaven and Earth have intercourse with one another, all things have free development. When superior and inferior are in communication with one another, they are possessed by the same aim. . . . " (p. 223).

" When Heaven and Earth act one upon the other, all things are transformed and produced " (p. 238).

" When Heaven and Earth have meeting with one another, the various things are all brought to manifestation " (p. 250).

" In the marriage of a young girl lies the great meaning of Heaven and Earth. If Heaven and Earth were without intercourse, all things would not flourish. (In the same way), the marriage of a young girl is the beginning and end of man " (p. 257).

Heaven and earth are the physical manifestations of the abstract first principles, *ch'ien* and *k'un*. They must be united to make things flourish. " Heaven and Earth are separate, yet their work is together. Man and woman are apart, yet they have a will in common. All things are separate, yet in their operations they fall into classes " (p. 243). Because of their union, Heaven and Earth, though separate, have their common work, just as man and woman, though separate, have a common will.

3—DEVELOPMENT AND CHANGE OF PHENOMENAL THINGS

Because of the union of *ch'ien* and *k'un*, all things exist, and hence there comes development and transformation. Appendix I says :
" When Heaven and Earth are released (from the grip of winter), we have thunder and rain. When these come, the buds of the plants and trees that produce the various fruits begin to burst " (p. 245).

" Heaven and Earth undergo their changes, and the four seasons complete their functions " (p. 254). And Appendix III :
" Shutting a door is called *k'un*. Opening a door is called *ch'ien*. One opening following one shutting is called change. The endless passing from one of these states to the other may be called the constant course (of things) " (p. 372).

Things in the universe ever change and become renewed, and these changes all follow a constant order. Appendix I says :
" Heaven and Earth act in concord, and hence the sun and moon make no error (in movement), and the four seasons do not deviate (from their order) " (p. 227).

" Heaven and Earth observe their regular terms, and the four seasons are complete " (p. 262).

" The way of Heaven and Earth is constant and unceasing. ' Movement in any direction whatever will be advantageous.' ¹ When there is end, there is beginning again. The sun and moon, pertaining to Heaven, can shine constantly. The four seasons, changing and transforming, can constantly give completion (to things). . . . When we see how they are constant, the nature of Heaven, Earth and all things can be seen " (p. 239). And Appendix III :

" Good and ill fortune are constantly overcoming one another. The way of Heaven and Earth is constantly to manifest themselves. The sun and moon constantly emit their light. All movements beneath the sky are constantly subject to one and the same rule " (p. 380).

The underlying idea in these quotations is that all things in the universe follow a definite order according to which they move everlastingly. The *Chung Yung* says : " The way of Heaven and Earth may be completely described in one sentence : They are not double-minded in their creation of things, and so they produce things inexhaustibly " (p. 322). This is exactly the idea conveyed in the quotation above : " All movements beneath the sky are constantly subject to one and the same rule." Because of this, evolution never ceases in the universe, so that Appendix VI says :

" Things cannot be exhausted, and therefore it is with *wei chi* 未 濟 ² that they (the sixty-four hexagrams) are brought to a close " (pp. 438-439).

4—THE ENDLESS CYCLE OF PHENOMENAL CHANGE

Things in the universe are ever changing according to an endless cycle. Thus the appendices say :

" Between Heaven and Earth nothing goes away that does not return " (p. 281).

" When there is end, there is beginning. Such is the movement of Heaven " (p. 229).

" His way is one of return and repetition. In seven days comes its return . . . . In this returning we see the mind of Heaven and Earth " (p. 233).

" When the sun has reached its meridian height, it begins to decline. When the moon has become full, it begins to wane. Heaven and Earth are now full, now empty, according to the flow and ebb of the seasons " (p. 259).

" When the sun goes, the moon comes. When the moon goes, the sun comes. The sun and moon thus take the place of one another in producing light. When the cold goes, the warmth comes, and when the warmth comes, the cold goes. Cold and warmth take the place of one another, and so the year is rounded out. That which goes contracts, and that which comes expands. It is by the influence,

---

¹ This is a quotation from hexagram 32 (p. 125), which is discussed here.—TR.
² Meaning ' not yet completed,' the name of the last and sixty-fourth hexagram.—TR.

one upon the other, of this contraction and expansion that what is beneficial is produced " (p. 389).

This ' return ' or constant round of the sun and moon and all other things in the universe constitutes a great universal law, according to which things change. Hence ' in this returning we see the mind of Heaven and Earth.'

Because of this principle, everything that reaches a certain peak, must then revert to its opposite. " When the sun has reached its meridian height, it declines, and when the moon has become full, it wanes." Thus in *ch'ien*, the first hexagram, the dragon, which is described in the first or lowest line as lying hidden, reaches its highest peak in the fifth line, when it is flying in the sky, but in the sixth or topmost line " the dragon exceeds the proper limits and there will be occasion for repentence " (pp. 57-58). In Appendix IV, Confucius is reported as commenting on this :

" This phrase, ' exceeds the proper limits,' indicates that he knows to advance, but not to retire ; he knows preservation, but not destruction ; obtaining but not losing. He only is the Sage who knows to advance and to retire, to preserve and to destroy, without ever acting improperly. Yes, he only is the Sage ! " (p. 417).

This principle of rise and fall is one taken from the *Lao-tzŭ*, and, according to the Appendices of the *I*, is illustrated in the arrangement of the sixty-four hexagrams themselves. Appendix VI says : [1]

" . . . . Treading leads to the hexagram *t'ai* 泰 (No. 11), after which there is peace. Hence this (hexagram 10) is followed by *t'ai*. *T'ai* denotes things having free course. They cannot forever have free course, and so this is followed by *pi* 否 (denoting things being shut up and restricted). Things cannot forever be shut up, hence this is followed by *t'ung jen* 同人 (denoting a union of mankind). . . . " (p. 434).

" . . . . Things should not be united in a reckless or irregular way, and hence this is followed by *pen* 賁 (No. 22). *Pen* denotes adorning. When ornamentation has been carried to the utmost, its progress comes to an end ; hence it is followed by *po* 剝. *Po* denotes decay and overthrow. Things cannot be done away with forever. When decadence and overthrow have completed their work at one end, re-integration commences at the other, and hence this is followed by *fu* 復 (meaning return) . . . " (pp. 434-435).

" . . . . *Chen* 震 (No. 51) is the idea of movement. Things cannot be in movement forever. They are stopped, and therefore this is followed by *ken* 艮. *Ken* denotes stopping. But things cannot be forever stopped, and so this is followed by *chien* 漸 (meaning advance) . . . " (p. 437).

---

[1] Some scholars have maintained that Appendix VI is of later origin than the other appendices. Yet it is quoted from in the *Huai-nan-tzŭ* (ch. 10, p. 7), indicating that in the time of the Prince of Huai-nan (died 122 B.C.) it was already known.

Because of this law, both good and evil must exist in the process of change in the universe. Therefore Appendix III says :

" Good and bad fortune, occasion for repentence or regret, all arise from movement " (p. 380).

" The lines (of the hexagrams) are patterned upon all the movements taking place beneath the sky. It is thus that good and bad fortune are produced, and repentence and regret appear " (p. 387).

Good and bad fortune are the invariable concomitants of any movement, and all phenomena in the universe consist in movement of some kind. Hence it is inevitable that there will be evil in the world. Thus Appendix III says again : " The eight trigrams serve to determine good and bad fortune, from which is produced great accomplishment " (p. 373). Such accomplishment must be closely connected with good and bad fortune. This is what Schopenhauer called ' eternal justice.' [1]

5—THE HEXAGRAMS AND HUMAN AFFAIRS

The things in the universe, and their production and change, all follow the universal laws described above. The *I Ching*, according to its Appendices, was composed so as to represent, through simple symbols, these universal laws, in order to be a model for human actions. In other words, the *I Ching* is a reflection in miniature of the entire universe. Appendix III says :

" As to the emblems (*hsiang* 象), the Sages used them in surveying all the complex phenomena under the sky. They then considered in their mind how these could be figured, and made representations of their appropriate forms, which are hence designated emblems " (p. 360).

" The appearance of anything is called a semblance (*hsiang*). When it has physical form, it is called an object. When we regulate and use it, this is called law. And when benefit arises from it in external and internal matters, so that the people all use it, it is called divine " (pp. 372-373).

That is, from the emblems (i.e., hexagrams) which the Sage has drawn to represent the things of the universe, he makes the utensils and laws that are used by the people. Therefore :

" Heaven produced the spirit-like things, and the Sages patterned themselves on them. Heaven and Earth have their transformations, and the Sages imitated them. Heaven suspends its emblems (i.e., stars, sun, moon, etc.) from which are seen good and bad fortune, and the Sages made semblances (*hsiang*) of them " (p. 374).

---

[1] A certain Chinese author writes : " An Immortal said : ' In playing chess, there is no infallible way of winning, but there is an infallible way of not losing.' He was asked what this infallible way could be, and replied : ' It is not to play chess.' For the playing of chess constitutes movement, and when there is movement there must result bad fortune as well as good, and consequent occasion for repentence or regret."

Things in the universe are ever in a state of flux and change, and the I Ching serves to represent these changes.   Appendix III says again :
" The lines (of the hexagrams) serve to imitate all the movements taking place beneath the sky " (p. 387).
" The I is a book which cannot be put far away.   Its method (of teaching) is that of frequent changing (of its lines).   They move and change without staying (in one place), flowing about into any one of the six places of the hexagram.   They ascend and descend, ever inconstant.   The strong and weak lines change places, so that an invariable and compendious rule cannot be derived from them. It must vary as their changes indicate " (p. 399).

Because of this constant movement, the Appendices often make references to what is ' timely ' (*shih* 時).   And because in their changes things must move from one extreme to the other, there is often reference to what is called ' central ' or ' the mean ' (*chung* 中).   The noted I Ching scholar, Hui Tung (1697-1758), points out how the word ' timely ' is used in Appendix I twenty-four times and in Appendix II six times ; while the word ' central ' occurs in Appendix I thirty-five times, and in Appendix II thirty-six times.   The word ' timely ' is used in many ways, such as waiting for what is timely, the timely movement, the timely completion, the timely change, the timely use, the timely meaning, the timely development, the timely release, and the timely standard.   The word ' central' or ' mean ' is also variously used in such phrases as the proper mean, the great mean, the central *Tao*, conduct according to the mean, the hard and the soft mean, etc. ; while in one place (commentary of Appendix I on hexagram 4), the terms ' timely ' and ' central ' are united in one phrase.   He also points out how these terms are also used in other early Confucian writings.[1]   Thus we see that in the I Appendices these terms, already of long standing in Confucianism (especially in the *Chung Yung*), are given a metaphysical meaning and that in the usage of these, as well as other expressions, Appendices I and II show certain similarities to that work.

Applying the principle that everything that reaches one extreme must revert to the other, the I Appendices offer mankind with ways of dealing with affairs, similar to those outlined in the *Lao-tzŭ*. Appendix I says :
" It is the way of Heaven to send down its beneficial influences below, where they are brilliantly displayed.   It is the way of Earth, lying low, to send its influences upward.   It is the way of Heaven to diminish the full and augment the humble.   It is the way of Earth to overthrow the full and replenish the humble.   Spiritual beings inflict calamity on the full and bless the humble.   It is the way of man to hate the full and love the humble.   What is humble is yet

---

[1] *Cf.* the *I Shang Shih Chung Shuo*, in his *I Han Hsüeh*, *chüan* 7, p. 4.

honored and brilliant. It is low but no man can pass beyond it. Thus the Superior Man reaches a good conclusion " (pp. 226). And Appendix III :

" Toiling laboriously yet humbly, the Superior Man will have good fortune in the end. The Master (i.e., Confucius) said : ' He toils but does not boast of it ; he achieves but takes no merit to himself from it : this is the height of generous goodness.' He was speaking here of the person who though having merit, puts himself below others. The virtue of the humble is overflowing, and his manners are respectful. Being most respectful, he is able to preserve his position " (pp. 362-363). Again :

" He who keeps danger in mind will rest safe in his seat ; he who keeps ruin in mind will preserve his interests secure ; he who sets the danger of disorder before him will maintain good order. Therefore the Superior Man, resting in safety, does not forget danger ; resting in security, does not forget disaster ; and when having good government, does not forget disorder. Thus his person is kept safe and his country is preserved. The *I* (hexagram 12) says : ' He perishes ! He perishes ! (If he thinks always on this) he will be as safe if bound to a clump of bushy mulberry trees ' " (pp. 391-392).

Here it is evident that the *I* Appendices are borrowing from the doctrines of the *Lao-tžŭ*.

Yet these methods for dealing with things in the world are only similar to, but not identical with, those in the *Lao-tžŭ*. The latter work advocates that extremes be synthesized so as to form a new blend or harmony, whereas the *I* Appendices simply advocate the taking of the mean or middle way between these two extremes. When the *Lao-tžŭ* says, for example : " Great skill is like clumsiness," this great or absolute skill is not something at a point midway between skill and clumsiness (meaning by this the skill that is ordinarily thought of when we speak of skill, and which, because is is not kept within bounds, may meet disaster). Rather it is a blend derived from the combination of ordinary skill with clumsiness.[1] The *I* Appendices, on the other hand, urge only to take the mean between the extremes (the Confucian doctrine of the mean), and in this respect remain Confucian documents.

As already seen, the position and relation of man and woman in the society of that time are extended, in the Appendices, by analogy to *ch'ien* and *k'un*. On the other hand, once the position and relationship of *ch'ien* and *k'un* in the universe have been established in the Appendices, they serve as a metaphysical interpretation of the relationship between man and woman in the actual world. Thus in Appendix I :

" In *chia jen* 家 人[2] the woman has her right place within, and the man his right place outside. The correctness of position of man

---

[1] See above, p. 185.
[2] ' People of the household,' the name of hexagram 37.—Tr.

and woman is the great principle of Heaven and Earth. In *chia jen* we have the idea of an authoritative ruler, that is, parental authority. When the father is father, the son, son; when the elder brother is elder brother, and the younger brother is younger brother; when husband is husband and wife is wife : then the way of the family is correct. When it is correct, all under Heaven will be established " (p. 242).

In this passage, the metaphysical support of ' the great principle of Heaven and Earth ' is brought forward to support the proper relationship that should exist between man and wife. Again Appendix III says :

" Heaven is lofty and honorable, Earth is low, and *ch'ien* and *k'un* are firmly fixed in this. Their lowliness and loftiness serve to display honorable and humble (social) position " (p. 348).

Honorable and humble position in society thus become things as natural as are the loftiness of Heaven and lowliness of Earth.

In addition to this, Appendix II, while describing the sixty-four hexagrams, points out how each can be used as a model by man :

" Heaven, in its motion, is vigorous. The Superior Man, in accordance with this, nerves himself to ceaseless activity " (p. 267).

" The power of Earth is denoted by *k'un*. The Superior Man, in accordance with this, supports things with his broad virtue " (p. 268).

Here man can apply the meaning of the hexagrams to self-cultivation. Again :

" Heaven above and a marsh below form *li* 履 (No. 10). The Superior Man, in accordance with this, discriminates between high and low, and gives fixity to the aims of the people " (p. 280).

" The intercourse of Heaven and Earth form *t'ai* 泰 (No. 11). The sovereign, in harmony with this, through his wealth gives completion to the way of Heaven and Earth, and assists what is appropriate to them, so as to benefit the people " (p. 281).

Here the hexagrams provide models for the conduct of government and society. Appendix III says :

" In the *I* there are four things characteristic of the way of the Sages. We should set the highest value on its explanations to guide us in speaking ; on its changes to guide our movements ; on its emblems (*hsiang*) for the making of utensils ; and on its prognostications for our practice of divination " (pp. 367-369).

The *I* was originally used for divination ; its words can be used as models for our own speech, and its hexagrams as models for our conduct. Appendix III gives a concrete explanation of how the emblems or *hsiang* may be used as models for the making of utensils :

" Of old, when Pao Hsi [1] ruled all beneath Heaven, looking up, he contemplated the emblems (i.e., sun, moon, stars, etc.) exhibited in Heaven, and looking down, surveyed the patterns shown on Earth.

---

[1] i.e., Fu Hsi, one of the earliest mythical emperors.—TR.

He contemplated the markings of birds and beasts and the suitabilities of the ground.   Near at hand, in his own person, he found things for consideration, and the same at a distance, in things in general.   Thereupon he first devised the eight trigrams to show fully the attributes of spirit-like intelligence (in its operations), and to classify the qualities of myriads of things . . . . . On the death of Pao Hsi, there arose Shen Nung.   He fashioned wood to make the share, and bent wood to make the plough handle.   The advantages of ploughing and weeding were then taught to all under Heaven.   The idea of this was taken, probably, from *i* 益 " (pp. 382-383).

I ䷩, the forty-second hexagram, which means ' advantage,' is composed of the trigrams *sun* ☴ above, and *chen* ☳ below.   *Sun* symbolizes wind and wood, while *chen* symbolizes thunder and movement.   Thus the hexagram *i*, composed of wood above and movement below, inspired the Divine Farmer, Shen Nung (one of China's culture heroes), to invent the share and plough-handle.   The same passage continues :

" They hollowed out trees to make boats ; they cut others long and thin to make oars.   Thus arose the benefit of boats and oars for the help of those who had no intercourse with others.   They could now reach the most distant parts, and all under Heaven were benefited.   The idea of this was probably taken from *huan* 渙 " (p. 384).

Huan ䷺, the fifty-ninth hexagram, is composed of the trigrams *sun* ☴ above, symbolizing wind and wood, and *k'an* ☵ below, symbolizing water.   Thus from the hexagram *huan*, composed of wood over water, Huang-ti (the Yellow Emperor) is supposed to have invented boats and oars.   Again :

" They harnessed oxen and yoked horses so as to draw heavy things to far-off places, thus benefiting all beneath the sky.   The idea of this was taken, probably, from *sui* 隨 " (p. 384).

Sui ䷐, the seventeenth hexagram, is composed of *tui* ☱ above, symbolizing marshes and contentment, and *chen* ☳ below, symbolizing movement.   Thus from the hexagram *sui*, composed of contentment over movement, was conceived the idea of utilizing oxen and horses for transport.

The *I*, in short, is a reflection in miniature of the entire universe, so that Appendix III says :

" The *I* is in a position of equality with Heaven and Earth, and is therefore able to give unity and order to their courses. (The Sage), looking up in accordance with it, contemplates the brilliant phenomena of Heaven, and looking down, examines the markings on Earth.   Thus he knows the cause of darkness and light.   He traces things to their beginning and follows them to their end.   Thus he knows what can be said about death and life " (p. 353).   Again :

" Wide is the *I* and great !   If we speak of it in its farthest reaching, no limit can be set to it.   If we speak of it with reference to what is near at hand, it is quiescent and correct. If we speak of it in connection with all between Heaven and Earth, it embraces all " (p. 358).

In short, if we model our conduct upon the *I*, we shall fall into no error. Appendix III says again :

" Therefore what the Superior Man peacefully rests in is the order shown in the *I*, and the study that gives him the greatest pleasure is that of the explanations of the lines. Therefore the Superior Man, when living quietly, contemplates the emblems and studies their explanations. When in activity, he contemplates their changes and studies their prognostications. It is thus that there is help extended to him from Heaven, with good fortune and nothing that is not beneficial " (p. 351).

In these lines the importance of the *I* is made evident.

6—The Cosmology of the *Huai-nan-tzŭ*

The book called the *Huai-nan-tzŭ* 淮 南 子 was written in the Former Han dynasty by the guests attached to the Court of Liu An 劉 安, Prince of Huai-nan, who after becoming implicated in a plot against the throne, committed suicide in 122 B.C. This book, like the *Lü-shih Ch'un Ch'iu*, is a miscellaneous compilation of all schools of thought, and lacks unity. Nevertheless it contains passages which explain the origin of the universe more clearly than do any earlier philosophic writings. This is because during the early period of Chinese philosophy interest was largely centered on human affairs, so that it was not until the beginning of the Han dynasty that cosmological theories assumed such fullness as found in the *I Ching* Appendices and in the *Huai-nan-tzŭ*. The second chapter of the latter work gives an example :

" (1) There was a beginning. (2) There was a beginning of an anteriority to this beginning. (3) There was a beginning of an anteriority even before the beginning of this anteriority. (4) There was Being. (5) There was Non-being. (6) There was ' not yet a beginning of Non-being.' (7) There was ' not yet a beginning of the not yet beginning of Non-being.'

" (1) The meaning of ' there was a beginning,' is that there was a complex energy which had not yet pullulated into germinal form, nor into any visible shape of root and seed and rudiment. Even then in this vast and impalpable condition the desire to spring into life was apparent ; but, as yet, the genera of things had not yet formed.

" (2) At the ' beginning of an anteriority to this beginning,' the fluid (*ch'i* 氣) of Heaven first descended, and the fluid of Earth first ascended. The *yin* and the *yang* united with one another, prompting and striving amidst the cosmos. They wandered hither and thither, pursuing, competing, interpenetrating. Clothed with energy and containing harmony, they moved, sifted and impregnated, each wishing to ally itself with other things, even when, as yet, there was no appearance of any created form.

" (3) At the stage, ' there was a beginning of an anteriority even before the beginning of anteriority,' Heaven contained the quality of harmony, but had not, as yet, descended ; Earth cherished the vivifying fluid (*ch'i*), but had not, as yet, ascended. There was a void, still, desolate, vapory, without similitude. The vitalizing fluid floated about without destination.

" (4) ' There was Being ' speaks of the coming of creation. The nuclei and embryos, generic forms such as roots, stems, tissues, twigs and leaves of variegated hues, appeared. Butterflies and insects flew hither and thither ; insects crawled about. This was a stage of movement with the breath of life everywhere. At this stage things could be felt, grasped, seen, followed, counted and distinguished.

" (5) The state of Non-being was so called because when it was gazed on, no form was seen ; when the ear listened, there was no sound ; when the hand grasped, there was nothing tangible ; when gazed at afar, it was illimitable. It was limitless space, profound and a vast void, a quiescent subtle mass of immeasurable translucency.

" (6) The state of ' there was not yet a beginning of Non-being ' wrapped up Heaven and Earth, shaping and forging the myriad things of creation. There was an all-penetrating impalpable complexity, profoundly vast and all-extending. Nothing extended beyond it, yet even the minutest hair and sharpest point could not be within it. It was a space uncompassed by any wall, and it produced the basis of Being and Non-being.

"(7) In the period of 'there was not yet a beginning of the not yet beginning of Non-being,' Heaven and Earth had not yet split apart, the *yin* and the *yang* had not yet become differentiated, the four seasons were not yet separated, and the myriad things had not yet come to birth. Vast-like, even and quiet ; still-like, clear and limpid ; forms were not yet visible. It was like light in the midst of Non-being which retreats and is lost sight of " (pp. 31-33).

Again (ch. 3) :

" When Heaven and Earth did not yet have form, there was a state of amorphous formlessness. Therefore this is termed the Great Beginning (*t'ai shih* 太 始). This Great Beginning produced an empty extensiveness, and this empty extensiveness produced the cosmos. The cosmos produced the primal fluid (*yüan ch'i* 元 氣), which had its limits. That which was clear and light collected to form Heaven. That which was heavy and turbid congealed to form Earth. The union of the clear and light was especially easy, whereas the congealing of the heavy and turbid was particularly difficult, so that Heaven was formed first and Earth afterward.

" The essences of Heaven and Earth formed the *yin* and the *yang*, and the concentrated essences of the *yin* and *yang* formed the four seasons. The scattered essences of the four seasons formed the myriad things. The hot force of *yang*, being accumulated for a long time, produced fire, and the essence of fire formed the sun. The cold force of *yin*, being accumulated for a long time, produced water, and the essence of water formed the moon. The refined essence of the excess fluid of the sun and moon formed the stars and planets. Heaven received unto itself the sun, moon, stars and planets, while Earth received water, rivers, soil and dust.

"Formerly Kung Kung contended with Chuan Hsü to be Emperor and, blundering in his rage against Mount Pu-chou, snapped the pillar of Heaven (at the northwestern corner) and the sustainer of Earth (at the southeastern corner). Hence Heaven dips downwards to the north-west, so that sun, moon, stars and planets travel toward that quarter. The Earth, on the other hand, cannot fill up the south-east, so that water, rivers, soil and dust flow in that direction. '

"The way of Heaven is to be round, while the way of Earth is to be square. Squareness dominates darkness, while roundness dominates light. Light is an ejection of fluid, and therefore fire is bright externally. Darkness is that which absorbs fluid, and therefore water is bright internally. That which ejects fluid, gives forth. That which absorbs fluid, transforms. Therefore *yang* gives forth and *yin* transforms.

"Among the irregular fluids of Heaven and Earth, that which is angry forms wind. Among the united fluids of Heaven and Earth, that which is in harmony forms rain. *Yin* and *yang* interact on one another and create thunder; excite each other and make thunder-claps; become confusedly mixed and make mist. When the *yang* fluid is dominant, it scatters (this mist) to make rain and dew. When the *yin* fluid is dominant, it congeals it to make frost and snow. Hence the furred and feathered classes of creatures, and those that fly and walk, pertain to *yang*; while the armored, scaled and hibernating classes of creatures pertain to *yin*.

"The sun is the lord of *yang*, and so in spring and summer the multitudes of quadrupeds shed (their hair). At the solstices of the sun the tailed and ordinary deer lose (their horns). The moon is the source of *yin*. Hence when the moon wanes the brains of fish become smaller, while when the moon is new snails and clams draw in. Fire floats upward, while water flows downward. Therefore birds move aloft, while fish move below. Different classes of creatures influence one another, and the root and topmost branches (of a tree) respond to one another. Therefore when a *yang sui* 陽 燧 (a kind of mirror) is put under the sun, it becomes hot and creates fire. When a *fang chu* 方 諸 (another kind of mirror) is put under the moon, it becomes moist and forms water. When the tiger roars, the valley wind comes. When the dragon arises, great clouds appear. When unicorns fight,

---

' This ingeniously explains why the heavenly bodies apparently move westward, and why the great rivers in China in general flow eastward.—TR.

the sun and moon are eclipsed. When whales die, comets come forth. When silkworms produce their silk, the string of the *shang* note (in the Chinese scale) breaks. When shooting stars descend, the great seas make inundations " (ch. 3, pp. 1-3).

This passage gives a unified system of cosmology to explain how Heaven, Earth and all created things came into being. It is curiously interrupted in the middle by the myth of Kung Kung struggling with Chuan Hsü to be Emperor, a section quite disconnected from the remainder of the passage, and probably an interpolation made by another visitor of Prince Huai-nan who belonged to a different school.

The *Huai-nan-tzŭ* also touches upon the relation and position of man in the cosmos, as in Chapter VII :

" Of old, before Heaven and Earth even existed, there were only images and no physical shapes, profound, opaque, vast, immobile, impalpable and still. There was a haziness, infinite, unfathomable, abysmal, a vasty deep to which no one knew the door. Then two divinities were born together, supervising Heaven and regulating Earth. Deep-like indeed ! No one could see where they ended. Great-like indeed ! No one knew where they ceased. Thereupon they divided into the *yin* and the *yang*, and separated to the eight extremes (of the compass). Hard and soft mutually completing each other, the myriad things acquired form. The murky fluid went to form reptiles, and the finer essence to form man. Hence what is spiritual belongs to Heaven, and what is physical belongs to Earth. When the spiritual returns to its door, and the physical reverts to its root, how can I continue to exist ? . . . .

" The spiritual is what is received from Heaven, while the form and body are what are drawn from Earth. Hence the saying : ' Oneness produced duality. Duality evolved into trinity, and trinity evolved into the ten thousand things. The ten thousand things support the *yin* and embrace the *yang*. It is on the blending of the breaths (of the *yin* and the *yang*) that their harmony depends.'[2] Therefore it is said : ' In one month there is an embryo ; in two months it has skin ; in the third and fourth it has tissue and more definite shape ; in the fifth there is muscle, and in the sixth bone ; it is completed in the seventh ; moves in the eighth ; is active in the ninth ; and is born in the tenth.' The bodily form being complete, the five viscera have form. Hence the lungs regulate the eye ; the kidneys regulate the nose ; the gall the mouth ; and the liver the ear. The senses are the outward, and the viscera the inward regulators. Their opening and closing, expansion and contraction, each has its fixed rule. Hence the roundness of the head imitates Heaven, and the squareness of the foot imitates Earth.

---

[2] *Cf.* the *Lao-tzŭ*, ch. 42.—TR.

" Heaven has the four seasons, Five Elements, nine divisions,[1] and three hundred and sixty days. Man likewise has four limbs, five viscera, nine orifices, and three hundred and sixty joints. Heaven has wind, rain, cold and heat, and man likewise has (the qualities of) accepting and giving, joy and anger. Therefore the gall corresponds to clouds, the lungs to vapor, the spleen to wind, the kidneys to rain, and the liver to thunder. Thus man forms a trinity with Heaven and Earth, and his mind is the master. Therefore the ears and eyes are as the sun and moon, and the humors of the blood as wind and rain. In the sun there is a bird standing on three legs, and in the moon a three-legged toad. Were the sun and moon to miss their course, there would be an eclipse and loss of light. Should wind and rain fail their proper time, there would arise disaster and calamity. Should the five planets fail in their course, continents and countries would suffer calamity.

" The Way (*Tao*) of Heaven and Earth is most great and boundless ; nevertheless they conserve their brilliant display and husband their spirit-like intelligence. How then can man's ears and eyes work long without rest ? How can his spirit ever speed on, without coming to exhaustion ? " (pp. 58-60).

In this passage, Heaven and Earth are described as a macrocosm, and man as a microcosm. Again (ch. 14) :

" Pervading Heaven and Earth, in confused Unwrought Simplicity, with nothing created : this is called the Great Oneness (*t'ai i* 太 一). All things issuing from this Oneness, each becomes differentiated. Insects, fish, birds and quadrupeds : these are the classifications of creatures. They are classified according to their varieties, and divided according to their groups, their natures and capacities being different, but all having physical embodiment. Cut off one from the other, they are divided each into its own particularity, and none can return to the common source. Hence moving, they are said to be animate, and at death they are said to be worn out. They are all creatures. They are not those that are not created, but those that create things. That which creates things is not amidst things. If we look back to antiquity, to the Great Beginning, man was there born out of Non-being to assume form in Being. Having form, he was regulated by things. But he who is able to revert to that state out of which he was born, so as to be as if he had never had physical form, is called the True Man (*chen jen* 眞 人). The True Man is he who is as if he had not yet separated from the Great Oneness " (ch. 14, p. 1).

Here is mysticism of the type that takes union of the individual with the universe as the highest state.

---

[1] i.e., the nine heavens that are mentioned elsewhere in the *Huai-nan-tzŭ* (ch. 3), consisting of the eight compass points, and the center as ninth.—Tr.

CHAPTER XVI

CONFUCIAN DISCUSSIONS ON THE SIX DISCIPLINES, AND THE ULTIMATE TRIUMPH OF CONFUCIANISM

1—Confucian Discussions on the Six Disciplines

A number of texts were used by Confucius for teaching purposes, comprising what I have already described as the Six Disciplines or Classics : the *Shih*, or Book of Poetry ; *Shu*, or Book of History ; *Li*, or Book of Rites ; *Yüeh*, or Music ; *Ch'un Ch'iu*, or Spring and Autumn Annals, and *I*, or Book of Changes.   But in his time the term, ' Six Disciplines ' (*liu i* 六 藝), was not yet in use, nor had any general statements appeared describing their merits as a group.   It was only toward the latter years of the Warring States period that such statements appeared, as for example in the *Hsün-tzŭ* (ch. 1) :

" The *Shu* records political events.   The *Shih* establishes the standard of harmony.   The *Li* sets forth the rules governing great distinctions, and is the regulator of social classes. . . . .The reverence and elegance of the *Li*, the harmony of the *Yüeh*, the comprehensiveness of the *Shih* and *Shu*, and the subtleties of the *Ch'un Ch'iu* are the epitome of all creation " (pp. 36-37).

In this passage, all the Six Disciplines save the *I Ching* are mentioned.   Though Confucius may have used the *I Ching's* moral teachings in his instruction, it is probable that he more frequently referred to the *Shih, Shu, Li* and *Yüeh*.   Mencius never once mentions the *I*, and though Hsün Tzŭ does refer to it, he never does so in the passages in which he makes general statements concerning the value of the other classics.   From this it would seem that though Hsün Tzŭ and the earlier Confucians may have used the *I Ching* in their teachings, they nevertheless regarded it as definitely less important than the *Shih, Shu, Li, Yüeh* and *Ch'un Ch'iu*.   Only after Hsün Tzŭ's time did the Confucianists begin to refer to the *I Ching* with increasing frequency, and not till then did it become equal in importance to the other classics.   The *Chuang-tzŭ* (ch. 33) says, for example :

" The *Shih* describes motives ; the *Shu* describes events ; the *Li* directs conduct ; the *Yüeh* secures harmony.   The *I* shows the principles of the *yin* and *yang*.   The *Ch'un Ch'iu* shows distinctions and duties (p. 439).

And the *Li Chi* (ch. 23) states :

" On entering a country, its teachings may be known. If its people are gentle and accommodating, sincere and honest, their teaching has been that of the *Shih*. If they have a wide comprehension and know what is remote and old, their teaching has been that of the *Shu*. If they are large-hearted and generous, indulgent and beneficent, their teaching has been that of the *Yüeh*. If they are pure and calm, refined and subtle, their teaching has been that of the *I*. If they are respectful and modest, earnest and attentive, their teaching has been that of the *Li*. If they are able to use their language carefully and to classify historical events correctly, their teaching has been that of the *Ch'un Ch'iu*. Therefore when the teaching of the *Shih* has been abused, there results a stupid simplicity. When that of the *Shu* has been abused, there results duplicity. When that of the *Yüeh* has been abused, there is wastefulness. When that of the *I* has been abused, there results violation of reason. When that of the *Li* has been abused, there results an over elaboration of ceremony. When that of the *Ch'un Ch'iu* has been abused, there is insubordination " (p. 255).

The *Huai-nan-tzŭ* states likewise :

" . . . . .The Six Disciplines are different in kind, yet all are the same in principle. Gentleness and kindness, accommodation and beneficence : these are the influence of the *Shih*. Simplicity and purity, sincerity and honesty : these are the teachings of the *Shu*. Clear-sightedness and logical comprehension : these are the meanings of the *I*. Respectfulness and modesty, veneration to others and humbleness : these are what are brought about by the *Li*. Magnanimity and simple ease : these are the transformations wrought by the *Yüeh*. The ability to make criticisms and argue about ideas : these are the results of the detailed analysis of the *Ch'un Ch'iu*. Therefore when the teaching of the *I* has been abused, demons appear. When that of the *Yüeh* has been abused, there is dissoluteness. When that of the *Shih* has been abused, there results a stupid simplicity. When that of the *Shu* has been abused, there is pedantry. When that of the *Li* has been abused, there is envy. When that of the *Ch'un Ch'iu* has been abused, there is slander. These six (disciplines), the Sage uses in co-ordination, and regulates according to their different merits " (ch. 20, p. 9).

The Han Confucianist, Tung Chung-shu (179?-104? B.C.), writes in his *Ch'un-ch'iu Fan-lu* (ch. 1) :

" The prince knows that he who is in power cannot by evil methods make men submit to him. Therefore he chooses the Six Disciplines through which to develop the people. The *Shih* and *Shu* make orderly their aims. The *Li* and *Yüeh* purify their fine qualities. The *I* and *Ch'un Ch'iu* illumine their knowledge. These six teachings are all great, and at the same time each has that in which it stands pre-eminent. The *Shih* describes aims, and therefore is pre-eminent for its unspoiled naturalness. The *Li* regulates distinctions, and therefore is pre-eminent in its decorative qualities. The *Yüeh* intones virtue, and therefore is pre-eminent in its influencing power. The *Shu* records achievements, and therefore is pre-eminent concerning events. The *I* takes Heaven and Earth as its bases, and therefore is pre-eminent in calculating probabilities. The *Ch'un Ch'iu* rectifies right and wrong, and therefore stands pre-eminent in ruling men " (*chuan* 1, p. 24).

Also Ssǔ-ma Ch'ien states in his autobiography in the *Shih Chi* : " The *I* records (the movements of) Heaven and Earth, the *yin* and the *yang*, the four seasons, and the Five Elements, and therefore stands pre-eminent in describing the mutations (of the universe). The *Li* correlates and regulates the classes of mankind, and therefore stands pre-eminent in the field of human conduct. The *Shu* records the affairs of the early kings, and is therefore pre-eminent in the field of government. The *Shih* contains records of mountains and rivers, valleys, birds and beasts, grasses and trees, and the male and female of the furred and feathered kind, and therefore is pre-eminent in its influencing power. The *Yüeh* is that whereby the feeling of joy is established, and therefore is pre-eminent in its harmonizing power. The *Ch'un Ch'iu* distinguishes between right and wrong, and therefore stands pre-eminent in ruling men " (ch. 130, p. 9).

Finally, the *I-wen Chih* in the *Ch'ien Han Shu* states : " As to the cultural value of the Six Disciplines, the *Yüeh* is intended to harmonize the (human) spirit, and is the manifestation of benevolence ; the *Shih* is intended to rectify words, and is the practice of justice ; the *Li* is intended to make clear the rules of bodily conduct, and the meaning here is so obvious that there is no need for an interpretive symbol ; the *Shu* is intended to broaden one's information, and is the practice of wisdom ; the *Ch'un Ch'iu* is intended to pass moral judgments on events, and is the symbol of faithfulness. These five are the way of the five enduring virtues ; they mutually support each other. The *I* is the source of all. Therefore it is said : ' When the *I* is not revealed, the activities of *ch'ien* and *k'un* are almost suspended.' ¹ This means that the *I* ends and begins with Heaven and Earth. But the other five teachings change in each period, just as the Five Elements succeed each other, one or another controlling affairs in each successive period " (*Aids*, p. 60).

Almost all of these passages about the classics are written by later Confucianists, and in them the term, ' Six Disciplines,' first becomes definitely established. At times, however, the classics were also spoken of as the Six Teachings (*liu hsüeh* 六 學), as in the chapter in the *Ch'ien Han Shu* which describes the Confucian school : " The Confucians of old studied widely the literature of the Six Disciplines. It was through these Six Teachings, which are the

---

¹ *Cf. I Ching*, p. 377.—TR.

texts of kingly teaching, that the former Sages made evident the way of Heaven, rectified human relationships, and brought to actuality the completed laws for perfect government " (ch. 88, p. 1).

The same chapter continues : " At this time the Confucians first devoted themselves to classical studies " (p. 3). The term, ' classical studies ' (*ching hsüeh* 經 學), here means the study of the Six Teachings or Six Disciplines.

It was when Wu-ti (140-87 B.C.) of the Han dynasty carried out (probably in 136 B.C.) the plan of the noted Confucianist, Tung Chung-shu, who asked that ' all not within the field of the Six Disciplines or the arts of Confucius, should be cut short and not allowed to progress further,' [1] that Chinese thought became largely centered around Confucianism ; while at the same time the teachings of the Confucianist school became definitely confined to those of the classics. From Tung Chung-shu's time down to that of the reformer, K'ang Yu-wei (1858-1927), most Chinese thinkers have endeavored to make the classics the foundation for their ideas (no matter how novel), since they have known full well that only in this way could they gain approval for them from the general public. Though the study of the classics has been undergoing constant modifications, yet the spirit of each age has continued to find chief expression in their study. The historical changes in Chinese scholarship and thought may therefore be summarized by saying that the age extending from Confucius down to the Prince of Huai-nan (died 122 B.C.) is that of the Philosophers ; while that from Tung Chung-shu down to K'ang Yu-wei has been the period of the study of the Classics.

2—CAUSES FOR THE ULTIMATE TRIUMPH OF CONFUCIANISM

The rise of the Confucian school marked the beginning of the Period of the Philosophers ; its supremacy over all other schools marked the close of the period. The turbulent thought of the epoch as a whole, together with its political, social and economic background, have already been described.[2] During the early part of the Han dynasty, a political unification of China was effected such as had hitherto been unknown, while the social and economic movements that had first begun during the Ch'un Ch'iu period, gradually crystallized into a new system. With this unification and settlement, it was natural enough that a corresponding unification of thought should occur. Both the earlier policy of Ch'in Shih-huang-ti and of his minister Li Ssŭ, which aimed at a unity of thought, and the latter one of Wu-ti and of his minister, Tung Chung-shu, were representative of the same historical tendency and hence were not the mere whim of one or two men.

---

[1] *Cf.* p. 17.
[2] *Cf.* ch. 2.

It is well known that when Ch'in Shih-huang created the title, ' scholar of wide learning ' (*po shih* 博 士), he conferred it not only upon Confucianists, but also upon scholars belonging to all other schools of thought.   In view of this fact it is rather surprising to see to what an extent he utilized Confucian ideas in his political organization. The great scholar Ku Yen-wu (1613-1682) has pointed this out clearly :

" Ch'in Shih-huang had a total of six tablets engraved with inscriptions, all giving accounts of his annihilation of the six kings (i.e., the six great states of the Warring States period), and unification of the empire.   Concerning the customs of the common people, the inscription at T'ai Shan stated : ' Man and woman (in their relations to each other) conform to the proper rites ; each fulfils his duty carefully ; the distinction between household and outside affairs is kept manifest ; there is nothing that is impure.' The Chieh-shih-men inscription stated simply : ' The men delight in their agricultural labors.   The women practise their regular occupations.'   And the words on the Kuei-chi inscription read : ' Cultivation is adorned and righteousness is made manifest.   When a woman who has children re-marries, she is (considered to be) disloyal to the dead (i.e., her dead husband) and unchaste.   The separation between household and outside affairs is distinct, dissipation is forbidden, and men and women are restrained and pure.   If a man commits adultery, he who kills him is without sin.   Thus the men observe the statutes of justice. If wives abandon (their married homes) to marry (another man), their children do not consider them as mothers, and so they all transform themselves to become pure.' '. . .

" Thus, then, although the Ch'in dynasty's use of punishments was too extreme, its purpose of restraining the people thereby and of correcting their customs, certainly differed in no way from that of the Three Kings." [2]

This use by the Ch'in dynasty of Confucian doctrines, and even its Burning of the Books and prohibition of private studies, were in no way at variance with the Confucian advocacy of a single system of morality and one social code ; the only difference was that the execution of these ideas was too extreme.   Li Ssŭ and Ch'in Shih-huang, by putting an end to all private teachings, made the first step toward a unification of thought.   By obliterating the various philosophic schools, Wu-ti and Tung Chung-shu took the second step toward this unification.   The fact, however, that even after the Burning of the Books many schools continued to exist until well into the Han dynasty, makes the question arise as to why it was that of all these schools, Wu-ti and Tung Chung-shu should have singled out Confucianism alone to be orthodox ?   Is it an accident that such a

---

[1] These tablet inscriptions appear in the *Shih Chi*, ch. 6, (*Mém. hist.*, II, 142, 166, and 188 f.).—Tr.
[2] *Cf.* his *Jih Chih Lu, chüan* 13, p. 2.

man as Tung Chung-shu should have been living during the Han
dynasty, and that the carrying out of his ideas by Wu-ti should have
led to such a result ?

Some scholars have said that Confucianism, because it advocates
reverence toward prince and restraint upon subjects, has gained
the support of would-be absolute monarchs ; yet if this were the
case, the doctrines most convenient for such rulers would be those of
the Legalists rather than the Confucianists. Many later rulers have,
as a matter of fact, been ' outward Confucianists but inward Legalists.'
It is easily understandable why they should believe in Legalism, but
why, in such a case, should they at the same time pretend to be
Confucianists ?

Perhaps the answer lies in the fact that despite the fundamental
changes occurring in political, social and economic conditions from
the Ch'un Ch'ui period down to the early Han dynasty, there were no
important mechanical developments or inventions, and hence anything
like industrial progress, and therefore commercial development, was
necessarily limited. The bulk of the population continued to be
agricultural as before, the only difference being that men who had
formerly been agricultural serfs now succeeded in becoming free
peasants. Because of this, most of the people remained grouped in
ancestral clans, within which they continued to cultivate their fields
as formerly. As a result, the ancient patriarchal social system
maintained itself without great deterioration, so that the ceremonial
teachings and regulations of the past continued, in part at least, to
find practical application. What only the nobles had formerly been
allowed to practise, however, was now in large measure practised by
the common people as well. This is explained by the fact that the
common people, after their liberation, eagerly appropriated the
ceremonial teachings and regulations that had once been restricted to
the nobility, so as in this way to gain self-importance and to divert
themselves.

Politically speaking, despite the changes made by the Ch'in and
Han dynasties from the past, the Ch'in imperial house still remained
the royal feudal family of early times, and even though Kao Tsu, the
Han founder, arose from the common people, his form of government
continued to be a hereditary monarchy. Hence in these respects, at
least, the Ch'in and Han dynasties did not wholly break with the past.

Man, moreover, can never wholly detach himself from his surroundings, so that no institution can ever be newly created in its
entirety. Hence when, after the Ch'in and Han unifications, it was
necessary to draw up in final form the new institutions that were to be
used in government and society, the services of Confucianists were
found necessary for their organization. For it was these Confucianists who were versed in the old records and regulations, and
who possessed records of every new form of political and social

institution that had appeared since the time of Confucius downward. The *Chuang-tzŭ* (ch. 33) says about these men :

" How perfect were the men of old ! They were equal with the spiritual and intelligent, they purified the world, they cultivated all things, they harmonized the empire. Their beneficent influence extended to the masses. They understood fundamental principles and connected them together with minute regulations reaching to all points of the compass, embracing the great and the small, the fine and the coarse. Their influence was everywhere. Some of their teachings which were concretely embodied in measures and institutions, are still preserved in ancient laws and the records of the historians. Those teachings that were recorded in the *Shih, Shu, Li* and *Yüeh*, are known to most of the gentlemen and teachers of the states of Tsou and Lu " [1] (p. 438).

The Confucianists were thus not only versed in the former records and institutions, but were able to idealize and revivify them through their expositions and discussions, and to give them order and clarity. The other philosophic schools, on the other hand, dealt only with political or social philosophy as such, and therefore lacked the broad outlook of the Confucianists and their unified system of approach toward the concrete problems of government and society ; or if these did exist among them, they were less complete than those of the Confucianist school. Hence during the ' reconstruction period ' that followed the Ch'in and Han political unifications, these other schools were quite unable to compete with Confucianism.

Still another factor for the success of Confucianism lies in the fact that the Six Confucian Disciplines did not originally belong to any one school, but contained the germs of many types of thought. As such they could readily undergo change or elaboration, and because of this flexibility toward various types of thought, it was possible for them to combine and assimilate many different elements. For this reason the ultimate supremacy of Confucianism did not mean the absolute extinction of other schools of thought, but only their perpetuation in a modified form within the frame of the Six Disciplines. The result of such a compromise was that Confucianism on the one hand did not have to engage in a death struggle with the other schools, nor did these on the other hand have to expend all their energy in opposing Confucianism—another reason which would go far to explain the eventual Confucian triumph.

The position of classical scholarship in later Chinese thought, as a result, has been like that of a constitutional ruler. Though the ruler stands always as the ' connecting link of a myriad genera-tions,' yet his policy of government must as certainly ever change

---

[1] i.e., of the Confucianists. Tsou and Lu were the respective states of Mencius and Confucius.—Tr.

with the succession of his privy councillors. Present-day China, since her contact with the West, has in her social, political and economic life once more been undergoing fundamental changes. And with these changes the study of the Classics, which for two thousand years has held a dominant position in Chinese thought, has for the first time suffered revolution and been forced to abdicate. At the same time the Chinese thought of the future is assuming a new aspect.

B.C.	WORLD THOUGHT	CHINESE HISTORICAL EVENTS	CONFUCIANS	MOHISTS	TAOIS
550—	Buddha (b. 567 ?)		Confucius (551-479)		
525—		536 First Written Law Code			
500—					
475—	Sophists	481 END of CH'UN CH'IU PERIOD	Tseng Tzŭ		
450—	Socrates (469-399)		Tzŭ Ssŭ (d. 402 ?)	Mo Tzŭ (c. 479- c. 381)	
425—	Plato (427-347)				
400—		403-221 WARRING STATES PERIOD			
375—	Aristotle (384-322)	(States of Ch'u, Ch'i, Ch'in, Yen, Han, Chao, Wei)	Mencius (372?-289?)		Yang C Lao-tzŭ Chuang (369?-28
350—	Epicurus (341-270)	334 Ch'u annihilates Yüeh			
325—	Zeno (336-264)				
300—			Hsün Tzŭ (c. 298- c. 238)		
275—		260 Ch'in defeats Chao, 400,000 soldiers killed		Later Mohists	
250—		CH'IN DYNASTY (255-207)			
225—		221 Unification of China			
200—		213 Book Burning HAN DYNASTY (206 B.C.-A.D. 220)	Li Chi compiled (?) Appendices of I Ching written (?)		
175—			Tung Chung-shu (179?-104?)		
150—					
125—		Reign of Wu-ti (140-87)	136 Confucianism made orthodox		
100—					

Note : Many of the dates here given are approximate

ECTICIANS	Yin-yang and Five Elements	Legalists	Miscellaneous	Literature	B.C.
				Materials of *Shu Ching* and *Shih Ching* existed though not in present form	—550 —525 —500
					—475
					—450
					—425
					—400
i Shih ung-sun ung	Tsou Yen	Shang Yang (d. 338) Shen Pu-hai (d. 337) Shen Tao	Kao Tzŭ Hsü Hsing and Ch'en Hsiang Ch'en Chung Tzŭ 'Hundred Schools' at Chi-hsia in Ch'i Yin Wen, Sung K'eng, P'eng Meng, T'ien P'ien, Shen Tao	*Tso Chuan* (?) *Kuo Yü* (?) Ch'ü Yüan's (d. 288 ?) *Li Sao*	—375 —350 —325 —300 —275
		Han Fei Tzŭ (d. 233)	*Lü-shih Ch'un Ch'iu* of Lü Pu-wei (d. 235)		—250 —225
				Chan Kuo Ts'e (?)	—200
					—175
					—150
			Huai-nan-tzŭ of Prince of Huai-nan (d. 122)	Ssŭ-ma, Ch'ien's (145-86 ?) *Shih Chi*	—125 —100

the traditional chronology prior to Confucius, see p. xx.

BIBLIOGRAPHY

The purpose of this bibliography is to bring together all the works referred to in the text. The numerals following each entry indicate where this is mentioned or quoted in the body of the book. The bibliography is arranged in the following divisions : I. Original Sources, divided into (*a*) Translations in Western Languages, and (*b*) Untranslated Sources ; II. Other works cited, divided into (*a*) Works in Western Languages, and (*b*) Works in Chinese.

I—ORIGINAL SOURCES

These are arranged according to title rather than author. Almost none of these sources is later than A.D. 100.

A—*Translations in Western Languages*

Aids, abbreviation for *Aids to the Study of Chinese Philosophy*, compiled by L. C. Porter, with translation by Fung Yu-lan and L. C. Porter. Yenching University, Peiping, 1934. See under *Chuang-tzŭ*, *Hsün-tzŭ* (*b*), *I-wen Chih* (*a*), *Shih Chi* (*b*).

Analects, see *Lun Yü*.

Book of Lord Shang, see *Shang Chün Shu*.

Changes, Book of, see *I Ching*.

Chou I, see *I Ching;* also see Index.

Chuang-tzŭ 莊 子, in 33 chapters. Supposedly by the Taoist, Chuang Chou 莊 周 (369 ?-286 ?), but much of it must have been written after his death. The first seven chapters are considered the most authentic. Chapter XXXIII, called ' The World ' (*T'ien Hsia* 天下), is of great importance because it is an early criticism, written by some Taoist writer, of several of the philosophic schools of the Warring States period. For several philosophers it is almost our sole source of information. A good translation of this chapter appears in *Aids to the Study of Chinese Philosophy*, compiled by L. C. Porter. For a good translation of the first seven chapters, see *Chuang Tzŭ*, by Fung Yu-lan (Shanghai, Commercial Press, 1933). All references in the present work are to Giles, H. A., *Chuang Tzŭ* (Shanghai, Kelly & Walsh, 2nd ed., 1926) : 14, 19, 47-48, 50-51, 62, 68, 78-80, 82, 103, 107, 132-133, 141-142, 148-159, 168, 172-176, 178-179, 182, 192-204, 207, 214-215, 217, 221-248, 269, 277, 283-284, 292, 331-334, 400, 406.

Ch'un Ch'iu, see *Tso Chuan ;* also see Index.

Chung Yung 中 庸 (Doctrine of the Mean), a small work of the Confucian school, now contained in the *Li Chi* (ch. 28). Commonly attributed to Tzŭ Ssŭ 子 思, grandson of Confucius, but probably made up of two portions : one an earlier portion showing similarities with the ideas of Confucius ; the other written either in the Ch'in or Han dynasty, showing the influence of Mencius. References to Legge, *The Li Ki*, in *Sacred Books of the East* (Oxford, 1885), Vol. 28, pp. 301-329 : 31, 359, 362, 365, 369-377, 388, 391.

See also Index.

Classic of Filial Piety, see *Hsiao Ching*.

Doctrine of the Mean, see *Chung Yung*.

Evolutions of Li, see *Li Yün*.

Forke, abbreviation for Forke, A., ' The Chinese Sophists,' in *Journal of the China Branch of the Royal Asiatic Society*, Vol. 34, 1901-1902. See under *Hsün-tzŭ (c)*, *Kung-sun Lung-tzŭ*, *Lieh-tzŭ (b)*.

Four Books, see *Ssŭ Shu*.

Grand Norm, see *Hung Fan*.

Great Learning, see *Ta Hsüeh*.

History, Book of, see *Shu Ching*.

Hsiao Ching 孝 經 (Classic of Filial Piety), commonly, but unjustifiably, attributed to Tseng Tzŭ 曾 子, a disciple of Confucius. Probably a Confucian work of the Ch'in or Han dynasty. References to Legge's translation in *Sacred Books of the East*, Vol. 3, pp. 465-488 (Oxford, 1899) : 337, 360-361.

Hsün-tzŭ 荀 子, in 32 chapters. A large part probably by the Confucian, Hsün Ch'ing 荀 卿 (*c*. 298—*c*. 238). Authenticity of other parts uncertain. References :

(*a*) For the greater part of the work, to H. H. Dubs, *The Works of Hsüntze* (London, Probsthain, 1928) : 14, 29, 31, 40, 56, 80-81, 102, 104, 133, 140, 143, 149, 151, 154, 159, 172, 193, 196, 246-247, 258, 280-292, 294-311, 315, 334, 339, 341, 344-353, 363, 366, 368, 400.

(*b*) For a portion of chap. 6 (' Against the Twelve Philosophers '), to *Aids to the Study of Chinese Philosophy*, compiled by L. C. Porter (quoted as *Aids*) : 280-281, 370-371.

(*c*) For a portion of chap. 2 referring to the Dialecticians, to Forke, A., ' The Chinese Sophists,' in *Journal of the China Branch of the Royal Asiatic Society*, Vol. 34, 1901-1902 (quoted as *Forke*) : 216.

(*d*) For quotations from untranslated portions, see Original Sources, Sect. B.

Huai-nan-tzŭ 淮南子, in 21 chaps.   A compilation of various schools of thought made by the guests attached to the court of Liu An 劉安, Prince of Huai-nan (died 122 B.C.).   See also Index. References to :

(*a*) Morgan, Evan, *Tao the Great Luminant* (Shanghai, Kelly & Walsh, 1934), for chaps. 1-2, 7-8, 12-13, 15, 19, see pages : 16, 134-135, 154, 395-396, 398-399.

(*b*) For quotations from other untranslated chaps., see Original Sources, Sect. B.

Hung Fan 洪範 (Grand Norm), one of sections in *Shu Ching*, and probably a product of the Five Elements school.   References to Legge's translation in *Sacred Books of the East*, Vol. 3 (Oxford, 1899) : 163-165.

I Ching 易經 (Book of Changes), also known as *Chou I* 周易. Consists of an original corpus dating from probably the beginning of the Chou dynasty, and used for divination, plus several appendices (known as the ' Ten Wings ' or *Shih I* 十翼) probably written by Confucians during the early years of the Han dynasty. References to Legge's translation in *Sacred Books of the East*, Vol. 16 (Oxford, 1899) : 16-17, 26-28, 44, 46-47, 49, 55, 65, 379-395, 400-402, 422.   See also Index.

I Li 儀禮, in 17 chaps.   A detailed account of rites and rules of etiquette, particularly as they should be practised by the individual. It possesses little philosophical value, and its materials probably antedate for the most part those of the *Li Chi*, the compilation of which was probably at least in part inspired by the *I Li*. Translation of John Steele, *The I-Li or Book of Etiquette and Ceremonial* (London, Probsthain, 1917), 2 vols. : 65.

I-wen Chih 藝文志.   The first extant Chinese bibliography, compiled by Pan Ku 班固 (A.D. 32-92) from materials first collected by Liu Hsiang 劉向 (77-6 B.C.) and his son, Liu Hsin 劉歆 (*c.* 53 B.C.-A.D. 23), and now found in the *Ch'ien Han Shu*, ch. 30. There are also other *I-wen Chih* chapters in some of the later dynastic histories, but it is only that of the *Ch'ien Han Shu* that is referred to in the present work.   References :

(*a*) For certain translated portions, to *Aids to the Study of Chinese Philosophy*, compiled by L. C. Porter (quoted as *Aids*) : 14-15, 48, 77, 144, 158, 171, 175, 194, 402.

(*b*) For untranslated portions, see Original Sources, Sect. B, under *Ch'ien Han Shu*.

Kung-sun Lung-tzŭ 公孫龍子, in 6 chaps.   By the Dialectician, Kung-sun Lung 公孫龍 (third century B.C.).   References to Forke, A., ' The Chinese Sophists,' in *Journal of the China Branch of the Royal Asiatic Society*, Vol. 34, 1901-1902 : 192, 204-214, 217-218, 261, 267, 269.

Lao-tzŭ 老子, in 81 chaps. Also known as *Tao Te Ching* 道德經. The question of its date and author is very uncertain, but it probably dates from the third century B.C. A good translation is Waley, Arthur, *The Way and its Power* (London, Allen & Unwin, 1934). Referred to by chapter numbers : 7, 133, 141, 152, 157-158, 170-190, 223, 225, 229, 276, 292, 315, 320, 334-335, 383-385, 389, 391-392, 398.

Li Chi 禮記 (Book of Rites), in 46 chaps. A Confucian compilation probably made during the early years of the Han dynasty. References to Legge's translation in *Sacred Books of the East*, Vols. 27 and 28 (Oxford, 1885) : 16, 44, 46-47, 49, 65, 108, 163, 298-299, 337-348, 350-364, 369-370, 400-402, 406..
See also *Chung Yung*, *Li Yün*, *Ta Hsüeh* and *Yüeh Ling*.

Li Sao 離騷, the most noted poem in the collection known as the ' Elegies of Ch'u ' (for which see Original Sources, Sect. B, under *Ch'u Tz'ŭ*). By Ch'ü Yüan 屈原 (died *c.* 288 B.C.). Many translations, including that of Lim Boon Keng, *The Li Sao* (Shanghai, Commercial Press, 1929) : 176, 221-222.

Li Yün 禮運 (Evolutions of *Li*). A short Confucian work showing strong Taoist influence, and now contained in the *Li Chi* (ch. 7). References to Legge, *The Li Ki*, in *Sacred Books of the East*, Vol. 27 (Oxford, 1885) : 377-378.

Lieh-tzŭ 列子, in 8 chaps. A Taoistic work. Chinese opinion holds it to be a production, in which earlier materials were incorporated, made in the Chin or Wei dynasties (third or fourth century A.D.). European scholars, however, hold it to date from the third century B.C. References :
(*a*) For the greater part of the work, to Lionel Giles, *Taoist Teachings* (London, John Murray, 1925) : 243, 256.
(*b*) For portion referring to the Dialecticians, to A. Forke, ' The Chinese Sophists,' in *Journal of the China Branch of the Royal Asiatic Society*, Vol. 34, 1901-1902 : 217.
(*c*) For chap. 7, supposedly representing the doctrines of Yang Chu 楊朱, an individualist living prior to Mencius, to Anton Forke, *Yang Chu's Garden of Pleasure* (London, John Murray, 1912) : 6, 19, 133, 135, 345.

Lü-shih Ch'un Ch'iu 呂氏春秋, in 26 books, each with a varying number of sections. A compilation of various schools of thought made under the direction of Lü Pu-wei 呂不韋 (died 235 B.C.). References to Richard Wilhelm, *Frühling und Herbst des Lü Bu We* (Jena, Eugen Diederichs Verlag, 1928) : 20, 77-78, 83-84, 133-134, 137-140, 151, 154, 156, 161-163, 167-168, 171, 176, 194-195, 203, 337, 384, 395.

Lun Heng 論衡, in 85 chaps. By Wang Ch'ung 王充 (died *c.* A.D. 97). References to Forke's translation in *Mitteilungen des Seminars für Orientalische Sprachen*, Vol. 10 : 147.

Lun Yü 論語 (Analects), in 20 books. A collection of sayings by Confucius (551-479) and some of his disciples, recorded by disciples of the Confucian school. Good translations by Legge, *The Chinese Classics*, Vol. 1 (2nd ed., Oxford, 1893) and Soothill, *The Analects of Confucius* (Yokohama, 1910). References to book and section numbers : 1, 7, 31-32, 44-60, 63-75, 77-78, 80, 84, 86, 112, 119, 128, 135-136, 145, 170, 175-176, 194, 247, 260, 311, 316, 337, 339, 341, 354, 361-362, 371-372.

Mencius 孟子, in six books. A collection of sayings of Mencius (372?-289?). Translation by Legge, *The Chinese Classics*, Vol. 2. References to book and section numbers : 10, 14, 31, 33, 46, 50-52, 56, 59, 61-62, 70, 72, 79-80, 95-96, 103, 107-129, 131-134, 136-137, 143-149, 168, 170, 175, 247, 281, 287, 339, 357, 359, 361-362, 364, 372.

Mo-tzŭ 墨子, in 71 chaps. A collection of writings of the Mohist school, which was founded by Mo Ti 墨翟 (*c.* 479—*c.* 381). References :

    (*a*) For those writings dealing with the early Mohist school of Mo Tzŭ himself, to Y. P. Mei, *The Ethical and Political Works of Motse* (London, Probsthain, 1929) : 19, 25, 77-79, 81-82, 85-102, 247, 256-257, 295, 316.

    (*b*) For the 'Mohist Canons' (*Mo Ching* 墨經) and 'Major and Minor Illustrations' (*Ta Ch'ü* 大取 and *Hsiao Ch'ü* 小取), comprising chaps. 40-45 of the *Mo-tzŭ*, and written by the Later Mohist school, probably of the third century B.C., to Alfred Forke, *Mê Ti des Sozialethikers und seiner Schüler philosophische Werke* (Berlin, *Mitteilungen des Seminars für Orientalische Sprachen*, Vols. 23-25, 1922) : 20, 47, 80-81, 246-278, 303-304, 308-310.

Monthly Commands, see *Yüeh Ling*.

Odes, Book of, see *Shih Ching*.

Rites, Book of, see *Li Chi*.

Shang Chün Shu 商君書, in 5 chaps., and many sub-sections. A Legalist work attributed to Shang Yang 商鞅 (died 338 B.C.), but really a compilation of various Legalist writings. References to J. J. L. Duyvendak, *The Book of Lord Shang* (London, Probsthain, 1928) : 315-316, 319.

Shih Chi 史記 (Historical Records), in 130 chaps. The first general history of China, extending from the beginnings down to the reign of Wu-ti (140-87 B.C.) of the Han dynasty. Begun by Ssŭ-ma T'an 司馬談 (died 110 B.C.), and completed by his son, Ssŭ-ma Ch'ien 司馬遷 (145—*c.* 86 B.C.). References :

    (*a*) For chaps. 1-47, to Ed. Chavannes, *Les Mémoires historiques de Se-ma Ts'ien* (quoted as *Mém. hist.*), 5 vols. (Paris, E.

Leroux, 1895-1905) : 13, 43-46, 51, 163, 169, 175, 320, 369-370, 404.

(*b*) For quotations from essay by Ssŭ-ma T'an on the six philosophic schools (found in *Shih Chi*, ch. 130), to *Aids to the Study of Chinese Philosophy*, compiled by L. C. Porter (quoted as *Aids*) : 21, 170, 193-194.

(*c*) For quotations from untranslated portions, see Original Sources, Sect. B.

Shih Ching 詩經 (Book of Odes). A collection of 305 court and folk songs, collected from the various feudal states of China during the early part of the Chou dynasty. A few may even antedate the Chou, though this is doubtful. Valuable for light they throw on early conditions and customs. Translation of Legge in *The Chinese Classics*, Vol. 4, in two parts. References to odes as numbered by Legge : xvi, 11, 22, 25, 28, 30-31, 34, 44-47, 49, 63-64, 66, 77, 107-109, 120, 160, 222, 342, 372, 375, 400-402, 406.

Shu Ching 書經 (Book of History). A collection of speeches, prayers, etc., given on various historical occasions. Many of these are later forgeries, but a few may go back to the first millenium B.C. References to Legge's translation in *Sacred Books of the East*, Vol. 3 (Oxford, 1899) : 22, 27, 30-31, 33, 44-47, 64, 77, 107-109, 163, 367, 400-402, 406.
See also *Hung Fan*.

Ssŭ Shu 四書 (Four Books). Under this general title are grouped 1. The *Lun Yü* of Confucius ; 2. The *Ta Hsüeh ;* 3. The *Chung Yung*, ascribed to the grandson of Confucius ; 4. The *Mencius*. See notices under individual titles. Pages 362, 369

Ta Hsüeh 大學 (Great Learning). A short Confucian work showing affinities with the thought of Hsün Tzŭ, and now contained in the *Li Chi* (ch. 39). References to Legge, *The Li Ki*, in *Sacred Books of the East*, Vol. 28 (Oxford, 1885) : 64, 121, 361-369, 373, 377.
See also Index.

Tao Te Ching, see *Lao-tzŭ*.

Tso Chuan 左傳 and *Ch'un Ch'iu* 春秋 (Spring and Autumn Annals). The latter is a very brief year-by-year chronicle history of the state of Lu extending from 722 to 481 B.C. The *Tso Chuan*, supposedly a commentary on the *Ch'un Ch'iu*, and covering the same epoch, is really a general history of the China of that time, and is enormously valuable for the detailed information it supplies. It was probably written or compiled in the third century B.C. References to Legge's translation in *The Chinese Classics*, Vol. 5, in two parts : xvii, 9-11, 13, 16, 22, 24-25, 28, 30-32, 35-38, 41-42, 47, 49, 54-55, 61, 78, 313-314, 380-382, 400-402.

Yang Chu chapter in *Lieh-tzŭ*, see under *Lieh-tzŭ*.

Yen T'ieh Lun 鹽鐵論 (Discourses on Salt and Iron), in 60 chaps. An economic treatise concerning state control of iron, salt, etc., by Huan K'uan 桓寬 (was alive *c.* 73 B.C.). References to Esson M. Gale, *Discourses on Salt and Iron* (Leyden, Sinica Leidensia Vol. 2, 1931) : 16.

Yin-wen-tzŭ 尹文子, a short work supposedly by Yin Wen (fourth century B.C.), but probably written much later. Translation by P. Masson-Oursel and Kia-kien Tchou in *T'oung Pao*, Vol. 15, 1914 : 150, 153.

Yüeh Ling 月令 (Monthly Commands), contained in *Lü-shih Ch'un Ch'iu* (sect. 1 of Bks. 1-12), and in *Li Chi* (ch. 4). An early Chinese almanac representing the thought of the Five Elements school. References to Legge, *The Li Ki*, in *Sacred Books of the East*, Vol. 17 (Oxford, 1885) : 163-165.

B—*Untranslated Sources*

See Section A for notices on works already mentioned.

Chan Kuo Ts'e 戰國策 (Plots of the Warring States). A collection of historical speeches by diplomats, statesmen, etc., arranged under states, and covering the period of the Warring States. Perhaps compiled in early years of Han dynasty. References to divisions according to states, and sections under these states : 143, 171, 192.

Ch'ien Han Shu 前漢書 (History of the Former Han Dynasty), in 120 chaps. By Pan Ku 班固 (A.D. 32-92). See also *I-wen Chih* under Sect. A. References to the *T'ung Wen Ying Tien K'an* 同文影殿刊 edition, 1903 : 12, 16-18, 26-28, 150, 168, 176, 370-371, 381, 402-403.

Ch'u Tz'ŭ 楚辭 (Elegies of Ch'u), a notable collection of poems of special type written chiefly by Ch'ü Yüan 屈原 (died *c.* 288 B.C.) and his followers. References : 176, 222.
Individual poems in this collection referred to in this work are : (*a*) *Li Sao* (see under Sect. A); (*b*) *T'ien Wen* 天問 (Questions about Heaven); (*c*) *Yü Fu* 漁父 ; (*d*) *Yüan Yu* 遠遊.

Ch'un-ch'iu Fan-lu 春秋繁露, in 82 chaps. By the Confucianist, Tung Chung-shu 董仲舒 (179 ?-104 ? B.C.). References to Su Yü 蘇輿, *Ch'un-ch'iu Fan-lu I-cheng* 春秋繁露義證 edition, 1910 : 401.

Elegies of Ch'u, see *Ch'u Tz'ŭ*.

Han-fei-tzŭ 韓非子, in 58 chaps. Supposedly by the Legalist, Han Fei (died 233 B.C.). Certain parts, such as chaps. 49-50, can reasonably be attributed to him, but others must be by other Legalist writers. References to *Ssŭ Pu Ts'ung K'an* 四部叢刊

edition, 1920-1922 : 19, 52, 79-80, 133-134, 150-152, 159, 171, 176-177, 179, 195, 202, 246, 312, 317-331, 335-337.

Han Shu, see *Ch'ien Han Shu*.

Hsün-tzŭ (see also under Sect. A). References to *Ssŭ Pu Ts'ung K'an* 四 部 叢 刊 edition, 1920-1922 : 250, 283-284, 293, 364-365, 368, 381.

Huai-nan-tzŭ (see also Sect. A and Index). References to Liu Wen-tien 劉 文 典, *Huai-nan Hung-lieh Chi-chieh* 淮 南 鴻 烈 集 解 edition (Commercial Press, 1933) : 56, 77, 82, 165, 389, 396-399, 401.

Kuan-tzŭ 管 子, in 86 chaps. Attributed to Kuan Chung 管 仲 (died 645 B.C.), but obviously much later, possibly third century B.C. Contains writings of many schools of thought, including Legalists, Taoists, Five Elements school, etc. References to *Ssŭ Pu Ts'ung K'an* 四 部 叢 刊 edition, 1920-1922 : 19, 78, 165-167, 275, 318, 321-322, 324, 334.

K'ung-tzŭ Chia-yü 孔 子 家 語 (Sayings of the Confucian School), supposedly a record of sayings by Confucius and his followers. Its authenticity is uncertain, some scholars saying it dates from the third century B.C., others saying it is a forgery of the third century A.D. References to *Ssŭ Pu Ts'ung K'an* 四 部 叢 刊 edition, 1920-1922 : 49-50.

Kung-yang Chuan 公 羊 傳, a Confucian commentary on the *Ch'un Ch'iu*. Written by Kung-yang Kao 公 羊 高 at beginning of Han dynasty. Interprets the *Ch'un Ch'iu* according to the ' praise and blame ' theory : 16, 65.

Kuo Yü 國 語 (Sayings of the States), a collection of historical conversations, arranged under states, and covering about the same period as does the *Tso Chuan*. The partial translation made into French by C. de Harlez, the first part of which was published in the *Journal Asiatique*, IX, ii (1893), 37, 373-419 ; iii (1894), 5-91 ; and the second part of which was published separately (*Le Koue yu*, Louvain, 1895), has not been available for consultation in Peiping. References to divisions according to states, and sections under these states : 11, 22, 24-25, 30-34, 39-42, 46, 49, 52, 62, 382.

Li Chi of elder Tai (*Ta Tai Li Chi* 大 戴 禮 記), a compilation of Confucian writings on the rites, etc., made by Tai Te 戴 德 about time of Christ. This was reduced by Tai Te's nephew, Tai Sheng 戴 聖, from 85 to 46 chaps., and in this form became the present *Li Chi* (Book of Rites). The work of the elder Tai has come down to us only in part. References to *Ssŭ Pu Ts'ung K'an* 四 部 叢 刊 edition, 1920-1922 : 337, 340, 354, 363, 374.

Shen-tzŭ 慎 子, a work attributed to Shen Tao 慎 到, but which in its present form is only a later compilation of fragments. References to *Shou Shan Ko Ts'ung Shu* 守 山 閣 叢 書 edition, 1889 : 155-156.

Shih Chi (see also Sect. A). References to *T'ung Wen Ying Tien K'an* 同 文 影 殿 刊 edition, 1903 : 56, 76, 84, 106-108, 132-133, 159-161, 171, 203, 221, 319-320, 334, 402.

Shuo-wen Chieh-tzŭ 說 文 解 字, composed by Hsü Shen 許 慎, about A.D. 100. The first Chinese dictionary to use the system of radicals for classification, being divided into 540 radical sections : 48.

Shuo Yüan 說 苑, by Liu Hsiang 劉 向 (77-6 B.C.). A rather uneven work dealing largely with the principles of good government, and containing much borrowing from earlier sources : 104-105.

T'ien Wen (Questions about Heaven), see *Ch'u Tz'ŭ*.

Yü Fu, see *Ch'u Tz'ŭ*.

Yüan Yu, see *Ch'u Tz'ŭ*.

2—OTHER WORKS CITED

These are arranged according to author rather than title.

A—*Works in Western Languages*

Aristotle, *Ethics* : 122, 371.

Bentham, Jeremy, *Introduction to the Principles of Morals and Legislature*, Oxford ed., 1907 : 96, 249.

Descartes, *Discours de la méthode*, Everyman's Library, London and New York, 1912 : 227.

Diogenes Laertius, *The Lives and Opinions of Eminent Philosophers* : translated by C. D. Yonge, London, 1915 : 80.

Dubs, H. H., 'The Conflict of Authority and Freedom in Ancient China,' in *Open Court Magazine*, Vol. 40, No. 3 : 69.

Dubs, H. H., *Hsüntze, the Moulder of Ancient Confucianism* (London, Probsthain, 1927) : 279.

Fung, Yu-lan, *Chuang Tzŭ, a New Selected Translation with an Exposition of the Philosophy of Kuo Hsiang* (Shanghai, Commercial Press, 1933) : 226, 240.

Fung, Yu-lan, 'Why China has no Science,' in *International Journal of Ethics*, Vol. 32, No. 3 : 3.

Hobbes, Thomas, *The Leviathan*, Everyman's Library : 101, 103.

James, William, *Essays in Radical Empiricism*, New York, 1912 : 239.

James, William, *A Pluralistic Universe*, New York, 1912 : 281.

Maspero, Henri, 'La chronologie des rois de Ts'i,' in *T'oung Pao*, 1927, No. 5 : 106.

Plato, *Dialogues :* 54.

Plato, *The Republic :* 117.

Richards, I. A., *Mencius on the Mind* (London, Kegan Paul, 1932) : 124.

B—*Works in Chinese*

Save for the CHIA I citation, all these works date from later than A.D. 100. They are all by Chinese scholars, except the one article by a Japanese scholar, Koyanagi Shikita. In cases in which only the date of birth is given, the author referred to is, so far as is known, still living.

Chang Hsüeh-ch'eng 章學誠 (1738-1801), *Wen-shih T'ung-i* 文史通義, in *Chang-shih I-shu* 章氏遺書 : 7, 19-20.

Ch'e Yü-feng 車玉峰 (lived *c.* 1274), and **Wang Po** 王柏 (1197-1274), *Lu Chai Chi* 魯齊集 : 368.
See also Wang Po.

Ch'en Chung-fan 陳鐘凡 (born 1892), *Chu-tzŭ T'ung-i* 諸子通誼 (Shanghai, 1926) : 206.

Ch'en Li 陳澧 (1801-1882), *Tung-shu Tu-shu Chi* 東塾讀書記 : 108, 121, 174, 287-288.

Cheng Ch'iao 鄭樵 (1104-1162), *T'ung-chih Hsiao-ch'ou Lüeh* 通志校讎略 : 15.

Ch'eng Fu-hsin 程復心 (fourteenth century), *Meng-tzŭ Nien-p'u* 孟子年譜 : 107.

Ch'eng Yüan-ying 成元英 (seventh century), *Nan-hua Chen-ching Chu-su* 南華眞經注疏 : 215.

Chia I 賈誼 (201-169 B.C.), *Lun Shih Cheng Su* 論時政疏, in the *Ch'ien Han Shu* 前漢書 (ch. 48) : 341.

Chiang Ch'üan 江瑔, *Lun Mo Tzŭ fei Hsing Mo* 論墨子非姓墨 (A Discussion that Mo Tzŭ was not named Mo), in *Tu Tzŭ Chih Yen* 讀子卮言 (Shanghai, 1917) : 79.

Chiao Hsün 焦循 (1763-1820), *Lun-yü Pu-su* 論語補疏 : 70.

Chiao Hsün, *Lun-yü T'ung-shih I-kuan Chung-shu* 論語通釋一貫忠恕 : 384.

Chiao Hsün, *Meng-tzŭ Cheng-i* 孟子正義 : 131.

Chiao Hung 焦竑 (1541-1620), *Lao-tzŭ I* 老子翼, in the *Chien Hsi Ts'un She* 漸西村舍 edition : 180, 225.

Ch'ien Mu 錢穆 (born 1895), *Mo-tzŭ* 墨子, in the *Kuo-hsüeh Hsiao-ts'ung-shu* 國學小叢書 (Shanghai, 1931) : 76, 79, 145, 150, 152.

Chu Hsi 朱熹 (1130-1200), *Meng-tzŭ Chi-chu* 孟子集註 : 121.

Fung Yu-lan (Feng Yu-lan) 馮友蘭 (born 1895), *Chung-kuo Che-hsüeh chung chih Shen-mi Chu-i* 中國哲學中之神秘主義 (Mysticism in Chinese Philosophy), in *Yenching Journal of Chinese Studies*, No. 1 : 244.

Fung Yu-lan, *K'ung Tzǔ tsai Chung-kuo Li-shih chung chih Ti-wei* 孔子在中國歷史中之地位 (The Position of Confucius in Chinese History), in the *Ku Shih Pien* 古史辨, Vol. 2 : 46, 52, 381.

Hsia Tseng-yu 夏曾佑 (died 1924), *Chung-kuo Li-shih* 中國歷史 (A History of China) : 11-12.

Hu Shih 胡適 (born 1891), *Chung-kuo Che-hsüeh Shih Ta-kang* 中國哲學史大綱 (An Outline History of Chinese Philosophy) : 9.

Hu Shih, *Hsiao Ch'ü P'ien Hsin-ku* 小取篇新詁, in *Hu Shih Wen Ts'un* 胡適文存, first collection : 261-262.

Huang Pai-chia 黃百家, (*c.* 1681) and his father, **Huang Tsung-hsi** 黃宗羲 (1610-1695), *Sung Yüan Hsüeh-an* 宋元學案 : 294.

Hui Tung 惠棟 (1697-1758), *I Shang Shih Chung Shuo* 易尚時中說 in *I Han Hsüeh* 易漢學, in the *Hsü Ching Chieh* 續經解 edition: 391.

K'ang Yu-wei 康有爲 (1858-1927), *Hsin-hsüeh Wei-ching K'ao* 新學僞經考 : 15.

Kao Heng 高亨 (born 1899), *Lao-tzǔ Cheng-ku* 老子正詁 : 179.

Koyanagi Shikita 小柳司氣太, *Bunka Shijo yori mitaru Kodai Sokoku* 文化史上所見之古代楚國 (The Ancient State of Ch'u as it appears in Cultural History), in the *Toho Gakuho* 東方學報, Tokyo, No. 1, March, 1931, pp. 196-228 : 176.

Ku Chieh-kang 顧頡剛 (born 1893), *Lun Shih Ching Ching-li chi Lao-tzǔ yü Tao-chia Shu* 論詩經經歷及老子與道家書 (A Letter concerning the History of the *Shih Ching*, and the Connection of the *Lao-tzǔ* with the Taoist School), in the *Ku Shih Pien,* 古史辨, Vol. 1 : 80.

Ku Chieh-kang, *Ts'ung Lü-shih Ch'un Ch'iu T'ui-tse Lao-tzǔ chih Ch'eng-shu Nien-tai* 從呂氏春秋推測老子之成書年代 (A Determination from the *Lü-shih Ch'un Ch'iu* of the Date of Formation of the *Lao-tzǔ* into a Book), in the *Ku Shih Pien,* Vol. 4 : 134, 150.

Ku Yen-wu 顧炎武 (1613-1682), *Jih Chih Lu* 日知錄 : 404.

Li Shan 李善 (died 689), commentary on the *Wei Tu Fu* 魏都賦 of Tso Ssǔ 佐思, in which he quotes from the *Ch'i Lüeh* 七略 ; commentary on *Ku An-lu Chao-wang Pei-wen* 故安陸昭王碑文, of Shen Hsiu-wen 沈休文, both contained in the *Wen Hsüan* 文選 (compiled *c.* 530) : 162.

Liang Ch'i-ch'ao 梁啓超 (1873-1929), *P'ing Hu Shih chih Chung-kuo Che-hsüeh Shih Ta-kang* 評胡適之中國哲學史大綱 (A Criticism of Hu Shih's *An Outline History of Chinese Philosophy*), in the *Liang Jen-kung Hsüeh-shu Chiang-yen Chi* 梁任公學術講演集, first collection : 9, 170.

Liu Chieh 劉 節 (born 1900), *Hung Fan Su-cheng* 洪 範 疏 證, in the *Ku Shih Pien* 古 史 辨, Vol. 5 : 164.

Liu Hsieh 劉 勰 (sixth century), *Hsin Lun* 新 論, in the *Han Wei Ts'ung-shu* 漢 魏 叢 書 : 50.

Liu Ju-lin 劉 汝 霖 (born 1903), *Chou Ch'in Chu-tzŭ K'ao* 周 秦 諸 子 考 (An Examination of the Chou and Ch'in Philosophers) : 171.

Liu Shih-p'ei 劉 師 培 (1884-1919), *Tso An Chi* 左 庵 集 : 62.

Lu Sheng 魯 勝 (alive in A.D. 291), *Mo Pien Chu Hsü* 墨 辯 注 叙 (Preface to a commentary on the Mohist Dialecticians), mentioned in the *Chin Shu* 晉 書 (ch. 94) : 247.

Lu Te-ming 陸 德 明 (died *c.* 627), *Ching-tien Shih-wen* 經 典 釋 文, containing commentary by **Ssŭ-ma Piao** 司 馬 彪 (died A.D. 306) on paradoxes of the Dialecticians : 200, 216, 218-219.

Ma Hsü-lun 馬 叙 倫 (born 1884), *Chuang-tzŭ Nien-piao* 莊 子 年 表, in his *T'ien Ma Shan Fang Ts'ung Chu* 天 馬 山 房 叢 著 : 222.

Ma Hsü-lun, *Lao-tzŭ Ho-ku* 老 子 覈 詁 : 182.

Ou-yang Hsiu 歐 陽 修 (1017-1072), *I T'ung Tzŭ Wen* 易 童 子 問 : 381.

Ssŭ-ma Piao, see **Lu Te-ming**.

Sun I-jang 孫 詒 讓 (1848-1908), *Mo-tzŭ Hou-yü* 墨 子 後 語 : 76-77.

Tai Tung-yüan 戴 東 原 (1723-1777), *Meng-tzŭ Tzŭ-i Su-cheng* 孟 子 字 義 疏 證 : 287.

T'ang Yüeh 唐 鉞 (born 1889), *Yin Wen ho Yin-wen-tzŭ* 尹 文 和 尹 文 子 (Yin Wen and the *Yin-wen-tzŭ*), in the *Ch'ing Hua Hsüeh Pao* 清 華 學 報, Vol. 4, No. 1 : 150, 153.

Teng Kao-ching 鄧 高 鏡 (born 1881), *Mo Ching Hsin-shih* 墨 經 新 釋 (Shanghai, 1931) : 273-276.

Ts'ui Shih 崔 適 (1851-1924), *Shih-chi T'an-yüan* 史 記 探 源 : 15.

Ts'ui Shu 崔 述 (1740-1816), *Chu-ssŭ K'ao-hsin Lu* 洙 泗 考 信 錄 : 170, 381.

Wang Chung 汪 中 (1744-1794), *Hsün-tzŭ Nien-piao* 荀 子 年 表, in his *Shu Hsüeh Nei Wai P'ien* 述 學 內 外 篇 : 280.

Wang Chung, *Lao-tzŭ K'ao-i* 老 子 考 異 : 170.

Wang Chung, *Mo-tzŭ Hsü* 墨 子 序 (Preface to the *Mo-tzŭ*), in his *Shu Hsüeh Nei Wai P'ien* : 247.

Wang Fu 王 符 (*c.* A.D. 76-*c.* 157), *Chien Fu Lun* 潛 夫 論, *Ssŭ Pu Ts'ung K'an* 四 部 叢 刊 edition : 261.

Wang Kuo-wei 王 國 維 (1877-1927), *Han Wei Po-shih K'ao* 漢 魏 博 士 考, in his *Kuan T'ang Chi Lin* 觀 堂 集 林 : 15.

Wang Ming-sheng 王 鳴 盛 (1722-1797), *Shih-ch'i-shih Shang-chüeh* 十 七 史 榷 : 192.

Wang Po 王柏 (1197-1274), *Ku Chung-yung Po* 古中庸跋, in the *Lu Chai Chi* 魯齊集, *Chin Hua Ts'ung Shu* 金華叢書 edition (see also **Ch'e Yü-feng**): 370.

Yü Cheng-hsieh 余正燮 (1775-1840), *Kuei-ssŭ Lei-kao* 癸巳類稿: 78, 121.

Yü Yung-liang 余永梁 (born 1901 ?), *I Kua Hsi-tz'ŭ ti Shih-tai chi ch'i Tso-che* 易卦爻辭的時代及其作者 (The Period and Authorship of the Hexagrams of the *I Ching* and Explanations on the Lines of the Hexagrams), in the *Ku Shih Pien* 古史辨, Vol. 3, pt. 1 : 380.

INDEX

In this Index the Chinese characters of all important names and places mentioned in the text will be found, except : (*a*) states given on the Map ; (*b*) books and articles listed in the Bibliography. The system of romanization followed is that of Giles, with the exception of the initial I when used as a proper name, which, because it might be puzzling to the non-specialist is spelled Yi.